Ce tems profane est tout fait pour mes moeurs
J'aime le luxe, et même la mollesse,
Tous les plaisirs, les Arts de tout espèce,
La propreté, le goût, les ornemans:
Tout honnête homme a de tels sentiments.

This profane era is perfectly tailored to my habits
I love luxury, and even indolence
All the pleasures, the Arts of every kind
Propriety, Taste, the ornaments,
Every gentleman has such sentiments

VOLTAIRE, *Le Mondain*, Paris, 1736

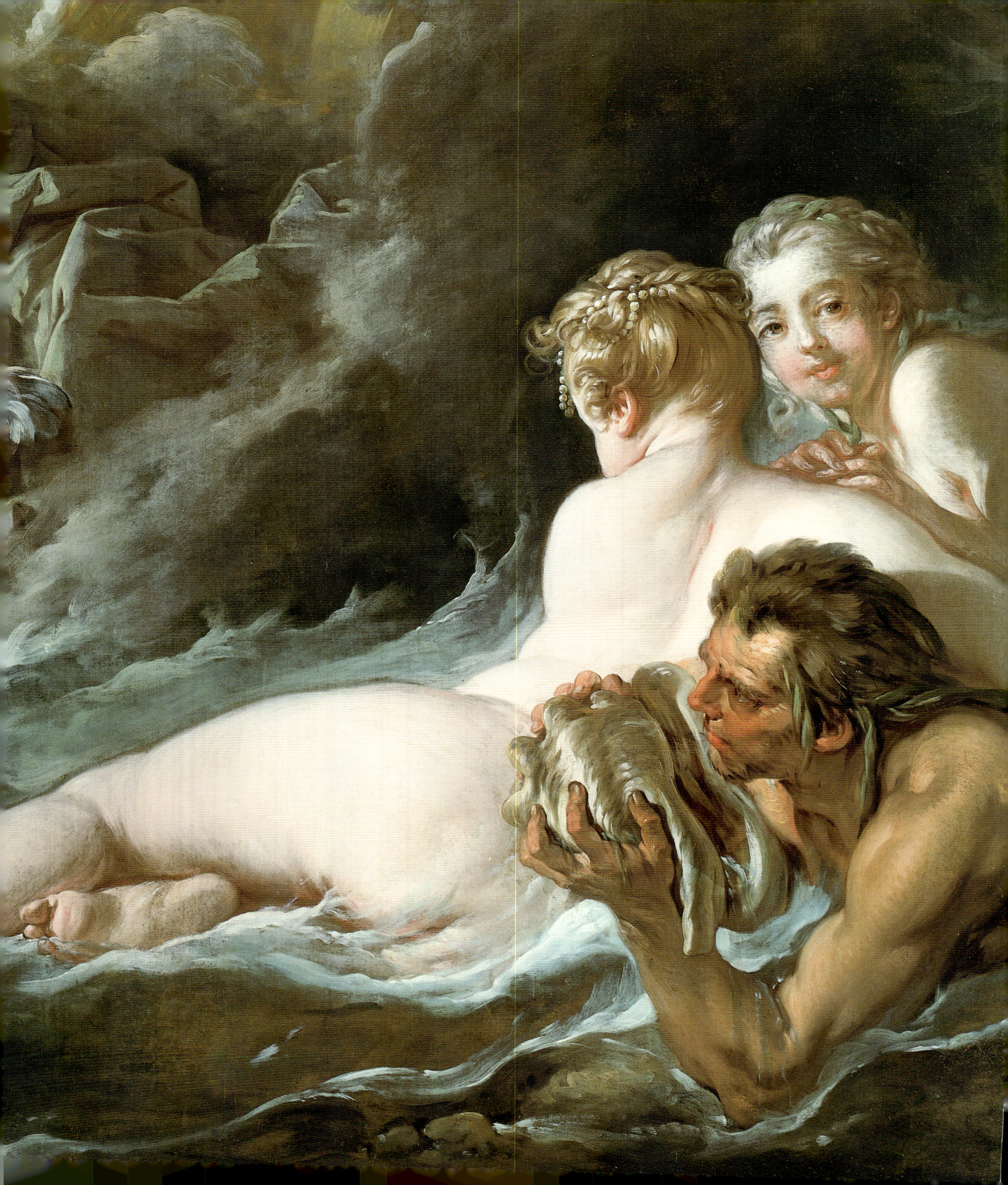

François Boucher

Seductive Visions

Jo Hedley

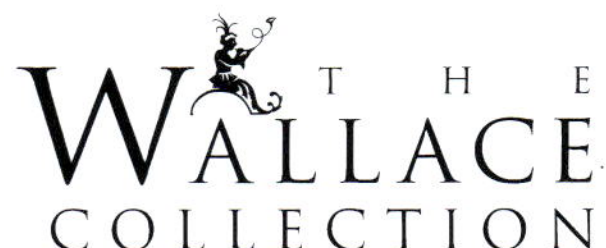

Published by the Wallace Collection to accompany the exhibition *Boucher: Seductive Visions* held at the Wallace Collection, London from 30 September 2004 to 17 April 2005, generously sponsored by the British Land Company PLC.

ISBN 0 900785 72 1

British Library Cataloguing-in-Publication Data
A catalogue record for this book is available from the British Library

Designed by Sally McIntosh
Printed by Graphic Studio, Verona, Italy

Front cover: Boucher, *Mars and Venus*, 1754, detail, Wallace Collection
Back cover: Boucher, *Mars and Venus*, 1754, detail, Wallace Collection
Frontispiece: Boucher, *The Rising of the Sun*, 1753, detail, Wallace Collection

Contents

Acknowledgements

This book celebrates Boucher in the Wallace Collection and accompanies a series of four exhibitions celebrating the artist's tercentenary at Hertford House: *Boucher: Seductive Visions* (30 September 2004 to 17 April 2005), *Boucher: Landscapes* (with the Bowes Museum, Barnard Castle; 30 September to 19 December 2004), *Boucher: Dutch and Flemish Inspirations* (with the Musée Magnin, Dijon; 6 January to 6 March 2005) and *Boucher: Seductive Re-Visions* (17 March to 17 April 2005).

My research greatly benefited from a series of related exhibitions held in 2003: *Boucher: hier et aujourd'hui* (Paris, Louvre), *Boucher et l'art rocaille* (Paris, École des Beaux-Arts *et al.*), *The Drawings of François Boucher* (New York, Frick Collection *et al.*) and *The Age of Watteau, Chardin and Fragonard: Masterpieces of French Genre Painting* (Washington, National Gallery of Art *et al.*). I was also able to hear the as yet unpublished papers given in 2003 at the Boucher conference at the École des Beaux-Arts, Paris and the C.A.S.V.A. conference on French Genre Painting held at the National Gallery of Art, Washington. Many have helped to form my ideas along the way and I am extremely grateful to the following for their assistance: Colin Bailey, Hans van Beck, Simon Bobak, François Borne, Andrew Cabrinovic, Jane Caplan, Hugo Chapman, Bart Cornelis, Jörg Ebeling, Alexandre Gady, Anne Hoguet, Nicolas Joly, Françoise Joulie, Alastair Laing, Christophe Leribault, John Lloyd, Miranda Lowe, Nicolas Milavanovich, Stephen Ongpin, Paul Raison, Lady Rosebery, Pierre Rosenberg, Kate de Rothschild, Martin Royalton Kisch, Charles Russell, Marie-Catherine Sahut, Xavier Salmon, Anna Sandén, Beverley Schreiber-Jacoby, Nicolas Schwed, Katie Scott, David Scrase, Joanna Selbourne, Jean-Pierre Selz, Julien Sereys de Rothschild, Andrew Shingleton, Perrin Stein, Jennifer Tonkovich, Jean Vittet, Kathie Way and Jon and Linda Whiteley.

Closer to home I would like to thank Alessandro Ghiglione, Peter Hughes, Saven Morris, Karine Sauvignon and my colleagues at the Wallace Collection, especially Rosalind Savill, Jeremy Warren, Stephen Duffy and Melanie Oelgeschläger, for their great support and for their careful reading of the text. A series of dedicated colleagues and volunteers also provided invaluable help in a variety of ways including Louisa Collins, David Edge, Barbara Lasic, Leanne Williams and the Wallace Collection Conservation Department, while Sally McIntosh was a wonderfully inspired designer.

Jo Hedley
Curator of Pictures Pre-1800

Director's Preface

François Boucher abounds in the Wallace Collection. This superlative display of his art combines balmy pastorals inhabited by shepherds and shepherdesses, mythological subjects gleaming with gods and goddesses, and a portrait of his great patron Madame de Pompadour. The sensuous ease and loveliness of these distant worlds seduce us into believing life was perhaps once like this, in stark contrast to our own world in 2004. But all too often his pictures are tossed aside as mere froth from a decadent and decorative age, rather than being celebrated as sparkling narratives revealing Boucher's affection for humanity and his quintessential painterliness. In the Wallace Collection, where his works hang on silk-covered walls in rooms furnished with the Sèvres porcelain and goldsmiths' work which embraced and absorbed his style, he can be seen perfectly as the very essence of the French Rococo.

As the Wallace Collection's Curator of Paintings pre-1800 and as a French specialist, Jo Hedley is perfectly placed to address Boucher's art. In this delectable book, she re-assesses him as an eighteenth-century man, imbued with history and tradition, not only in his art but in his life, a man of learning and culture, whose interests, tastes and instincts confirm him as an artist of the Enlightenment. Yet this monograph serves and enhances our understanding of more than just Boucher the painter, it also sets him in his historical context and offers a refreshing view of his sources of ideas and inspiration.

This book owes so much to the sponsorship of British Land PLC, whose Chairman John Ritblat, is also about to become Chairman of the Trustees of the Wallace Collection. In thanking him and his company for their great generosity, I also want to welcome him in his new role here, where he too will be an enlightened man of his time in the future fortunes of the Wallace Collection.

Rosalind Savill
Director of the Wallace Collection
July 2004

Key to Map of Central Paris

From the *Plan Turgot*, 1739, commissioned by Michel Etienne Turgot, marquis de Sousmons and Mayor of Paris in 1734

From the Church of St-Gervais to Les Halles

1 *Cemetery of St-Jean*
2 *Church of St-Gervais* Boucher's parents married here in 1698.
3 *Rue de la Verrerie* Boucher's birthplace, 29 September 1703.
4 *Hôtel de Ville & Place de Grève*
5 *Le Grand Châtelet*
6 *Rue des Foureurs* Boucher's parents living here at the time of his marriage, 1733.
7 *Cemetery of the Innocents*
8 *Les Halles*

The Isle de la Cité and the Quais

9 *Quai Pelletier* Home of Pierre Sirois.
10 *Pont Notre-Dame* Site of Gersaint's main shop.
11 *Pont au Change* Site of Gersaint's first shop.
12 *Cathedral of Notre-Dame*
13 *Place Dauphine* Site of annual open-air Corpus-Christi picture exhibition.
14 *Quai des Orfèvres* Street of the silver- and gold-smiths.

The Louvre

15 *Church of St-Germain-l'Auxerrois* Where Boucher's children were baptised, his daughters married and he and his father were buried.
16 *Vieux Louvre* Ancient Parisian residence of the Kings of France, home to the French Royal Academies and where Boucher lived 1752–70.
17 *Salon Carré and Galerie d'Apollon* Home to the French Royal Academy of Painting and Sculpture and the Salon.
18 *Place du Louvre* Where Boucher's father lived and dealt in prints shortly before his death in 1743.
19 *Rue Fromenteau* Traditionally inhabited by prostitutes.
20 *Grande Galerie of Louvre* Artists given lodgings on the ground and mezzanine floors; Boucher probably had a studio mid 1740s–1752.
21 *Rue St-Thomas du Louvre* Boucher living here at the time of his wedding in 1733; his three children born here.

The Rue St-Honoré

22 *Church of St-Eustache* Parish church of the rue de Richelieu.
23 *Rue St-Honoré* One of principal streets in Paris, upper reaches near the Halles inhabited by petit bourgeois shop keepers; increasingly smart from the rue du Foin to the Palais Royal, eventually giving way to the grand hôtels of the aristocracy and the wealthy haute-bourgeoisie.
24 *Rue de Grenelle (St-Honoré)* Boucher and family lived here, opposite the Rue des Deux Ecus, 1743–50.
25 *Palais Royal* The seat of the Court of the Regent 1715–23.
26 *Place du Palais Royal* One of the main social focuses in eighteenth-century Paris; cafés in the daytime and prostitution at night.
27 *Rue de la Boucherie* Traditionally inhabited by prostitutes.
28 *Rue de Richelieu* Street of the Royal Bank, then the King's Library, the Hôtel Crozat, and the Boucher family 1750–2.
29 *Rue de l'Evêque* Home of Marie-Jeanne Buzeau at the time of her marriage to Boucher.
30 *Church of St-Roch* Boucher and Marie-Jeanne Buzeau married here in 1733.

Off the Map

The book and print district, where Boucher lived (rue St-Jacques) *c.*1723–1728, to the South of the river Seine

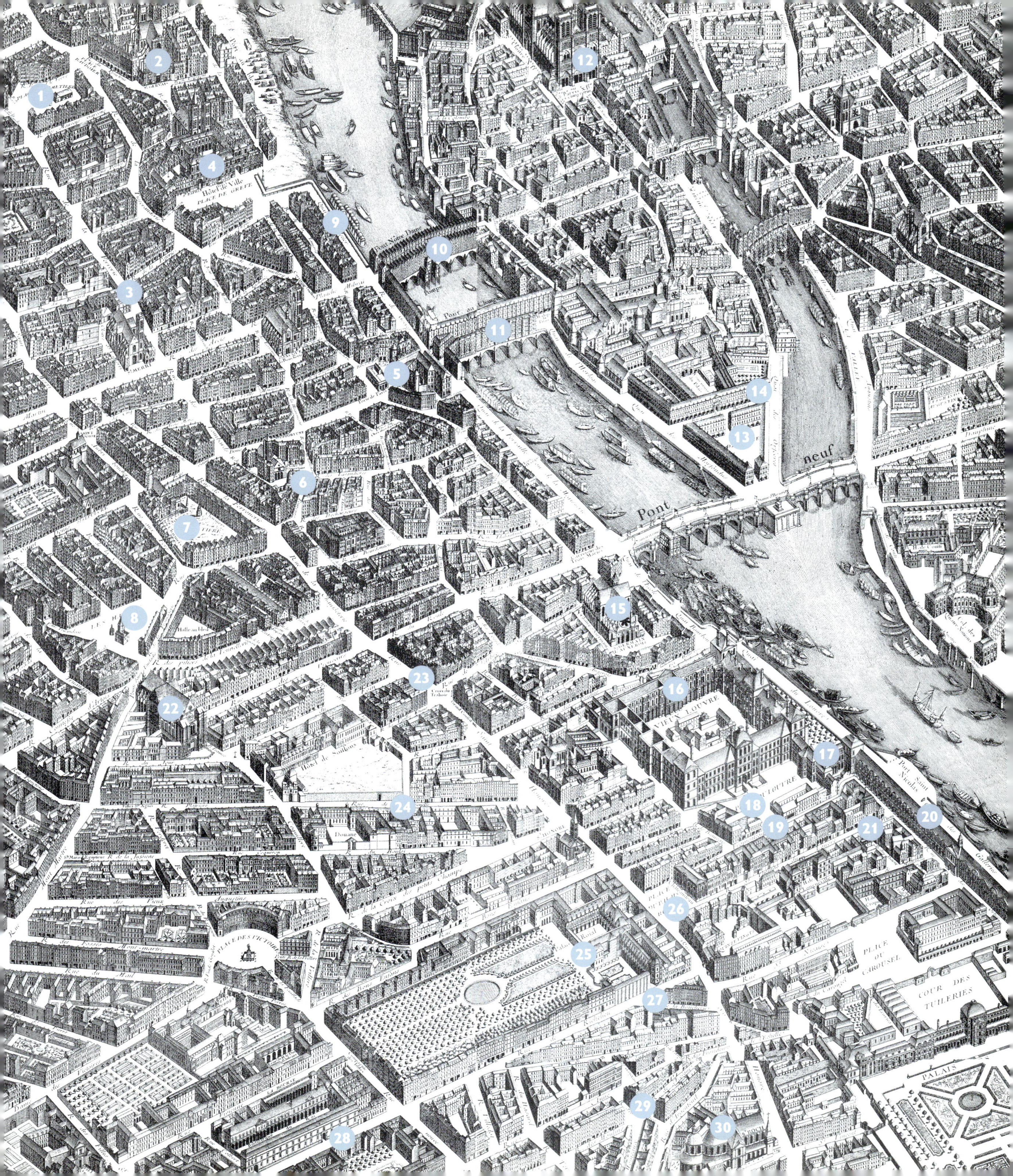

1
2
3
4
5
6
7
8
9
10
11
12
13
14
15
16
17
18
19
20
21
22
23
24
25
26
27
28
29
30
Pont
neuf
VIEUX LOUVRE
PLACE DU CAROUSEL
COUR DES TUILERIES
PALAIS

Key to Map of Paris and its Environs

From Hurtaut & Magny, *Dictionnaire historique de la ville de Paris et de ses environs*, 1, Paris, 1779.

1 *Paris*
2 *Gobelins* Royal Manufacturies of tapestry and furniture.
3 *Vincennes* Site of Vincennes porcelain manufactory until 1756.
4 *Château of Saint-Ouen* Leased by Mme de Pompadour from 1759.
5 *Château of La Muette* Royal residence.
6 *Château of Meudon* Royal residence.
7 *Château of Bellevue* Site acquired by the King in 1748, ceded to Mme de Pompadour in 1749, sold back to the King in 1757.
8 *Sèvres* Site of Sèvres porcelain manufactory from 1756.
9 *Château of Saint-Cloud* Residence of the Orléans family.
10 *The Pavilion of Louveciennes* Built for Mme du Barry.
11 *Château and Forest of Marly* Built as a retreat from Versailles by Louis XIV, used similarly by Louis XV.
12 *Château and Forest of Saint-Germain* Royal residence remodelled under Louis XIV.
13 *Versailles* Built as a hunting lodge by Louis XIII, lavishly enlarged and embellished by Louis XIV, principal residence of the French Court 1682–1715 and from 1722 to the Revolution of 1789.
14 *Château of Montigny* (destroyed) Country residence of the financier Trudaine de Montigny.
15 *Jouy* From 1760 the site of the production of toile de Jouy.
16 *Château of Sceaux* Alternative 'Court' of the duchesse de Maine, wife of Louis XIV's legitimised son, the duc de Maine.
17 *Arcueil* Site of the château, gardens and aqueduct of Arcueil.
18 *Château of Choisy* Royal residence and favourite haunt of Louis XV.
19 *Château of Étiolles* Residence of Madame Lenormand d'Étiolles, future Mme de Pompadour.
20 *Château and Forest of Fontainebleau* Royal Residence; due to its excellent hunting one of Louis XV's favourite châteaux.
21 *Rambouillet* Site of Marie-Antoinette's dairy.

Off the Map

Château of Crécy to the West of Rambouillet; first residence acquired, in 1746, by Mme de Pompadour.

Beauvais to the North-West of Paris; site of the Beauvais tapestry manufactory.

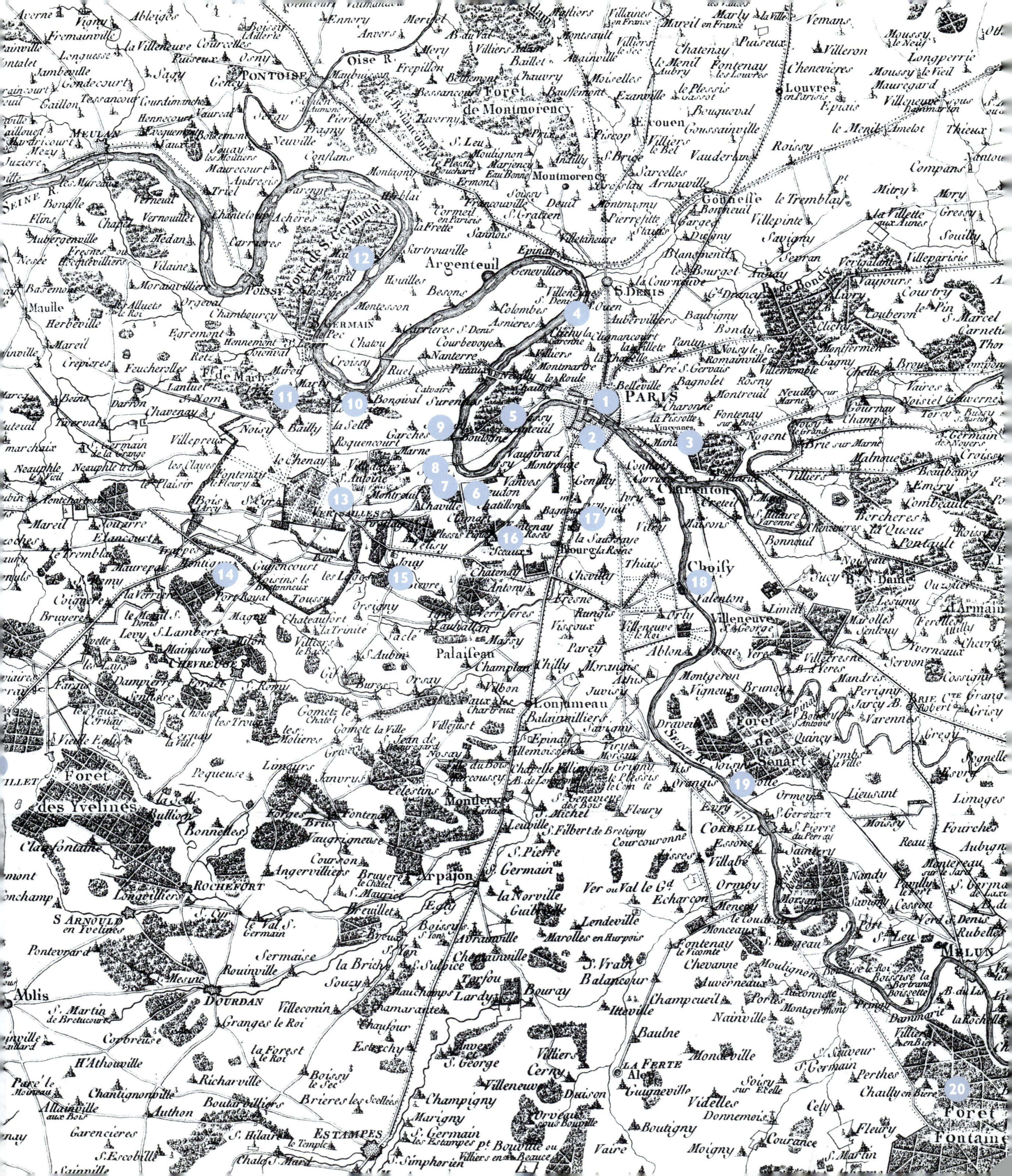

Avernes Vigny Ableiges Ennery Meriel Valmondois Maffliers Villaines en France Mareil en France Marly la Ville Vemans
Fremainville la Villeneuve Courcelles Boissy l'Aillerie Anvers B. du Val Villiers Adam Montsault Villiers le Sec Puiseux Moussy le Neuf Villeron
Longuesse Puiseux Osny PONTOISE Oise R. Mery Baillet Attainville Chatenay le Menil Aubry Fontenay les Louvres Chenevieres Longperrie
Jambeville Sagy Gency Maubuisson Frepillon Bethemont Chauvry Moiselles Louvres en Parisis Moussy le Vieil Mauregard
Gondecourt Tessancourt Courdimanche Vaureal Cergy S. Ouen l'Aumone Pierrelaie Bessancourt Forêt de Montmorency Baussemont Ezanville le Plessis Gassot Epiais Villeneuve sous Dammartin
Gaillon Hennecourt Evequemont Boisemont Neuville Pontoise Taverny Ecouen Bouqueval
MEULAN Vaux Pragny Conflans S. Leu Moutignon Piscop S. Brice Villiers le Bel Goussainville le Menil Amelot Thieux
Mezy Juziere Jouy les Moutiers Maurecourt Andresis Montigny le Plessis Bouchard Margency Eau Bonne Andilly Montmorency Sarcelles Arnouville Vauderlan Roissy Compans
SEINE R. Les Mureaux Triel Carenne Herblai Ermont Soisy Deuil Groslay Gonesse Mitry Mory
Bonafle Verneuil Vernouillet Chanteloup Achères Cormeil en Parisis Francouville S. Gratien Montmagny Pierrefitte Stains Bonneuil le Tremblay la Villette aux Aunes Gressy
Flins Chapet Medan Forêt de S. Germain la Frette Sannois Villetaneuse Garges Dugny Villepinte Souilly
Aubergenville Carrieres Vilaine Sartrouville Argenteuil Epinay Blanmenil Savigny
Nesée Fresnes ou Ecquevilliers Poissy le Mesnil Houilles Besons Genevilliers le Bourget Aunay Sevran Vertgalant Villeparisis
Morainvilliers Orgeval les Loges Montesson Colombes Villeneuve S. Denis S. Ouen S. DENIS la Cournuve Drancy Bondy Vaujours Courtry
Basemont Les Alluets le Roi Maule Chambourcy S. GERMAIN Carrieres S. Denis Asnieres Aubervilliers Baubigny Livry le Pin S. Marcel
Herbeville Egremont Hennemont le Pec Chatou Courbevoye Clichy la Garenne Clignancourt Pantin Clichy Couberon
Mareil Retz Fourqueux Croissy Nanterre Villiers la Villette la Chapelle Noisy le Sec Romainville Montfermeil Gagny Carnetin Thorigny
Crepieres Feucherolles F. de Marly Marly Ruel Calvaire Puteaux Neuilly Montmartre le Roule Pré S. Gervais Bagnolet Villemomble Chelles Brou
Beine Lanluet S. Nom Bougival Surennes Belleville PARIS Charonne Rosny Neuilly sur Marne Vaires Noisiel
Darron Chavenay Louveciennes la Selle Passy Montreuil Gournay Champ Torcy Bussy
Tiverval Villepreux Noisy Bailly Garches Boulogne Auteuil la Pissotte Vincennes Fontenay sur Bois Noisy le Grand Nogent Brie sur Marne S. Germain des Noyers Croissy
S. Germain de la Grange Neauphle le Chat. les Clayes Roquencourt Marne Vaugirard Montrouge S. Mandé Malnoue
Neauphle le Vieil Fontenay le Fleury le Chenay Ville d'Avray S. Antoine Sèvres Issy Vanves Gentilly Conflans Carrieres Villiers Beaubourg Emery
Pontchartrain Bois d'Arcy S. Cyr Montreuil Meudon Chatillon Arcueil Ivry Charenton Creteil S. Maur Combeault
Mareil Jouarre Elancourt VERSAILLES Chaville Clamart Bagneux Villejuif Vitry S. Hilaire la Varenne Bercheres la Queue Roissy
le Tremblay Trappes Guyancourt Velisy Plessis Picquet Fontenay aux Roses la Saussaye Maisons Chennevieres Pontault
Maurepas Montigny Voisins le Bretonneux Buc Jouy les Loges Sceaux Bourg la Reine Thiais Choisy Bonneuil Noiseau
S. Remy Coignere la Verriere Port Royal Toussu Bievre Chatenay Antony Chevilly Valenton Sucy B. N. Dame Ozouer
Magny Chateaufort Orsigny Fresne Rungis Orly Limeil Lesigny Armainvilliers
Bruyeres le Mesnil S. Denis Levy S. Lambert la Trinité Villiers le Bacle Saclé Lauhallan Verrieres Massy Wissous Villeneuve le Roi Villeneuve S. George Yeres Marolles Santeny Ferolles Attilly Chevry
Mainvour Milon CHEVREUSE S. Aubin Palaiseau Paray Ablon Crosne Villecresne Servon Yverneaux
Dampierre Senlisse Forges S. Remy Gif Champlan Chilly Morangis Athis Montgeron Brunoy Mandres Cossigny
Cernay les Vaux de Cernay Chousé Bures Orsay Villebon Juvisy Vigneux Epinay Perigny Jarcy B. Brie Cte Robert Grisy
Vielle Eglise Gometz le Chatel les Troux Saux les Chartreux LONJUMEAU Savigny Draveil Boussy S. Antoine Quincy Varennes Gregy
Forêt des Yvelines Cheney la Ville les Molieres Gometz la Ville Villejust Balainvilliers Viry Forêt de Senart Combs la Ville Soignolle
Grivery S. Jean de Beauregard Nozay Villemoisson S. Epinay Morsan Seine Soisy Etiolles Evry
Limours Janvrus la Ville du Bois Marcoussy Chapelle Villiers B. de Longpont Grigny le Plessis le Comte Ris Orangis Ormoy Lieusant Limoges
Pequeuse Celestins Montlhery S. Genevieve des Bois Fleury S. Germain S. Pierre du Perray Moissy Fourches
Bullion Bonnelles Forges Briis Fontenay Linas S. Michel Courcouronne CORBEIL Essonne Saintry Reau Aubigny
Clayfontaine Vaugrigneuse Leuville S. Filbert de Bretigny Villabé Nandy Montereau sur le Jard
Courson S. Pierre Lisses Ormoy Forêt de Rougeau Savigny Pouilly le Fort Cesson S. Germain
Rochefort Angervilliers Bruyere le Chatel S. Maurice Arpajon S. Germain Ver ou Val le Gd Echarçon Morsan Verd S. Denis Rubelles
Longvilliers S. Cyr Breuillet Egly la Norville Guibeville Lendeville Menecy le Coudray S. Port S. Leu MELUN
S. ARNOULD en Yvelines le Val S. Germain Breux Boissy S. Yon Avrainville Marolles en Hurpois Monceaux Pringy
Pontevrard Sermaise S. Yon Cheptainville Fontenay le Vicomte S. Vrain Chevanne Moulignon Boissise le Roi Boissise la Bertrand Boissette
Rouinville la Briche S. Sulpice Torfou Bouray Balancour Auverneaux Ponthierry
Ablis S. Mesme Souzy Mauchamps Chamarante Lardy Champcueil Nainville Portes Auxonnette Montgermont B. du Lys
S. Martin de Bretoncourt DOURDAN Villeconin Itteville Baulne Dammarie Villiers en Biere la Rochelle
Granges le Roi Chaufour Estrechy Mondeville
Corbreuse la Forest le Roi Janville S. George Villiers Cerny LA FERTE Alais Guigneville S. Sauveur S. Germain
H'Athouville Richarville Boissy le Sec Villeneuve Daison Soisy sur Ecolle Perthes
Chantignonville Boutarvilliers Brieres les Scellées Champigny Orveau sous Bouville Videlles Chailly en Biere
Allainville aux Bois Authon Marigny Donnemoit Cely Forêt Fontaine
Garencieres S. Hilaire le Temple ESTAMPES S. Germain les Estampes Pt. Bouville ou Villiers en Beauce Vaire Boutigny Moigny Courance Fleury
S. Escobille Chalo S. Mard S. Simphorien S. Martin

1 2 3 4 5 6 7 8 9 10 11 12 13 14 15 16 17 18 19 20

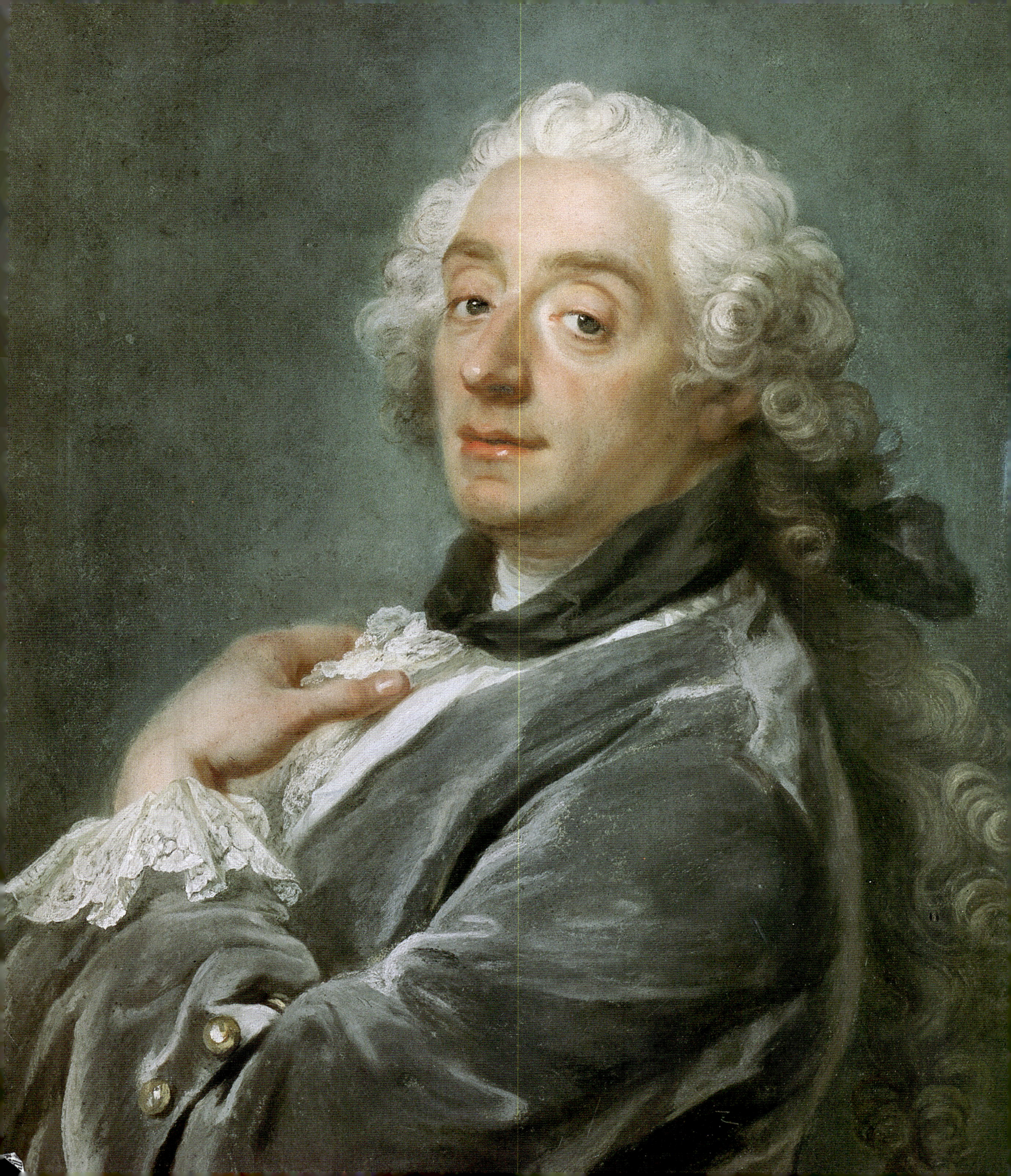

I

To be born in Paris is to be doubly French because there one receives the flower of urbanity that is found nowhere else MERCIER[1]

Boucher's Beginnings: 1703–1731

The art of François Boucher is instantly recognisable: its rococo palette, luscious female nudes and be-ribboned pastorals have been both praised and dismissed as light, sensual and elitist. For some it is the visual archetype of decadent *ancien régime* frivolity, thankfully swept away by David and the French Revolution. Others, nostalgic for a lost era of aristocratic elegance untrammelled by utilitarian concerns, see Boucher's work as the embodiment of a 'moment of perfection in French Art', conceived in essentially decorative terms. Both points of view, coloured by political and teleological approaches to pre-Revolutionary France, have undermined impartial evaluation of Boucher's achievement as a major artist working in the Western European tradition. This book is a general account of Boucher's career, focussing upon his works in the Wallace Collection, which aims to demonstrate how Boucher's artistic vocation was every bit as serious and ambitious in the eighteenth century as that of Titian or Rubens in their eras. Boucher worked extremely hard to acquire and refine his craft. Combining technical virtuosity with an imagination rarely equalled, he created a unique vision that could meet the specific demands of individual clients but also satisfy the new and expanding public market for imagery. His work reflects and anticipates many of the cultural preoccupations of the eighteenth century. Boucher was not an unthinking tool of a reactionary and decaying régime, but a man and artist of the Enlightenment, an age which believed, often naively and in many differing and contradictory ways, in the progress of man and the pursuit of happiness. We must re-examine his life, times and work to help us understand how this most unashamedly hedonist and Parisian of artists came to be so superbly represented in the centre of London at Hertford House, and what his art means to us today.

The Personality of the Artist

François Boucher, resplendent in his velvet coat and fashionably curled wig, raises an elegant hand to his breast, the better to show off his magnificent lace cuff and jabot, and turns nonchalantly towards his viewers (fig.1). Lundberg's 1743 pastel of Boucher won him membership of the French Royal Academy of Painting and Sculpture and is one of the few indications of how Boucher himself wanted to be seen.[2] In our celebrity-obsessed time it is surprising to find how little else there is to tell us directly of Boucher's personal life and ambitions. Boucher was no great political or military figure and did not come from an illustrious ancient family; so, according to the tenets of eighteenth-century historiography, his life was not considered of interest. It was his work that made him famous, so eighteenth-century commentators argued that 'the best way to praise this great man is to speak of his work'.[3] Unfortunately for Boucher's reputation, towards the end of his life, and after his death, criticism became increasingly informed by moral and aesthetic codes very different from those under which he grew up and his art came to be judged immoral. Later ages, hungrier for intimate details, invented an appropriate persona to fill the biographical void, a libertine, whose reputation in turn undermined serious consideration of the formal qualities of his work.

FIG.1 *facing previous page*
GUSTAV LUNDBERG (1695–1786), *Portrait of François Boucher*, 1743, pastel, 67.2 × 51cm, Paris, Musée du Louvre

The personality we can reconstruct from contemporary sources is very different from the one Boucher has often been saddled with. Those who knew him all agreed that he was straightforward, kind and generous, good fun in company as well as pleasure loving.[4] The abbé de Fontenay, in his dictionary of artists, published only six years after Boucher's death, said that 'envy never troubled him; and no one admitted the ability of his rivals more freely. Games and intrigue might sometimes harm him; but he was as unaware of them as he was of avarice. He was noble and disinterested to the point of enriching his friends and to the detriment of himself, by freely giving them those of his works which they seemed to desire'.[5] This professional generosity, rare in the ambitious milieu of the Academy, is demonstrated by Boucher's friendship with Vien (1716–1809), whose neo-classical artistic vision rivalled and ultimately supplanted Boucher's own. Even Madame Geoffrin noted with some surprise that 'the two men are friends, which is rare among artists'.[6] Something of the reciprocal esteem and affection in which Boucher was held by his colleagues is indicated by the Academy Secretary Cochin's comment to an unknown correspondent: 'You are like M. Boucher, who has effortlessly performed fine actions throughout his life: such are the truly great masters'.[7]

Considering the moralising that Boucher's 'love of pleasure' has inspired, it is worth trying to understand what this might have meant in practice and what contemporaries thought. The Swedish envoy, Carl Frederick Scheffer, used it with Queen Louise-Ulrika of Sweden to explain Boucher's delay in completing the original version of *The Milliner* (Stockholm; see fig.58). Although admitting he had no hard evidence to support his assertion, he complained that 'Boucher's *libertinage* has to be seen to be believed ... Boucher never renounces his pleasures for one client or the next'.[8] Later in the eighteenth century, *libertinage* came to be associated with sexual excess, but in the early eighteenth century it denoted a more general pursuit of pleasure. Such behaviour was not only socially acceptable but even a mark of social distinction for men of Boucher's generation, such as his friend, the portraitist Tocqué, who was also noted for his pleasure-loving ways.[9] As the moral climate gradually changed from the late 1740s onwards, there is still no hint of Boucher exhibiting any specifically sexually compromising behaviour. By the 1760s Boucher's pupil Mannlich, while regaling us in some detail with his own sexual conquests, describes Boucher's marriage as idyllic and insists on Boucher's 'utter probity on all counts'.[10] Although from the 1730s onwards Boucher lived a stone's throw from the Place du Palais Royal, the centre of Parisian prostitution, there were many other ways a man could enjoy himself in that world, drinking and gambling being the most conspicuous.[11] Boucher, who apparently 'enjoyed himself with those who cultivated literature'[12], may have been a member of the 1730s literary dining society, the *Cellar Dinners*, run every Sunday by the caterer Landelle in the cellars of the cabaret in the rue de Buci. There he would have found cultural stars of the era such as the writer, Crébillon *fils*, the opera-singer, Jelyotte, and the composer, Rameau.[13] His association with the noted antiquarian and art world luminary, the comte de Caylus, might also have taken him to another club, the *Society of the End of the Bench*, whose name alone implies a fairly light-hearted approach. A letter provides a tantalising glimpse of such conviviality. Written by the collector Mariette it was sent with two Boucher drawings to his fellow-collector, Gabburri, in Florence: 'The one in watercolour represents a lunch in the country. I am sure it will please you. You will find written on the bottom: 'Boucher's Lunch', because he drew it during a gathering of painters where each agreed to pay for their lunch with a drawing'.[14] Mannlich also mentions that Boucher was a freemason, and one can imagine him enjoying the mixture of rationality and spiritual brotherhood that attracted many artists to the movement in the eighteenth century.[15] There is no doubt of Boucher's addiction to opera, ballet and the theatre in general; he was not just an avid spectator but also an active participant, producing

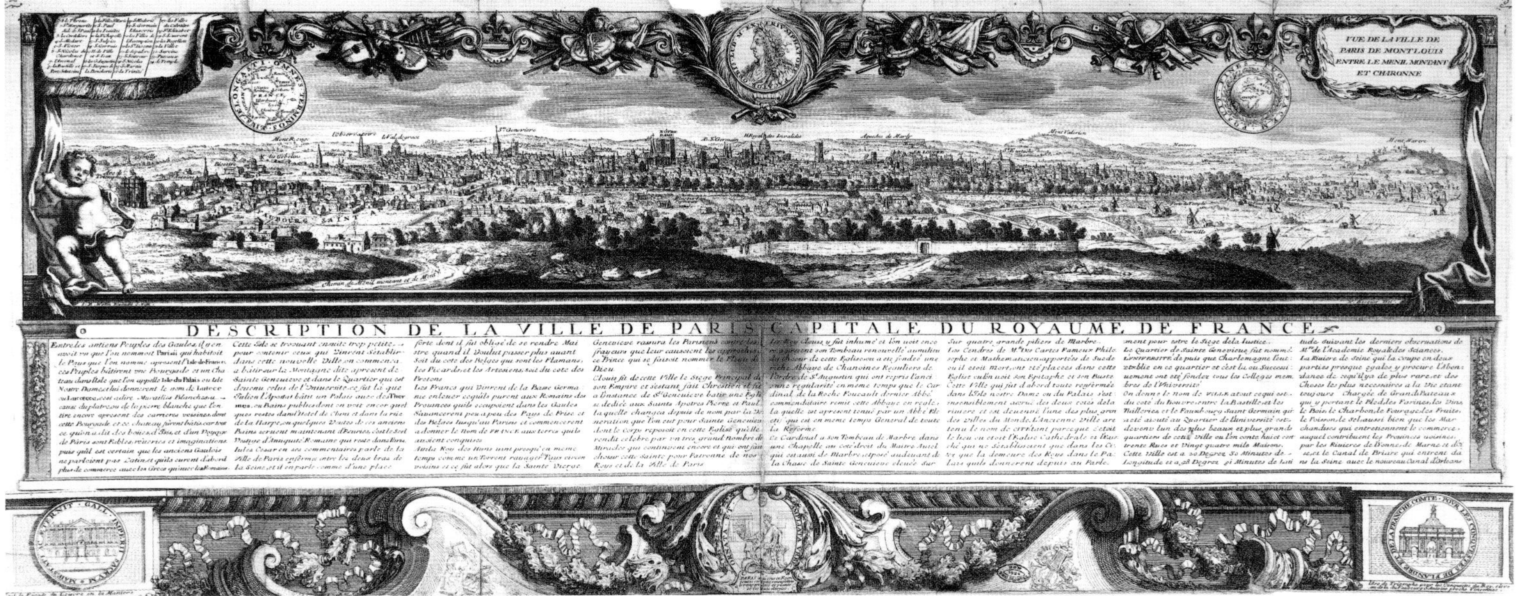

FIG.2
JEAN BAPTISTE NOLIN after NICOLAS BOCQUET, *View of Paris*, c.1700, engraving, 25 × 75cm (with text), Paris, Bibliothèque Nationale de France

lavish sets for the elite Paris Opéra and for the more popular Opéra Comique. The catalogue of Boucher's astonishingly rich and varied sale in 1771 reveals that he also thoroughly enjoyed another of the great diversions of the eighteenth-century luxury capital of the world: he loved to shop.[16]

The important thing to note is that however enthusiastically Boucher pursued these 'pleasures' they rarely deflected him from his artistic ambition. Scheffer's comments notwithstanding, most commentators marvelled that Boucher's love of life never affected his immense capacity for hard work, recalling how he regularly spent ten to twelve hours a day at the easel. His greatest passion was his art, and this artistic vocation is summed up in the abbé de Fontenay's comment that the 'taste which he always had for pleasure did not stop him from being the most prolific painter of his time. His imagination was always active and love for his art, did not allow him to lose a single day for his glory'.[17]

Boucher's Paris

Looking at Lundberg's debonair portrait it seems scarcely credible that Boucher, who ended his life as First Painter to the King in a luxurious apartment in the Louvre, was born 'in poverty',[18] on a busy thoroughfare in the centre of Paris on 29 September, 1703 (fig.2). Boucher's thirty-year old father, Nicolas, was a master-painter, a member of the Corporation of Painters and Image-Makers, one of the hundred and twenty-seven guilds in Paris.[19] It is thought that Boucher's grandfather had been an artist too, so Boucher probably had little option but to be 'born with a brush in his hand'.[20] His mother, Elisabeth Lemesle, was twenty-five and illiterate.[21] The couple were living on the rue de la Verrerie, one of the main East-West axes of Paris and the traditional street of the stained-glass makers.[22] The baby was born close to the Place de Grève (today's place de l'Hôtel de Ville), where unemployed labourers congregated in the mornings and public festivities and executions attracted crowds in equal measure. He was christened at the nearby church of Saint-Jean-en-Grève, with a minor legal functionary, François Prevot, and Marie-Louise Boullenois, the daughter of another legal official, acting as his godparents. So Boucher began his life as a member of the highly traditional petit-bourgeois artisan class (a sort of upper-working class) of Paris. His subsequent rise seems impressive, even by today's

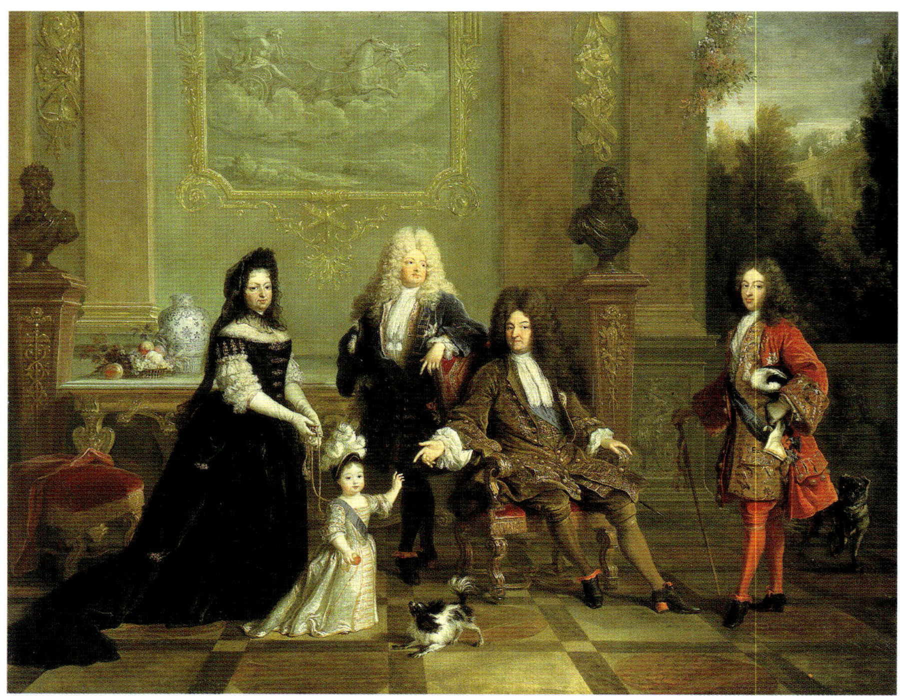

FIG.3
FRENCH SCHOOL,
Louis XIV and his Heirs,
*c.*1715, oil on canvas,
127.6 × 161cm,
Wallace Collection

standards, although in this Boucher would prove himself a man of his age, for such advancement was to become increasingly common, helping to confirm the Enlightenment belief in social progress.[23]

Although his art would later be seen as quintessentially *Louis Quinze*, Boucher was actually born in the closing years of Louis XIV's reign, which had seen France become a superpower, with a population of over twenty million, more than the rest of Europe put together. The Sun King, as he was termed, had dominated European politics for nearly half a century. When he moved the Court from Paris to his magnificently rebuilt château at Versailles in 1682, France had appeared invincible both militarily and culturally, but by the time of Boucher's birth the sun was beginning to set on the reign of the greatest absolute monarch Europe had ever seen. The War of the Spanish Succession (1702–13), the conflict Churchill called 'the real First World War' which was sparked by Louis's expansionist attempt to unite the crowns of France and Spain, had plunged France into an expensive and ultimately unsuccessful conflict against the Emperor, England, the United Provinces, Portugal and the Duke of Savoy. During Boucher's infancy military defeats, as well as internal rebellion in the Cévennes (1702–5) and freezing temperatures and famine (1709), rocked French confidence and undermined Louis's royal mythology. A growing spirit of rational enquiry as manifested in the writings of Descartes, Newton, Locke and Bayle began to undermine orthodoxy.[24] Meanwhile at Court, a series of deaths from a smallpox epidemic robbed Louis of all his direct heirs except a great grandson born in 1710.[25] Something of the solemnity of these later years of Louis XIV's Court is recalled by the stiff posthumous portrait of the old king and his heirs in the Wallace Collection (fig.3).[26]

Louis XIV died on 1 September, 1715, the month of Boucher's twelfth birthday. As the five-year-old Louis XV ascended the throne, Boucher was probably already hard at work apprenticed to his father. In stark contrast to Versailles, Paris at the beginning of the eighteenth century was an exciting place to be. Even before the self-appointed Regent, Philippe d'Orléans, moved the Court to Paris, it had provided a welcome escape for younger aristocrats eager to enjoy the less formal pleasures on offer in the developing capital.[27] The new Regent, now usually remembered for his own sybaritic behaviour, astutely ensured the good times would continue. He made peace with France's enemies (most importantly with Britain, whose rise was to be a continual thorn in the flesh of French foreign policy throughout the eighteenth century), and neutralised any potential revolt from the old aristocracy or the Parisian bourgeois parliamentarians, both of whom hoped for more influence following Louis XIV's death. Religious dissent between the Jesuits (the Catholic high church, supported mainly by the aristocracy) and the Jansenists (the austere low church supported by the Gallican Parlement) was dealt with similarly. Meanwhile the flamboyant Scotsman, John Law, gave the stagnant French finances a boost by introducing paper currency and encouraging speculation on the expanding colonial markets. As inflation rose to giddy heights, debts were cleared, spending increased, but the property-owning classes and money-lending bourgeoisie found their assets plummeting in value. With its tumbling gold coins and cornucopia, the intricate iron balustrade from Law's Royal Bank in the former Hôtel de Nevers on the rue de Richelieu provides a vivid symbol of these boom and bust years (fig.4).[28] Although some lost everything, others, such as Voltaire, profited from financial speculation to such a degree that they were able to indulge their taste for luxury objects, thus providing more work for the artisans of Paris and contributing to the boom that propelled the French economy into the modern age.

The fall of Law's bank in 1720 coincided with the arrival in Marseilles of the last great plague to reach Europe. Once that had died away there was nothing to halt French economic expansion. The three horses of the Apocalypse that had ravaged Europe in the seventeenth century, War, Famine and Pestilence, were beaten, and the early years of Louis XV's reign even basked in unusually good weather and harvests. By accident of birth, Boucher found himself at the epicentre of the richest and most powerful nation on earth. Marivaux's observation that 'Paris is the world, the rest of the earth is only the suburbs'[29] in part explains why, apart from his youthful trip to Rome and a brief foray to the Netherlands at the end of his life, Boucher never felt the need to search out other markets like Rubens or Tiepolo. Parisians have difficulty living anywhere other than their city today; how much more difficult would it have been to leave Paris in the eighteenth century, when to be civilised was to speak French.[30] Formed under the pleasure-loving Regency, and a Parisian through and through, one of Boucher's most notable qualities as an artist was his ability to reflect and exploit his environment. Boucher's interests and insider knowledge helped him ensure that his paintings became one of the most chic and desirable luxuries Paris could offer and, where Paris led, the world followed.

Where his great-grandfather had been a man of action and conquest, Louis *Le Bien-Aimé*, the well-loved, was initially associated with peace, prosperity and above all, pleasure. The comedies of Dancourt and Saint-Yon, popular at the beginning of the century, depict a society addicted to modish gambling and stylish adultery, where everything was permitted except lack of *esprit*, or wit. Less witty and more hell raising were the drunken antics of Regency rakes like those Buvat's journal describes abducting a recently deceased lawyer's corpse with the cry: 'poor Nigon, come with us, drink as much as you like and then we'll bury you like the duc d'Aremberg, who has drunk so much already that he's sleeping content'.[31] A more measured sociability found outlets in the growing number of cafés, while ideas were discussed in comfort in the fashionably intimate interiors of the private salons, which became an increasingly influential channel for new cultural and political theories under the watchful eyes of formidable

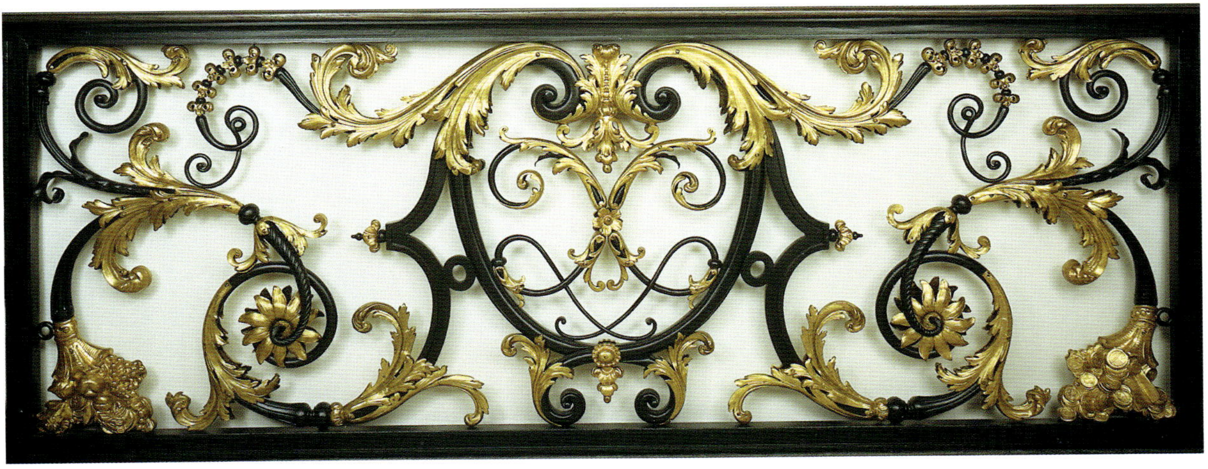

FIG.4
Balustrade of the Royal Bank of France, detail, *c.*1719–20, wrought and cast iron and gilt brass, height 91.5cm, Wallace Collection

hostesses like *Mesdames* Lambert, Geoffrin and du Deffand.[32] Balls and masquerades abounded, from public free-for-alls in the Champs-Élysées, to ticketed masked balls at the Opéra and Comédie Française, to select invitation-only affairs in the châteaux of the urban elite.[33] Meanwhile at the fairs in the Paris suburbs all classes rubbed shoulders to see the lewd pantomimes of the *commedia dell'arte*, all the more exciting since their official banishment by the old King in 1686, or, in later years, to enjoy one of the charming, but still subversive, operettas of the Opéra Comique. English visitors were amazed to see even grand ladies enjoying such plebeian pleasures. Apparently such elegant *Parisiennes* required little encouragement to transgress: 'one tells a woman she is pretty three times, more is not necessary: from the first, she will surely believe you, she will thank you the second time, and will pay you back in full on the third'.[34] And while the permissive morality and availability of prostitutes reduced the number of rapes in Paris,[35] the number of abandoned children rapidly increased;[36] D'Alembert the *encyclopaedist* was one such, abandoned by the former nun and salon hostess, Madame Tencin. An encounter between the young Louis XV and the Neapolitan ambassador, Domenico Caraccioli, perfectly sums up the fine line between wit and vulgarity that distinguished the studied insouciance of the French gentleman, or *honnête homme*, in the first half of the eighteenth century. As the King graciously asked the hard-working ambassador if he at least had time to make love, Caraccioli quickly replied: 'No Sire, I buy it ready made'.[37]

A more down-to-earth perspective on daily life in the streets of Boucher's Paris is provided by Louis-Sébastien Mercier. He writes 'At seven in the morning all the gardeners, baskets empty, go to their allotments … one sees hardly any carriages about. One meets only the office-clerks, who are dressed and curled at that hour. At nine, one sees the wig makers running covered in powder from head to foot … carrying in a grip of iron a toupée and a wig. The café boys, always in jackets, carry coffee and infusions of tea, sugar and milk to the rented rooms …around ten, a black cloud of men of law move towards the Châtelet and the Palais … at midday the dealers go in a crowd to the stock market, and the leisured to the Palais Royal. The *quartier* of Saint-Honoré, home to the financiers and men of rank, is very full … it is the hour of solicitations and all types of requests. At two dinners are held in the town … all the carriages run at this hour … At three one sees very few in the streets as everyone is eating … At quarter past five there is a terrible, infernal din. All the streets are full, all the carriages are running in all directions to different spectacles or to go on promenades. The cafés fill up. At seven calm … it is also the most dangerous period as the watch is not yet in place …The day falls; and as the decorations of the opera are in movement, the crowd of workmen, carpenters, stonecutters regain their suburbs … at nine in the evening the noise starts again: it is the procession to the theatres … high society pays short visits before supper. It is the hour also when all the prostitutes…pursue you in the mud in their silk stockings and flat slippers … At eleven o'clock, again silence. It is supper-time. It is the hour when the cafés throw out the indolent …At a quarter past midnight one hears the carriages of those who, not gambling, are retiring … At one in the morning, six thousand peasants arrive carrying vegetables, fruit and flowers. They make their way to the Halles … this non-interrupted tumult contrasts with the sleep of the rest of the town; for at four in the morning there is only the brigand and the poet awake. At six the bakers of Gonesse, the food-providers of Paris, twice a week bring a great quantity of bread … soon the workmen tear themselves away from their pallets, grab their work tools and go to their workshops … in the morning the libertines leave the prostitutes, pale and dishevelled … the gamblers, paler still, leave the famous or obscure gambling dens; some beating their head and stomach, throwing desperate looks to heaven; others promising to return to the table that favoured them, but which will betray them tomorrow'.[38]

One sees in this description the gap between rich and poor also noted by Montesquieu in 1721, when he wrote that 'Paris is perhaps the most sensual city in the world and the one where one is most meticulous in the refinement of pleasure; but it is perhaps also the city where one has the hardest way of life. For one man to live deliciously, a hundred others must work without rest'.[39] Average male life expectancy was only forty-two years, and the perils of childbirth made it even shorter for women.[40] Yet such materialism also enabled a new social mobility; the lawyer Barbier observed: 'today luxury is considerable and money is everything, all is confused in Paris, the well-off artisans and the rich merchants have risen above their station and are no longer to be counted among the people'.[41] As the bourgeois aped the wealthy financier, and the financier tried to imitate or even marry into the aristocracy, appearance was all: 'the increased confusion of the conditions and ways of life, the preponderance of the criteria of splendour and personal pleasure lead one to judge primarily on appearances'.[42] Boucher's portrait confirms the importance of appearances at this time, but how differently we view it on reading Mercier's description of how 'clerks, musicians, painters, engravers and poets buy woollen cloth, braid, and even lace; but they do not buy linen. A fine gentleman only puts on a clean shirt every fifteen days; he sews lace cuffs onto a dirty shirt, powders his neck to the point where one can see the mark on his velvet coat. There you have the Parisian in gross; he goes to the wigmaker every day; but to the laundry only once a month'.[43]

Artistic Trends during Boucher's Youth

Boucher was to become one of the masters of illusion, whose sensual vision continues to inform our ideas of eighteenth-century France today. But the brilliant surface, so convincing and beguiling, belies the material and artistic struggle behind it. As for most painters of the period, there is little information about Boucher's early artistic development; it is only once a person becomes famous that his activity is recorded.[44] The teenage years and early twenties would have been crucial to Boucher's formation as an artist, and although we have virtually no facts about his life in this period, we are able to describe the artistic milieu of contemporary Paris. Artistically, the later years of Louis XIV's reign were marked by the retreat from public virtue to private pleasure outlined above.[45] As the last great decorative team efforts of the school of Le Brun were completed at the church of the Invalides (1702–6) and the chapel at Versailles (1707–10), a series of more intimate royal retreats had been designed to provide respite from the punishing schedule of Court. Their interiors reflected a new mood of repose, intimacy and gallantry in contrast to the bombast of the Grand Château at Versailles. At the Grand Trianon, for example, the themes of Boucher and his contemporaries were anticipated in a series of twenty-seven canvases illustrating the loves of the gods from Ovid's *Metamorphoses*, painted by the fashionable artists of the day, including Charles de La Fosse (1636–1716), Jean Jouvenet (1649–1717) and Louis de Boullogne (1654–1733). Youth and fantasy were even more in evidence in the decorations at the *Ménagerie* for Louis XIV's grand-daughter-in-law, the duchesse de Bourgogne, mother of Louis XV, where pretty mythological overdoors and chimney-pieces mingled with humorous arabesques by Claude II Audran (1658–1734). This shift in painting from a medium of public display and message to one of private delight was articulated in the writings of the art theorist, Roger de Piles (1635–1709).[46] His work earned him honorary membership of the Academy and his aesthetic theories greatly influenced painting in the first half of the eighteenth century. It was De Piles who first clearly defined painting as an independent art whose main purpose was to charm the eye rather than satisfy the intellect. This in turn led him to stress its purely formal qualities.

De Piles's sensualist aesthetic fitted perfectly with the social and cultural developments in Paris. The intimate apartments of the new Parisian *hôtels*, or town-houses, were increasingly designed for comfort as much as show. Architects created

FIG.5
ANONYMOUS EIGHTEENTH-CENTURY FRENCH ARTIST, *View of the End Wall of the Second Cabinet of Jean de Jullienne*, c.1756, watercolour, detail, New York, Pierpont Morgan Library. 1966.8.f.50

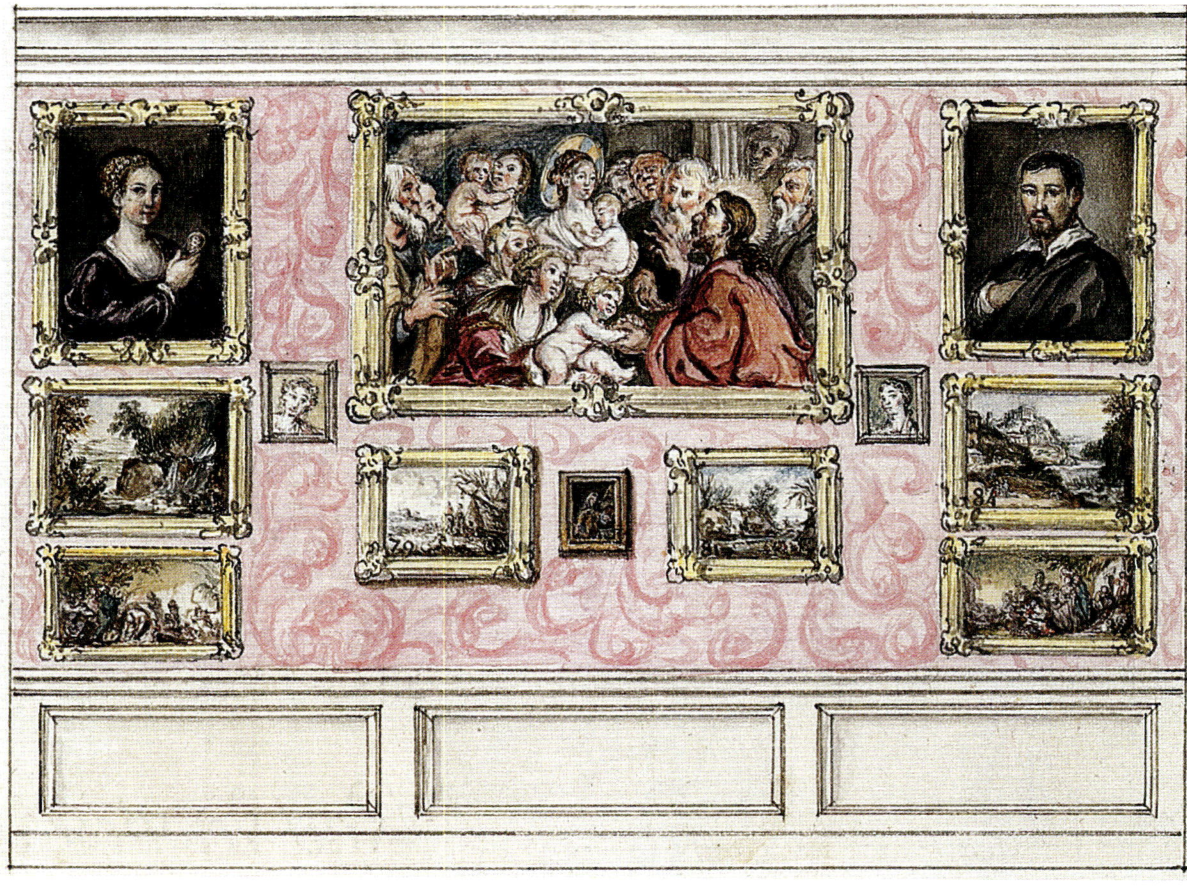

interiors with elegant architectonic panelling; painters, if not filling these panels with arabesques, provided decorative pictures for the spaces above doors and mirrors, and in the covings of ceilings.[47] Although evolving from a grander Italian and French Baroque tradition, painting in this context needed to match the new and lighter architecture and to discreetly attract the viewer's attention without upsetting the delicate balance of the ensemble. A separate room, the collector's *cabinet*, was set aside for the special appreciation of pictures acquired on the rapidly expanding art market. Here one might see many different types of painting hung together regardless of subject, almost frame to frame, in an arrangement where considerations of symmetry and overall effect were as important as the individual merits of any particular work (fig.5).[48] As in the Wallace Collection today, a picture competed with its neighbours for the viewer's interest, inviting judgements of technical merit. This focused attention on the formal abilities of the artist and encouraged the fashion for pictures with pleasing colours, surprising picturesque effects or exquisite surfaces such as those painted by the Dutch and Flemish in the seventeenth century.[49] Among the early eighteenth-century elite this stimulated the growth of connoisseurship, where the *honnête homme* could demonstrate his taste and discernment through his response to such works of art.[50] Some collectors and patrons, like the Regent, even took up art themselves – drawing in particular became part of an eighteenth-century lady's or gentleman's education.[51] In stressing the formal qualities of art, drawings and oil sketches also came to be appreciated, not just as mere preparations, but as independent works of art.[52] It is this attitude that lies behind the words of Voltaire quoted at the beginning of this book, and that led to the formation of private collections such as Pierre Crozat's.[53] Crozat came from a wealthy family of financiers and amassed a vast collection of drawings and paintings which artists and art lovers were welcome to consult. He held regular cultural gatherings in his hôtel in the rue de Richelieu and in his château at Montmorency, both noted for their congenial interior decorations by La Fosse and Jean-Antoine Watteau (1684–1721). The Venetian pastellist, Rosalba Carriera (1675–1757), describes an evening at Crozat's in her journal where, in addition to the Regent and Law, Watteau, Mariette, the comte de Caylus and M. and Mme Jullienne were present, all of whom were to prove influential in Boucher's career.[54]

Something of the ideal of connoisseurship is reflected in Watteau's *Shop Sign* painted for his friend, the dealer Edme Gersaint (fig.6).[55] Gersaint's aunt bought the picture and frame business 'At the Sign of the Great Monarch' for her nephew in 1718, on the occasion of his marriage to the daughter of one of Watteau's early dealers, Pierre Sirois.[56] When the ailing Watteau went to live with Gersaint briefly in 1720 he painted a sign as an advertisement for both his friend's shop and his own talent. The sign depicts the interior of Gersaint's shop with a portrait of Louis XIV being packed away; a reference not only to the name of the shop, now on the Pont Notre-Dame, but also to the replacement of the grand manner with the new styles of paintings adorning the shop walls. These include Flemish and Dutch-style landscapes and portraits, Venetian-looking mythologies and a prominent oval picture of nymphs being pored over by connoisseurs. Fashionably dressed shoppers gaze at themselves in a mirror while a gentleman gallantly invites a lady in from the street. Like Boucher's pastel portrait, it is an idealised image. In reality Gersaint's shop was a pokey affair, built in a muddy street on an overcrowded bridge within sight of the Grand Châtelet – 'the most stinking place that exists in the entire world', according to Mercier.[57] His stock lists reveal what Gersaint actually dealt in at this period: small anonymous religious pictures, the odd landscape and copies such as those Watteau himself had been forced to paint at the beginning of his artistic career in Paris, around the time of Boucher's birth. The contrast between the vision and the reality must have seemed extraordinary when the picture was exhibited outside Gersaint's shop for two weeks in 1720. Boucher would have

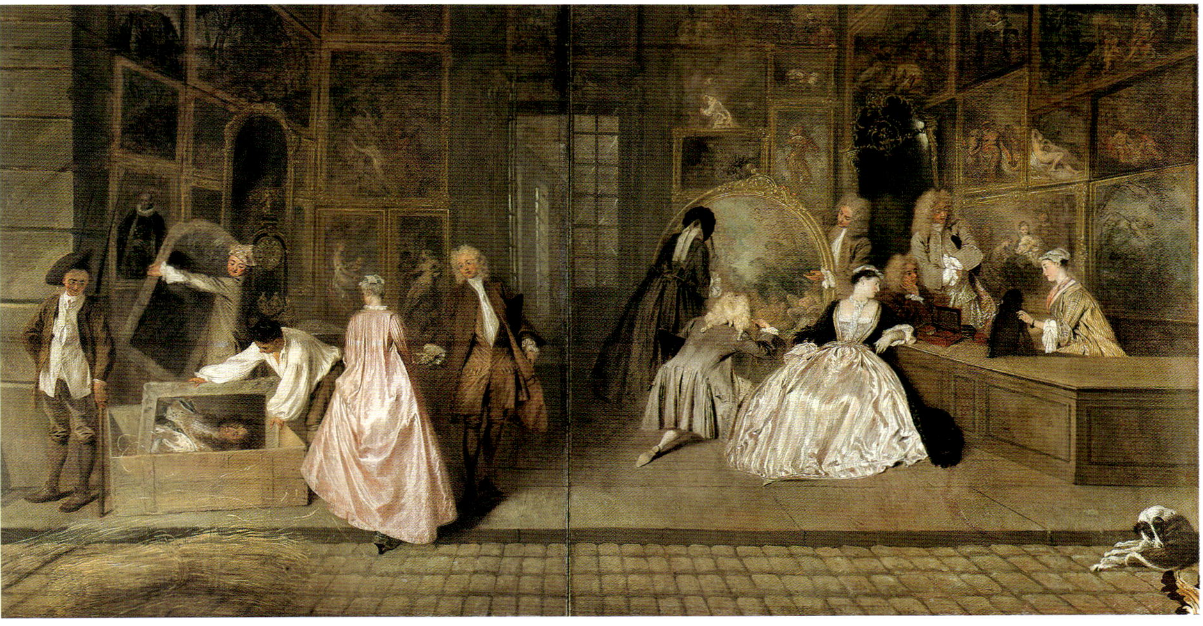

FIG.6
JEAN ANTOINE WATTEAU (1684–1721), *Gersaint's Shop Sign*, 1720–1, oil on canvas, 166 × 306cm, Berlin, Schloss Charlottenburg

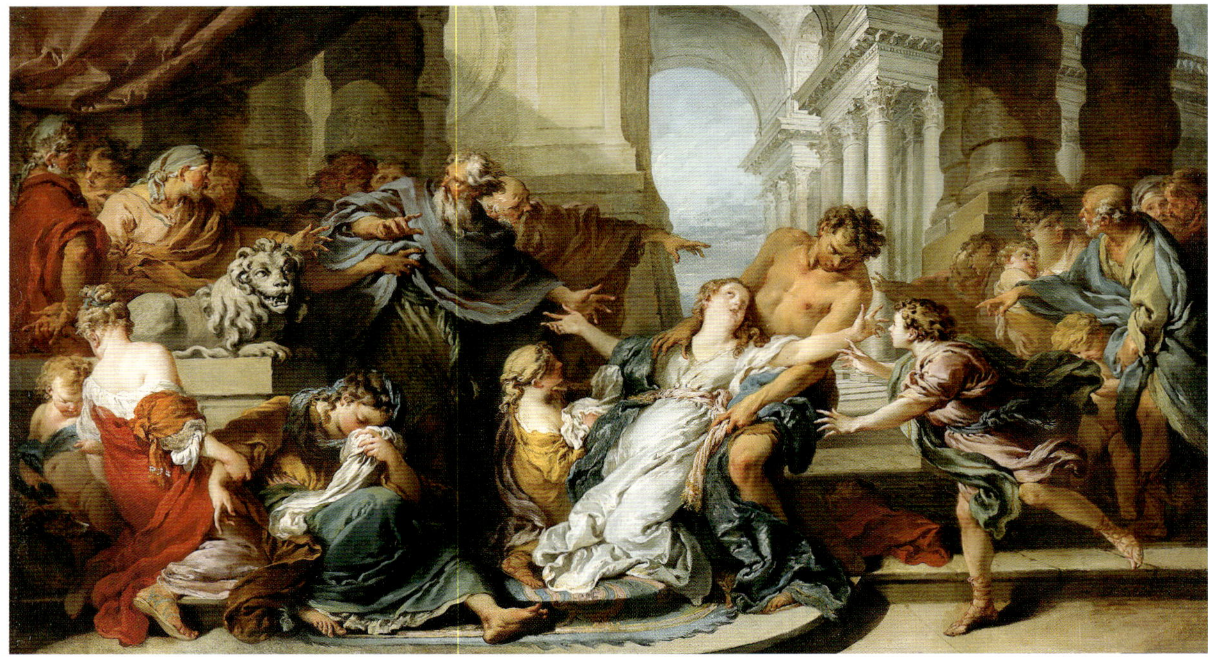

FIG.7
François Boucher (1703–1770), *The Judgement of Susannah*, *c.*1721, oil on canvas, 82.5 × 145.2cm, Ottawa, National Gallery of Canada

FIG.8 *opposite*
François Lemoine (1688–1737), *Perseus and Andromeda*, 1723, oil on canvas, 183 × 149.7cm, Wallace Collection

been seventeen at the time and it is tempting to believe that he saw the picture and, along with most artists of his generation, preferred the dream to the reality.

Boucher's Early Training

Watteau's example would have proved to Boucher that no matter how humble his birth the doors of salons such as Crozat's would open for talent. If he aimed beyond his father's world of the guild-system and the Pont Notre-Dame, at becoming a member of the Royal Academy and attracting royal patronage, riches and even ennoblement were possible.[58] An artist's initial training was not, however, easy. Chardin, who was four years older than Boucher, later complained bitterly about the apprenticeship young painters had to undergo: 'The chalk holder is placed in our hands at the age of seven or eight years. We begin to draw eyes, mouths, noses, and ears after patterns, then feet and hands. After having crouched over our portfolios for a long time, we're placed in front of the *Hercules* or the *Torso*, and you've never seen such tears as those shed over the *Satyr*, the *Gladiator*, and the *Medici Venus*, and the *Antinous* ...After having spent entire days and even nights, by lamplight, in front of an immobile inanimate nature, we're presented with the living thing and suddenly all the work of the preceding years seems reduced to nothing: it's as though one were taking up the chalk for the first time. The eye must be taught to look at nature; and many are those who've never seen it and never will.'[59] When Boucher was coming towards the end of his apprenticeship, *c.*1720, he painted his earliest known works: a series of small devotional images of which two, depicting *Saint Andrew* and *Saint Bartholemew*, survive in private collections.[60]

The next stage in an ambitious young artist's career was to train with a prominent member of the Academy, whose students had the right to compete for one of the Academy's prizes. The most prestigious, the *Prix de Rome*, was to encourage history painting, considered the highest branch of the profession because of the increased imaginative and intellectual demands it made of the artist.[61] The prize was an all expenses-paid trip to the French Academy in Rome. There the fledgling artist finished his education by looking at classical statuary and the great masters of Renaissance and Baroque painting. This prepared him, on his return to Paris, to become an associate member (*agréé*) and then a full member of the Academy (*reçu*) on presentation of a reception piece. The rising stars of the Academy in Boucher's youth were François Lemoine (1688–1737) and Jean-François de Troy (1679–52) and he appears to have studied with both. Restout, the author of one of the biographies published after Boucher's death, noted that 'a picture representing *The Judgement of Susannah*, that he did at the age of seventeen years, attracted the praise of Le Moine, who foretold great success for him'.[62] As most eighteenth-century commentators thought that Boucher was born in 1704 (including the artist himself, who told Mariette that he was sixty-three in 1767) this would date the picture (fig.7) to *c*.1721.[63] Not only is it an extremely assured painting for an eighteen-year old, but it also demonstrates an astute appeal to the formal canons of the Academy combined with an awareness of the latest trends. Taking the Old Testament subject of the false accusation of adultery made against Susannah, Boucher portrays the scene in a legible and dramatic manner, full of action and emotion as befitting a grand history painting. He deliberately quotes from the most eminent French models of the previous generation, the recently deceased La Fosse and Antoine Coypel (1661–1722), the First Painter to the King and Director of the Academy. The overall colouring and composition, however, evoke fashionable contemporary Venetian painters, especially Sebastiano Ricci (1659–1734), who had been in Paris in 1716 and accepted into the Academy in 1718, and Antonio Pellegrini (1675–1741), who had made repeated visits to Paris, 1719–21, to decorate the ceiling of the Royal Bank before it folded.

Impressed, Lemoine took Boucher into his studio, but despite the fact that Lemoine proved an important influence (fig.8), Boucher was later loath to acknowledge this.[64] Mariette recalls Boucher's own comments that 'although it is true that he studied under Lemoine, he did not profit much under such a master, who took little care of his students and with whom he stayed for such a short time'.[65] Boucher was happy to acknowledge Lemoine's skill, as shown by his later comments when asked to enlarge a Lemoine picture now in the Wallace Collection, *Time Revealing Truth*: 'I would be very wary; such works are like sacred vessels to me: I would fear to profane them by adding my hand'.[66] But, reading between the lines, it would appear that Boucher did not find the depressive and sarcastic Lemoine a congenial teacher. Mariette goes on to comment: 'M. Boucher assured me that he did not stay longer than three months with M. Lemoine. But of whom is he then the disciple?'[67] The sale catalogue of one of Boucher's main patrons, Sireul, gives us a clue in that it describes an '*Armida visiting Rinaldo during his sleep in the forest*. This picture is a sketch copied by M. Boucher after M. Detroy, while he was in his school'.[68] No other evidence of Boucher's time with De Troy exists and Boucher's biographers, keen to emphasize the original genius of their subject, insist that 'he owed everything to himself' and that 'Boucher was a born painter; they are few that surpass him in facility'.[69]

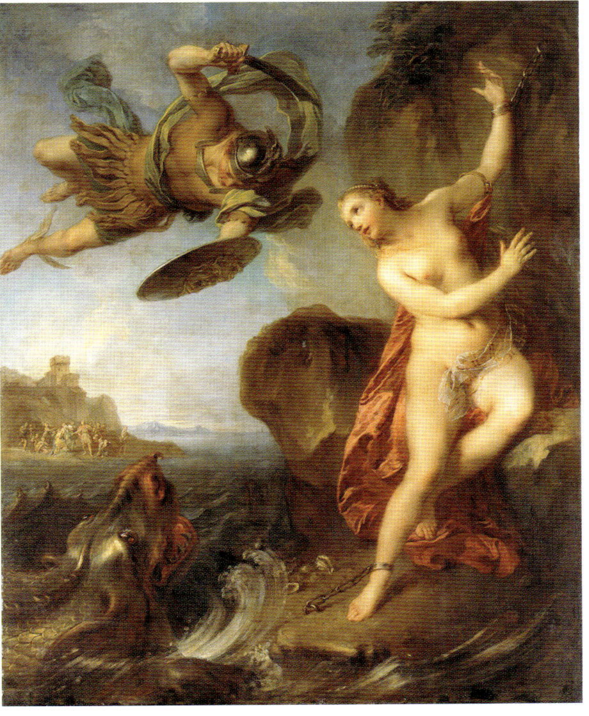

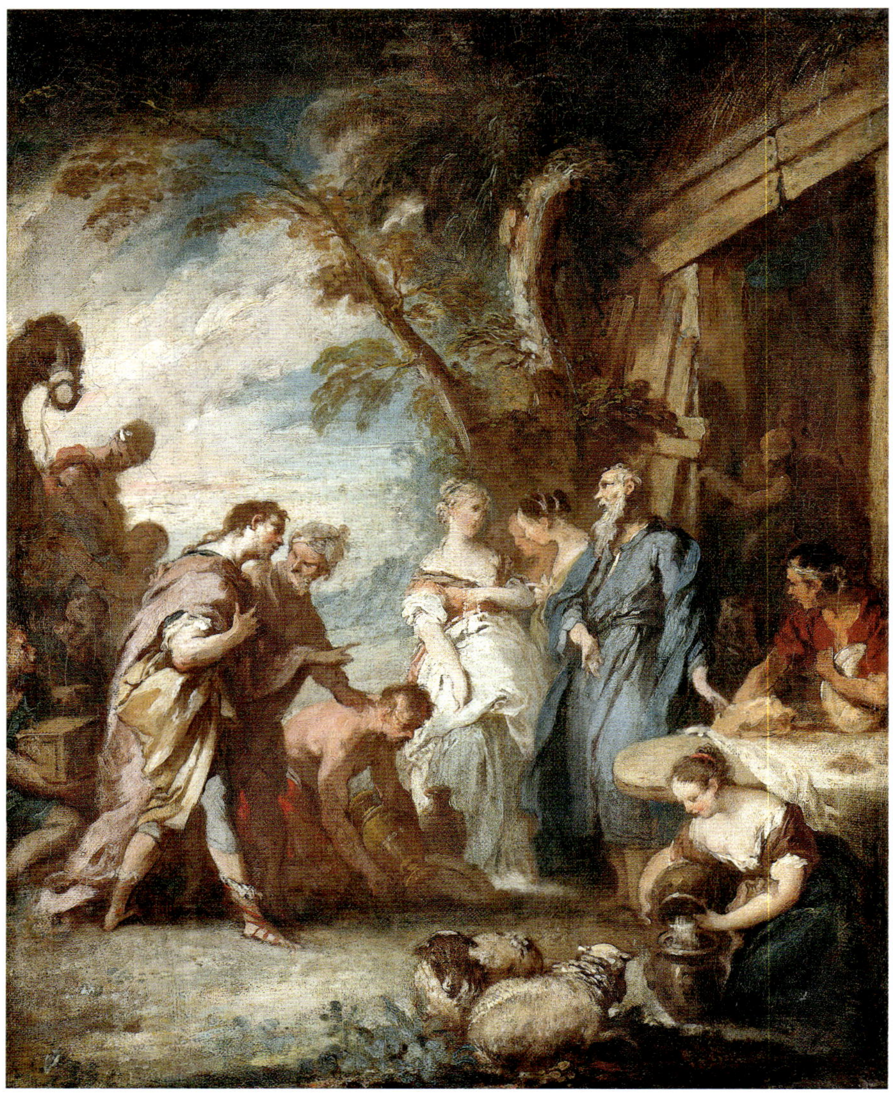

FIG.9
BOUCHER, *Bethuel Welcoming the Servant of Abraham*, c.1725, sketch, oil on canvas, 46.5 × 37cm, Paris, Musée du Louvre

Boucher was, however, listed as a pupil of Lemoine when he won the coveted *Prix de Rome* in 1723 with a now lost picture on the unusual subject of *Evilmerodach Releasing Jehoiachin from Prison*. Unluckily for Boucher, the *Surintendant des Bâtiments du Roi*, or Minister of the Arts, the duc d'Antin, had never heard of the young artist and a favourite was sent to Rome instead. As Cochin later noted, 'M. le duc d'Antin placed much importance on patronage … excellent students such as Vanloo, Boucher and others were passed over and not sent to Rome'[70]. This must have been a cruel disappointment and have provided an early lesson to Boucher that the professional artist in eighteenth-century France needed not only to be talented but also to court the right people. Thus when in 1743 the comte de Caylus tried to replace the young Cochin with Boucher on a commission to engrave the frontispiece for the *Mémoires de l'Académie Royale de Chirurgie* (*Memoirs of the Royal Academy of Surgeons*), Boucher sympathised with Cochin but also pointed out that 'it's your own fault; you never go to see M. Caylus'.[71] Meanwhile Boucher's ambition to move from the artisan world of his father into the professional world of the Academy was temporarily stalled. He continued to paint, but, rather than being commissioned to paint large decorative canvases or histories like a professional artist, Boucher was limited to painting small canvases in the hope of finding a purchaser on the open market.

As a non-member of the Academy, its official art exhibition, the Salon, was closed to him. He could, however, show his work at the Corpus Christi exhibition. This took place in the open air on the place Dauphine; it was open to all comers and a lively affair according to contemporary accounts: 'it is a most interesting picture to see on that day, at nine in the morning, a crowd of young artists, hardly out of their infancy, assembling in that place; one carries his own works under his arms himself, another follows with attention a porter who carries *his entire fortune*, and of whom he makes sure not to lose sight; all hang their pictures with care and thus abandon them to the judgement of the curious. The great masters, the Academicians are at the crossroads beneath the tapestries, and their presence further spurs on the emulation of the young folk. You will see them, down there, coming and going, examining all the faces, questioning all the eyes and catching all the indirect opinions that they receive from a crowd of art lovers whom they do not know and who reason each according to his own degree of knowledge'.[72] Before the regularisation of the Salon (held bi-annually from 1735), Academicians also regularly participated in the Place Dauphine exhibition; it was here, for example, that Lemoine exhibited *Perseus and*

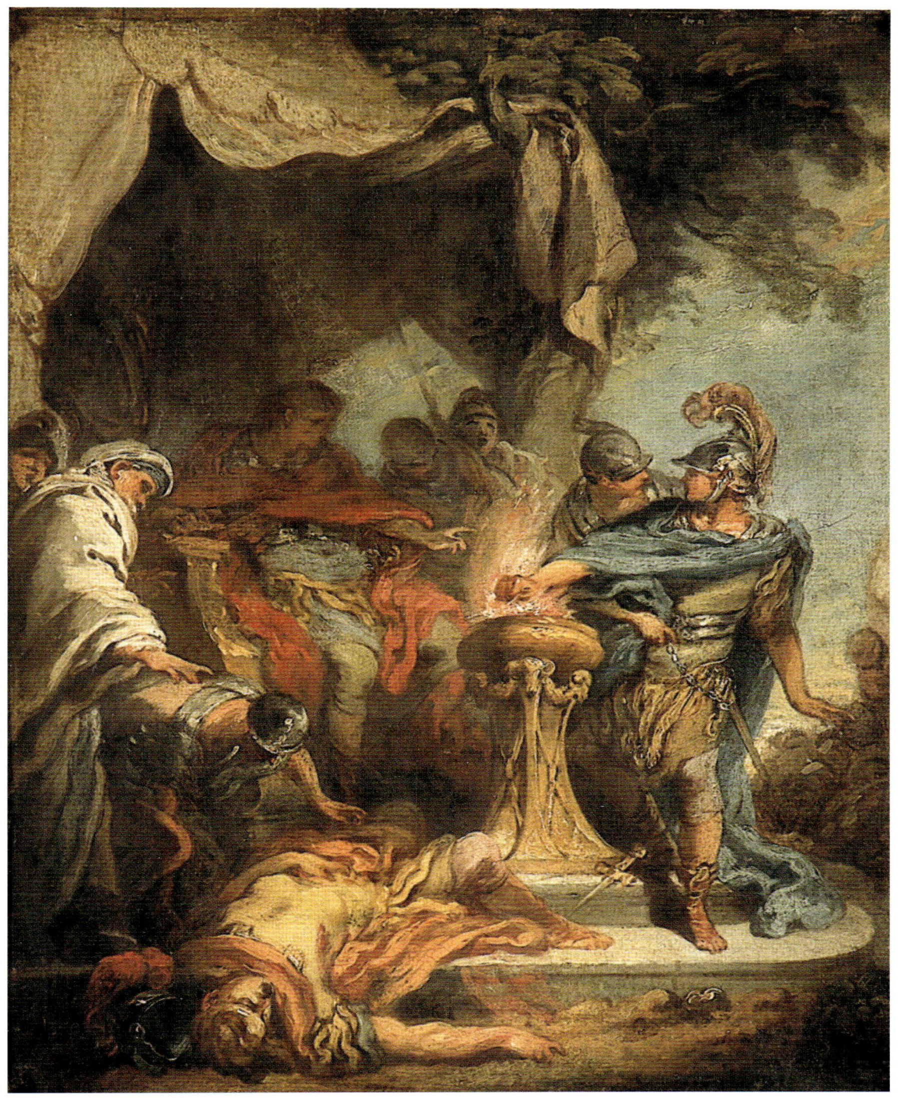

FIG.10
BOUCHER, *Mucius Scaevola putting his hand in the fire*, *c.*1727, oil on canvas, 59 × 48cm, Saint Omer, Musée de L'Hôtel Sandelin

Andromeda (fig.8) and a *Rebecca Receiving the Presents sent by Isaac* (lost) in 1723. The critic of the *Mercure de France*, reviewing the exhibition two years later, noted that 'one sees with pleasure lots of little pictures by sieur Boucher, pupil of sieur Lemoine, painted with a very good taste for colour, which makes one hope that this young man could excel in this art.'[73] Boucher's own version of the Old Testament story of Rebecca, with Abraham's servant being welcomed by her father, Bethuel (Strasbourg), may have been among this group.[74] Its small and jewel-like preparatory oil sketch (fig.9) reveals a tendency, following the contemporary taste for cabinet pictures, to concentrate on scintillating surface effects, and a tonality reminiscent of Pellegrini and of another Venetian artist, Pittoni (1687–1767), who may also have been in Paris *c.*1720.[75] The composition, with its elongated graceful figures set against a bright and atmospheric landscape with exotic slanting palms, is also influenced by Lemoine and, according to an early sale catalogue, the finished picture was painted under Lemoine's supervision.[76]

The Print-Maker's Apprentice

Although painting was where Boucher's main ambition lay, like many young artists he found it hard in these early years to make a living from his pictures alone and this impelled him to diversify. He was probably encouraged to do so by the example of his own father. Members of the Corporation of Painters could be found painting anything from devotional images to shop signs (considerably more modest than Watteau's), restoring pictures, dealing, and working in the print trade. Nicolas Boucher had been working as a draughtsman when he married Boucher's mother in 1698 and he may have been dealing in prints at the end of his life in the Place du Vieux Louvre.[77] So, according to Mariette, Boucher 'went to live with father Cars the engraver who printed and designed theses and who employed Boucher to do drawings for the plates that he then had engraved. He gave him board and lodging plus 60 *livres* a month, which Boucher then regarded as a fortune'.[78] By going to live with Jean-François Cars, the father of his future collaborator Laurent Cars (1688–1771), in the rue Saint-Jacques on the left bank, Boucher was plunged into the academic milieu around the university of the Sorbonne. In addition to thesis plates, Boucher also started to draw book illustrations, an activity for which his imagination fitted him perfectly. He continued to provide illustrations and frontispieces throughout his career, even when he certainly had no financial need to do so, and was careful to maintain contact with his friends in the print-trade long after his elevation to

FIG.11 *below*
BOUCHER, *Reclining female Nude seen from behind*, *c.*1725, black, red and white chalk on brown paper, 25 × 43cm, Paris, École Nationale Supérieure des Beaux-Arts

FIG.12 *opposite, above*
BOUCHER after WATTEAU, *Landscape*, 1728, etching, 17 × 23.2cm, London, British Museum

FIG.13 *opposite, below*
BOUCHER after CAMPAGNOLA, *Landscape in the Veneto*, *c.*1726, red chalk on cream paper, 22.2 × 34.9cm, Cambridge, Fitzwilliam Museum

the Academy, thereby ensuring the engraving and promulgation of his work. His practice as an illustrator was also a catalyst for his ideas in painting, tapestry and set design, and he proved adept at transferring images between all media. Although certainly not scholarly, he was not the untutored genius of popular legend: Boucher 'loved literature' and the company of literary men; at his death he owned a substantial library worth 6,843 *livres*.[79] As Papillon de La Ferté commented 'The prodigious quantities of sketches of sacred and profane subjects, which came from his hands, prove as much the richness of his imagination, as his literary knowledge'.[80]

One of the projects Boucher worked on during this period was the illustrations for a new edition of père Gabriel Daniel's *L'Histoire de France depuis l'établissement de la Monarchie française* (*The History of France since the Establishment of the French Monarchy*).[81] This was advertised in 1727 and published two years later, so the album of lively little pen and wash drawings Boucher produced for the project (Louvre) is dateable *c.*1726–7.[82] That this was Boucher's first recorded book commission is in keeping with the growing interest in history during the Enlightenment, where the past was analysed in much the same way as far-away cultures in an attempt to increase knowledge and ensure material progress. Analysis of dealer's stock, such as Gersaint's, reveals that in addition to the usual religious tomes he also sold increasing numbers of history books (as well as a discreet number of risqué novels from under the counter).[83] So it is not surprising to find that Boucher tried his hand at painting vivid episodes of classical history such as *Mucius Scaevola* thrusting his right hand into the flames to demonstrate his fidelity to the Roman Republic in the face of the enemy king, Porsenna (fig.10).[84]

Watteau, Boucher and the Cult of Celebrity

Boucher's *Prix de Rome* disappointment brought unexpected advantages: not just the extra string that working with the print trade added to Boucher's artistic bow, but also the opportunity it gave the young history painter to study a model normally beneath the attention of those studying

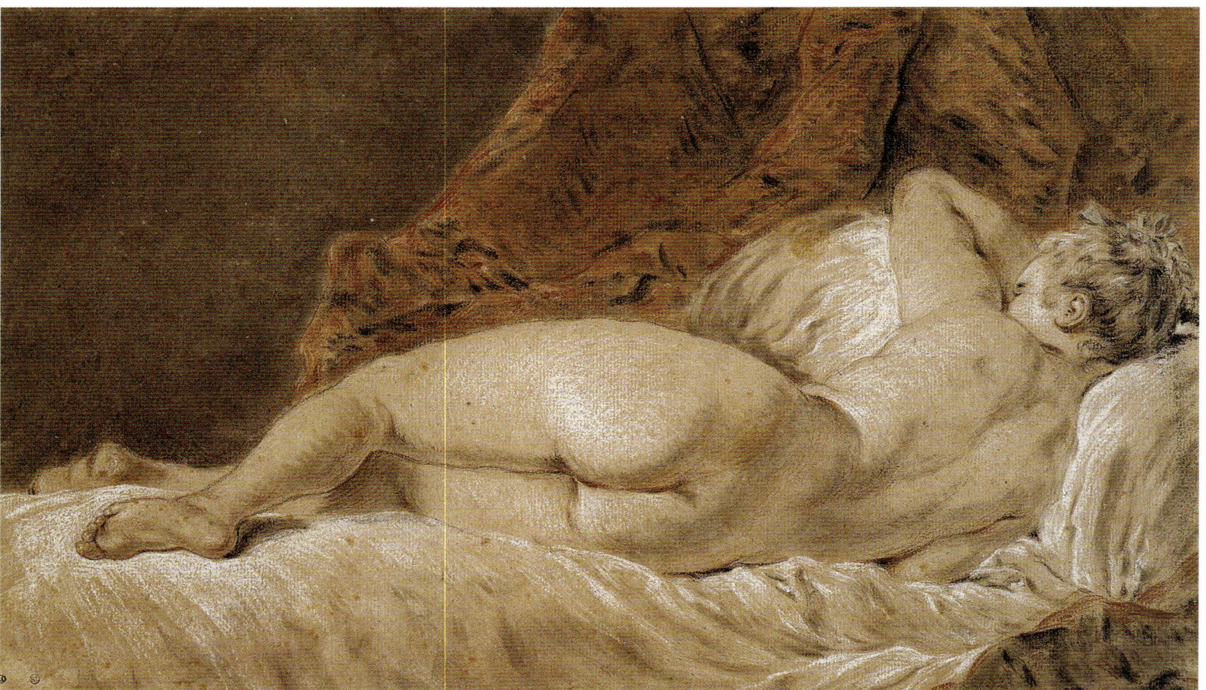

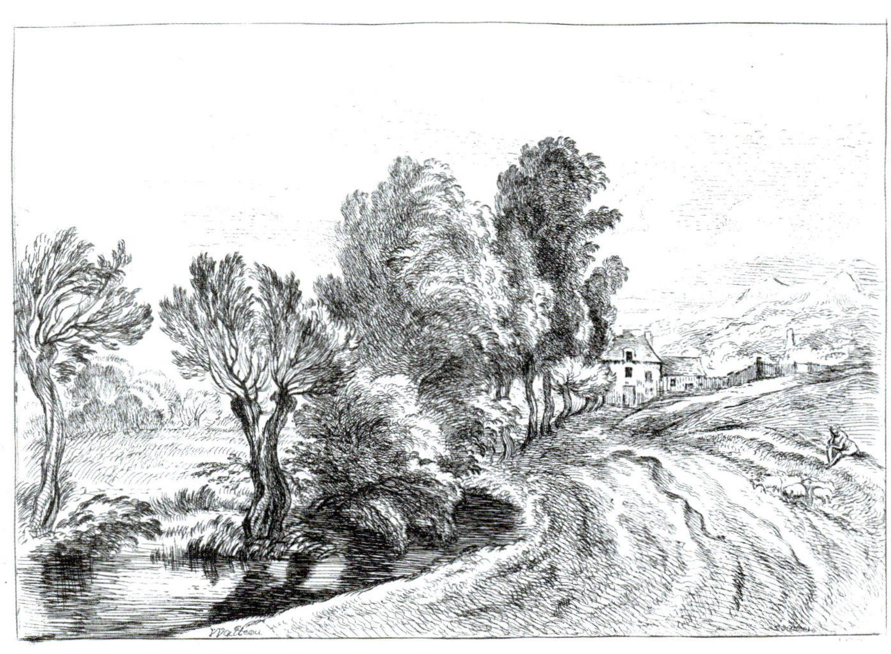

for the *grand genre* in the 1720s. As Mariette records: 'he soon got to know M. de Jullienne who, wanting to have Watteau's drawings engraved, distributed many of them to Boucher, who acquitted himself perfectly well. His light, spirited touch seemed made for this work. M. Jullienne gave him 24 *livres* a day, and both were content, because Boucher was very fast, and engraving was just a game to him'.[85] Jean de Jullienne (1686–1766), whose fortune derived from his cloth and dying business and who from 1718 was Director of the Gobelins tapestry manufactory, was a friend of Watteau's and a collector-dealer of his works. After Watteau's death in 1721 Jullienne conceived the idea of having all of his friend's works, both drawings and paintings, engraved as a monument to their friendship, ensuring Watteau's fame and increasing market value. The *Recueil Jullienne*, as it became known, was the first complete visual catalogue raisonné of an artist's oeuvre, very much in tune with the Enlightenment taste for cataloguing and classifying, as seen in the work of the natural historian, Linnaeus, or the encyclopedists, Diderot and D'Alembert. Boucher etched 119 out of 350 plates of the *Figures de différents caractères de Paysage, et d'Etudes dessinées d'après nature par Antoine Watteau*, the prints after Watteau's

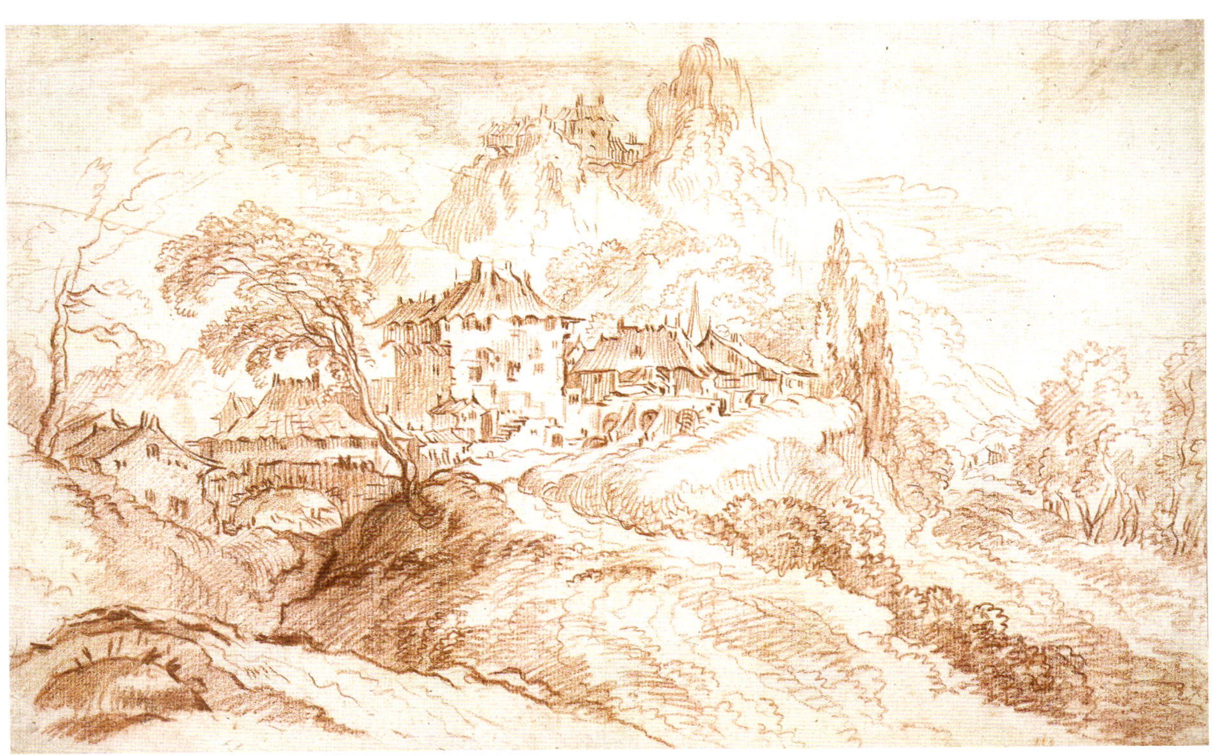

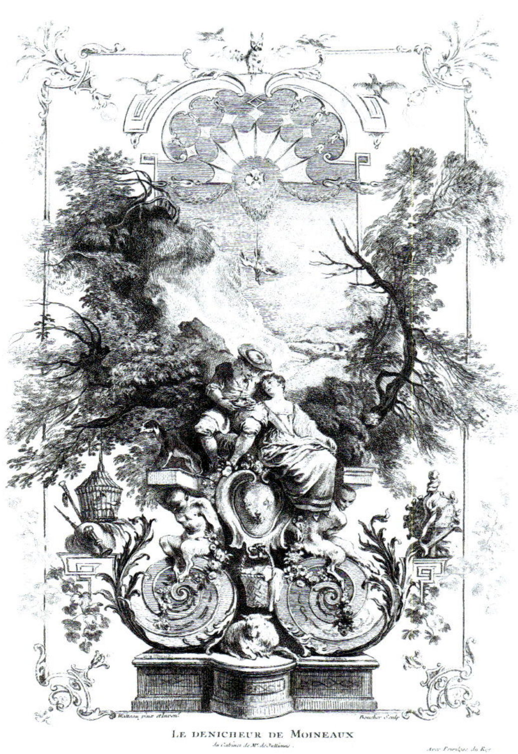

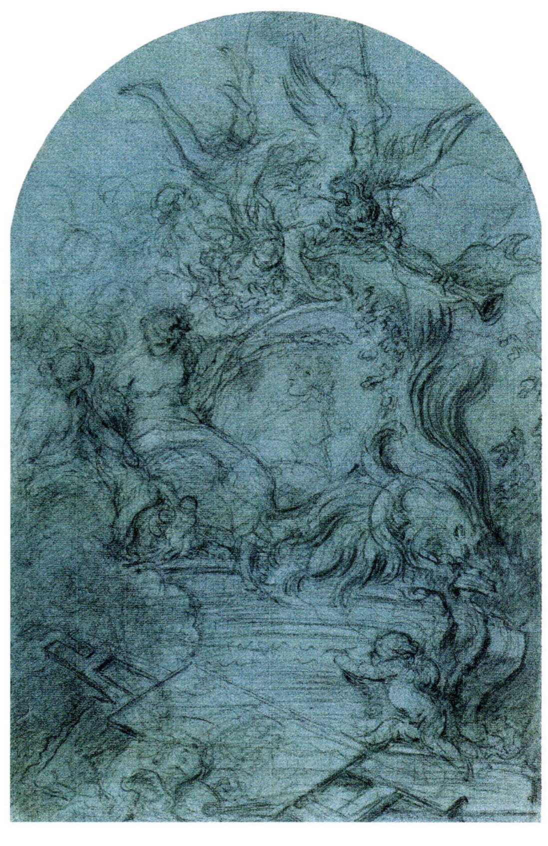

FIG.14 *right*
BOUCHER after WATTEAU, *The Sparrow-Nesters*, 1727, etching, 40.5 × 28cm, London, British Museum

FIG.15 *far right*
BOUCHER, *The Graces at the Tomb of Watteau*, *c*.1725–6, black and white chalk on blue paper, 46.2 × 27.6cm, Windsor, Collection H.M. The Queen

FIG.16 *opposite*
BOUCHER after WATTEAU, *Portrait of Watteau*, 1727, etching, 33.3 × 23cm, London, British Museum

drawings published in two volumes in 1726 and 1728. He worked on 5 etchings after Watteau's paintings, printed in 1727 and subsequently gathered together into *L'Oeuvre d'Antoine Watteau*, and another four arabesque designs of *The Four Seasons*.[86] He also etched 12 of the 30 *Figures Chinoises*, after Watteau's chinoiserie decorations for the château of La Muette which, although published in 1731, had probably been completed before his trip to Italy.[87] Watteau, after his death, became Boucher's most important teacher. Boucher may even have helped Watteau's former pupil, Pater (1695–1736), to complete some of Watteau's last works, which remained unfinished following his untimely death at the age of thirty seven.[88] One wonders to what extent Boucher himself might actually have also identified with Watteau. Coming from a modest background, Watteau, too, had failed to make the longed-for journey to Rome despite winning second prize in the *Prix de Rome* in 1709. Nonetheless he went on to attract a prestigious clientele and became a member of the Academy, as a painter of *fêtes galantes*, in 1717. Watteau's interest in the quotidian, his love of fashion, his observation of the mores of *honnêteté* and his technical finesse in both painting and drawing were to have a profound influence on Boucher, ultimately helping him to succeed where Watteau had failed: in inventing a seductive historical idiom in tune with developing rococo fashions.

Watteau's influence is clearly seen in a number of drawings produced by Boucher around this time, some previously wrongly attributed to Watteau, where Boucher experiments with the more sensual chalk techniques used by Watteau. Boucher's drawing of the *Reclining female Nude seen from behind* is drawn in Watteau's favourite three-crayon manner of black, red and white chalk on brown paper (fig.11) and shows Boucher trying to imitate Watteau's staccato strokes especially in the hair and drapery.[89] The subject recalls Watteau's life studies of semi-clad women as well as his pictures of contemporary nudes such as *The Remedy* (Norton Simon Museum) and *The Toilette* in the Wallace Collection.[90] Boucher already prefers to depict a more voluptuous figure type, while the viewpoint from behind the model, full of suggestive possibilities, allows him to concentrate on her ample bottom; one of the parts of the female anatomy that attracted him the most throughout his career. The somewhat uncertain anatomy, however, underlines the fact that Boucher would have had limited opportunities to draw from live models at this point, as he was not a member of the Academy.

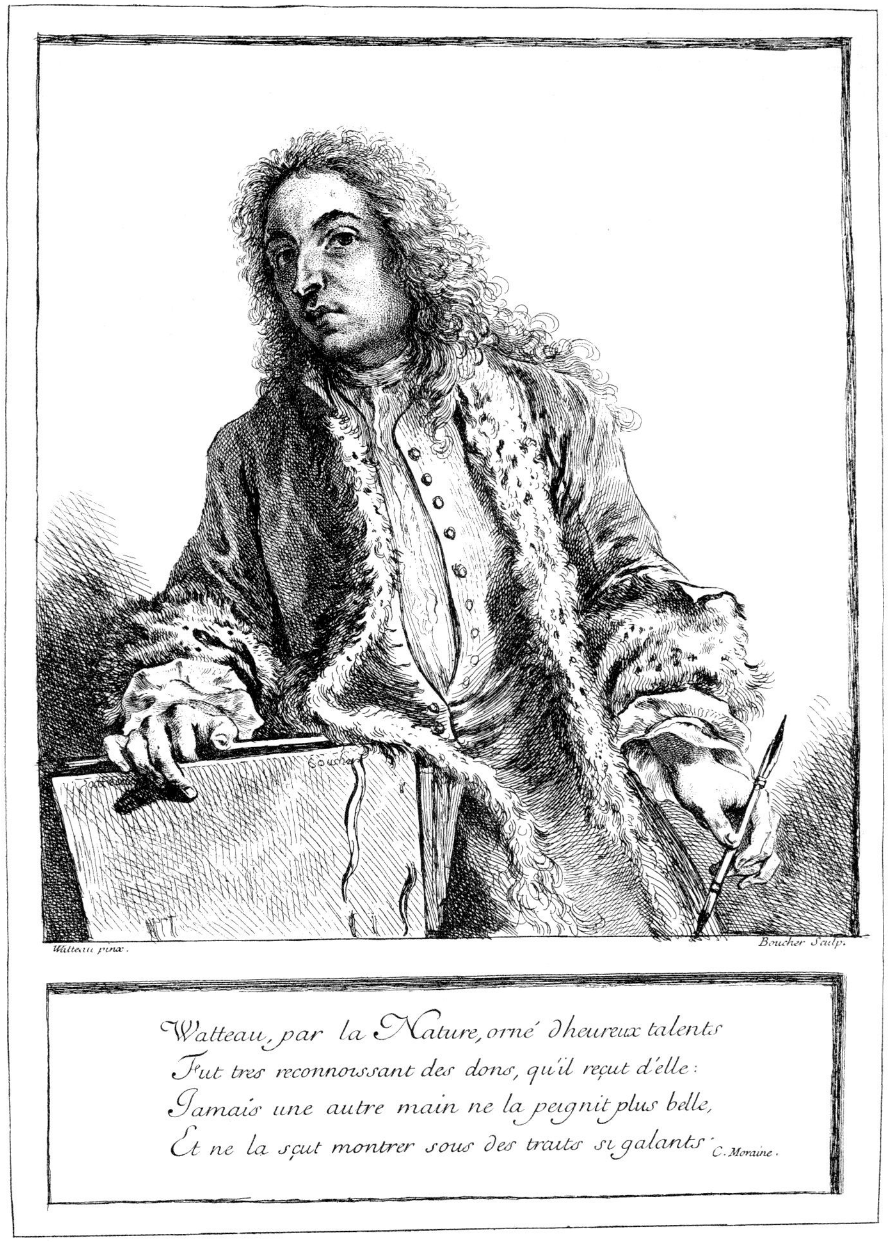

All the landscapes in the *Figures de différents caractères* were etched by Boucher, unlike the figure studies, which were engraved by a variety of artists. Boucher was acknowledged as the specialist in this genre; following Watteau's example he came to study landscape more thoroughly and in many different guises. Watteau was born in the Franco-Flemish border town of Valenciennes and was actually described as a Flemish artist in the dedicatory poem of the *Figures*. Among the landscapes Boucher engraved, many were extremely northern in character and helped Boucher to absorb such influences into his own work. No. 167 (fig.12) from the second volume of the *Figures*, for example, depicts a muddy track with a pond, pollard willows, bushy trees and a distant view of a cottage, all archetypal elements of the seventeenth-century Dutch landscapes Boucher would later collect. Boucher was also inspired to study Venetian landscape drawing, especially Campagnola (1500–64), through Watteau's example. Watteau had studied such drawings in Crozat's collection and Boucher did the same, although Boucher's interpretations are noticeably more fluid and picturesque.[91] The landscape in the Fitzwilliam Museum (fig.13) was copied by Boucher after an etching by the comte de Caylus after a drawing by Campagnola (Louvre). Its Italiannate character in turn recalls the landscape, no.8, etched by Boucher for the first volume of Jullienne's *Figures*.[92] Such Venetian-inspired landscapes also reappear in the backgrounds of Boucher's *Tame Sparrow* (*c.*1730; lost) and *The Geese of Brother Philippe* (*c.*1727; Besançon), notable for the Watteauesque charm of its female figures.[93] The further transformation of the northern rustic view of nature into the quintessentially French *champêtre* approach, which links Watteau's *fêtes galantes* to the *genre pittoresque* Boucher was to practise in the 1730s, can clearly be seen in one of Boucher's etchings, *The Sparrow-Nesters*, etched for *L'Oeuvre d'Antoine Watteau* (fig.14). This demonstrates the commercial uses to

FIG.17
BOUCHER, *Study of a Cockerel*, *c.*1727–8, black, red and white chalk on brown/grey paper, 17 × 20cm, Stockholm, Nationalmuseum.

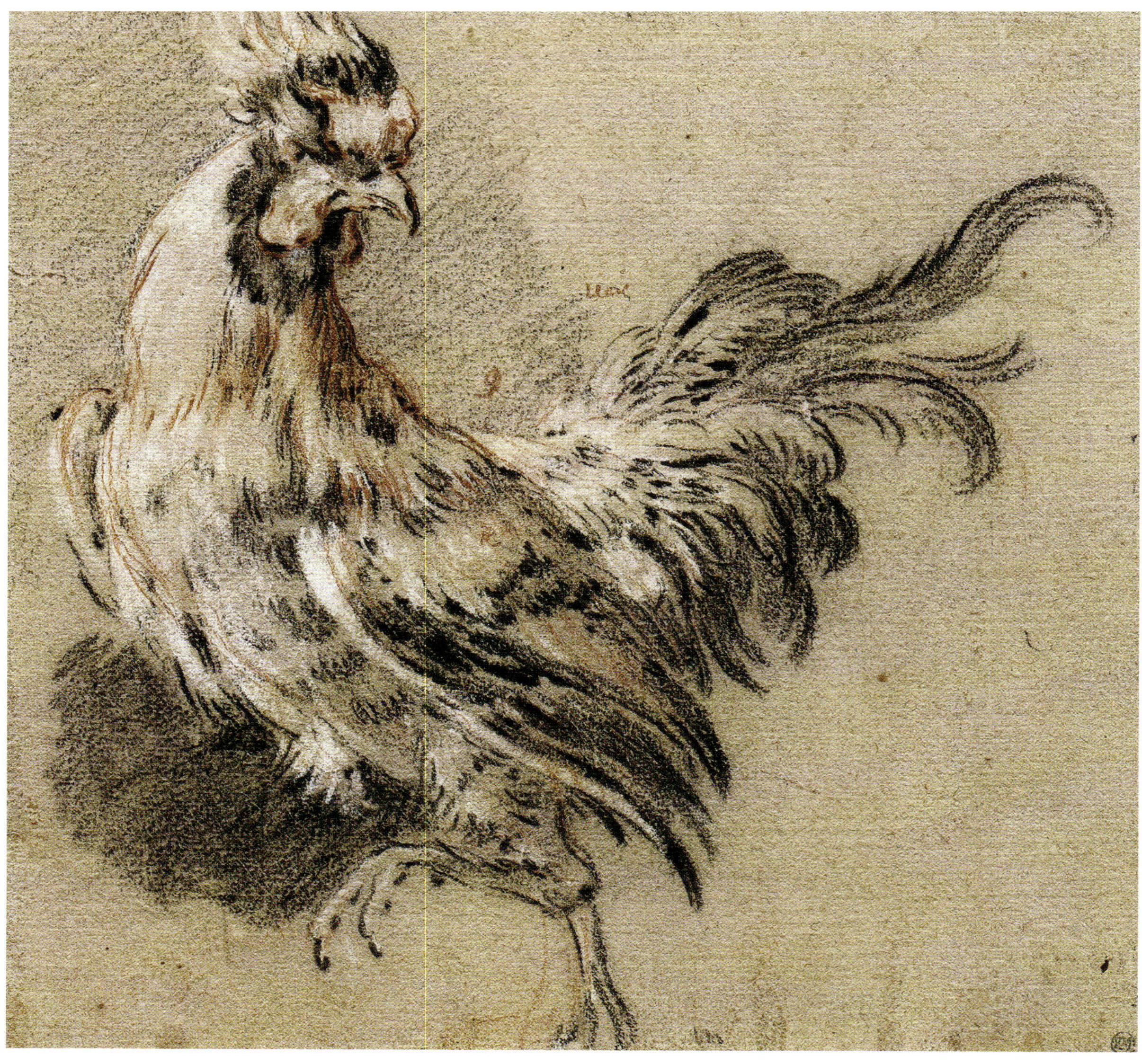

which *recueils*, or groups of engravings of this sort, could be put; they were perfect for reproduction in the decorative arts, and indeed the top of the arabesque that surrounds *The Sparrow-Nesters* is just visible on a screen in the background of Jean-François de Troy's *Reading from Molière* (fig.49).

Boucher also engraved two frontispieces for the two volumes of the *Figures de différents caractères*; one after Watteau and one after a design of his own. His preparatory drawing for the frontispiece of volume II, *The Graces at the Tomb of Watteau* (fig.15), again shows the decorative arts milieu with which Boucher was coming into contact through his work for the print trade. The swirling movement, curling fronds of vegetation and playful putto of Boucher's drawing recall the development of rococo design seen in the work of the ornamentalist, Juste-Aurèle Meissonnier (1695–1750), who was later to serve as godfather to Boucher's son.[94] Working in the rue Saint-Jacques, Boucher would have become aware of the connection between the wider audience reached by the print trade and the creation of artistic reputation.[95] He seems to have foreseen the fame the wide dissemination of Watteau's work through engravings would bring and, when he etched the frontispiece for the first volume of the *Figures de différents caractères* (print published in 1727), he featured his own name prominently (fig.16). Not only are the names of Watteau and Boucher placed below the image in the conventional manner, with Watteau as the original artist on the left and Boucher as the engraver on the right, but Boucher has also incorporated the names within the image itself. Half in shadow to the left of Watteau's hand on the portfolio is Watteau's name while to the right in full view is Boucher's. It almost looks as if the portfolio belongs to Boucher rather than Watteau, and stakes his claim to be Watteau's artistic heir.

Boucher also arranged for some of his own pictures to be engraved, namely the set of fifteen small devotional images painted at the beginning of the 1720s, which were published in 1726 by one of Boucher's collaborators on the *Figures Chinoises*, Edme Jeaurat (1688–1738).[96] As no contracts have been discovered between Boucher and his engravers, it is not clear how much Boucher stood to gain financially from such collaborations. The fact that he later publicly denounced the engraver Duflos for stealing his images suggests, however, that he normally received a percentage of the profits, as well as the right to control the quality of the reproductions.[97] Ensuring his drawings and paintings were reproduced in print would gain Boucher a wider audience than the picture trade. In addition to the trade audience, who proved highly receptive and adept at copying Boucher's designs onto a variety of media from screens to porcelain and from gold boxes to textiles, Jeaurat's print series shows how Boucher also aimed to break into the increasing market of bourgeois print buyers.

Working as a draughtsman-engraver for Jullienne would have brought Boucher into regular contact with the collector and his milieu, and he naturally exploited the situation by trying to impress Jullienne with his painterly skills. This explains the presence of two early Bouchers in Jullienne's collection, which we can just see on the view of the end wall of the second cabinet (fig.5). Boucher's *The Sacrifice of Noah* and *Noah Entering the Ark* balance each other at the extreme bottom left and right of the wall.[98] They vie for attention with two landscapes by Bril (1554–1626), two portraits by Annibale Carracci (1560–1609) above them, a large Nativity ressembling Jordaens (1593–1678) in the centre, two small pastel heads by Boucher just visible to either side and below, two landscapes by Wouwermans (1619–68) flanking a tiny self-portrait by Watteau.[99] Painted on panel with a bright sparkling finish, they deliberately aim to complement Jullienne's beloved Dutch and Flemish pictures.[100] They include lively and picturesque

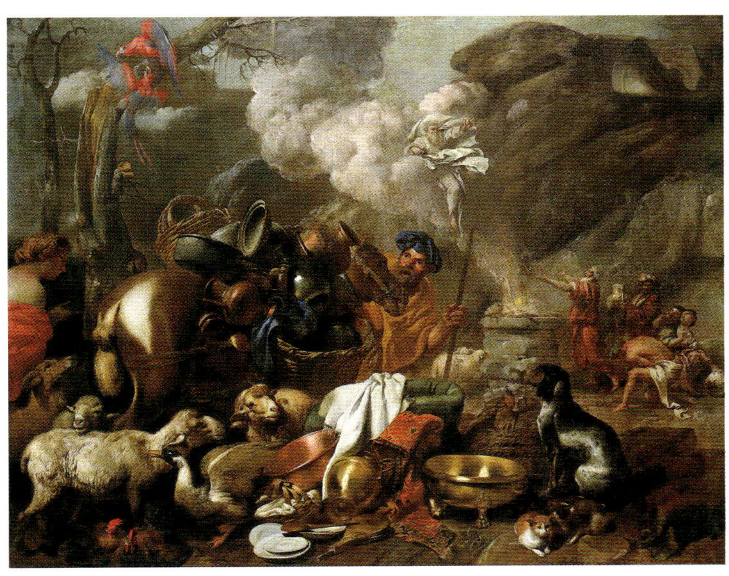

FIG.18 *below, left* GIOVANNI BENEDETTO CASTIGLIONE (1609–1664), *The Sacrifice of Noah*, *c.*1640, oil on canvas, 106 × 133cm, Genoa, Palazzo Bianco

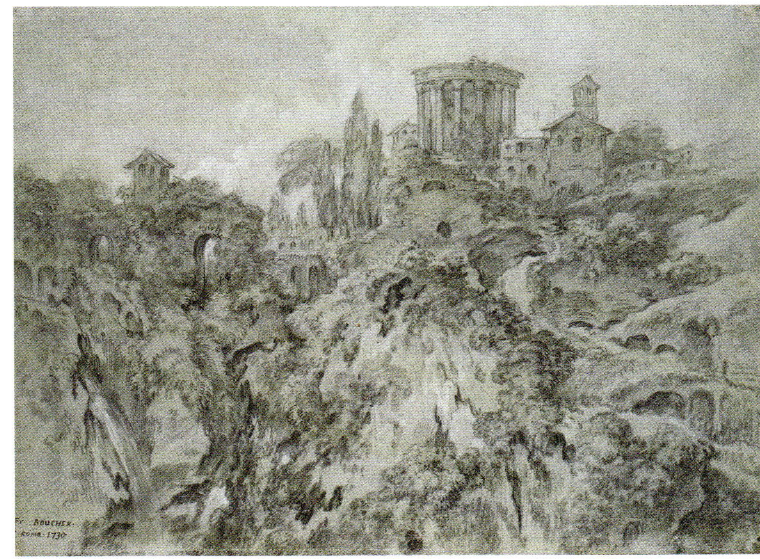

FIG.19 *below, right* BOUCHER, *The Circular Temple at Tivoli*, 1730, black and white chalk, stumped on blue paper, 30.4 × 40.6cm, Amsterdam, Rijksmuseum

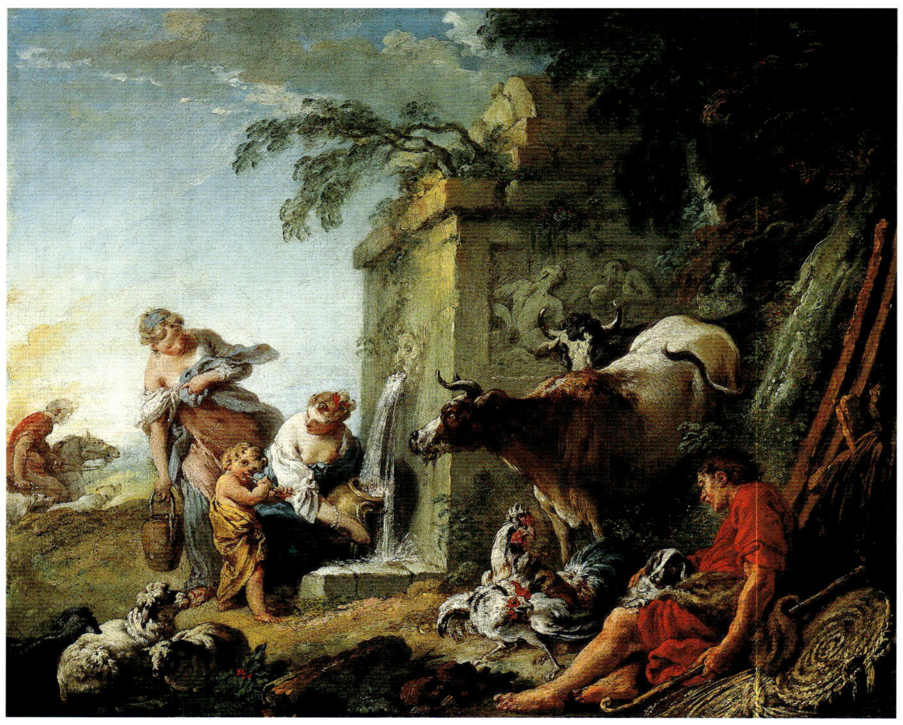

FIG.20
BOUCHER, *La Fontaine*, *c.*1730, oil on canvas, 54 × 65cm, Louisville, The J.B. Speed Art Museum, Mrs Blakemore Wheeler Fund, 1969.12

details such as cooking utensils and copper pans similar to those in the work of Teniers (1610–90), while a hen and cockerel, which seem to be copied from nature, are actually taken from a picture by the Dutchman, Hondecoeter (1636–95; fig.17).[101] Dezallier d'Argenville in 1727 claimed that 'the Flemish are the only real painters, and if their drawing were as accomplished as their colour they would be the leading painters of the universe'.[102] Boucher then adds the excitement of Venetian colouring to this northern template. The pictures are distinguished by a bright turquoise tonality, accented with splashes of red and yellow, while their compositions and subjects recall an artist who worked in Venice in the seventeenth century, Giovanni Benedetto Castiglione (1609–64; fig.18), whose rustic processions were to become a recurrent theme in Boucher's work.[103]

Boucher in Italy

Such were Boucher's artistic influences and the type of work that enabled him to save up enough money to finance his study trip to Italy in 1728. It seems, however, that Boucher's arrival in Rome with Carle Van Loo (1705–65) and his nephews, Louis-Michel (1707–71) and François (1708–32), came as something of a surprise to Vleughels (1668–1737), then Director of the French Academy. He wrote to the duc d'Antin on the 27 May that 'there came with Srs Vanloo (who should have arrived) a young man who has quite a bit of talent; he is so open and he shows much promise. It will be a pleasure to try to help him as it will be with the others'.[104] He wrote again a few days later that 'there is also [a student] called Boucher, a simple lad with lots of merit; I've stuck him in a little hole of a room, nearly outside the house ... it's true it's only a hole; but it's covered'.[105] Little wonder, perhaps, that Boucher soon fell ill; as Papillon de La Ferté noted in his biography of the artist: 'during the time that he stayed there, the poor state of his health prevented him from doing all the studies that were proposed to him. He could not even work on the subject that was given to the young artists, in order to compete for the grand prix that the Pope gave out at the Capitole'[106]. Mariette, presumably informed by Boucher himself, claimed that in any case Boucher went to Italy 'more to satisfy his curiosity than to gain any real profit. Also he did not stay long in that country'.[107] In this way Boucher's biographers, with their tendency to stress the natural genius and originality of their hero, underplay the fact that Boucher actually spent about three years in Italy, probably studying not only in Rome but in Venice and Florence as well. More and more copies by Boucher after Italian originals are now being recognized. In contrast, however, to the classical and Renaissance models a regular student at the Academy would have been set to copy, Boucher's works reveal that, avid for ideas he could translate into his own art for fashion-conscious Paris, he was attracted more to the sensual and decorative art of the Italian Baroque. What Boucher found in the work of artists such as Baciccio (1639– 1709), Bassano (*c.*1510/18–92), Bernini (1598–1680), Caravaggio (1571–1610), Guercino (1591–1666), Lanfranco (1582–1647), Solimena (1657–1747) and above all

FIG.21
BOUCHER, *The Rural Life*, *c*.1730, oil on canvas, 61 × 48cm, Lincolnshire, Belton House, National Trust

Pietro da Cortona (1596–1669), was not only a useful repertoire of forms from which he would quote throughout his life, but also a compositional monumentality, achieved through the sophisticated interplay of light, shade and colour, which had been lacking in his work to date.[108] No wonder, then, that Boucher's final advice to his pupil, Mannlich, setting off for Rome forty years later, was to look more to Baroque models like Albani (1578–1660) and Reni (1575–1642) than to Raphael (1483–1520) or Michelangelo (1475–1564): 'Raphael despite his great reputation is a sad painter, and Michel Angelo makes one cry ... look at them, but I would not advise you to imitate them, you would become cold as ice'.[109]

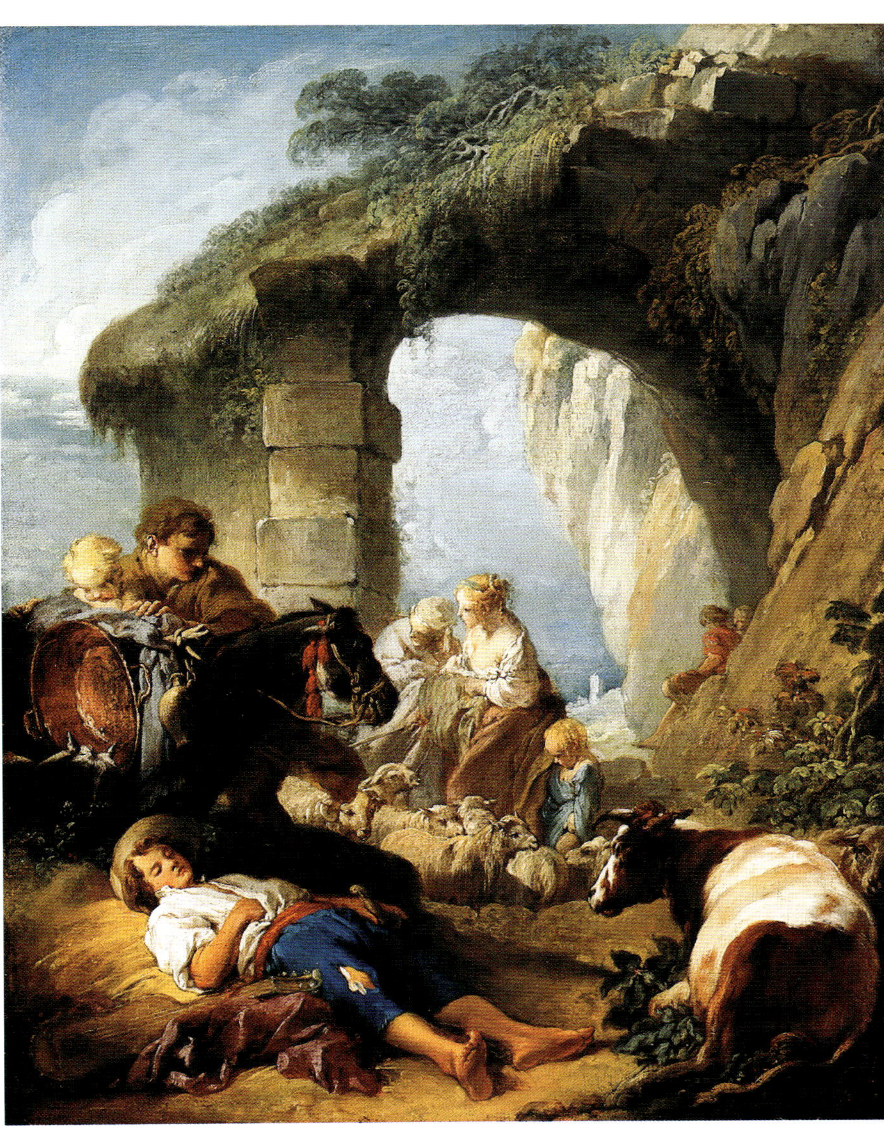

Baroque art was not the only major influence on Boucher at this period. Vleughels, an old friend of Watteau's and advocate of *plein-air* landscape drawing, encouraged his students to go out into the suburbs of Rome and sketch landscape from nature. Despite his extensive study of northern and Venetian landscape paintings and drawings, it was probably the first time the inveterate city-dweller Boucher had actually gone outside and drawn from the real thing. Along with his fellow-students, he produced a series of black chalk drawings on blue paper of the most picturesque monuments in the environs of Rome (fig.19), which he would later re-use as the basis for decorative landscape compositions in paintings and tapestries.[110] Something of his excitement at this encounter with nature is captured in a paradoxically artificial drawing, *The Genius of the Artist Torn Between Nature and the Antique* (whereabouts unknown).[111] It shows a languid youth reclining in bored reverie against a classical plinth while Venus's emissaries, the amours, beckon him to follow a jolly procession out into the countryside. Despite advocating the superior claims of nature, it is a vision based on a well known etching by Castiglione, *The Genius of Castiglione*. The procession, too, reminds us of Castiglione's own rustic cavalcades, which Boucher now could study at first hand, as well as the Italian's fluid handling which helped Boucher to broaden his own painterly technique.

It was also during this period that Boucher and his fellow-students encountered another influential model who was to provide a mine of picturesque motifs that could be used to enliven landscapes, namely the Dutch painter Abraham Bloemaert (1564–1651). It appears that Boucher and his colleagues had access in Rome to a sketch-book of Bloemaert's, containing numerous studies of rural figures, which Boucher and his fellow-students copied.[112] In 1735, after his return to Paris, Boucher typically used these to his commercial advantage, publishing a set of engravings after his copies called the *Livre d'Étude d'après les Dessins*

FIG.22 *opposite*
BOUCHER, *Hercules and Omphale*, *c*.1730, oil on canvas, 90 × 74cm, Moscow, Pushkin Museum

Originaux de Blomart.[113] The influence of Bloemaert and Castiglione's rustic oeuvre on Boucher's work at this period is combined in a series of 'precious little pictures, in the Flemish manner' which Papillon de La Ferté described Boucher painting in Rome.[114] *The Fountain* (fig.20) incorporates a Bloemaert-like seated young man with a staff, plus the Hondecoeter cockerel (fig.17) and hen and other animals apparently drawn from life.[115] The smaller figures of the women and child on the left are comparable to the picturesque little figures found in Vleughels's paintings, while the jumble of people, objects, animals and fluid handling are reminiscent of Castiglione.[116] The subject itself, a gathering at a public fountain, in contrast to the fragile inventions of Watteau, is given a new physicality, reflecting the lively Italian scenes Boucher probably observed while sketching fountains such as Bernini's at the Palazzo Antamaro in Rome.[117] Comparable in approach and handling is *The Rural Life* (fig.21).[118] 'Immature artists imitate, mature artists steal', as Lionel Trilling remarked, and while quoting from Bloemaert for the sleeping figure in the foreground and recalling Castiglione in the group with the heavily laden mule, Boucher's picture has a charm of its own. The appeal of such exquisite rustic visions, even outside Boucher's intended clientele in Paris, is borne out by the presence of such works in English collections in the eighteenth century.

Boucher aimed, however, to be a history painter and it was evidently to make a mark in this most demanding of genres that he embarked upon an intentionally eye-catching version of the story of *Hercules and Omphale* (fig.22).[119] The year before Boucher set off for Rome the unabashed sensuality of Nöel-Nicolas Coypel's (1690–1734) *Rape of Europa* (Philadelphia) had greatly impressed the public at the 1727 Salon.[120] That year the duc d'Antin, worried about the increasing frivolity of much contemporary French history painting, had organized a competition to encourage a more serious and didactic approach. The exercise backfired when the official winners, Lemoine and De Troy, were outshone by the sheer brilliance and verve of Coypel's masterpiece. With this in mind, Boucher cast about for a similarly erotic subject, ambitiously choosing Hercules's effective emasculation by his all-consuming love for Omphale. The story had been popularised in France through an opera by André Destouches in 1701 and, more significantly, had been painted by Lemoine during the latter's sojourn in Italy in 1724.[121] Lemoine's image made a big impact on the younger generation: Dumont Le Romain (1701–81), for example, depicted the same subject in his reception piece for admission to the Academy six months after Boucher's departure for Rome and Charles Coypel (1694–1752) painted the scene in 1731.[122] In conscious rivalry, Boucher embarked on the same theme. Eschewing the lyrical landscape setting of his predecessors, he moved the action to Omphale's bedroom, a confined Baroque interior whose rich draperies and furnishings underscore the atmosphere of claustrophobic sexual desire. The attributes of club and distaff, usually placed in the protagonist's hands to symbolise their role reversal, here are not allowed to impede their love-making but left instead to the care of the Amours who play with them at the foot of the bed. Meanwhile, the raunchy pose of the embracing couple, so seemingly spontaneous, is carefully researched and based on artistic precedent, recalling Annibale Carracci's *Hercules and Iole* on the frescoed ceiling of the Palazzo Farnese, Rome (*in-situ*), and Veronese's canvas of *Venus and Adonis* (Vienna). It was this contact with Italian art and the fact that probably for the first time he was able to draw regularly from the life-model in the Academy school that gave Boucher the confidence to paint large-scale nude figures for the first time.[123] Boucher never painted another picture as sexually explicit again, but it helped to establish his reputation as *the* painter of seductive visions for his generation. There could be no clearer example of his artistic ambition and the lengths to which he was willing to go in order to get his work noticed on the eve of his return to Paris.

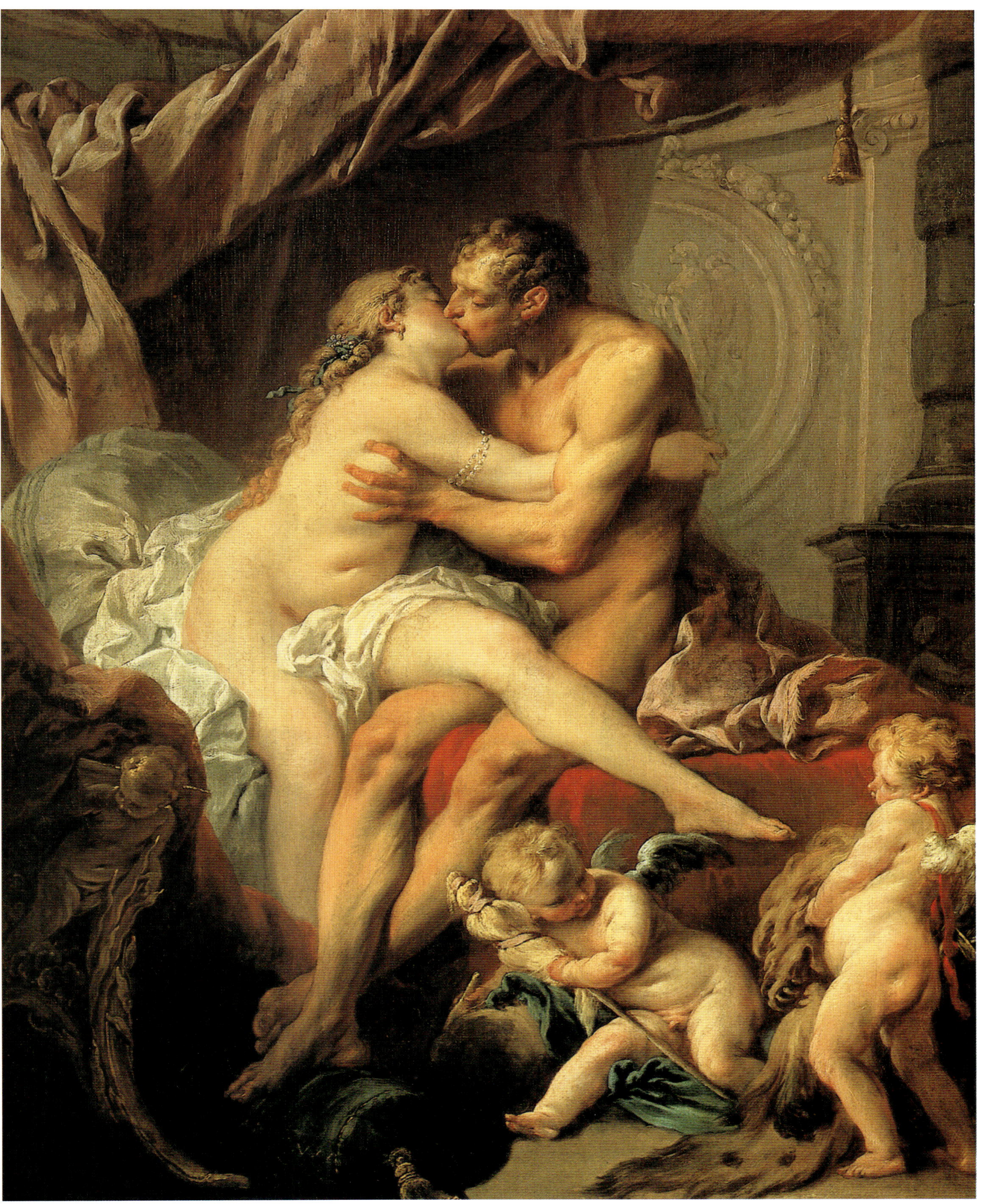

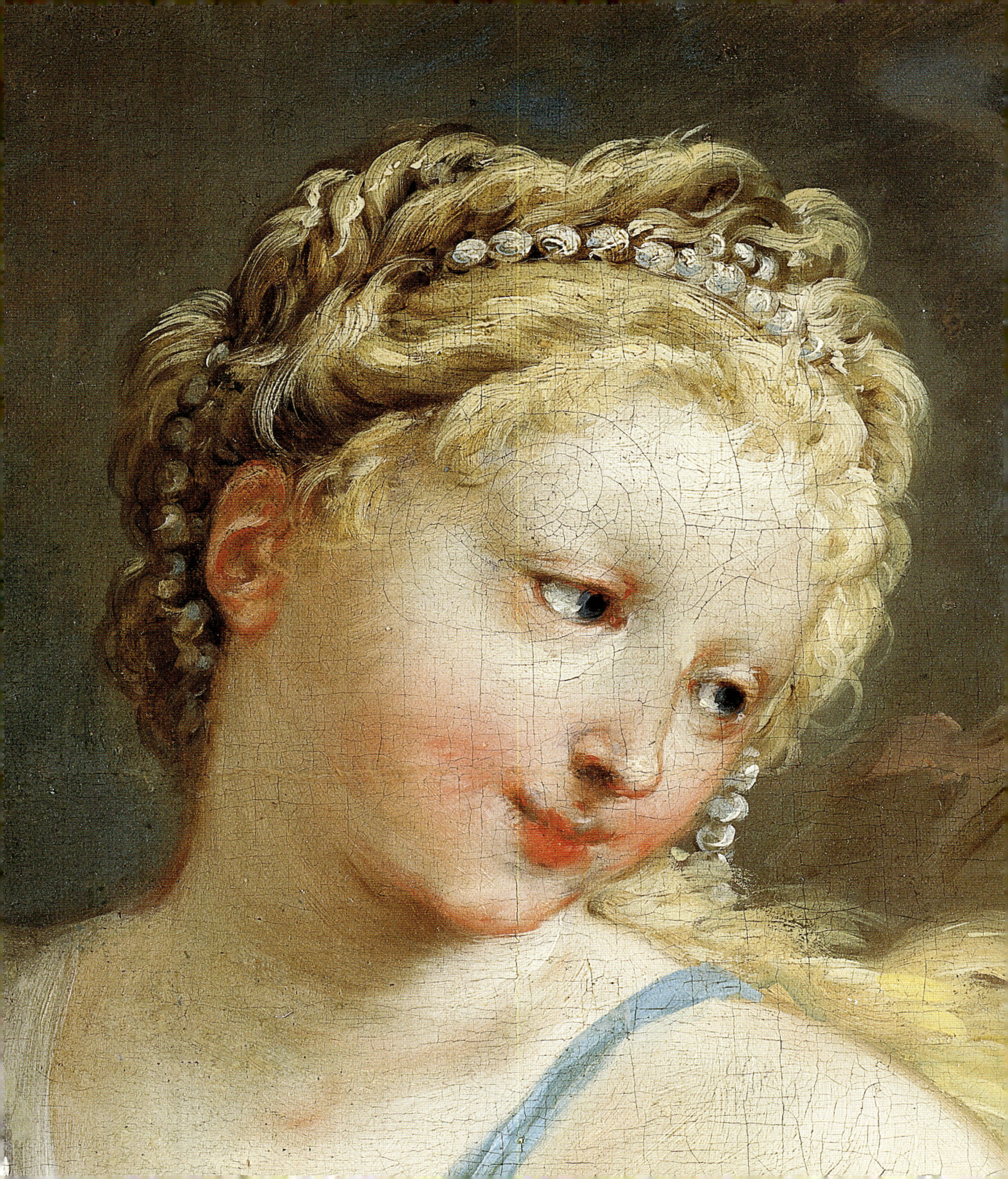

II

The painter of the Graces and the most ingenious artist of our century BASTIDE[1]

The Rising Star of the Rococo: 1731–40

When Boucher returned to Paris in 1731, France, under the guidance of Louis XV's First Minister, Cardinal Fleury, 1726–43, was continuing to enjoy an unprecedented period of peace, stability and material progress. The arts were flourishing and, as the quotations from Voltaire's *Mondain* demonstrates, they formed a vital element in eighteenth-century Parisian culture: they reflected the wealth and taste of their owners, created congenial interiors in which to meet, and provided material for conversation. After his period in Rome, and now at the relatively mature age of twenty-eight, Boucher would have been keener than ever to make his mark as a serious painter. He did not return to the print world of the rue St-Jacques, but in all likelihood moved immediately to the rue St-Thomas du Louvre, in the *quartier* of professional painters around the Louvre and the Academy, where he was recorded in 1733 living next door to one of his rivals, Charles Natoire (1700–77). One of his first acts was to approach the Academy for membership, something that had been unthinkable before his time in Rome. Following the reports of his progress sent back to Paris by Vleughels, Boucher was now a known quantity. The proceedings of the Academy in 1731 describe the straightforward manner in which 'sieur François Boucher, of Paris, Painter of History, presented himself and showed his works; by verbal consent of the members he was accepted as an associate [*agréé*]'.[2]

However, to be accepted as a history painter, and to survive as a practitioner in a market that commissioned primarily portraits and preferred to buy old masters rather than contemporary French history paintings, were two very different things. Even a painter as competent as Nattier (1685–1766) had been forced to abandon the higher calling and accept a living as a portraitist.[3] Boucher had to make an impact quickly if he was not to be dragged back to the print trade or forced to specialise in a minor genre such as landscape. At this point it must have seemed virtually impossible for him to attract a large-scale historical commission when he had no previous track-record for painting such works. His extraordinary solution was to paint a series of major historical paintings for free, including the Wallace Collection's *Mercury confiding Bacchus to the Nymphs* and *The Rape of Europa* (figs. 23–5), just to get himself noticed.[4] Echoes of the effect this daring move had in 1730s Paris can be felt in Mariette's account: 'One only has to see what he painted in his youth, and in particular that *Rape of Europa* ... which is part of a number of large pictures which he did for a marble mason called Dorbay to adorn his entire house, which was very easy, as Boucher at that time, looking only to become known, did them, I believe, for nothing rather than pass up the opportunity.'[5] The 'Dorbay' Mariette mentions was in fact a lawyer called Derbais who owned an *hôtel* on the rue Poissonnière. His father had been a sculptor (two bronze casts after his marble busts of Louis XIV's generals Condé and Turenne are in the Wallace Collection) which probably made him sympathetic to Boucher's predicament and willing to let him use the hôtel as a gallery. Boucher's gamble paid off and Papillon de La Ferté records how 'these ingenious compositions attracted a throng of admirers, who publicised the talents of the young artist'.[6]

FIG.23
BOUCHER,
The Rape of Europa,
*c.*1733–4, oil on canvas,
detail, Wallace Collection

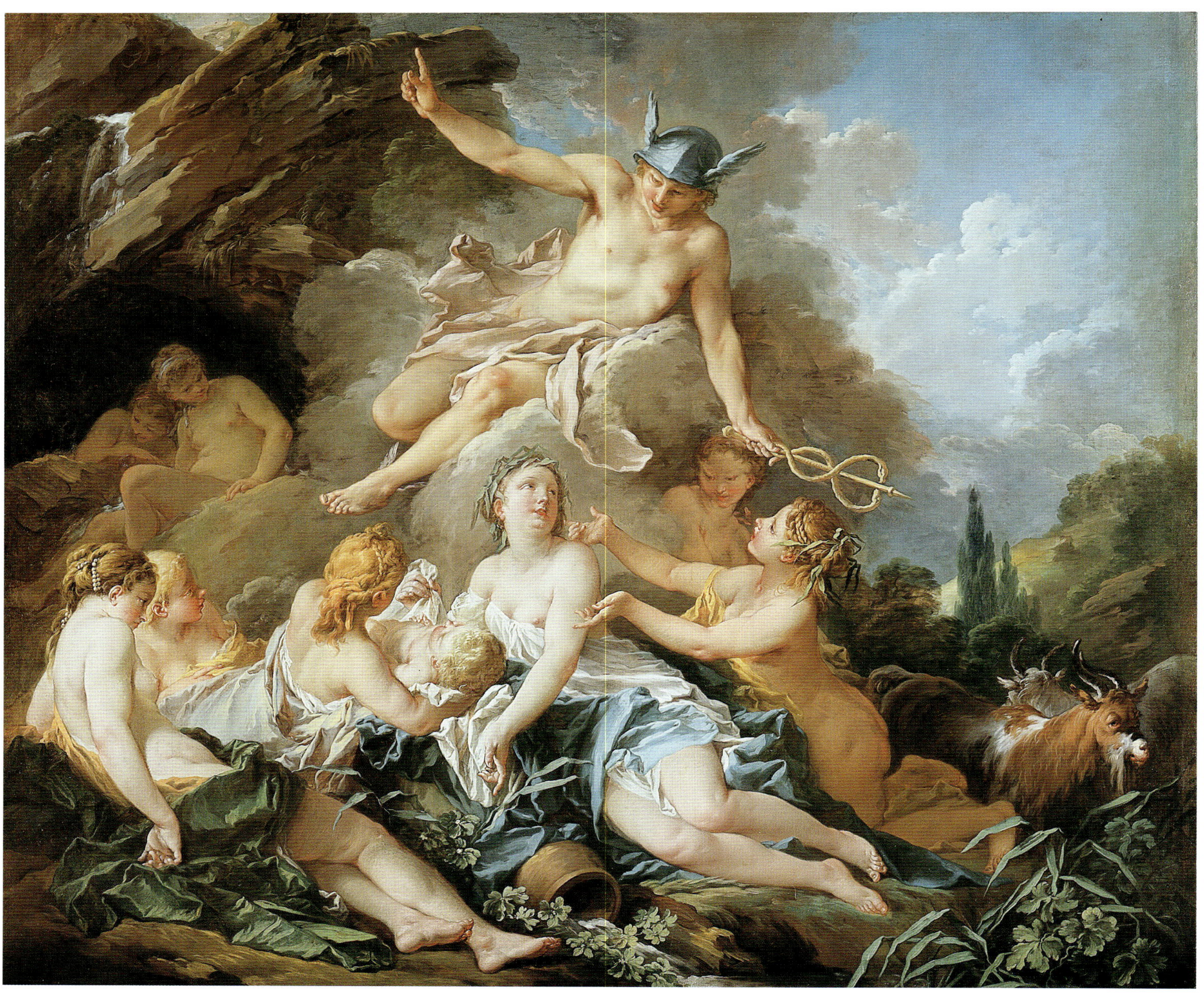

FIG.24
BOUCHER, *Mercury confiding Bacchus to the Nymphs*, *c*.1732–3, oil on canvas, 230 × 273cm, Wallace Collection

The pictures are listed in Derbais's posthumous inventory as hanging in his billiard room,[7] alongside a large *Birth of Venus* (*c*.1731; Romanian Embassy, Paris), two smaller vertical canvases showing the pairs of lovers *Venus and Vulcan* (1732; Louvre) and *Aurora and Cephalus* (1733; Nancy) and two overdoors of *Putti*.[8] The subjects, mainly illustrating amorous episodes from Ovid's poem *Metamorphoses*, were a radical departure from the historical and religious subjects of Boucher's youth. As they were not strictly commissioned they probably reflect the type of subject Boucher was drawn to and the sort of painter he aspired to be: namely a purveyor of decorative mythology to the elite of Paris. One wonders to what extent he was inspired by the example of his teacher, Lemoine, who had provided a similar set of mythologies for François Berger (1684–1748). This financier and

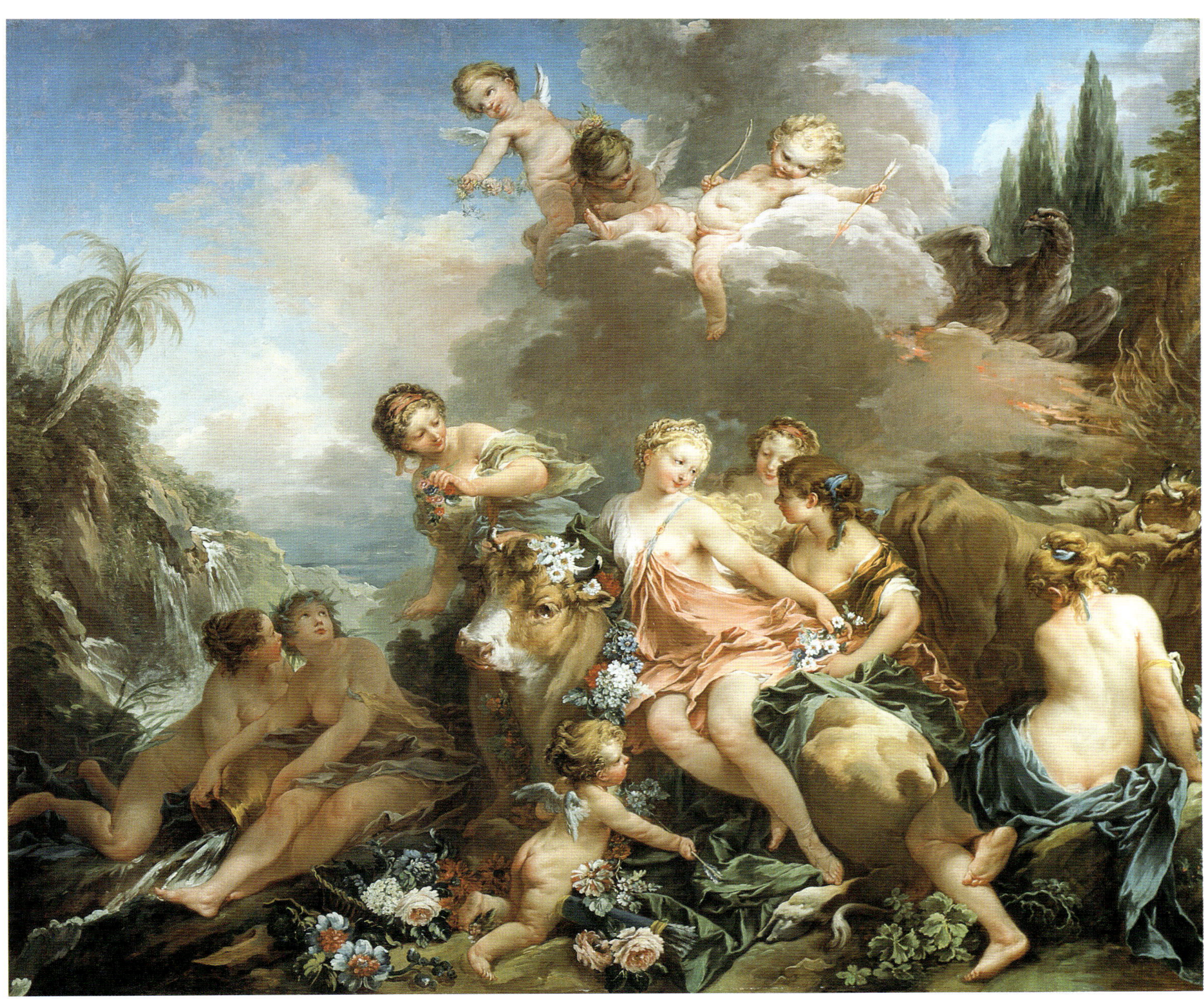

FIG.25
BOUCHER,
The Rape of Europa,
*c.*1733–4, oil on canvas,
230.8 × 273.5cm, Wallace
Collection

friend of the duc d'Antin had 'proposed to decorate an entire cabinet with pictures by M. le Moine' in 1722 and seven of these, including the *Perseus and Andromeda* (fig.8), had been delivered by 1731.[9] Berger was certainly the type of wealthy client whom Boucher hoped to attract with his publicity stunt at the rue Poissonnière and he later did work for him indirectly, designing sets at the Opéra (1737–48) during Berger's directorship.

Boucher also deliberately chose to invite formal comparison with illustrious precedents. His depictions of Venus, the goddess of love and beauty, requesting arms for her illegitimate son, Aeneas, from her estranged husband Vulcan, and of Aurora, the nymphomaniac goddess of the Dawn, seducing the newly married Cephalus, not only recalled a well-known picture by Van Dyck in the Royal Collection (*c.*1626–32; Louvre) but also

FIG.26 *below*
BOUCHER, *Mercury confiding Bacchus to the Nymphs*, *c.*1732, sketch, oil on canvas, 59.7 × 73.7cm, Cincinnati, Art Museum

FIG.27 *opposite*
BOUCHER, *The Rape of Europa*, *c.*1733, grisaille sketch, oil on canvas, 49.9 × 58.7cm, Amiens, Musée de Picardie

echoed Charles de La Fosse's pairings such as *Venus and Vulcan* and *The Deification of Aeneas* (*c.*1700; Nantes).[10] Boucher takes up La Fosse's cloud-borne goddess looking down on her male counterpart but stretches the space between them, invests the figures with a new elongated elegance, relegates all subsidiary figures to the background and lightens the overall tonality resulting in a new decorative elegance focusing on the naked goddess. The *Venus and Vulcan* may also have been painted in deliberate rivalry with Natoire, who was given the same subject in 1731 for his Academy reception piece. Natoire's resultant composition (1734; Montpellier) was heavily influenced by Boucher's example as was another composition painted by Carle Van Loo (private collection).[11] Marine triumphs, with their scope for depicting a variety of putti and nudes frolicking in the waves, were a common theme in French art before Boucher. Poussin had painted a coldly monumental version of Venus's birth from the foam of the sea (*c.*1635; Philadelphia), while La Fosse and Antoine Coypel had painted sensual triumphs of the sea-nymph Galatea (*c.*1700; Agen; Coypel's version lost but known from an engraving by Simonneau). Antoine Coypel also depicted a *Triumph of Venus* in his decorations for the *Ménagerie* showing Venus borne aloft by Tritons on a shell-like throne (1700; Louvre) which in turn inspired his step-brother, Noël-Nicolas, to paint a more elaborate rococo version of the same subject (1732; St Petersburg).[12] It is intriguing to speculate whether Coypel was responding to Boucher's picture in the rue Poissonnière, or whether Boucher with his own *Birth of Venus* was deliberately challenging Coypel's position as the most avant-garde painter of sensual mythologies. Certainly, Coypel's death two years later removed a rival from Boucher's path. Boucher invests the subject with a new originality for, in contrast to other recent versions of the subject, he brings the figures closer to the picture plane and concentrates attention on his elegantly twisting female nudes.[13]

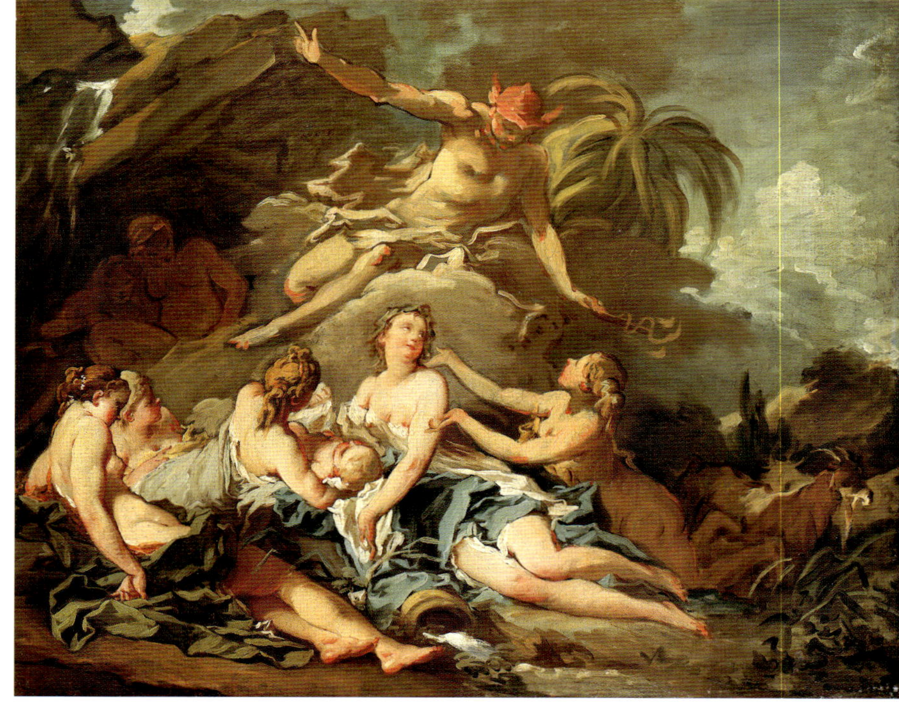

Jupiter's transformation into a bull in order to deceive and abduct Europa was another favourite subject in French art. Around the start of the eighteenth century many French artists, such as La Fosse (*c.*1690; Basildon Park) and Lemoine (1725; Moscow) had produced pictures recalling the fashionable sixteenth-century Venetian model, Veronese (1528–88), by depicting similarly lavishly dressed Europas, surrounded by attendants in rich landscapes with views of the sea beyond.[14] As Boucher was already depicting the *Birth of Venus* for Derbais, he avoided the marine setting of Noël-Nicolas Coypel's 1727 *Rape of Europa* and looked to these more sedentary depictions. He invested his picture, however, with a light colouring, sharper line and crisp use of light and shade influenced by the great Baroque artists Pietro da Cortona (1596–1669) and Simon Vouet (1590–1649). Boucher's facial types recall both artists, while the pose of Europa follows Dorigny's 1642 engraving after Vouet's *Rape of Europa* (1641–2; Madrid) as well as Aveline's 1730 engraving after Watteau's picture on the same subject.[15] Again he seems to have been consciously rivalling Natoire who painted the same subject in 1731 (St Petersburg). Boucher obviously had Natoire in mind when he executed his oil sketch (fig.27) for he copied the

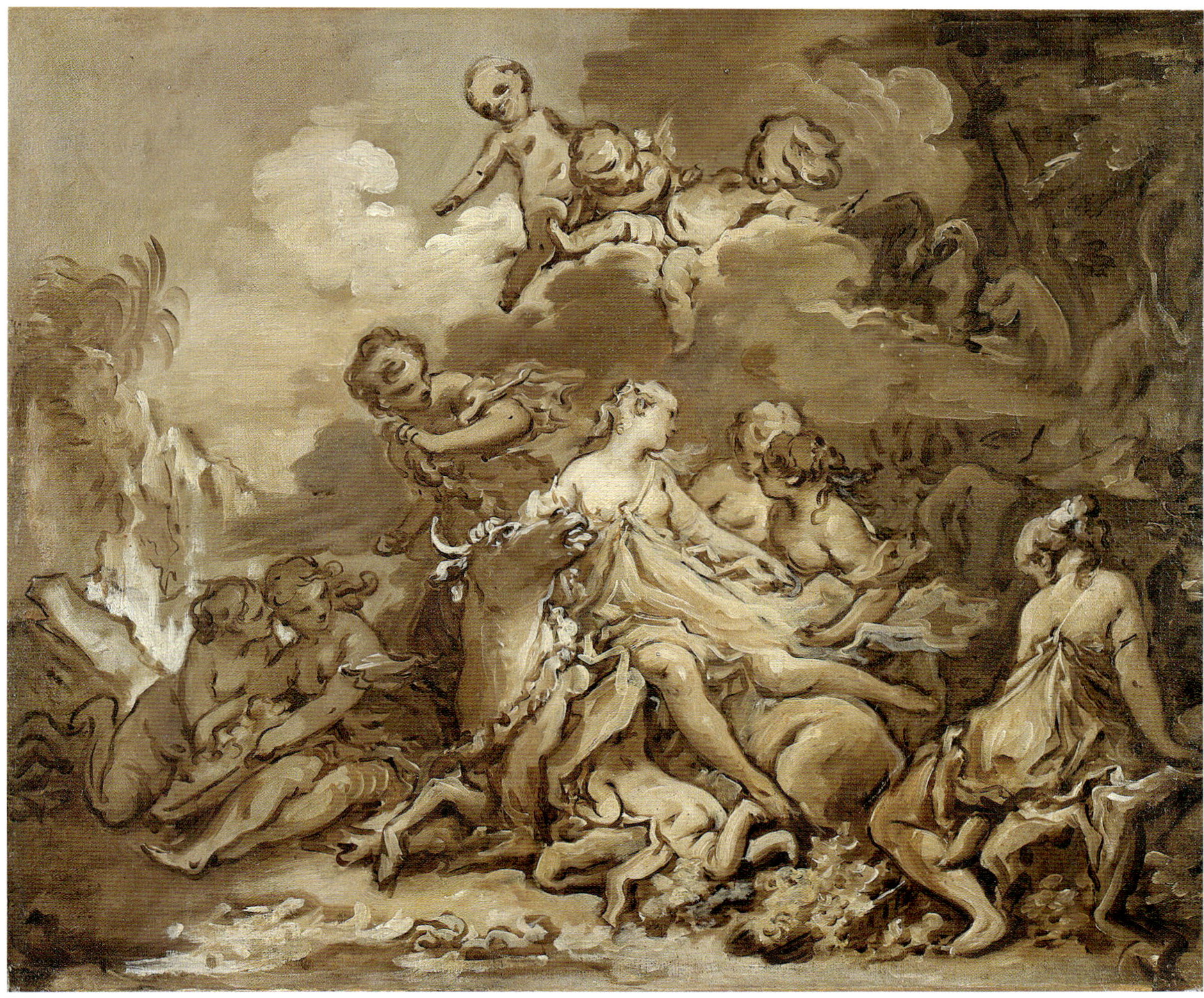

pose of the head of Natoire's bull, later altering it in favour of a frontal pose in the picture as finally executed.[16] Natoire's ideas of the herd of cattle returning in the background and Jupiter's eagle with putti in the sky remain, but Boucher reduces the number of subsidiary figures in his picture. Then by expert use of light and shadow, as on the face of Europa's attendant to the right, he further relegates their importance in the composition, fixing our attention even more closely on the radiant central figure of Europa. The story of Mercury entrusting the nymphs of Nysa with the care of the infant Bacchus, illegitimate child of Jupiter and Semele, is less frequently depicted and Boucher's slightly ungainly pyramidal composition reflects this fact. However, he again treats the figures in a monumental manner close to the picture plane, linking them with diagonal movement and dramatic foreshortening and unifying the whole composition through a balanced use of colour, light and shade. The canvases in the Wallace Collection were mistakenly attributed to Lemoine in the nineteenth and early twentieth centuries, but they brilliantly demonstrate Boucher's ability to create his own highly identifiable visual world, the sensual power of which even his later detractors had to admit.

A series of preparatory sketches and drawings attest to the care with which Boucher worked on the series. To work out the overall composition and effects he painted sketches rapidly in oil on canvas to capture his initial ideas (figs. 26–7). The sketch

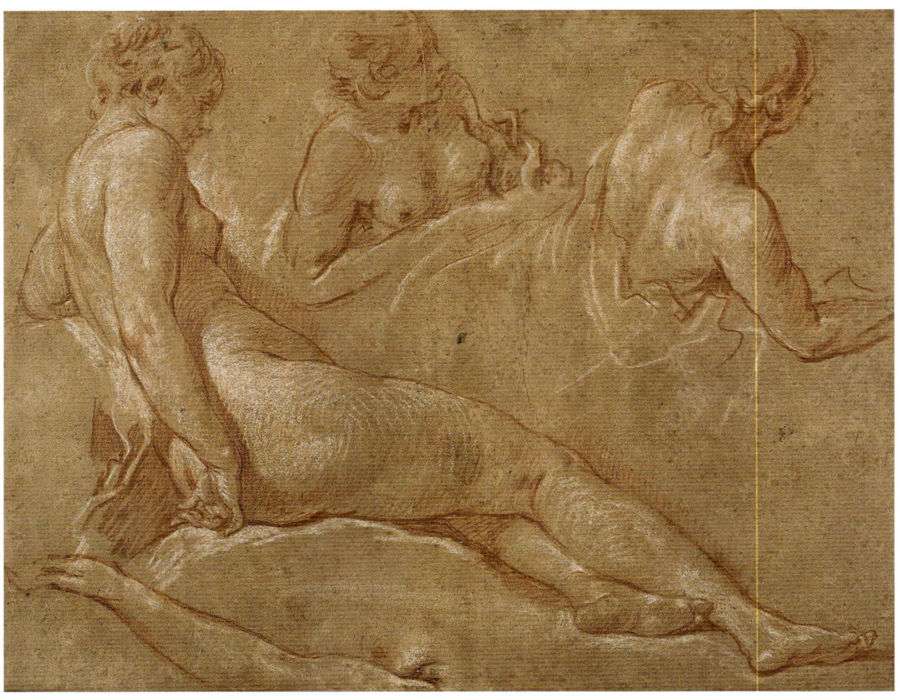

FIG.28
BOUCHER,
Study of Nymphs,
*c.*1732, red and white chalk on brown paper, 25.8 × 32.9cm, Tours, Musée des Beaux-Arts

FIG.29 *opposite*
BOUCHER, *Study for Mercury*, *c.*1732, red and white chalk on light brown paper, 33.6 × 35.4cm, photo courtesy of Christie's

for *Mercury confiding Bacchus to the Nymphs* is dated slightly earlier than that of *The Rape of Europa* due to its more nervous fractured technique, more straightforwardly picturesque use of colour and odd anatomical inaccuracies like the legs of Mercury. Comparing the sketch to the finished picture one can see how Boucher refined the colours to harmonize the overall effect, eschewing the use of red on Mercury's helmet for example. He also eliminated the rather distracting feathery palm to the right of Mercury's head in order to focus our attention on the basic, traditional pyramidal composition. The sketch for *The Rape of Europa* is more fluid and assured. Executed in contrasting tones of brown *grisaille* with the figures strengthened with black lines, Boucher has used the technique to plan the basic forms and light and shade. He already used grey *grisaille* to prepare thesis plates for engraving and this sensitivity to *grisaille* sketching may date from his monochrome work for the print trade. The sketch barely bothers to indicate the landscape detail, concentrating instead on the general transformation from light to dark from left to right in the background. The foreground figures are quickly brushed in with fluid strokes, the main differences between canvas and sketch being the more frontal poses of Europa and the bull and the changed position of the foreground putto who, in the sketch, appears to be burrowing his way beneath Europa's drapery. Boucher's interest in the overall effect of his final canvases is also revealed by his experimentation with the unifying effects of coloured grounds, using a blue ground for the grotto of Mount Nysa and a pink ground for the festive shore of Europa.

Each individual figure was based on a live model, or, as in the case of the seated girl on the right in the *Europa*, taken from a previous artistic model.[17] Figure 28, for example, shows the red and white chalk study for the nymphs on the left-hand side of *Mercury confiding Bacchus to the Nymphs*, demonstrating Boucher's increased confidence and ability with female nudes compared to his early Watteau-style study (fig.11).[18] Like Watteau before him, he tended to keep such drawings to form a repertoire on which he could call when working on other compositions. The seated figure of the girl on the left reappears, for example, semi-clothed in the sketch for *The Toilette of Psyche* (private collection) and fully clothed in two Italianate landscapes, *The Farmer's Children* and *The Tame Sparrow* (both now lost).[19] Boucher often reversed such figures to disguise these self-borrowings or to fit differing compositional needs. Thus a counterproof[20] of the same girl (Besançon) was probably used as the basis for the figure of Venus in a small cabinet picture of *Venus and Cupid* acquired by Watteau's former friend and patron, Antoine de La Roque (lost). This composition in turn then became known to a wider audience through engravings by Aubert, Dufour and Lépicié.[21] From now on, such female nudes would become an acknowledged speciality; Papillon de La Ferté could claim at the end of Boucher's career that 'No artist has drawn the female nude with more correction, none has better expressed the flexibility of the muscles and the softness of the skin'.[22]

The early female nudes seen in the two Wallace Collection mythologies very much reflect the then fashionable ideal of the feminine form which, according to contemporary accounts, was about five feet in height, quite plump, with wider hips than shoulders, a well defined waist, plump firm white arms, dimpled skin, full firm thighs which thinned to small knees and small round breasts. In an era when even the children of the bourgeoisie were despatched at birth to the wet-nurse, too much bust was considered common, as were large hands and feet which implied that the owner had to work and walk rather than ride in a carriage. A pretty face was described as being round with a jutting chin, with round cheeks, a large forehead, a straight nose (a snub nose being considered less disfiguring than a long nose), a small mouth, good teeth and medium-sized well modelled ears.[23] Although we might find this far from the twenty-first century ideal of whippet-thinness, it does in fact represent a significantly slimmer, more elegant female form than that promulgated in the seventeenth century. Unlike the ample Rubensian nude, the Boucher model reflects the new dietary habits of the French upper classes where 'Parisian ladies … are desperate when they start to gain weight and drink vinegar to keep their figures' and the word 'dondon' or 'fatty' was invented to refer to 'girls of the people, meaning a large and fat girl, of squat proportions'.[24] Boucher's nudes are not merely idealised: any notion that they might be sexually abandoned is quashed by their lovingly detailed coiffures. With their hair entwined in ribbons, pearls or garlands of leaves, Boucher's goddesses and nymphs look like an Olympian equivalent of Legros de Rumigny's eighteenth-century hairdressing handbook or a carefully studied Bloemaert engraving.[25] Although often overlooked beside his female nudes, a similar elegance informs Boucher's depiction of the male, as seen in the preparatory chalk drawing for *Mercury* (fig.29).[26] The long-limbed, slim and almost adolescent figure recalls classical depictions of Apollo and again indicates an ideal of male beauty associated with peace, leisure and refinement rather than war, work or action.

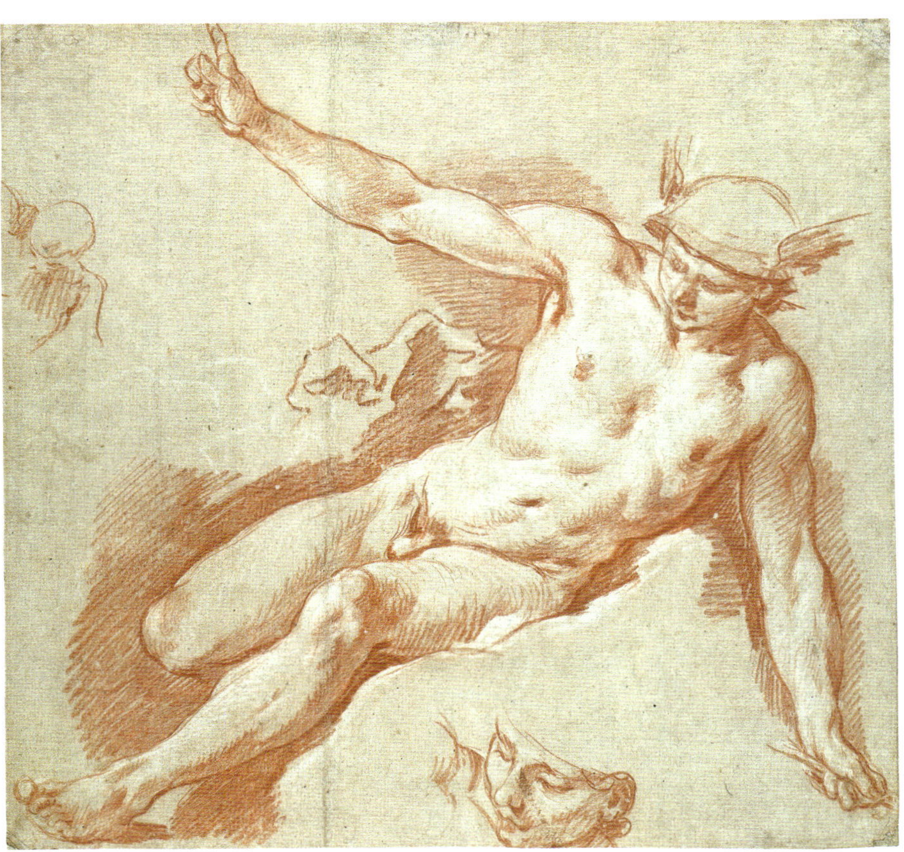

Although Boucher, following De Piles's theories, wanted his pictures to make a striking initial impact through their overall effect, he also aimed to retain the viewer's attention through picturesque detail. Contemporaries were particularly impressed by the landscape backgrounds of the Derbais pictures, with their slanting palms, rocky escarpments and cascades. The connoisseur, Bachaumont, when discussing a projected series of paintings illustrating the story of Psyche, wrote to Boucher exclaiming 'You do Landscape like an Angel – I can hear from here the sound of the waterfall; remember well what you have done for M. Derbais'.[27] Boucher deliberately combines elements from nature, artistic precedent and his own invention to create a parallel visual universe to capture the viewer's attention and stimulate his imagination. Drawings for the realistic-looking goats appear to have been done from nature and after models such as Roos da Tivoli (Stockholm and private collections); the landscapes in general recall Castiglione and the profusion of flowers in the *Europa* recalls the garlands of Cortona. The vigorous brushwork, noted by Mariette for being 'as strong as it is gracious' also provides surface interest to enthral the observer.[28] The connoisseur is invited, for example, to marvel at the broadly painted foliage, the exuberant painting of the flowers, the thickly painted shaggy coat of the bull and the creamy flesh of Europa offset with piquant little touches of red on her nose and chin (fig.23).

This stylistic bravura is so visually overwhelming that it tends to overshadow the mythological subjects of the canvases. It is Boucher's technical virtuosity, as much as the stories he illustrates, that transports the viewer. Stylistically Boucher's pictures parallel the vivacity and seemingly improvisatory quality of early Enlightenment literature, where it is not just what one says but how one says it that is important. As Duclos explained 'the most sought after men of letters are those whom one commonly calls *beaux esprits* (fine wits) ... Society prefers the writer whose wit is used more variously, and with a less decided and wider application'.[29] Pedantic displays of learning or didacticism are as alien to Boucher's artistic approach as they were to thinkers such as Condorcet, who wrote that 'one must be a philosopher, but not appear to be one', or Voltaire, who predicted 'unhappiness to the author who always wants to instruct'. This is not to say that Boucher's picture series for Derbais had no iconographic programme, just that it was worn with the same apparent insouciance and charm as the latest fashions. Yet, like the latest fashion, it was pursued with the same covert seriousness of purpose. We find, for example, that contemporary educators such as Charles Rollin advocated the use of fable and mythology to sweeten the pill of moral education.[30] Studying the amorous tales of the *Metamorphoses* could thus civilise people by teaching the virtues of regulated love and courtship, thereby ultimately contributing to the sum of human happiness. Far from inciting troubling sexual desire with their nudity, the pictures Boucher painted for Derbais were actually intended to illustrate the eighteenth-century civilising concept of 'the erotic'. This was defined as the birth of love; a moment of suspense and equilibrium between reason and feeling, when the first emotional stirrings could still be analysed in the manner of a Marivaux comedy.[31] In *The Rape of Europa*, for example, there is no sense of the fear and impending sexual violation movingly portrayed by Titian's painting on the same theme (Boston, Isabella Stewart Gardener Museum). Indeed the title in French, *L'Enlèvement d'Europe*, implies a gallant abduction rather than a rape. As Rousseau later advised: 'one easily forgets a love that frightens/ In favour of one that flatters./ Let the care of charming/ Be your unique concern./ Remember that the art of loving/ Is only that of pleasing./ Do you want in passion/ To find lasting happiness?/ Be less amorous./ Become more amiable'.[32] So Boucher charms our eyes and invites amusement at Jupiter's predicament; transformed into a dumb animal, comically bedecked with flowers and overwhelmed by female attention as he peers at us dolefully from beneath fringed lashes. One is reminded of the anonymous words of the eighteenth-century Opéra Comique: 'When one desires,/ One is always gallant,/ Active and obliging;/ One is everywhere the lover;/ An hour appears a moment;/ One cherishes one's martyrdom'.[33]

The subject of *Mercury confiding Bacchus to the Nymphs* also helps us understand how the Derbais series might have been read by contemporaries. At first sight, it does not appear to fit with the other pictures, since it depicts the result of an amorous encounter rather than the birth of love seen in all the other pictures. But its significance resides in the fact that Bacchus was to provide the world with one of its greatest pleasures, wine. Indeed, at the very moment Boucher's picture was being painted, Parisians were enjoying the recent invention of champagne, 'the King of Wines and Wine of the King'.[34] Wine appeals to our sense of taste, and the subjects of the other pictures broadly fit into an allegory of the senses: sight is symbolised by the visual beauty of Venus and the naked sea-nymphs,

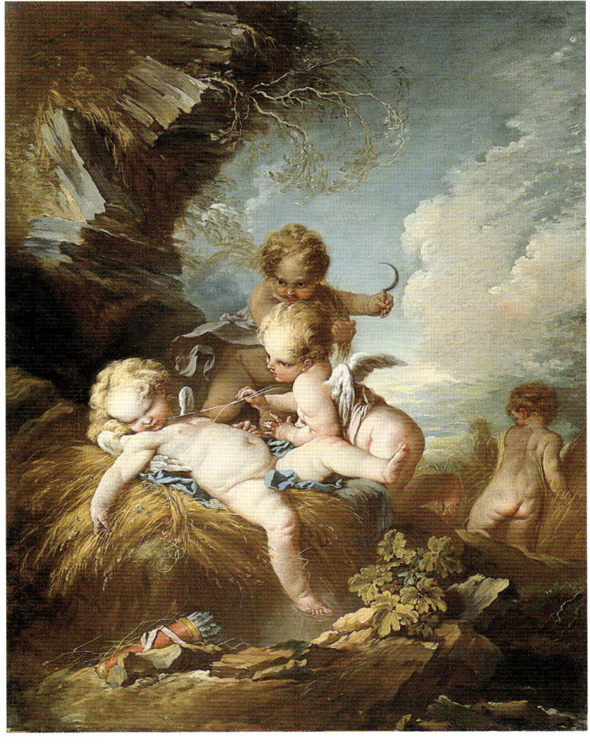

FIG.30
BOUCHER,
Love the Harvester,
c.1733, oil on canvas,
125.5 × 95.5cm, Houston,
Sarah Campbell Blaffer
Foundation

smell is denoted by the extraordinary flowers in the *Europa* and touch by Vulcan fingering his suggestively phallic sword. The most oblique reference for a modern audience is the connection between *Aurora and Cephalus* and hearing; but in addition to Cephalus's listening pose, his hunting horn is prominently displayed at the bottom of the canvas and recalls the hullabaloo of an *ancien régime* hunt. The Derbais series is thus a celebration of sensual pleasure painted in a sensually satisfying manner. It aimed to create the feelings of *douceur de vivre*, sweetness of life, pursued by contemporaries such as Voltaire who believed that 'Happiness is an abstract idea, composed of various sensations of pleasure' and that 'sight is the fore-runner of pleasure'.[35] Standing in Derbais's billiard room, transported by Boucher's paintings, one might well have believed in Voltaire's vision of terrestrial paradise.[36]

The playful allegorical nature of the early Enlightenment aesthetic also helps to explain the popularity of Boucher's infant compositions, which seem so alien to us today. Unlike Chardin's visions of children rooted in observed reality, or the increasingly moralistic images of Greuze (1725–1805) which parallel and reflect the new educational theories of Rousseau, Boucher's flying babies belong to an earlier aesthetic which appreciated such subjects for their poetic allusions to the birth of wit or genius and for their ability to surprise and delight the eye. In addition to the overdoors in the billiard room, Boucher also painted four such pictures, representing the seasons, for Derbais's staircase. One of these, *Love the Harvester*, breathes new life into the traditional imagery of Autumn, by taking the airborne Cupid of the *Rape of Europa* and depicting him in the same pose but now reversed and asleep on a pile of new hay (fig.30). Boucher was not the first artist to paint children in such a way; Albani (1578–1660) was renowned for such depictions, Lemoine had experimented with similar imagery and Boucher himself later owned a sculpted bas-relief of children playing with a goat by François Duquesnoy (1594–1643).[37] Boucher, however, invented particularly witty and charming combinations, continually delighting and surprising his contemporaries and inspiring Papillon de La Ferté to claim that no artist had ever 'given more finesse and spirit to the characters of children and Amours'.[38]

Of course, all this was only available to the minority with the money to commission a Boucher painting. But Boucher was more than ready to adapt his vision for other markets. The compositional invention displayed in Boucher's pictures made them perfect for engraving as source material for the decorative arts. Both the *Rape of Europa* and the *Mercury confiding Bacchus to the Nymphs* appear in reverse on the lids of two gold boxes in the Louvre.[39] As, however, much of the pictorial meaning of Boucher's original canvases resided in their colour and painterly handling, contemporaries felt that new meaning was needed to compensate for its absence in prints that were to be enjoyed as objects in themselves. Engravings after Boucher paintings are thus often accompanied by moralising verses, sometimes at odds with the picture's original connotations and deliberately

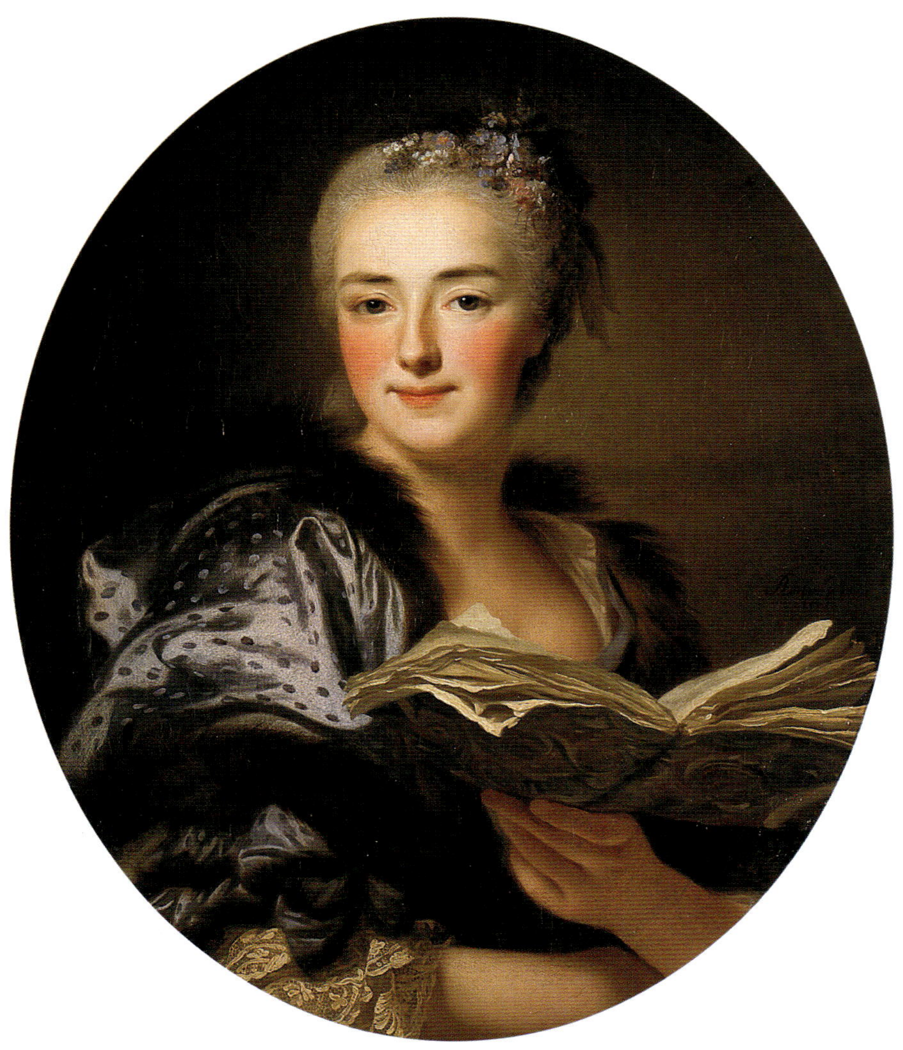

calculated to appeal to a more conservative bourgeois buyer. So, rather than celebrating courtly love, the verses attached to Aveline's 1748 engraving of *Europa* see the story as a warning of love's deceit: 'Love is, beautiful Europa, an impostor./ Take care, believe me, of this flattering bull:/ His sweetness might cause you some misfortune:/ Flee, and with those flowers cease to embellish him./ I predict that he wants to relieve you of only one,/ One which no Spring will ever bring back again'. Alcohol was appreciated all the way down the social scale, however, so the verses for the pendant engraving of *The Birth of Bacchus* are more positive: 'Come, Nymphs, come and receive from Mercury/ This child who smiles with such a gracious air./ Guard him well this son of the Heavens:/ One day he will pay back his keeping:/ And give in exchange for his milk a precious nectar;/ Which will be the happiness of men and Gods'.[40]

Marriage and Establishment Recognition

The Derbais project must already have been yielding results by 1733, for the thirty-year-old Boucher felt secure enough to take a wife. In an era when marriage was as much about property as attraction, Boucher was lucky or prudent enough to satisfy both criteria. His seventeen year old bride Marie-Jeanne Buzeau (fig.31) was not only beautiful but from a significantly more comfortable background. In contrast to Boucher's parents, now living in the rue des Fourreurs between the Châtelet and the Halles, Marie-Jeanne's father was a 'bourgeois de Paris', the class of commoners who often lived off rents from property as well as enjoying other financial advantages. Her brother was a musician, and the family lived in the rue de l'Evêque at the fashionable end of the rue St-Honoré. The wedding took place nearby, in the society church of St-Roch, with its newly resplendent Servandoni-designed façade. Marie-Jeanne received a comfortable dowry from her father of 6000 *livres*, paid in cash, but what is perhaps more surprising is that Boucher was able to match this sum, settling 3000 *livres* on his wife and having 6000 *livres* worth of property himself.[41]

Considering Boucher's highly developed aesthetic appreciation of the female form, it is unsurprising to find that his new wife was a legendary beauty. Even in her forties she appeared 'beautiful and fresh' in her morning negligée, when seen by Boucher's former student Mannlich during his first visit to the artist at the beginning of the 1760s. He describes how 'descending the stairs of the old Louvre, I couldn't stop myself eulogising over the great beauty of Madame Boucher – 'You should have seen her twenty years ago my dear Mannlich' replied the duke [of Zweibrücken, his patron] 'not only was she the most beautiful woman of Paris but even of the whole of France.

FIG.31 *opposite*
ALEXANDRE ROSLIN (1718–1793), *Portrait of Marie-Jeanne Buzeau*, Madame Boucher, 1761, oil on canvas, 63 × 51cm, Munich, Schloß Nymphenburg

My brother as well as many others were madly in love with her; they sighed in vain, the young woman was as good as she was beautiful and made every one esteem as well as love her. She must be at least forty now, and still counts as one of the most beautiful women of Paris; that's the result of youthful good conduct'.[42]

In addition to the picture illustrated, Madame Boucher's beauty was recorded in a pastel by Quentin de La Tour (1737; lost), another by Lundberg (Salon 1743; lost) and in an earlier portrait by Roslin, which depicted her in a ball-gown (Salon 1753; lost). Although the ideal of female beauty seen in Boucher's paintings may have resembled his wife's looks, it is very unlikely that Boucher ever used her as a studio model. Comments such as Bachaumont's that Boucher should 'above all study Madame Boucher' when looking for artistic inspiration are indications of eighteenth-century gallant manners rather than studio practice.[43] The abbé de Fontenay's comment that Boucher 'was in the happy position of having chosen a companion who could retrace the idea of the Graces unceasingly for him, and he knew how to make happy use of this in his art' should be treated with similar caution.[44] The closest Marie-Jeanne came to the studio was through her own ability as an amateur artist and miniaturist, an accomplishment common to many ladies of breeding as well as to the wives of artists such as Fragonard (1732–1806) and Vien.[45] She also acted as Boucher's secretary, as a group of letters written by her on Boucher's behalf to the theatrical impresario, Favart, prove. The couple's affectionate complicity is demonstrated by Boucher dictating a letter, via his wife, joking that their mutual friend the abbé de La Garde had become such a courtier that 'the women will lose their heads over him and I am not without worries for Madame Boucher'.[46] Roslin's 1761 portrait of Marie-Jeanne, unbound book in hand, emphasises her accomplishments and has a pendant portrait of Boucher holding a crayon holder (1761: Versailles). Beautiful, fashionable and cultivated, Madame Boucher also appears significantly younger than her husband whom all commentators describe as looking like an old man by the 1760s.[47]

The couple's three children were all born in their apartment in the rue St-Thomas du Louvre: Jeanne-Elisabeth in 1735, Juste-Nathan in 1736 and Marie-Émilie in 1740. All three were baptised in the artists' church of St-Germain-l'Auxerrois, their increasingly distinguished godparents marking the Bouchers' social ascent. Boucher's mother and Marie-Jeanne's brother acted as godparents to Jeanne-Elisabeth; Juste-Nathan had the ornamentalist Meissonnier and his wife as godparents; Oudry (1686–1755), Inspector of the Beauvais and Gobelins tapestry works and animal painter to the King, was godfather to Marie-Émilie.[48] With a fashionable wife, a growing family and his own 'pleasures' to fund, Boucher seems to have been increasingly driven as much by financial necessity as by artistic ambition to establish his reputation and to diversify into any artistic areas that might prove lucrative.

The seal of establishment approval came the year after his marriage, with Boucher's full acceptance into the Academy on presentation of his reception piece of *Rinaldo and Armida* (fig.32).[49] The theme had been specified at the time of his *agrément* when it was recorded that 'he will go to Mr De Boullogne, Director, who will give him the subject of the picture which he will do for his reception'.[50] Although he was thus restricted in theme, one had been chosen which perfectly complemented his talents and interests. The story of the seduction of the Christian knight, Rinaldo, by the Saracen witch, Armida, and his subsequent repudiation of her was an edifying tale from the Counter-Reformation epic poem, Torquato Tasso's *Gerusalemme Liberata*. Lully and Quinault's popular opera, *Armide*, first performed in 1686, stressed the more amorous features of the story, however, and in turn inspired notably sensual depictions of the subject by La Fosse, Antoine Coypel and Boullogne.[51] Boucher's version is both sensual in the manner of the Derbais pictures and also appropriately theatrical in its grandiose architectural setting. It clearly marks out Boucher

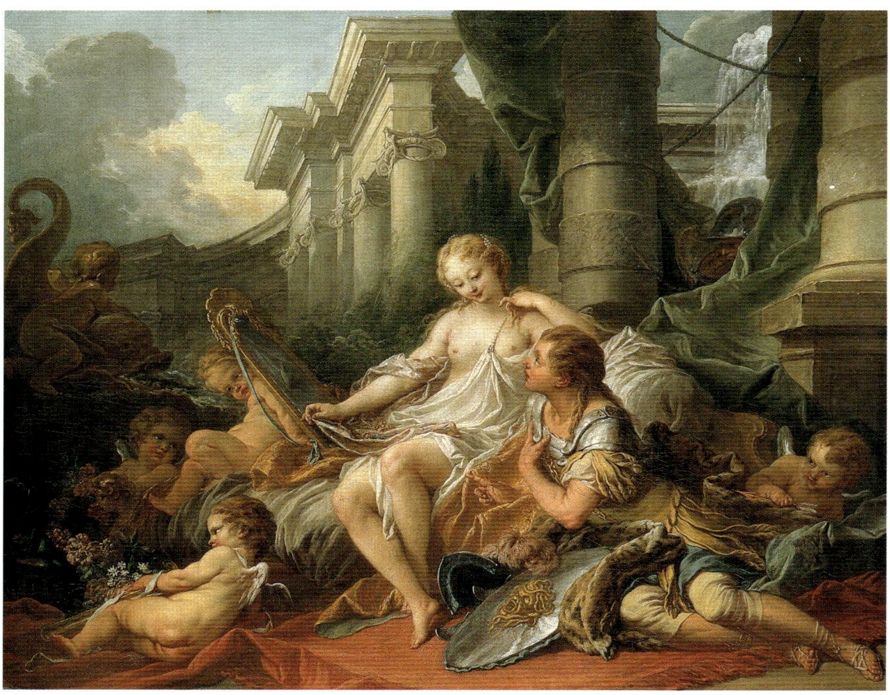

FIG.32
Boucher,
Rinaldo and Armida, 1734,
oil on canvas, 135 × 170cm,
Paris, Musée du Louvre

to his colleagues as a painter of poetic and amorous themes treated in an imaginative and technically accomplished manner.

Boucher became a member of the Academy on the same day as the portraitist Tocqué and the two were given seats next to each other at meetings, which presumably suited them both as Tocqué's widow later noted that her husband shared Boucher's 'pleasures and tastes'.[52] Thereafter the Academy became a central feature of Boucher's life: he steadily rose through the hierarchy, becoming assistant professor in 1735, professor in 1737, assistant rector in 1752 and rector in 1761. He was a conscientious teacher, regularly attended Academy meetings and was noted for the fairness of his professional conduct.[53] His general amiability, however, made him no less ambitious to attain the highest honours of Director and First Painter to the King than his main rivals Charles Natoire, who became an academician later the same year, and Carle Van Loo, who was made a member the year after.[54] Boucher won the battle as foremost decorative artist when Natoire was despatched to direct the French Academy in Rome on the death of Jean-François de Troy in 1752. His own ambitions for the top spot dashed, Natoire was able to imagine with wry amusement 'all the discussions about *Boucher* and *Vanloo*' which the death of the Director and First Painter, Charles Coypel, would have inspired a few months after Natoire's departure. 'Both must be in a fine state of suspense' he observed with understandable *schadenfreude*. When Boucher was finally made First Painter in 1765, his pride in achieving the longed-for honour even overcame his customary love of financial gain. Cochin suggested he would be ready to accept a salary cut occasioned by an increased pension to the previous incumbent's widow, Madame Van Loo: 'what will flatter him the most will not be the money, but the title'.[55]

Ironically, in view of his famous later connection with Louis XV's official mistress, Madame de Pompadour, Boucher's first royal commission was actually for the Queen, Marie Leszczynska. In 1735 he was commissioned to paint decorations for the Queen's Bedchamber at Versailles (fig.33).[56] This was the largest room in the Queen's State apartment, where she spent the greater part of her time, receiving the ladies of Court at her awakening and giving private audiences during the day. The room had been built in the time of Louis XIV to mirror the King's bedchamber, thereby stressing the claim of his Queen, Marie Thérèse, to the Spanish throne. In 1730–5 the room was remodelled to reflect the new lighter fashions of interior decoration, under the direction of the royal architects Robert de Cotte and Jacques Gabriel. Being a royal interior of such significance the previous decoration could not be completely swept away: the room retained its seventeenth-century-coffered ceiling and the design of the new wall panelling was somewhat conservative compared with developments in the private interiors of Paris. A note of modern grace was added, however, by the set of *grisailles* by Boucher which were designed to complement new curvilinear frames inserted into the coving of the ceiling. The subjects of Boucher's four paintings, the Virtues of *Charity*, *Abundance*, *Fidelity* and

FIG.33 *below*
BOUCHER, *Charity*, 1735, grisaille, oil on canvas, Versailles, Queen's Bedchamber

FIG.34 *right*
PHILIPPE JACQUES LE BAS (1707–1783) after BOUCHER, *Paris in Autumn: Charity and the Pont Neuf*, engraving, 18.6 × 11.5cm, for the *Bréviaire de Paris* published in 1736, Paris, Musée du Louvre

Prudence, were standard iconographic choices to illustrate the necessary qualities of a Christian queen, qualities for which the pious and homely Marie Leszczynska was renowned. The pictures themselves demonstrate how Boucher's graceful forms and fluid style fitted superbly into their decorative context and how Boucher was able to endow the most conventional of iconographies with an intimate visual charm so beguiling that it almost undermined the message he was officially required to convey. So, while one is drawn to admire the pretty pointed face (recalling Armida) and elegant twisting figure of *Charity* one tends to forget her moral significance.

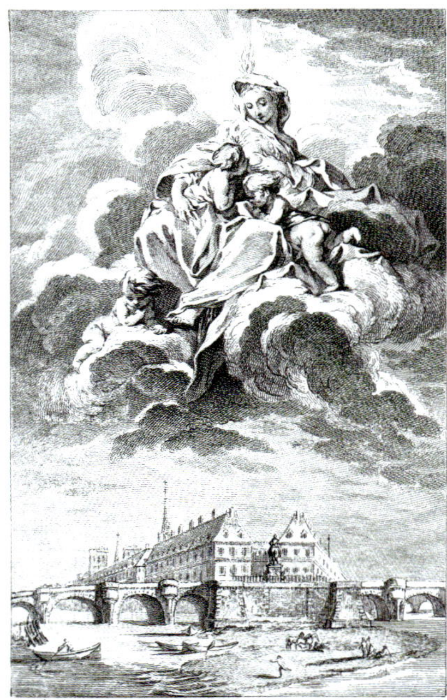

Such an unashamedly aesthetic approach, while endearing Boucher to those who wished to create congenial private interiors, did not mark him out as an appropriate artist for institutions that wished to use painting for public and didactic ends. This helps to explain the paucity of religious pictures by Boucher following his return to Paris. Despite the growing secularism of the eighteenth century, Paris remained a profoundly Catholic city, where debates between religious groups such as the Jansenists and the Jesuits were of central concern to all levels of society.[57] Churches were well-frequented public places and artists who painted major altarpieces, like Carle Van Loo or Jean Restout (1692–1768), were assured of an instant audience.[58] Even Natoire, Boucher's main rival as a decorative painter of mythology, felt the need to make his mark in the religious sphere, later providing a series of pictures for the illusionist theatrical interior of the church of the *Enfants Trouvés* (*Foundlings;* 1750; destroyed).[59] Yet Boucher, despite beginning as a painter of devotional images, produced relatively few religious pictures for the rest of his career. He seems to have had no wish to return to subjects which may have reminded him of his artisan beginnings and that, while assuring renown amongst the Parisian public, did not necessarily pay well nor attract the type of private work that would. He made an exception, however, in the field of book illustration. As we have noted, turning out drawings for engraving was child's play for an

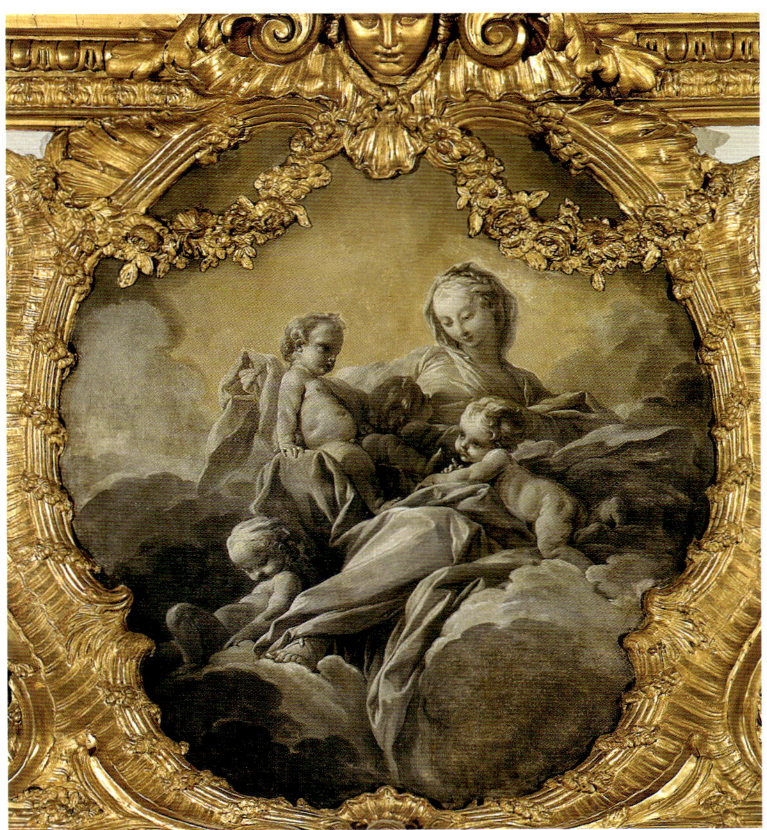

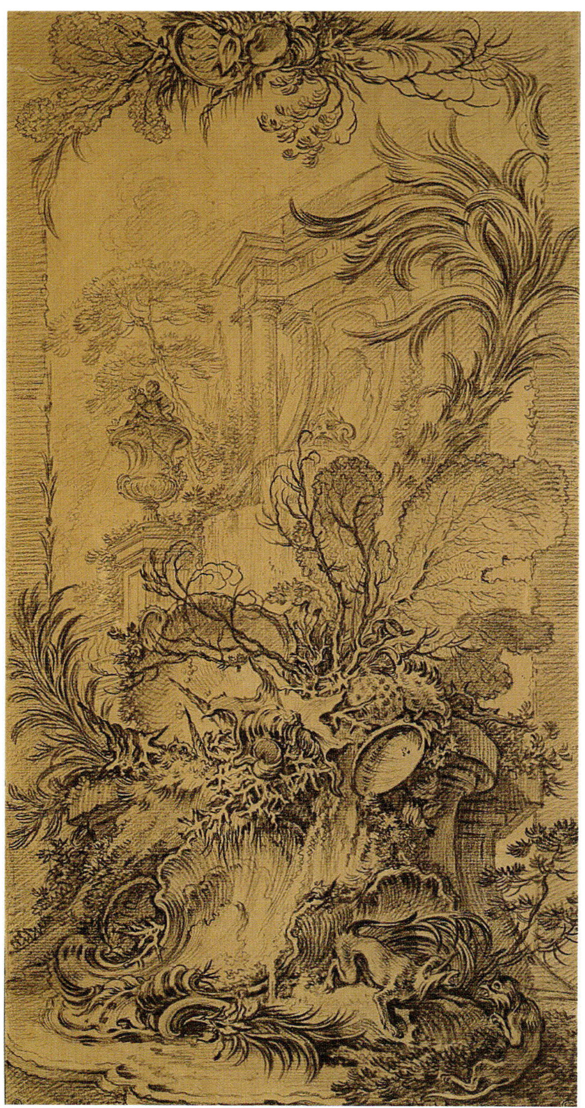

FIG.35
BOUCHER,
Rocaille, *c.*1735–6, black chalk on brown paper, 49.1 × 24.8cm, Paris, École Nationale Supérieure des Beaux-Arts

FIG.36 *opposite*
JACQUES DE LAJOUE (*c.*1687–1761), *Decorative Screen*, *c.*1734–40, oil on paper laid down on panel, each panel 162 × 57.5cm, Paris, Musée du Petit Palais

artist with such a fecund imagination. At the same time he was singularly adept at re-using his inventions across several media, thus the Versailles *Charity* reappears hovering elegantly above the Pont Neuf in an illustration engraved by Le Bas after Boucher for the *Bréviaire de Paris* (fig.34). This sumptuous prayer book was commissioned by the Archbishop of Paris and published in a limited edition in 1736. Boucher must have been working on the illustrations at the same time as he was painting the decorations for the Queen's Bedchamber, and it is typical that he should exploit his ideas for the royal commission in a spin-off venture. It is also worth noting that the *Bréviaire*, while religious in subject and available to a wider audience, was a work of private devotion. Here Boucher's delicate images were intended to combine with the words of the prayers to aid and inspire the reader's personal journey closer to God. The little vignettes of the city, locating the beginnings of this spiritual progression in the real world, add a distinctly picturesque note of Parisian style.

Rocaille

Boredom was one of the main threats to the happiness of the man of leisure in the eighteenth century; as Voltaire wrote, 'boredom and vapidity are a cold poison against which few people find an antidote'.[60] The arts came to be seen as a means of staving off this evil. The playwright Houdar de La Motte warned that 'boredom was born one day from uniformity', so the arts were required to be constantly new, inventive and surprising.[61] This approach encouraged the development of the playful and ever more fantastical style now called the rococo; then referred to by the adjective *rocaille*, which conveys the idea of picturesque decoration recalling the stone and shell-encrusted grottoes of the Renaissance.[62] Boucher's exceptional visual imagination perfectly matched the increasing demand for ever-changing *rocaille* imagery. As Papillon de La Ferté explained 'the ease with which he drew, made it more of an agreeable amusement than a terrible laborious task; he possessed to a superior degree the happy art of embellishing nature, and of giving grace to beauty'.[63] Boucher's instinct for the trends of Parisian fashion, his immersion in the Watteauesque idiom of the arabesque, his fascination with the decorative and his continuing links with the print world soon placed him at the centre of developments in rococo ornament. We have already mentioned Boucher's friendship with the leading rococo ornamentalist, Meissonnier, and Boucher's sale catalogue reveals that he also collected the type of decorative arts for which he provided designs.[64] Inventing *rocaille* designs thus

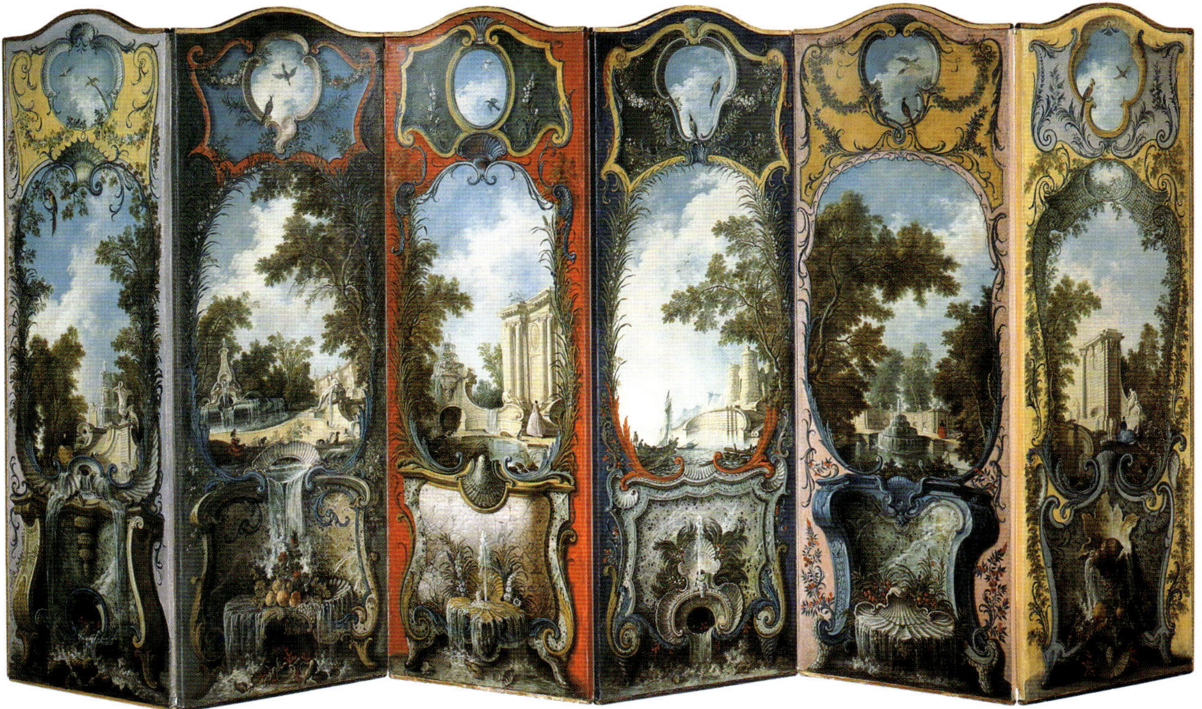

seems to have provided Boucher not only with a useful alternative source of income but also an amusing *divertissement* much to his own taste.

Figure 35 shows the type of rococo ornamental drawing Boucher produced.[65] It is marked by the same organic asymmetry that one finds in other rococo designs of the period. Two monkeys play on an assemblage of shells, corals and palms which seem to grow from an architectural pediment and to disappear into an imaginary vista with a fantastically curving façade, a fountain, vase and even a pyramid in the distance. It was engraved by Claude Duflos (1700–86) as one of a series of five decorative panels, published by Larmessin in 1737, which could be copied onto a screen in the manner of Boucher's own engraving after Watteau's *Sparrow-Nesters* (figs. 14 and 49).[66] Few rococo screens of this sort survive but the exquisite nature of such luxury objects is conveyed by a rare surviving example painted by another major rococo artist, Jacques de Lajoue (1686?–1761; fig.36).[67] A picture recently acquired by the Musée de la Chartreuse, Douai, also reveals that Boucher collaborated with Lajoue, providing picturesque figures for his landscapes.[68] Boucher's screen designs were sold by the engraver and print dealer Gabriel Huquier (1695–1772), another major figure in the dissemination of rococo ornament. Huquier published several series of prints after Boucher for fountains (1735–6), children (1735–40), cartouches (1736–38), *The Cries of Paris* (1737), vases (1738–49), Chinese subjects (1740s), male academies (1740s) and pastorals(1750s–60s).[69] Little wonder then that when he came to design a new address card in 1749, he classified prints after Boucher with those of Meissonnier, Oppenord and Lajoue (fig.37).[70]

Art, Science and the Enlightenment Collector

The celebration and imaginative translation of the beauty of the natural world which lies at the heart of rococo design was paralleled in Enlightenment thought by an equal fascination with nature. It was the meticulous observation of nature that led to the rapid development of the sciences during the period. Art, science and philosophy were not regarded as separate disciplines in the eighteenth century, but were all pursuits for the cultivated gentleman who increasingly preferred investigating

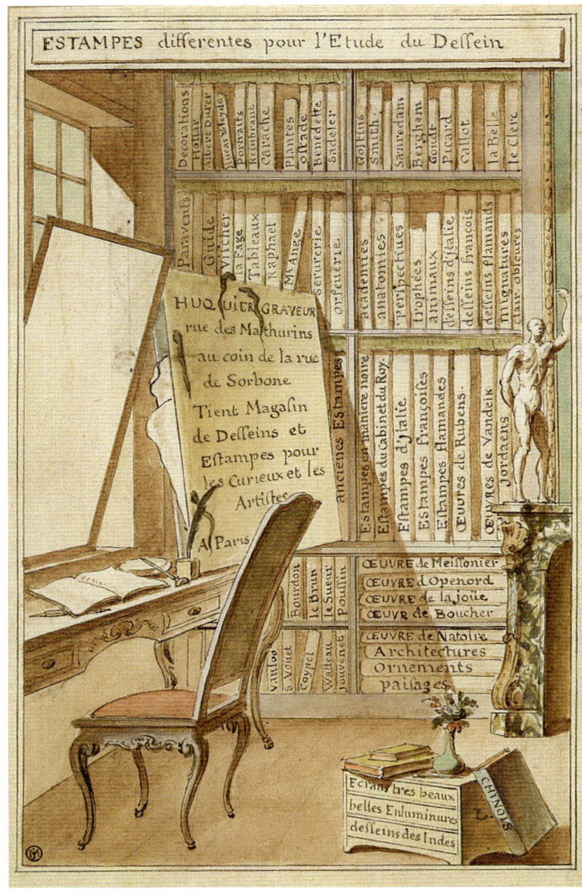

FIG.37
GABRIEL HUQUIER (1695–1772), *Project for an Address Card for Gabriel Huquier's Shop*, 1749, black chalk, pen and brown ink, brown wash and watercolour, 23.5 × 14.8cm, Paris, École Nationale Supérieure des Beaux-Arts

FIG.38 *opposite, left*
JEAN-BAPTISTE COURTONNE (1711–81), *The Second Natural History Cabinet of Bonnier de La Mosson*, detail, *c.*1739, pen and ink and coloured wash, height 37cm, Paris, Institut national d'Histoire de l'Art (collection Jacques Doucet)

FIG.39 *opposite, right*
CLAUDE DUFLOS (1700–1786) after BOUCHER, *Still life of Shells, Corals etc.*, 1736–44, engraving, 13 × 8cm, first used as frontispiece to Gersaint's *Catalogue raisonné de Cocquilles et autres Curiosités Naturelles* in 1736, this example taken from Gersaint's catalogue of the Bonnier de La Mosson Sale, 1744, London, Natural History Museum

and enjoying the terrestrial world to hypothesizing about the workings of heaven. An increasing number of periodicals reflected the combined interest in the arts and sciences such as *Observations sur l'histoire naturelle, sur la physique et sur la peinture*, 1752–6 and *Observations périodiques sur la physique, l'histoire naturelle et les arts*, 1756–7. Art might be defined in scientific terms as 'Nature operating with the aid of the instruments she has made'[71] and science in aesthetic terms, as in Dezallier d'Argenville's comment that 'France gives precedence to no nation in taste and curiosity; there one regards beautiful things, above all the productions of Nature, as the true food of the sciences'.[72] At the *Jardin du Roi* (Royal Botanical Gardens) on the Faubourg Saint-Victor, where regular public lectures were held on botany, pharmacology and chemistry, art was brought in to aid and embellish science, with a series of portraits by Oudry of the animals from the Royal *Ménagerie* (1739–45; Schwerin, Staatliches Museum).[73] Voltaire's materialist linking of art and science via the physiological workings of the senses also helps to explain the emphasis on a formalist, feel-good approach to art in the first half of the eighteenth century.[74] Science, meanwhile, was required to be as entertaining as art. Abbé Jean Antoine Nollet's popular scientific demonstrations were as much salon *divertissements* as scientific lectures, while the eloquent literary descriptions of animals in Buffon's *Histoire naturelle* (1749–89) are every bit as vivid and imaginative as the depictions of corals and shells in a Boucher *rocaille*. Something of this spirit of discovery and delight in nature and the imaginative arts it inspired is seen in Courtonne's view of the natural history cabinet of the collector Bonnier de La Mosson (fig.38).[75] Here shells and other curiosities are displayed in an elaborate display case in a rococo interior with decorative boiserie, pier glass and console table and an overdoor by Lajoue that depicts an artistic re-creation of the ideal *Cabinet of Physical Sciences* (1734; Russborough).[76]

Enlightenment collections were given further impetus by the commercial diversification of enterprising dealers such as Gersaint.[77] Finding it hard to survive as a local picture dealer, he began to travel to Holland in 1733 to search out new merchandise for the Parisian market. While purchasing the obligatory Dutch cabinet pictures he also started to acquire shells, corals, minerals and eventually art objects brought from the Indies by Dutch traders. Such diversification allowed him to attract a more distinguished clientele. He also publicised his activities by arranging public auctions for which he provided the first written *catalogues raisonnés*, or complete catalogues, whose rational ordering and clear descriptions of the merchandise on offer parallel other Enlightenment compendia of organized knowledge. Boucher designed the frontispiece for Gersaint's very first sale catalogue of this type, the *Catalogue raisonné de Cocquilles et autres Curiosités Naturelles* of 1736, which Gersaint re-used in 1744 for his catalogue of the Bonnier de La Mosson sale (fig.39).[78] Duflos's engraving after Boucher symbolises the interrelationship of knowledge, art, connoisseurship and commerce in eighteenth-century Paris and Boucher's central position in this world. The design does not aim to illustrate the contents of the catalogue, but rather to pique the potential buyer's curiosity and imagination by a deliberately ornamental presentation of the objects. As in the *Rocaille* Boucher uses his observation of corals and shells as a stimulus for his imagination, enabling him to portray a variation on nature which alludes to, but does not exactly reproduce, reality. In this it differs, for example, from Vallayer-Coster's famous still life of corals and shells (1769; Louvre), which records every detail of the objects with immense care, investing them with a gravity far removed from Boucher's witty approach.

As his earnings increased towards the end of the 1730s Boucher also became one of Gersaint's clients. His natural history cabinet, which represented a quarter of the value of his posthumous sale catalogue, was widely admired for both scientific and aesthetic reasons by contemporaries. A list of its contents demonstrates the eighteenth-century drive to catalogue the natural world as comprehensively as possible. In addition to minerals, precious stones, fossils, polypers, corals and shells it also included eight framed displays of sea-weed 'forming a sort of marine herbarium', a quantity of butterflies, 'a stuffed pheasant and a sparrowhawk with a little bird in its talons that it is about to devour' and 'a serpent from the Indies in a jar'.[79] Boucher shared the Enlightenment passion for engraved gems, a number of which are also listed together with four hundred and eighty copies in sulphur of classical intaglios and two imperial medals including one of Pope Alexander VIII.[80] Something of the naïve enthusiasm of the Enlightenment collector comes down to us in Mannlich's description of Boucher 'in his natural history cabinet which, by the beauty

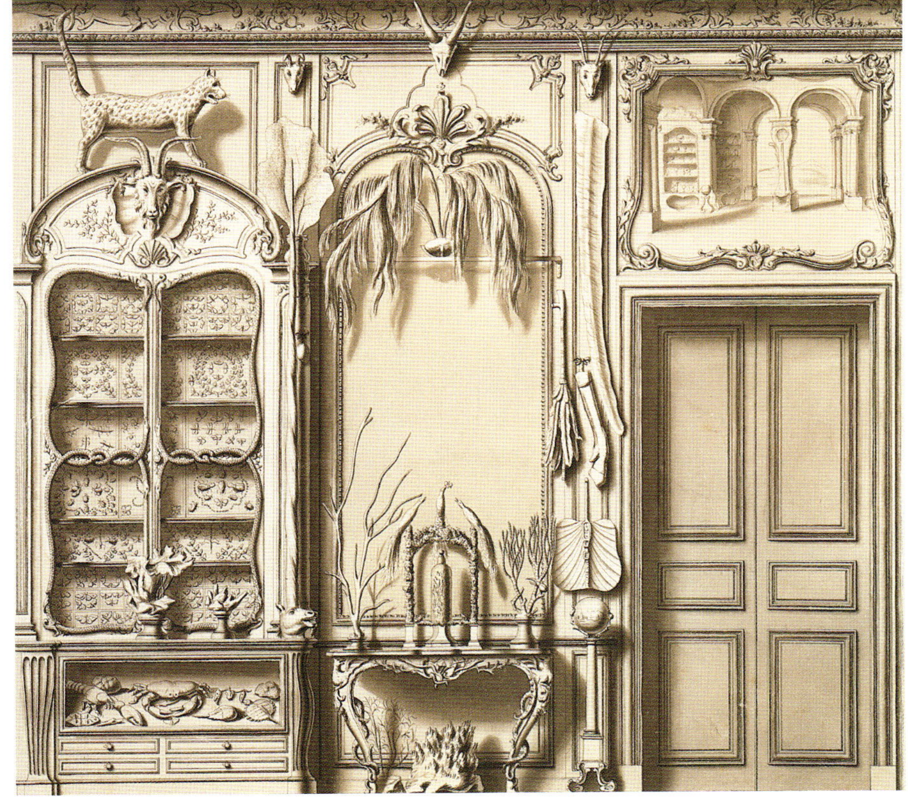

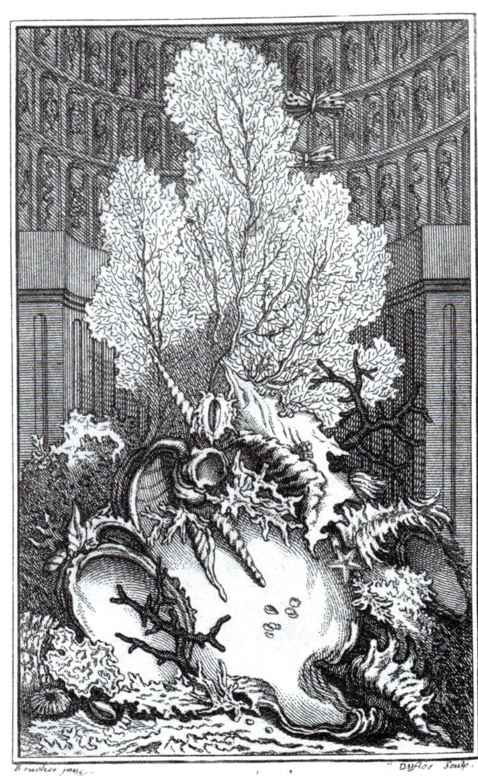

and the choice of objects it contained, and above all by its arrangement was unique'.[81] He later describes the elderly Boucher's excitement on receiving a case of minerals: 'decrepit as he was, he couldn't wait to undo it. At each rare and well-chosen piece, he cried and was happy as a child. Yet of all the case he kept only seven pieces for his cabinet, putting the rest aside to barter with the collectors and dealers with whom he had spent his life doing business. He told me that he had shells which, without being very rare, had cost him more than 600 *livres* each, having bartered them again and again against more beautiful examples of the same species; and giving each time one or two *louis* (gold coins) in addition. His mineral collection was unique, he had natural and polished solitaires of considerable worth and all types of precious stones, marbles, agates etc. down to cobbles from the street'.[82] A pocket-guide for shell-collectors, published in 1767, stressed the combined aesthetic and educational value of Boucher's collection: 'This emulator of Albani, whose brush guided by the Graces, offers only smiling images, possesses a curiosity cabinet, as agreeable as it is instructive. This ingenious painter has placed his shells on tables covered with glass. They present to the eyes of the onlooker an enamelled parterre which rivals with nature. On the left on entering, one finds a glass fronted case richly filled with madrepods, minerals, precious stones etc. which are all very beautiful'.[83] Like those of Bonnier de La Mosson, Boucher's display cabinets were every bit as precious as their contents, as lot 1863 of his sale catalogue reveals: 'a shell case veneered in violet wood by Oeben and with bronze mounts by Philippe Caffiéri'.[84] Something of the sheer visual beauty of such eighteenth-century natural history cabinets can still be seen today in the Cabinet Lafaille, preserved in the Natural History Museum at La Rochelle.[85]

Boucher's sale catalogue, a copy of which is in the Hertford House library, also reveals that he shared the eighteenth-century enthusiasm for mechanical toys and models, while his collection of objects from the Indies, to which we shall return in the following chapter, reflects his interest in far-away peoples and their customs. He also collected arms and armour from different countries including Spain, Italy, Turkey, Arabia and China. He had a large collection of oriental porcelain, which he could compare with European versions by Meissen and the local Vincennes-Sèvres factory. These stood alongside vessels in crystal, amber, jade and other semi-precious stones, plus glass and enamel ware, vases, gold boxes and jewels. He owned fine furniture, including examples of Boulle marquetry, wall lights, candelabra, display pedestals, bronzes, marble bas-reliefs and statues. As one might expect, over half of his collection consisted of paintings, drawings and engravings and was particularly rich in Dutch and Flemish landscapes and genre pictures. The visual effect of all these beautiful, educational and amusing objects must have been quite stunning and can only have further stimulated Boucher's fertile imagination. A final touch of rococo wit was added by the presence of objects such as 'a lamp after the antique made out of a man with his head between his legs holding his thighs and sticking out his tongue' and twenty-five Chinese fireworks.[86]

Boucher's estate at his death was valued at 152,618 *livres* 11 *sols*; 110,388 *livres* 15 *sols* of this was raised by the sale of his collection. Over seventy per cent of his wealth was thus tied up in his collection. Dezallier d'Argenville in 1727 had described the ideal curiosity cabinet as 'filled with everything that might amuse a gentleman (*honnête homme*), without incurring extraordinary expense'.[87] Commentators increasingly criticised those collectors who instead let their spending run out of control. Thus Fréron, criticising Antoine de La Roque, asked 'is it really necessary to live in sad and straitened circumstances, to be badly lodged, to renounce all the comforts of life … in order to accumulate curiosities, drawings etc. without ceasing'.[88] One of Boucher's most noted patrons, the comte de Tessin, did indeed ruin himself financially through his collecting habit[89] and Metra described the contents of the sale of another of Boucher's major patrons, Randon de Boisset, as 'terrible temptations for the amateur'.[90] So perhaps it was to such uncontrollable enthusiasms that Natoire was referring in 1754 when he wrote from Rome asking 'and Boucher, is he being reasonable?'.[91]

The Rococo Interior

Rococo art at its best is a supremely civilising, humane and sophisticated aesthetic. Like early Enlightenment learning it aimed to contribute to human happiness. Smaller and exquisitely embellished interiors added comfort and beauty to the lives, not just of sovereigns, but of whomever could afford them. Boucher's pictures were the perfect complement to ensembles conceived to delight the senses and engage the intellect through the use of mythology and fable, through the careful selection of the most picturesque in nature and through witty and surprising visual juxtapositions. Reason and control were always present, each element in the decoration being designed to work towards the equilibrium of the ensemble. In the architectural theorist Blondel's novel, *L'Homme du monde Éclairé par les Arts*, or *The Man of the World Enlightened by the Arts*, Blondel's hero describes an ideal interior as one where 'all the charming Arts were found together. There the gallant was in no way frivolous, the beautiful was not serious ... never was an ensemble better formed'.[92] His descriptions, recalling the rococo interiors of the 1730s and 1740s, are designed to seduce the senses and stimulate the imagination in much the same way. Hence his vivid description of the Hôtel de T***: 'The interiors ... are the most agreeable, the most interesting, the most varied that I have ever seen... one does not see a single straight line, either in the plans or in the elevations. Symmetry is banished here ... Imagine the enchanting spectacle of the lightest of ornaments, allied with the most gallant paintings, Bouchers and Natoires, mixed with bas-reliefs, trophies, flying dragons, and the prettiest little monkeys in the world. Everywhere one sees flowers, garlands, palms, *rocailles*, *pagodes*; finally, charming nothings mixed with curvilinear frames, moulded panelling, which dissimulate their origin with infinite art and disappear at their summit in picturesque contours beneath sculptures as admirable as they are interesting'.[93] Rather than trying to impress or teach through excessive public display or moral didacticism, the art of the rococo interior is one of allusion and illusion where observation and discovery in the real world are used to inspire the viewer to embark upon an imaginative journey, in which there could be no more inspiring guide than Boucher.

An eighteenth-century *appartement*, or suite of rooms, was basically arranged *en filade*, with one room opening on to another. An *appartement* usually consisted of a vestibule, decorated in a sober architectonic manner with a tiled floor, an *antichambre*, where the servants would wait and where Blondel advised the decorative use of mirrors rather than paintings, a richly decorated *salon* which might be used as a dining room, a *salle de compagnie*, room for entertaining or games room, and *chambres* or bedrooms with their associated *cabinets* and *garderobes*, wardrobe rooms. A grander house might also have a library, gallery, chapel and one of the new bathroom suites, possibly including a new-fangled flush toilet.[94] Different types of painting and subject were considered appropriate to each type of room. Boucher's first picture for the King, *The Leopard Hunt* (fig.40) was one of a series of exotic hunting pictures commissioned from the leading artists of the day to decorate the gallery of the King's private apartments at Versailles.[95] The contributions of the individual painters would have invited comparison amongst them, while the rich frames and panelling by Verberckt presented them as a unified ensemble. Boucher's picture with its dynamic composition, recalling Baroque models such as Rubens and Cortona, and its observation of nature, copying the animal studies of Oudry, displays his characteristic combination of detail and theatricality.[96] Large hunting pieces, picturesque landscapes and hunting still lifes were also considered appropriate decorations for grand

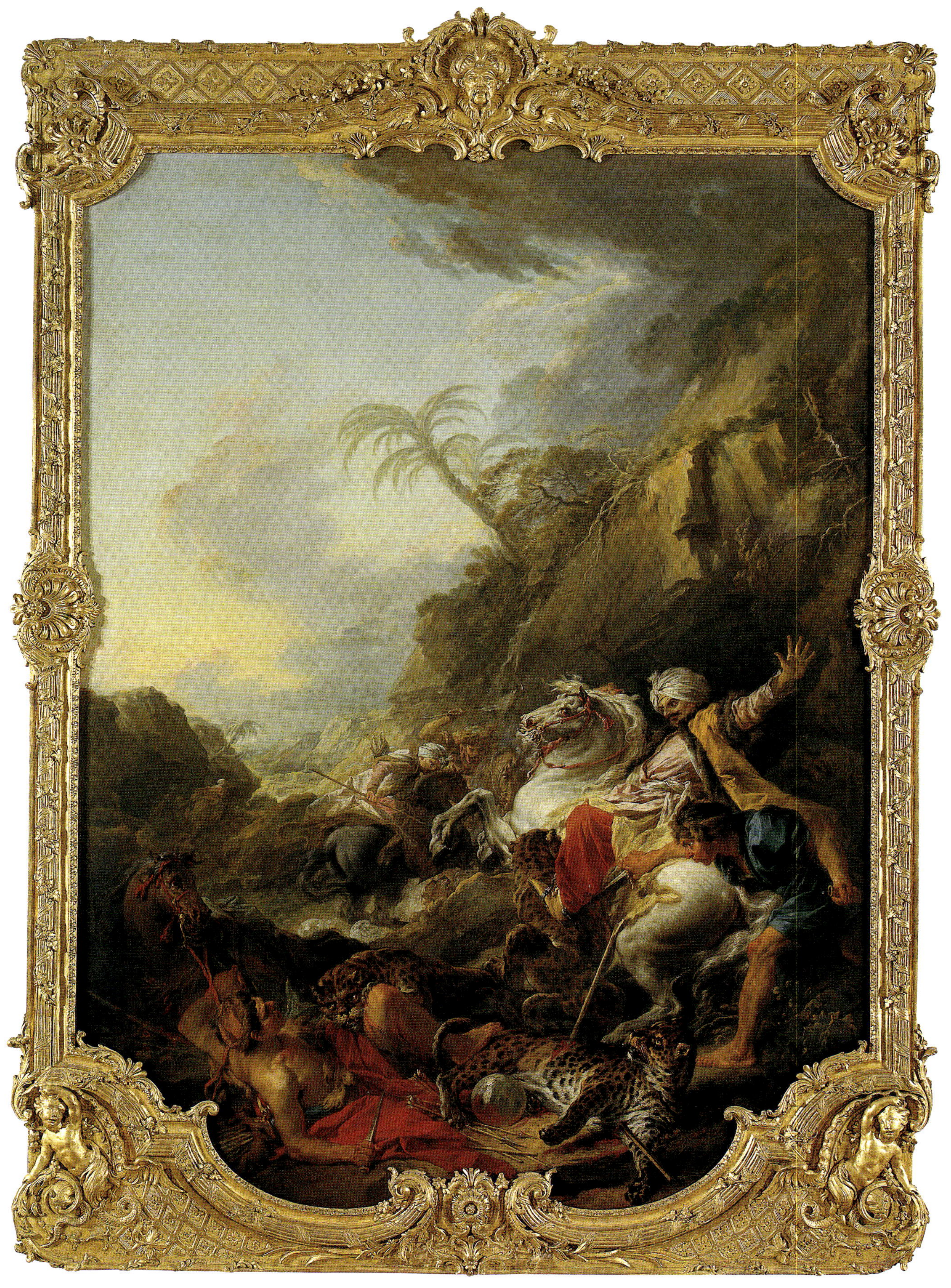

FIG.40 *opposite*
BOUCHER, *The Leopard Hunt*, 1736, oil on canvas, 174 × 129cm, Amiens, Musée de Picardie

FIG.41 *below*
Elevation of a large Salon with view of the Fireplace, engraving, 21 × 34.7cm, from J.-F. Blondel, *L'Architecture des Maisons de Plaisance*, vol.II, part II, Paris 1738, Library of Hertford House

salons (fig.41). These subjects reflect the all-pervasive influence of hunting, the 'noble exercise reserved for the pleasure of kings and the nobility', as the chief leisure pursuit of the elite from the King downwards.[97] Immense sums of money were expended on this costly activity, which on a royal hunt might involve as many as eighty horn-blowers, nine hundred hounds and a thousand horses.[98]

This type of picture represented one of the few instances where a painter was given scope to work on the grand scale in a rococo interior and Boucher was understandably keen to make his mark as a supplier of such works. As Oudry dominated the hunting and monumental still life market at the time, Boucher, an altogether more urban individual, combined his observations of Italian landscape with Dutch and Flemish rural anecdote and the verve of Castiglione's rustic processions to produce a new type of large picturesque landscape (*c.*1735; Munich, Norfolk (Virginia) and Pittsburgh).[99] The panache displayed in such pictures attracted Oudry's attention, and rather than have Boucher as a rival he enlisted his help to provide designs for the Beauvais tapestry manufactory, the royal industry that produced low warp tapestries for the private market.[100] Tapestries were an expensive luxury item, redolent of aristocratic prestige and tradition, which had embellished the country seats of the French

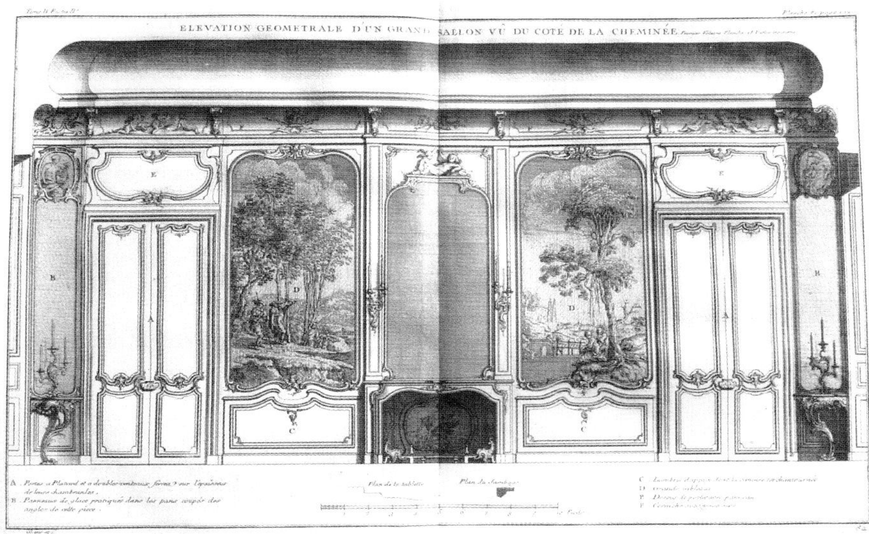

nobility for centuries. Boucher's great achievement was to transform the tapestry into yet another desirable piece of Parisian chic. The abbé de Fontenay noted that the depiction of landscape was 'appropriate to the tapestries of our apartments' and that the secret of Boucher's appeal lay in his creation of a particularly successful brand of 'nature embellished by the imagination'. [101] This is seen in *The Charlatan and the Peep-Show* (fig.42), one of the first tapestries of the *Fêtes Italiennes* (*Italian Festivities*) series, designed in 1736.[102] In addition to the elements already found in his large landscapes Boucher adds the fun of the fair by including fairground characters, familiar to his Parisian clientele from the popular Foire Saint-Germain and Foire Saint-Laurent, and a sprinkling of *fête galante* chic with courting couples such as those seen in the bottom right. The large scale of tapestries provided Boucher with a chance to work on the monumental scale and he proved himself more than equal to the challenge. Although the life-size cartoons from which the tapestry weavers worked were cut up to insert under the low-warp tapestry frames, a series of enchanting drawings in a variety of techniques attests to the care with which Boucher treated these commissions.[103] Papillon de La Ferté describes how 'the brilliant and luminous effect' of Boucher's Beauvais designs 'were so successful, that this manufactory, which was as if forgotten up till then, raised itself, and appeared to merit comparison with that of the Gobelins'.[104] Indeed the Gobelins, the royal manufactory of mainly high-warp tapestries for the King, requested that Boucher's talents be transferred to them in the 1750s, arguing that 'the Manufacture of Beauvais has sustained itself close on twenty years through the gracious pictures of Sr. Boucher alone ... Whether his works are good or bad, the most knowledgeable private clients will always give preference to novelty and will be pleased with subjects treated in the composition and taste of the said Sr. Boucher'.[105]

Such beguiling idealisations of the leisure pursuits of the Parisian elite immediately attracted a distinguished clientele, including Hercule-

FIG.42
BOUCHER, *The Charlatan and the Peep-Show*, first weaving 1736, wool and silk Beauvais tapestry, 324 × 417cm, from the series *Fêtes Italiennes*, New York, The Metropolitan Museum of Art, The Jules Bache Collection, 1949 (49.7.119)

FIG.43 *opposite, above*
GERMAIN BOFFRAND (1667–1754), Wall-elevation of the formal Bedchamber of the Prince de Rohan in the Hôtel de Soubise, *c.*1737, black chalk, 29.1 × 52.4cm, New York, Cooper Hewitt Museum of Design

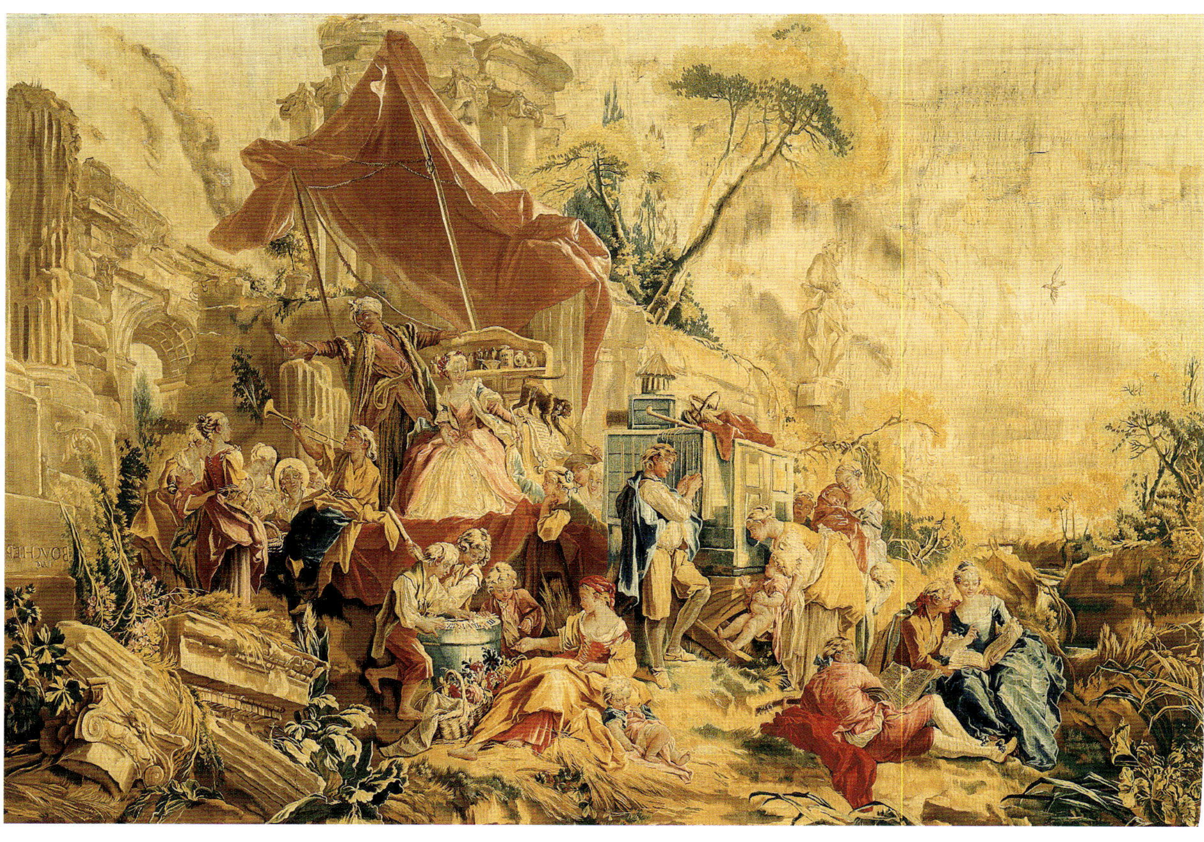

Mériadec de Rohan, prince de Soubise. In 1732, on the occasion of the prince's marriage to Marie-Sophie de Courcillon, the Hôtel Soubise, now home to the Archives Nationales in Paris, was completely remodelled by the architect Boffrand. An iconographical scheme was designed for the interior which celebrated both the position of the Rohans as *princes étrangers*, a rank close to that of princes of the blood, and also the nuptials of the head of the household.[106] The most famous ensemble was the series of pictures depicting the story of *Cupid and Psyche*, symbolising the union of spiritual and physical love, painted by Natoire in the *salon de la princesse*.[107] Boucher formed part of the team, including Carle Van Loo, Restout and Trémolières (1703-39), who were commissioned to paint overdoors for the rest of the hôtel. Boffrand's elaborate interior panelling left little space for paintings, as can be observed from the wall elevation of the prince's formal bedchamber (fig.43). Here Boucher painted the picture of *Aurora and Cephalus* seen on the right while Van Loo interpreted Boffrand's vision of *Mars and Venus* on the left; elsewhere in the same room Restout and Trémolières provided pictures of *Neptune and Amphitrite* and *Hercules and Hebe* (all the overdoors remain *in-situ* today, but in different rooms). Boucher, whose powers of invention and speed of execution won him the lion's share of the overdoors, went on to paint more mythologies in the princesse's apartments where the Graces could be seen educating Cupid in the formal bedchamber (version fig.141) while Venus descended from her chariot and perfected her toilette in the private bedroom. He also provided one of his pretty landscapes for the *cabinet vert* (green cabinet) in the apartments of the prince's grandchildren. His most original contributions, however, were his decorations for the prince's audience chamber, including two gallant pastoral overdoors (fig.44).[108] Here Boucher's rustic protagonists have been transformed into silk-clad shepherds in settings

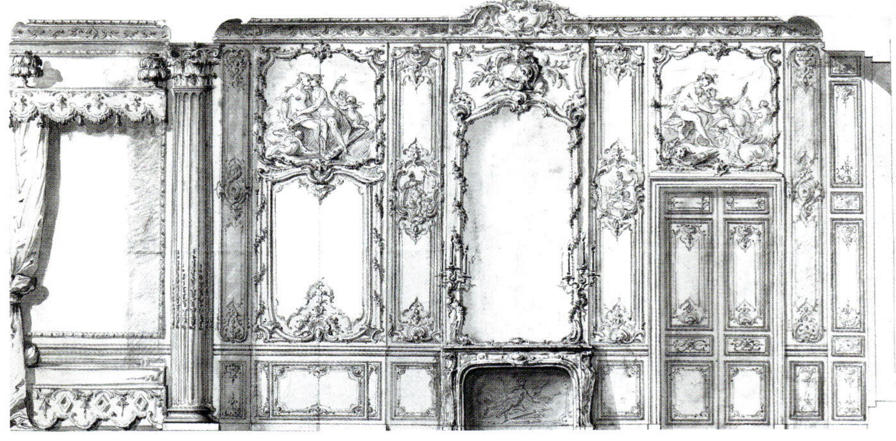

FIG.44 *below*
BOUCHER, *The Gallant Shepherd*, 1738, oil on canvas, 125 × 167cm, formerly Audience Chamber of the prince de Rohan now in the formal Bedchamber of the princesse, Paris, Hôtel Soubise

reminiscent of Watteau's park-landscapes. Their subjects anticipate another fairground phenomenon, the pastoral pantomimes of the Opéra Comique that were to have such a hold on the public imagination in the following decade. This shift from the rustic to the pastoral can also be followed in a series of coloured wash drawings for overdoors in Stockholm, the Louvre and the Metropolitan Museum, New York, which recall the delicacy of Boucher's preparatory drawings for his first tapestries, demonstrating how inter-linked such projects were in his mind.[109] The prince de Soubise placed his *Fêtes Italiennes* tapestries in the same room, which together with the overdoors created an original themed space that played with ideal representations of the country in an urbane and theatrical manner. It must have been an impressive demonstration of the prince's wealth, prestige, courtly values and impeccable modern taste.

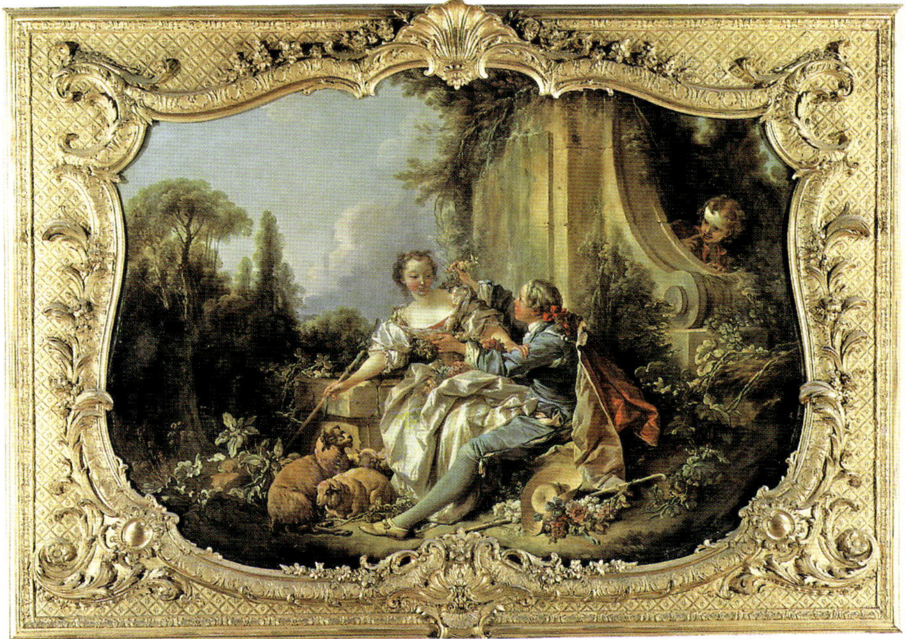

Art Versus Nature in Rural and and Urban Visions

Pascal in the seventeenth century had damned painting in general with the platonic comment 'how vain painting is, exciting admiration by its resemblance to things which we do not even admire in the original!'[110] The idea of the artist as the ape of nature was more humorously portrayed in pictures such as that of the monkey painter on copper commissioned from Watteau by the Regent to complement a Pieter Breughel, which presumably depicted exactly the kind of lowly subject despised by Pascal.[111] The Regent's evident appreciation of such works derived from the artist's power to transform even the lowliest subject into a work of art which pleased the senses more than the original. The artist did not aim, therefore, at the beginning of the eighteenth century to record base reality, the dirty shirt beneath the lace cuffs, as it were, but to use nature as inspiration for an alternative world of artistic beauty that would contribute to the onlookers' enjoyment and sense of well-being. Modern philosophers such as Locke acknowledged this when pointing out 'tis in vain to find fault with the arts of deceiving wherein men find pleasures in being deceived'.[112] Artists accordingly stressed their imaginative and technical capabilities. The self-portrait of Watteau flanked by two Wouwermans and Bouchers in Jean de Jullienne's collection (fig.5), for example, showed the artist in an interior posed before a landscape he had painted from his imagination. In his variation on the same subject (fig.45) Boucher exaggerates the contrasts between reality and fiction to humorous effect. Instead of an elegant self-portrait, Boucher envisages a down-at-heel young artist, surrounded by the clutter of his trade. The dim glow of a fire can just be seen

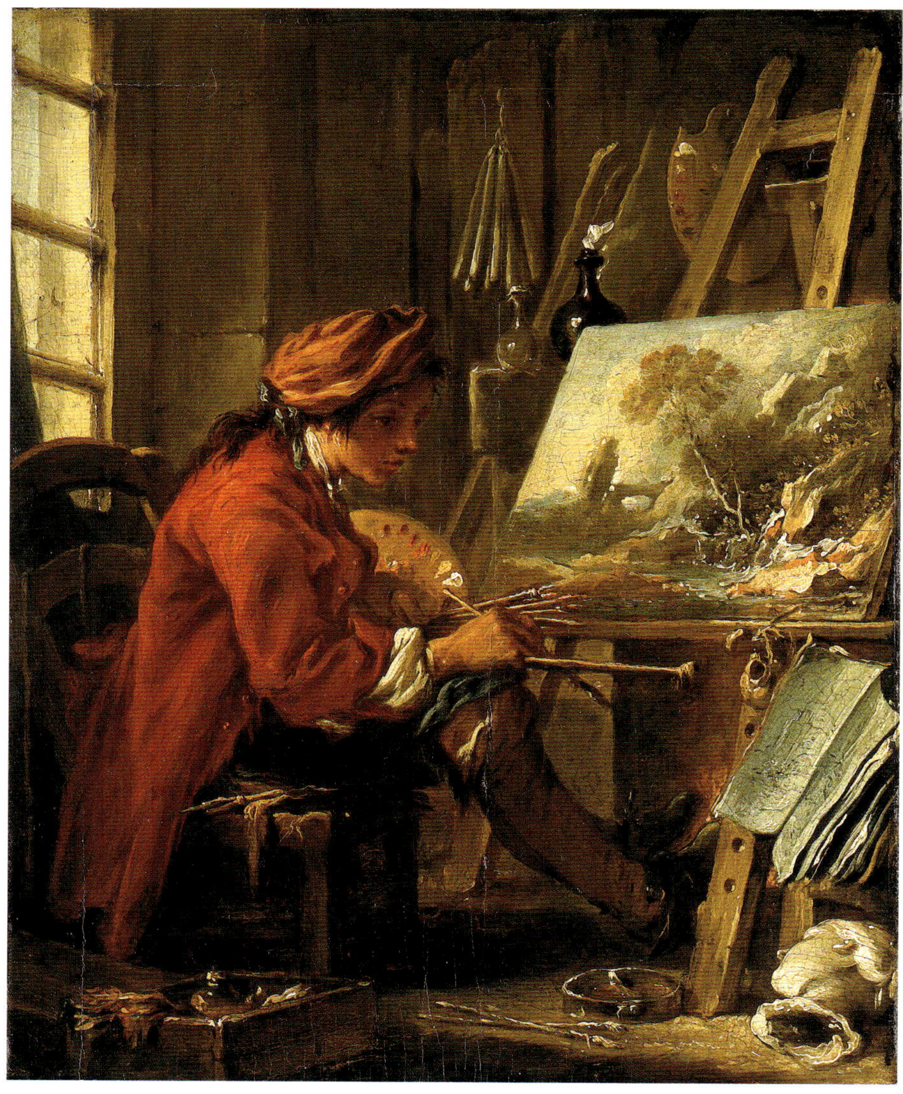

FIG.45
BOUCHER, *Young Artist in his Studio*, *c*.1732–5, oil on canvas, 27 × 22cm, Paris, Musée du Louvre

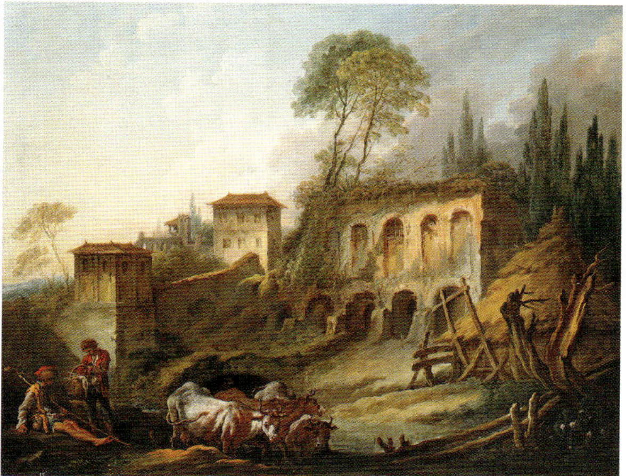

FIG.46 *right*
BOUCHER, *Capriccio Landscape with View of the Farnese Gardens*, 1734, oil on canvas, 63.5 × 81cm, New York, The Metropolitan Museum of Art, The Jack and Belle Linsky Collection, 1982 (1982.60.44)

beneath the easel on which, in stark contrast, the inspired child-painter is completing one of Boucher's own radiant Italianate views.[113] Boucher's highly artificial but nonetheless charming souvenir landscapes obviously proved a lucrative sideline to his large scale decorative paintings. Like the small Flemish-style pictures he painted in Italy, they were probably painted speculatively to attract buyers of cabinet pictures. Figure 46 shows one such view painted in 1734, the background landscape of which is based on a drawing Boucher did in Rome of the Palatine Hill, while the figures quote from his studies of Bloemaert.[114] Boucher thus combined art and studies after nature, and his continuing interest in the exact depiction of things is revealed by the fact that he owned and used a camera obscura and by Mannlich's assertion that he 'painted the smallest accessories from nature: something which, neither I, nor my friend Ménageot nor any collector however enlightened would have been able to know had we not seen it every day'.[115] Mannlich was in Boucher's studio just before the visit of the English portraitist, Reynolds, in 1768. One cannot help but detect an element of studied Gallic insouciance in the face of Reynolds' earnestness, when Reynolds found Boucher 'at work on a very large Picture, without drawings or models of any kind. On my remarking this particular circumstance, he said, when he was young, studying his art, he found it necessary to use models; but he had left them off for many years'.[116]

The rage for Dutch and Flemish cabinet pictures, a passion which Boucher shared with other contemporary collectors, also prompted him to try his hand at interior views inspired by artists like Kalf and Teniers. Like his seventeenth-century counterparts, Boucher, in the expanding picture market of contemporary Paris, needed to distinguish his productions from those of his competitors and create a fashion for his works. Using the gallant decorative approach he was known for elsewhere, he developed a charming French take on the northern cabinet picture, of which *The Beautiful Kitchen-Maid* (fig.47) is a good example.[117] Although rooted in the

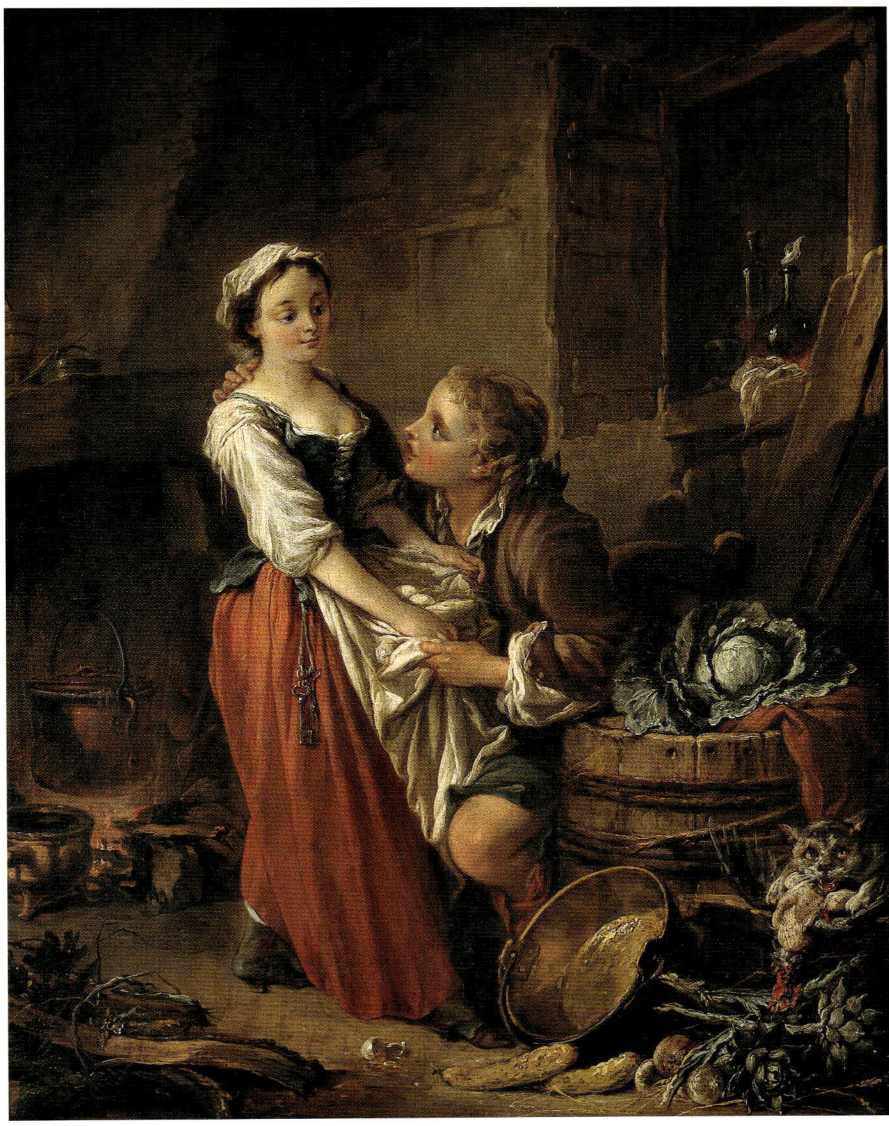

FIG.47
BOUCHER,
The Beautiful Kitchen-Maid, *c*.1733–4, oil on panel, 55.5 × 43.2cm, Paris, Musée Cognacq-Jay

traditional world of northern bawdy symbolism, where cracked eggs function as a metaphor for sex, Boucher's scenes deliberately veil any potential vulgarity with an overlay of French sophistication.[118] This also explains the French eighteenth-century practice of prettifying Dutch and Flemish interiors and landscapes by adding picturesque figures, which Boucher was recorded as doing on a number of occasions.[119] The finished pastel of a *Boy holding a Parsnip* (fig.48) is another variation on the theme of the deceptiveness of appearances. To a modern audience it may at first appear to be a drawing from life; the model, who resembles the little painter, is certainly one used by Boucher in the 1730s. His pose, however, is actually copied from an earlier picture by the artist, *Kitchen Maid and Young Boy* (*c*.1735, private collection).[120] In the 1738 pastel, Boucher has replaced the boy's ragged hat with a becoming blue bow, presenting a more appealing prospect for the growing number of connoisseurs of drawings whose custom Boucher obviously hoped to attract. Indeed the pastel is an example of the type of highly-prized presentation drawing by Boucher that collectors such as Jullienne hung on their walls (fig.5). The beautiful kitchen maid is also wittily re-used as a model for Ravenet's print after Boucher of the seller of *Des Radis des Raves*, radishes and celery, a well known eighteenth-century aphrodisiac which one would hardly need on catching sight of such a ravishing purveyor. This was one of the series of *The Cries of Paris* engraved by Le Bas and Ravenet and advertised by Huquier in 1737.[121] The picturesque vignettes, delightful as they are, provide a contrast to Mercier's description of the cries of the itinerant tradesmen in Paris in the eighteenth century: 'There is no town in the world where the criers in the street have more bitter or piercing voices. One has to hear them throwing their voices beyond the rooftops; their cries rise above the tumult of the crossroads. It is impossible for a foreigner to understand; the Parisian himself would not distinguish them were it not out of habit ... all these discordant cries form an ensemble ... the servants have an ear more practised ...they know how to distinguish them from the fourth floor and from one end of a street to another ... it is an inexplicable cacophony for every one else'.[122]

À la Mode

Boucher's concern with new ways of interpreting the traditional cabinet picture and his love of Paris, fashion and luxury in general came together at the end of the 1730s in his experiments with another genre, the *tableau de mode*, or fashion picture. He may have been encouraged in this by the departure of Jean-François de Troy in 1738 to take up the

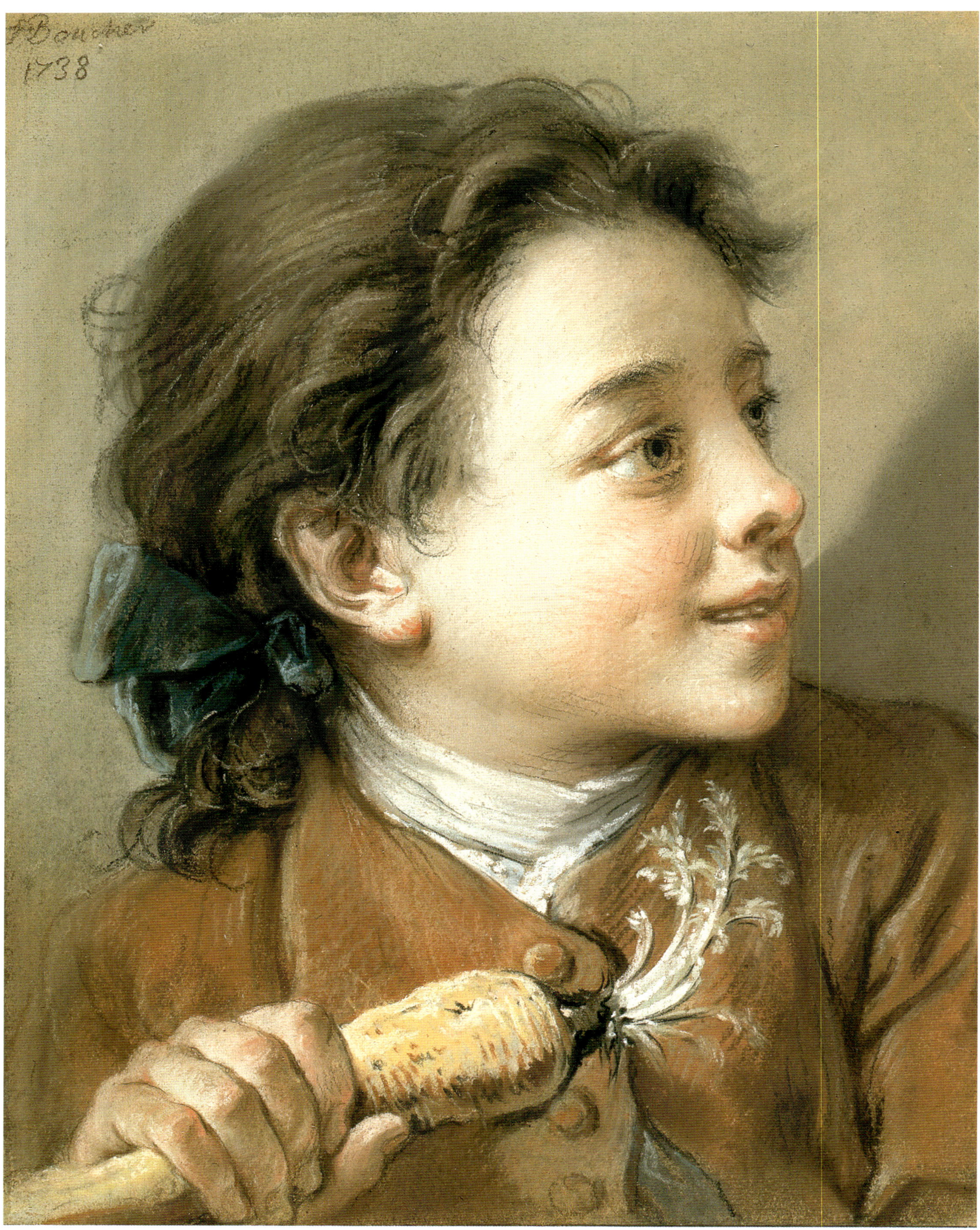
F Boucher
1738

FIG.48 *opposite*
BOUCHER, *Boy holding a Parsnip*, 1738, pastel, 30.6 × 24.1cm, Chicago, Institute of Art

FIG.49 *below*
JEAN FRANÇOIS DE TROY (1679–1752), *A Reading from Molière*, 1731, oil on canvas, 72.4 × 90.8cm, private collection

FIG.50 *right*
LAURENT CARS (1699–1771) after BOUCHER, *Dom Garcie de Navarre* or *The Jealous Prince*, 1734–35, etching and engraving, 19.4 × 14cm, London, British Museum

post of Director of the French Academy in Rome following the death of Vleughels. De Troy, in works such as *The Reading from Molière* (fig.49), had brilliantly encapsulated and idealised the preoccupations of the elite.[123] His meticulous depiction of material detail particularly endeared him to the financial classes, who sought his paintings as the visual expression of their wealth, tastes and aspirations. When Boucher was commissioned to provide illustrations of Molière, for an edition published 1734–5, he updated the scenes from their original seventeenth-century context to a refined version of the present day in order to make them more relevant and appealing to the contemporary reader.[124] The illustration to *Dom Garcie de Navarre* (fig.50), for example, depicts the jealous prince of the title watching the lovers embracing in front of a magnificent rococo pier glass and mirror. When Boucher was called upon to illustrate La Fontaine's tale of the haughty courtesan Constance's voluntary servitude to her beloved Camille (fig.51), he similarly transposed the scene to a fashionable Parisian interior.[125] Boucher follows De Troy in creating a convincing contemporary atmosphere through the inclusion of fashionable dress, furnishings and paraphernalia that would be immediately familiar to his audience. It is evident from their costumes that Camille and

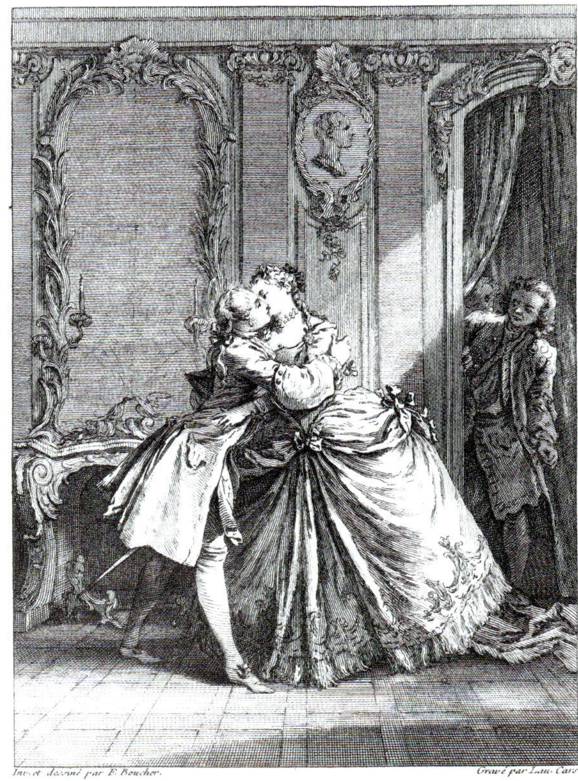

Constance have just returned from a masked ball. Constance wears a *costume espagnol*, Spanish fancy dress, and a mask lies abandoned on the parquet. From the clock, we can see that it is twenty to one in the morning and the light of the fire, in front of which stands a fashionable screen, illuminates the room. A note of humour and animal desire is added by the watchful cat snuggling up to the rococo fireplace. As in *The Reading from Molière*, interest is added by the inclusion of mirror, wall lights, objects on the mantelpiece, folding screen and drapery, exactly the type of luxury and clutter absent from Chardin genre pieces of the same period.

It was at precisely this period that Voltaire was defending such luxuries in *Le Mondain*, or *The Man of the World*, not only as desirable manifestations of the progress of civilisation but also as necessary stimuli for economic growth. He argued that 'above all ... Luxury enriches/ A great State, even if it ruins a small one./ This splendour, this Worldly Pomp/ Is the certain mark of a happy Reign/ The rich man is born to spend;/ The poor

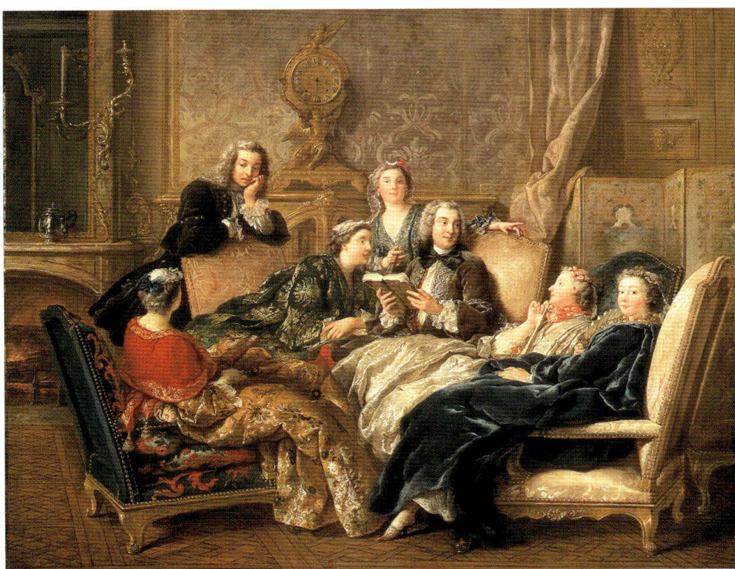

man is made to accumulate'.[126] Voltaire's poem was a paean to that seemingly effortless blend of the chic, the beautiful, the sexy and the expensive which is still the Parisian ideal. Voltaire also indicated the spread of such tastes through all levels of society: 'The taste for luxury enters all the social classes;/ The poor see in it the vanity of the Great;/ And work, thus guaranteed by indolence,/ Opens by slow steps the way to riches'.[127] The way to riches was indeed opening up to Boucher at this time and when he painted his first individual contribution to the *tableau de mode* in 1739 (fig.52), the well-to-do bourgeois interior was of the type in which Boucher himself was probably living.[128] Nowhere near as grand as De Troy's palatial rooms or as spartan as Chardin's vision of the bourgeoisie, Boucher's interior charms with its clutter of objects, children and people. We can see from the rococo clock that it is two, the time for dinner as it was then termed, and the family appears to be taking its post-prandial hot chocolate which is also being offered to the children. We know that Boucher's eldest children were about the age of those in the picture, and that he had two servants, Rentaut and his wife, who, together with Boucher's wife, have been identified as the characters in the picture. Boucher, however, was no ape of nature. His genius was for idealisation and he generally avoided specific characterisation, and normally even the lucrative practice of portrait painting. The interior, nevertheless, has an immediacy that derives from observation of real objects and people. Indeed many of the little touches that render the picture so charming, such as the fat Chinese figurine, or *magot*, representing the Chinese god of Happiness, the silver tea pot, the wall lights, the lacquer nest of tables and the mounted oriental porcelain pot-pourri are items which can be found in Boucher's sale catalogue.[129] With yet another genre mastered, by the end of the 1730s Boucher was indeed well on the way to becoming 'the Painter of the Graces and the most ingenious artist of our century'.

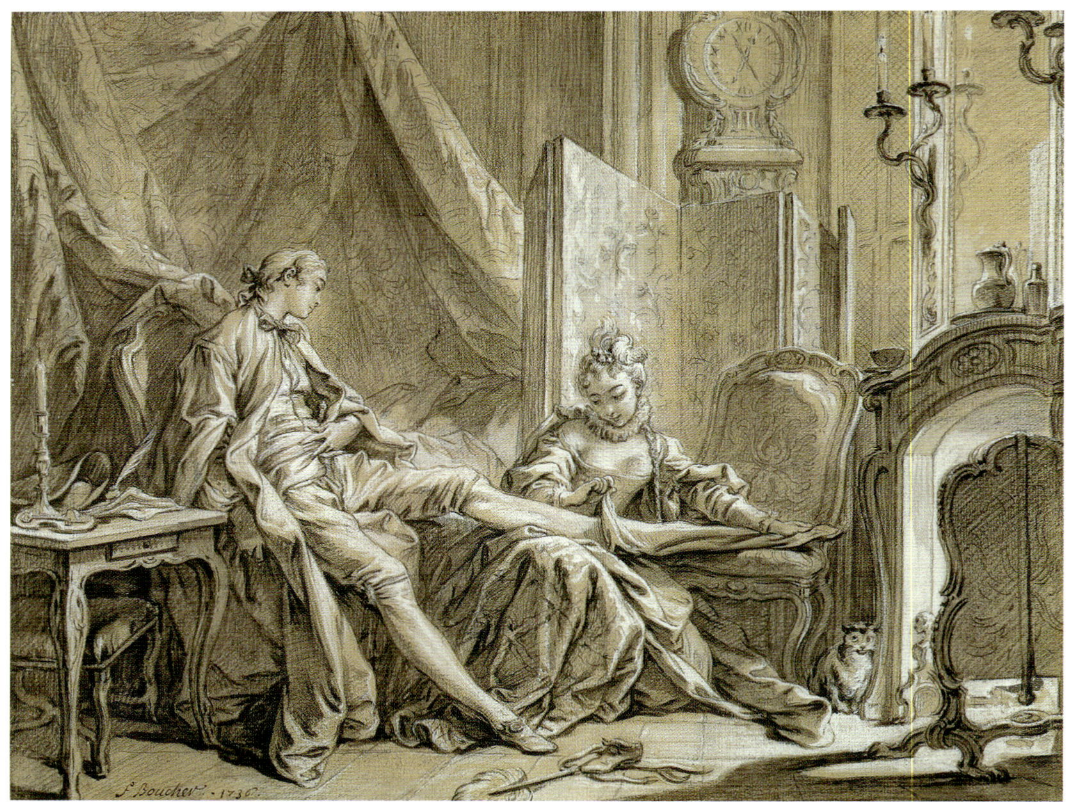

FIG.51
BOUCHER,
The Amorous Courtesan, 1736, black chalk, grey wash heightened with white, 74 × 93cm, Buckinghamshire, Waddesdon Manor, National Trust

FIG.52 *opposite*
BOUCHER,
The Luncheon, 1739, oil on canvas, 81.5 × 65.5cm, Paris, Musée du Louvre

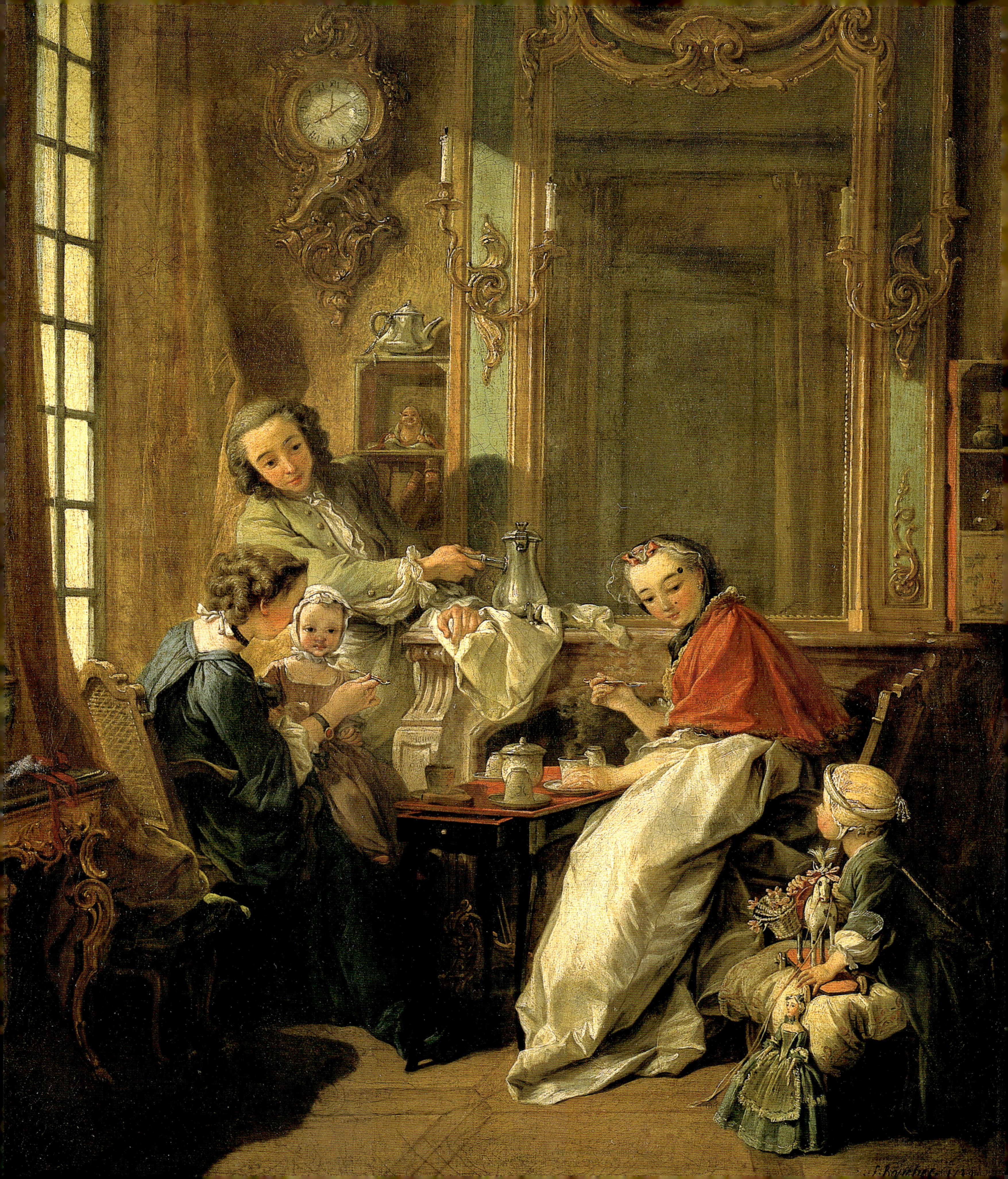

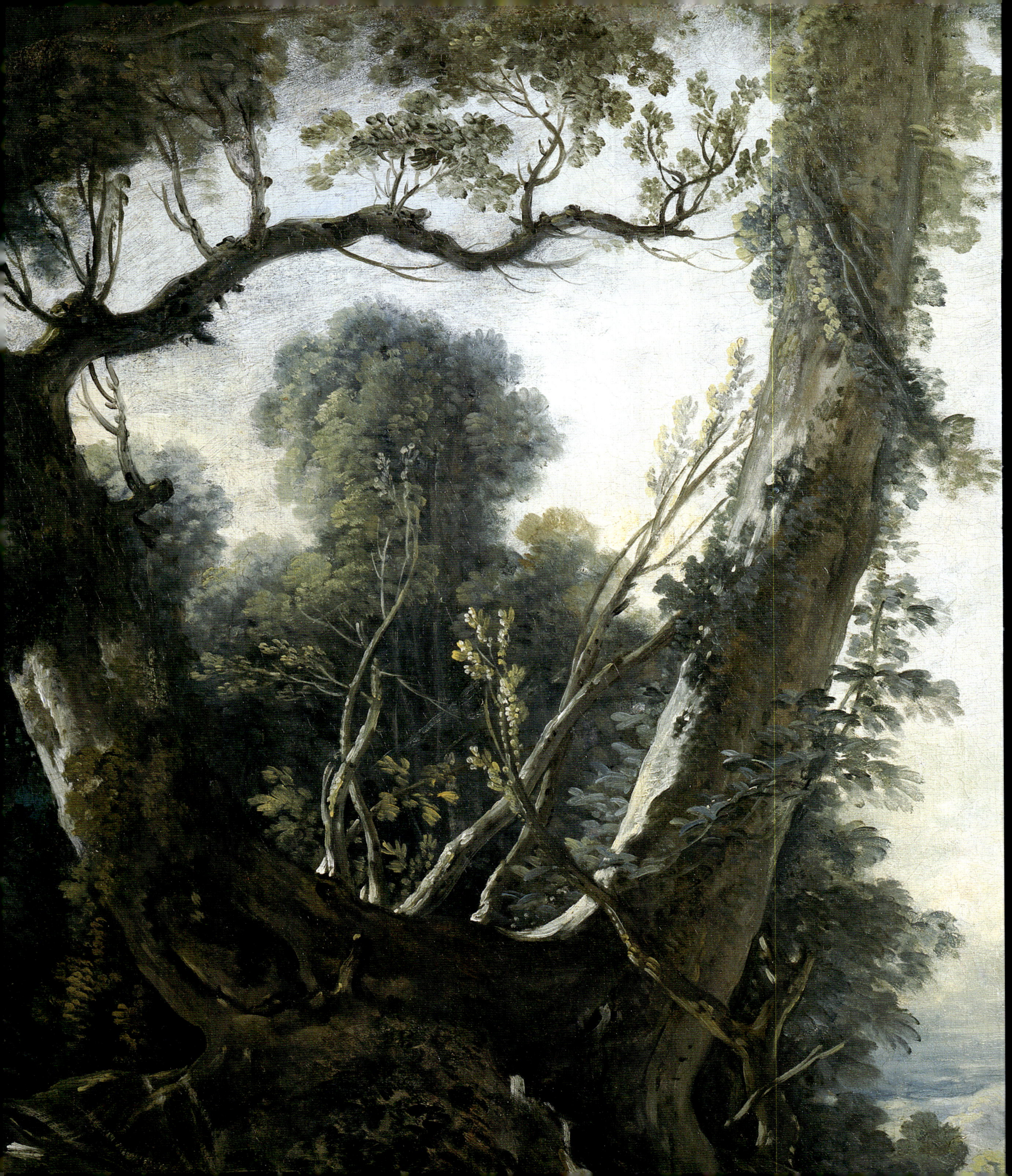

III

I look only for elegance, grace and beauty, sweetness, kindness and gaiety – in a word all that which breathes either flirtation or sensuality – all without too much liberty, draped with a veil which, in its scrupulous honnêteté, veils even the truth: a gauze which the imagination easily tears PIRON[1]

Goddesses, Princesses, Odalisques and Shepherdesses; Boucher in the 1740s

In 1742, Boucher provided a delightfully imaginative frontispiece to Dezallier d'Argenville's important treatise, *L'Histoire Naturelle éclaircie dans deux de ses parties principales, la Lithologie et la Conchyliologie*, or *Natural History explained in two of its principal parts, Mineralogy and Conchology* (fig.54). No incompatibility was perceived by contemporaries between Boucher's fanciful evocation of the book's theme and the scientific texts and engraved plates of minerals and shells. Boucher creates a rococo vision of the elements: a triton and siren bearing shells and corals from the sea, birds flying in the air, a camel, elephant, serpent, frog and tortoise on the earth, together with bees, presumably smoked out of their hive by fire. The 1780 edition of the same book recalled with admiration Boucher's own natural history cabinet describing how 'it was above all the shells that attracted the attention, either by their rarity, or by their size, or finally by their brilliance and variety of colour joined to the finest state of preservation'.[2] Perhaps this interest in conchology attracted Boucher to marine mythology; allowing him to marry his fascination with the fruits of the sea and rococo grottoes to his preference for gallant subjects and the female nude.

In 1740, Boucher painted the definitive rococo Venus (fig.55) for one of his most sympathetic patrons, the Swedish ambassador, Carl Gustaf, comte de Tessin (1695–1770), who in 1739–42 received artists regularly at his magnificent hôtel on the quai des Théatins in Paris.[3] Tessin wrote excitedly to his friend, Hårleman, in Sweden, 'Boucher has done a birth of Venus for me: an apparition! What a beautiful thing! Only eyes like yours are worthy of it'.[4] The picture was admired at the Salon, although found somewhat shocking by the more conservative visitors such as the abbé Desfontaines, who complained that 'there is in the picture by monsieur Boucher representing the birth of Venus too much grace, the vaunting of which stricter morals would have prevented'.[5] Tessin, nevertheless, was quite happy to pay Boucher his asking price of 1600 *livres* for this large and exquisitely finished historical canvas (a considerable sum when the salary of a professor at the Sorbonne was 1900 *livres* and the annual income of a bourgeois living off bonds and rents about 3000 *livres*).[6] Tessin regarded the work as a superb example of contemporary French history painting and later railed against those 'mad, ignorant people who imagine that one should place such liberal arts on the same level as the mechanical arts and artists on the level of artisans', adding that 'too many people are enslaved by a profound ignorance of the arts in general, of which they know neither the worth, nor the quality'.[7]

The Birth of Venus depicts a deliciously relaxed goddess emerging from the foam before a rocky

FIG.53 *facing previous page*
Boucher, *Daphnis and Chloé*, 1743, oil on canvas, detail, Wallace Collection

FIG.54 *below*
Pierre Quentin Chedel (1705–1763) after Boucher, engraving, 25.5 × 17.5cm, frontispiece to A.-J. Dezallier d'Argenville, *L'Histoire Naturelle éclaircie dans deux de ses parties principales, la Lithologie et la Conchyliologie (Natural History explained in two of its principal parts, Mineralogy and Conchology)*, Paris, 1742, London, Natural History Museum

cave, surrounded by gambolling cherubs, naiads lolling on frosted velvet waves and tritons energetically blowing fantastical shells; it perfectly illustrates those artistic objectives described in Piron's verses above. Alexis Piron wrote a petition in verse in 1746 requesting on Boucher's behalf a lodging in the Louvre from the new Minister of the Arts, Lenormand de Tournehem, uncle-in-law of the King's new mistress, Madame de Pompadour. The poem, written with Boucher's knowledge and agreement, provides us with valuable insights into Boucher's sense of artistic mission: what interested and motivated him and how he expected his pictures to be understood. Looking at *The Birth of Venus* today it is obvious that Boucher looked 'Only for elegance, Grace and Beauty/ Sweetness, kindness and gaiety/ In a word all that which breathes/ Either flirtation or sensuality'. Less clear, perhaps, to our more sexually explicit age is the

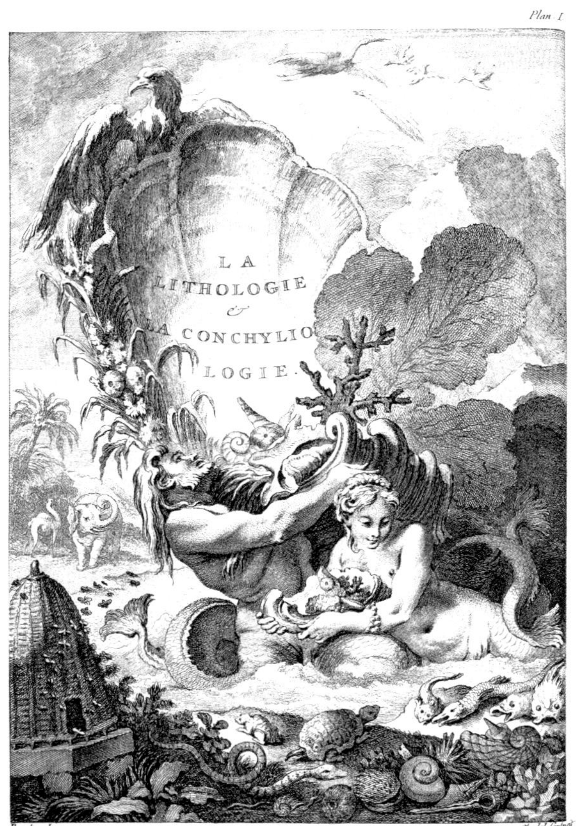

fact that Boucher's picture was not intended as a crude pornographic display, but was arranged and refined to create a highly sophisticated type of visual seduction, designed to please both the senses and the intellect. Thus whatever Boucher depicts is painted 'without too much liberty/ Draped with a veil/ which in its scrupulous *honnêteté*/ veils even the truth': the excitement lies in the power of Boucher's dazzling visuals to stimulate the imagination to tear the veil. As the century progressed, Boucher's art was cited in novels as a potential weapon in the lover's arsenal of seduction. Thus, Blondel's *Man of the World Enlightened by the Arts* imagined himself in his lady-love's 'house, in her cabinet even at her feet, explaining the beauties by which she was surrounded, using their voluptuous sensuality to my advantage'.[8] Unsurprisingly he goes on to describe 'a day cabinet, where Boucher had painted the Graces and the Loves, with that voluptuous sensuality so well known, and always so new'.[9]

Piron's poem also states that in response to those who might consider it an embarrassment to work only for the Muses (Paphos) or for the Graces (Cythère), Boucher, on the contrary, saw no disgrace in this; others could paint gods, kings and heroes, he preferred to paint the child, Cupid, who deceived them all. Moreover, Venus's conquest of Mars, the god of war, was considered a parable of the civilising force of peace and love. Accordingly, to be considered a 'painter of Love and the Graces' in the first half of the eighteenth century was a good thing; Piron used the same complimentary description for the poet Gentil Bernard.[10] Boucher's preoccupation with Venus was actually in keeping with the rôle of the post-Renaissance professional secular artist, for Venus, the goddess of beauty, was the patron deity of painting and sometimes seen as its personification.[11] For the ambitious member of the Royal Academy she occupied the place that the Virgin held for the artisan of the Parisian Guild of Saint Luke.[12] Even when the critical tide was beginning to turn against Boucher, towards the end of the 1740s, Baillet de Saint-Julien characterized him positively as 'the painter of the Graces'.[13]

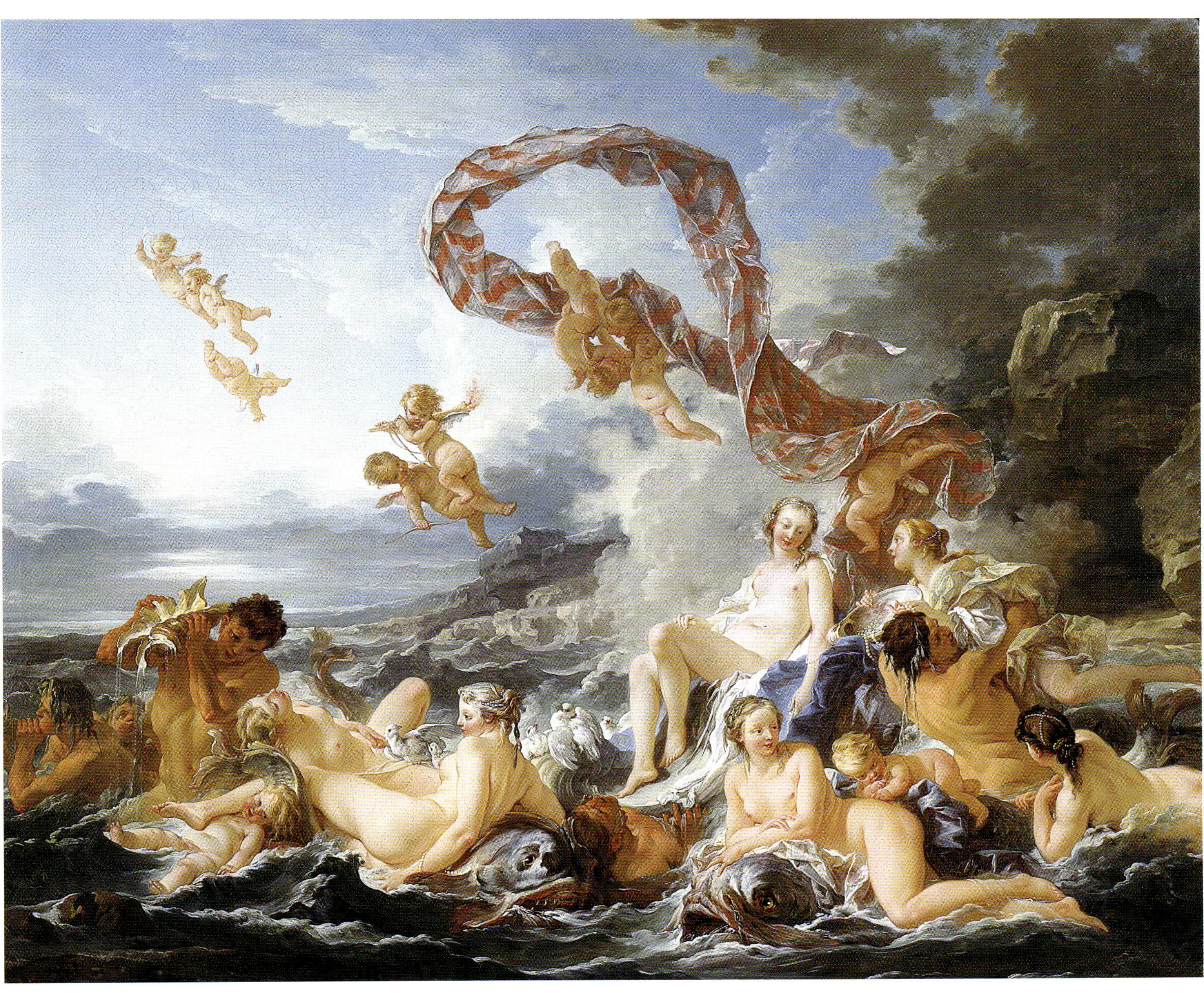

FIG.55
Boucher,
The Birth of Venus,
1740, oil on canvas,
130 × 162cm, Stockholm,
The National Museum of
Fine Arts

Saint-Yves went so far as to describe him as 'the most agreeable artist there ever was, the only one worthy to paint Venus, Love and the Graces'. He also notes, tongue-in-cheek, that Boucher's 'heroines … more agreeable [than Albani's], would make charming mistresses; but one would rather that one's wife resembled those painted by the Italian. The latter should paint only Virgins, and M. Boucher Venus, and the frivolous Court of Cythera'.[14] Piron's verses also mention a practical imperative behind Boucher's approach: 'I have children and needs/ To please is my taste, and there one runs less/ To Michael Angelo than to Albani'.[15]

The cost of fashion today exceeds that of the table and of one's stable MERCIER[16]

Boucher received his first modest pension of 400 *livres* from the Crown in 1742, which was increased to 600 *livres* two years later. The pension was both

FIG.56 *below*
BOUCHER, *Lady Fastening her Garter*, 1742, oil on canvas, 52.5 × 66.5cm, Madrid, Thyssen-Bornemiza Collection

FIG.57 *opposite*
BOUCHER, *Study of a Young Woman seen from Behind*, c.1742, black, red and white chalk on brown paper, 35.3 × 19.9cm, Paris, Fondation Custodia, Institut Néerlandais

an acknowledgement of Boucher's rising reputation and an encouragement in his work for the King which at that date included a commission to paint four overdoors for the Medal Cabinet of the King's Library on the rue de Richelieu and the first of a series of fifteen pictures for the Château de Choisy. The following year the Boucher family moved to an apartment in the rue de Grenelle, off the rue St-Honoré, although Piron's petition implies that even larger lodgings were needed. The situation may have been alleviated by Boucher gaining a separate studio in the Great Gallery of the Louvre, which he is recorded as relinquishing to Restout in 1752. Meanwhile Boucher's financial needs prompted him to diversify and Tessin became one of a number of connoisseurs anxious to commission a variety of different works from the artist. However, Tessin's interest in Boucher may not have been purely artistic. A manuscript note of 1767 by the bookseller M. Paulmy, inside a copy of Tessin's fairytale, *Faunillane ou L'Infante Jaune*, records that: 'this book is by the comte de Tessin, Swedish Ambassador in France, who, being enamoured of Madame Boucher and in order to have the excuse to see her more often, commissioned the illustrations from her husband, the painter, Boucher'.[17]

Tessin also commissioned another of Boucher's masterpieces of the 1740s, the *Lady Fastening her Garter* (fig.56), a highly finished cabinet picture comparable to *The Luncheon* (fig.52).[18] Unlike Jean-François de Troy's upper-class version

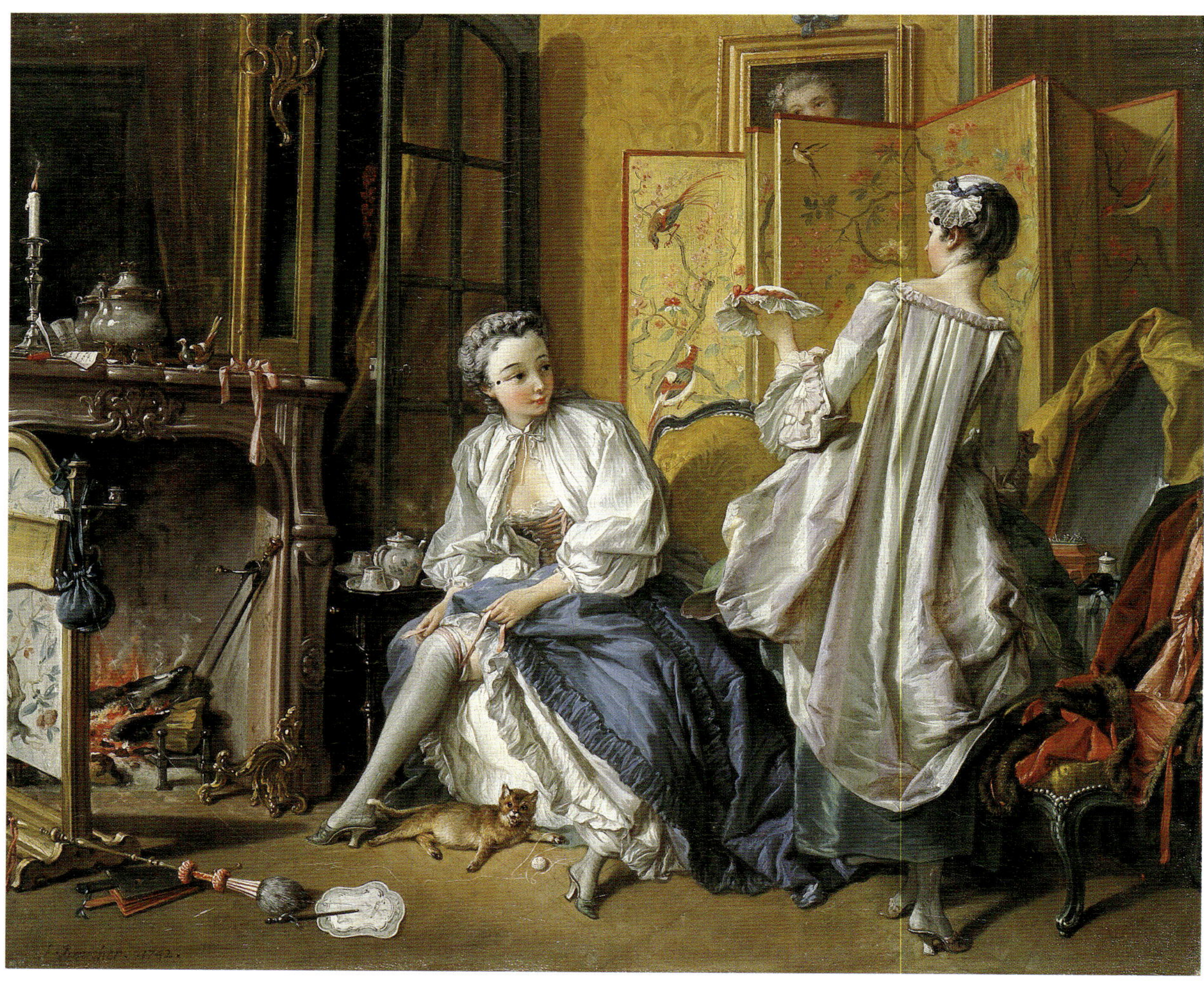

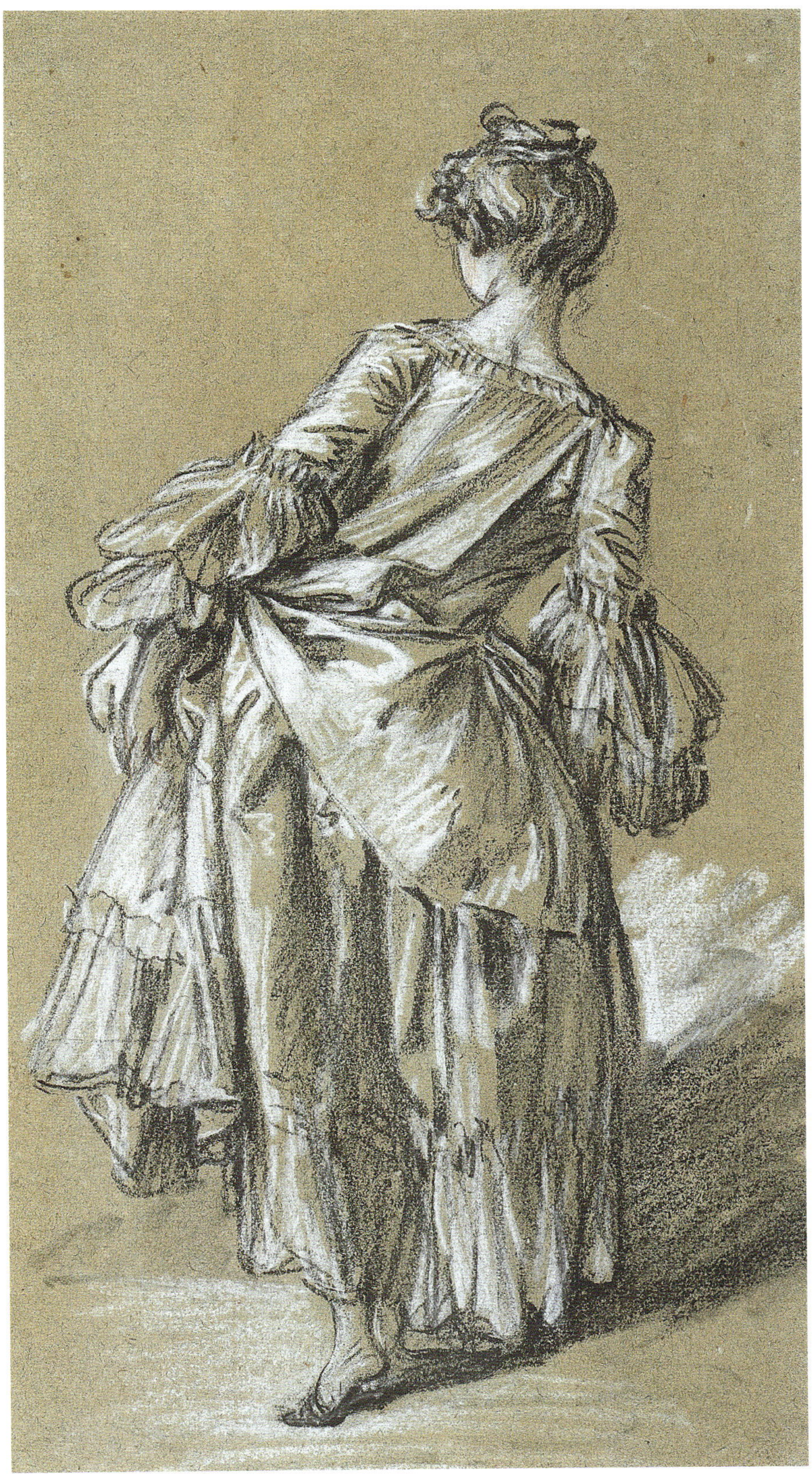

(1724, private collection),[19] where a lady is shown attempting to tie her garter while fending off an over-eager courtier, Boucher's picture is an altogether more cosy affair. It is in part a male fantasy about how women behave in the absence of men. The lady is preparing her toilette, her hair already dressed in the fashionable 'sheep's head' style, her face made up and her beauty-spots in place. But she still wears the *peignoir*, a type of negligée used to protect the clothes during the toilette, and, as she absent-mindedly ties her garter and flashes her thigh, she anticipates her next action which will be to don the *commode*, a lace cap worn by married women, held by her maid. She is not yet ready for the active coquetry implied by this; by depicting such an unselfconsciously intimate moment Boucher renders the scene all the more seductive. One is reminded of Mercier's comment that 'a pretty woman regularly does two toilettes every morning. The first is very secret, and lovers are never admitted there; they enter only at the specified hour. One can deceive a woman; but one must never surprise her: that's the rule'.[20] Like his contemporary Marivaux, however, Boucher was fascinated by such moments of surprise.[21] Among the paraphernalia of the scene are hints of sexuality, derived from the emblematic tradition of Dutch art – the cat with splayed legs, the open letter on the mantelpiece, the warning fire in the grate – but none of these elements is allowed to obtrude or to preach at us. We can take them or leave them as we survey the domestic clutter of the room on a winter's morning.

Boucher here proves himself to be the first artist since Watteau able to convey the allure of physical intimacy; a quality lacking, for example, in the charming but doll-like confections of Pater and Lancret, in the fashionable pretentiousness of De Troy or the silent gravity of Chardin. The picture flirts with our expectations and makes us wonder what happens next. Even the back-view of the fully-dressed maid is tantalising; with her pretty ankles, graceful *profil-perdu* and beauty spot she is every bit as attractive and elusive as Watteau's lady in pink in Gersaint's shop sign (fig.6). Indeed her figure is based on an exquisite study (fig.57) whose scintillating handling recalls Watteau's own chalk studies.[22] Her shoes, in an age long before Manolo Blahnik, recall Restif de La Bretonne's description of the allure of high heels: 'Look, Monsieur, what grace in that noble walk, and what majesty Madame is given by two or three additional inches'.[23] The link between fashion and sexuality was as clear to Boucher and his contemporaries as it is to devotees of *Sex and the City* today: 'everything of a woman should have a sexuality, clothes, hairstyle, shoes, above all shoes'.[24]

Montesquieu described the Parisian obsession with fashion at a time when 'a woman who leaves Paris to spend six months in the country comes back looking as out of date as if she had been abandoned there for thirty years'.[25] Mercier wrote that this obsession continued to affect all levels of society even on the eve of the Revolution: 'fashion is an extremely successful branch of commerce. Only the genius of the French could rejuvenate the most common things in a new manner ... No one dreams of disputing this incontestable superiority with us but what is most alarming, is that the *petite-bourgeoise* wants to imitate the marquise and the duchesse. The poor husband is obliged to sweat blood and water to satisfy the caprices of his wife'.[26] Boucher could easily have based his observation of the fashions in the picture on his own wife's clothes, for Madame Boucher's exquisite wardrobe, at the time of her husband's death, was worth 4880 *livres*.[27] The fur-trimmed red velvet cape draped on the chair to the right was certainly the latest 'must-have': Tessin's wife had been portrayed wearing one in her portrait by Nattier the previous year.[28] It is not just the female protagonists and their dress, however, but every intimate detail of the interior that combines to seduce and stimulate. As in *The Luncheon*, part of the picture's sense of immediacy depends on its detailing of the fashionable interior and the wealth of covetable objects it contains. We know that Boucher owned such items as the red lacquer dressing-table mirror and matching chinoiserie screen with red lacquer frame.[29] Other objects, such as the coloured porcelain bird and mounted crackled porcelain *cassolette* on the mantelpiece, are also found in Boucher's sale catalogue.[30] One wonders if Blondel would have classed Boucher among the gentlemen he criticises when he commented that 'pretty women are distracted by the desire to please ... and their taste is generally quite frivolous. How many men have the misfortune to resemble them!'[31]

After Tessin's return to Sweden in 1742, he was replaced in Paris by his friend Hårleman who later wrote how 'poor Boucher, his pretty wife, the good Oudry, Van Loo and lots of other artists, ask me with tears in their eyes to find Your Excellency in Sweden'.[32] The departure of such a generous patron, however, brought Boucher to the attention of a wider clientele, for the collection Tessin took with him to Sweden was admired by Frederick of Prussia's sister, Crown Princess Louisa Ulrika, wife of the heir to the Swedish throne. France's alliances with Sweden and Denmark and, during the war of the Austrian succession (1741–48), with Bavaria, Prussia and Spain, encouraged the export of French art to Scandinavia and Germany. Boucher was friendly with Swedish artists in Paris, numbered Swedish and Danish pupils among his students, was commissioned to paint works for the Swedish Court and the Danish and German aristocracy and was even invited to become First Painter to Frederick the Great in 1748.[32]

Frederick's sister, avid for Parisian chic and details of day-to-day life in the capital of fashion, instructed her agents to acquire genre pictures from the leading French artists of the day. The original of Boucher's *Milliner* (1746; Stockholm), of which the Wallace Collection picture (fig.58) is a copy probably painted by Boucher's studio assistants and later used as an engraver's model, was one of a series of four cabinet pictures commissioned by Tessin on Princess Louisa Ulrika's behalf.[34] The secretary to the Swedish embassy in Paris, Carl Reinhold Berch, wrote of the subjects initially agreed with Boucher: 'Morning will be a woman who has finished with her hairdresser, is still

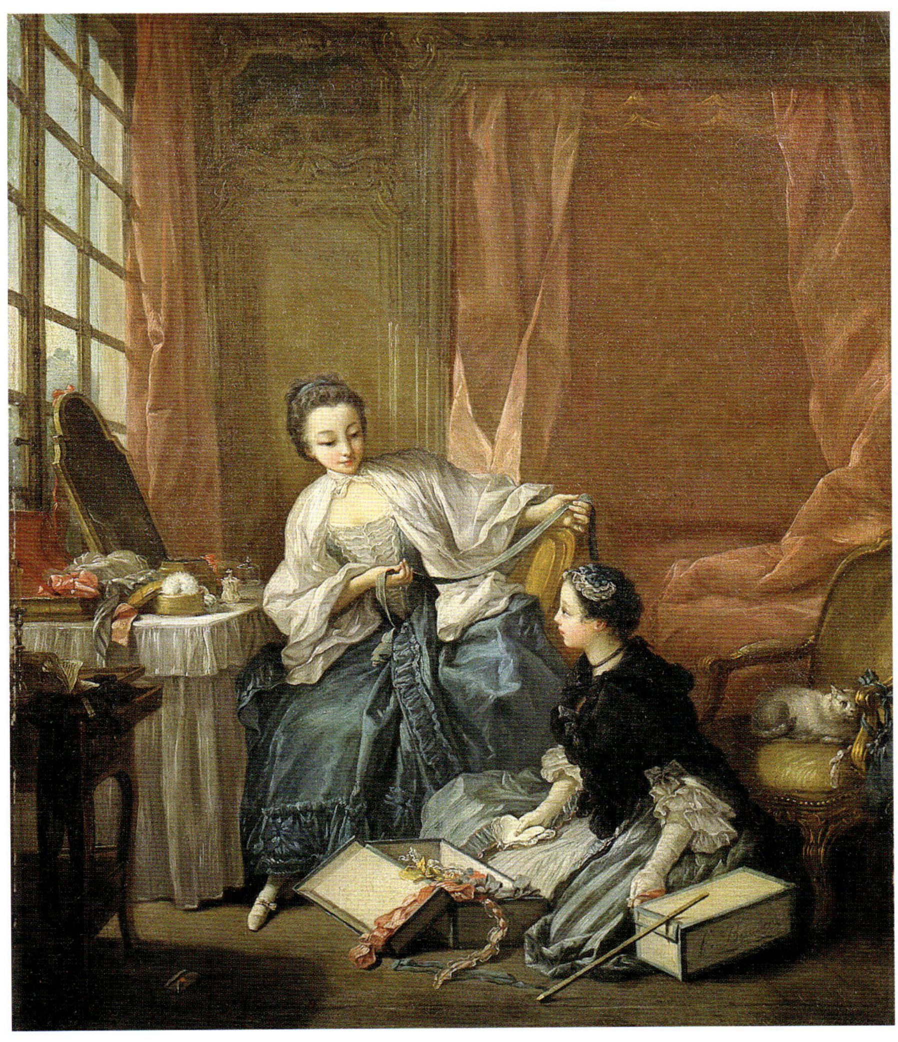

FIG.58
Studio of Boucher, *The Milliner*, 1746, oil on canvas, 63 × 51.8cm, Wallace Collection

wearing her negligée, and is enjoying looking at the furbelows a milliner is proposing to her. Midday, a conversation in the Palais-Royal between a lady and a fine wit who is reciting some dreadful poem, boring the lady who shows the time on her watch ... After Dinner or Evening is the trickiest: the chambermaid bringing letters arranging a rendez-vous, or cape, gloves etc... for her mistress who wishes to pay a visit; Night can be represented by frivolous young things in ball dresses mocking one who has fallen asleep. One will try to depict them in such a way that the Four Times of the Day might also represent the Four Seasons'.[35] Berch explains in the same letter why Boucher might be preferred to Chardin, who also painted pictures for the Princess: 'Boucher is quicker' he wrote, optimistically stating that the four proposed paintings would be finished by the end of March 1745.[36] We learn from the same letter that Boucher's standard fee for such small cabinet pictures was '600 *livres* ... when there is a high degree of finish', but might be reduced in the case of a good customer like Tessin – Boucher nevertheless stipulating that he would like to be paid more promptly than on previous occasions! In the event, Boucher only painted the first picture, using failing eyesight as an excuse for his repeated delays. Given the time it took to paint a highly finished cabinet picture and the fact that Boucher could command 800 *livres* apiece for more rapidly executed overdoors for the King's bedchamber at Marly, it is unsurprising that he tried to increase his price for the Swedish pictures, and then abandoned both the commission and the painting of genre pictures in general.[37]

The Milliner is thus Boucher's last direct observation on contemporary mores. Its subject, together with those of its intended companions, demonstrates that the appeal of such genre pictures lay in their depiction of fashionable behaviour as much as in the depiction of fashionable objects. Montesquieu claimed that 'the role of a pretty woman is much more serious than one thinks' and that 'there is nothing more serious than that which happens every morning at her toilette'.[38] This was an age where appearances were so important that an entire room might be devoted to the daily spectacle of the long transformation necessitated by the dictates of fashion. The interior seen in Boucher's picture is less opulent; the lady is receiving her morning visit in her bedchamber, as can be seen from the presence of the alcove bed with its silk drapery in the background. The plain panelled room, with its landscape overdoor, appears to be a fashionable and comfortable bourgeois interior. Boucher's lady is seated before a draped toilet table where she would apply her makeup. In the seventeenth century, women at Versailles had used cosmetics in a highly stylised way to signify their membership of the elite. As

FIG.59 *opposite*
COMTE DE CAYLUS (1692–1765) after BOUCHER, *At the Sign of the Pagoda*, 1740, engraved trade card, 27.4 × 18.5cm, Paris, Bibliothèque Nationale de France

distinctions between the Court and the rich of Paris became blurred at the beginning of the eighteenth century, cosmetics were taken up by fashion-conscious Parisiennes. Makeup remained a conscious artifice, applied publicly during the morning toilette, but was increasingly seen as a way to embellish nature rather than as a mask and became another technique of seduction for the fashionable lady.[39] Hair fashions were equally artificial and the lady in Boucher's image wears a *peignoir* to protect her clothes from the flour mixture used to powder her hair. It was the perfect moment for milliner to call and tout her ribbons and furbelows to a client already at the dressing table. This second public toilette, according to Mercier, was 'a game invented by coquetry'. It was one of those social moments when the theatre of amorous intrigue, whose echoes reach us today in the comedies of Marivaux or the operas of Mozart, came to the fore. Caraccioli vividly describes how it was at the toilette that one 'receives *billets doux*, returns them, introduces love and dismissal, the caress and the complaint, provocation and rebuttal; it is there that the Marquis disputes the conquest of the pretty Widow or the divine Comtesse with the Chevalier, making their assaults with fine wit; it is there that the Parrots, the Canaries and the Dogs come to be admired, kissed and licked; it is there that the chamber maids are sent away trembling, are recalled, and always told off, and there that a poor hairdresser, comb in the air for two hours, waits until the twisting head comes to a stop, so that he can finally put a curl in place'.[40] At the core of Boucher's picture, therefore, is the seductive image of a woman planning her own strategy of seduction.

To transform China into one of the Realms of the Rococo GONCOURT[41]

In 1740 Gersaint renamed his shop *At the Sign of the Pagoda*. The new name was meant to arouse the interest of a more elegant clientele than would normally be seen on the Pont Notre-Dame. It deliberately evoked the glamour of the Indies and of China in particular. Like Watteau before him, Boucher now helped the enterprising Gersaint to advertise by providing a drawing (lost) for a trade card which was then engraved by the comte de Caylus (fig.59).[42] Both Boucher and Caylus were clients of Gersaint and the card was probably something of a joke, as the aristocratic Caylus would certainly not have viewed the task as a commission and still less have expected to be paid.[43] The personal nature of the commission perhaps also explains the beauty and wit of the image, easily the most lavish and exquisite trade card of the eighteenth century. Indeed, it seems to have had a certain amount of success as a work of art in its own right. Tessin, for example, commissioned the Swedish artist Olaf Fridsberg to copy it onto a corner cupboard, seen in a watercolour of Tessin's wife in her room in the château of Äkero.[44] The objects depicted on Gersaint's card reflect the diverse merchandise in which he now specialised and the type of object that Boucher himself collected. The inscription tells us that *At the Pagoda* one could find 'all sorts of new and tasteful bibelots, jewels, mirrors, cabinet pictures, *pagodes*, Japanese lacquer-ware and porcelains, shells and other objects of natural history, stones, agates, and generally all curious and strange merchandises'. Here we find one of Boucher's fat *magots*, peeking out from beneath a fringed curtain, perched on top of a lacquer cabinet on a rococo stand and holding another *pagode* in his hand. Shells, corals, *pagodes*, a porcelain bird, lacquer boxes, a tray and cups, fans, tea and coffee pots, a coffee grinder, arrows and a Chinese scroll are arranged in an artfully careless manner in the foreground. Just visible in the background are a group of canvases on the left and to the right a screen and a bundle of walking sticks with funny faces. From Watteau's ideal vision of connoisseurship, we have moved to an exquisitely trendy visiting card advertising a delightful clutter of fine and decorative art presided over by the Chinese god of happiness.

In the preface to his play *Bajazet* (1676) Racine commented that, 'people barely distinguish between that which is a thousand years away from them, and that which is a thousand leagues away'.[45]

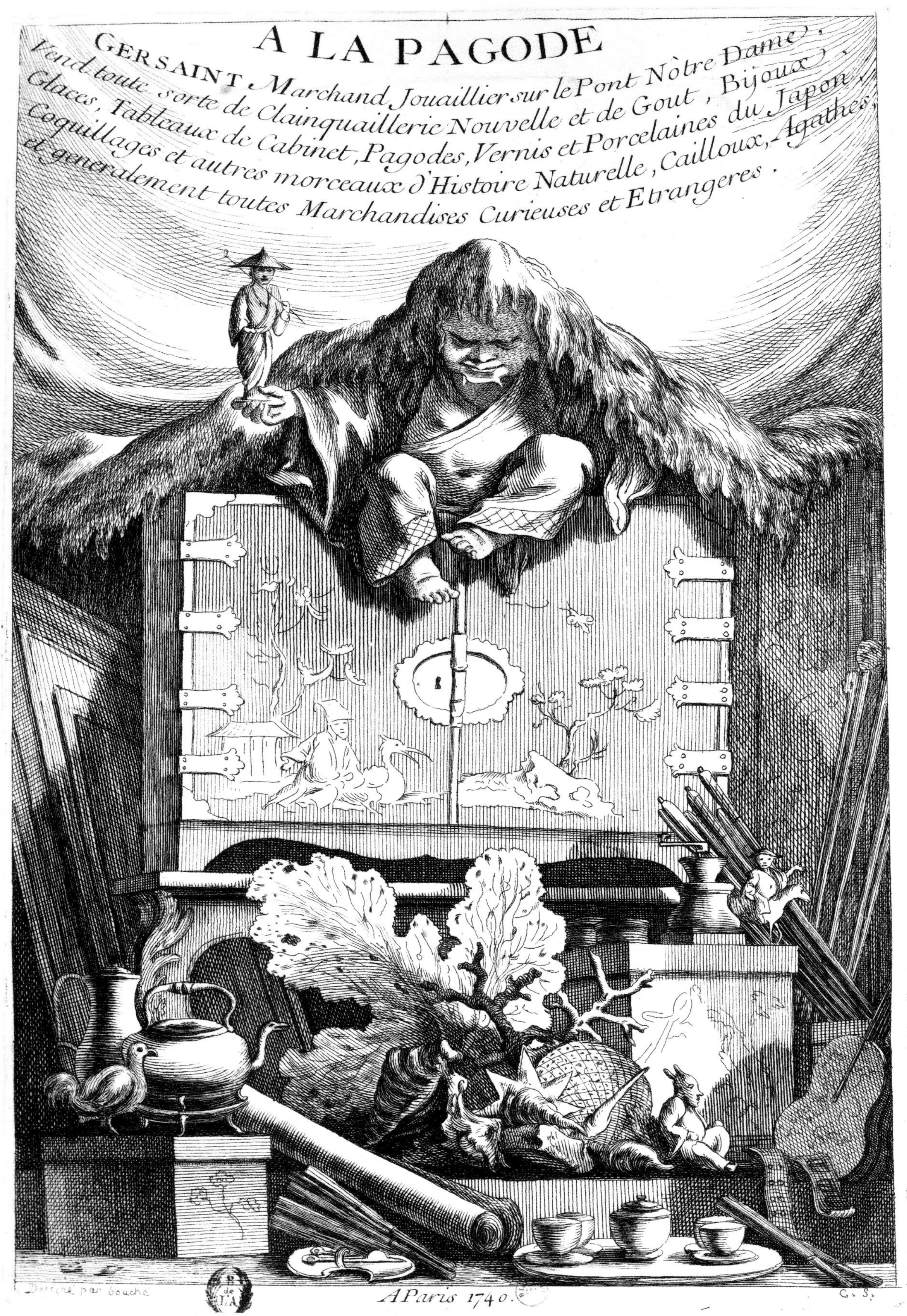
A LA PAGODE
GERSAINT, Marchand Jouaillier sur le Pont Nôtre Dame,
Vend toute sorte de Clainquaillerie Nouvelle et de Gout, Bijoux,
Glaces, Tableaux de Cabinet, Pagodes, Vernis et Porcelaines du Japon,
Coquillages et autres morceaux d'Histoire Naturelle, Cailloux, Agathes,
et generalement toutes Marchandises Curieuses et Etrangeres.
Dessiné par boucher
A Paris 1740.
C. S.

FIG.60 *opposite*
BOUCHER, *The Element of Fire*, *c.*1739–40, red chalk on cream paper, 35 × 28.8cm, New York, The Metropolitan Museum of Art, Van Day Truex Fund, 1984 (1984.51.1)

FIG.61
H. CHEVAL, gold box with scenes after GABRIEL HUQUIER's engravings after BOUCHER, *Scènes de la Vie Chinoise*, Paris, 1749–50, 7.2 × 5 × 3.2cm, Wallace Collection

In an age when few travelled beyond the borders of their own country and it took months for a ship to return from a transatlantic voyage, one can understand the fascination of the strange goods that arrived in Paris from trading posts as far away as China, Japan, Ceylon, India and Siam. A mythical idea of the Indies was created which conflated the West Indies, including South America, with the East Indies, which included the territories bordering the Indian and Pacific oceans.[46] This fascination is reflected not only in the growing interest in collecting objects from the Indies, shown in Gersaint's trade card, but also in the inclusion of related motifs and styles in the arts of the time. Hence the craze for chinoiserie decoration, exotic genre painting, and works such as Montesquieu's *Lettres Persanes* (Persian Letters) or Goudar's *L'espion chinois* (The Chinese Spy).[47] Although this coincided with a growing Enlightenment interest in foreign cultures, the fanciful appeal of these exotic elements in the first half of the eighteenth century is also captured in Rameau's 1735 opera-ballet *Les Indes Galantes* (*The Gallant Indies*).[48] Here the amorous concerns of eighteenth-century French society are thinly disguised in exotic dress as we are taken on a journey through an Indies of the imagination, from Turkey, via the Incas of Peru to the 'savage' Indians of America. Although Boucher did not provide the set for this production, only starting working for the Opéra two years later, he did design Favart's pastiche of *Les Indes Galantes*, *L'ambigu de la Folie ou Le Ballet des Dindons* (*The ambiguity of Madness or the Ballet of the Turkeys*) which amused the audience of the Opéra Comique in 1743.

Of all the Indies the country that most fascinated Boucher was China. His interest was probably first aroused when he engraved some of Watteau's *Figures Chinoises* as described in chapter I. This interest can only have been fuelled by the oriental objects flooding onto the market through the efforts of dealers such as his friend Gersaint. Boucher was not just an observer but also a major collector of oriental objects. His sale catalogue details a treasure trove of Eastern art and curiosities. He had a collection of oriental mounted and unmounted porcelain and bronzes,[49] a quantity of lacquer furniture, boxes, trays, a medal cabinet, a screen, cups and saucers, tea-pots and a black lacquer shield with golden dragons.[50] His ivories included tea caddies decorated with flowers, plants, pagodas, animals and chimerae, a quantity of exquisitely decorated Chinese baskets, boxes, trays, chopsticks and even a mechanical boat.[51] His love of the picturesque and amusing was represented by over forty *pagodes* and *magots*, some of which had nodding heads, one with moveable hands and one on a horse with a mechanism to make it walk.[52] His collection of Chinese earthenware included 'a box with a little man inside with a nodding head who looks as if he is trying to catch a crab'.[53] He also owned a quantity of jade[54] and Chinese silverware including teapots, cups and saucers, an egg cup and most spectacular of all, a silver head-dress decorated with semi-precious stones and pearls and hairpins with coloured pompoms.[55] Such items were not only fascinating curiosities from a far-off land, but also stimuli for his imagination: they included a Chinese lantern, a parasol, a house on a stand, screens, fans, Chinese fruit, a pearl collar, pretty purses, padlocks, a little game bag, two belts, a silver cord, a weighing scale, back-scratchers, an ear trumpet, a measure, a pipe case, slippers and a collection of Chinese musical instruments.[56] The descriptions read like a prop-list for Boucher's Chinese re-enactments.

The early-eighteenth century passion for chinoiserie also provided a commercial opportunity for those able to copy or reinterpret such styles, particularly in the decorative arts, something which Boucher was eminently capable of doing.[57] Another reason that Boucher became particularly attracted to re-inventing Chinese subjects was that China, far away and relatively unknown, allowed much greater scope for the imagination than countries such as Turkey. The creative freedom Chinese subjects allowed the European designer is acknowledged by Boucher's contemporary Antoisne Fraisse who, in the preface to his book

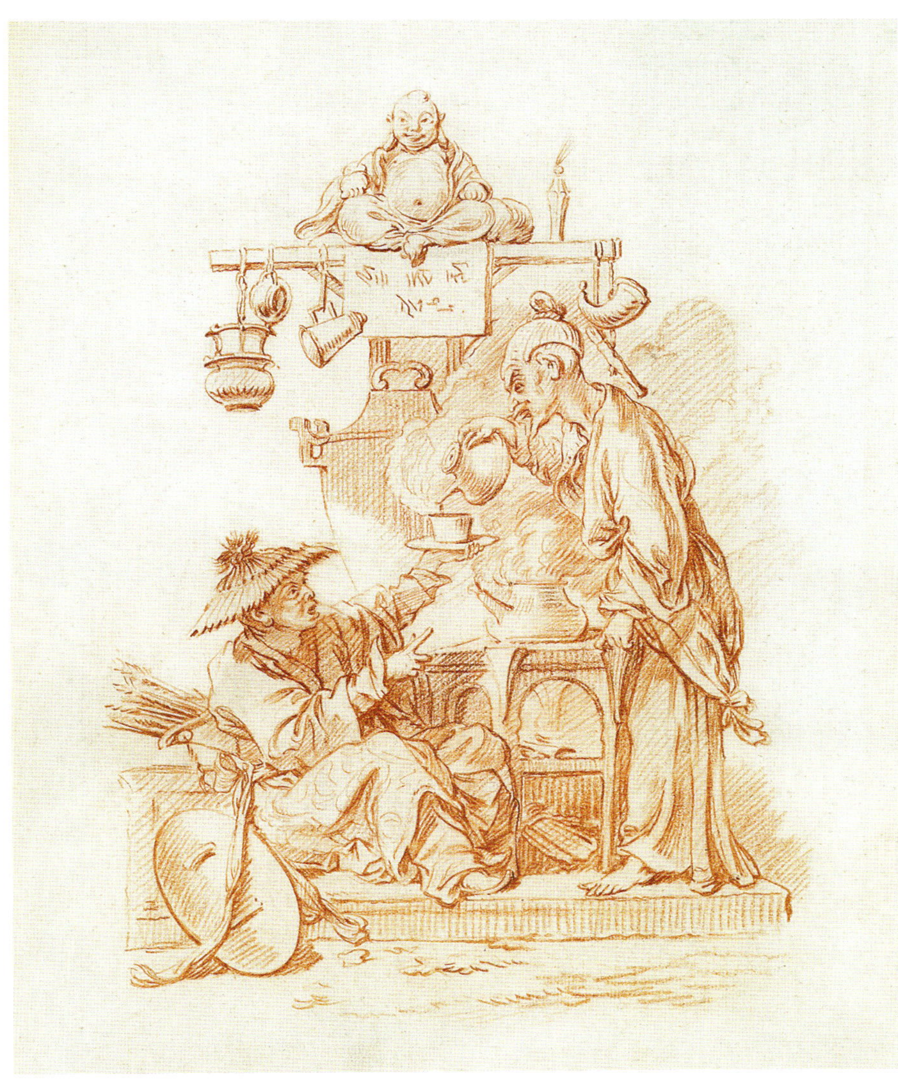

of Chinese designs, wrote that rather than merely copying he thought it better to 'absorb from Chinese works that taste which we have been so eager to acquire'.[58] Robert Sayer expressed a similar opinion in 1750: 'With Chinese objects greater liberties may be taken because luxuriance of fancy recommends their Productions more than Propriety, for in them is seen a Butterfly supporting an Elephant or a thing equally absurd; yet from their gay colouring and airy disposition they seldom fail to please'.[59]

Propriety, however, was central to the code of *honnêteté* which Boucher absorbed during his youth. Thus, while the Chinese designs he created are inventive in their use of costume and accoutrements, they are not allowed to stray too far from an acceptable Western ideal. Elegant Western-featured figures are shown engaged in the same civilised pursuits as their eighteenth-century French audience. The technique of many of Boucher's chinoiserie drawings and paintings is remarkable for its restraint, delicacy and exactness, as is seen, for example, by comparing the vigorous handling of the chalks in figure 57 with the fine lines and hatching of *The Element of Fire* (fig.60).[60] Boucher may have been trying to imitate not just Chinese subjects but also something of the sophistication of Chinese watercolours. He was certainly knowledgeable about such things: his sale catalogue reveals that he owned a number of Chinese paintings, including four large landscapes on paper in gilt frames, four vases of flowers painted on paper cut out and laid on canvas, thirty-six little painted sheets of paper, four Chinese engravings of landscapes and marines, and a large scroll depicting a Chinese landscape.[61]

The Element of Fire depicts a smiling *magot* presiding over a Chinese kitchen with a cook pouring a tea for a seated warrior. Tea, coffee and chocolate were popular imports from the Indies whose appeal, according to Mercier, stretched to the workmen of Paris, whom he describes as being addicted to the milky coffee of the street vendors. By depicting Fire in this manner, with a kettle bubbling merrily on a stove, Boucher was reminding

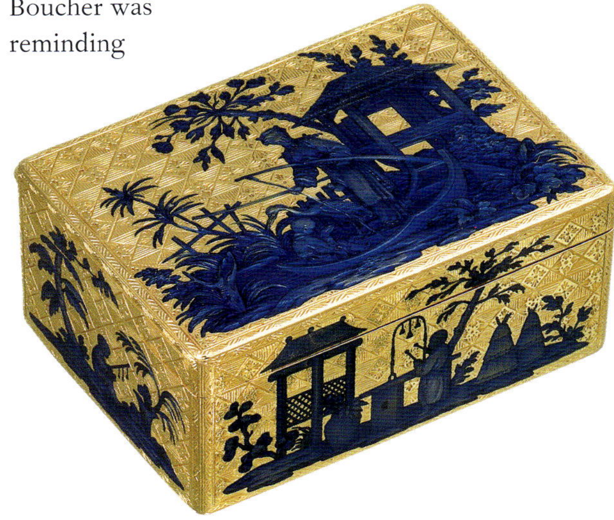

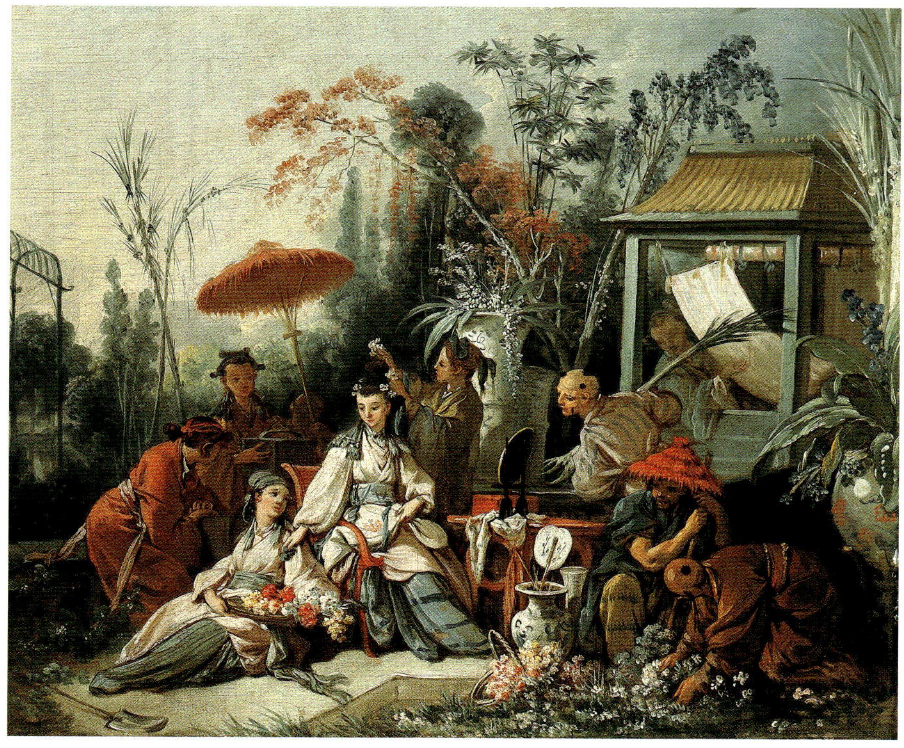

FIG.62
BOUCHER,
The Chinese Garden, 1742, sketch, oil on canvas, 40.5 × 48cm, Besançon, Musée des Beaux-Arts

FIG.63 *opposite*
After BOUCHER,
The Morning Toilette, wool and silk low warp Beauvais tapestry, 318 × 244cm, from *The Chinese Tapestry* series first on the loom in 1743; Dalmeny House, Earl and Countess of Rosebery

contemporaries of the exotic origins of one of their favourite beverages. The drawing was one of a series representing the elements as Chinese scenes engraved and published by Huquier *c.*1740.[62] Its precise technique must have greatly facilitated the engraver's task. One use to which such chinoiserie engravings might be put is illustrated by a card fan (private collection) of a similar shape to that seen abandoned on the floor in *The Garter* (fig.56) which is decorated with the engraving after Boucher's *Fire* within an ornamental border by Huquier.[63] The demand for such material is borne out by other engravings after Boucher chinoiserie designs, including the *Scènes de la vie chinoise* (1737), the *Recueil de diverses figures chinoises du Cabinet de monsieur Boucher* (1738) and the *Suite des Cinq Sens*, all published by Huquier, and the *Figures chinoises* (1744–6) and *Les Délices de l'enfance* (1748), published by Audran.[64] A gold box in the Wallace Collection (fig.61) shows how such scenes might then be re-interpreted in the decorative arts as it incorporates anecdotes from the *Scènes de la Vie Chinoise* on its different faces.[65] The attempts of the Vincennes porcelain factory to rival oriental porcelain make it particularly appropriate that one of the earliest Boucher designs to be copied by the factory was inspired by a fishing scene in Boucher's *Chinese Tapestry*.[66] A pair of chinoiserie overdoors painted in *camaïeu bleu* by Boucher in 1742 (fig.95), while demonstrating the delicacy of his chinoiserie technique in general, also recall oriental porcelain with their blue design on white.

The first *Chinese Tapestry* woven at Beauvais was begun in 1664, using designs by Vernansal, Monnoyer and Blin de Fontenay. It was conceived as an exotic parallel to the magnificent celebration of Louis XIV's reign, *The King's History*, already on the high warp looms of the Gobelins from 1662.[67] The incidents depicted were Chinese versions of the ritual of Versailles, including scenes such as *The Emperor's Audience* and *The Emperor's Embarkation*. The tapestry was extremely popular, as was another series, *The Indies Tapestry*, begun in 1687 and woven after designs by Desportes, based on a series of paintings by Eckhout and Frans Post given by Prince Maurice of Nassau to Louis XIV, illustrating his travels in South America. It was virtually inevitable that Boucher should be commissioned when a second *Chinese Tapestry* series, reflecting the more intimate ethos of the eighteenth century, was proposed for Beauvais. *The Chinese Garden* (fig.62) is one of the preparatory oil sketches for the series that Boucher exhibited at the Salon of 1742 and again shows the delicate touch he felt appropriate to his Chinese subjects.[68] Although Boucher derived inspiration from his collection of oriental artefacts and the illustrations of seventeenth-century voyages to the Orient by writers such as Nieuhoff, Kirchner and Montanus, his recreation of China for the Rococo has nothing archaeological about it.[69] *The Chinese Garden*, for example, is a delicious masquerade of themes dear to the eighteenth-century disguised in Chinese fancy-dress. The toilette, the *fête champêtre*, the park landscape are all subjects already encountered in his work, but here they are given a completely new twist to send the eighteenth-century imagination on yet another journey away from boredom.

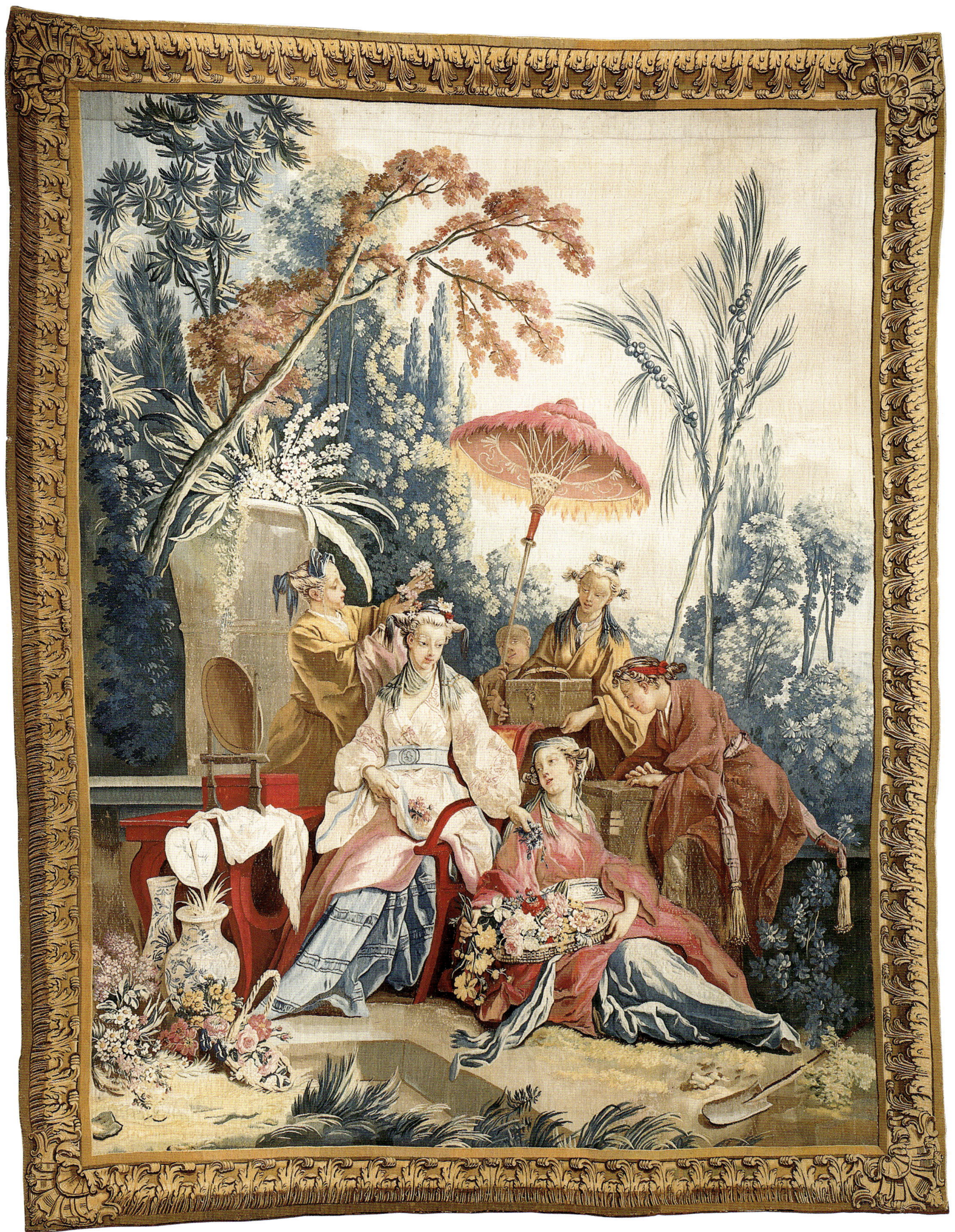

The sketches were worked up into cartoons by Jean-Joseph Dumons (1687–1779), a friend of Boucher and Oudry and studio painter to the tapestry manufactory at Aubusson (1731–55) which later produced its own pirated version of the Beauvais series.[70] Weaving started on the second *Chinese Tapestry* in 1743. *The Morning Toilette* (fig.63) is from a set at Dalmeny House, others of which are inscribed with the Beauvais co-directors' names, 'Besnier et Oudry', allowing us to date them to 1743–53, although it is still unclear for whom they were woven.[71] *The Toilette* demonstrates how Boucher's composition might be adapted to an interior with smaller walls than allowed for in the original design. It is in reverse, as usual with Beauvais tapestries, and depicts only the Chinese princess and her immediate attendants, omitting the gardeners and male attendants seen in the right of Boucher's sketch. The simulated 'frame' tapestry border shows that the composition was intentionally reduced. There is still a wealth of detail to enjoy, from the picturesque costumes to the exuberant foliage and flowers, the fashionable oriental porcelain and fan and the wonderful Rococo red lacquer dressing table. The tapestry weavers excelled themselves in translating Boucher's Chinese Rococo vision into luxurious textile hangings despite their restricted range of colours. A delightful postscript is added to Boucher's imaginary Chinese journey by the fact that a set of his tapestries made the real voyage to China, being presented to the Chinese Emperor Qianlong in 1767. One wonders how much the Emperor recognized in Boucher's vision of China; the set certainly pleased or amused him for it was displayed prominently in the Summer Palace, Peking, the following year.[72]

Parisian fashions were notoriously fickle and by the end of the 1740s Boucher's Chinese vision was beginning to fade. Saint-Yves sounded the warning bell when he wrote in 1748 that 'those who take a keen interest in him fear that the habitual study of the Chinese taste, which seems to be M. Boucher's favourite passion, will eventually alter the grace of his contours. They will no longer have the same softness if he continues to draw figures in this manner'.[73] Boucher, ever sensitive to trends, took note. Although he continued to amass Chinese objects for his pleasure, even acquiring in the last years of his life a copy of William Chambers's 1767 book of engravings after Chinese 'buildings, furniture, costumes, machines and utensils', he produced few Chinese subjects thereafter. Instead he turned to explore other realms of the Rococo.[74]

Luxe, calme et volupté BAUDELAIRE[75]

One exotic realm that attracted Boucher less than many of his colleagues, but which he evokes in one of his most memorable pictures (fig.64), was the Ottoman Empire, which included present-day Turkey, Arabia, Iran and much of North Africa.[76] The visit of the Ottoman ambassador, Mehmet Reza Bey, in 1715 had been one of the last great spectacles of Louis XIV's reign and his entourage had been drawn by Watteau and then engraved by Boucher in the *Figures de différents caractères*.[77] At the same time the fashion for turquerie was fuelled by the distribution of *One hundred Engravings Representing the Various Nations of the Levant*, published 1707–8, after paintings by Jean-Baptiste Van Mour commissioned by Ferriol, the French ambassador to Constantinople. Boucher also later engraved two of Van Mour's Turkish compositions.[78] The year 1721 saw both the publication of Montesquieu's *Lettres Persanes* and the visit of the new Ottoman Ambassador, Mehmet Effendi. Pictures in the Wallace Collection, such as Nattier's *Mademoiselle Clermont as a Sultana* (1733), Lancret's *Beautiful Greek* (*c.*1735), pendant to an *Amorous Turk* inspired by Voltaire's tragedy *Zaïre* (1732), and Carle Van Loo's *The Grand Turk Giving a Concert to his Mistress* (1737) attest to the contemporary vogue for *turquerie*.[79] Added impetus came in the 1740s from the work of Jean-Étienne Liotard (1702–89), whose engravings after drawings executed during his first trip to Constantinople (1738–42) started to circulate in Paris from 1743. Liotard himself arrived in Paris at the beginning of 1746 and Boucher was immediately influenced by his work,

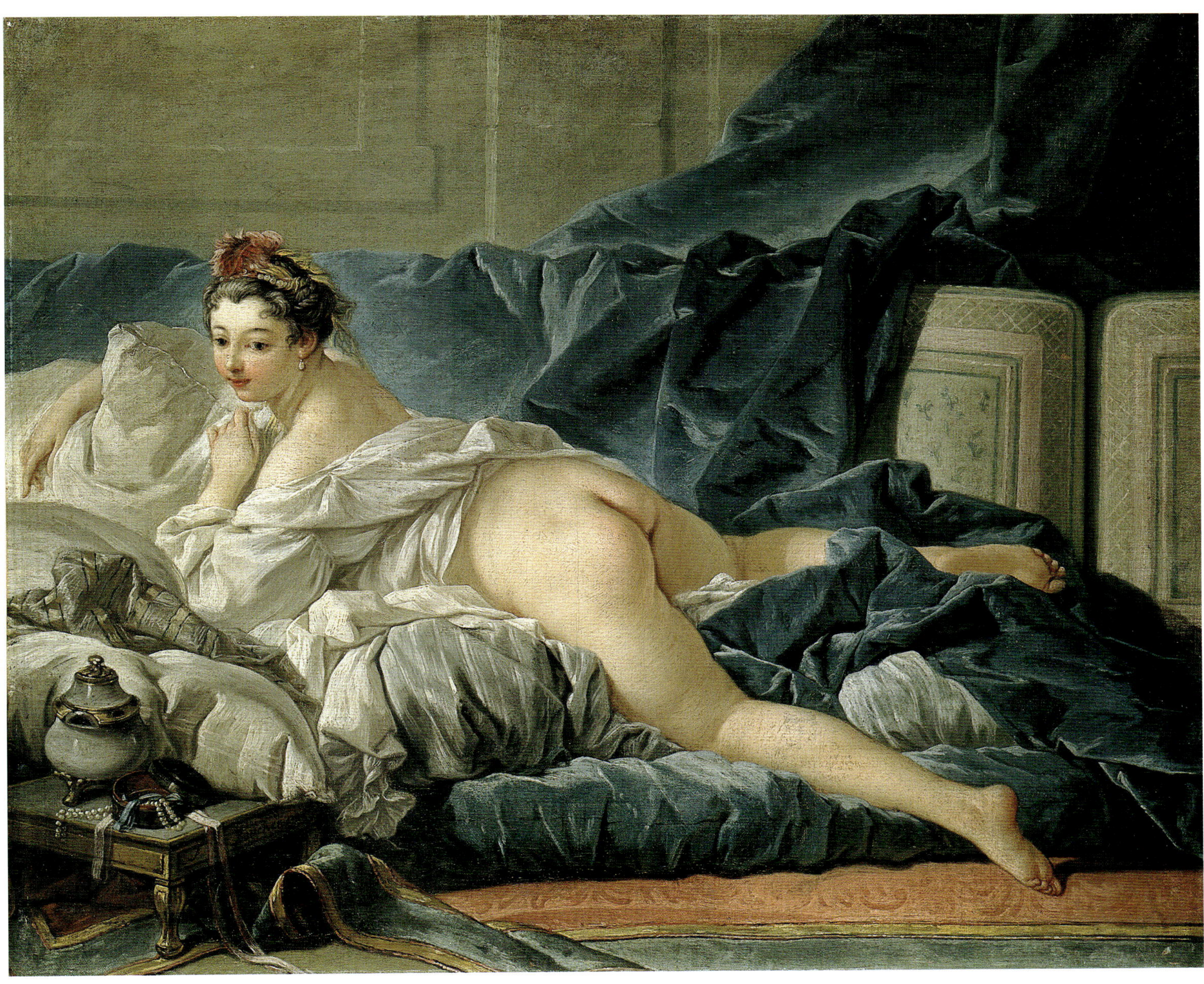

FIG.64
Boucher,
The Brunette Odalisque,
1743, oil on canvas,
53.5 × 64.5cm, Paris,
Musée du Louvre

basing his *Sultana Reading*, one of his illustrations for Jean Antoine Guer's *Moeurs et Usages des Turcs* published the same year, on a Liotard prototype.[80] But, in general, *turquerie* did not hold the same fascination for Boucher as did *chinoiserie*. He owned a few Ottoman objects, including some Persian faience (pottery), a silver hookah pipe and Turkish and Arabian trophies, sabres and daggers, but nothing to match the number of his Chinese artefacts.[81] Such an omission seems all the more surprising given the erotic fascination Turkey had for the eighteenth century imagination.[82] With its stories of seraglios and harems, and with *A Thousand and One Nights* (translated into French by Galliard in 1704), the Ottoman Empire might have provided endless inspiration for Boucher. But his friend and rival, Carle Van Loo, had already rather cornered the market, and Boucher fought shy of direct competition with his former travelling companion to Rome.

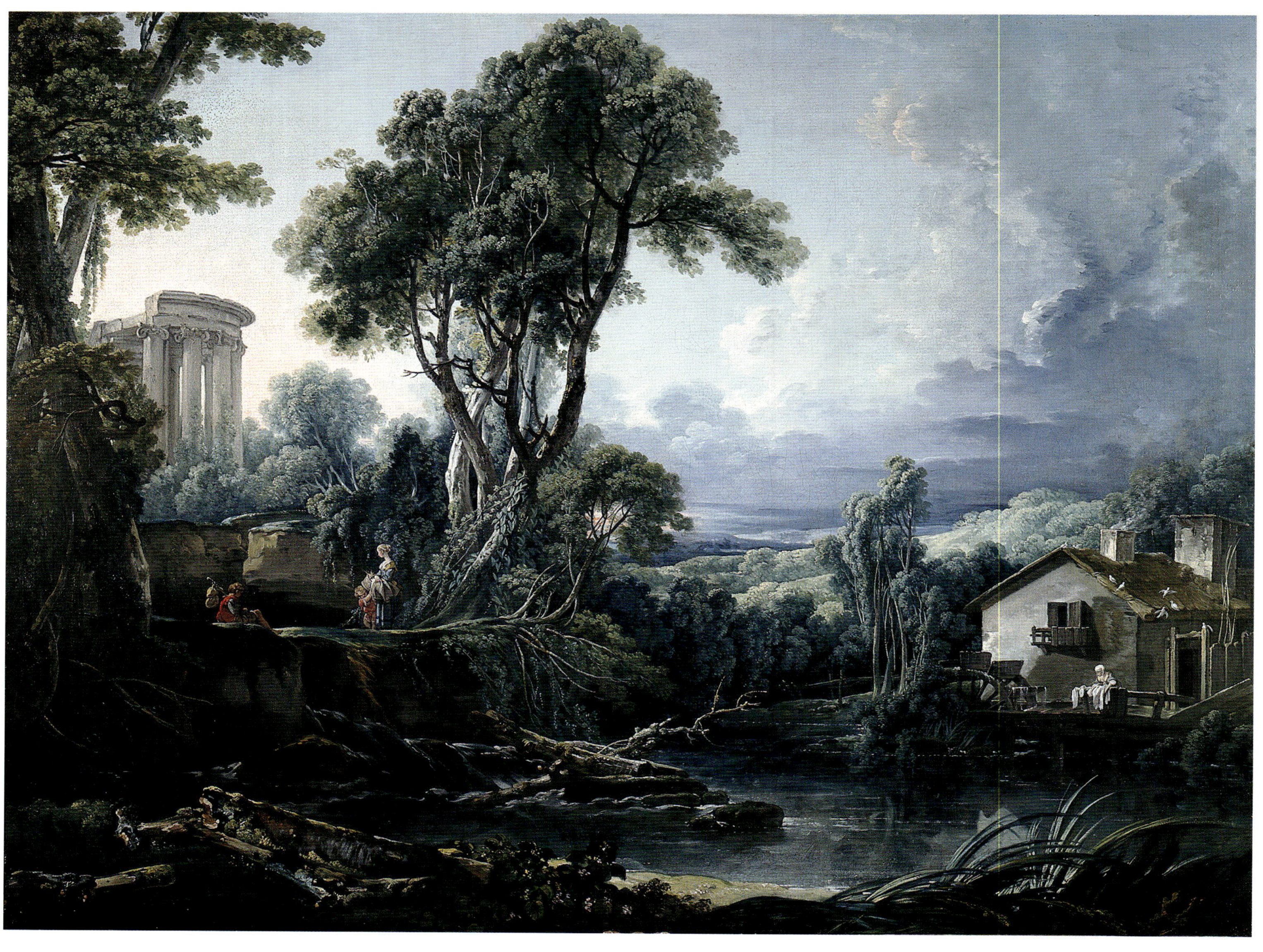

FIG.65
BOUCHER, *Landscape*, 1743, oil on canvas, 90.8 × 118.1cm, Barnard Castle, Bowes Museum

The Brunette Odalisque, often cited as a prime example of Boucher's style, thus ironically stands alone in his oeuvre. The model's pose derives from the female academies Boucher started drawing at the beginning of his career (see fig.11) and which had previously been incorporated into his mythological works' nymphs and goddesses (see, for example, fig.55).[83] This is the first time, however, that he depicts an almost naked female figure on her own with no mythological accoutrements and virtually filling the canvas. Watteau apparently regretted the contemporary nudes he painted during his lifetime and instructed that they be destroyed on his death, the *Toilette* in the Wallace Collection being a fortunate exception.[84] The narrow dividing line in the eighteenth century between the acceptable mythological nude and the seemingly obscene or libidinous contemporary nude, was one that Boucher was understandably nervous of crossing. So he added an exotic gloss, to 'veil' and excuse the image in an *honnête* manner. The interior is a hastily cobbled-together vision of the seraglio, with a few cushions thrown on the floor, a rumpled carpet, a low stool and the same

FIG.66 *below*
PIERRE PATEL (1605–76), *Landscape with a Colonnade, Washerwomen and Shepherds*, c.1645–6, oil on canvas, 59 × 85.5cm, Springfield, Massachusetts, Museum of Fine Arts

grey pot-pourri or *cassolette* as seen on the mantelpiece in *The Garter* (fig.56). The blue velvet drape, with its chalky white highlights to indicate where the folds catch the light, is also curiously reminiscent of the watery bed of the naiads in Boucher's *Birth of Venus* (fig.55). The model has been given a pearl earring and a coiffure set off with a jaunty feather to complete her translation into an odalisque, thus placing her at the head of an eminent artistic tradition in France which stretches through Ingres and Delacroix in the nineteenth century to Picasso in the twentieth.

Boucher's image might have been partly inspired by the appearance the previous year of Crébillon's *Le Sopha*, claimed to have been published in Peking by the printer to the Chinese Emperor, and also using the Indies as a backdrop to justify a catalogue of sexual encounters. Amanzée, a courtier of the Prince of the Indies, Schah Baham, while distracting his master from the boredom of court, tells him the tale of his former life as a sofa. He had been punished by the god, Brama, for his own lax morals by being thus transformed until the moment when two people freely made love on him. Amanzée then becomes witness to a variety of sexual couplings which demonstrate that 'as there are few heroes for those who see them close up, I can only say that for sofas there are few virtuous women'.[85] This viewpoint was not necessarily considered negative. Voltaire considered it 'amusing that a virtue is made out of the vice of chastity' while Vivant Denon, the first director of the post-Revolutionary Louvre museum, and himself a student in Boucher's studio in 1769, explained in his libertine tale of a one-night stand, *Point de lendemain* (*No Tomorrow*), that 'the desires are reproduced by images of desire'.[86] Despite Boucher's attempts to justify his image with exoticism, and the fact that his odalisque is not strictly an image of desire, but rather a desirable image, the sight of a pretty girl proffering her ample buttocks, painted with such convincing technical mastery, is perhaps too sexy for its own good. Diderot could barely restrain his pen at the sight of this, or another similar picture, when he described the girl's pose as 'an invitation to pleasure, inviting to it with the easiest attitude, the most comfortable – from what they say the most natural even, or at least the most advantageous'.[87]

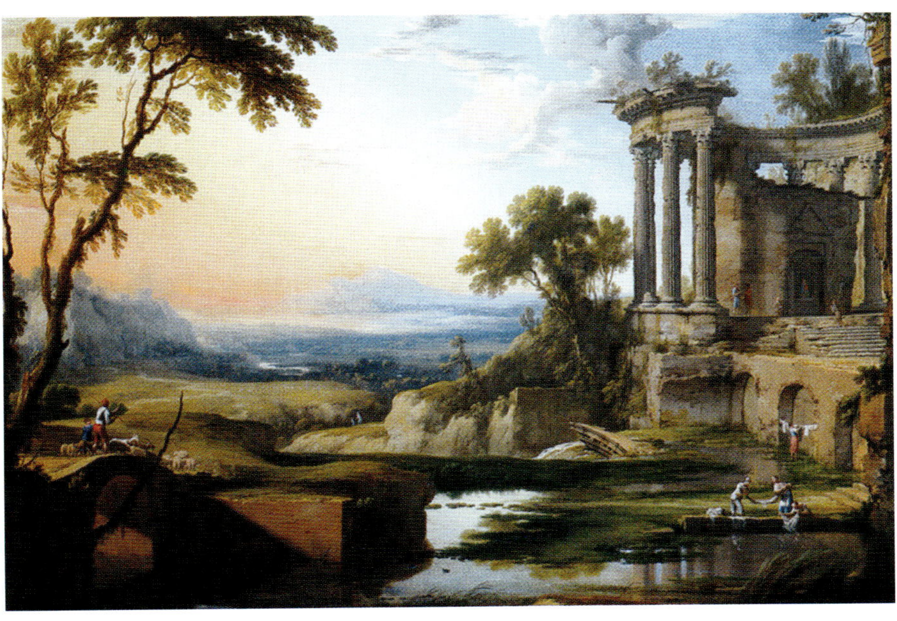

Pictures such as the *Brunette Odalisque* attracted and continue to attract a disproportionate amount of attention within Boucher's oeuvre, despite the fact that he painted few pictures of this sort. Their achievement in provoking a response has led commentators to interpret them rather crudely as evidence of Boucher's own sexual incontinence. In the eighteenth century, the female life model was regarded as little better than a prostitute, but an anecdote recounted by a woman to Restif de La Bretonne exonerates Boucher from any accusations of improper conduct: 'I was taking washing back to M. Boucher; he saw me; proposed that I work for him and for his students as a model: he offered me in a day four times what I earned as a laundry maid, giving me the ability to extract my husband from the terrible state he was in, because he was working as a water-carrier; I accepted; it was worked out that I should pretend to be the reader of an old lady, a neighbour of the painter. That's my history. I have little to suffer from the students, because of the great care taken by the painter to keep them under control.'[88]

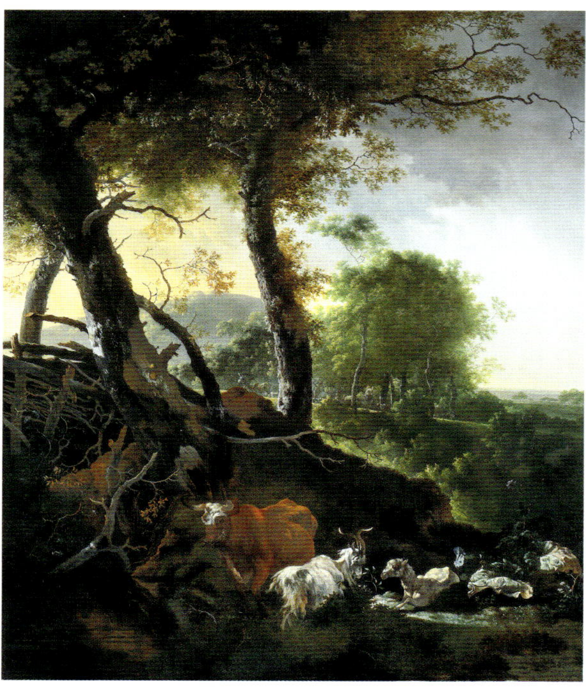

FIG.67
ADAM PYNACKER (*c*.1620–1673), *Landscape with Animals*, oil on canvas, 117.5 × 102.5cm, Wallace Collection

The theatrical landscape

Boucher's interest in landscape took a new turn in the 1740s when the rural and Italianate visions of the 1730s, with their warm browns and reds, were gradually replaced by landscapes displaying blue and green tonalities, akin to those of Boucher's mythological canvases of the period (see fig.55), and more in keeping with the pastel shades favoured by the interior decorators of the day. Boucher's work at this time recalls a variety of increasingly sophisticated landscape models. In 1740 he painted a pair of pictures one of which, *The Forest* (Louvre) is reminiscent of Oudry and De Troy's forest scenes and of Salvator Rosa's shattered tree trunks and Italian soldiers. Its pendant, *The Mill* (Kansas City), combines a distant view of the Temple of the Sibyl at Tivoli, which Boucher had sketched in Italy (fig.19), with a pollard willow rather like those Boucher engraved after Watteau and with a new identifiably French motif, a watermill.[89] Through his work for Beauvais Boucher would have become aware of Oudry's sketches of the French landscape and would have had reason to visit the environs of Paris.[90] This combination of influences prompted him to incorporate prettified versions of the cottages, dovecotes, and mills of rural France into his pictures. Boucher became a member of Oudry's sketching parties to Arcueil in the 1740s and, like Oudry, produced a number of drawings on blue paper of the aqueduct and park of the prince de Guise. The park's state of picturesque abandon seems to have had the same stimulating effect on the imaginations of Boucher and his companions as the dilapidated gardens of the Villa d'Este would have on Fragonard, Saint-Non (1727–91) and Hubert Robert (1733–1808) in the following decade.[91]

A landscape in the Bowes Museum (fig.65) beautifully demonstrates the appeal of Boucher's exquisite, if consciously artificial, landscape style during this period. Rosa's influence is again found in the tree trunks in the foreground, while another distant view of the Temple of Tivoli, on the left, is combined with an impossibly tidy French mill, rendered all the more charming by the addition of tiny doves and a woman washing, on the right.[92] A seated Bloemaert-like peasant boy has been relegated to the mid-ground beside a girl and child on the left; no detail is allowed to dominate or unbalance the compositional equilibrium. The painterly finesse, tonality and expert depiction of light show that Boucher was now turning to the lyrical French landscapes of the previous century for inspiration. He seems to have been particularly attracted to the decorative approach and elegance of Pierre Patel (1605–76). Patel's *Landscape with a Colonnade, Washerwomen and Shepherds* (fig.66), also containing a reference to the temple at Tivoli, is similarly bathed in a luminescent pink and blue glow.[93] The Patel, and other pictures like it, formed part of the celebrated seventeenth-century interior of the Hôtel Lambert, which belonged in the eighteenth century to the wealthy financier, Marin de La Haye, who also owned the pair of 1740 Boucher views mentioned above. By the time of his death, Boucher himself owned a view by Patel.[94] Boucher's landscape in the Bowes adopts the compositional technique, typical of the seventeenth century, of suggesting depth by

FIG.68 *below*
BOUCHER,
Design for a Stage Set (Issé?), 1741, oil on canvas, 68 × 112cm, Munich, on loan to the Alte Pinakothek

painting the foreground in shade, the mid-ground bathed in light and the distance with a bluish tonality. The same approach is used, for example, in the work of Dutch Italianates such as Adam Pynacker (*c*.1620–1673).[95] If one compares Pynacker's *Landscape with Animals* (fig.67) with the background detail of Boucher's *Daphnis and Chloé* that opens this chapter (fig.53) one can also see how Pynacker's treatment of plants and foliage, his twisting silver birch trunks, calligraphic branches and large cabbage-like leaves, affected Boucher's own treatment of such elements.

Boucher's decorative approach to landscape proved perfect for his work as a set designer. Opera and ballet were central to the eighteenth-century social round, as Saint-Yves stresses: 'Every man with a reasonably comfortable fortune goes out a great deal in society; and the Opéra of all the spectacles is the most frequented by people of this sort'.[96] Voltaire also commented in one of his poems that 'We trouble the order of the heavens./ We take Venus for Mercury/ For you know that here/ To examine the planets/ Instead of telescopes/ We use opera-glasses'. Working as a set designer was, for Boucher, a personal passion and another way of reaching a wider audience. It also seems to have been quite lucrative to judge from the payment of 5000 *livres* he received from the Opéra for designs produced between 1744 and 1748. His work at the Opéra, dating from 1737, was suspended in 1748, when the extravagant Berger was replaced as director by Tréfontaine, who promptly sacked Boucher. Boucher complained so bitterly at losing his free pass that Madame de Pompadour wrote to the comte d'Argenson that she feared his despair would cause him to paint crippled one eyed nymphs in the pictures he was painting for her at Bellevue![97] He is again recorded

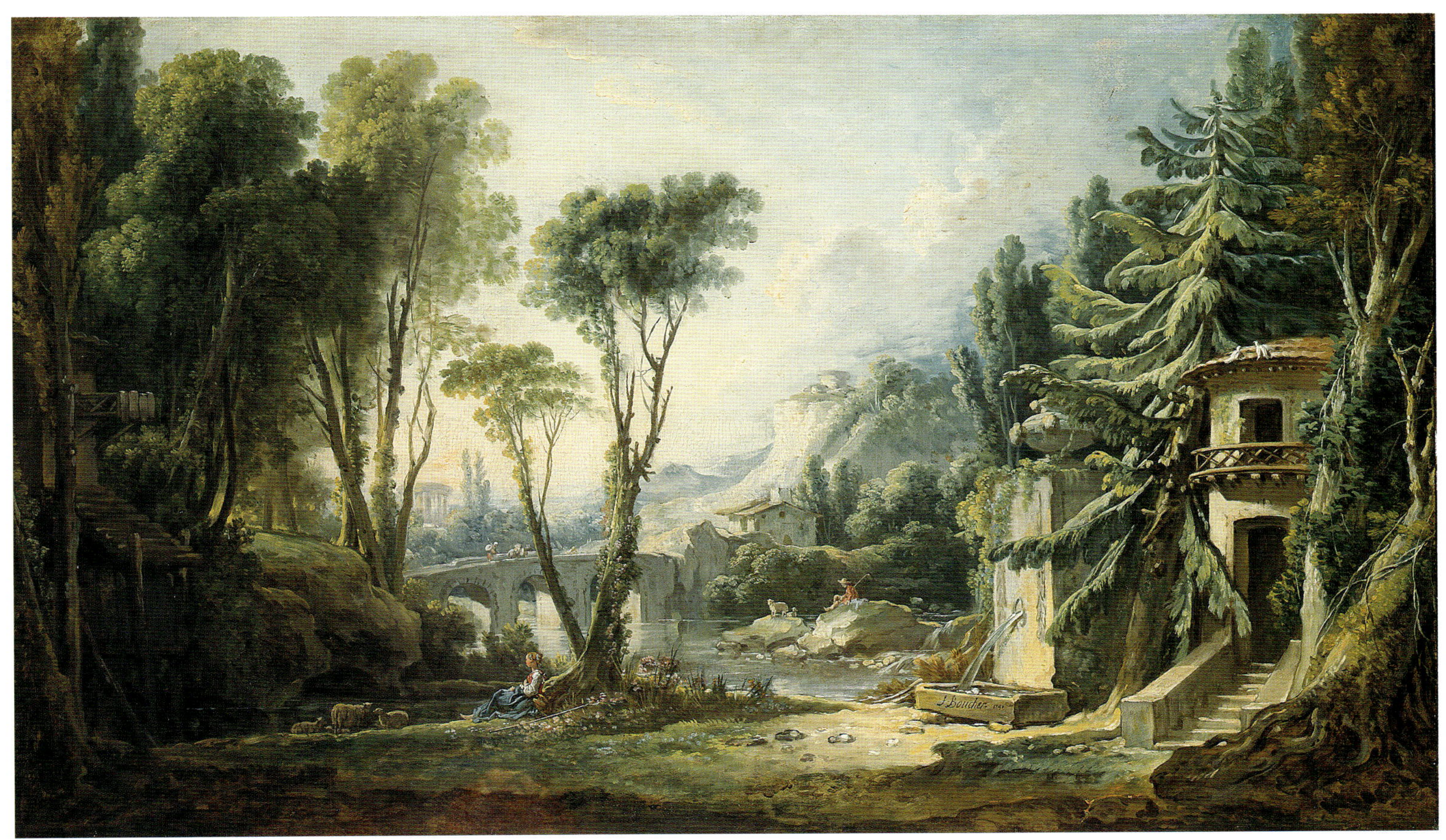

working regularly for the Opéra from 1761, when he provided designs for a revival of Lully's *Armide*.[98] Boucher was also one of a dozen 'famous artists' including Cochin and Lemoine, listed as having free entry at the Comédie Française by the actor Kain.[99] Meanwhile he also worked for Jean Monnet at the Opéra Comique, which produced operettas or musical pantomimes for a more diverse public at the popular Foire Saint-Laurent.[100] Here he was involved with a team that included Rameau, Favart and the dancer Jean-Georges Noverre, in an enterprise that challenged the Opéra so successfully that it was closed down by the Royal Academy of Music in 1745. When Monnet re-opened the Opéra Comique in 1751, Boucher rushed to his aid and, according to the impresario's memoirs, 'took pleasure in composing the ceilings, the decorations, even the ornaments, and in overseeing all aspects of the painting that were undertaken in the theatre'.[101] Boucher's work even inspired the subject of one of the spectacles performed at the Opéra Comique. The bizarrerie of his illustrations for Tessin's novel, *Faunillane ou L'Infante Jaune*, prompted the members of the *Society of the End of the Bench* to invent alternative stories to match them. The best, by Duclos, was printed under the title *Acajou et Zirphile* in 1744 and was then turned into a successful comic opera by Favart.

Boucher's set design (fig.68), thought to be for the 1742 revival of André Cardinal Destouches's opera *Issé*, demonstrates how Boucher's new refined landscape style went hand-in-hand with similar developments on the stage. Here we find the blue tonality and elegantly etiolated trees of the Bowes picture already prefigured. The round rustic French building on the right, with its staircase, was obviously intended to provide a dramatic entrance for the protagonists. Considering that Issé, the heroine, was a shepherdess, one can see that once she was on stage the effect would have been like seeing a Boucher landscape come alive. What was held to constitute the key to a successful stage set is revealed in the comments of Baillet de Saint-Julien, who maintained that 'Decoration [set design] is one of the things one must least neglect, because it is principally by theatrical spectacles that Nations publicise their magnificence'. Keeping this didactic purpose in mind, he disliked Boucher's architectural set-designs where 'he sins by too much imagination', preferring the less fantastical and easy to realise visions of Servandoni, an actual architect.[102] But when it came to non-architectural decorations and landscapes he unreservedly accorded Boucher pre-eminence: 'Who better than M. Boucher could render such beautiful gardens, beautiful grottos and beautiful landscapes where one recognises with pleasure a happy mixture of views of Rome and of Tivoli with those of Sceaux and Arcueil'.[103] The relatively high esteem in which Boucher's sets were held is also reflected in the higher values placed on them in the 1748 inventory of the Opéra taken following the death of Charles-Louis Perronet.[104] Unsurprisingly, Baillet de Saint-Julien was also a fan of Boucher's landscape cabinet pictures and regretted their absence in the 1748 Salon: 'why does he no longer exhibit his beautiful landscapes, such as he showed us a few years ago? Is he leaving us only the memory of having seen them, with no hope of their return?'[105] Later Mannlich, with an ear attuned to the beauties of German music, described how, during his first visit to Paris in 1762–3, Boucher's costumes and decorations were one of the main attractions of the Opéra: although they 'had much more taste, elegance and richness, than truth and purity; it is, however, these, and above all the ballets in which Vestris, the God of Dance, performs, that make the greatest if not the only merit of the Opéra. If by the grace of Apollo one could become deaf during the singing or the exclamations of the actors, and short-sighted so as not to see the hideous grimaces which disfigure their efforts, the Spectacle would be more brilliant and voluptuous'.[106]

The Anacreon of Painting SAINT-YVES[107]

After Boucher's death, commentators often equated his landscapes with his pastorals, the genre with which he became particularly identified in the latter part of his career. The success of both depended

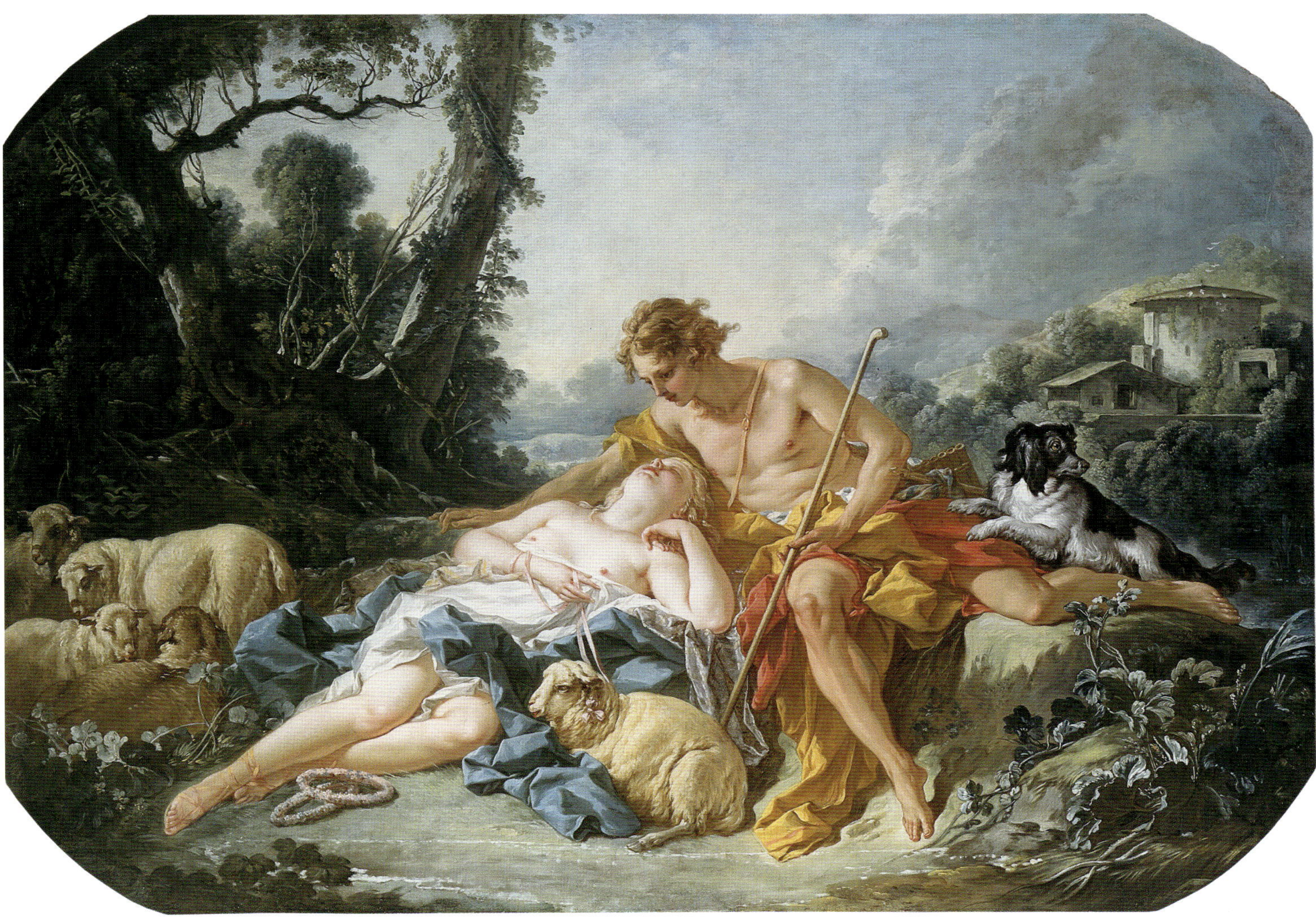

FIG.69
BOUCHER, *Daphnis and Chloé*, 1743, oil on canvas, 109.5 × 154.8cm, Wallace Collection

on the originality of Boucher's theatrical and decorative reinterpretation of nature. Papillon de La Ferté, after discussing Boucher's artistic influences, maintained that he could be compared 'only to himself in his Pastorals and Landscapes, whose backgrounds he knew how to embellish, with a taste and an art which are particular to him alone'.[108] The picturesque foliage and blue and green tonalities of the landscape in *Daphnis and Chloé* (fig.69) illustrate this quality and we can also see, in the background on the right, one of the rural buildings that Boucher increasingly introduced into his landscapes during the same period.[109] The figures, however, unlike the rustics of the landscapes, and despite their dog and flock of sheep are very reminiscent of Boucher's mythological groupings and their poses even appear to have been based on a seventeenth-century bronze statuette attributed to Francesco Fanelli (fl.1609–*c*.1665). This reflects the classical source of Boucher's theme, which tells how the orphaned protagonists grow up unaware of their noble origins, become shepherd and shepherdess and fall in love. Typically, Boucher chooses the symbolic moment when Daphnis is surprised by love and desire on seeing the semi-naked body of the sleeping Chloé. The sensuality of Boucher's picture reflects the poetry of the story, but rather undermines the moral meditation on the rites of passage to adulthood found in Longinus.

FIG.70
BOUCHER, *Spring*, 1745, oil on canvas, 98.5 × 132cm, Wallace Collection

FIG.71 *opposite*
BOUCHER, *Bacchus and Erigone: Autumn*, 1745, oil on canvas, 99 × 134.5cm, Wallace Collection

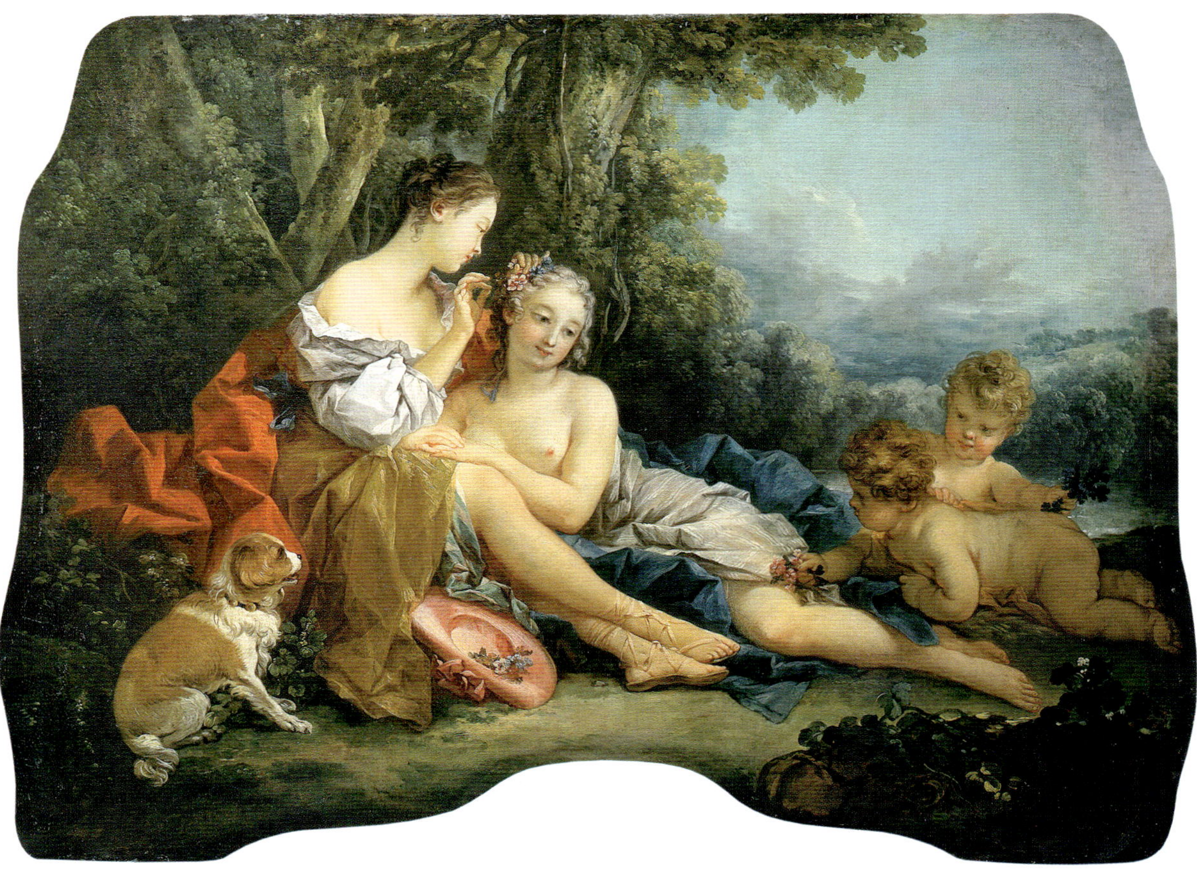

Longinus's poem follows the pastoral mode of classical antiquity, which preached the virtues of the simple life from the sophisticated point of view of a literary elite. Gresset in his poem *Le Siècle Pastoral* explained in 1744 how the gentleman of his era, worn out by the social round of Court and capital, might be similarly attracted to this imagery of a pre-lapsarian idyll, when 'All the universe was rural/ All the men were Shepherds;/ The names of subject and of master/ Were still strange to them…In their rural republic/ Order reigned, image of the heavens/ Man was what he should be/ He thought less, he lived better'.[110] Many opera-ballets, such as Rameau's *Fêtes d'Hébé*, premiered while Boucher was working for the Opéra in 1739, also depicted a similar refined Arcadian ideal, where shepherds and shepherdesses mingled with the gods of Olympus in a courtly celebration of the gallantry and sincerity which had formed the ideal of aristocratic behaviour since the seventeenth century.[111] Watteau's *fêtes galantes* and Boucher's reworkings of the *fête champêtre* at the Hôtel Soubise (figs. 42 and 44) reflect the same codes of *honnêteté*, but *Daphnis and Chloé* is one of the few paintings that mix the mythological and pastoral modes so common on the eighteenth-century operatic stage; this results in an original eye-catching overdoor, painted in a rapid fluid manner, with a contemporary resonance for the eighteenth-century patron and (most probably) opera-goer. In the same way a set of four 1745 overdoors represents *The Seasons* with a mixture of mythological and pastoral imagery. *Spring* places the toilette in a pastoral setting, with one shepherdess adjusting the coiffure of another in a landscape accompanied by amours, a dog and a straw hat (fig.70). *Autumn* is represented by an Ovidian tale of seduction: that of the nymph Erigone, here again represented as an Arcadian shepherdess. Her would-be lover, the god Bacchus,

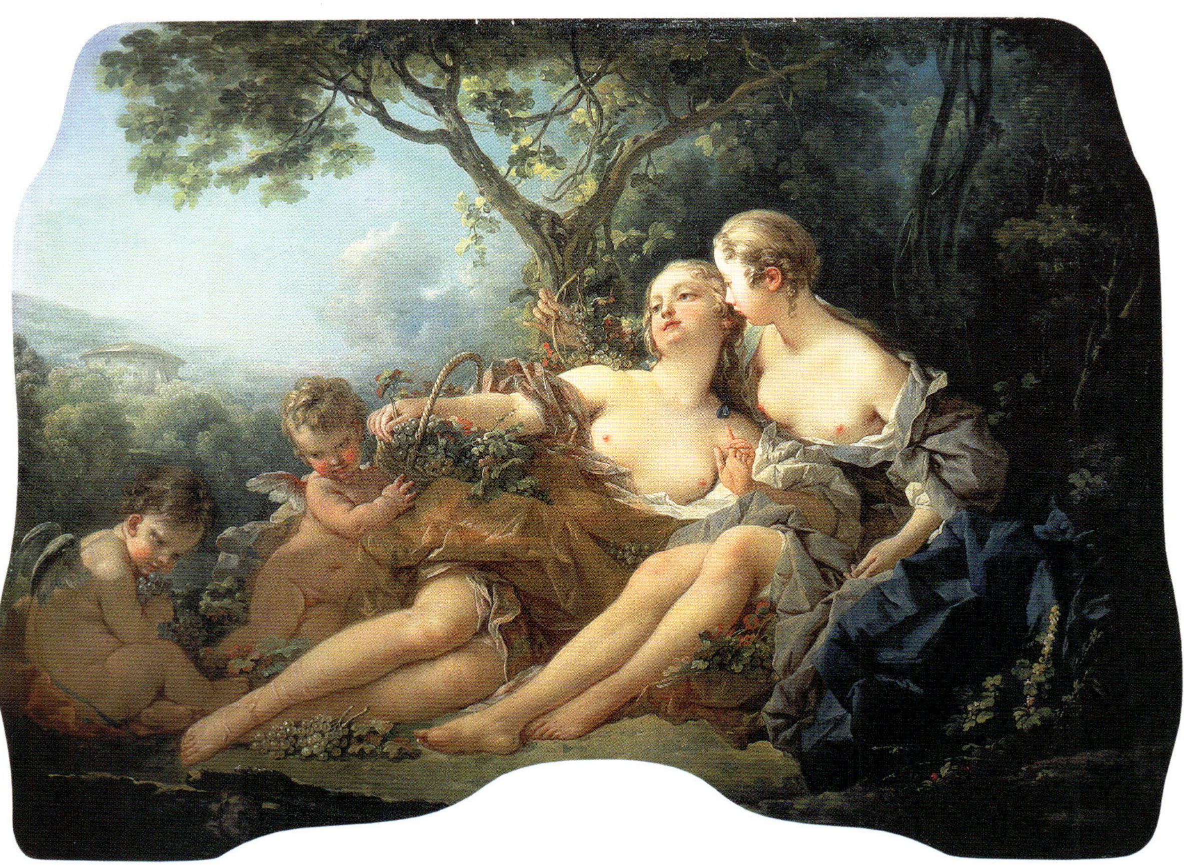

lies in wait, transformed into the bunch of grapes offered to her in a basket by an amour (fig.71). *Summer* has three shepherdesses with their flock conversing in a landscape (Musée Cognacq-Jay), while *Winter* returns to the mythological mode by depicting *Diana Returning from the Hunt* (Los Angeles).[112]

A strikingly new pastoral, meanwhile, was being invented by Boucher's friend Favart at the Opéra Comique. Like Boucher in his landscapes, Favart made the pastoral more relevant to a wider French audience at the Foire Saint-Laurent by re-locating his Arcadia, not in mythological Italy, but in an idealised never-never land supposedly located in the environs of Paris, the valley of Tempé or Montmorency as it became known. At the same time his more straightforward and sentimental stories of the love of French shepherds and shepherdesses, such as Lisette, Babette and the Little Shepherd from his most famous work *Les Vendanges du Tempé* or the *Grape-Harvest of Tempé* (1745), reflected a growing sentimentalism in the arts. This evolved in reaction to the cynicism of libertine literature where love was reduced to a stylised battle between the sexes: 'one knows today that taste alone exists, and if one still says that one loves, it is less because one believes it, but rather because it is a more polite way of asking reciprocally for that which one needs physically'.[113] In contrast, sentimental novels, such as abbé Prévost's *Manon Lescaut*, extolled the virtues of love and emotional sensitivity: 'persons of a more noble character can be moved in a thousand different ways; it seems as if they have five senses and that they can receive ideas and sensations which pass beyond the ordinary bounds of nature; and, as they have a feeling of such a grandeur that it lifts them above the vulgar, there is nothing of which they are more jealous'.[114] This sensitivity, in its purest sense, was associated by other writers,

FIG.72
LE BAS after BOUCHER, *Madame Favart in the role of Ninette*, engraving, 13.9 × 9.3cm., which first illustrated C.-S. Favart, *Ninette à la Cour*, Paris, 1755; this version taken from *Théâtre de M. Favart ou recueil des comédies, parodies, opéra comiques* ..., Vol.III, Paris, 1763, London, British Library

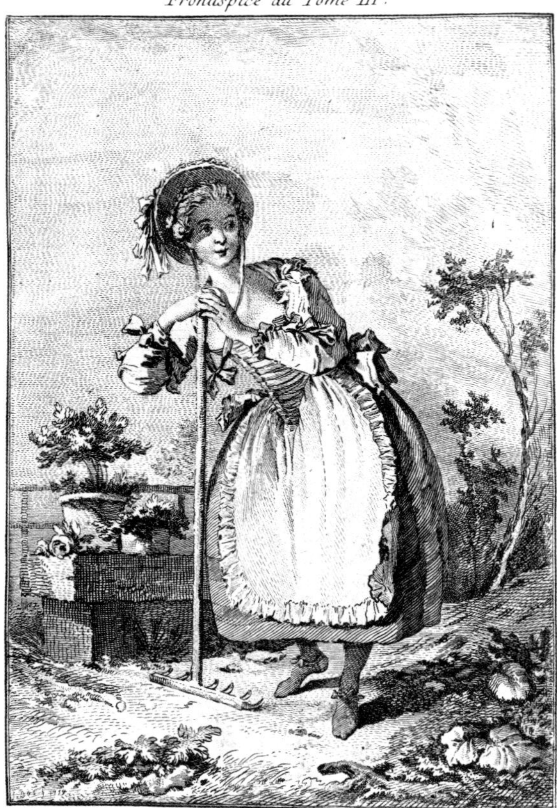

such as Voltaire's friend Vauvenargues, with youth, innocence and simplicity: 'The spirit is the eye of the soul, not its strength. Its strength is in the heart, that is to say in the passions. The most enlightened reason does not inspire one to act or to want ... in the infancy of all peoples, as in that of individuals, feeling has always preceded thought and has been the first to be born'.[115] Favart's shepherds and shepherdesses became the theatrical embodiment of such ideas. But it was not just Favart's subjects that ensured the success of his sentimental rustic tales. The pretty rural costumes invented by his wife (fig.72) were much applauded by contemporaries and Boucher's landscape sets must also have contributed greatly to the overall spectacle. One of the most unexpected compliments the new pastoral mode received came from the pen of the young Jean-Jacques Rousseau, better known today for his radical Enlightenment philosophy, who wrote his own pastoral opera, *Le Devin du village*, in 1751. The great egalitarian apparently fled after its perfomance at Fontainebleau the following year, too overawed to accept the congratulations of the King.[116]

Boucher, already part of the team responsible for the success of Favart's pastoral pantomimes, soon started to reproduce their theatrical imagery in his canvases, as usual experimenting with the themes across a variety of media. His borrowing was also immediately recognized by contemporaries: 'M. Boucher, famous for his gracious compositions, borrowed the idea of some of his pictures from them, and that is by no means the only honour that the *Pantomime of the Harvest of Tempé* has received'.[117] The Wallace Collection's *Shepherd Piping to a Shepherdess* (fig.73) is typical of the type of Favart-inspired overdoor he produced from 1745 onwards, showing a seated shepherd and shepherdess in bright costumes, painted in a broad manner. The depiction of the shepherd serenading his beloved on a flute would have immediately recalled the music of the Opéra Comique. The pastoral mode also allowed Boucher to concentrate once again on his favourite subject of the birth of love; to 'search the human heart for all the corners where love might hide' as Marivaux said of his own work. Indeed, in a century noted more for its ideas than its poetry, Boucher was recognised as *the* poetic painter of his day. Many of his concerns reflect those of Marivaux, considered the most poetic writer of the first half of the eighteenth century, and Boucher was the first choice as illustrator for *Julie, ou la nouvelle Héloise* by Rousseau, who represents the poetic response of French literature in the second half. Something of the originality and power of Boucher's pastoral vision, in an age not yet blunted by centuries of tawdry repetitions, is conveyed by Baillet de Saint-Julien's enraptured description of the pastorals exhibited by Boucher at the 1748 Salon: 'Can one describe his pastoral subject with more tenderness and naivety? It is a shepherd who teaches a young shepherdess to play the flute. What happy attitude? What noble simplicity? Nevertheless the characterization of the shepherdess is much

FIG.73 *below*
BOUCHER,
Shepherd Piping to a Shepherdess, 1745, oil on canvas, 94 × 142cm, Wallace Collection

FIG.74
following pages, left
BOUCHER, *Summer Pastoral*, 1749, oil on canvas, 259 × 197cm, Wallace Collection

FIG.75
following pages, right
BOUCHER, *Autumn Pastoral*, 1749, oil on canvas, 259 × 198.6cm, Wallace Collection

superior in beauty to that of the shepherd. In effect, in the delicacy of his traits, he does not appear to be sufficiently masculine. The accessories of the Picture match the subject perfectly; the landscape is admirable; the eye wanders there agreeably, and seems to leave such a beautiful place with regret; the Fountain is excellently treated (one reads above it the inscription FOUNTAIN OF TRUTH), and the Animals are of a spiritual touch; but the goat and sheep in the foreground appear not to have been done after nature'.[118] Even Saint-Yves, often critical of the frippery of much of the art of his time, describes one of Boucher's pastorals as 'one of the most agreeable inventions that has come from the brush of this Anacreon of Painting. In this picture, of which the expressions are of a great naivety, and of the most up-to-date elegance, everything carries a *champêtre* character which enchants ... which inspires such sweet ideas'.[119]

One of the great advantages of the pastoral was that its subject was appropriate to both town and country. It referred to one of the most fashionable recreations of the capital and therefore did not look out of place in a chic Parisian salon, while its rural subject matter made it just as apt for the decoration of a country château as a hunting picture by Oudry. Indeed, Boucher pastorals and Oudry overdoors, all now in the Wallace Collection, were used to decorate the new *maison de plaisance* near Versailles of the financier Daniel-Charles Trudaine de Montigny (1703–69).[120] Boucher may have met Trudaine de Montigny at Madame Geoffrin's as both men frequented her salon.[121] The financier also became involved with the Beauvais manufactory in 1748 in repairing a set of Boucher's *Fêtes Italiennes* tapestries.[122] Perhaps it was the sight of the tapestries that inspired him to commission the only two large-scale theatrical pastorals known by Boucher (figs. 74 and 75). They were displayed, as one might expect, in a large salon on the ground floor; the sort of room illustrated in Blondel's *L'Architecture des Maisons de Plaisance* (fig.41). The *Summer Pastoral* is a grand re-working of a cabinet-picture, *Shepherd and Shepherdess* (private

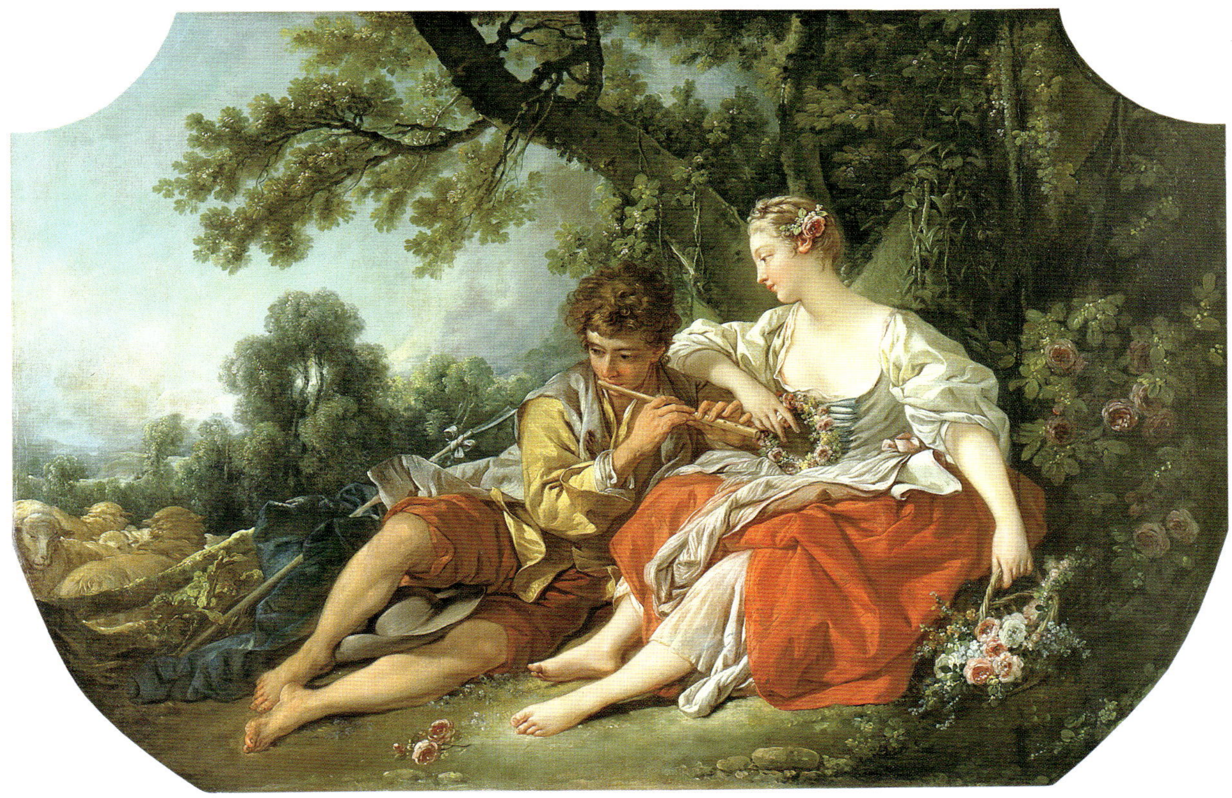

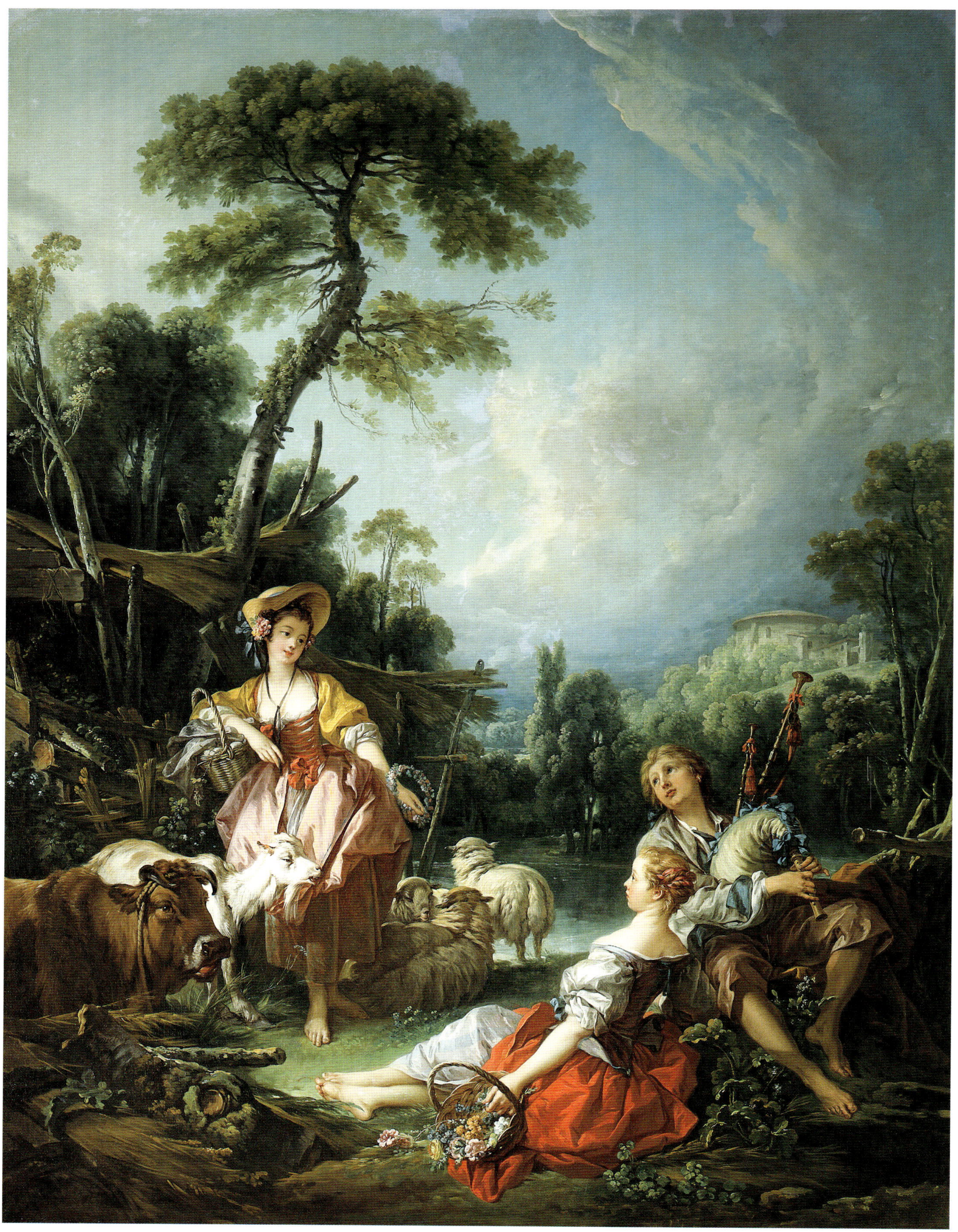

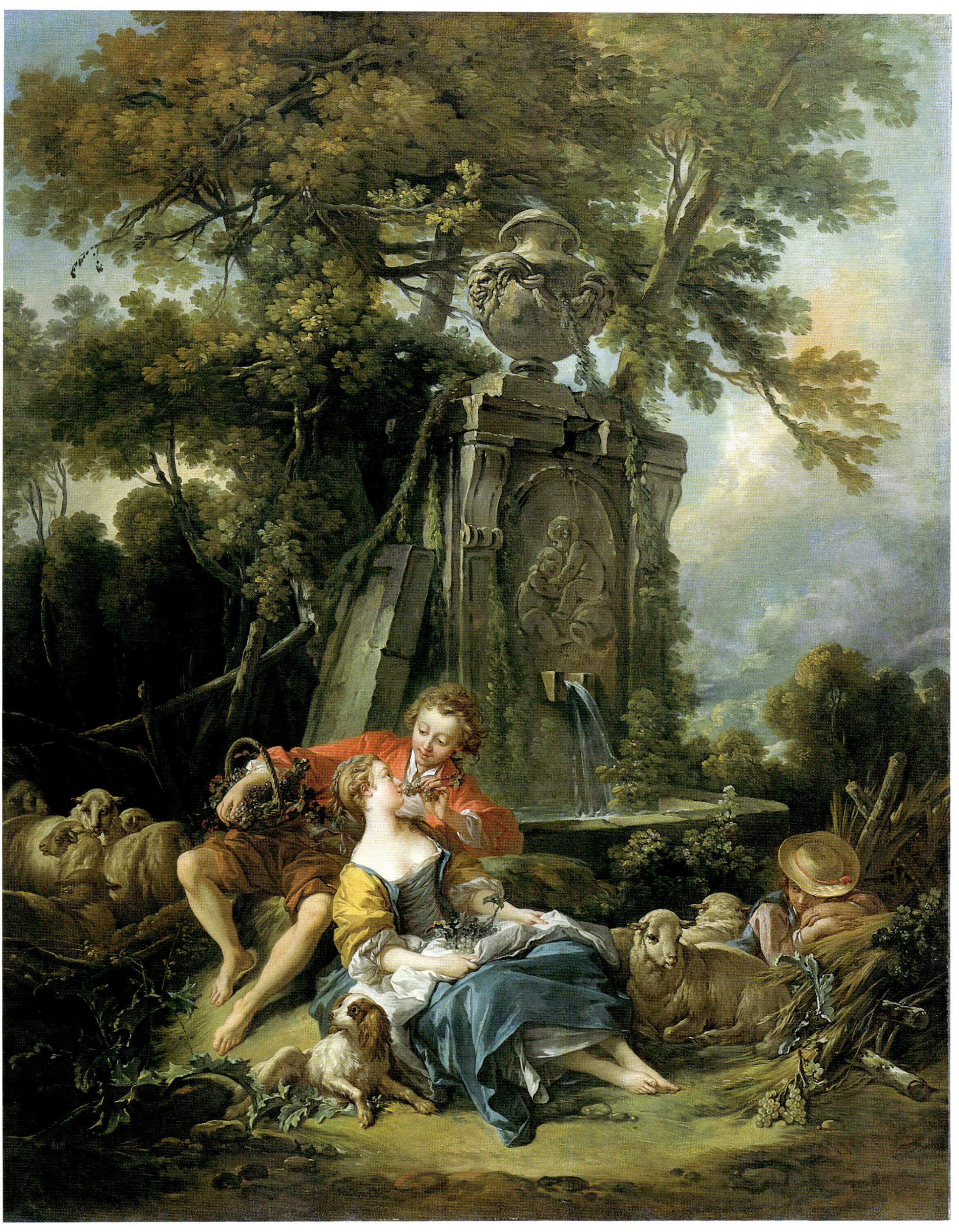

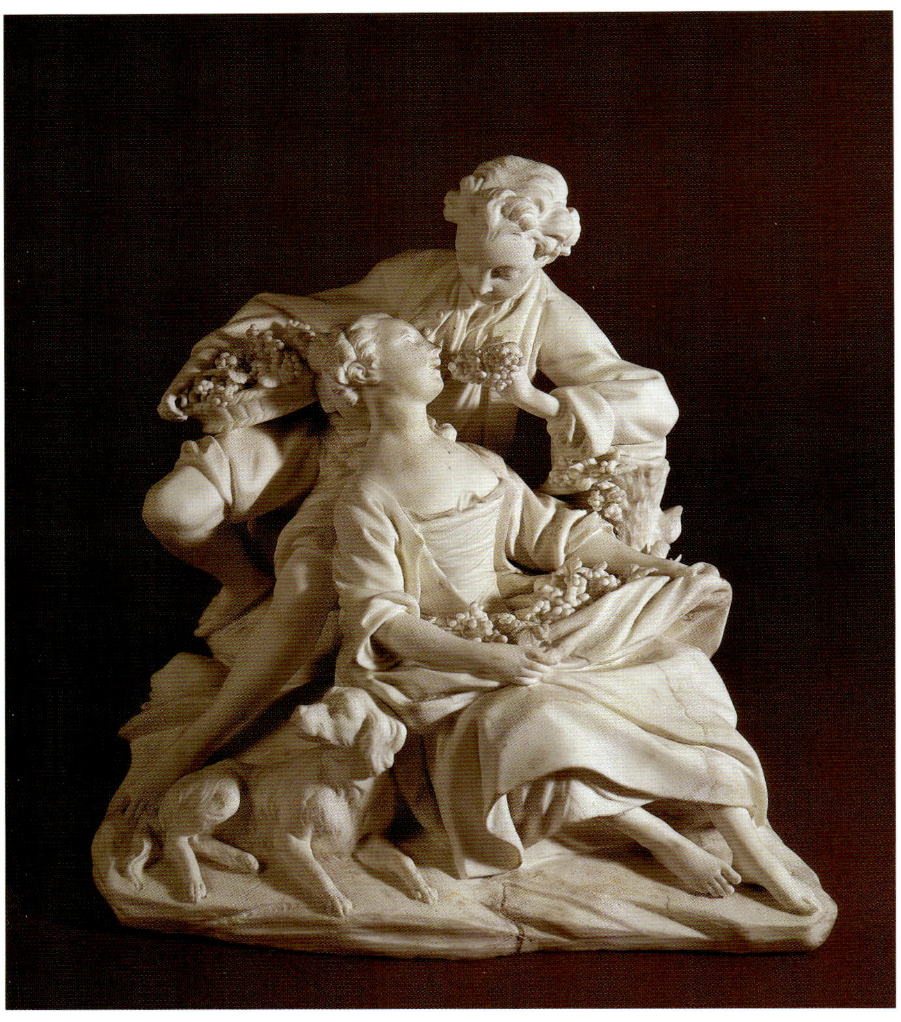

collection), painted the previous year as part of a series which included three other pastorals: *The Surprise* (lost), *The Mysterious Basket* and *The Agreeable Lesson* (both in Melbourne). The subject of the *Autumn Pastoral* recalls both an anecdote from *Les Vendanges du Tempé* and Boucher's oval cabinet-picture *Is he Thinking About Grapes?* (1747; Chicago; variant in Stockholm).[123] In the cabinet picture, however, the girl feeds the boy grapes, while the situation is reversed in the *Autumn Pastoral*, which places the figures in a far more monumental setting, seated below a magnificent fountain, symbol of the sincerity of their relationship. X-rays show that Boucher, returning to a pastoral on this scale, at first thought to include on the right the type of Castiglione-like mule that had appeared in his large pastorals painted in the early 1730s. Instead he rejected this too-rustic reminder of Italy and inserted the wittier, and more French, peeping-Tom; a direct quotation from a picture by Watteau.[124] The dog, meanwhile, is a self-quotation and appears in a number of pictures by the artist including *Daphnis and Chloé* (fig.69). The especial care taken by Boucher over the *Autumn Pastoral* may reflect the fact that Trudaine's new domaine, four and a half leagues from Paris, was particularly noted for its vineyards.[125] Trudaine also seems to have been involved with the new Vincennes porcelain manufactory, which helps to explain why the couple eating grapes were reproduced by 1752 as a biscuit group (fig.76).[126] Boucher's *Autumn Pastoral* was never engraved but it became a source of inspiration for the Vincennes-Sèvres factory for many years to come. Indeed Boucher's pastorals in general proved perfect for adaptation across the decorative arts and appeared on a variety of objects including porcelain, tapestry, gold boxes and fans, and were reproduced in numerous sets of engravings, including four books of pastorals published by Huquier.[127]

Criticism

As the eighteenth century approached its mid-point a rare note of anxiety began to creep into the writings of critics and philosophers. A feeling of sensory overload can be detected in reaction to the pursuit of pleasure in the capital. Commentators adopted an increasingly moralistic stance when discussing Parisian materialism. There was a feeling that the Parisian taste for frivolous and costly luxuries was threatening the moral health of the nation. Despite the expense, nothing of lasting value seemed to be produced, as Saint-Yves noted in 1748: 'We love the pleasures of the flesh and everything that makes life sweeter and more comfortable, brilliant equipages, jewels and amusements of every kind … Our luxury is found in fragile things that cost much and last little'.[128] In contrast to Voltaire's earlier defence of luxury, the excessive consumption of luxury goods was

FIG.76 *opposite*
AFTER BOUCHER,
The Grape-Eaters, 1752,
soft-paste Vincennes biscuit porcelain, height 22.5cm,
Sèvres, Musée National de la Céramique

now branded as irrational, hence the abbé Desfontaines's comment 'is it not madness to ruin oneself for a shell?' when describing the collecting obsession of Quentin de Lorangère.[129] Artists like Boucher, whose art was based on a sensualist aesthetic and who were connected in people's minds with the consumption of luxury goods, naturally came under increasing attack, initially for moral reasons and then for stylistic ones. As early as 1738, the marquis d'Argens had warned that 'a great number of people think that in twenty years time in France one will swap two pictures by Raphael for a fan by Watteau'.[130] Boucher might not have thought this a bad exchange, but for the first time he was out of step with the avant-garde. His approach is displayed by the fact that he devoted time in 1747 to decorating Easter eggs for Louis XV and designing cut-out dolls, called *pantins*; precisely the type of frivolities that inspired Diderot in the same year to refer disparagingly to 'giddy young people … talking of everything and knowing nothing, finding finesse in frivolities … interrupting to talk of politics, and concluding with profound reflections on a hairstyle, a dress, a Chinese figurine, a Meissen nude or jug, a pantin by Boucher …'.[131]

The sense of grandeur and civic duty so lacking, according to critics, in contemporary selfish hedonism was rediscovered by some in nostalgia for the great achievements of the age of Louis XIV. This attitude informs Voltaire's *Siècle de Louis XIV*, recalling Charles Perrault's 1687 eulogy, *L'Age de Louis le Grand*, which claimed that the age of Louis XIV was superior even to classical civilisation.[132] The public and didactic role of art was also stressed in La Font de Saint-Yenne's 1749 pamphlet *L'Ombre du Grand Colbert, le Louvre et la Ville de Paris*. This again invoked the 'great works' of the age of Louis XIV while covertly accusing the current administration of laxity and negligence: pointing out that the Louvre was still not architecturally complete, that the King's collections at Versailles could not be seen by the public and that the urban development of Paris was pretty much where it had been at the death of Louis's great minister Colbert. A remedy to the frivolity of the age was suggested by Saint-Yves when he regretted the contemporary 'progress' away from classical models, claiming that: 'one notices … that the more one advances the more one distances oneself from the antique, from that simplicity so noble, so majestic, so touching, and from the correction in drawing that made such a great name for Raphael, Poussin or Le Sueur'.[133] Over the coming decades the return to the grand manner and to antiquity was eventually to evolve into the heroic style of David (1748–1825).

Meanwhile the regular establishment of the Salon had already led to the development of art criticism by writers more concerned with subject, polemic and moral, as opposed to the technical merits of painting. Although Boucher's ability to respond to the demands of the rococo interior may have endeared him to a wealthy private clientele, his works, removed from their decorative context, did not always elicit the same response from critics at the Salon. What appeared colourful and charming above a door did not necessarily impress when placed lower down and in full view of a more middle-class public. Indeed, it was virtually impossible to please the two audiences, and Boucher sided with those who paid well now rather than with those who would revise his reputation for posterity. La Font de Saint-Yenne was typical of the new breed of critic whose yearning for a return to the seeming certainty and grandeur of Raphael and the Baroque led to ambivalence towards Boucher's technically brilliant productions. When discussing *Eloquence* and *Astronomy*, two of Boucher's overdoors for the Medal Cabinet of the King's Library in the rue de Richelieu (*in-situ*) exhibited at the 1746 Salon, he admited that Boucher 'has reputation' and that 'their composition is agreeable, their drapery well-thought out and light, their tones varied and quite well contrasted'. But he went on to say that 'it would be quite difficult to identify *Eloquence* from the physiognomy of the figure that symbolises her, which is extremely cold and characterless. What fire! What vehemence should strike us in the traits which announce this powerful Art which subdues the spirits, and masters our passions as it pleases! One would desire a stronger more vigorous colouring in the flesh tints: more nobility and expression in the heads, above all in those of the young girls, and that they would bear some resemblance to the dignity and decency of those of Raphael, the Carracci, Guido Reni, Carlo Maratta, Le Brun, Poussin and Mignard, etc., which are all of a noble and devout character without resembling each other. One would ask of him also a little more truth and nature in his attitudes, above all in those of the children, or Genii who accompany his Subjects, and which are for the most part unnecessarily topsy-turvy and violent without being beautiful'. Boucher was not alone in being criticised like this, for La Font de Saint-Yenne points out that the 'public' thought the same of Natoire, whom he criticises even more severely for his faded flesh tints, adding that 'today nearly all our productions in Literature and Painting are tinted the colour of roses and last about the same length of time'.[134]

The following year La Font de Saint-Yenne linked the decorative approach of artists like Boucher and Natoire to the unfortunate manner in which painting had become subject to the dictates of private patrons and their frivolous interiors. Art had been condemned 'beyond the reach of sight and confined by the lack of space to insipid and uninteresting depictions: the four elements, the seasons, the Arts, the Muses, and other such formulations, the common triumphs of a plagiarizing and labouring Painting, which require neither genius, nor invention and which have been turned and turned about over the past twenty years'.[135] Saint-Yves proposed that art should instead resume a civic role such as it had enjoyed under Louis XIV: 'It is much more important than one thinks that Painting, Sculpture, Architecture and Music are carried to the highest point of perfection possible for the glory of the nation. They are a universal language, understood by foreigners, and give them a high opinion of the people who cultivate them'.[136] The public role of art in the capital was, accordingly, of even greater importance and he bemoaned the fact that currently 'one sees nothing imposing in France'.[137] He also proposed that the best examples of painting and sculpture should be displayed publicly in churches to encourage a taste in the arts; a church, of course, being the last place one expected to encounter a painting by Boucher.

Ironically, Lenormand de Tournehem's administration became the most active since Louis XIV in countering the decorative style of painting his niece initially patronised. He adjusted the price paid for histories according to their size, reduced the price of portraits and then announced a history competition in 1747: 'to revive the art, which seems to have fallen not only in France, but even in countries where painters formerly excelled'. The two most critically acclaimed pictures, Dumont Le Romain's *Mucius Scaevola* (Besançon) and Restout's *Alexander with his Doctors* (Amiens) clearly evoked the tradition of seventeenth-century history painting and marked the revival of the elevated academic manner. No outright winner was nominated, however, and the prize money was divided equally among the eleven contestants and the secretary of the Academy, Lépicié. Boucher's picture, another *Rape of Europa* (Louvre), elicited mixed responses. The abbé Le Blanc, for example, acclaimed Boucher as 'the Painter of sensuality and the graces' who 'instructed by nature … has stolen Venus's girdle' and admired both 'the Nature and the Art' of his picture.[138] He nevertheless had to admit that many people found it too pink, an observation repeated by Baillet de Saint-Julien who confessed himself surprised by 'the division of public opinion over the two paintings by MM. Natoire and Boucher. The rose tonality, which dominated the work of the latter, may have been the cause'. Baillet de Saint-Julien went on to state that 'the pictures by these two art-lovers are well composed, although that by M. Boucher is superior in genius and imaginative power. They are equally well-drawn … looking in detail at these two knowledgeable productions, is one not obliged to acknowledge the current superiority of the

French Masters above all other schools?'[139] The fact that *The Rape of Europa* was subsequently acquired by the Crown for 1,500 *livres* demonstrates the tension between the new moralistic art themes and the actual art market of the time.[140] While De Tournehem and his successor, Pompadour's brother, Monsieur de Vandières, the future marquis de Marigny, might promote the virtues of civic art to the glory of France, in private the King and most of the wealthy elite understandably preferred to live with a seductive vision by Boucher, rather than some morally edifying canvas by one of the new neo-classical artists like Vien. Boucher's response, meanwhile, was to concentrate on the visuals. Borrowing an image from Salvator Rosa, he produced a witty satirical frontispiece to Le Blanc's generally sympathetic account of the 1747 Salon, showing Painting gagged in front of her easel unable to defend herself against the unfair criticisms of Envy, Ignorance and Stupidity.[141]

Boucher's imaginative power was increasingly viewed as suspect by critics stressing the public mission of art. This led to a developing concept of artistic truth linked to a more direct representation of nature and accompanied by a return to genre specialisation. To the new intelligentsia, Boucher's technical versatility and formal brilliance undermined any notion of artistic truth or seriousness and his artisan connections fatally compromised his status as a professional artist. In 1745 Bachaumont noted approvingly Boucher's ability to depict 'Landscapes, *Bambochades*, and Grotesques and Ornaments in the manner of Watteau. He also paints flowers, fruits, animals, architecture, and little gallant and fashionable subjects equally well'.[142] He is more critical by 1750, when he points out that despite his versatility Boucher's figures have 'little expression', an absolute requirement of the grand manner, and that his approach is too picturesque: 'his female heads are more pretty than beautiful, more coquette than noble. His draperies are nearly always too full of folds, the folds sometimes too broken and somewhat heavy and unflattering to the nude'.[143] Although Saint-Yves was similarly unable to deny Boucher's technical accomplishment, he nevertheless perversely insisted that 'with a genius less vast, M. Boucher would have been a still greater man'.[144] One is reminded of Diderot's acerbic judgement on Voltaire: 'That man is the second in all the genres'.

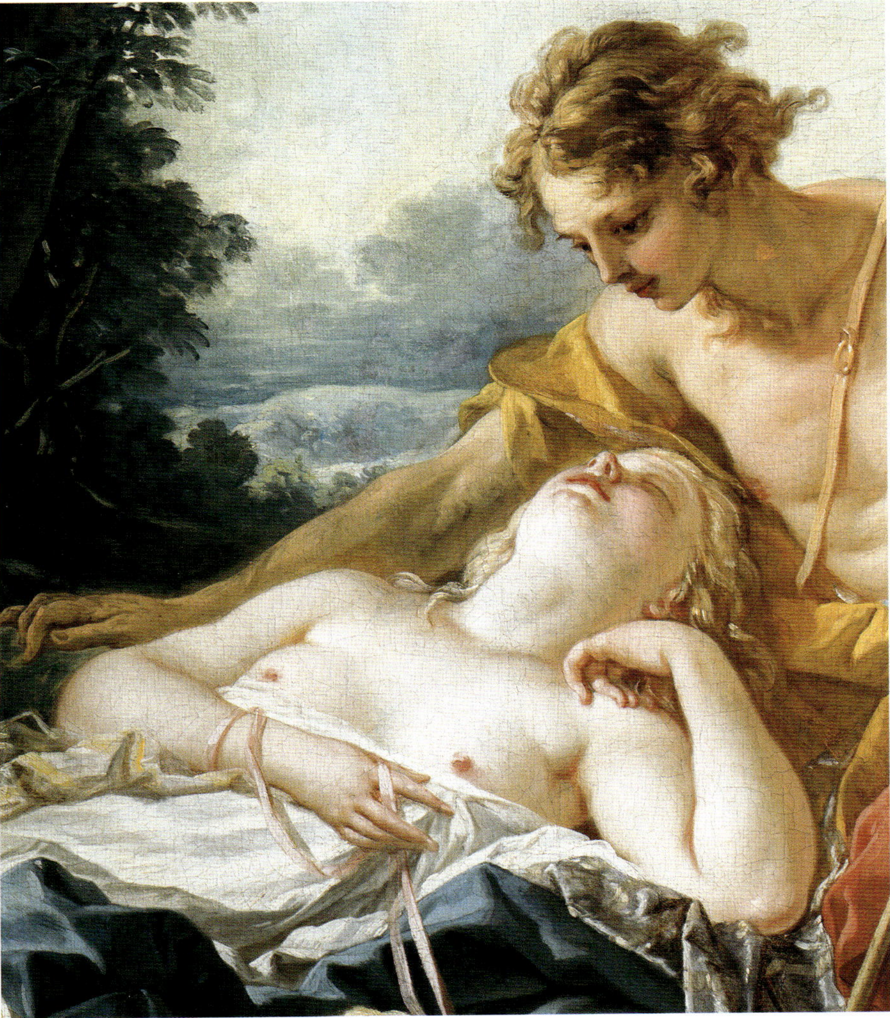

Detail, FIG.69

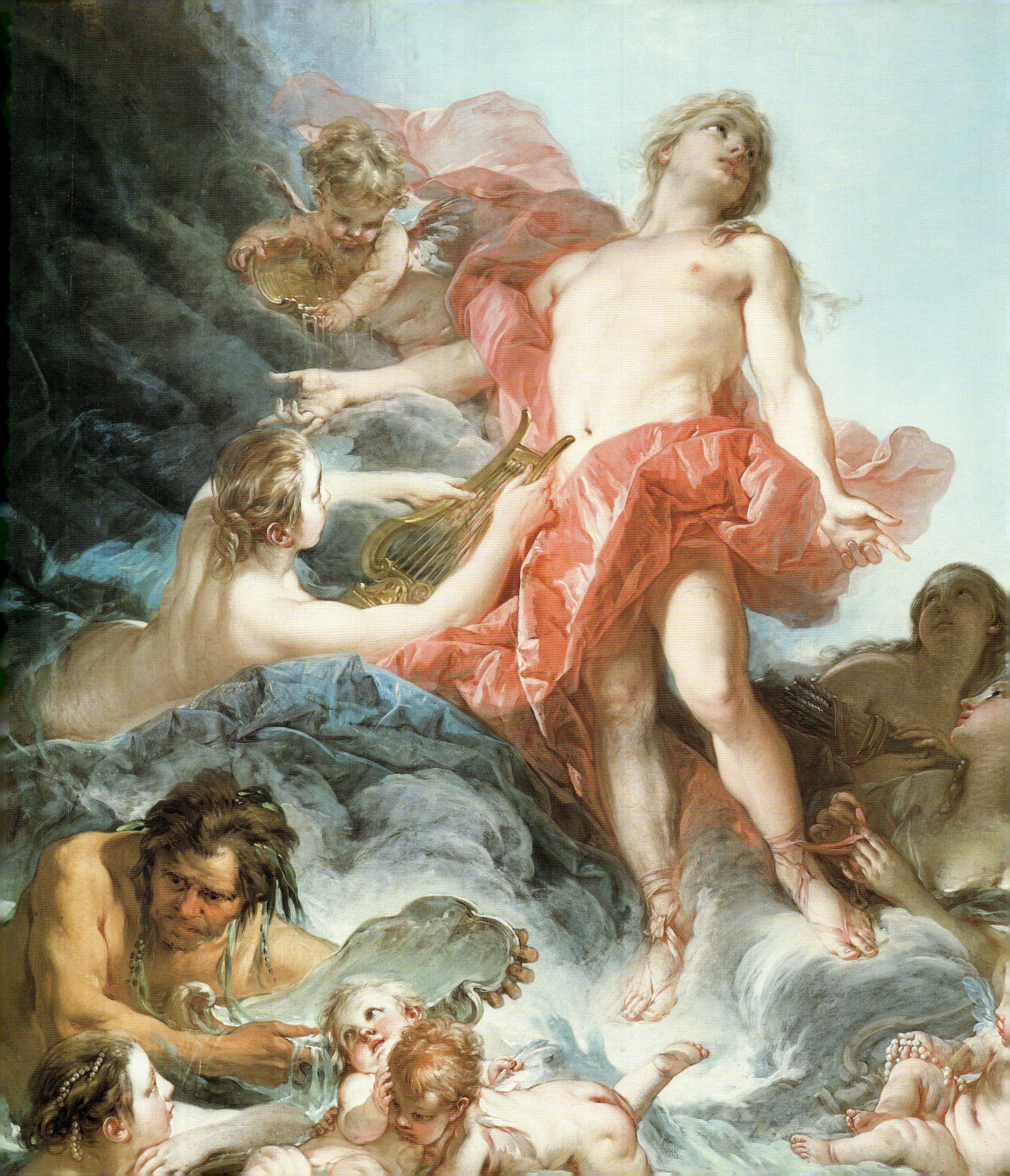

IV

No longer a painter, but Painting Itself JOURNAL ENCYCLOPAEDIQUE[1]

Pompadour's Painter: 1750s

A punning series of verses by Panard celebrating and satirising the most famous poets, intellectuals, musicians, artists, dancers, actors and composers of France appeared in the *Nouveau Logogriphe* in 1744. Boucher was celebrated with a riddle playing on 'butcher', the meaning of his name in French: 'He does not have sausage-like fingers/ This painter whose name contains/ The merchant who every Friday/ Closes his shop and his door'.[2] The following year marked the arrival at Court of a new mistress to the King. To the horror of many aristocratic commentators, for the first time this role was taken by one of the daughters of the nouveau riche Parisian bourgeoisie, whose name, often similarly lampooned, refers to the merchant who did a roaring trade on Fridays. Jeanne-Antoinette Poisson, the Miss Fish who had become Madame Lenormand d'Étioles in 1742, was created marquise de Pompadour by the infatuated King and installed at Court in 1745.[3] Two years later La Font de Saint-Yenne warned of the increasing feminisation of the arts in France, complaining that 'it is chiefly the ladies one should blame if our products so often descend to the level of trifles and trinkets'.[4] At the time, Madame de Pompadour was enjoying the first idyllic years of her affair with the King, caught up in a whirl of hunting parties, amateur theatricals and *petits soupers*. As their sexual relationship waned around 1750, however, Madame de Pompadour turned increasingly to the arts for help in her great patriotic task of continuing to amuse and seduce the King.[5] Her single-minded devotion recalls the limitations of female influence in the eighteenth century where 'Man enjoys the happiness that he himself feels, while woman enjoys that which she creates in others'.[6] Like many cultured *arrivistes* before and since, Madame de Pompadour probably hoped that her genuine interest in the arts would demonstrate her nobility of taste and deflect attention from her actual lack of breeding, thus confirming her right to her new status.

Madame de Pompadour was to become Boucher's highest profile client after the King and one of his most inspiring patrons. Of the four painters described by Bachaumont as the leading artists in 1750, namely Carle Van Loo, Natoire, Boucher and Pierre (1713–89), it was Boucher who clearly excelled in imagination and pleasing approach, making him the perfect choice to help Madame de Pompadour carry out her artistic agenda.[7] In addition, he was as thoroughly Parisian as her, his wife was only five years older than the marquise, and his interest in opera and the latest Parisian fashions made him a source of information to the royal mistress lamenting her isolation at Court. Boucher's paintings helped Madame de Pompadour to invest her interiors at Court with something of the luxurious chic and intimacy of the Parisian capital, while in return, her patronage of Boucher clearly singled him out as the first decorative painter of the day. Pierre was still a relative youngster and Natoire was dispatched to direct the French Academy in Rome in 1752, leaving only Carle Van Loo as Boucher's main rival. Although Madame de Pompadour patronised both men she obviously preferred Boucher, commissioning more works from him and stretching him artistically by ordering historical and religious subjects more challenging than those

FIG.77 *previous page*
BOUCHER, *The Rising of the Sun*, detail, 1753, oil on canvas, Wallace Collection

FIG.78 *opposite*
BOUCHER, *Madame de Pompadour*, 1759, oil on canvas, 91 × 68cm, Wallace Collection

with which he had been previously identified. Madame de Pompadour's patronage of Boucher was thus crucial in encouraging him to develop a grander manner and allowing him to demonstrate his ability in direct comparison with Van Loo.

The trust which developed between painter and patron is borne out by a series of portraits Madame de Pompadour commissioned from Boucher between 1750 and 1759, culminating in the portrait in the Wallace Collection (fig.78).[8] Madame de Pompadour was acutely aware of the precariousness of her position at Court, even more so once the cessation of her sexual relationship with the King had become public knowledge. Keen to project a confident and attractive image, clearly demonstrating her continuing role as the King's confidante, she commissioned a series of portraits stressing her friendship, loyalty, spiritual and intellectual accomplishments and beauty. In the 1740s, like most ladies of Court, she had employed the portraitist Nattier to depict her in fashionable mythological guise as a modern Diana, referring to her lover's passion for the hunt which she then shared (1746; Versailles).[9] By 1750, aware of Nattier's homely portrait of the Queen reading the bible (1748; Versailles) and wishing to imitate the Queen's respectable image, she turned to portrait specialists, the draughtsman, Jean-Etienne Liotard, and the pastellist, Maurice-Quentin de La Tour, to execute her portrait in modern dress. She soon grew exasperated, however, with the former's unflattering realism and the latter's slowness and perfectionism.[10] The appeal of the marquise evidently lay as much in her vivacious disposition as in her physical appearance and contemporaries felt that few artists were capable of capturing her essential allure. One described her as 'taller than average, slim, graceful, supple, elegant; her face well matched to her height, of a perfect oval, with beautiful light brown hair, quite large eyes, with fine eyebrows of the same colour, the nose perfectly well-formed, the mouth charming ... the most beautiful skin in the world rendered all her traits all the more striking. Her eyes have a particular charm, which perhaps derives from their uncertain colour; ... the ensemble of her person seems to hover between the last degree of elegance and the first of nobility.'[11] Boucher was not noted for his talent as a portraitist, but his acknowledged ability to paint children led to a royal commission in 1749 which may have suggested him as a portraitist to the marquise. The delightful portrait of the infant *Duc de Montpensier* (1749; Waddesdon), son of Louis XV's cousin, the duc d'Orléans, who became the future regicide, Louis-Philippe Égalité, could not have failed to charm the notoriously sentimental marquise.[12]
By March of the following year Boucher had completed his first portrait of Madame de Pompadour, and she wrote to her brother: 'I am going to send you the copy of one [portrait] by Boucher, which is charming, and which he will finish on me'. In April she wrote 'I am sending you at last the copy of my portrait by Boucher; it greatly resembles the original, but little myself; nevertheless quite agreeable'.[13] The first comment illustrates how a person as busy as the marquise would not sit for an entire portrait: instead the pose, setting and dress would be worked out in advance while the sitter would only pose for the head to be finished from life. The construction of the image was almost as imaginative and artificial a process as composing a history painting. The marquise's comments also reveal that she was concerned that Boucher's portrait should project an attractive image rather than an exact resemblance so, despite her reservations regarding the accuracy of Boucher's likeness, she went on to commission at least a further eleven portraits.[14]

The Wallace Collection portrait is the last image Boucher painted of his illustrious patroness and demonstrates how they devised an iconography that would have had a charming and intimate significance for the marquise's immediate circle including, most importantly, the King. It celebrates her friendship with Louis, while also delighting the viewer as an exquisite representation of a beautiful and fashionably dressed woman. Unusually, it depicts her full face (she is normally shown looking to the right) leaning elegantly, fan

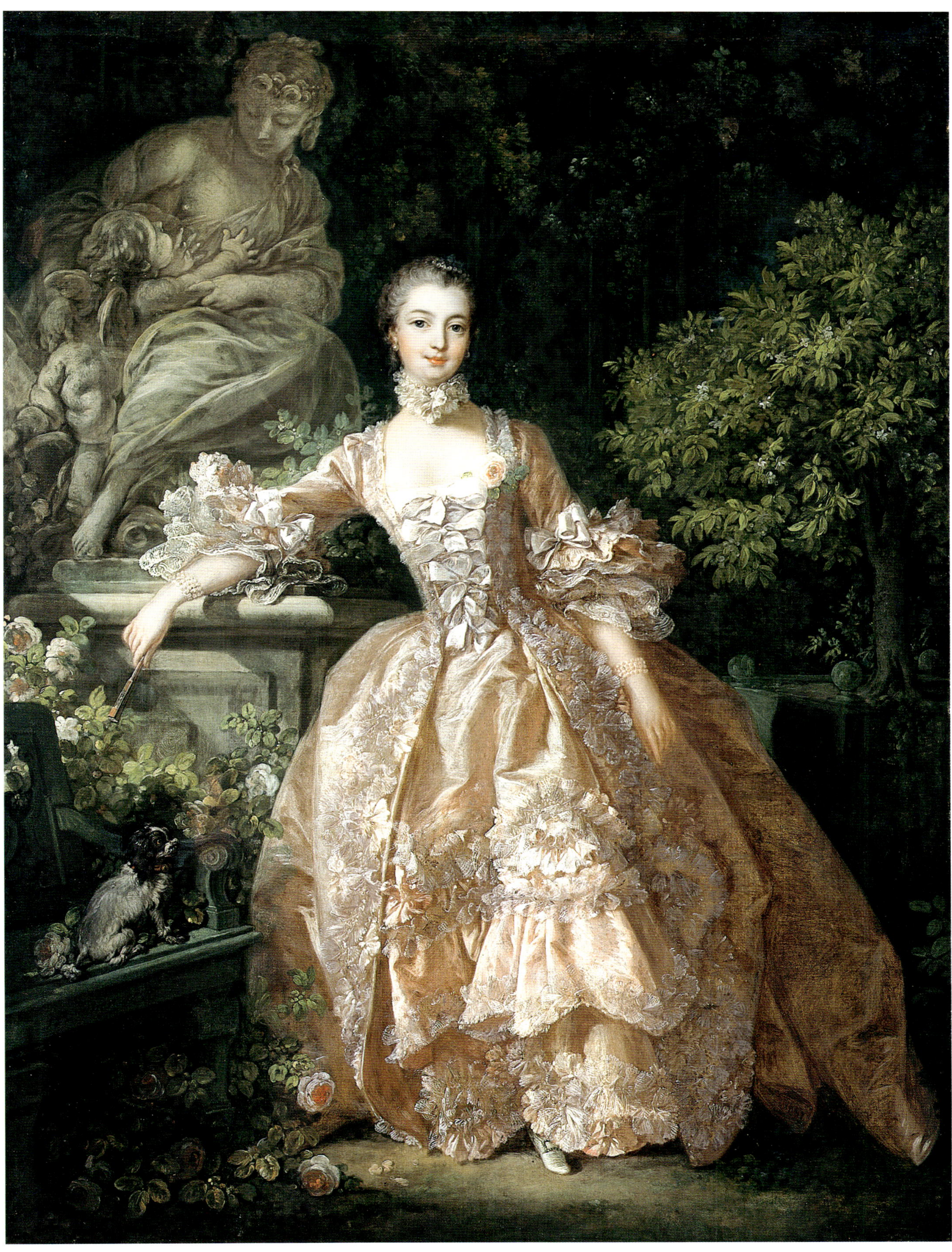

FIG.79
MADAME DE POMPADOUR after BOUCHER, *Love and Friendship*, *c*.1752–3, engraving, 15.3 × 13.1cm, Paris, Musée du Louvre

FIG.80 *opposite*
BOUCHER, *Apollo and Issé*, 1750, oil on canvas, 129 × 157cm, Tours, Musée des Beaux-Arts

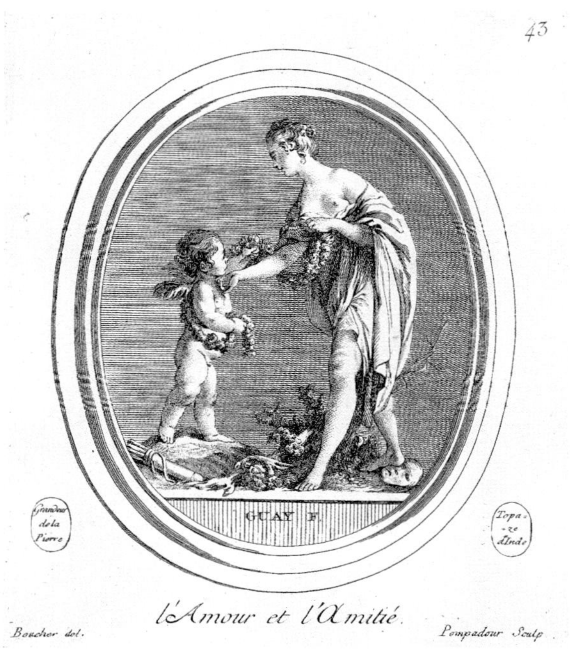

in hand, against a statue which evokes the ideals of friendship and platonic love, recalling the statue of *Friendship embracing Love* which the marquise had commissioned from Jean-Baptiste Pigalle in 1755 (completed 1758; Louvre).[15] Faithfulness is implied by the presence of Madame de Pompadour's pet spaniel, Inès, who had been engraved by Étienne Fessard and Augustin de Saint-Aubin after Christophe Huet as a symbol of *Fidelity* in 1755–56, while love is symbolized by the orange blossom and roses.[16] The portrait's setting recalls the shared passion of the marquise and King for gardening evoking the park at Bellevue, Madame de Pompadour's most spectacular country residence, where 'roses, jasmine and even orange trees… seemed to spring from the bosom of the earth'.[17] The portrait is a reminder of the *Grove of Friendship* in the centre of which stood a statue by Pigalle of Madame de Pompadour as *Friendship* (1753; Louvre).[18] In the picture Madame de Pompadour stands, a living rose in her sumptuous pink dress, planted against the dark green trellis of the grove. Boucher depicts every detail of her finery, painting the silk taffeta of her robe in a thin pink wash over a grey ground which shows through the upper layer and lends the picture a silvery cast almost impossible to reproduce in print. Paradoxically, as war and unpopularity took their toll on the marquise's reputation, such stylistic sensuality was probably deemed increasingly inappropriate by a mistress keen to stress her virtue. Subsequently she turned to the more staid Carle Van Loo and François-Hubert Drouais for images that were less flattering, but more respectable.[19] Today, however, the Wallace Collection portrait, with its ravishingly attired subject teasingly extending a dainty satin-slippered foot, remains one of the most reproduced images of the marquise.

Boucher served as teacher to his patroness, who shared the eighteenth-century amateur passion for drawing and also learnt to engrave under his tutelage. The same iconography of *Love and Friendship*, therefore, appears in an engraving by Madame de Pompadour after Boucher (fig.79). This formed one of a series of designs which were both engraved by the marquise and cut onto semi-precious stones by Jacques Guay (1711–1793). *Love and Friendship* was number 43 of the *Suite des estampes Gravées par Mme la marquise de Pompadour d'après les Pierres gravés de Guay Graveur du Roy*, first published in 1755, and, in an expanded version, in 1758.[20] It was also engraved by Guay in 1753 onto one of the three intaglio decorated faces of an Indian topaz which was made up into a seal for Madame de Pompadour's personal use (Medal Cabinet, Bibliothèque Nationale de France). The other two faces of the seal depict the related subjects of *Love Sacrificing to Friendship* and the *Temple of Friendship*.[21] In this way, the Enlightenment fashion for engraved stones, intaglios and cameos led Boucher to experiment with neo-classical forms and subjects, depicting classically-draped girls sacrificing to Love, long before such themes appeared in the work of Vien and Greuze.[22] It seems that Boucher was among the first to recognise the formal potential of classical themes as applied to the decorative arts. They did not, however, affect his painterly aesthetic, which was too firmly rooted in an appreciation of the Baroque and in the theories of De Piles to be able

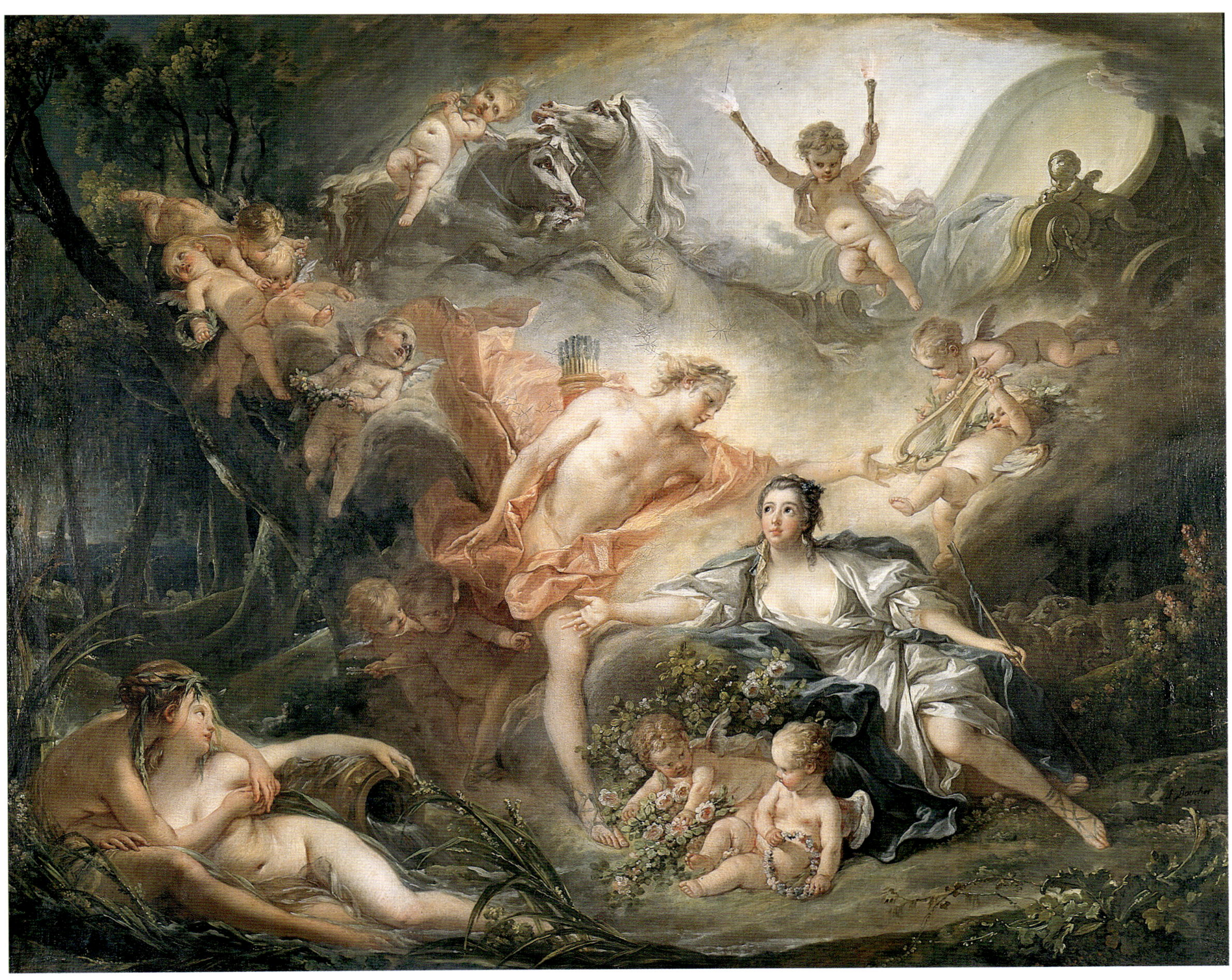

to recognise the antique as a source for the moral and formal rejuvenation of painting advocated by contemporary critics.

Lux ex Tenebris: Out of Darkness Light

FREEMASONS' MOTTO

As Madame de Pompadour's artistic choices were predicated on her need to please the King, she was naturally keen to employ artists he liked. The increasing number of royal commissions that Boucher had received in the 1740s would already have marked him out as potentially useful to the marquise. These included: four overdoors for the Medal Cabinet of King's Library(1741); fifteen pictures for the Château de Choisy, including landscapes and mythological works suited to a country residence used for hunting; overdoors depicting *Venus and Vulcan* (Louvre) and *The Apotheosis of Aeneas* (private collection), rejected by the prudish Dauphin but accepted by the King for his bedchamber at Marly (1746); an overdoor

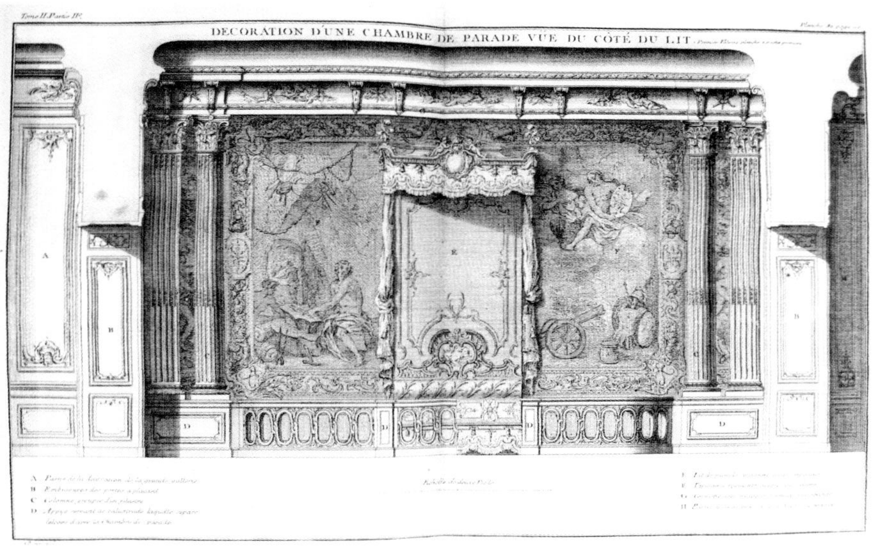

FIG.81
Decoration of a Formal Bedchamber, engraving, 21 × 34.7cm, plate 82, from J.-F. Blondel, *L'Architecture des Maisons de Plaisance*, Vol.II, part II, Paris, 1738, Library of Hertford House

depicting *The Return from the Hunt* for Fontainebleau (1748; lost); two overdoors of mythological subjects symbolising the Seasons, *Arion on the Dolphin* (Princeton) and *Vertumnus and Pomona* (Ohio), plus a set of tapestries after Boucher for La Muette (1749) and the *Rape of Europa* (1747; Louvre) acquired by the Crown in 1747.[23] The seal of royal approval came with a commission from the Crown in 1749 for Boucher to depict *Apollo and Issé* (fig.80).[24] That same year Madame de Pompadour had delighted the King as Issé in a revival of Destouches's opera of the same name. In view of the traditional identification of the King with the Sun god, the story of the shepherdess Issé's love for Apollo would have hinted at a parallel with Madame de Pompadour's love for Louis. It seems that Pompadour's rendition of Issé inspired the King to return the compliment by commissioning a picture on the same theme which included her portrait, and is described in a memorandum of November 1749: 'This picture represents Apollo and Issé … Issé, semi-reclining on a bed of flowers, seems to be recovering from a swoon and looks tenderly at Apollo at the moment when the God leaves off his shepherd-like disguise, which is shown by the Amours who play with the different shepherding attributes. With one hand the God holds the Goddess's hand, with the other he shows her the Glory he shares with her'. Boucher, who had already designed sets for the same opera (fig.68), was a natural choice to paint such a theatrical subject and he received the substantial sum of 2,400 *livres* for his pains. A note added to the memorandum by the then First Painter to the King, Charles Coypel, points out that 'the order did not pass through my hands', underlining the unusual nature of the commission.[25] Boucher's involvement in such a private gift from the King to his mistress could not have recommended him more highly to Madame de Pompadour.

In the same year, 1750, that Boucher finished painting *Apollo and Issé*, Madame de Pompadour embarked on her next great interior decoration project at the newly built Château of Bellevue, which the King had ceded to her the previous year. Of all Madame de Pompadour's residences, Bellevue was the only one she was able to oversee from construction to completion, and was by all accounts the most exquisitely furnished.[26] With its splendid view overlooking the Seine, near the royal Château of Meudon and not too far from Versailles, Bellevue became one of Madame de Pompadour's pet projects. Boucher was employed to decorate some of the most prestigious rooms in the château, providing overdoors and tapestries for the King's apartment, and an altarpiece for the chapel, as well as decorative overdoors elsewhere.

While Madame de Pompadour's own bedroom on the ground floor at Bellevue might be decorated with embroidered fabrics and *turquerie* overdoors by Carle Van Loo, protocol demanded a more magnificent scheme for the King's bedchamber on the first floor.[27] Formal bedchambers were often decorated with tapestry (fig.81) and we have already seen how Boucher's designs for Beauvais had rejuvenated this traditional medium. At the end of the 1740s Boucher provided a set of designs for a new and yet more grandiose Beauvais tapestry series, *The Loves of the Gods*, first on the loom in 1749. In scenes such as *Apollo and Clytie* (fig.82), Boucher re-invented well-known subjects from Ovid with a panache and elegance calculated to appeal to the wealthy private buyer. Studying

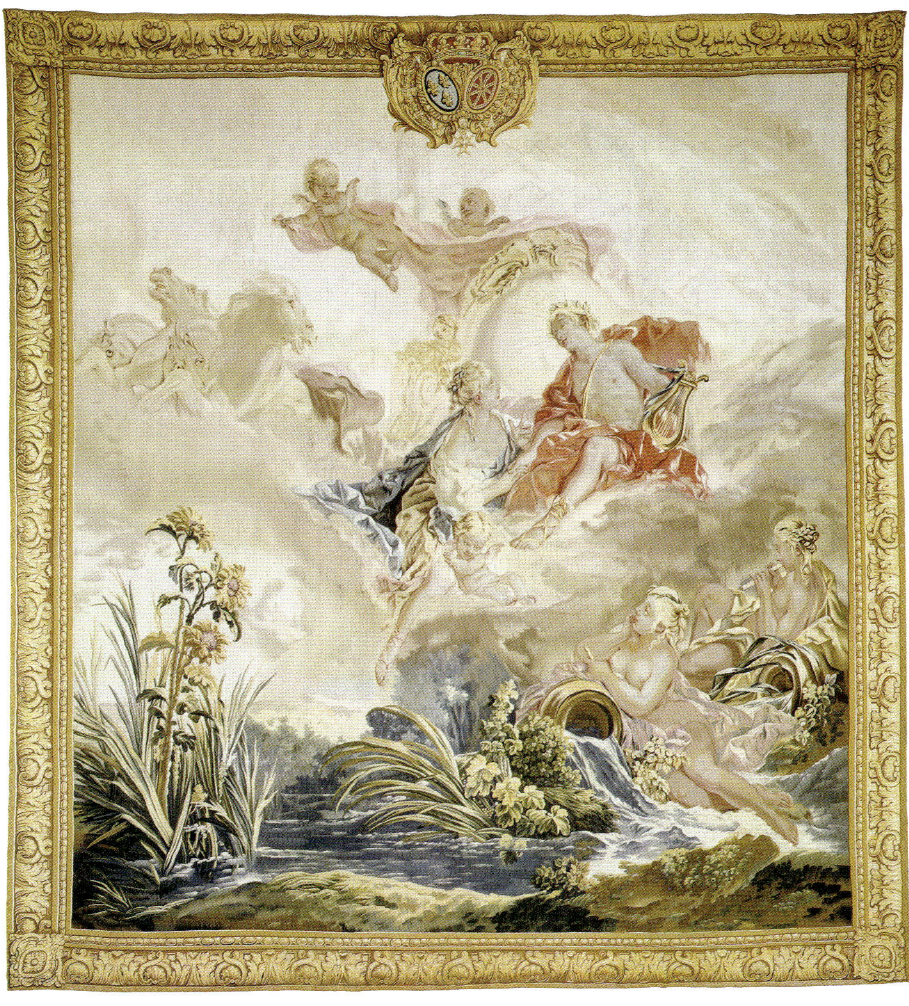

FIG.82
After BOUCHER,
Apollo and Clytie, wool and silk low warp Beauvais tapestry, 353.3 × 302.3cm, from the series *The Loves of the Gods* first on the loom in 1749, Cambridge, Fitzwilliam Museum

the large-scale works of illustrious Baroque predecessors, such as Rubens and La Fosse, Boucher effortlessly incorporated visual references to their work and learnt from their manner of organising large compositions without compromising his own sensuality and grace. Thus while the horses in *Apollo and Clytie* may recall a drawing by Rubens (Dresden) and the figure of Apollo is reminiscent of La Fosse's Apollo in his ceiling for the *Cabinet des Muses* of Charles Perrault (version, private collection; engraved by Chastillon), the overall effect is lighter and more engaging.[28] Boucher's ability to design such visually sumptuous yet modern tapestries prompted the marquise to commission from him a set for the King's bedchamber at Bellevue intended to be both monumental and yet also new, witty and personal in the manner of *Apollo and Issé*.

This is why Boucher's most ambitious paintings, widely regarded as his masterpieces, *The Setting* and *The Rising of the Sun*, were actually commissioned as tapestry cartoons in 1752 (figs. 83–84).[29] A memorandum of 1747 demonstrates how lucrative tapestry designing could be for a painter. Members of the Academy were required to produce 'small originals' from their own hand and 'large copies from their hand or supervised by them to a standard which they would vouch for'. The large copies were used as models by the weavers while the small pictures were kept by the chief-weaver, 'who should always have an overall view of the tapestry he is supervising to hand'. The artist was paid the same price for a cartoon, which was 6,000 *livres* for a large cartoon (about 7 x 6m), 5,000 for a medium cartoon (about 5½ x 4m) and 4,000 for a small cartoon (about 4 x 3m), regardless of whether it was an original or copy, as it was the overall quality of the design rather than an individual artist's hand that mattered.[30] This was at a time when (admittedly smaller) overdoors painted by Boucher, such as those for the King's bedchamber at Marly, were priced at 800 *livres* apiece, *The Return from the Hunt* for the dining room at Fontainebleau cost 600 *livres* and the two overdoors for La Muette 700 *livres* each.

We do not know how much Boucher was paid for the cartoons of *The Setting* and *The Rising of the Sun*, but they were part of an extraordinarily lavish commission first mentioned in 1752.[32] They were the first major tapestry designs painted by Boucher for the high warp looms of the Royal manufactory of the Gobelins, which was more prestigious than the Beauvais manufactory. The tapestries took over three years to weave and at a cost of 8,160 *livres* were described as the most expensive ever woven at the factory. The complexity of the figures and compositions required a team of specialist weavers; indeed the illness and death of one particularly talented artisan, who was working on the heads, caused a severe delay.[33] The special nature of the

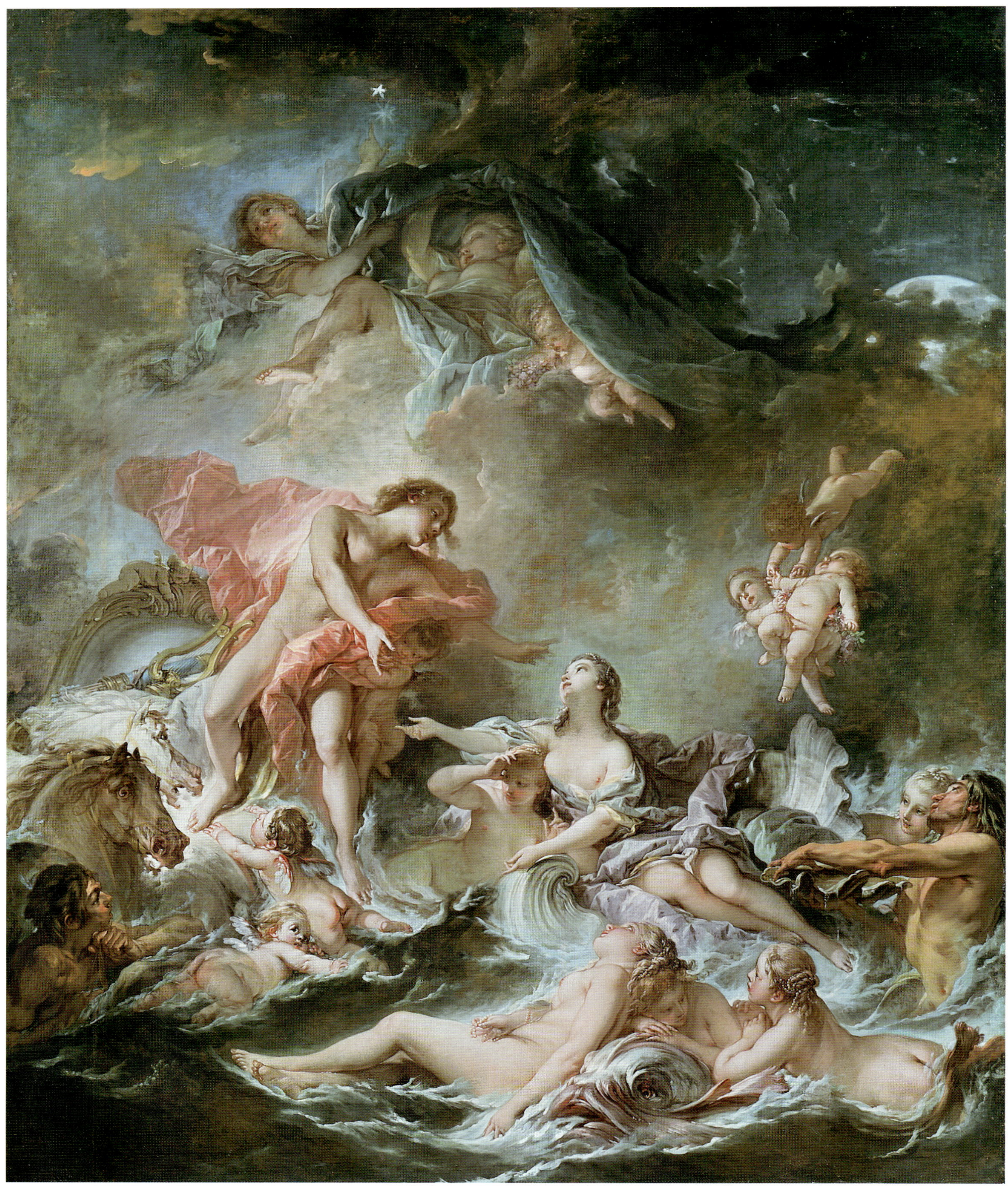

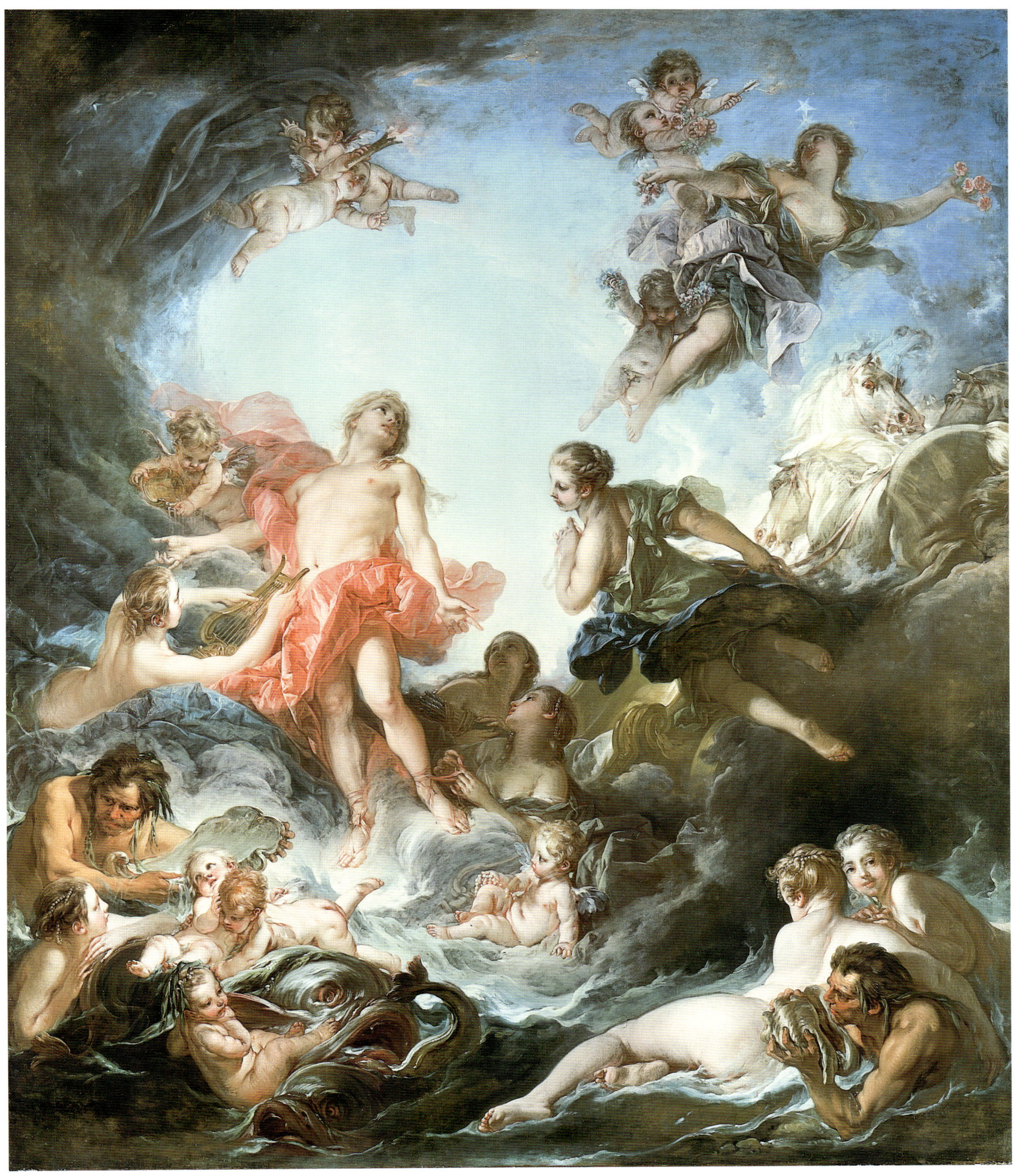

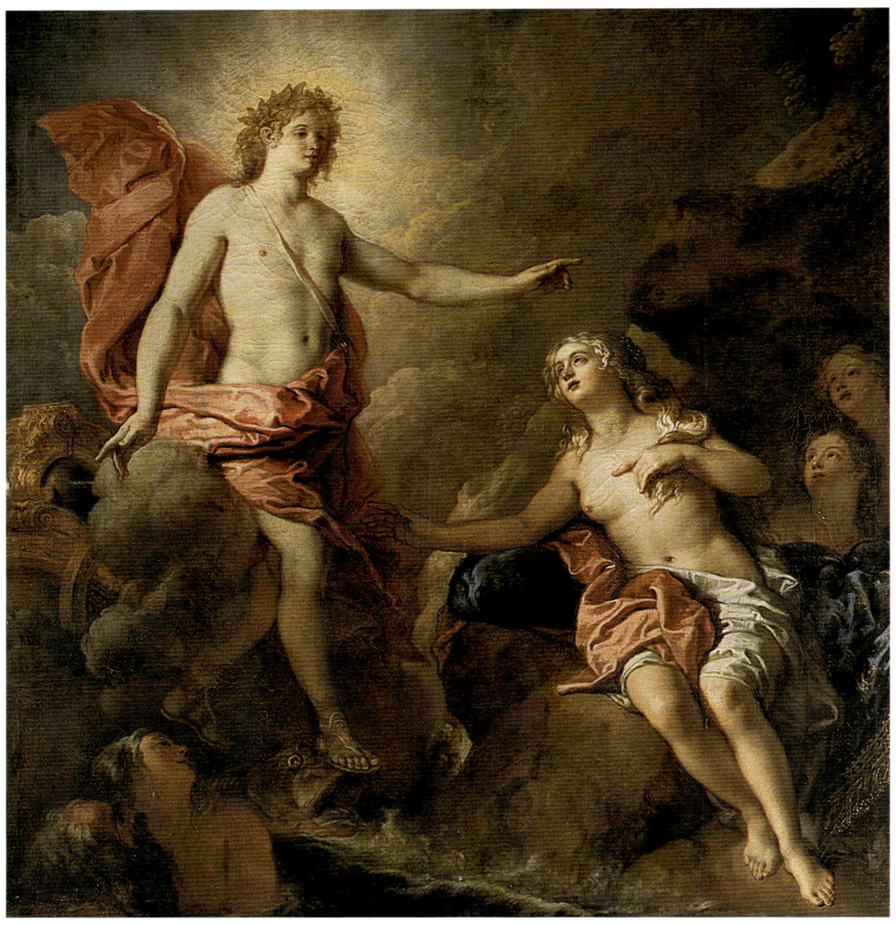

FIG.83 *previous page, left*
BOUCHER,
The Setting of the Sun, 1752, oil on canvas, 318 × 261cm, Wallace Collection

FIG.84 *previous page, right*
BOUCHER,
The Rising of the Sun, 1753, oil on canvas, 318 × 261cm, Wallace Collection

FIG.85 *above*
CHARLES DE LA FOSSE (1736–1716), *Apollo and Thétis*, 1688, oil on canvas, 168 × 149cm, Versailles, Grand Trianon

commission is underlined by the fact that the cartoons, normally retained by the manufactory and re-used as models for subsequent weavings, were withdrawn half way through production in order to be shown at the Salon of 1753, and also immediately reclaimed by the marquise once the tapestries were finished in 1755. The cartoons were subsequently used to decorate the room of the King's bodyguards, the Swiss Guards, on the ground floor at Bellevue.[34] The tapestries of *The Setting* and *The Rising of the Sun* actually formed part of a set of five commissioned to decorate the King's bedroom at Bellevue. One of these was a small piece depicting a simulated sky, which was placed on the wall above the King's bed; described as *à la duchesse* and surmounted by a curtained canopy, similar to that seen in fig.81. The other four tapestries were placed directly to either side of the bed, and then on the return walls, forming a tapestry alcove around the bed. The plans for Bellevue show that the bed was positioned facing the two windows, which looked out onto the terrace and view of the Seine.[35] Immediately to the left of the bed, was a door leading to a wardrobe room, which thus reduced the space available to display a tapestry. *The Setting* and *Rising of the Sun* were thus placed in frames on the equally proportioned return walls where they would have been visible from the bed, probably with *The Setting* on the right showing Apollo moving towards the bed and *The Rising* on the left with Apollo moving away. The geographical orientation of the room would also have meant that in this position *The Setting* would have caught the evening light from the West while *The Rising* would have been illuminated by the morning light from the East.

The Setting of the Sun was the first of the two compositions to be painted. Boucher and Madame de Pompadour collaborated to create an iconography and style which deliberately referred to the age of Louis XIV, at a moment when the Grand Siècle was again fashionable, and invested that august tradition with an operatic contemporaneity and private meaning, highlighting the marquise's mission to amuse and support the King. The story of *The Setting* and *The Rising of the Sun* derives from Ovid's *Metamorphoses* (II, 1–160). According to Ovid, Apollo rose every day in his chariot from the Ocean, drove across the heavens, bringing light to the world, and returned to the sea in the evening where he was attended by Queen Téthys, wife of the sea-god Oceanus. An amorous dimension was added to the story at the Court of the Sun King, Louis XIV, when Téthys was conflated with the nymph Thétis, Apollo's lover.[36] A grotto, the *Grotte de Thétis*, was built next to the main Château of Versailles, with a sculptural group by Girardon representing Apollo relaxing after his day's labours (Versailles).[37] This idea was later elaborated in a picture painted by Charles de La Fosse for the bedroom of Louis XV's mother, the duchesse de Bourgogne, in the Grand Trianon (fig.85).[38] Here Apollo is shown returning to the arms of Thétis, who, with drapery decorated in *fleurs-de-lis*, is now identified with France. Both Girardon's and La Fosse's works thus implied that the grotto of Versailles and the Grand Trianon were, like Thétis's grotto, places where the new Apollo, Louis XIV, could rest after a hard day driving the chariot of state. This was in direct contrast to the formal life of Court where even Louis XIV's going to bed and rising were public ceremonies: *Le Coucher du Roi* and *Le Lever du Roi*. Madame de Pompadour was fully conversant with the implications of the myth of Apollo, Téthys and Thétis and had already played the roles of Aurore and Égine in Collin de Blamont's *Les Fêtes de Thétis* in the theatre of the *petits appartements*.[39] In *The Setting of the Sun* her presence is implied in the figure of Thétis herself, who is shown awaiting her lover Apollo/Louis with open arms, eager to relieve him of the cares of state at her grotto of Bellevue. The decoration of the rest of the room deliberately continued the grotto theme: the mirror over the grey marble chimney-piece, for example, had an elaborately decorated frame incorporating shells, flowers and putti. At the same time, by deliberately evoking the Grand Siècle, Madame de Pompadour clearly hoped to give her relationship with the King a gravitas recalling the liaisons of Louis XIV, one of which had resulted in his morganatic marriage to Madame de Maintenon. *The Rising of the Sun* again recalls the glories of seventeenth-century Versailles, namely La Fosse's Apollo ceiling and Tuby's fountain of the same subject (both *in-situ*).[40] Although Thétis is absent from the scene, Madame de Pompadour's theatrical alter-egos, Aurore and Égine, are present, flying in the sky and handing Apollo the reins of his chariot, leaving us under no illusion as to who has enabled the radiant god to face the day.

Considering the prestige of Madame de Pompadour's commission it is no surprise to find that Boucher was inspired to create a new gallant-heroic style, especially tailored to the scale and operatic nature of his subjects. He also seems to have responded to recent criticisms of his work, which attacked his overly-picturesque approach. As Saint-Yves wrote in 1748: 'According to some people, in order to be brilliant M. Boucher often goes over the edge: he scatters his light effects; they no longer form coherent masses, and are not contrasted enough by the shadows which support them: that which dazzles the eye, no longer finds that harmony, that repose, which is one of the greatest charms of painting ... It is not thus ... that Rubens proceeded, whose pictures have an eclat which one does not even find in nature. Everything there is simple, everything is in accord, through the great attention he pays to light and shade, which none has understood better than he: this is the painter whose manner M. Boucher, who loves the brilliant, should study'.[41] In *The Setting* and *The Rising of the Sun* Boucher deliberately reduces the individual picturesque effects, the overloading of detail and exuberant colouring found, for example, in the Derbais pictures, and concentrates instead on nudes unencumbered by drapery and on the orchestration of the whole to form a satisfying and monumental visual ensemble. Already in assessing the current nostalgia for the Grand Siècle, Voltaire had claimed that 'one is reduced either to imitate it or to go astray'.[42] In a similar way, Boucher was now further drawn to the aesthetic theories of Roger de Piles, which drew parallels between painting, music and poetry, to the example of De Piles's great model, Rubens, and to the acknowledged French champion of *Rubenisme*, La Fosse.

De Piles's *Cours de peinture par principes* was the first major aesthetic theory in post-classical art that stressed the value of art for its own sake, independent of any pre-existing literary text or didactic purpose.[43] For De Piles, if art did not succeed from the first in a visual sense, any associated meaning was irrelevant. What mattered was a picture's instant visual power, its ability to seduce the eyes as music did the ears. He explained how 'enthusiasm lifts us without our realising it, and carries us, as one might say, from one country to another, which we perceive only by the pleasure that it causes us. It seems, in a word, that enthusiasm seizes us, and we seize the Sublime. It is

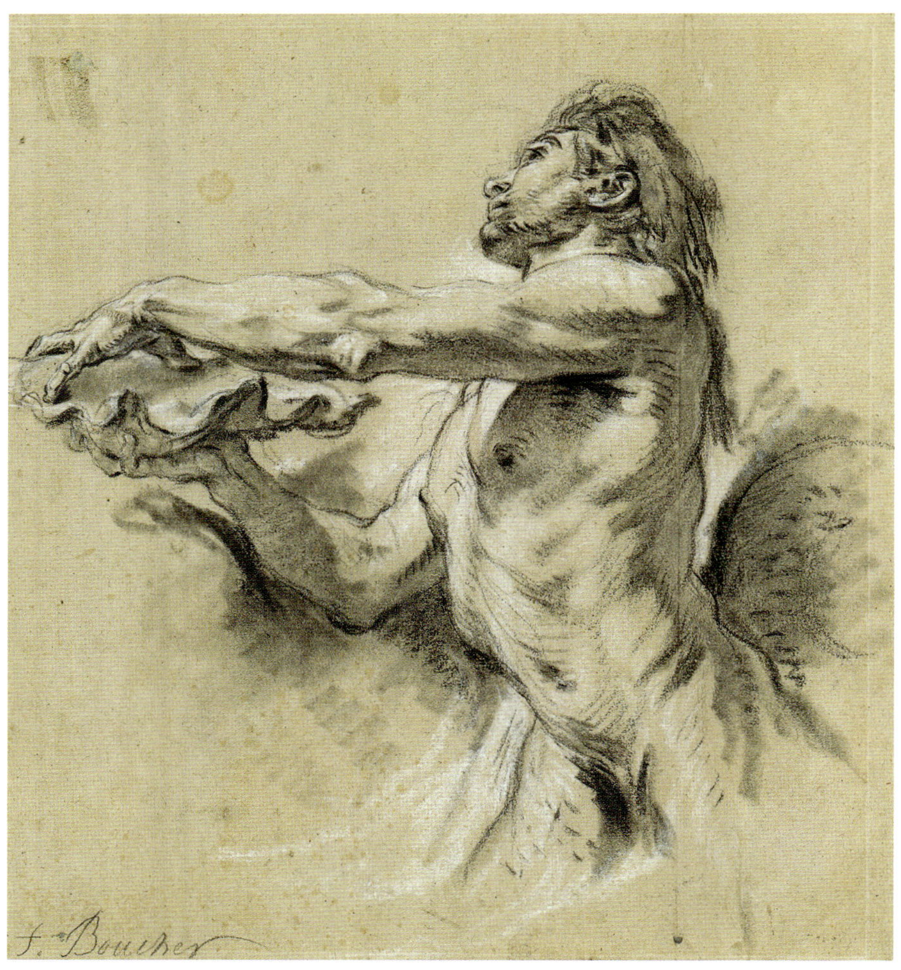

FIG.86
BOUCHER, *Study for a Triton holding a Shell*, *c.*1751, black and white chalk with some stumping, on light brown paper, 33 × 30cm, Weimar, Staatliche Kunstsammlungen

to this surprising, but just and reasonable, elevation that the painter and the poet must carry his work; if they each want to arrive at this extraordinary 'truth' which moves the heart, and which is the greatest merit of painting and poetry'.[44] Painting's unique ability to fire the imagination through the eyes led De Piles to advocate that the true aim of the artist was to concentrate on the purely visual means by which this might be achieved. He stressed in particular the importance of the overall effect of a picture, *le tout ensemble* as he termed it, which should capture the viewer's attention and transport him to the imaginative parallel world of art. This in turn led him to concentrate on examining the effects of light and shade and colour, all of which should work together in harmony to create that initial dramatic visual impact. The continuing enthusiasm for De Piles's theories among practitioners and lovers of art at this time is demonstrated by the new edition of his *Éléments de Peinture Pratique*, re-edited and re-published in a considerably expanded version by Charles Jombert in 1766.[45] Even Caylus, the noted antiquary whose collection, work and patronage provided one of the main inspirations for the new neoclassical decorative idiom in the mid-eighteenth century, remained very much an *honnête homme* of his generation through his faithful adherence to the precepts of Roger de Piles.[46]

The Setting and *The Rising of the Sun* in composition and tonal arrangement are the quintessential visualisations of De Piles's theories. Their organisation in dramatic vortices of movement which draw the eye into the fictive world of the canvas adhere closely to De Piles's theory that the most satisfying visual compositions gave the illusion of a concave or convex space. Light, shade and colour are all designed to contribute towards this initial dramatic impact. As De Piles had illustrated with the shading on a bunch of grapes, the extremities of the canvas are darker in tonality moving towards a bright centre, which, in accordance with Boucher's theme, is the figure of Apollo himself, from whom all light radiates. Other shadows in the picture, while beautifully observed, are never allowed to become too contrasted and risk upsetting this overall balance. All colour is similarly subject to this unified approach, displaying the new 'silvered' manner noted by Papillon de La Ferté in Boucher's later works.[47] Such tonal subtlety, playing on shades of pink, blue, green and grey, would have looked particularly stunning translated into tapestry, and displays an almost abstract approach to design far removed from any wish to replicate nature. If we look at the two pictures together we can see how each has its own tonality appropriate to its subject, for *The Setting of the Sun* is deliberately darker in tone than *The Rising*. Originally Boucher must have worked out his compositions in oil sketches similar to those known for *The Rape of Europa* and *Mercury Confiding the Infant Bacchus* (figs. 26–27).

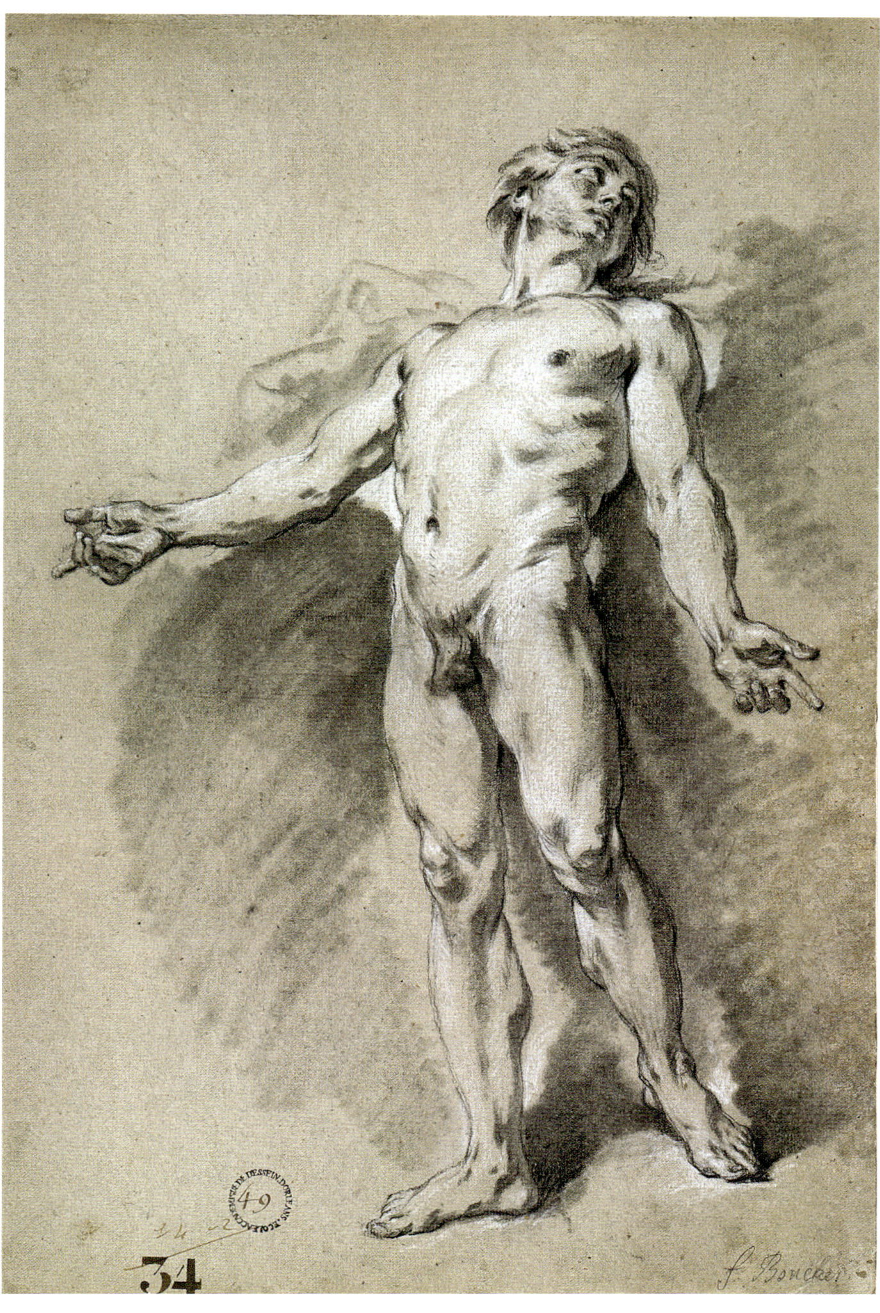

FIG.87
BOUCHER, *Study for Apollo*, *c.*1753, black and white chalk with stumping on light brown paper, 54.6 × 36.6cm, Washington, National Gallery of Art, Gift of Robert H. Clarice Smith

Unfortunately the originals are now lost, but two studio copies imply that *The Setting of the Sun* was probably preceded by a *grisaille* sketch reflecting its shaded subject, while the more nervy copy of the oil sketch of *The Rising of the Sun* is brightly coloured (both private collection).[48]

The figures in *The Setting* and *The Rising of the Sun* are all orchestrated to create a sweep of centrifugal movement. Apollo's twisting descent from his chariot, leaning towards Thétis's outstretched arms, adds an appropriately balletic note to the gallant poses of the protagonists. Their relationship is told through body language rather than facial expression, in much the same manner as in the earlier works of La Fosse or Watteau which use conversational attitudes to 'civilise and harmonise' their pictures.[49] While Apollo in *The Rising of the Sun* recalls the Apollo Belvedere, Rubens's *Medici Cycle* and Le Brun's *Apollo leaving Téthys*, it is primarily theatrical precedent that explains his self-consciously elegant pose.[50] With streaming golden locks, he turns from the naiad handing him his lyre, symbol of his role as god of the arts, to gaze at the goddess of the dawn who announces his arrival in the sky. It is typical of Boucher's playful approach that, even in such a major mythological canvas, he should translate the Homeric concept of 'the rosy fingered dawn' into a flying maiden, quoted from Pietra da Cortona, with roses literally falling from her hands.[51] Similarly, the myth of the creation of the foam of the sea and the dew of the dawn is wittily attributed in both canvases to the vapour snorting from the nostrils of Apollo's horses. In *The Setting of the Sun* the winged figure of Sleep threatens to envelop his voluptuous mother, Night, with the velvet curtain he draws over her, the same curtain which is playfully pushed away by cupids in *The Rising of the Sun*. Meanwhile the naiads, tritons and amours in both pictures are arranged in graceful curving attitudes, mostly looking towards the central figure of Apollo, and adding to the feeling of repose through their relaxed and unabashed sensual poses. The fluid rapid handling of the paint, whose thinness now allows the grey ground to show through in many places, is characteristic of Boucher's *fa presto* approach to painting large compositions, especially tapestry cartoons. It was a technique already noted by Bachaumont in 1750 when describing Boucher's 'many extremely rich pictures after which excellent tapestries have been made at Beauvais. These pictures are not particularly finished, they are painted almost in one

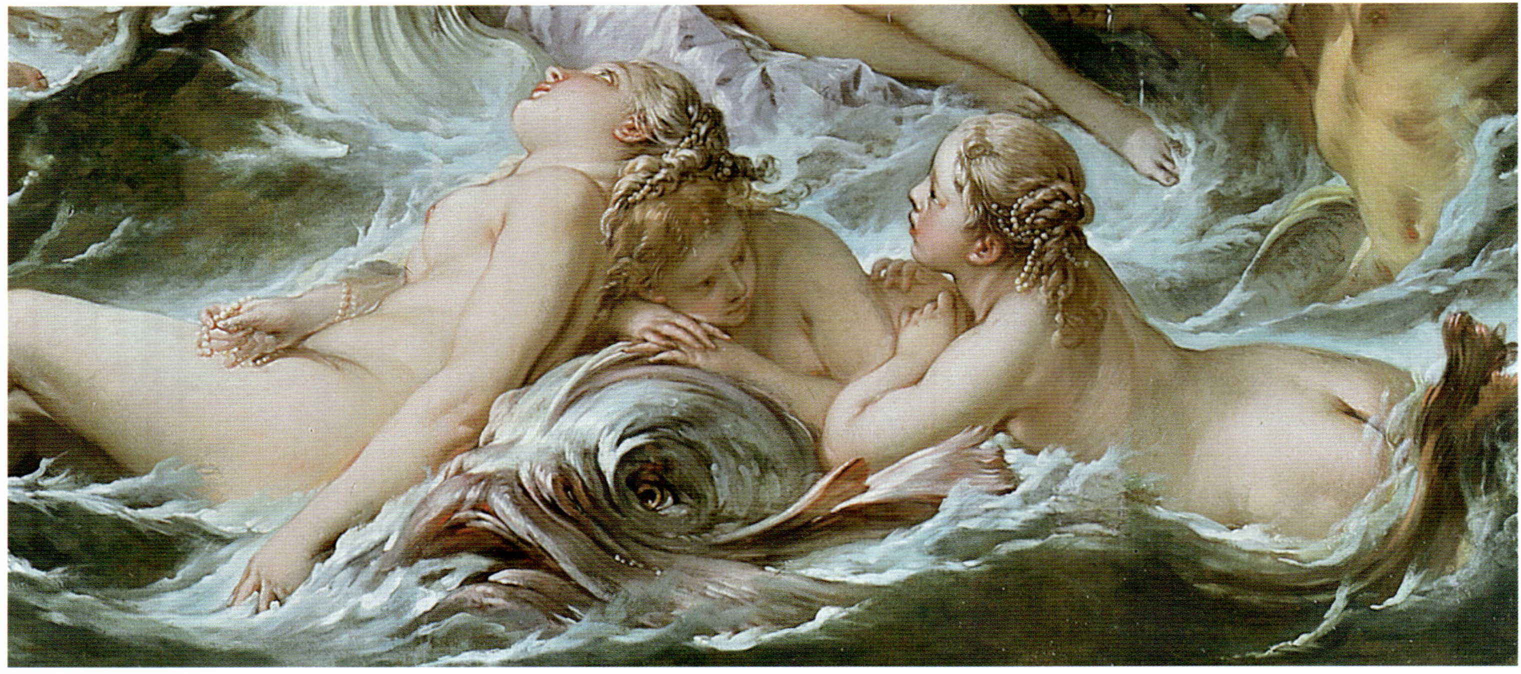

FIG.88
BOUCHER, *The Setting of the Sun*, detail, 1752, oil on canvas, Wallace Collection

go, but that is sufficient for tapestries'.[52]

This is not to say that Boucher did not prepare very carefully for both compositions. The wealth of drawings associated with the works, preparing the compositions or later recording their most popular elements, demonstrate both his artistic ambition and his pride in the final result. Figure 86 is a typical study for a triton. Executed in black and white chalk with some stumping, achieved by dabbing a damp cloth or sponge onto the chalk to obtain a more fluid shading, it shows Boucher's increasingly monumental treatment of the figure and his ability to depict the muscular male body in action. Prefiguring the triton holding a shell on the extreme right in *The Setting of the Sun*, it recalls both Boucher's male academies of the period and the other figures of tritons in both *The Setting* and *The Rising of the Sun*: all appear to have been drawn from the same model, Jean-François Deschamps, who worked at the Academy from 1725 to 1773.[53] Boucher's friend, Watelet, described how at this period 'nearly all of the figures of the pictures of the French School have been studied after him ... sometimes Deschamps was the ever-youthful Mercury, sometimes the terrible Mars, sometimes Neptune, Pluto, Jupiter ... one was astonished to see his somewhat Bacchic face become that of a hero or a God'.[54] Indeed one sees the same Bacchic face reappearing throughout *The Setting* and *The Rising of the Sun* where, in addition to his muscularity, shaggy brown hair and craggy face, his active masculinity is denoted by a tanned body which contrasts vividly with the pearly skin of the naiads and the luminous form of Apollo (fig.77). Apollo's figure is more elegant and graceful, with a more youthful, aristocratic countenance, befitting his divine status and role. Such a characterisation is also intended to flatter Apollo's alter-ego, the supremely civilised Louis XV. Boucher was pleased with this figure and did not hesitate to repeat it in a carefully worked-up presentation drawing (fig.87) which found its way into the collection of one of Boucher's admirers, the amateur artist Aignan-Thomas Desfriches (1715–1800).[55] Desfriches founded the Orléans Academy of design in 1786 and the drawing entered the Academy's working collection. Boucher's ideal male thus became a model for students at a time when his paintings had long been out of fashion.

It was the female forms in *The Setting* and *The Rising of the Sun*, however, that attracted most comment from contemporaries (fig.88). Boucher here reveals a new, more classically proportioned form which contributes towards the overall ideal effect of his pictures. Less dependent on current fashionable models, it recalls artistic precedent, namely the plump nymphs of Rubens and La Fosse. The coquettish pointed faces of his earlier nymphs are replaced by the softer rounded heads of the naiads whose figures are given a new monumentality by their more regularly proportioned and smoothly voluptuous bodies which are broadly painted, rarely veiled, and presented in unabashed, languorous glory. There is greater smoothness and amplitude in the figure of the reclining naiad in *The Setting of the Sun*, for example, than in her earlier incarnations as a *Sleeping Venus* (1735; Musée Jacquemart-André) or as one of the *Companions of Diana* (1745; San Francisco).[56] This new hour-glass aesthetic was described by Mannlich who related that towards the end of his life Boucher believed 'one should almost doubt that the body of a woman contains bones … without being fat they should be dimpled, delicate and with a slim waist without being thin'.[57] The studies that survive for the female figures in *The Setting* and *The Rising of the Sun* tend to be executed in red chalk which adds to their sensuality.[58] Moreover, the obvious appeal of this new brand of Boucher beauty to the private collector is borne out by the finished drawings Boucher worked up from his original sketches and copied from the groupings of naiads in the pictures. Thus the naiads and triton seen in the bottom right of *The Rising of the Sun* (detail opposite the title page to this book) reappear in a particularly fine presentation drawing by Boucher in the Louvre (fig.89) which belonged first to the engraver Huquier, then to the great Boucher drawings collector Blondel d'Azaincourt. The same group was frequently copied by other anonymous artists and engraved in the new chalk manner by Demarteau (1722–76).[59]

Mannlich goes on to write that Boucher claimed to have encountered the ideal female form in only one model: 'Of the hundreds that I have had undress for me … I have found only one who had

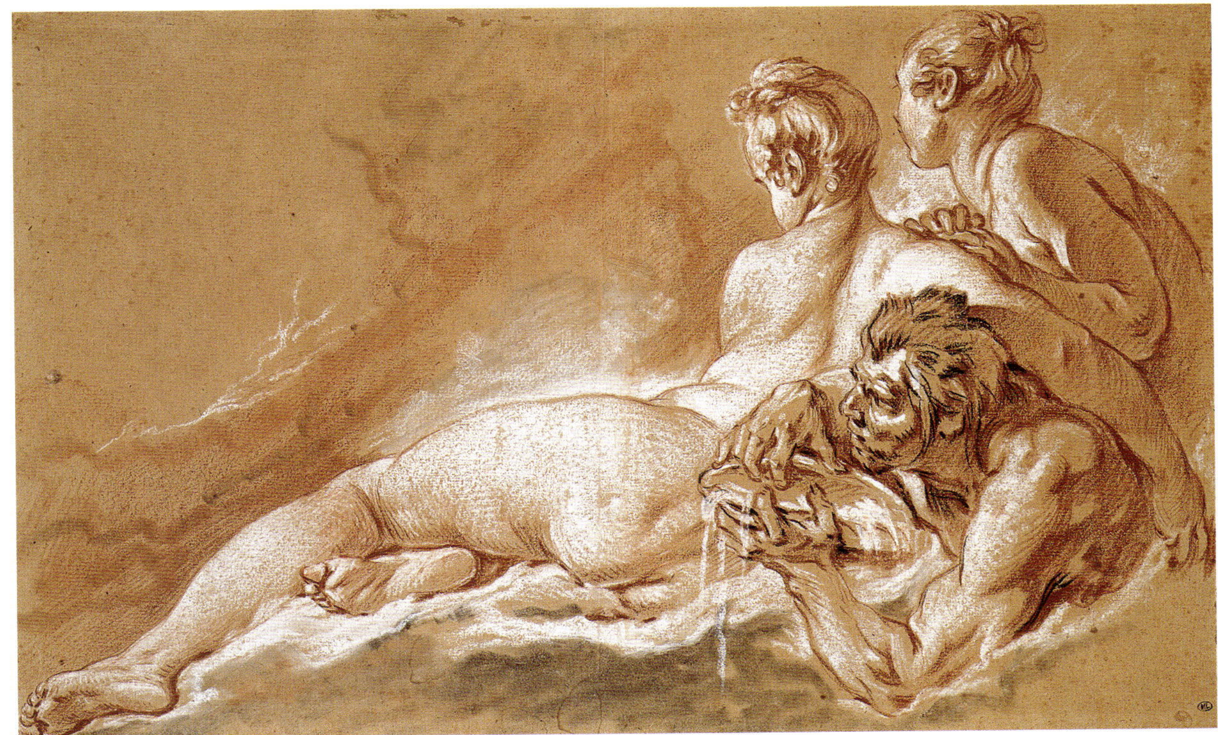

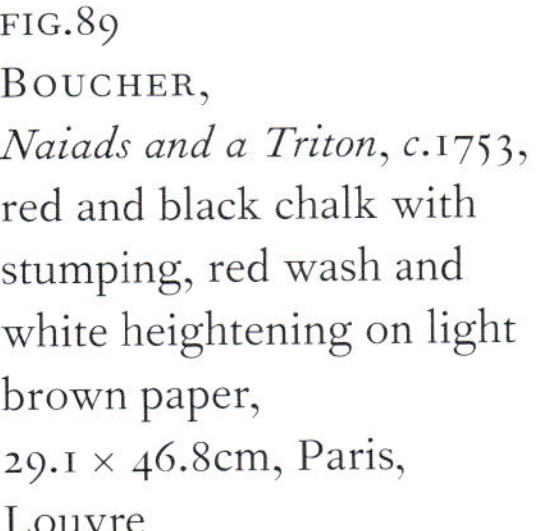

FIG.89
BOUCHER,
Naiads and a Triton, c.1753,
red and black chalk with stumping, red wash and white heightening on light brown paper,
29.1 × 46.8cm, Paris, Louvre

FIG.90
BOUCHER,
Blonde Odalisque, 1752,
oil on canvas, 59 × 73cm,
Munich, Alte Pinakothek

FIG.91 *opposite*
STUDIO OF BOUCHER,
Triton, black and white chalk with some stumping on light brown paper, 21.6 × 26.7cm, Library of Hertford House

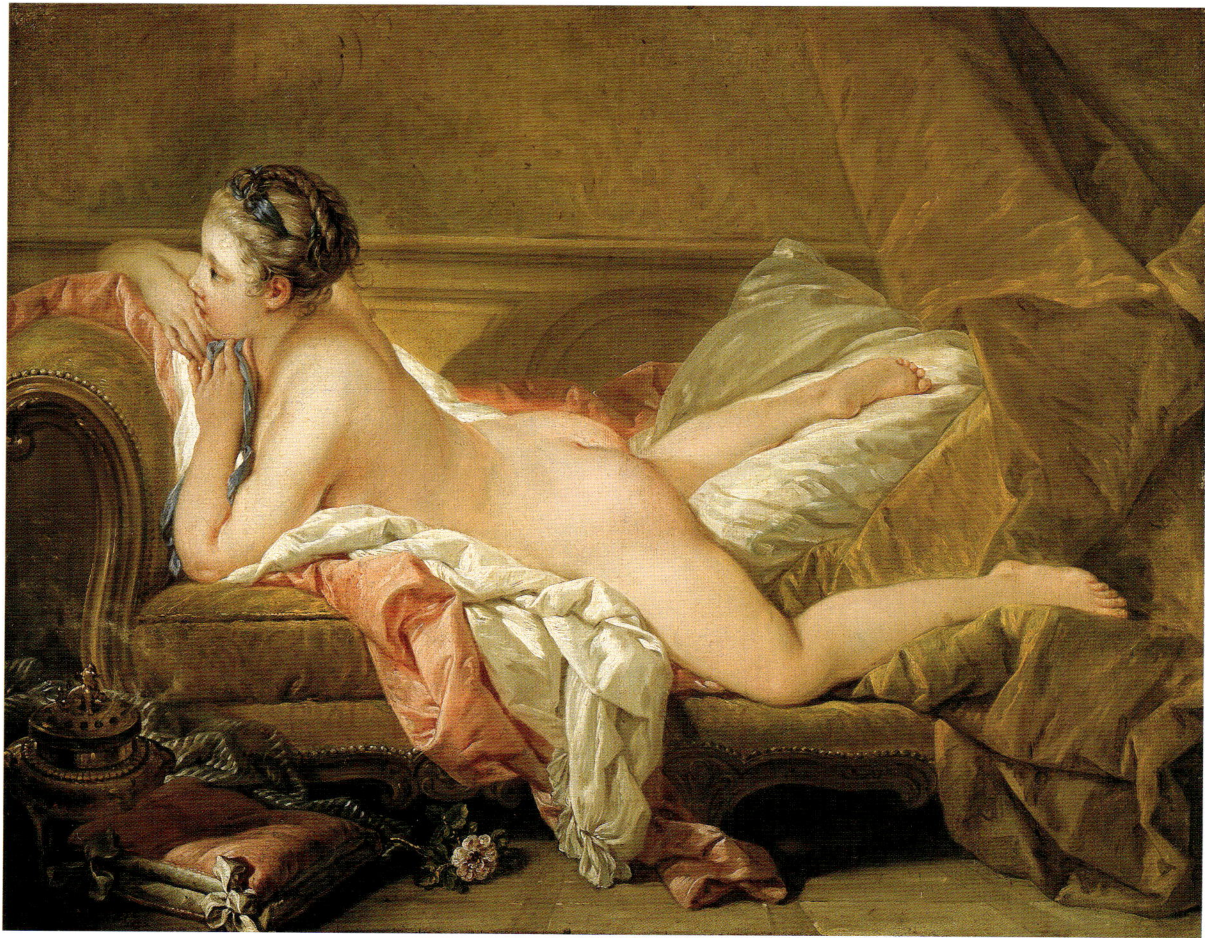

this high degree of beauty. She is a perfect model! She has served me for many years, and was only fifteen when she gave me the first sitting.'[60] His description of the plump adolescent recalls one of Boucher's most famous pictures, painted at the same time as *The Setting of the Sun*: the *Blonde Odalisque* (fig.90), a version of which belonged to Madame de Pompadour's brother, Monsieur de Vandières.[61] A letter from De Vandières to Natoire in Rome explains how such an intimate cabinet picture might be displayed and appreciated: 'I have a particular cabinet that I want to enrich with four pieces from the most talented painters of our school. I have already placed there a *Vanloo*, a *Boucher* and a *Pierre*; you well judge that I am missing a *Natoire* … I have to add that, as this cabinet is very small and very hot, I only want nudes: the picture by Carle depicts *Sleeping Antiope*; that of Boucher, a *Young Woman Lying on her Stomach*, and that of Pierre an *Io*. Choose any subject you want, as long as it is not the same as any of the ones named, and that it contains no or nearly no drapery'.[62] Clearly, Boucher's removing the veil to depict the contemporary female nude was sanctioned and encouraged by the establishment. The model's age reminds us of the libertine De Nerciat's comment that 'in Paris, a young girl of thirteen or fourteen years already receives some marks of attention, when she is pretty'.[63] The following year, 1753, the duc de Croÿ commented in his journal that 'the greatest news I left at the Court was the taste the King has for a young beauty … whom it is claimed that the painter Boucher, who often has beautiful models, has procured for the King'.[64] This has led in the past to Boucher's model, and indeed many of the naiads in *The Setting* and *The Rising of the Sun*, being identified with Louise O'Murphy. *La petite Morphile* was the most famous inmate of the Parc aux Cerfs.[65] This was a small *hôtel* in Versailles, housing a succession of young girls engaged to meet the King's sexual needs. It seems unlikely that Madame de Pompadour's brother would have acquired such a delectable image of a girl who, although tolerated by his sister, would hardly have been welcome to her. Similarly, the idea that Boucher was acting as pander to the King seems far-fetched when one reads the rest of Mannlich's account of Boucher's description of his ideal model, whose form by the 1760s had 'developed' and was 'now in all her beauty'. Boucher commented approvingly that the same girl 'is good, and never comes to me without her mother. She was recently married to a relatively aged but comfortably off man who only allows her to sit for me'.[66] This is not to deny that Boucher was certainly willing to provide sexy imagery for important clients. Thus, in addition to the ravishing picture of the teenager stretched out on her sofa, Boucher also provided a drawing for an unknown client which was clearly a fetish piece and depicted only her right foot in pastel (Musée de Carnavalet).[67]

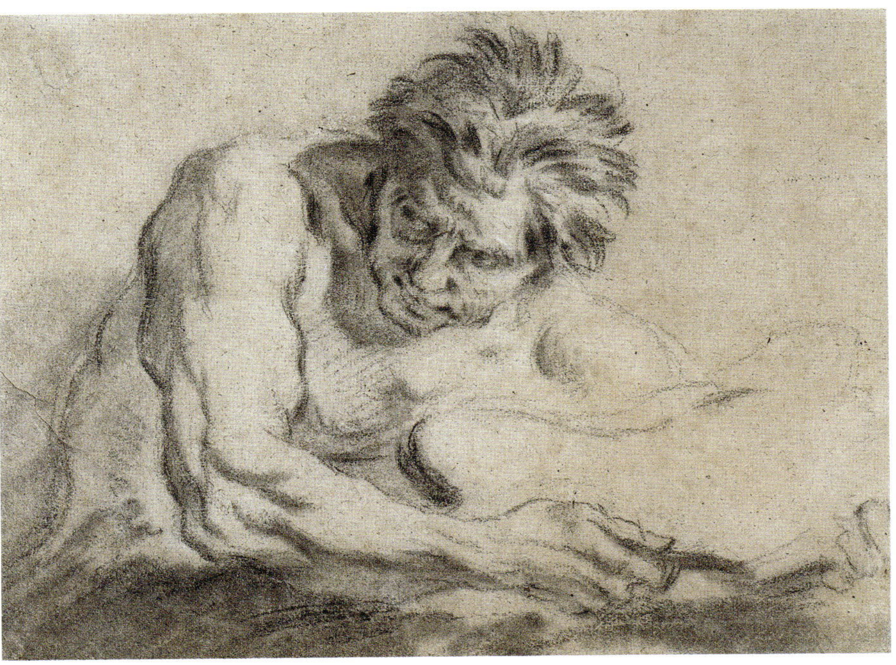

The success of *The Setting* and *The Rising of the Sun* is convincingly demonstrated by the number of art-lovers keen to buy drawings and prints associated with the paintings. They were painted during a period when Boucher had been forced to expand his studio in order to meet the growing demand for his work and some of the drawings relating to the pictures were copied by Boucher's students. Mannlich recalled how Boucher 'in the morning, while taking his chocolate in his cabinet, amused himself making or retouching a drawing. He couldn't do enough of them for the collectors or the minor dealers, who paid two *louis* [48 *livres*] a piece for them ...for a long time he made us copy the most beautiful drawings which he wanted to keep in his portfolio. These copies we were required only to prepare, without putting the final touches, which he would then add during his breakfast, thereby creating 'originals' which he sold for two *louis* each'.[68] The study related to the triton holding a shell on the extreme left of *The Rising of the Sun*, in the Library of Hertford House (fig.91), appears to be one of these studio copies. Although executed in the same technique as Boucher's triton studies, it is noticeably weaker in handling and of lesser quality than an identical study, by Boucher himself, which is in a private collection.[69]

The Setting and *The Rising of the Sun* remain breathtaking examples of Boucher's ability as a painter. They magnificently expound the formal tenets of De Piles and visually recreate the poetry of Ovid in a manner as original as Titian or Rubens. Boucher's vision may be less intellectually profound or demanding but it engages the senses as no artist had done before. He was justly proud of his achievement as noted by Pierre Remy in Madame de Pompadour's sale catalogue of 1766: 'The ingenious composition, the graces, and everything that could contribute to render these pieces of the first distinction is found reunited in these two pictures. I have heard the author say on many occasions that they were among the works he was most pleased with. The judgement of an artist as modest and diffident about his own talents as Monsieur Boucher should be believed'.[70]

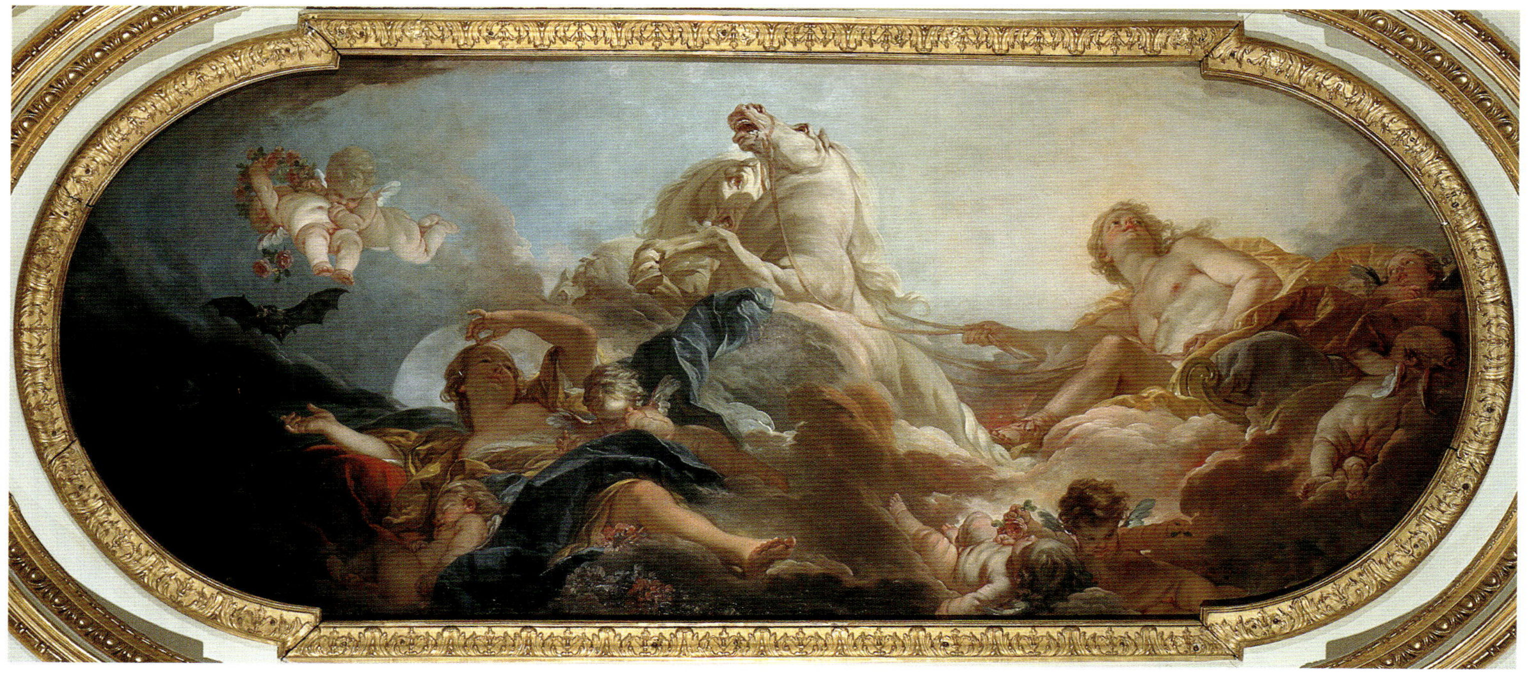

FIG.92
BOUCHER,
Apollo in his Chariot, 1753,
oil on canvas, 130 × 250cm,
Fontainebleau, Council
Chamber

FIG.93 *opposite*
View of the Council
Chamber, Fontainebleau

The Gallant-Heroic in Public

Boucher re-used the association of Thétis and her marine environment for an *Allegory on the Education of Louis XV* etched by Laurent Cars in 1753.[71] This formed the tenth plate of the *Histoire de Louis XV par les Médailles* started under the direction of Cochin in 1753, and depicted the infant Louis XV, here associated with the young Achilles, leaving the care of Thétis and being placed under the tuition of the centaur Chiron. At the same time Boucher's brilliant renewal of the Apollonian tradition in *The Setting of the Sun* attracted a prestigious commission from the Crown. To date he had only been commissioned to provide decorative overdoors, tapestry designs and the occasional history painting, but *The Setting of the Sun* and *The Loves of the Gods* tapestries clearly demonstrated Boucher's ability to provide more monumental yet still attractive mythological decorations. In 1751, as part of a major refurbishment programme at one of the King's favourite châteaux, Fontainebleau, the decision was taken to redecorate the Royal Council Chamber. The newly appointed Minister of the Arts, Monsieur de Vandières, was keen to make his mark by creating a decorative ensemble worthy of the symbolic role of the room and pleasing to the King's sensual tastes. An iconographic scheme was devised that deliberately evoked the great decorative interiors of Versailles.[72] Moreover, Vandières insisted that the architectural structure of the room should remain untouched thereby stressing the continuity of the royal house of Bourbon.

Boucher was commissioned to do the 'noble' part of the decorations by providing an appropriately majestic ceiling. It was to represent *Apollo and the Seasons*: the same subject that had been painted by Charles de La Fosse nearly a century earlier on the ceiling of Louis XIV's formal Bedchamber and Throne Room at Versailles (*c.*1671; *in-situ*).[73] At his death, Boucher owned a substantial collection of paintings, oil sketches and drawings by La Fosse, including a circular *modello*, for the Versailles ceiling (Rouen).[74] This was probably already in Boucher's collection by the 1750s, as he had quoted from La Fosse's ceiling in his design of *The Marriage of Cupid and Psyche* for the *Psyche* tapestry series (commissioned by Beauvais in 1737).[75] At Fontainebleau, Vandières insisted that the old compartmented ceiling structure,

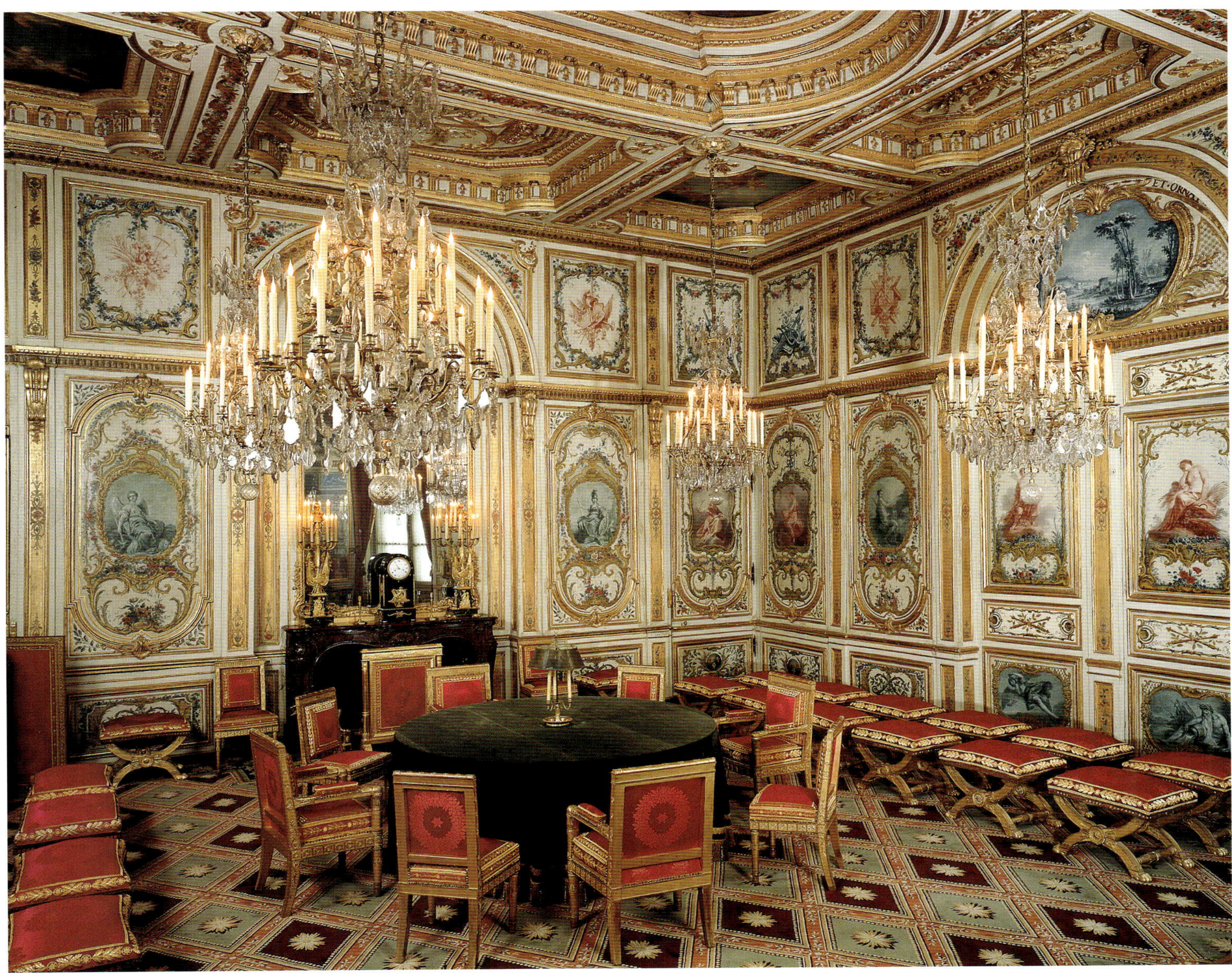

with its heavy beams, be retained in the Council Chamber, so Boucher was unable to treat the space as a single span. However he ingeniously lightened and modernized its appearance by depicting *Apollo in his Chariot* alone in the central compartment (fig.92), symbolizing the enlightenment the modern Apollo, Louis XV, brought to the world. The cosmological and universal nature of the King's reign was then wittily denoted by separating *The Seasons* from Apollo and representing them as gambolling putti in the subsidiary compartments. The shared genesis of Madame de Pompadour's tapestries and the King's Council Chamber ceiling is made clearer when one considers that *The Seasons* were shown alongside *The Setting* and *The Rising of the Sun* at the Salon of 1753.

Elsewhere in the room the cosmology and divinity of kingship was conveyed by depictions of the *Virtues*, the *Seasons* and the *Elements*, derived from the traditional symbolism laid down by

FIG.94 *opposite*
BOUCHER, *The Light of the World*, 1750, oil on canvas, 175 × 130cm, Lyon, Musée des Beaux-Arts

seventeenth-century French re-interpretations of Cesare Ripa's *Iconologia*.[76] These were executed in the lightest and least pedantic manner possible, however, using delicious *grisaille* figures painted on to the panelling of the walls: those in *camaïeu bleu* by Carle Van Loo and those in *camaïeu rose* by Pierre (fig.93). The leading serious history painters of the day were thus employed to paint witty vignettes in the tradition of the arabesques of Audran and Watteau to suit the decorative tastes of the King. Alexis Peyrotte (1699–1769), a rococo decorative painting specialist and not even a member of the Academy, was employed to paint the additional flowers, trophies of the Arts and Sciences, overdoors, and grisaille scenes at the top and bottom of the panelling together with a chinoiserie passage leading to the room.[77] Today, this delicious ensemble remains marooned among the imperial pomp of the Napoleonic interiors of Fontainebleau. It is one of very few major eighteenth-century French decorative interiors that has survived together *in-situ*, and even then in a form determined by a pre-existing seventeenth century room with beamed ceiling. It is only in a room like the Council Chamber at Fontainebleau that one comes close to understanding the delicate balance of public virtue, private pleasure and careless wit that lies behind the deliberately transient charm of much rococo art and which informs even the more monumental paintings of Boucher.

Enlightened Religion

Light is the subject of another of Boucher's most famous works, also commissioned by Madame de Pompadour, which again marked a new departure in his art. *The Light of the World* (1750; fig.94) is the first picture Boucher is recorded as painting for the marquise, and ironically, in view of their later reputations, is a religious picture.[78] So, long before the lightburst of the Apollo tapestries symbolised the King's temporal power in his bedchamber, the celestial light of the Infant Jesus was illuminating the chapel at Bellevue. Madame de Pompadour's decision to commission a religious picture from Boucher again demonstrates her sensitivity to existing royal taste. Boucher's first royal commission had a moral, quasi-religious significance when he painted the charming series of *Virtues* for the Queen's bedchamber at Versailles, which reappeared as emblems safeguarding views of the capital in the *Bréviaire de Paris* (figs. 33–34). Boucher's comforting, feminine vision of religion, centred on charming female images of the Virtues and the Virgin, was bound to appeal to Madame de Pompadour whose increasing religious sentiment was noted by contemporaries throughout the 1750s. It is no surprise to find that she owned an exquisite prayer book of the *Office of the Holy Virgin*, printed in 1757 and bound in two volumes in blue Morocco leather, which was adorned with original drawings by Boucher. These included two frontispieces and scenes from the *Life of the Virgin* illustrating each day of the week. The characterisation of the Virgin in *The Immaculate Conception*, the illustration for Sunday, is particularly close to that of *Charity* in the Queen's bedchamber and in the *Bréviaire*.[79]

Critics had been much impressed by a small *Nativity* (lost) that Boucher had exhibited at the Salon of 1748. Baillet de Saint-Julien described it as 'a little picture representing a Nativity, which also shines with fire and genius. In order to better express in his Child Jesus the birth of the Word, principle of the Light, he has cleverly made all the daylight in his picture come from this Child, as if from a new Sun which seems to rise in order to enlighten the world'.[80] Even Saint-Yves had praised the work noting that 'it is well composed, of a finish and sweetness with admirable brushwork, and of a colour to make one feel what the author could do, if he wished to apply himself to this important area of Art'.[81] It is a mark of Madame de Pompadour's intelligence as a patron and her foresight regarding Boucher's capabilities as a history painter that she gave the artist his first commission to paint a monumental altarpiece. The picture was to be placed at the heart of the château of Bellevue, in a central salon, which acted as a passage-way between all the different apartments

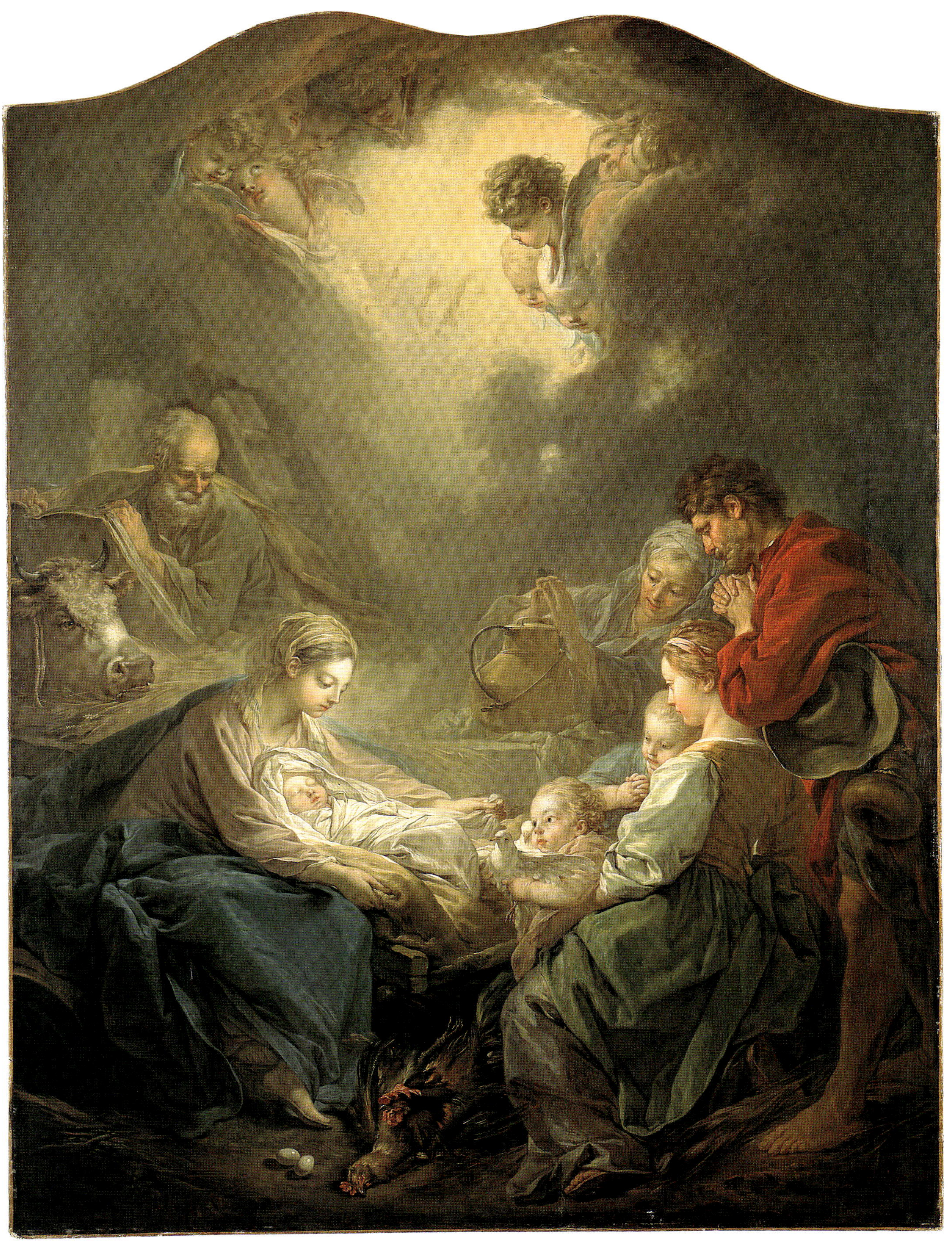

of the first floor. An altar was constructed in the room, which could be hidden from view behind double doors, but which when opened revealed the altarpiece dramatically lit from above by a lantern ceiling.[82] Naturally, the marquise did not wish to commission a religious image that would prompt the King, whose apartment was next door, to brood on the state of mortal sin in which his soul languished while he continued to enjoy adulterous relationships and refused to go to confession and accept the sacrament. Boucher was thus a clever choice for the altarpiece, for his work in the Queen's Bedchamber and his 1748 *Nativity* had already intimated that his talent for rendering any subject attractive and seductive might even be extended to religious works.

The Light of the World projects an exceptionally comforting, intimate, and positively enlightened view of the redemptive power of Christ. No hint of the Passion is allowed to disturb this vision of joy brought to the world. Despite its intentionally 'light' approach, Boucher took the commission very seriously, as is attested by the surviving drawings and oil sketches associated with the picture.[83] The conceit of the Christ child providing the illumination is obviously inspired by serious sixteenth and seventeenth-century Italian precedents such as Correggio's *The Night* (1530; Berlin) and Guido Reni's *The Adoration of the Shepherds* (*c*.1640; The National Gallery). But the characterisation of the different ages of man, the peculiar charm of the graceful Madonna and the vivid portrayal of the children is very much Boucher's own. The picture, exhibited at the Salon of 1750, attracted virtually unanimous praise. Baillet de Saint-Julien's evaluation is typical: 'His devotional picture, which is a Nativity, is treated in the most interesting manner in the world. One does not find what one usually sees; but the subject, although treated so often, here appears absolutely new … All is remarkable in this work: the fine seductive air of most of the figures, the elegant naivety of their attitudes, and the singular variety of the characterisations. Its colour matches its drawing and makes an admirable union in the whole … the background is filled with an indefinable Glory of light: which adds marvellously to the subject: it seems to represent the Dawn which the Saviour of the world announces; it is the pure light of the rising Sun'.[84]

Madame de Pompadour increasingly turned to religion following the death of her daughter Alexandrine in 1754. At the same time, she hoped to protect her position at Court by investing it with some form of moral validity. This prompted her to curry favour with the pious coterie surrounding the Queen, leading to her investiture as one of the Queen's ladies-in-waiting in 1756. Considerably younger than the Queen, Madame de Pompadour clearly hoped to outlive her and, following in the footsteps of Madame de Maintenon, persuade her royal lover into marriage. The Austrian Minister, Kaunitz, for example, noted that: 'the plan of the marquise is formed on the example of Madame de Maintenon. If the Queen were to disappear, one would soon see her pious and the King would not think it too dear to buy peace for his conscience, following the example of his great-grandfather'.[85] She was thus inspired to order an increasing number of religious paintings from Boucher, which share the same theatrical but nonetheless charming sentimental devotion that characterized the marquise's own public displays of piety.[86] These, together with the pastorals and landscapes popular with private clients during the period, formed the core of Boucher's exhibits at the Salon in the late 1750s. It was the sight of one of these, *The Rest on the Flight into Egypt* (Saint Petersburg), exhibited at the Salon of 1757, that prompted an anonymous critic to exclaim that 'one admires the ardour and spirit of this genius independent of the rules, of whom someone talking to the author said that he was no longer a painter but painting itself'.[87] The abbé de Fontenay noted at the end of Boucher's life that 'among the devotional pictures he painted, the Nativity and Holy Families are the subjects he chose by preference, because they did not draw him away from the graces or the beauty that he liked to paint, and which he found easily in the figure of the Virgin and in that of the infant Jesus'.[88] Boucher's

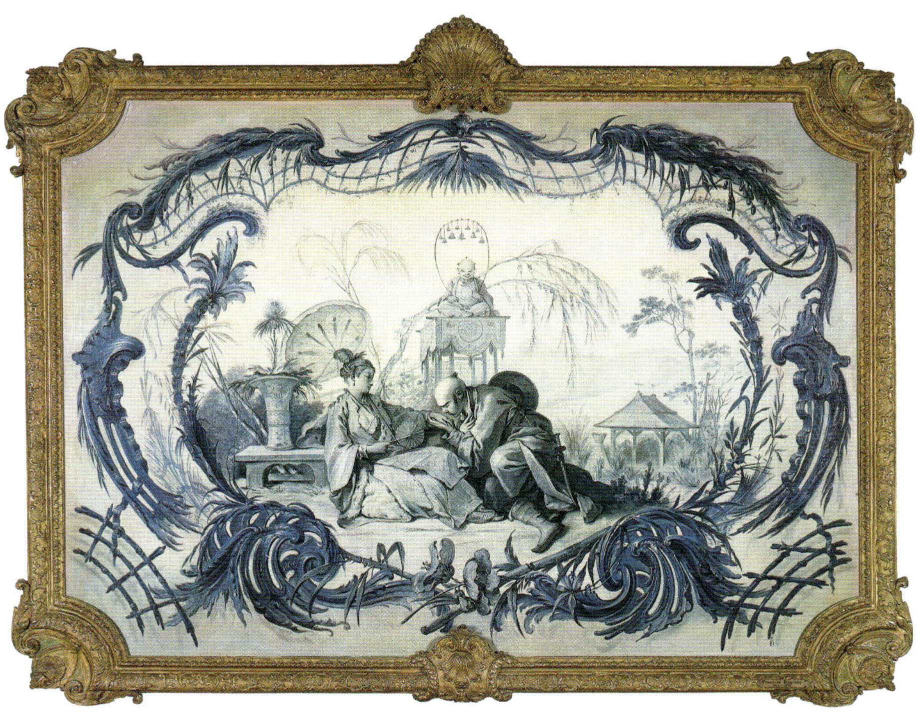

FIG.95
BOUCHER,
The Chinese Gallant, c.1742,
oil on canvas, 104 × 145cm,
Copenhagen, The David
Collection (B275)

natural predilection was matched and encouraged by Madame de Pompadour who was his major client for this type of picture.

Seductive Spaces

Blondel believed that 'gallantry precedes love; love itself cannot save me from the seductions of frivolity, and frivolity dies in my heart under the traits of boredom. But, in inconstancy, in boredom itself, I am never insensible to the charms of the Fine Arts…the ideas which I gain from the Arts, enrich my imagination, perfect my *sensibilité*'.[89] A similar belief lies behind Madame de Pompadour's creation of a series of ever changing intimate interiors calculated to entrance and relax the King and stave off his dreaded boredom. Boucher, already the master of invention and seduction, created a series of exquisite images to match the luxury of Madame de Pompadour's fashionable interiors and add to the blend of intimacy and fantasy with which the mistress hoped to distract and amuse her royal lover. Piganiol de La Force describes how after the glories of the King's bedroom in Bellevue, 'one finds a gallery of an elegance and delicacy which honours the taste of Madame de Pompadour who imagined and traced the designs herself. All the carving forms garlands of flowers, worked with the greatest lightness by Monsieur Verbeckt and painted by Monsieurs Dinant and Dutout; the garlands enclose pretty pictures by Boucher' depicting playing putti.[90] The King's gilded cabinet also contained two unspecified overdoors by Boucher and a picture decorating the top of the mirror over the fireplace. Everything else in the room was of an exquisite costliness, from the gilded panelling varnished by the Martin brothers to the matching furniture upholstered in expensive silk, hand painted by Peyrotte. Meanwhile exoticism reigned in Madame de Pompadour's own apartment on the ground floor at Bellevue. As she employed the most fashionable painter of *turqueries*, Carle Van Loo, to provide overdoors for her own harem-like bedroom, she also employed Boucher, the most sought-after painter of chinoiserie, to decorate her neighbouring Chinese-themed *cabinet de toilette or boudoir*.[91] Although the picture illustrated in fig.95 was painted almost a decade earlier, it shows the type of delicate gallant scene Madame de Pompadour would have enjoyed and which would have matched items such as her bidet upholstered in white material with blue and silver flowers.

One of the most luxurious, intimate and modern aspects of the château at Bellevue was the bathroom suite contained in one of the separate wings of the château. This included a ground floor room with appropriately chosen mythological overdoors by Boucher depicting *The Toilette of Venus* (fig.96) and *Venus Bathing* (1751; Washington). Bathing, regarded as suspect in the Christian medieval tradition and associated with the exotic frissons of the harem, had recently become a luxury for the rich, reflected in new suites of rooms, called *cabinets des bains*. For the rich, used to the omnipresence of servants and hangers-on, the *cabinets des bains* became the most intimate spaces in their homes. Here, ladies of fashion could indulge in the new sensual pleasures of cleanliness, anointing their bodies with perfumes that replicated

FIG.96
BOUCHER, *The Toilette of Venus*, 1751, oil on canvas, 108.3 × 85.1cm, New York, The Metropolitan Museum of Art, Bequest of William K. Vanderbilt, 1920 (20.155.9)

the scents of the fresh flowers used to protect their private apartments against the invasive odours of the street.[92] French artists from Watteau onwards celebrated this advance in *l'art de vivre* in intimate pictures of women bathing in or out of doors, Boucher himself producing some of the more voluptuous images. *The Toilette of Venus*, with its roses and perfume burner, reminds us that where previously the unpleasant odours of unwashed (and often unhealthy) bodies and uncleaned teeth had simply been masked by even heavier animal based perfumes, in the eighteenth century a revolution was brought about by the importation of perfumes from the orient and the invention of subtler plant-based scents, making the sense of smell another potential pleasure zone.[93] Boucher's picture recalls the sensuality of the *Toilette of Psyche* which Bachaumont proposed he should paint in 1737: 'Oh what beautiful vases of gold and cristal; What beautiful perfume burners! How the bedchamber of Psyche is beautiful and rich, in the background one sees an alcove beneath which is a canopied bed which brings water to the mouth'.[94]

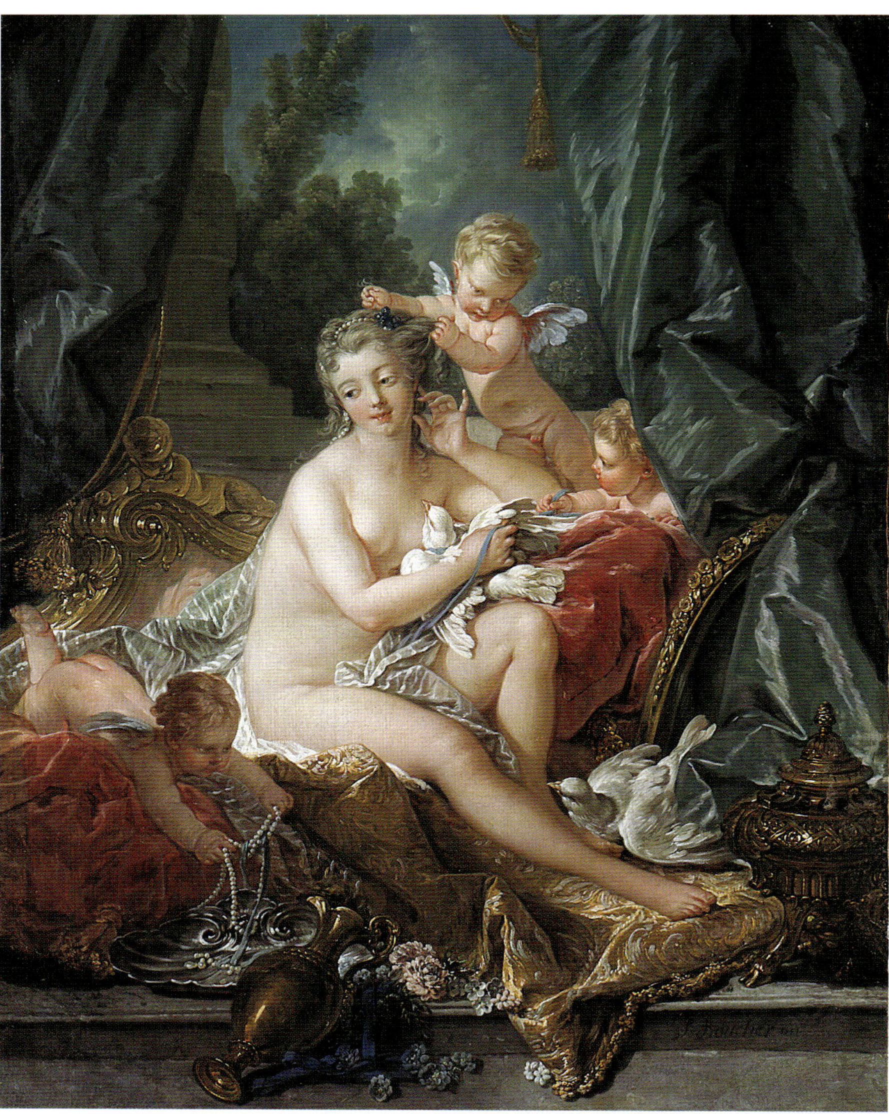

Other subjects by Boucher that appeared in Madame de Pompadour's châteaux included pastorals and contemporary fashionable genres such as *Winter* (fig.97). This was one of four Seasons, painted in 1755, whose shape and relatively small size imply that they were incorporated into decorative panelling or above mirrors.[95] *Spring* and *Autumn* are represented by pastoral scenes, *Summer* by a bathing scene and *Winter* by this fashionable young lady being pushed in a sleigh by a rather Cossack-looking gentleman. The subject recalls the skating scenes of Watteau and his followers but also, through its inclusion of the Russian figure, anticipates the type of Russian subject that would gain wide currency in the following decade in the work of Boucher's pupil Jean-Baptiste Le Prince (1734–81).[96] It is typical of Boucher that he should be one of the first artists to reflect the emergence of Russia as a force on the European stage in the eighteenth century and that he should do so in such a quintessentially picturesque and French manner.

Infant Pleasures

Madame de Pompadour's deceptively light technique of attraction was memorably described by the duc de Croÿ in his journal: 'she mingled in many things, without seeming to do so … whether naturally or politically, she seemed more occupied with her little comedies or other bagatelles … She was very teasing with the King and employed the art of the most delicate flirtatiousness to seduce him'.[97] In view of her deliberate playfulness and also of her sentimentality, as described by her friend the abbé de Bernis, it is unsurprising to find that Madame de Pompadour was greatly attracted to Boucher's allegorical use of infants (see fig.30). At about the same time as Boucher was painting the infant *Seasons* for the ceiling of the King's Council Chamber at Fontainebleau, the duchesse de Luynes admired 'Boucher's pink and blue children representing the Arts' in one of Madame de Pompadour's boudoirs.[98] The marquise also ordered a set of Gobelins tapestry designs for seat furniture depicting putti representing the arts, woven after designs by Boucher between 1754 and 1756.[99] A re-working of the *Loves of the Gods*, peopled with infant divinities, was later ordered from the Gobelins by her brother in 1757, with designs provided by Boucher, Pierre, Vanloo and Vien. This inspired Madame de Pompadour to commission a second set in 1761, expanded to include two new larger designs after Boucher and Noël Hallé (1711–81) depicting infant *Geniuses of the Arts* and *Geniuses of Poetry, History, Physics and Astronomy*.[100]

Meanwhile a shocking series of events in the capital had made Parisians value their children all the more. Barbier recounts how, between November 1749 and May 1750, panic spread among the lower classes as children were abducted from the streets: 'They say in Paris that for the last eight days disguised agents of the police have been roaming the different quarters and abducting children, boys and girls, from about five or six years to around ten years old, putting them in waiting covered wagons; they are the little children of artisans and others who are in the neighbourhood, sent to church or on errands'.[101] Rumour abounded as to the causes of the

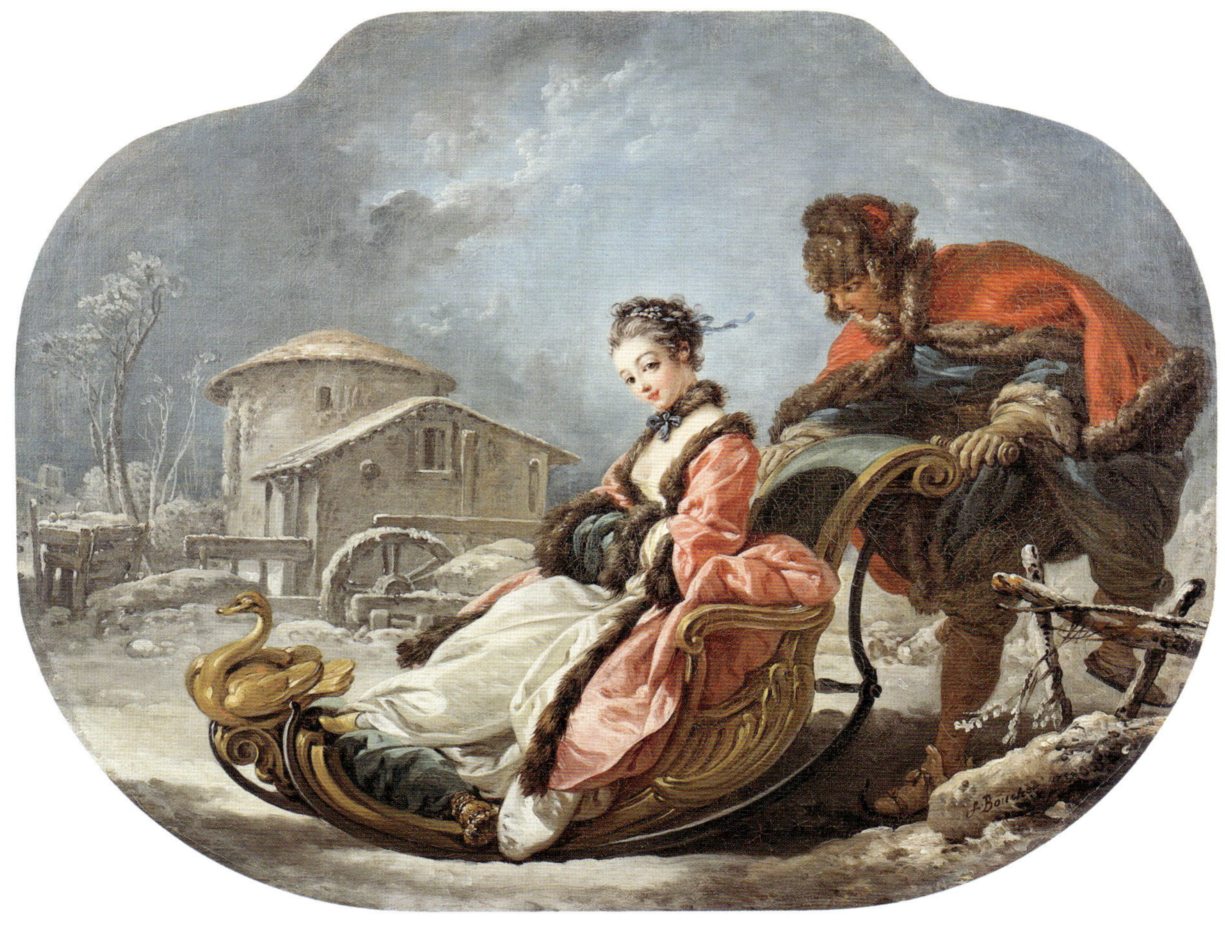

FIG.97
BOUCHER, *Winter*, 1755, oil on canvas, 56.8 × 73cm, New York, The Frick Collection

FIG.98 *opposite*
After BOUCHER, decorative panelling with children representing *The Arts and The Sciences*, mid-late 1750s, oil on canvas laid down on panel, height 217.2cm, New York, The Frick Collection

abductions, the most horrifying being the belief that children were being sacrificed so that a decrepit prince might bathe in their blood, but Barbier states that the most likely reason for the disappearances was the demand for child labour in the Mississippi silk sheds. Whatever the motivation the people rose up in protest and Paris saw its first major revolt of the eighteenth century. At the same time, the overload of adult sensual pleasures noted at the end of the 1740s, which had contributed to the return to Nature movement of which Boucher's pastorals were one of the most artificial examples, also led to an increasing fascination with concepts of innocence and childhood.[102]

Boucher was prompted to create a new subject to reflect this feeling and started to depict small children of school age a decade before the publication of Rousseau's *Emile, ou de l'Éducation* (1762) and the first depictions of Greuze.[103] They were initially associated in Boucher's mind with his ideas on the pastoral, for they often appear dressed up as shepherds, shepherdesses, little farmers or gardeners and they were intended from the outset to be transferable across the range of the fine and decorative arts.[104] Madame de Pompadour was immediately attracted to this new subject, ordering, in 1751, her very first set of Gobelins low-warp furniture tapestries for Bellevue, after models by Boucher depicting children engaged in country pursuits.[105] Boucher's *Children* were depicted in a growing variety of occupations which, while reflecting the contemporary interest in education, were never allowed to become didactic but were primarily intended to charm. The success of Boucher's infants is borne out by the decorative panelling with children representing *The Arts* and *The Sciences* painted after Boucher's designs now in the Frick Collection, New York (fig.98).[106] With their cartouches containing Boucher *Children*, small landscapes in *camaïeu bleu* and decorative flowers all painted on a cream background, probably by specialist artists associated with the Gobelins, they appear like a witty child-like version of the decorations for the Royal Council Chamber at Fontainebleau (fig.93).

From the outset Boucher seems to have been keen to see his new creations realised in three dimensions and as early as 1749 produced a drawing of a *Little Gardener* which was used as the basis for a Vincennes biscuit figure.[107] Although providing drawings for Vincennes was not particularly lucrative, it was precisely the type of *divertissement* that Boucher enjoyed and was also a way to gain favour with Madame de Pompadour and the King, who were both notable protectors of the factory. In 1753, the year Duflos advertised his first set of pirated engravings after Boucher's *Children*, Blondeau was paid by the Vincennes factory for eight models of *Children* after Boucher, while Allegrain, Falconet, Coustou and Vassé were commissioned to make small statues after Boucher *Children* for Madame de Pompadour's dairy at Crécy; these were also later modeled in porcelain by Fernex and Suzanne for Vincennes.[108] The following year, when Duflos produced his second set of unofficial engravings of Boucher's *Children*, Boucher himself was paid 300 *livres* for drawings supplied to Vincennes, while Fernex and De La Rue were paid for models. The latter were paid for more of the same in 1755, while Boucher received 485 *livres* for drawings in 1756, in which year the Vincennes factory relocated to Sèvres. Boucher's last consignment of drawings, now for Sèvres, appears to have been in 1757. Although a set of Boucher drawings of *Children* was copied by Falconet *fils*, engraved by Tardieu and published by Jollain in 1761, by the beginning of the 1760s Boucher was no longer working for Madame de Pompadour and had discovered a new outlet for his talents as a draughtsman: the new crayon and wash-manner engraving techniques practised by engravers such as Demarteau and Floding.

Nevertheless, between 1752 and 1766 many of the designs copied or adapted to embellish the surfaces of a variety of Vincennes and Sèvres porcelain, from vases to tea wares, were derived from Boucher. Figure 99 shows a tray, with matching cups, saucers, sugar bowl and cover, called a *déjeuner 'Courteille'*, thought to have been bought by Madame de Pompadour in December

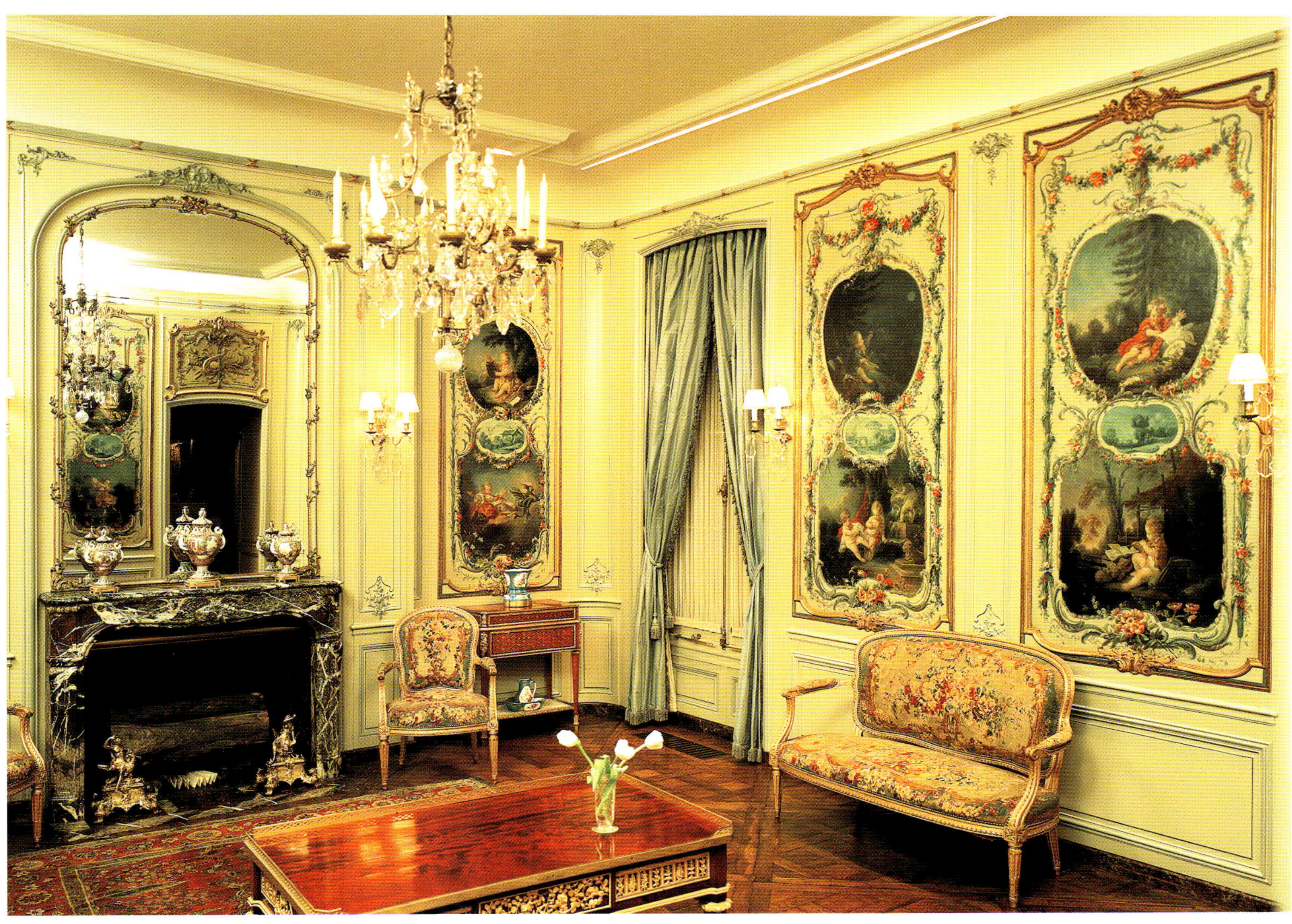

1759 for 720 *livres*, and incorporating children inspired by Boucher.[109] The imagery chosen reflects the advancing technical abilities of the factory in producing more complicated polychrome designs and tends to be slightly behind taste in the fine arts. This time lag is easily explained when one considers that many of the designs were copied from engravings executed some time after the original works, or from pictures commissioned from Boucher some time previously by collectors, like Trudaine, who were also associated with the factory. By his death Boucher himself had amassed a small collection of Vincennes/Sèvres, including blue and green vases, a flowered coffee pot, a flowered teapot with matching cups, a number of large cups and saucers and a small collection of biscuit-ware including two figures after his own designs.[110]

Criticisms and Rewards

Madame de Pompadour's strategy, in which Boucher's art played a major role, was successful with the King and she remained the official royal mistress until her death in 1764. Unfortunately disputes between the Crown and *Parlement*, losses to the British in the colonies, and the unpopular alliance with Austria in the costly and unsuccessful Seven Years War (1756–63) caused increasing political dissent in the capital. Much of the criticism was levelled at Madame de Pompadour, whose lavish spending, so successful in winning over the King, was universally decried in Paris which saw little lasting public benefit in the art she promoted. She was considered, moreover, to be a pernicious influence on the King's own taste, as is revealed by the duc de Croÿ's observation that 'the marquise [has] given him all these little tastes…all is executed at great cost, all the more unfortunate as they are doing almost as much at all the King's houses, as well as those of the marquise; this unfortunate taste for little building and for little details is immensely expensive, without anything fine remaining'.[111] There was much criticism, for example, of the fact that one of the glories of the School of Fontainebleau, the Ulysses Gallery decorated by Nicolò dell'Abate after the designs of Primaticcio, had been allowed to fall into disrepair and then destroyed to make way for the new interiors.[112] A letter of a clerk of the King's Building Works (the *Bâtiments*) is typical of the aesthetic approach which was now being criticised. He wrote ordering that one of the cabinets 'must be painted the same colour as the little toilet commode near this cabinet, that is to say a clear grey'.[113] Questions naturally arose over the propriety of royal interiors whose appearance was determined not by some glorious propagandist scheme but by the colour of a toilet commode! Despite Vandières's attempt to stress links with the glorious royal past at Fontainebleau, the exquisite decoration of the King's Council Chamber was deemed inappropriately intimate by many observers. Indeed its appearance recalls the imaginary interiors described in Jean-François Bastide's account of the perfect love-nest, *La petite maison*, such as the *cabinet de toilette* with 'panelling painted by Huet, with fruits, flowers and foreign birds, interlaced with garlands and medallions in which Boucher has painted little gallant subjects in *grisaille*, as well as overdoors'.[114] Bastide warned that to the uninitiated such appearances might 'give us an air of superficiality and perfidy' and this is exactly how it seemed to those who were increasingly censorious both towards the ruling regime and towards the type of art it patronised.[115]

The works that Boucher created for Madame de Pompadour, many of which were paradoxically more monumental than anything he had produced before, were fatally compromised by their association with the royal mistress. Something of the variety of the different audiences for art in this period and their conflicting aesthetic, moral and political viewpoints is implied by the differing reactions to *The Setting* and *The Rising of the Sun* at the Salon of 1753.[116] Madame de Pompadour was obviously pleased with the paintings as she approved stopping work on the tapestries in order that the pictures should be shown at the Salon. The secretary of the Academy, Cochin, demonstrated his solidarity with Boucher by defending the paintings in formal aesthetic terms citing arguments in accordance with the principles of De Piles.[117] He claimed that 'I do not think that you have ever seen from this Master, nor from any other, two Pictures filled with more grace and agreeableness. They are of an admirable wealth of genius, whether in their poetic composition, or in their picturesque details … Their overall effect is marvellous, with a tone full of sweetness, without the affectation of contrasting harsh colours, which might have the power to shock, but which do not satisfy those who know the enchantment of harmony'. He pointed out in particular Boucher's ability to depict light and shade in 'the group of the night which is one of the most excellent parts of the picture, as well as the figure of the woman who supports Thétis. Among all the beauties that find themselves united in this figure, the effect of the light is one of the most piquant; she only receives a fugitive light on her face, which produces a vigour in the shadows, while the rest of the figure is in reflected shade painted without the use of black and with an admirable intelligence and freshness of colour. In general one has to admit that M. Boucher excels in the art of depicting flesh in sweet shadows.' Cochin ends by lauding Boucher's originality: 'one can say in his praise that he imitates no one; Painter of the graces, he sees in

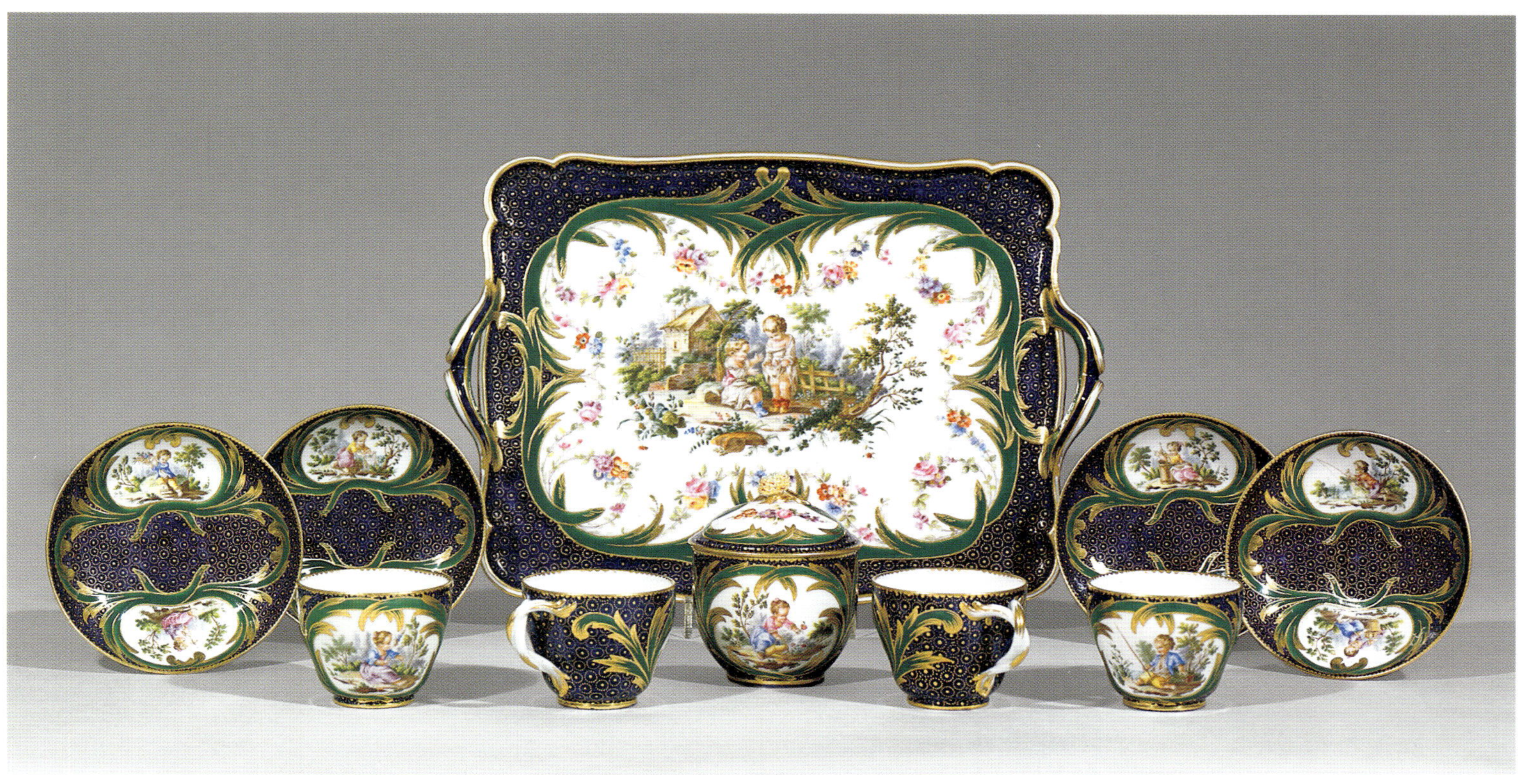

FIG.99
Tea Service (*déjeuner 'Courteille'*), 1758–59, soft-paste Sèvres porcelain, dimensions of tray 30 to 36.2 × 23 × 26.5cm, Wallace Collection

Nature what no other artist has ever perceived'.

Other observers were less convinced. The mythological subjects seemed of dubious value in an age that increasingly advocated that knowledge and art should be founded on a rational study of nature. As Holbach wrote 'If ignorance of nature gave birth to the Gods, Knowledge of nature is destined to destroy them'.[118] In similar vein Gautier Dagoty maintained that 'the true connoisseur does not search to delude his eyes, and by the help of art to trace on his retina objects foreign to those which Nature presents to us, but he desires only to observe to what point a canvas covered in colours might modify the incidental rays, and send them back under different modulations, with the same accord as do the real objects which surround us and which the Painter wishes to imitate'.[119] As sight resulted from the action of light on the retina, the natural depiction of light in a painting became of prime concern, with Gautier Dagoty warning against the artistic manipulation of light in a canvas and advocating instead the direct translation of light and shade as seen through a camera obscura.[120] Colour should be treated in a similarly rational manner as 'colour is born in light and shade; the two parts are inseparable'.[121] When he came to review Boucher's *Setting* and *Rising of the Sun* he found them difficult to assess as their subjects were outside the boundaries of nature: 'What can M. Boucher do to compose a man in the clouds, women in the waves, children in the air, a light in a subject, a day in another, has he models for all these phenomena? … the imagination alone is the dominant part of his productions'. Although he admits that 'they are beautiful dreams', he implies that their subjects are not the most appropriate for an artist to depict.[122]

Others took an increasingly moral stance believing that it was the duty of the history painter not to please, as Boucher did, but 'to depict great events', favouring 'the grand, the noble, the majestic, the sublime'.[123] This attitude informs one of Boucher's fiercest critics, La Font de Saint-Yenne: 'I am going to talk to you about the pictures

FIG.100 *opposite*
MAURICE JACQUES (1712–1784), design for a decorative border for the Gobelins tapestries of *The Setting* and *The Rising of the Sun*, *c.*1757, oil on paper, 130 × 76cm, corner 128 × 128cm, Paris, Mobilier National

of another painter whom I have always warned you against. It is M. Boucher. You like neither his colour, nor his composition, nor his taste in drawing, nor his thoughts. You even carry your antipathy to the point of saying that he has enervated the progress of our school with his seductive make-up, by his flesh-tints which are not at all those of nature, being nearly all the colour of rose and violets. You have even made an unflattering comparison with the songwriter of pretty ditties as opposed to the good epic and tragic poet. Finally, you reduce his talents to the pastoral genre and the shepherd's crook.' While admitting that Boucher's 'brush has a freshness and suavity that pleases many people', he criticises the impropriety of subject and treatment in *The Setting* and *The Rising of the Sun*. He complains that although 'some are painted with strength and with good tone' the naiads and tritons appear to be indiscriminately arranged 'without much choice or order' and are impossibly relaxed despite the agitation of the sea. Although he admits the voluptuousness of the naiad who regards the spectator in *The Rising of the Sun* he complains that she detracts from the true subject of the picture and that the other characters also show insufficient respect for Apollo. With *The Setting of the Sun* he feels that Thétis and Apollo do not show enough emotion towards each other while their marine Court is similarly uninterested and lacking in action. Finally, unable to deny the seductiveness of Boucher's vision he attacks it in moral terms for precisely this quality: 'Many people who are not ridiculously severe either in business or sentiment, but who still respect the mores and proprieties of correct behaviour, have been astonished to see such a display of scarcely veiled nudity exhibited to the public. They have prevented good churchmen, the truly religious from seeing the Salon due to the description relayed to them. Many persons of the fair sex, who still have some modesty, have felt it proper for the same reason not to bring their daughters. A painter, like a poet, should never defy decency in his works. Their indecencies are surely applauded and admired by libertines, but decent people will always disdain them.'[124] At the same time, even the cleanliness of the naked bodies in Boucher's canvases might be viewed as suspect. For in Paris cleanliness was an expensive luxury. All water had to be carried from the Seine by water carriers. It was not simply charged for by quantity, but increased in price the further from the Seine it came and the higher the floor of the building to which it had to be carried. As luxury in general came under attack, cleanliness bought at such a price came to be perceived as unnatural and associated with libertinism. The clean body might be seen as a morally deflowered body and associated with promiscuity.[125] So in *Emile* Rousseau's Sophie 'disdained that excessive cleanliness of the body which sullies the soul; she is better than clean, she is pure'. By association the clean naked bodies of Boucher's canvases contributed to an impression of moral degeneracy. So painters were now discouraged from appealing to the senses and were exhorted to paint for 'the soul, the rest only paint for the eyes'.[126]

The financial crisis following the outbreak of war forced Madame de Pompadour to sell Bellevue back to King in 1757. *The Setting* and *The Rising of the Sun*, tapestries and paintings, which had only been delivered to Bellevue in 1754–5, were now taken to her Parisian residence, the Hôtel d'Evreux. It is unclear where Madame de Pompadour displayed the pictures, but it was decided to show the tapestries in her audience chamber, or *salle de dais*. They were too small for the new room so special borders were ordered from the Gobelins to enlarge them. These were designed by Maurice Jacques (1712–1784), in consultation with Boucher (fig.100).[127] In this year the establishment was shocked to the core by Damiens's assassination attempt on the King, no longer as divine and invulnerable as previously thought. The Royal mistress meanwhile was ageing, ailing and increasingly pious. Boucher's luscious nymphs must now have appeared poignantly inappropriate to a woman who no longer held court at her dressing table but received visitors at her embroidery frame. The new borders

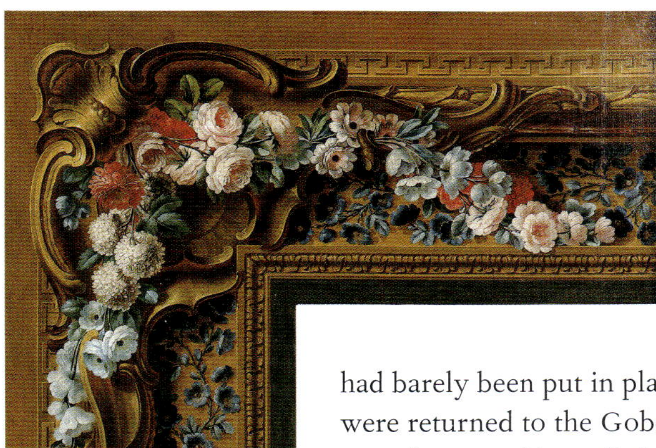

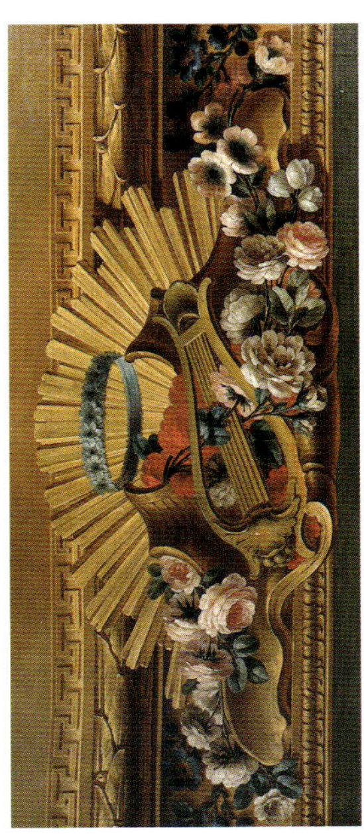

had barely been put in place before the tapestries were returned to the Gobelins and exchanged in 1760 for something a little more discreet: a set of *Infant Gardeners* woven between 1706–20 after designs by Charles Le Brun. Meanwhile they were replaced in the *salle de dais* by the marquise's less audacious infant *Loves of the Gods* tapestries and in particular by the two new designs after Boucher and Hallé of the infant *Geniuses of the Arts* and *Geniuses of Poetry, History, Physics and Astronomy*.[128] *The Setting* and *The Rising of the Sun* tapestries were last mentioned in 1768 when re-sold by the Gobelins for just over 6,966 *livres* to the financier Pierre-Jacques-Onésime Bergeret, a notable patron of both Boucher and his pupil Fragonard.

Luckily for Boucher, as Gautier Dagoty noted, 'the amateur public of sciences and arts does not carry its zeal far enough to worry about artistic debates', and his private practice continued to thrive.[129] He had profited greatly from his association with Madame de Pompadour. It was probably her delight at *The Light of the World* and *The Setting of the Sun* that had led, in 1752, to Boucher receiving a pension of 1,000 *livres* on Jean-François de Troy's death. In that year, on the death of Charles Coypel, he was also awarded the spacious apartment in the Old Louvre which had been occupied by two generations of the Coypel family, Antoine and then Charles, both of whom had been First Painters to the King and Directors of the Academy. On the death of Oudry in 1755, Boucher became his successor as artistic supervisor at the Gobelins, thereby adding another 1,200 *livres* to his annual income. All this was at a time when Madame de Pompadour's own pension from the King was reduced after 1750 to 4,000 and then 3,000 *livres*![130] Together with what he earned from his paintings, drawings and prints, Boucher probably now enjoyed an annual income of around 50,000 *livres* a year, the equivalent of a noble's or a bishop's income.[131] This enabled him to carry out a series of lavish improvements to his apartment, for which he was reimbursed 4,000 *livres*, with 4,800 *livres* still owed to him from the Crown on his death.[132] His financial ease is also revealed by his ability to endow each of his daughters with dowries of 6,000 *livres* each, the same as their mother had received from her father twenty-five years previously. Boucher's expensive way of life, however, led to irregular and incomplete payment of the dowries; thanks to the good relations of the Boucher family neither daughter nor son-in-law ever pursued him for what was owing.[133] Mannlich recounts how 'Mme the marquise de Pompadour loved and esteemed Boucher, not only as a famous man, but also as her painting teacher, her colourist and even her friend' and even proposed to find him two rich tax farmers as husbands for his pretty daughters. Bearing in mind that Madame de Pompadour was the supreme example of the successful financial classes, Boucher's supposed reply seems highly unlikely: 'Ah! Madame what are you thinking of? My daughters will be rich without being happy; and I shall be very afflicted seeing them drink the blood of the unfortunate in goblets of gold'.[134] Nevertheless Boucher's social ascent is demonstrated by the fact that Madame de Pompadour along with her brother, now marquis de Marigny, Madame Geoffrin and the writer, the abbé de Lagarde, all acted as witnesses at the double wedding of Boucher's daughters to his pupils Pierre-Antoine Baudoin (1723–1769) and Jean-Baptiste Deshays (1729–1765) in 1758.

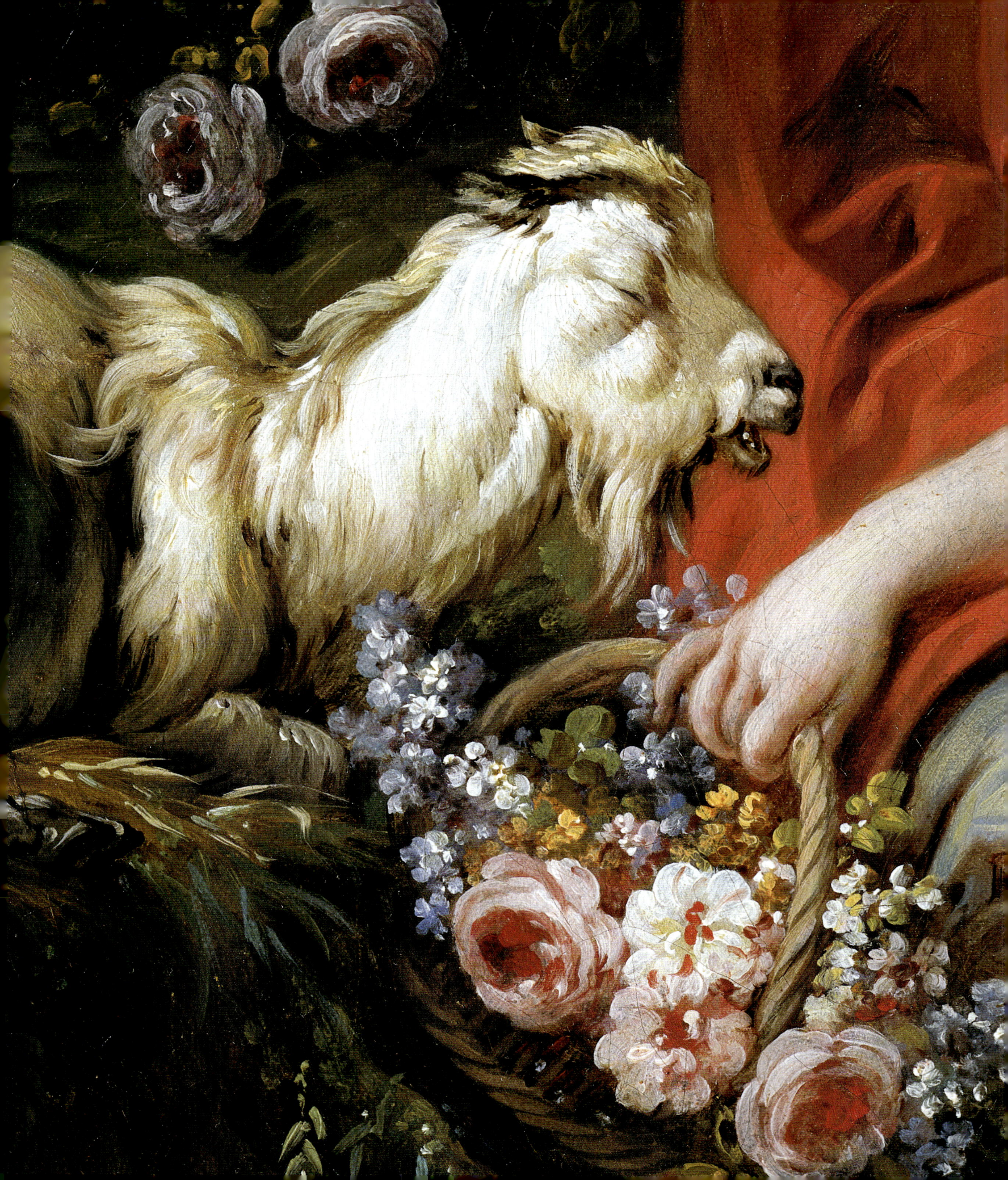

V

Criticism is easy, and art is difficult DESTOUCHES[1]

Copyists and Critics: Boucher mid-1750s to 1770

FIG.101 *opposite*
BOUCHER, *Shepherd and Shepherdess*, 1761, oil on canvas, detail, Wallace Collection

following pages
FIGS.102–4
BOUCHER, *Mars and Venus*, 1754, oil on canvas, 164 × 71cm, Wallace Collection

BOUCHER, *Judgement of Paris*, 1754, oil on canvas, 164 × 76.6cm, Wallace Collection

BOUCHER, *Venus and Vulcan*, 1754, oil on canvas, 164.5 × 71.5cm, Wallace Collection

According to Shakespeare 'Beauty is bought by judgement of the eye', a belief often symbolised in Western art by the story Boucher portrays in *The Judgement of Paris*.[2] The shepherd Paris, bribed with the promise of possessing the most beautiful woman in the world, awarded the golden apple, the prize inscribed 'to the fairest', to Venus, rather than to Minerva, goddess of wisdom, or to Juno, Queen of the gods.[3] Artists from the Renaissance onwards had identified with Paris's task of deciding between competing forms of beauty, while the subject also provided the opportunity to depict three different female nudes, thereby inviting the viewer to make similar aesthetic choices. The subject perfectly encapsulates Boucher's own artistic preoccupations, and features as the central panel in a series in the Wallace Collection celebrating the goddess of love and the power of visual beauty (figs. 102–104).[4] The curving chain of figures in *The Judgement of Paris* (fig.103) starts with a leopard-skin clad Paris, seated on the earth, and moves to a cloud-borne Venus, shown frontally so that her beauty might be fully admired, via a tantalising back view of Minerva up to the disgruntled Juno in the heavens. The cloud formations in the other two canvases suggest that Vulcan's discovery of his wife, Venus, in bed with Mars, god of war (fig.102) would have been placed to the left of *Paris* with Venus persuading her husband to forge weapons for her son, Aeneas, on the right (fig.104).[5] These two canvases focus yet more closely on Venus and her lovers, revealing the luscious, pearly female figures of Boucher's maturity offset by the bronzed Mars and Vulcan whose similarities derive from the fact that Deschamps probably served as model for both. Mannlich described in the 1760s how, having already posed for the Academy and for artists privately for twenty-five years, 'the famous Deschamps served me for my Vulcan and my Cyclops. Of all the models that I have had in my life Deschamps was the only one who had the talent to penetrate the person that he had to represent; he was old but still vigorous and in good shape'.[6]

In addition to his sensual, fluid handling of the figures, Boucher's canvases delight with their carefully painted accoutrements. In *Mars and Venus*, he is careful to distinguish between the blue velvet, the peachy striped-silk taffeta, the white silk satin sheets and transparent veil of Venus's hair, while the flowers, putti and weapons abandoned at the foot of the bed all add to the picturesque interest. Similarly, in *Venus and Vulcan*, once one's gaze has been sated by the form of the goddess, carefully slimmed down, as retouchings on her left side reveal, one's eyes are invited to linger on details such as the weapons destined for Aeneas, and on the superbly painted anvil and vice. While both canvases laud the sexual attraction of the goddess of love, Boucher is careful to deflect any accusations of obscenity with humour: hence the witty bow tied in the god of war's hair, echoing Hercules's emasculation by Omphale (fig.22), and hence the replacement of Vulcan's workers, the Cyclops, with Amours industriously forging weapons of love rather than war. As Bret observed, if Boucher 'painted Venus coming to demand from Vulcan weapons for her son, it was not to the burning forge of this god, it was not to the terrible Cyclops that he gave the principal role in his canvas: but to the mother of the Amours, and her enchanting cortege'.[7]

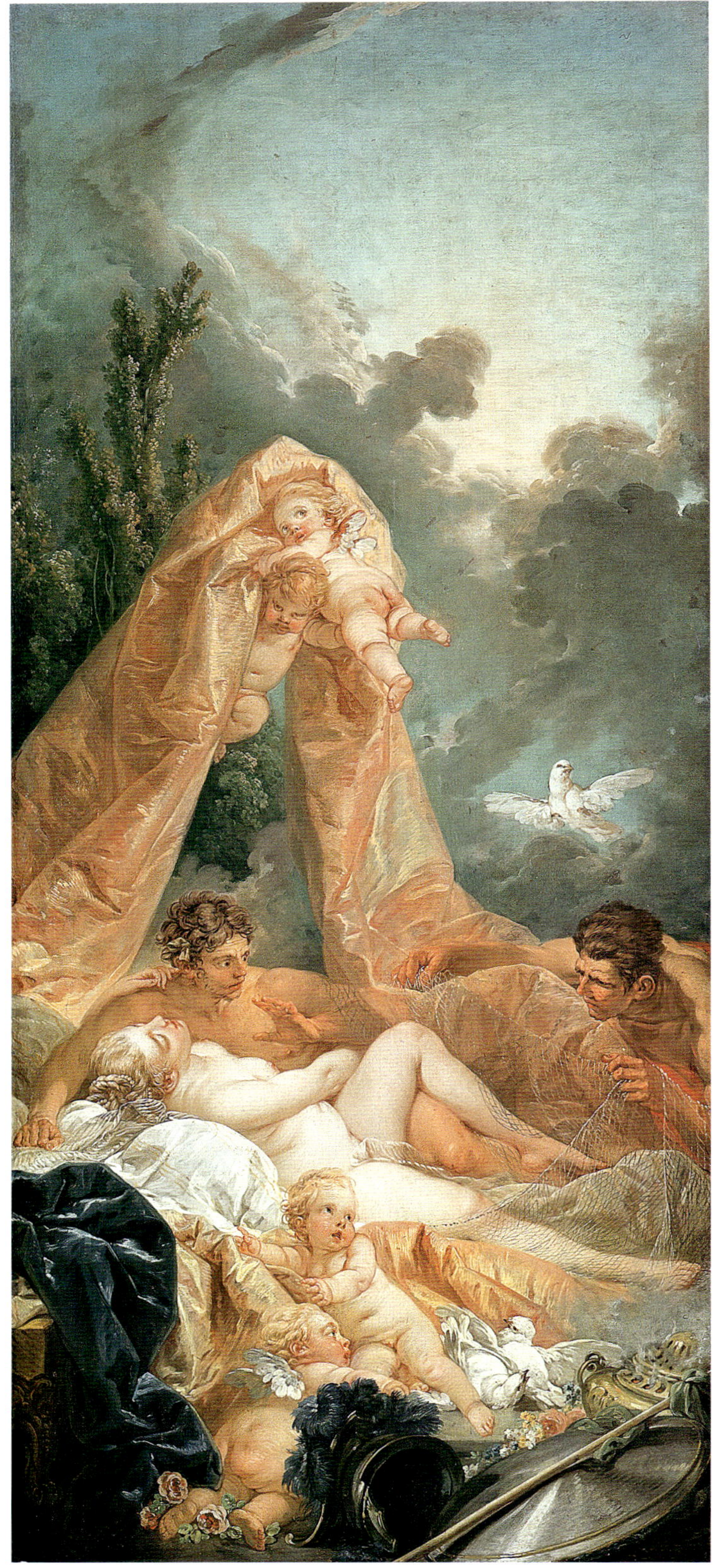

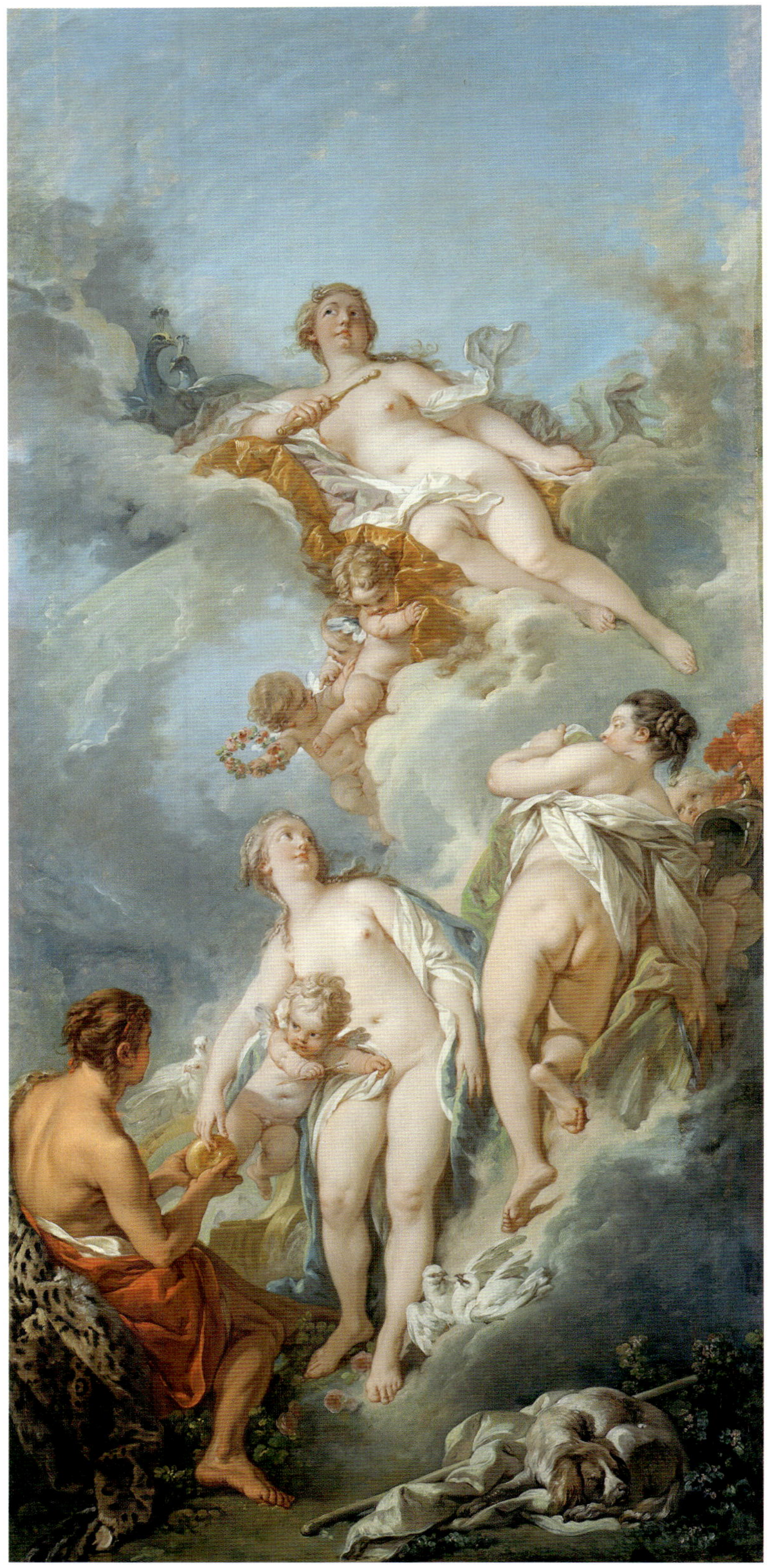

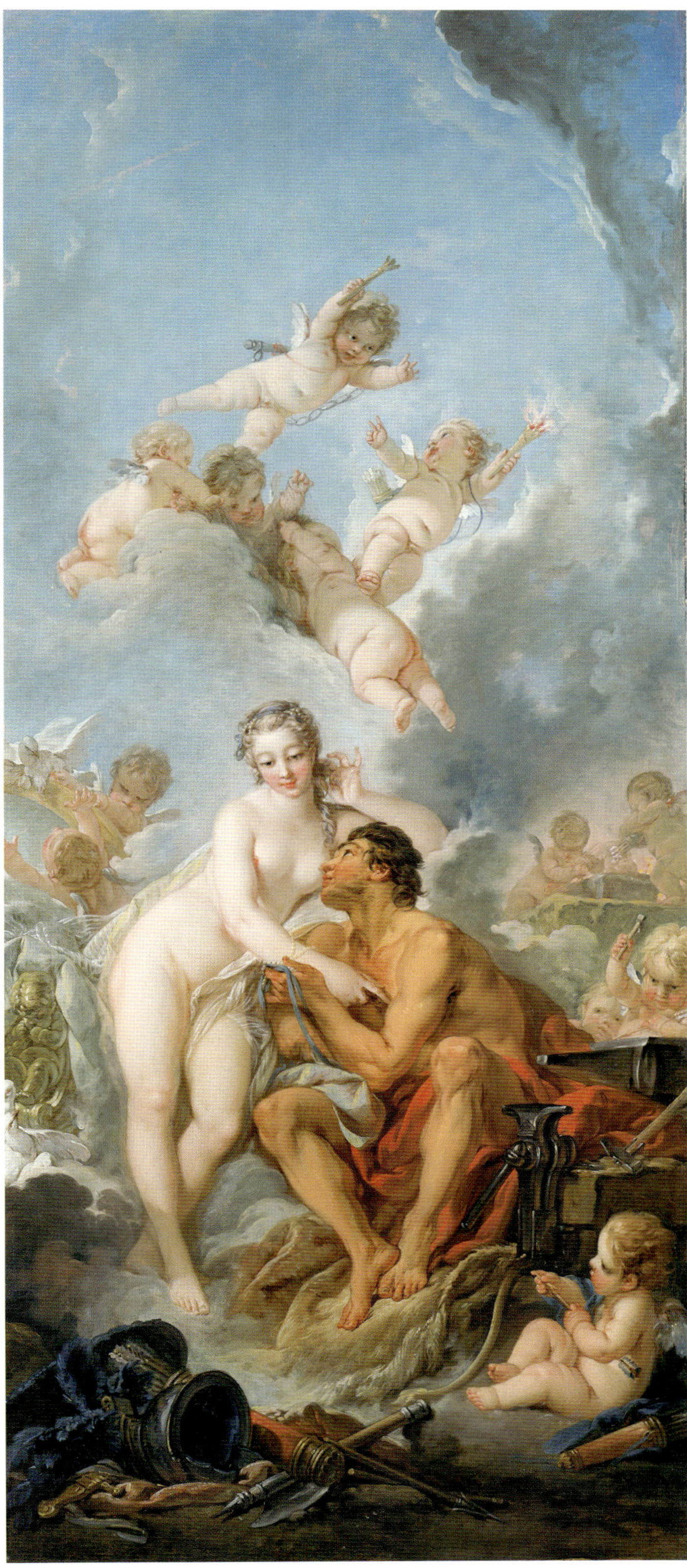

Although they are decorative paintings the vertical format of the Wallace Collection's Venus series implies that they were to be inserted in panelling at eye level, which would have demanded greater care from the artist than that required, for example, in an overdoor. Unsurprisingly in view of their quality, subject and date (1754) they were later associated with Madame de Pompadour although there is no evidence that she commissioned them from the artist. Even in 1757, another *Venus demanding arms for Aeneas* (Louvre), commissioned for the Gobelins, inspired the comment 'What, yet more Graces, Venus and *Amour* [Love]! Have you not already, Boucher, painted Pompadour!'[8]

A fourth canvas in the Wallace Collection, *Cupid a Captive* (fig.105), was later incorporated with the Venus series into a screen acquired in the nineteenth century by the 4th Marquess of Hertford.[9] Cleaning of the Venus pictures revealed, however, that they were originally of narrower dimensions than *Cupid a Captive*, which, together with their different iconography, prove they were not part of the same commission, although dating from about the same period. *Cupid a Captive* is distinguished by the absence of Venus and illustrates a passage in one of Anacreon's *Odes* where Venus's power failed to retrieve her errant son, willingly held captive by the Graces.[10] The Graces symbolise the three stages, chastity, desire and consummation, through which love progressed in a civilised society, as opposed to the abandoned erotic feeling displayed by the infant Cupid, whom the Graces had already been set to 'educate' in a picture by Boucher of the 1730s (version fig.141).[11] The Wallace Collection's picture represents a mature flowering of this elevated theme, but was precisely the type of picture that appeared increasingly out of date to Salon audiences, ignorant of or uninterested in such suggestive meanings, and captivated or shocked instead by the display of naked bodies. The artistic initiative was finally wrested from Boucher by works such as Jean-Baptiste Greuze's *Reading from the Bible* (1755; Louvre), painted about the same time, which indicated a new moral and aesthetic approach that

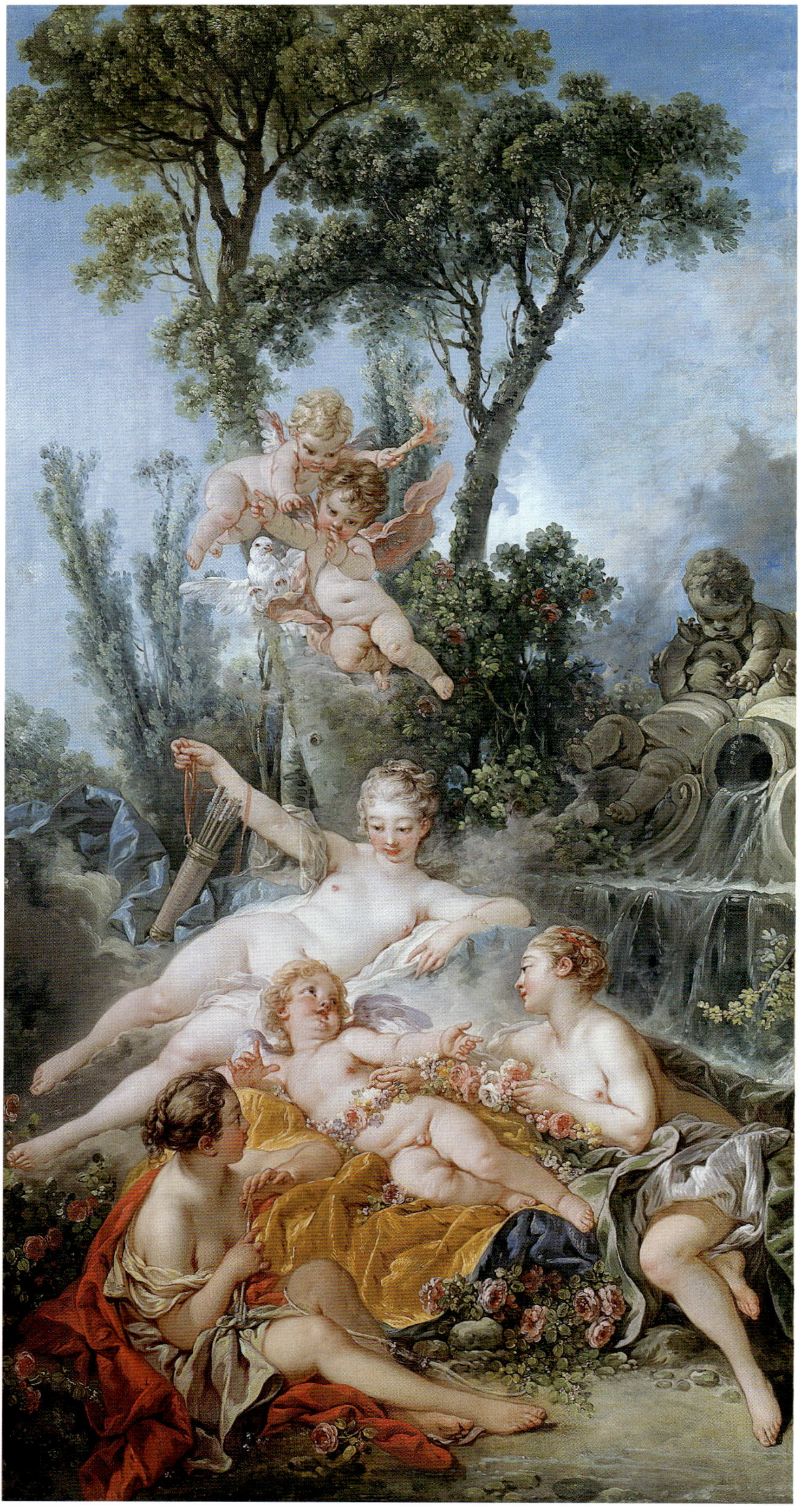

sounded the death knell for Boucher's allusive mythologies.

Cupid a Captive, nevertheless, demonstrates how Boucher, now in his fifties, was still capable of executing brilliant paintings. Its recent cleaning has revealed a pastel tonality previously obscured by a thick, yellowed varnish. Infra-red photography shows how, despite the rich composition, Boucher suppressed details such as a tree in the background on the right (fig.106) in order to maintain overall clarity. The detail of the Grace's profile, delicately silhouetted in shadow in the foreground leading the eye to the brightly illuminated figure of Cupid in the centre of the picture (fig. 107), demonstrates Boucher's still-expert use of light and shade and his virtuoso handling of paint. Indeed Boucher's later mythological works, which include a large number of tapestry cartoons and larger decorative schemes, are distinguished by their increasingly rapid, loose and painterly handling.[12]

Venerating Venus and the Muses with help from the Studio

Boucher's artistic output was legendary, estimated at about a thousand pictures and ten thousand drawings at the end of his life. If he worked at a steady pace from his twenties onwards, this would have been equivalent to around two pictures and sixteen drawings a month.[13] As official commissions from the crown and Madame de Pompadour added to growing private demand for his pictures from the mid 1740s, he was able to sustain this punishing workload only with the help of studio assistants. Later commentators, like Bret, also mentioned that Boucher was forced to increase his output 'in order to meet his spending and his different tastes'. This obliged him to 'accept the resource of mediocre talents' and to lower himself, as Bret saw it, to painting all manner of minor decorations including 'overdoors, carriage panels, and even *Pantins*'.[14] Figures 108 and 109 show the type of rapidly executed and somewhat repetitive formulas that Boucher devised to decorate the increasingly rectilinear overdoor spaces of the interiors of the

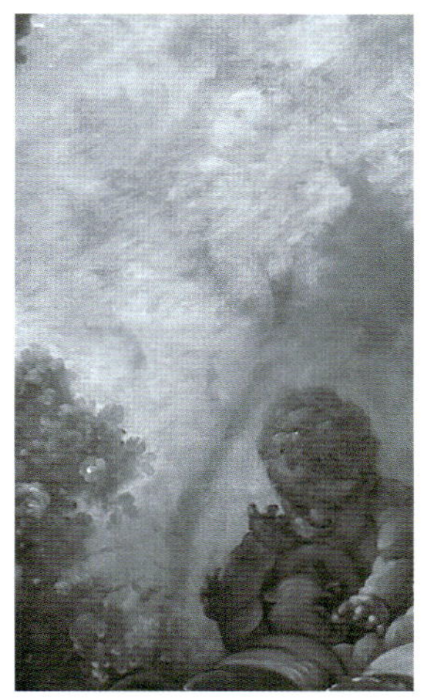

1750s and 1760s, as these became more sober and classically influenced.[15] Gone are the curving Rococo spaces with their complementary twisting figures, and in their place Boucher depicts a goddess or muse in a pose following the angle of the frame, with Amours to provide narrative and picturesque detail. The formula was easily imitated by Boucher's students, assistants and followers, leading to a rash of banal productions (figs. 110–112) which further undermined his reputation.[16]

Boucher's active role as a teacher was noted by contemporaries such as the abbé de Fontenay: 'he formed many students of whom he took especial care. His custom was not to overburden them with precepts, quite often of no use. 'I do not know how to teach' he said, 'unless it is with a brush in my hand'; and so, taking the work of his disciple, he would correct it with four strokes, and add there those charms of which only he knew the secret'.[17] Restout also describes Boucher as 'a sincere friend' to young artists with talent, 'always ready to direct their studies and contribute to their progress' and keen to help them, never employing them without also rewarding them with pictures, or money, or both.[18] Boucher's studio, according to Bret, functioned as an open house for talented beginners and amateurs: 'Friend of youth, as he was of pleasure, he was often surrounded by it; and as he had none of those incertitudes in his manner of painting, none of those mysteries which render some studios inaccessible, his hours of work were useful lessons for those he judged able to profit by them'.[19] Unlike the nineteenth-century romantic idea of the solitary artist painting in a garret, Boucher's studio must have appeared very much like the illustration of an artist's studio in Diderot

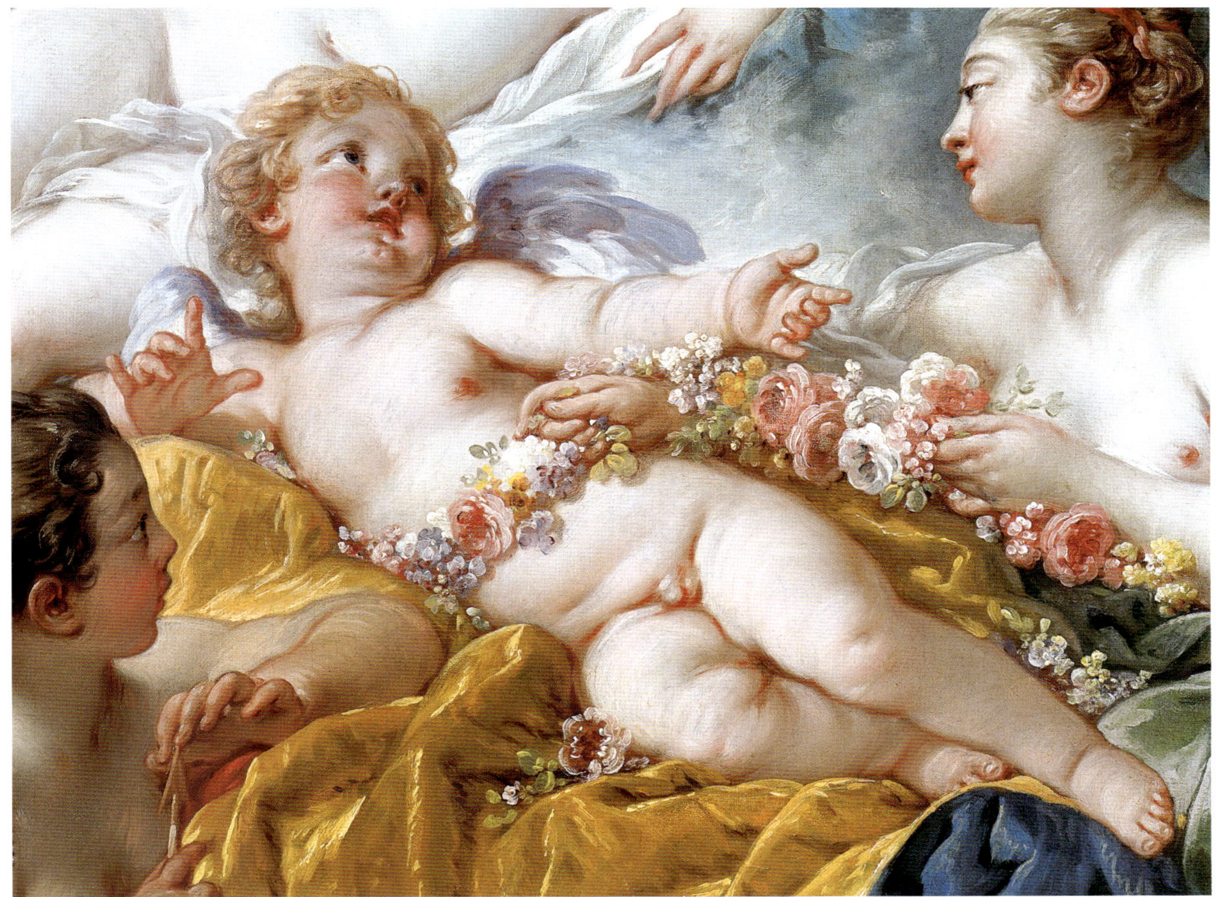

FIG.105 *opposite*
BOUCHER, *Cupid a Captive*, *c*.1754–5, oil on canvas, 164.5 × 84.5cm, Wallace Collection

FIG.106 *above*
BOUCHER, infra-red photograph of detail taken from *Cupid a Captive*, *c*.1754–5, oil on canvas, Wallace Collection

FIG.107 *right*
BOUCHER, *Cupid a Captive*, *c*.1754–5, oil on canvas, detail, Wallace Collection

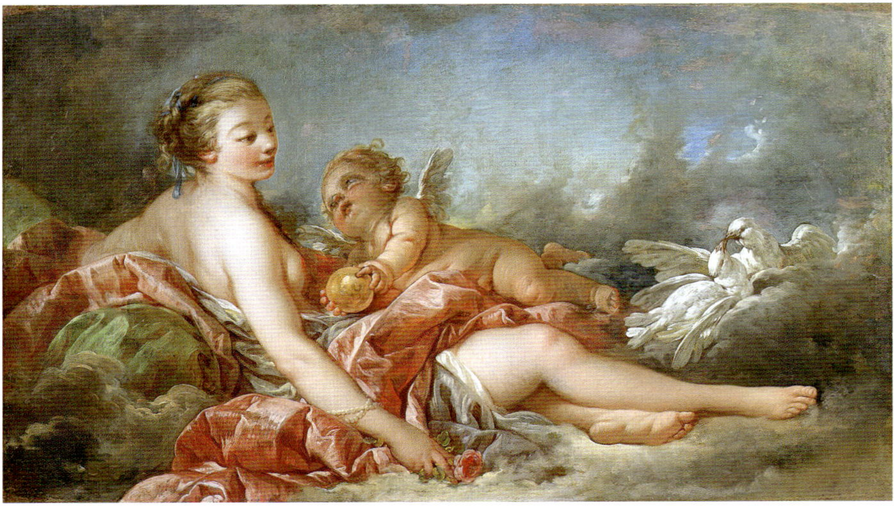

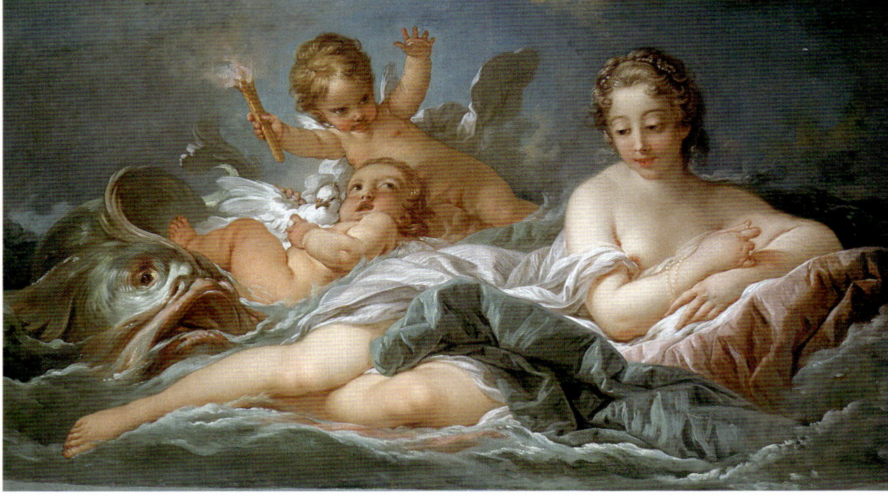

FIG.108 *top*
BOUCHER, *Cupid Offering Venus the Golden Apple*, 1754, oil on canvas, 79.2 × 139cm, Wallace Collection

FIG.109
BOUCHER, *Venus*, 1754, oil on canvas, 79.2 × 138.7cm, Wallace Collection

and D'Alembert's *L'Encyclopédie* which shows a lively community of painters occupied in different tasks, drawing, copying posed models, perched on ladders painting larger canvases or producing smaller repetitions.[20] Even as the critical tide turned against Boucher, and his work was damned not only for its artificiality but also for corrupting the young, one commentator pointed out that 'M. Boucher is perhaps of all our masters, the one who has formed the largest number of good Students, which is a necessary result of the fecundity of his genius, and of his good principles of colour, which even his censors cannot fail to recognise'.[21]

It is still surprising quite how many of the next generation of artists passed through Boucher's studio as pupils or assistants.[22] The Academy prize lists for the 1750s and 60s are full of artists described as former pupils of Boucher. His pupils Le Mettay and Hutin won first prizes and La Traverse a second prize at the Academy in 1748. In 1750 it was the turn of Melling to win first prize, then Deshays the following year and Fragonard the year after that. In 1753 Brenet was awarded a special prize and Gabriel de Saint-Aubin won second prize. Finally, his pupil Saint-Quentin gained first prize in 1762 and Ménageot in 1766. Meanwhile, although not a pupil, the young Vien was championed by Boucher at his reception by the Academy in 1754, and from the end of the 1750s Boucher's own former pupils began to be accepted as members of the Academy: Deshays and Julliar in 1759, Baudouin in 1763, Fragonard (as an associate member) and Le Prince in 1765 and Brenet in 1769. Although Robert was not a pupil, his landscapes in Boucher's collection suggest that Boucher certainly took an interest in Fragonard's friend.[23] At the same time, the derivative work of artists like Jean-Baptiste Huet, a pupil of Le Prince who specialized in Boucher-like pastorals, shows how the pupils of Boucher's students in turn spread his influence. Moreover, the presence of foreigners such as Mandelberg (Danish), Müller (Swedish), and Baldrighi (Italian) who were in Boucher's studio at the beginning of the 1750s, and the German, Mannlich, who was there between 1765 and 1768, attest to the cosmopolitan nature of Boucher's *atelier*. In 1764, even David's uncle, Buron, tried to use family influence to place the eighteen-year-old artist in Boucher's studio. Despite, or perhaps because of the fact that they were related, Boucher, pleading old age, recommended him to the care of his young friend, Vien; David's early works nevertheless attest to the pervasive influence of Boucher on the younger generation.[24] Unfortunately, like many high-achieving fathers, Boucher had less success with his own son. In contrast to Boucher's own beginnings and as a special favour to his father, Juste-Nathan Boucher was sent to study in Rome by Marigny,

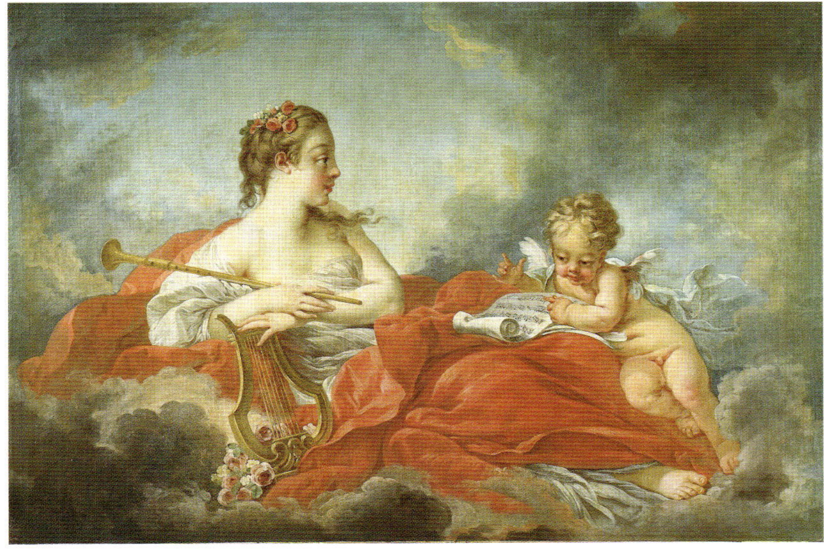

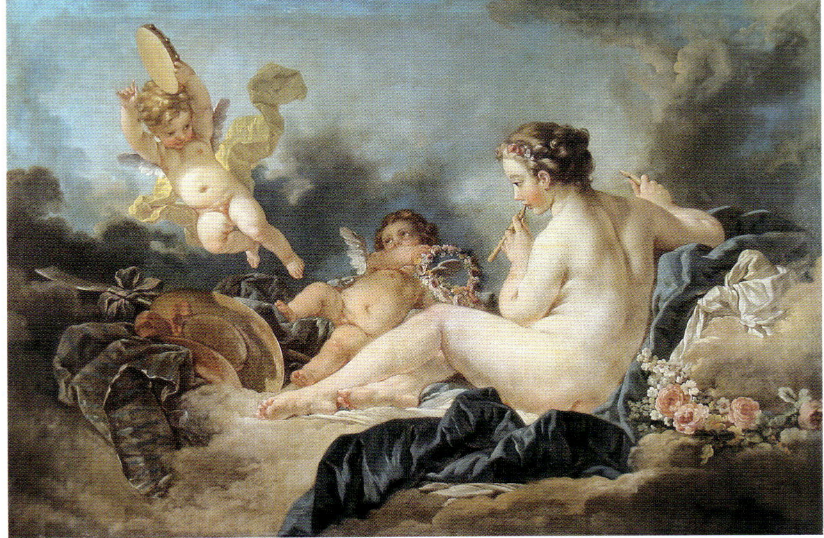

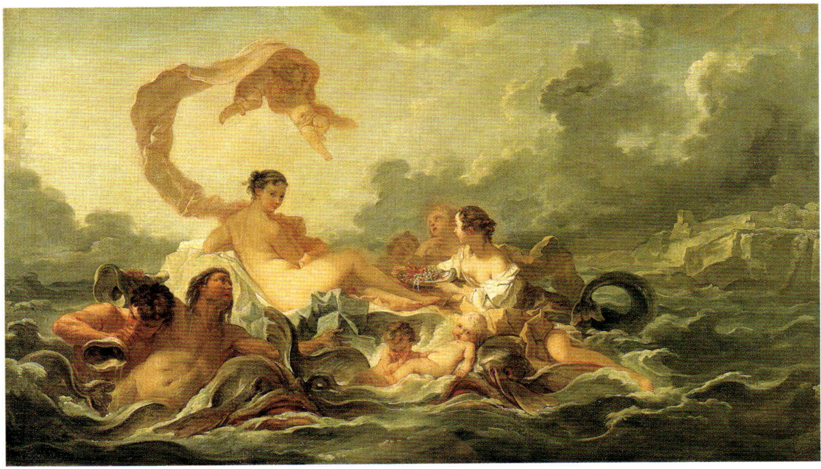

who took a special interest in his young protégé's progress. Natoire describes Juste-Nathan as 'working hard and making progress. He is very well behaved and I hope he will honour his father'.[25] But, despite such help, Juste-Nathan did not distinguish himself, becoming an unremarkable draughtsman and architect.

Another reason for Boucher's increasing reliance on studio assistance in the 1760s was his age and frailty. He already appears an old man in Roslin's portrait (Versailles) painted at the same time as that of his 'still beautiful' wife (fig.31).[26] Moreover, his recurrent infirmity is attested by his absence from his teaching duties at the Academy in 1763, and his rejection, the following year, of the post of Director of the King's Drawings Collection because of failing health.[27] He was seriously ill again at the beginning of 1765, the same year that saw the death of his thirty-five year old son-in-law, Deshays. According to Restout he suffered from asthma, 'which had tormented him for a long time' and the *Correspondance littéraire* described how before his death 'he had for a long time the air of a spectre, and all the inevitable infirmities of a life consumed by work and unregulated pleasures'.[28] As well as being a fashionable accoutrement, the fine ebony and silver cane sold after his death was probably used in

FIG.110 *top*
STUDIO OF BOUCHER, *The Muse Clio*, *c.*1755, oil on canvas, 96 × 140cm, Wallace Collection

FIG.111
STUDIO OF BOUCHER, *The Muse Euterpe*, *c.*1755, oil on canvas, 96 × 140cm, Wallace Collection

FIG.112
After BOUCHER, *The Birth of Venus*, third quarter of the eighteenth century, oil on canvas, 67.3 × 119.2cm, Wallace Collection

earnest.[29] Little wonder that, as Mannlich described, towards the end of his life 'M. Boucher rarely went out – his responsibilities required him to go from time to time to Versailles, to the Gobelins where he was the Director, to the opera ... and to the dealers and lovers of natural history'.[30]

The French Picturesque

Most of Boucher's Salon exhibits in the 1760s consisted of landscapes and pastorals. Bret noted that 'M. Boucher could not ignore that all the Cabinets were full of exact, but servile, imitations of nature, and that an inn scene by Wan-Ostade [sic] was covered in gold, while one hardly threw a glance at our best French Pictures'.[31] Boucher, as already mentioned, was a notable collector of Dutch and Flemish landscapes and even made an artistic pilgrimage in 1766 to the Netherlands with his friend and patron, the financier Randon de Boisset.[32] Boucher, while influenced by Northern models, aimed to create his own identifiably French brand of landscape painting; thus 'with the aid of his light and gallant compositions, he knew how to keep his buyers, which more essential works made for his glory would have retained with more difficulty'.[33] His landscapes seem to have been profoundly influenced from the 1750s onwards by his own pastorals and his rural sets for Monnet's revived Opéra Comique, plus the success of his old friend Oudry's visions of French rural life, such as *The Farm* (1750; Louvre).[34] The Dauphin had dictated the subject of the latter in detail, and Boucher may have seen these instructions as well as the picture. Oudry's picture was extremely popular with the Royal Family; the Queen herself painted a very competent copy of it in 1753 (Versailles).[35] Similarly rustic farmhouses, mills and dovecotes thereafter increased in Boucher's own works, accompanied by whirling doves or pigeons to provide a more decorative but still specifically French picturesque feel. A detailed drawing (Boston) of the same view depicted in the *Landscape with a Watermill* (fig.113) suggests that such scenes might be related to actual places, but the turquoise palette, feathery trees and pretty figures are products of Boucher's idealising imagination.[36] Oudry died in 1755, leaving Boucher the undisputed master of the picturesque French landscape, which led to his being commissioned the following year to paint four landscape overdoors for the Dauphin's cabinet at Versailles, only two of which were actually delivered (unidentified). Boucher continued to be resolutely attached to the picturesque despite the fashionable verisimilitude of younger contemporaries such as Joseph Vernet (1714–89) and the movement towards the 'sublime' historical landscape signalled by the publication the same year of Edmund Burke's *A Philosophical Enquiry into the Origins of the Sublime and the Beautiful*. Burke's brother, William, visited Boucher's studio with Reynolds, but it is interesting to note that the only British work owned by Boucher was an engraving after Gainsborough, which probably depicted one of Gainsborough's similarly picturesque early landscapes.[37]

Bret noted that Boucher only painted 'nature embellished by the imagination perhaps because the rich folk, for whom they were destined, would not look with pleasure on the crude and suffering condition of our Peasants ... or because he shared the ideas of M. d'Urfé and M. Fontenelle, who wanted to transform the history of our countryside into an ingenious novel ... [His] shepherdesses have more the airs of nymphs than women destined to guard herds of animals ... it was always as a poet of taste that he painted our countryside ... after the delicious illusions of the antique valley of *Tempé*'.[38] Although Boucher's landscape subjects remained unchanged in the 1760s, his painterly handling grew noticeably freer, as we can see in the *Landscape with a Young Fisherman* of 1768 (fig.114), one of a pair of pictures which belonged to the duc de Caylus.[39] Boucher's freer handling would have been encouraged by his interest in oil sketches, his later work as a tapestry designer and his return to designing and painting sets for the Opéra in the 1760s. In addition, Boucher's late landscape drawings, such as black and white chalk studies

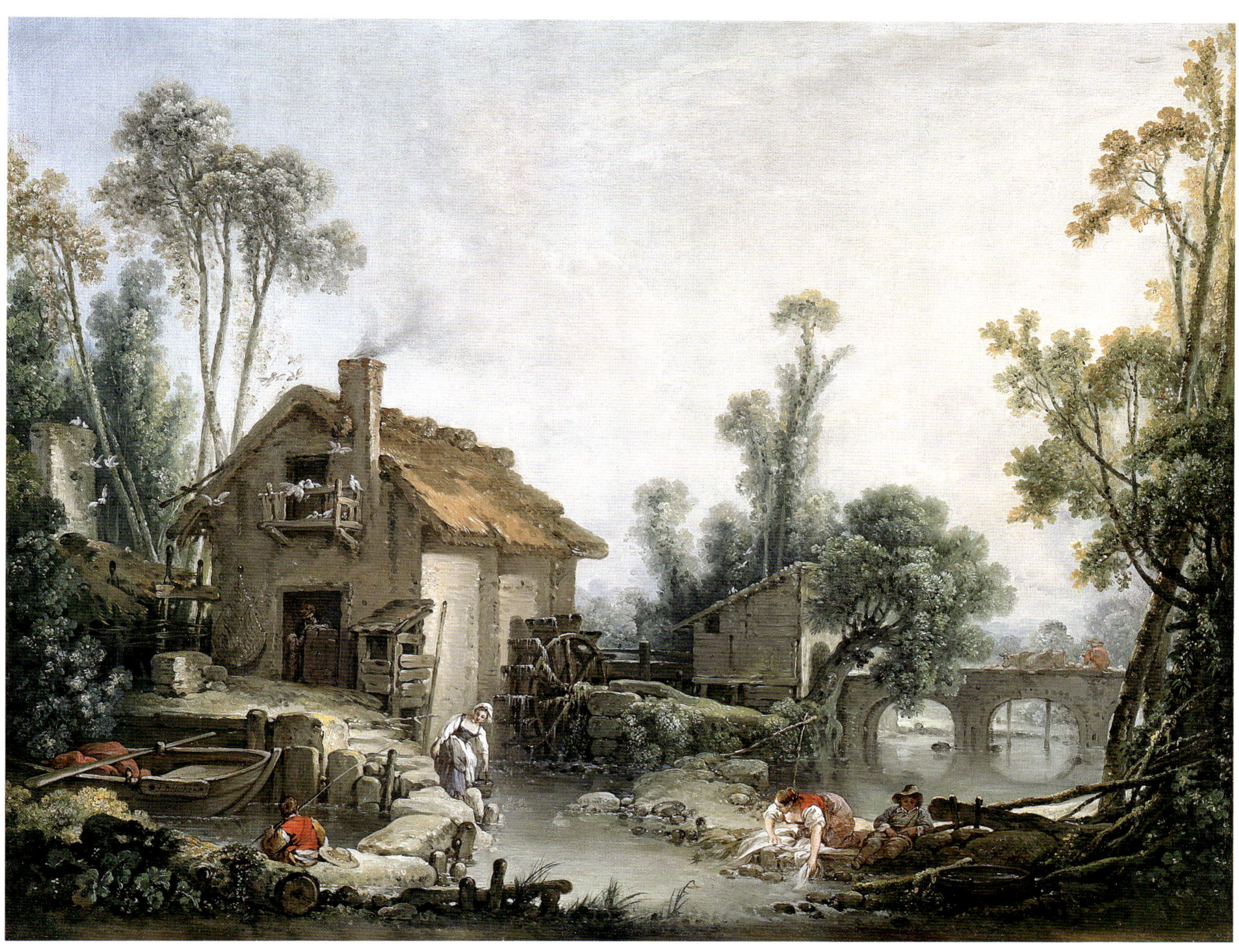

FIG.113
BOUCHER, *Landscape with a Watermill*, 1755, oil on canvas, 57.2 × 73cm, London, National Gallery

on blue paper in Frankfurt and Hamburg, demonstrate his interest at this period in the broader landscape styles of Dutch models such as Anthonie Waterloo (1609–90), whose drawings also figured very prominently in his collection.[40]

Boucher's picturesque approach to landscape was developed in the work of pupils such as Nicolas Jacques Julliar (1719–90), Jean-Baptiste Le Prince and Jean-Honoré Fragonard, while Hubert Robert, who owned prints and drawings of Boucher figures (Courtauld Institute), included them as staffage in his own landscapes.[41] Boucher's landscape compositions also gained a wider audience through the works of professional and amateur engravers such as Le Bas, Chedel, Basan (1723–97), Blondel d'Azaincourt (1719–94) and Papillon de La Ferté (1727–94).[42] A group of landscape engravings after Boucher was even acquired by the porcelain factory in Berlin in the eighteenth century as a source for decoration.[43] Meanwhile, the intimate milieu that linked landscape-painter, engraver, amateur and the theatre is recalled by Wille who dined on 13 February 1769 'at M. Basan's'. There he found that

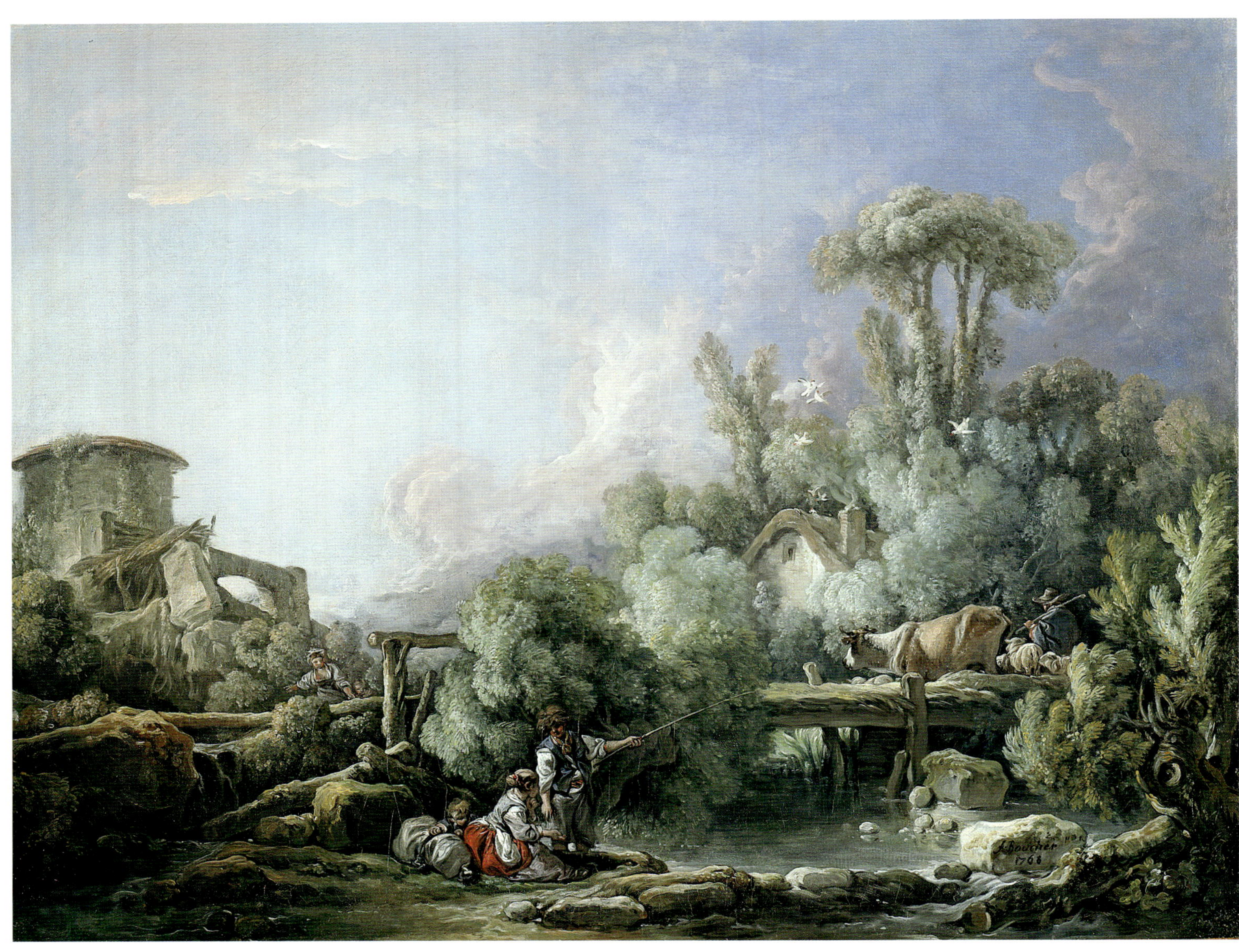

FIG.114
Boucher,
Landscape with a Young Fisherman, 1768, oil on canvas, 49.5 × 64.5cm, Manchester, City Art Gallery

'M. Boucher, First Painter to the King, my old friend, was there, as well as M. Monnet, Director of the old Opéra Comique, M. de Valois, art-lover, and M …., attached to the service of Monseigneur the duc de Choiseul'.[44]

The New Pastoral

Boucher's development of the pastoral genre was closely related to his work as a landscapist. The pastoral continued to be favoured by Boucher's private clients in the 1750s and prompted the Beauvais manufactory to commission a tapestry series from the artist, *The Noble Pastoral*, which was first on the looms at Beauvais in 1755. The series was extremely popular and demonstrated how the disparate Italian and *fêtes galantes* elements of Boucher's earlier *Fêtes Italiennes* series were now thoroughly assimilated and transformed into the quintessentially Boucheresque *fête champêtre*. Meanwhile, the changing fashions in interior decoration in the 1760s led to larger wall spaces becoming available for paintings, prompting Boucher to transfer the monumental pastoral back to canvas. The large pastorals he produced in the 1760s recall the early essays in the genre he produced on his return from Italy, but display a more elegant and theatrical approach in keeping with his new landscape style. Indeed, landscape occupied an increasingly dominant role in pictures such as the *Washerwomen* and the *Shepherds' Idyll* (1768; New York), where the figures are relatively small compared to the broadly painted landscape backdrops.[45] Such decorative subjects were ideally suited to Boucher's wealthy clientele who were not very keen to adorn their walls with the moralising histories advocated by the Ministry of the Arts and by critics such as Diderot. The King refused to live with one such edifying series, the *Sovereign Acts of Generosity*, depicting such acts by famous rulers of antiquity, commissioned to decorate his gallery at Choisy.[46] Boucher was initially chosen to paint one of the scenes but eventually excused himself from the prestigious commission by claiming he was 'too busy'. In the event, the series, according to Mannlich, 'did not amuse the voluptuary, Louis, who awaited with impatience for the heroes to be replaced by amiable shepherdesses in amorous conference with their tender lovers'. Boucher accordingly started work on a set of large replacement pastorals which, although 'considered rather like wall-paper [*meubles*], were truly enchanting'.[47] They were never completed or delivered, however, as the Ministry of the Arts seems to have been unable to pay for them and in Pierre's words, 'M. Boucher … was unable to devote himself to them because his own position was as [financially] embarrassed as that of the Ministry'.[48] Pierre, independently wealthy, suffered from no such constraints and fulfilled the commission after Boucher's death. It was only when the King's new mistress, Madame du Barry, rejected Fragonard's *Progress of Love* series (1773; Frick Collection) in favour of Vien's classical maidens sacrificing to Love (Louvre and elsewhere) that the pastoral finally became out-moded at Court. Even so, Louis XVI's Queen, Marie-Antoinette, was still playing the shepherdess at her *Hameau* at Versailles on the eve of the Revolution.

Boucher also developed a lucrative line in exquisite and detailed pastoral cabinet pictures of which the Wallace Collection's *Shepherd and Shepherdess* is a prime example (figs. 101 and 115).[49] This belonged to Boucher's friend, Randon de Boisset, and originally had a pendant depicting *The Badly Defended Bird* (private collection).[50] It is typical of a number of small pastorals and mythologies that Boucher painted at the end of the 1750s and the beginning of the 1760s, remarkable for their much thicker use of paint and fluid handling. This is seen, for example, in the staccato dabs of paint used to depict the flowers in the basket and the foliage, or the rich treatment of the thick fleece of the sleepy goat. Boucher's technique may have been influenced by his pupil, Fragonard, who worked in Boucher's studio at the beginning of the 1750s, before he became a pupil at the Academy school in 1752. During this period he painted a number of pastorals influenced by Boucher, including the Wallace Collection's *Musical Contest* (fig.116), which was attributed to Boucher when acquired by the 4th Marquess of Hertford in 1842.[51] The subject clearly recalls works such as Boucher's *Summer Pastoral* (fig.74) but the handling of the paint is radically different: in place of the smooth fluid technique of Boucher's pastorals of the late 1740s and early 1750s, one finds a much more detailed, impastoed and calligraphic touch, especially in the treatment of the foliage. This would become a signature technique of Fragonard whose painterly freedom and originality soon attracted connoisseurs and collectors of cabinet pictures. The closeness of Boucher and Fragonard's working relationship at the beginning of the 1750s is also illustrated by a page of sketches that Gabriel de Saint-Aubin made when viewing the Randon de Boisset sale in 1777.[52] On the same page that he sketched the Wallace Collection's *Shepherd and Shepherdess* with the annotation 'pastorale very beautiful' he also sketched four other pastoral subjects, including versions of *Blind-Man's Buff* (Toledo) and *The Sea-Saw* (Madrid). These he described as 'seen with Remy [the auctioneer] 4 pictures by M. Boucher, clerk, and

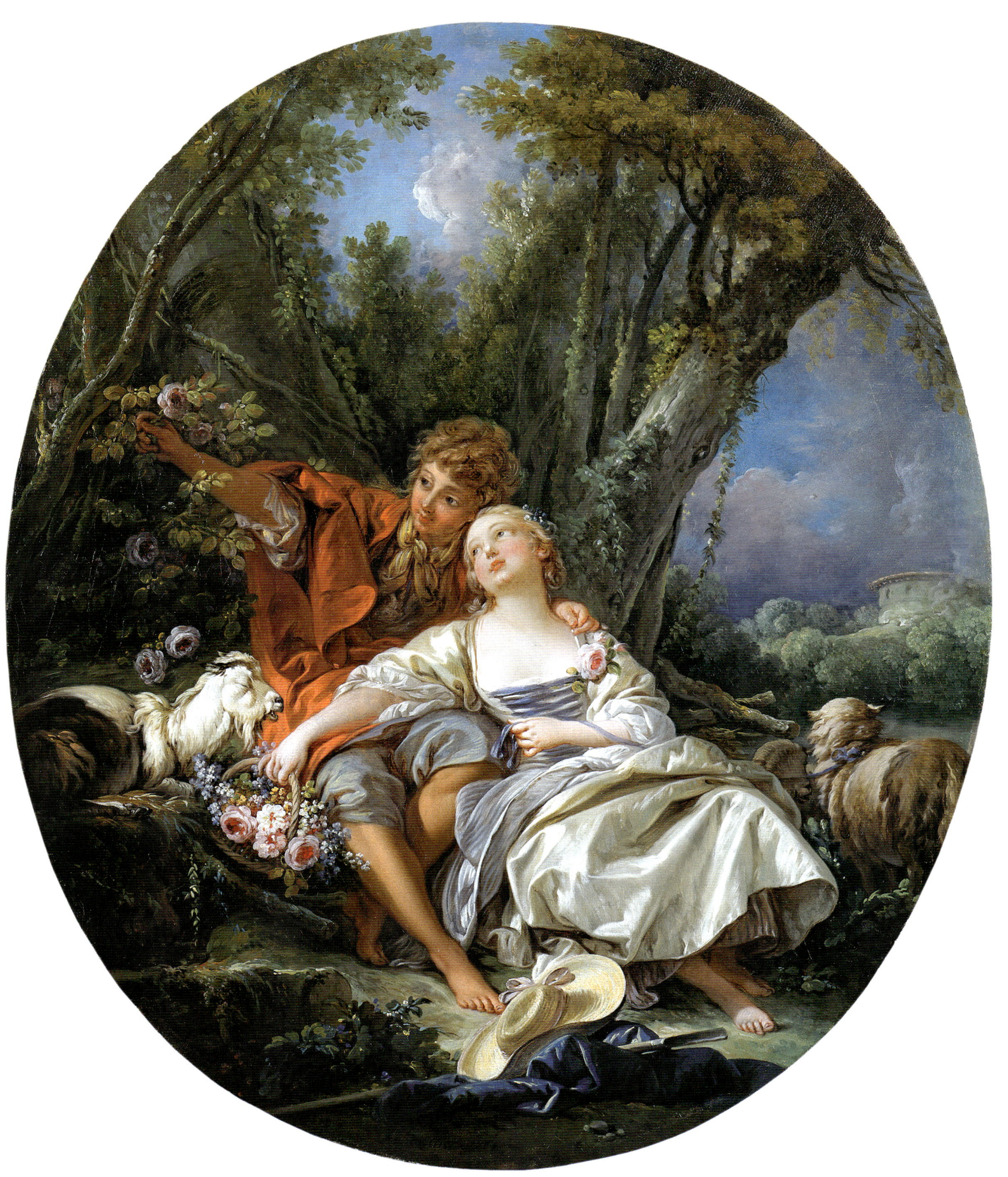

M. Fragonard, pupil who does not like them at all. Remy says that the invention came from Deshays'. The Toledo and Madrid pictures are now generally given to Fragonard but engravings exist attributing the pictures to both artists.[53]

Nature Unleashed

While continuing to paint landscapes and pastorals for the *cabinet* of the discerning connoisseur, Boucher was not further attracted to the *tableau de mode* or genre picture. His followers Baudouin and Fragonard, however, made something of a speciality out of their increasingly risqué cabinet pictures and gouaches, such as Fragonard's *Swing* and Baudouin's *The Night* (figs. 117 and 118).[54] Their work developed the suggestive character of Boucher's earlier genre scenes, which Bachaumont may have had in mind when writing his 'List of agreeable genre subjects' in 1756. Bachaumont's descriptions anticipate Fragonard and Baudouin's work of the following decade and represent a movement away from the deliberately veiled erotic towards an erotic more overt and more as we would define it today. The list included subjects such as *Clothing*, envisaged as a woman in front of a mirror in 'a white corset and a little white short skirt, both emphasizing her naked body and allowing us to see the back of her legs, her white stockings, her fine thighs, and her little feet'.[55] Fragonard's *Swing*, which, according to the writer Collé, was commissioned by the unknown young man depicted looking up his mistress's skirts, is both a cheeky reworking of one of Boucher's favourite concerns, gallantry and courtship, and also a homage to his theatrical vision of nature. Fragonard deliberately adopts the turquoise and pink tonalities of his mentor but, through his overabundance of curling foliage and flickering lights, banishes the equilibrium found in Boucher's canvases. Nature overwhelms Fragonard's picture in the way that it did Enlightenment thought in the latter part of the eighteenth century: 'Nature was too rich in its composition, too complex in its attributes, too potent in its effects to be imprisoned in a formula and the formula gave way under the strain ... Conscious of all this, they began to hold in Nature the reappearance of that Mystery which they were bent on banishing from the world'.[56] Meanwhile, Falconet's *Cupid*, which by the 1760s was erroneously believed to have decorated Madame de Pompadour's *Grove of Love* in the park at Bellevue, watches over both Fragonard's and Baudouin's scenes of illicit passion, wittily demanding our complicit silence.[57]

FIG.115 *opposite*
BOUCHER, *Shepherd and Shepherdess*, 1761, oil on canvas, 76.6 × 63.6cm, Wallace Collection

FIG.116
JEAN-HONORÉ FRAGONARD (1732–1806), *The Musical Contest*, c.1751, oil on canvas, 62 × 74cm, Wallace Collection

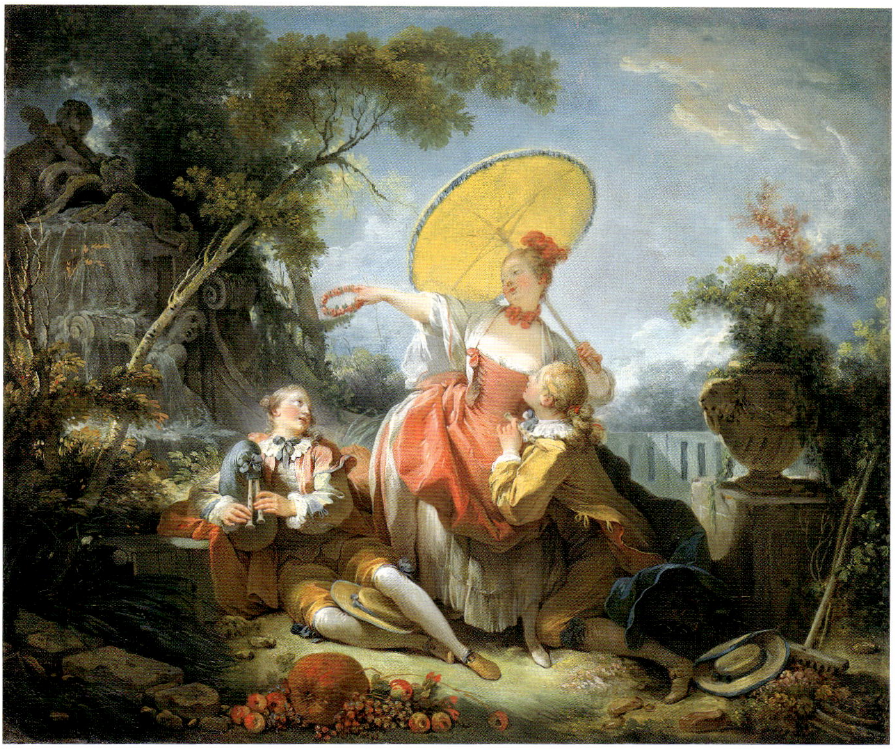

A fantastical park-like vision of nature also decorated the saleroom of Boucher's collaborator, the engraver Demarteau, in the rue de la Pelleterie on the Île de la Cité. Boucher, assisted by Fragonard and Huet, devised a decorative scheme of trelliswork, statues and park views with birds and animals, which was painted in oil on canvas, laid down on panel, in about 1765. Figure 119 shows a wall of the room (now in the Musée Carnavalet) with a statue of Cupid with a crown of flowers painted on the door to the left by Fragonard, a statue of a Cupid with grapes painted on the door to the right by Boucher and overdoors

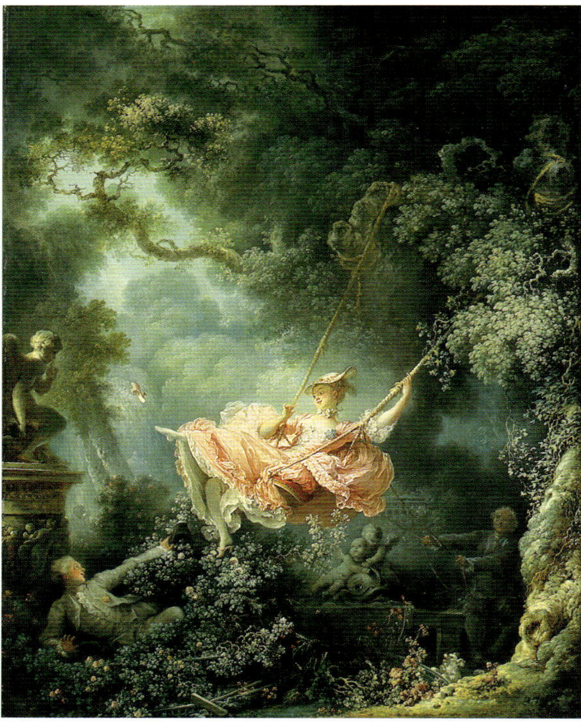

FIG.117
FRAGONARD, *The Swing*, 1767, oil on canvas, 81 × 64.2cm, Wallace Collection

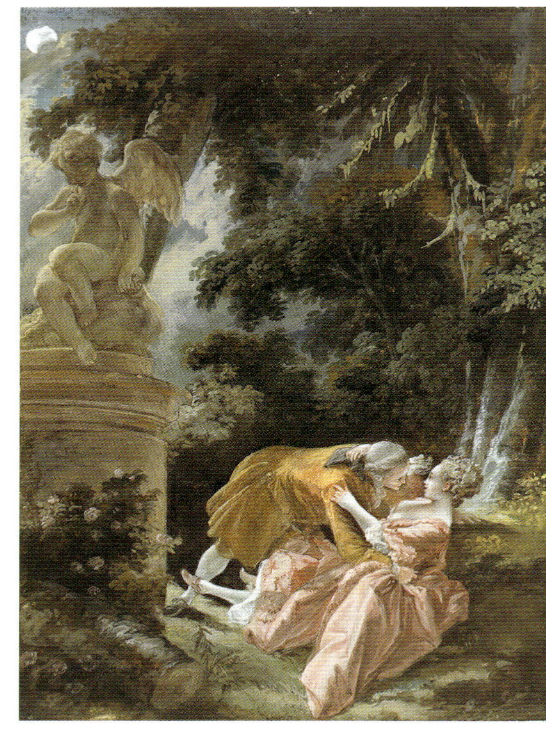

FIG.118 *right*
PIERRE-ANTOINE BAUDOUIN (1723–69), *The Night*, *c.*1767, gouache on paper pasted on board, 25.9 × 20cm, New York, The Metropolitan Museum of Art, Gift of Anne Payne Blumenthal, 1943 (43.163.20)

of doves and a wall panel with birds painted by Huet.[58] The decoration recalls that suggested in 1749 for the Queen's small *cabinet* at Versailles, where it was originally proposed that Oudry and Boucher should paint imaginary perspectives on the walls with trellis and foliage mixed with flowers, and that Boucher should also provide landscape and pastoral overdoors.[59] In the end, Oudry decorated the room with a series of canvases illustrating the five senses, but Boucher clearly did not forget the idea.[60] Walpole, who was also visiting Paris in 1765, noted the continuing vogue for garden design exclaiming 'I am in love with *treillage* [trellis] and fountains, and will prove it at Strawberry [Hill]'.[61] Demarteau's salon, although recalling much earlier projects by Huquier and Boucher, was still highly fashionable.[62] The collaborative nature of Boucher's working practice is further borne out by the fact that he may have taken his idea for the Cupid eating grapes, also engraved by Demarteau, from a statue by Pajou in his collection.

Affordable Visions

Demarteau became the main engraver and publisher of prints after Boucher in the 1760s, so by decorating his salon Boucher was helping create a congenial atmosphere where more of his own works might be purchased. In 1744, Gersaint had pointed out the potential of prints for selling art to the masses when he noted that 'one must be rich in order to make a delicate choice in pictures; drawings, whose appeal is all spirit, demand a profound knowledge if one is to be sensitive to them and to taste all their pleasure; but engravings are for all ages, all levels and all abilities'.[63] Charles-François Joullain maintained that they 'compensate for the inequality of fortunes by satisfying amateurs of every sort. Sovereigns, grandees and opulent men possess paintings and the public enjoys them in turn by way of an exact imitation acquired at little expense'.[64] As prints came to be seen less as souvenirs of an artist's oeuvre or as a useful repertoire for the decorative arts and more as cheap substitutes for paintings for the general

FIG.119
View of the salon of the engraver Gilles Demarteau (1722–76), *c.*1765, Paris, Musée Carnavalet

market they came to be displayed in a similar manner, framed on walls, rather than kept in portfolios by their buyers. The quantity of framed engravings in her posthumous sale proves that even a patron as wealthy as Madame de Pompadour found them a cheap and attractive way to cover the walls of her numerous properties. As the demand for such affordable imagery increased, so did the ingenuity of the print makers who devised new techniques for imitating the sensual effects of colour and handling seen in the original works of art.[65] Following the fashion for collecting Boucher drawings, in 1757 Delafosse and Magny, followed by Demarteau in 1759, produced their first engravings after Boucher in the new crayon manner, which imitated chalk drawings by printing in either red ink or in combinations of red, black and white ink. In 1762 Floding engraved an *Apollo and Daphne* and *A Guardroom* after Boucher in the new wash manner, imitating the effects of wash drawings, a process adopted by Fragonard's friend the abbé de Saint-Non, who produced a number of wash engravings after Boucher in 1766. The following year Bonnet and Demarteau started to print complicated multi-colour engravings after Boucher, imitating his pastel studies. Bonnet's

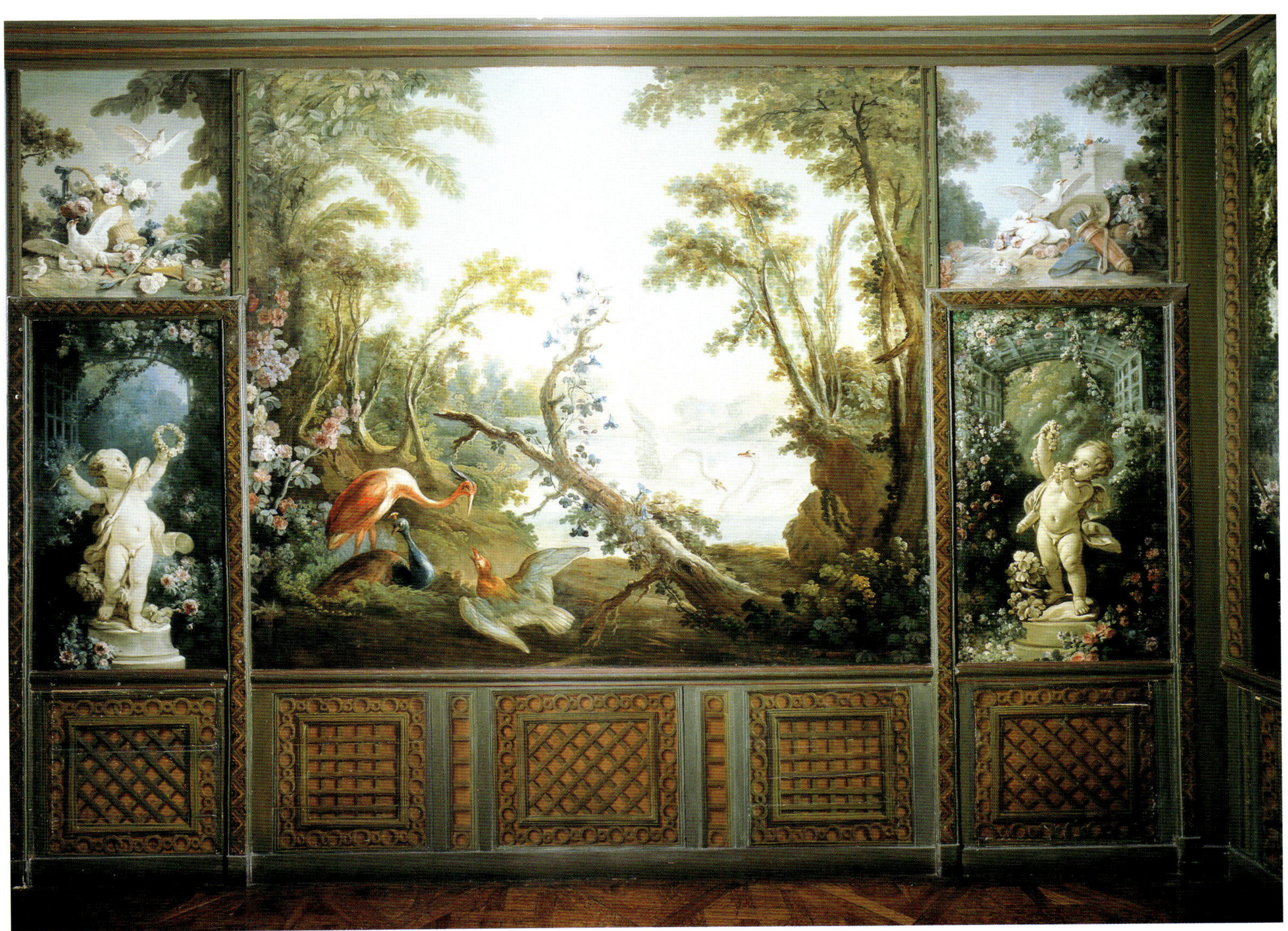

engraving of *Flora* (fig.120), printed in red, green, yellow, a variety of blues, black, tan, brown, white and pink inks is generally considered the masterpiece of the pastel manner and copies a pastel by Boucher, said to depict his daughter, Marie-Émilie, the year before her marriage to Baudouin (private collection).

The new engraving techniques are typical of the Enlightenment obsession with manufacturing, whereby technical advances increased commercial opportunities that in turn increased the wealth of the nation. The eighteenth-century market was fascinated with the translation of images via some technical process, which accounts for the popularity of framed tapestry pictures during the same period, a number of which after Boucher were listed in Madame du Barry's collection. The prints in the new chalk, pastel and wash manners, by virtue of their stress on formal ingenuity, also demanded an aesthetic rather than a narrative response from their audience. Thus, unlike black and white line engravings, the prints in the new manners were less likely to carry moralising inscriptions explaining their images, which in turn were deliberately chosen for their sensuality. At a time which saw a proliferation of printed erotic imagery,[67] Boucher's art provided a source of female nudes and head studies for engraving in the new manners, while the success of such prints also encouraged an increase in traditional engravings after Boucher's paintings.[68] By 1762, the *Mercure de France* was able to state that: 'Engravings after the famous Boucher, are very sought after today, and his taste seems to have become that of all the Amateurs'.[69]

The market for Boucher prints and that for Boucher's drawings were linked in the minds of commentators at the end of the eighteenth century. The abbé de Fontenay wrote that Boucher 'increased the number of his sought after drawings to over ten thousand, which the happy inventions of Demarteau have popularised even more'.[70] The situation had been different earlier in the century when Gersaint, hoping to encourage, via snobbery, a trend for collecting drawings, commented that 'there are few connoisseurs of drawings, which normally interest only those who have acquired the knowledge necessary to make them feel their beauty'.[71] Boucher, although encouraging the taste for drawings, by flooding the market with his work ultimately demystified them to his own critical detriment. Figure 121 shows a typical Boucher coloured chalk drawing of this period.[72] It relates to the figure of Venus in *Venus and Vulcan* (fig.104), one of his trademark sensual female nudes, which was drawn not in preparation for the picture, but copied from the canvas or an original figure study and carefully worked up as a presentation drawing for sale. Gersaint noted that connoisseurs were particularly attracted to 'carefully finished and coloured' drawings and Boucher's use of pastel at this period is aimed at the collector who wished to frame his drawings and display them in the same manner as the collector of prints.[73] Boucher has rendered his drawing still more presentable by sketching in a target with heart and arrows, clouds, doves and a cupid. Boucher also had a number of his drawings mounted in order to make them more attractive to potential buyers. In the 1760s he often employed the mounter, Jean-Baptiste Glomy, whose professional seal or mark appears on many Boucher drawings of this period.[74] Important collections of Boucher drawings were formed by private buyers, often from the wealthy financial classes, impressed not only by Boucher's work but also by his court connections as draughtsman and painter to Madame de Pompadour. They included men like M. de Sireul, whose collection was referred to as 'the Portfolio of M. Boucher', and the financiers, Blondel d'Azaincourt and Bergeret de Grancourt. Both Restout and Bret describe how 'for a long time the most discerning art-lovers besieged his studio and fought over his fine drawings of one or two figures which, being always so well thought out, so gracious, so svelte and piquant, would be sure to attract every gaze in their *Cabinets*'.[75]

Closely associated with the marketing of Boucher's drawings and prints was the production from the 1750s onwards of miniatures after Boucher models. Miniatures accorded perfectly

FIG.120
Louis-Marin Bonnet (1736–1793) after Boucher, *Head of Flora*, 1769, print in the pastel manner, 41.8 × 33.6cm, Washington, National Gallery of Art, Rosenwald Collection

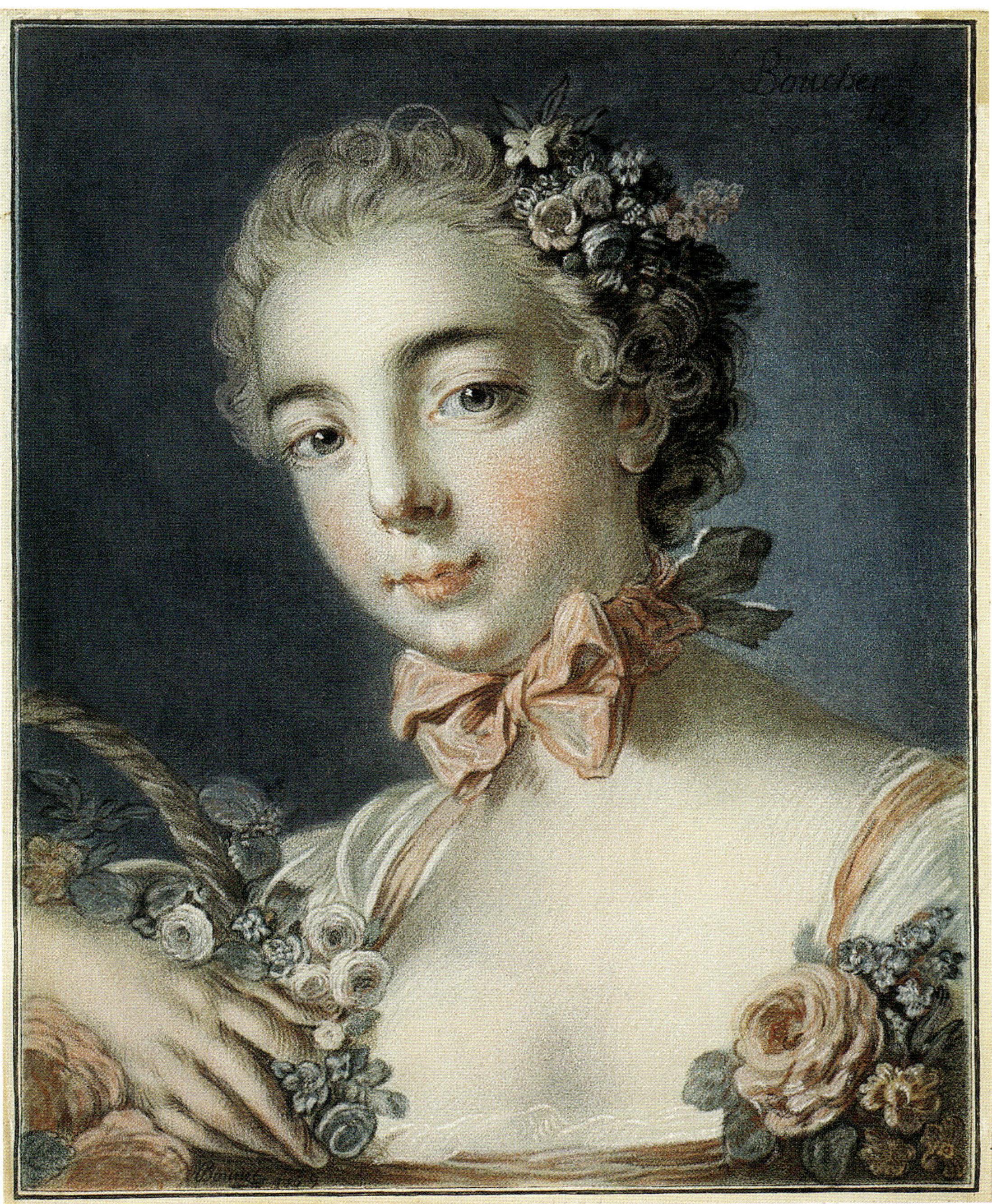

with the eighteenth-century love of the intimate, the gallant and the bijou. Goudar in *L'Espion chinois* extolled the virtues of the miniature as a portable pleasure, allowing one to imprison a beauty in one's pocket: 'whereas previously, two hearts united by love could not leave each other, if they wanted to be together, today a lover can leave his mistress a thousand leagues away, but still enjoy her company and even sleep with her'.[76] Boucher himself did not paint miniatures, but his wife did, and also made drawings and prints after her husband's work. Baudouin, similarly, was an accomplished miniaturist (see fig.139). Some of the finest re-interpretations of Boucher's work in miniature were done by Jacques Charlier (*c*.1725–1790), who is thought to have spent a period working in Boucher's studio in the 1750s and was linked with Boucher and described as 'hot-headed' by Natoire in 1754. Charlier's more ambitious works after Boucher, like *The Birth of Venus* (fig.122), appear to have been special commissions from collectors anxious to have small and exquisite reproductions of well-known compositions, in this case after a work known from an oil sketch in the Detroit Institute of Arts.[77] The miniatures which Charlier painted on a more speculative basis for the open market were simpler, generally depicting only a few figures, revealing a taste for the female nude paralleled by that in the print trade from the mid-1750s. Indeed most of the female nudes in his miniatures were also depicted (usually in reverse) in contemporary prints, both prints and miniatures deriving from models in Boucher's mythological paintings and figure drawings.[78] Miniatures by artists such as Charlier and Baudouin provided yet another way in which a wider group of collectors could afford a Boucher nude, while their small scale meant that they could be acquired by those without the space for large-scale decorative paintings. Painted for the private delectation of the connoisseur, the success of these miniatures can be gauged by the fact that they spawned many imitations, both in Boucher's day and during the rococo revival of the nineteenth century. Their widely varying quality and frequent anonymity suggest that they were bought as much for their subject matter as for the skill of the artist. The proliferation of such semi-pornographic imagery, obviously based on Boucher prototypes, further undermined Boucher's own reputation.

Criticising the Dream

In the early years of Louis XV's reign, artists, as the comte de Caylus complained, were held in low esteem by the aristocracy who 'regard the glory of talent as the merit of the vulgar and applaud them as *inferior* qualities which cease to be acceptable in a distinguished rank'.[79] It was only when Boucher was in his late forties that the salons of Paris began to open their doors to artists, and that a gentlemen like the marquis de Marigny 'made it his job to live in the milieu of artists, and to communicate with them, less as a superior than as a friend'.[80] This encouraged social and intellectual ambition amongst the new generation of artists and critics, reflected in the chevalier de Valory's lecture to the Academy in 1763 on the question of 'Whether it is more advantageous for artists to live in retreat or in the commerce of the world?' His answer was overwhelmingly yes to the latter, but the ideal milieu defined by Valory was very different from the free society that had existed under the Regency in Boucher's youth. Boucher belonged rather to the '*bureaux d'esprit*' or witty gatherings described as old-fashioned by journals such as the *Nouvelle Bigarrure* of 1754. Valory's ideal society was, in contrast, a more serious didactic affair – a gathering of 'taste', based on the utilitarian ideal of salon society in the second half of the eighteenth century, where men of high birth and high talent learned from each other, and raw talent was polished into a more useful and socially acceptable form.[81] The 'new men' of the cultural elite who attended salons such as Madame Geoffrin's found the ageing Boucher's Regency humour uncouth. It was in vain that Restout claimed that the envious, unable to attack his work, had censured Boucher because of his love of pleasure and that 'he never used the resource of seduction. He knew how to respect innocence and *honnêteté*, and he was never out of place even in the best of company; his tone was always very decent; his candour, his gaiety and his witty remarks often rendered his company as correct as it was agreeable'.[82] Marmontel still prudishly complained that Boucher had 'inspiration in his imagination, but little truth, and even less nobility; he had not met the graces in a good place; he painted Venus and the Virgin from back-stage nymphs; and his language and pictures revealed the mores of his models and the tone of his studio'.[83] At the end of the eighteenth century, Mercier considered the artisans the happiest of all the classes: 'gaining a living from their industry and

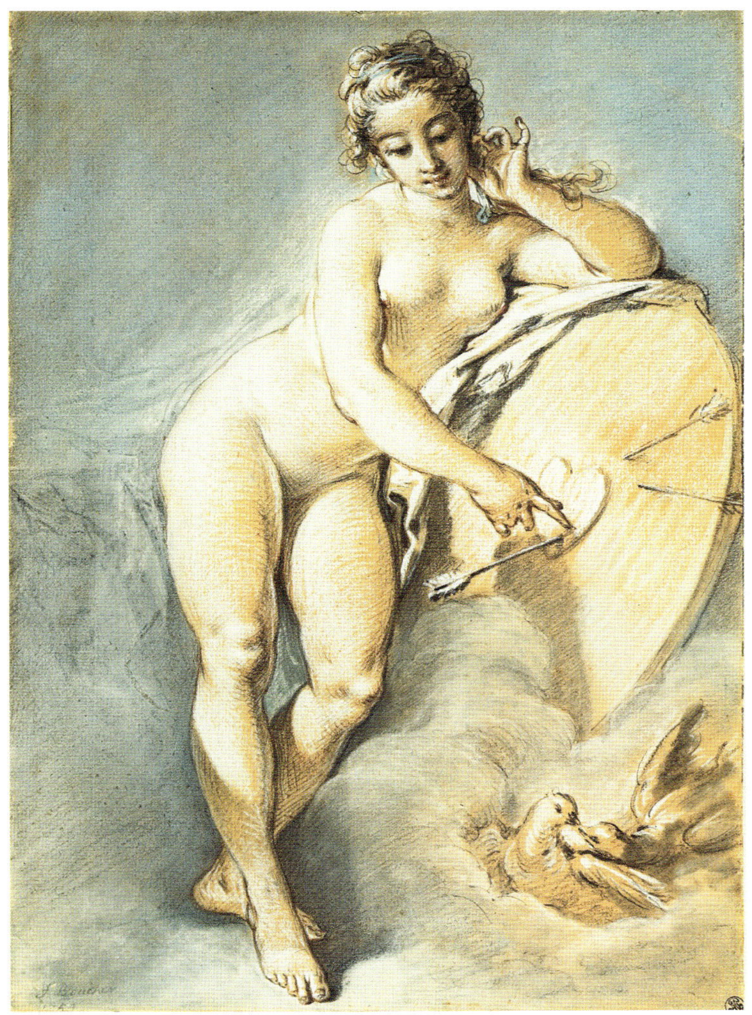

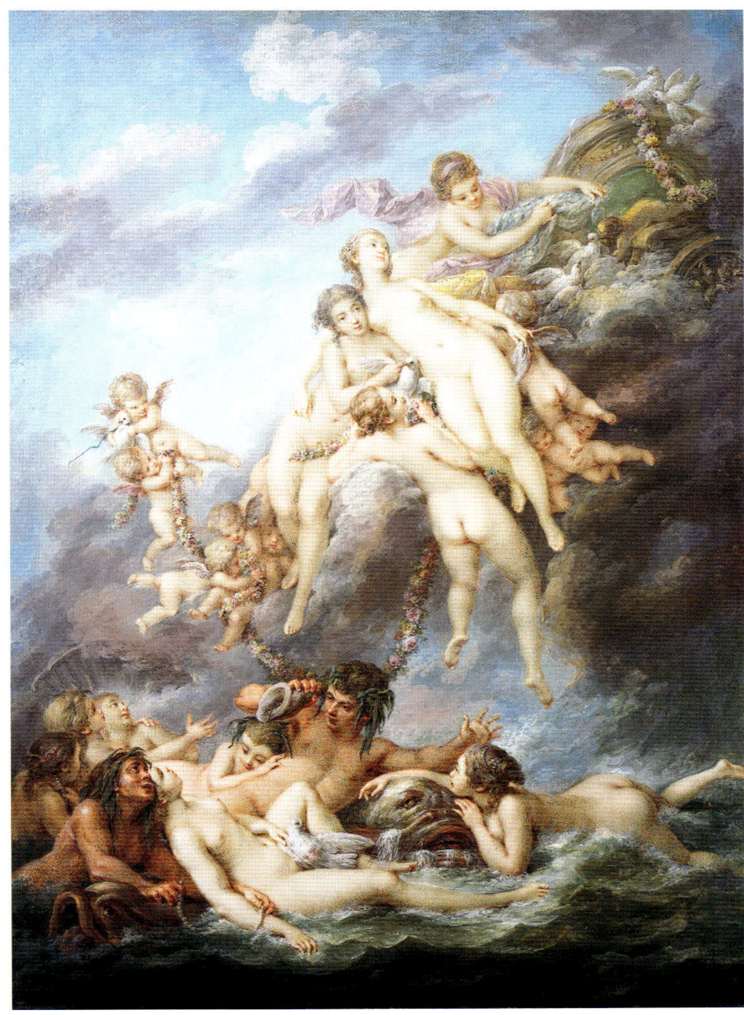

FIG.121
BOUCHER, *Venus*, 1754, black chalk and pastel on light brown paper, 42.8 × 30.3cm, photograph courtesy of Christie's

FIG.122 *above, right*
JACQUES CHARLIER (*c.*1720–1790), *The Birth of Venus*, *c.*1770, gouache on vellum stretched over laminated board, 65.7 × 50.6cm, Wallace Collection

manual dexterity, they stay in their place, which is wise and extremely rare'.[84] Despite the jibes of the younger generation, Boucher, although coming from this class, had moved far beyond it. His artistic preoccupations, way of life, interests and even his old-fashioned manners were marks of the gentleman, but a gentleman of an earlier time. Remy stresses this last point in his introduction to the Boucher sale catalogue, saying that however much one was struck by the extraordinary beauty of Boucher's collection one was seduced even more by the '*honnêteté*, natural politeness, affability, fine wit and cheerfulness of the owner'.[85]

At the same time the debate about what art was and for whom it was intended, became increasingly imbued with moral overtones. Thus the *connaisseur* was criticised as a practitioner of art whose judgement was affected by manual considerations of craft and the *curieux* as an untutored enthusiast, while the *amateur* was upheld as the true art-lover, combining a love of painting with superior taste and cultural and intellectual discernment.[86] Critics, lacking the wealth to form extensive collections themselves, were frustrated by the inaccessibility of private collections and thereby moved to criticise private patrons and private styles of art such as Boucher's. One such commentator noted of the Randon de Boisset sale that 'at least the public will see his pictures which he kept locked away'.[87] Similarly, Boucher, who by this date had an established clientele for his work and was in no need of the publicity offered by the Salon, was attacked for his lack of enthusiasm for exhibiting to the public. He was accused of 'affectation' by the *Observateur littéraire* in 1759, for example, when his one exhibit, a *Nativity*, was not included in the Salon *livret*.[88] When he showed no works in 1767 Diderot wrote scathingly 'What! Monsieur Boucher, you to whom the progress and the presence of art should be especially dear in your capacity as First Painter to the King, is it at the moment you obtain this title, that you give your first slight to one of our most useful institutions, and that because of the fear of hearing the hard truth?'[89]

Meanwhile, natural disasters like the Lisbon earthquake (1755) and man-made crises like the Seven Year's War (1756–63) provoked frustration at the moral vapidity of the age. In the ensuing debate over French nationalism, some looked back with nostalgia to the time of Louis XIV, while others saw medieval France as worthy of emulation.[90] At the same time contemporary art, of which Boucher's paintings were the quintessential expression, was attacked by writers like Rousseau for being feminine and superficial in its concentration on pleasure and its failure to celebrate great men or virtue.[91] In *Émile* Rousseau stated that the only justification of painting was to give moral lessons through the visual embodiment of history.[92] A similar sense of moral responsibility was at the heart of the cult of *sensibilité*, which suffused Rousseau's best-selling novel, *Julie, ou La Nouvelle Héloise*, where the reader was moved by the emotional outpourings of the lovers, Julie and her tutor Saint-Preux, but edified by Julie's rejection of her lover in favour of her father's choice of husband.[93] *Émile* further stressed the importance of the family as the basis for a moral society and focused on the part that children and their education should play in ensuring society's future. All this coincided with a condemnation of the intimate type of architecture Boucher's paintings had often been designed to embellish. Thus Mercier deplored the fact that 'architecture, once majestic and which did not demean itself, has been subjugated to the licence of our mores and our ideas. It has anticipated and satisfied all the intentions of debauchery and libertinage; the secret passage-ways and hidden staircases are in the taste of some popular novel. Finally, architecture, complicit in our disordered way of life, is no less licentious than our erotic poetry'.[94]

Diderot's vivid accounts of the *Salons* (1759–1781), the forerunners of modern art criticism, further attacked the lack of relevant and edifying subjects in contemporary painting.[95] Diderot felt that art should be true to nature and emotionally engaging. He exhorted artists to 'look in the streets, gardens, markets, houses, for that is where you will get the right idea of the true movement and action of life'. 'Modern moral subjects', such as *The Village Betrothal* (1761; Louvre), of the genre painter, Jean-Baptiste Greuze were the visual embodiment of Diderot and Rousseau's ideals. 'Now this is moral painting ... Has not the brush been consecrated to debauchery and vice long enough? Should we not feel satisfied at last to see it dealing with dramatic poetry to touch us, to teach us, to correct us to virtue?'[96] Although Greuze's sentimental images of children and of the sexual awakening of young girls may now appear ambiguous and mawkish, for contemporaries they were a moving visual testimony to the growing social conscience of the age, which eventually prompted reforms such as the abolition of child-labour and slavery. To Diderot, fired by his mission to re-establish the didactic rôle of painting, Boucher's amoral sensualities and formal aesthetic approach were dangerously subversive. He was forced to recognise Boucher's talent, but, as it was directed to an aesthetic of pleasure with which he fundamentally disagreed, he interpreted its allure as misleading and even corrupting.

Diderot's first extensive criticism of Boucher appeared in response to the latter's exhibits at the Salon of 1761. His delight in the artist's painterly ability, despite himself, comes across very clearly in his description of the landscapes and pastorals, which included the Wallace Collection's *Shepherd and Shepherdess* (fig.115): 'What colours! What variety! What richness of objects and ideas! ...

There is no part of his compositions which, separated from the others, does not please you; the ensemble even seduces you'. But this powerful attraction exasperated him and made him condemn Boucher's untruthfulness all the more: 'That man has everything except truth' and 'One asks oneself: But where has one actually seen shepherds dressed with such elegance and luxury? ... What a din of disparate objects!' The danger as Diderot perceived it was that, despite one's rational repulsion, 'one cannot leave the picture. It fixes you. One comes back to it. It is such an agreeable vice, an extravagance so inimitable and rare! There is so much imagination, of effect, of magic and of facility!' Diderot also censured that elite audience which had a taste for Boucher: 'he is made for turning the heads of all sorts of people ... who are strangers to true taste ... how could they resist the prominence, the libertinage, the brilliance, the pompoms, the breasts, the buttocks, the epigrammatic style of Boucher'. While he might admit that 'no-one understands the art of light and shade as does Boucher', this technical merit had no virtue for Diderot when not directed to moral ends. Diderot poured scorn on Boucher's fellow artists, who, admiring how Boucher 'has surmounted the difficulties of painting and for whom this is the only merit understood by them, bend their knees before him. He is their god.'[97]

As the decade advanced Diderot delivered ever more frenzied warnings against the seductive falsehoods of Boucher's works, even stooping to spite and libel in the process. During Boucher's lifetime Diderot's salon criticism was read only by the select subscribers to Baron Grimm's *Correspondance littéraire*, including rulers such as Frederick the Great and Catherine the Great. This may have increased the author's sense of impunity because it probably took some time for the objects of his attacks to become aware of them. In 1763 he railed against Boucher's 'abuse of talent! What a waste of time! ... but how can one say that to a man corrupted by flattery and praise of his talent, he would just disdainfully raise his head'. He goes on: 'this man will be the ruin of all young students of painting. They hardly know how to a wield a brush or hold a palette before they torment themselves enchaining garlands of putti, painting puffed up pink bottoms, throwing themselves into all sorts of extravagances, unredeemed by the warmth, originality, amiability or magic of their model: they only have his defects'.[98] Diderot claimed that Boucher's sexuality was too obvious to attract him: 'That man there only takes up his brush to show me tits and arses. I am quite happy to see them; but I can't bear having them shown to me'; he actually reveals a fascination with Boucher's nudes all the more prurient for being repressed.[99] Diderot excused his own salivating descriptions by couching them as moral condemnation, inventing an immoral persona for Boucher and using the sensuality of his pictures as evidence. Thus, in 1765 Diderot responded to Boucher's pastorals, landscapes and an earlier version of *Jupiter and Callisto* (see fig.127), with the exasperated comment 'I do not know what to say about that man there. The degradation of his taste, colour, composition, characterisation, expression, and drawing follows step by step the depravity of his morals. What would you want this artist to throw down on canvas? That which he has in his imagination. And what can he have in his imagination, such a man who has spent his life with prostitutes of the lowest order?' Having compared Boucher to the libertine writer Crébillon *fils* he admits that 'he is not an idiot, however. He is a false good painter, as one can be a false fine-wit. There is no thought in his art; only concepts'.[100] However, Diderot's criticism was neither as impartial nor as concerned with realism as he would have us believe: while criticising Boucher's other works in the same Salon he inexplicably changed direction and praised four of his pastorals. These he describes as 'a charming little poem' demonstrating that 'the painter for once in his life had a moment of reason'.[101] Diderot's *volte-face* is explained when one reads in the Salon *livret* that the pictures belonged to the celebrated salon hostess, Madame Geoffrin, whose power to make and break reputations could not be ignored, even by Diderot. Diderot was back on scurrilous form in 1767 when, despite Boucher's absence from the Salon, he did not hesitate to libel the artist's wife: 'Didn't we see in the Salon seven or eight years ago, a woman, completely nude, stretched out on some pillows, one leg here, another there, presenting the most voluptuous head, the finest back, the most beautiful thighs, ... No offence to Boucher who didn't blush to prostitute his wife, from whom he painted this voluptuous figure'.[102] Boucher's *Gypsy Procession, or Caravan in the taste of Benedetto di Castiglione* (Boston), his last Salon exhibit, shown in 1769, prompted the usual conflicting responses and caused Diderot to remark spitefully that 'the old athlete didn't want to die without exhibiting himself once more in the arena'.[103]

Return to the Grand Manner

In 1768 Gabriel de Saint-Aubin cheekily noted that 'If Boucher in his sweet pastiches/ Refrains from harsh accords/ It's out of pity for the rich/ And out of love of their treasure'.[104] In the 1760s, however, Boucher was stimulated by the criticism of his work to experiment with new themes and styles more in keeping with the increasingly moral and classical attitude of the times. He was probably also spurred on by his omission from the list of painters (Carle Van Loo, Pierre and Restout) commissioned to produce a series of grand history paintings for Frederick the Great of Prussia in 1757, and by his failure to be named First Painter to the King in 1762, when Carle Van Loo was appointed to that coveted position, vacant since the death of Charles Coypel in 1752. Such factors help explain the stoic subject and return to the baroque manner of his youth seen in Boucher's surprising oil sketch of *The Death of Socrates* (fig.123).[105] In 1762 this theme had been set as the subject for the *Prix de Rome* competition in which Boucher's son took part. The competition was won by another of Boucher's pupils, Saint-Quentin, and it was perhaps post-competition discussion in his studio that inspired the ageing artist to try the subject. The bravura handling of the *grisaille* recalls Boucher's youthful studies influenced by Castiglione (fig.18, 20–21), to whose example he again returned while aiming to demonstrate his ability in more serious, monumental canvases such as *The Rest on the Flight into Egypt* (1757; Saint Petersburg) and a *Halt at a Spring* (exhibited 1761; Boston).[106] The louring foreground, the dramatic subject and the characterisation of the standing bearded figure on the left of *The Death of Socrates* also remind us that Boucher increasingly studied and collected the works of Rembrandt during this period. Towards the end of his life he produced a number of figure drawings of Rembrandtesque turbanned men and women in exotic dress, sometimes drawn in a scratchy pen and ink manner deliberately imitating Rembrandt's own technique.[107] Boucher evidently shared his enthusiasm for Rembrandt with his pupils and assistants: two copies by Fragonard after Rembrandt *Holy Families* were listed in Boucher's collection after his death and these in turn may have inspired Boucher's own *Peasant Family* of 1762 (private collection).[108]

The same serious approach and grand manner are also found in an oil sketch of *The Marriage of the Virgin* (fig.124), once thought to be by Boucher but now attributed to his pupil and son-in-law, Deshays.[109] Deshays worked closely with Boucher at the beginning of the 1760s and both artists seem to have influenced each other. Although Deshays eschewed the light subjects favoured by his father-in-law, concentrating on weighty historical themes such as his *Iliad* tapestry series designed for Beauvais in 1761, his style as seen in this sketch was heavily influenced by Boucher. The fact that Diderot's quarrel with Boucher arose from the artist's subject matter rather than his technique is also demonstrated by Diderot's unreserved admiration for Deshays whom he regarded as an 'inspired prophet'. Unfortunately, Deshays's premature death in 1765 and Fragonard's specialisation in light-hearted genre left no artist capable of continuing Boucher's formal aesthetic and applying it to the new moralising subjects.

Boucher finally attained the coveted position of

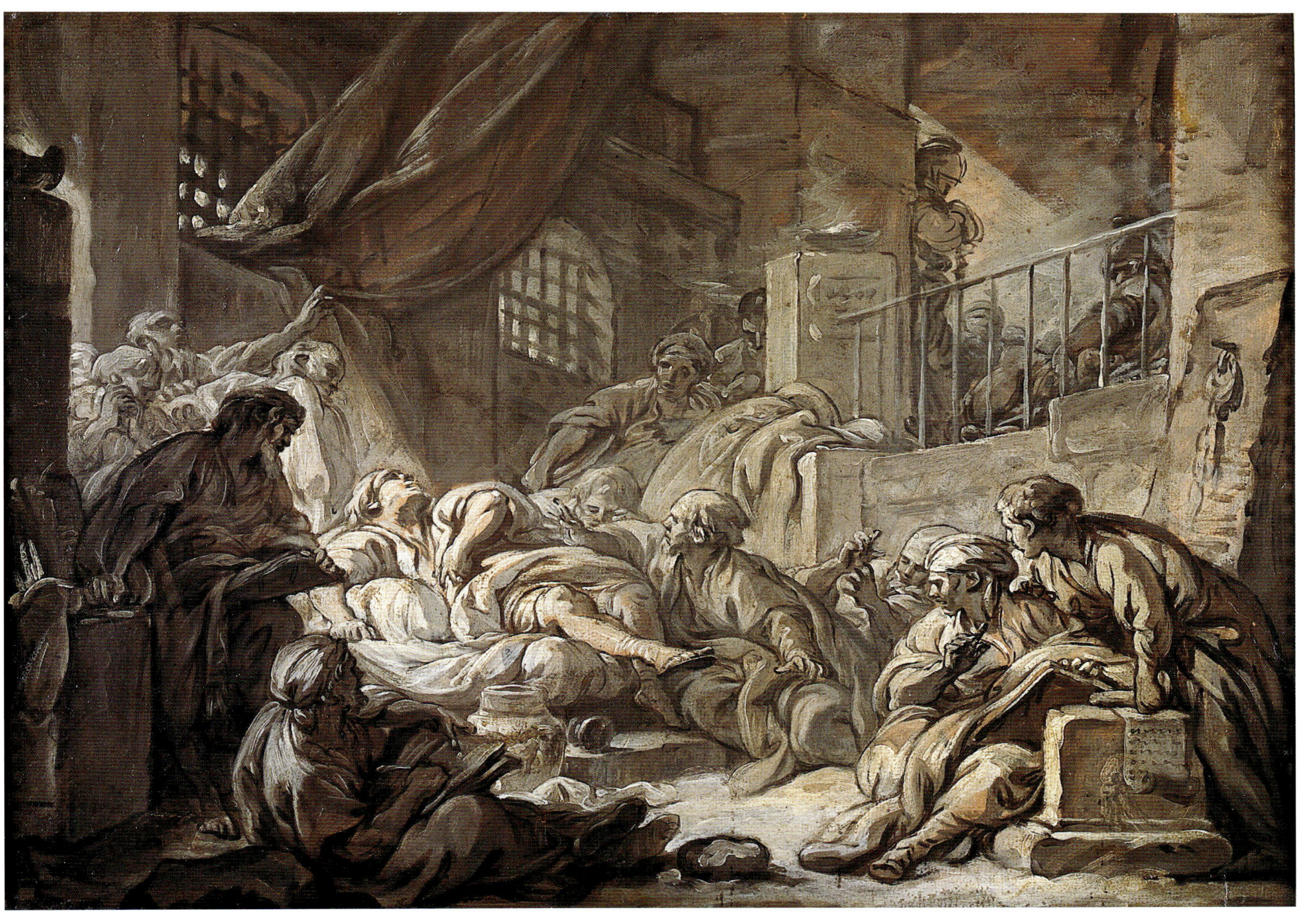

FIG.123
BOUCHER, *The Death of Socrates*, *c.*1762, sketch, oil on canvas, 41 × 55cm, Le Mans, Musée Tessé

First Painter on the death of Van Loo in 1765. The position had been a long time coming and, according to Restout, 'when he was presented to the King, this Prince, who had apparently judged his age from the warmth and vivacity of his works, was astonished to find him much older than he had imagined. 'Sire' replied Boucher, 'the honour with which your Majesty is covering me will rejuvenate me'.[110] Such old-fashioned gallantry did not earn Boucher ennoblement like other holders of the office, such as Louis de Boullogne, the Coypels, and Van Loo before him or Vien after. He was, however, awarded the previous incumbent's pension of 6,000 *livres* and his pension of 1,200 *livres* as Inspector of the Gobelins was continued, despite the fact that the post now passed to Pierre.[111] Pierre, meanwhile, showed 'nothing at the Salon this year. It is said that it is out of disappointment at seeing M. Boucher named First Painter to the King'.[112] Pierre was not the only one disappointed, as Diderot complained 'and so! My friend, it's at the moment when Boucher ceases to be an artist that he is named First Painter to the King'.[113] The artistic community, however, generally felt Boucher's new honour was merited and he was immediately voted Director by the Academy as well. A poem by Bret stressed Boucher's merit, originality and probity: 'Intrigue with its hidden

FIG.124
JEAN-BAPTISTE DESHAYS (1729–1765), *The Marriage of the Virgin*, c.1763, sketch, oil on canvas, 104 × 62cm, Douai, Musée de la Chartreuse

FIG.125 *opposite*
BOUCHER, *The Continence of Scipio*, c.1765–7, brown chalk, brush and brown and grey wash heightened with white with touches of pen and ink, 40.5 × 25.9cm, Quimper, Musée des Beaux-Arts

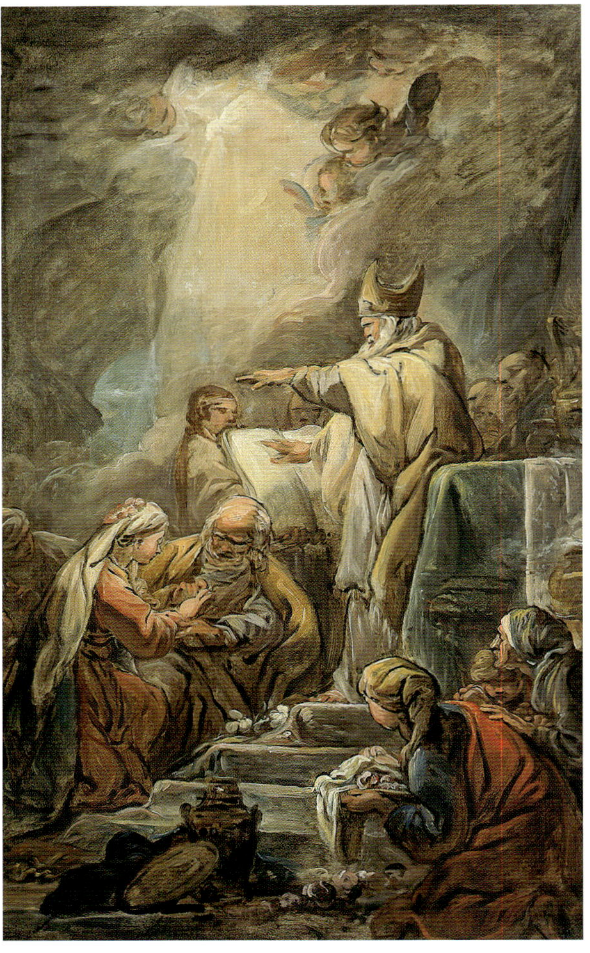

face, agitating cabal; will no longer find any opportunity ... Boucher, you disdain from following any footsteps;/ You walk alone; your brilliant daring/ Serves as example and rule; A thousand divine pictures have consecrated your rights;/ And as the Painter of the Graces/ You are also the most beloved by Kings'.[114] Even Natoire, writing to Marigny from Rome, said he was 'charmed that my colleague Boucher replaces M. Vanloo'.[115]

Walpole, who was visiting Paris the same year, noted that 'the *bon ton* here is to be grave and learned' while 'Crébillon is entirely out of fashion, and Marivaux a proverb: *marivauder* and *marivaudage* are established forms for being prolix and tiresome'.[116] In this context Boucher probably felt obliged to try and paint the new type of improving history considered appropriate to his position. An opportunity came with a commission in 1766 to paint one of four Roman histories for Madame Geoffrin's protégé, the newly elected King of Poland, Stanislas Poniatowski.[117] Boucher was requested to paint *The Continence of Scipio* and figure 125 shows the last of a series of drawings elaborating his ideas on the theme.[118] It combines the brown chalk manner often used in his late drawings with the use of pen and ink inspired by his study of Rembrandt.[119] Compared to the earlier drawings in the series, it also demonstrates how Boucher was attempting to invest the scene with increased monumentality and fashionable classical detail, such as the bas relief on the base of Scipio's throne. Boucher did not, however, find the task easy and this, combined with the constant interference of Madame Geoffrin, forced him to abandon the work. Diderot recounts how '*A Continence of Scipio* was commissioned from Boucher; but one wanted this, one wanted that, and then again this; in short, our artist was peppered with so many suggestions that he refused to work. He is wonderful to hear on the subject'.[120] When Prince Galitzin approached Boucher, on behalf of Catherine the Great of Russia, for a similar subject a couple of years later, Diderot wrote to Falconet that 'It is no good expecting anything ... from Boucher, who is flighty, old, and lazy ... It will cost the Empress money – but less than it did the King of Poland – and I hope that she will be better served. That is because we let artists go their own way, whereas Mme Geoffrin wants them to go hers. It was to remove himself from her despotism that Boucher, who was originally charged with painting *The Continence of Scipio*, passed on the commission to Vien'.[121] There is, nevertheless, some irony in the fact that the projects the 'Painter of the Graces' was working on when he died included a *Mausoleum*, a series of decorations for the palace of the archbishop of Paris and a *Presentation in the Temple* (sketch 1770; Louvre).[122]

As early as 1756 Grimm, however, had expressed doubts regarding the grand manner, which Boucher's late attempts at serious histories employ, as an appropriate style for the new

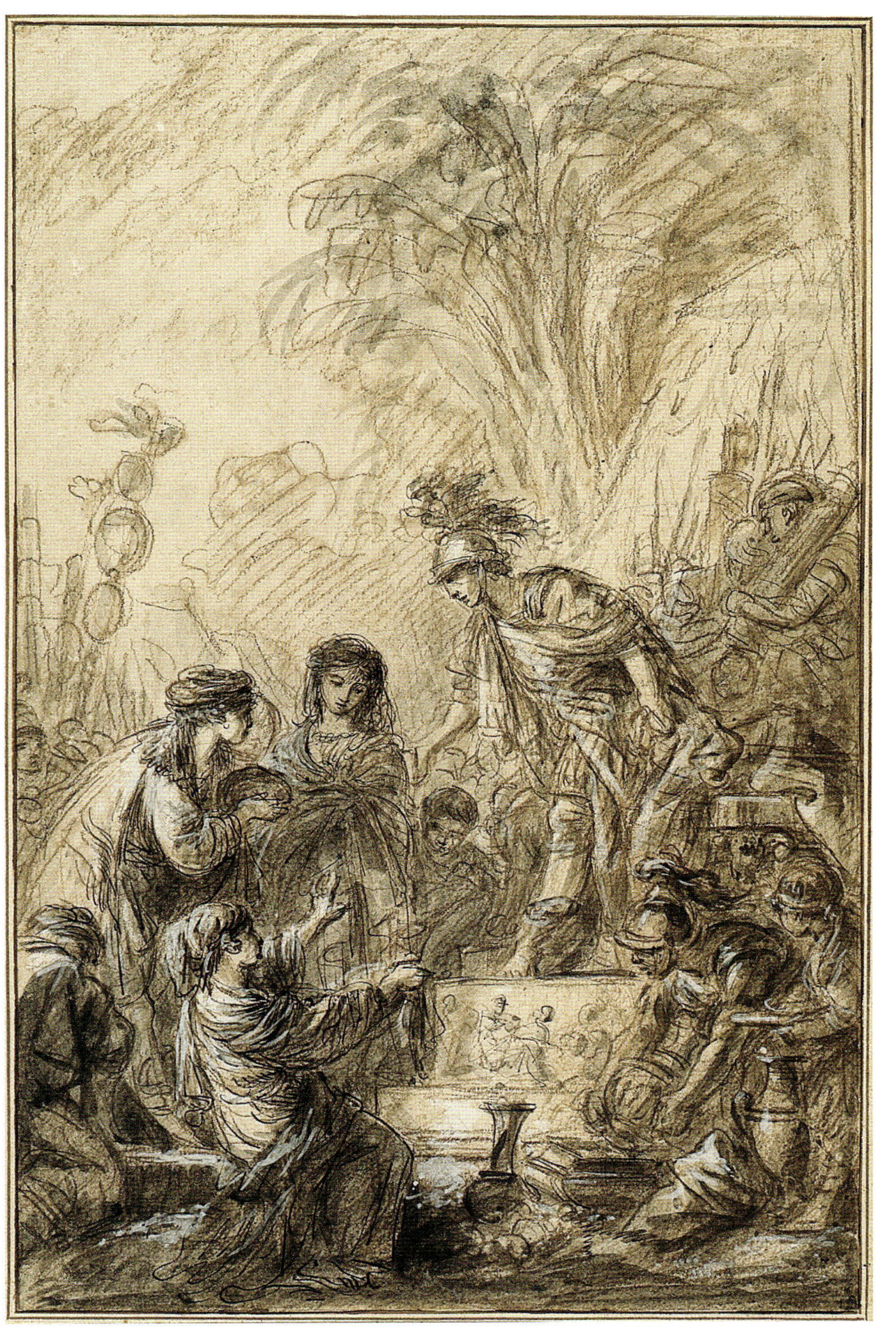

moralism. He called instead for 'simplicity of subject and unity of action'.[123] At the same time an alternative 'neo-classical' style, recalling antique ornament, was appearing in the decorative arts, while interest in ancient Greece and Rome increased.[124] In 1769, when attempting to gain admittance to the Academy as a history painter, Greuze exhibited a number of classical subjects in the Salon, including the first eighteenth-century French painting to marry classical form with an edifying subject from classical history: *Septimius Severus and Caracalla* (1769; Louvre). His attempt was ahead of its time and his application was rejected. Boucher apparently thought it looked like a bas-relief rather than a painting, thus revealing that he drew a distinction in his own mind between what was appropriate to fine art and to the decorative arts. For Boucher the power of painting resided so much in its visual sensuality that he was incapable of recognising that a rejection of such effects might produce a more arresting image. The didactic moral vision of neo-classical history painting was also a world away from that of the ageing sensualist artist. He might sympathise with the desire to produce more lasting and monumental art, leading to the grand manner and scale of some of his last canvases, but it seems unlikely that he identified with the moral zeal of his younger compatriots. So it was left to his young kinsman, David, to find the perfect fusion of classical form and moral message in his *Oath of the Horatii* (1784; Louvre).[125] Every bit as attention grabbing as Boucher's *Hercules and Omphale* (fig.22), David's picture marked the death of the Boucher aesthetic in painting.

Nonetheless, the neo-classical style was another fashion that Boucher was very happy to incorporate into his own designs for the decorative arts, as in his spirited chalk drawing for a clock for the marquis de Marigny (fig.126).[126] The same group of caryatids also served as the basis for an engraving in the new wash manner by Demarteau, transformed into statues holding a disc observed by spectators with a classical temple beyond.[127] Boucher also devised a series of classically-inspired statue, tomb and vase designs during the same period including a *Vase Design with Putti* (*c*.1761–62; present whereabouts unknown) which inspired Clodion to produce a model on which a white marble vase, *c*.1790, in the Wallace Collection is based.[128] Interestingly, Boucher's own collection also included wall lights and candelabra in the neo-classical taste.[129]

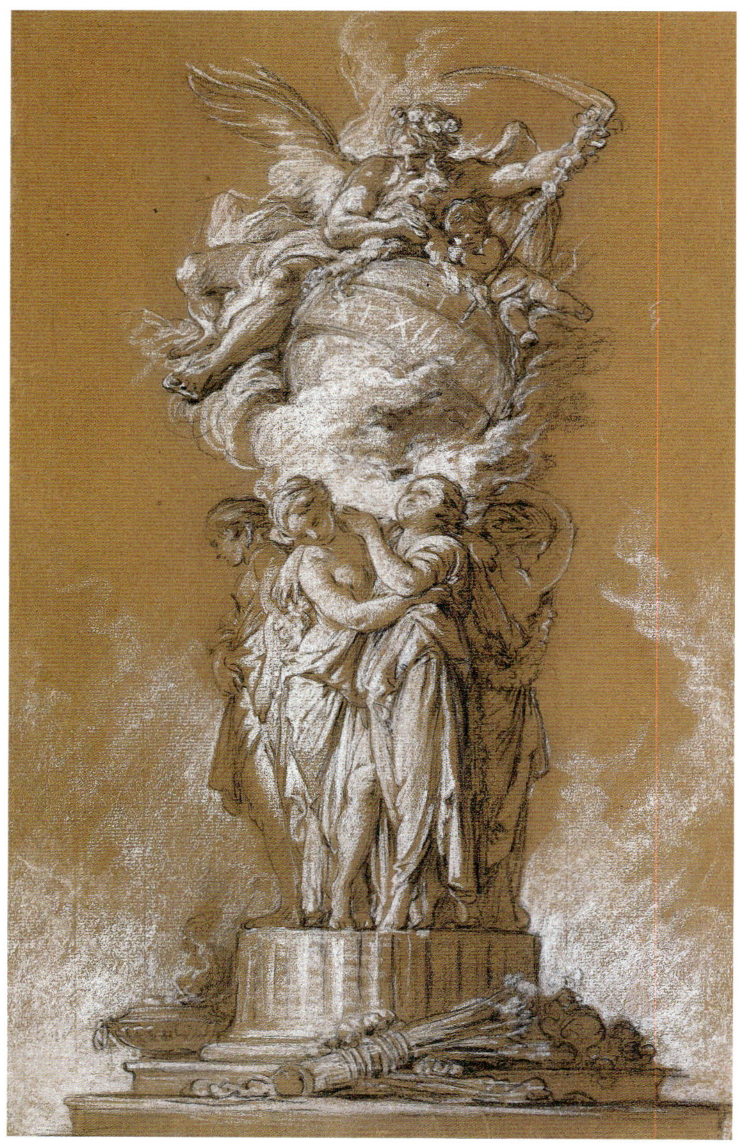

Death of the Artist

In 1768 Boucher, increasingly infirm, resigned his position as Director of the Academy. In 1769, as a new mistress, Madame du Barry, was presented at Court, Boucher was made an honorary member of the Academy of Saint Petersburg. That same year his son-in-law Baudouin died and Boucher painted the *Jupiter and Callisto* (fig.127) in the Wallace Collection which relates to a series of pictures on the same theme painted in the 1760s.[130] The subject also appears in one of the medallions of the *Boucher Tapestry* devised by Boucher and Jacques (see fig.137).[131] Although not neo-classical in itself, the *Jupiter and Callisto* in the tapestry, framed in an oval medallion suspended on a pink background embellished with flowers, birds and cornucopia, recalls the appearance of eighteenth-century classical print rooms and medallion decorations at Pompei. In 1770 Boucher received payment from the prince de Condé for an oval painting of *Jupiter and Calypso* [*sic*] which might be identified with the Wallace Collection's picture. The picture's sloppy execution demonstrates how Boucher's eye problems were now affecting his work. As Restout commented: 'his last compositions, tend towards purple, and his flesh-tints seem to reflect the effects of a red curtain: he excused this weakening of his sight himself by explaining that he saw only an earth colour where others saw vermilion'.[132] The tortoiseshell and silver lorgnette and the tortoiseshell magnifying glass listed in his sale catalogue probably had a practical as well as ornamental value.[133]

In 1770, the year of Tiepolo's death and Marie-Antoinette's marriage to the future Louis XVI, Boucher died in his apartment in the Old Louvre at five in the morning on 30 May. He was buried the following day in the artist's church of St-Germain-l'Auxerrois. Witnessing the scene were his son, Juste-Nathan, his grandson, François-Jean Baudouin, Charles Etienne Cuvillier, the chief clerk of the Royal Buildings who went on to marry Marie-Émilie Boucher, and the elite of the Academy: Pierre, who was to become Boucher's successor as First Painter to the King, Vien, a future Director of the Academy in Rome and First Painter to the King and Louis-Michel Van Loo, the only surviving member of that band of students with whom Boucher had set off for Rome some forty years earlier. Although a pension of 1,200 *livres* was accorded to Madame Boucher, it was significantly less than Carle Van Loo's widow had received five years earlier and she had to move out of the spacious apartment in the Old Louvre. But as Boucher's estate was worth over 150,000 *livres*, she was not in any immediate hardship. Boucher left no will and no detailed inventory was made of

FIG.126 *opposite*
BOUCHER,
Design for a Clock, *c*.1766,
black chalk, heightened
with white on brown paper,
49.5 × 30.5cm, Paris,
Musée des Arts Décoratifs

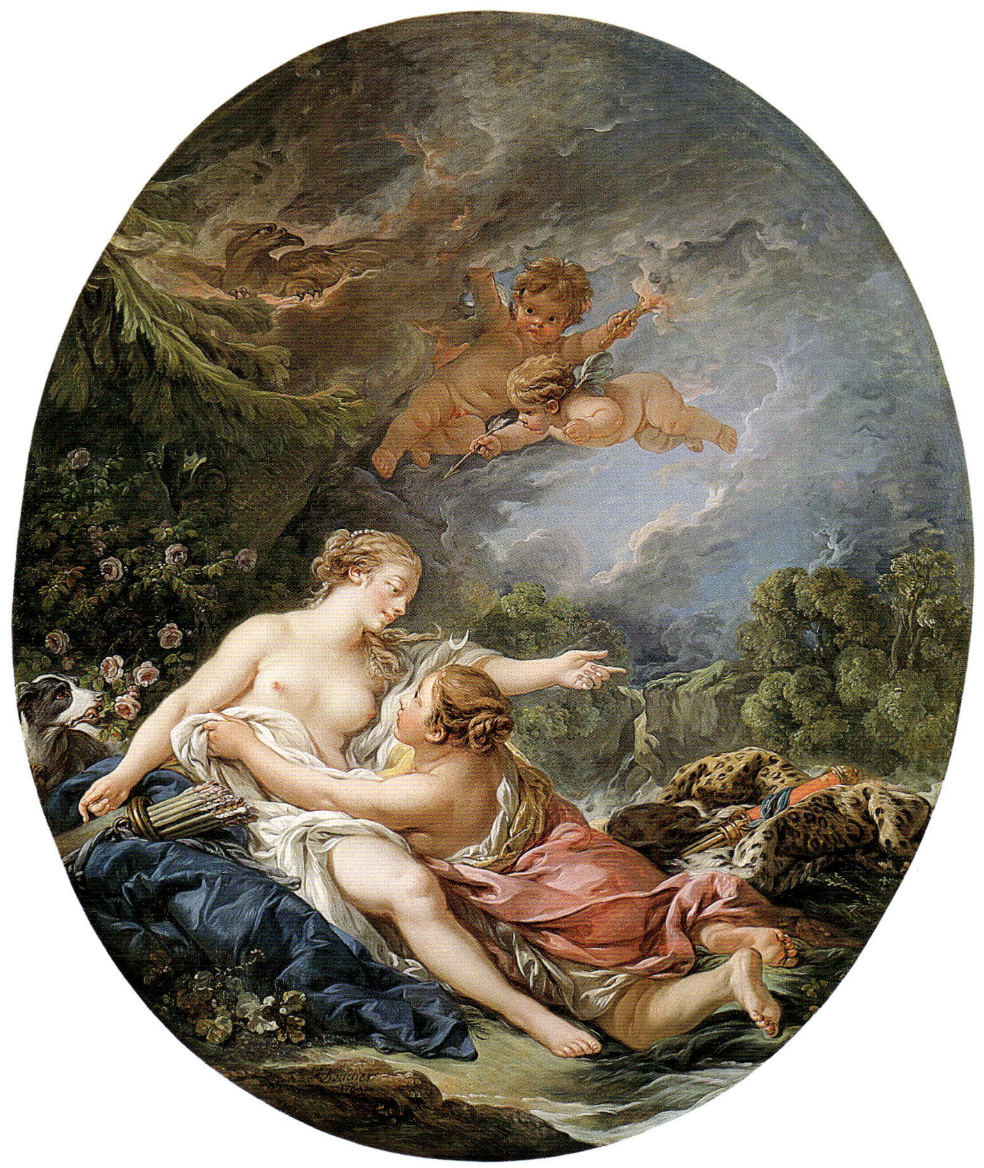

FIG.127
BOUCHER,
Jupiter and Callisto, 1769,
oil on canvas, 160 × 129cm,
Wallace Collection

the estate, implying that the family was close and unlikely to quarrel over the succession. The debts Boucher owed at the end of his life provide a poignant testimony to the life of the artist. In addition to the sums his estate owed to the organisers of the sale of his collection the following year, Boucher owed money to his patron Bergeret, to a framer, an upholsterer, an engraver, a merchant, a locksmith, a carpenter and a timber merchant as well as to his tailor, his wig-maker and to the two doctors who had attended his last illness.[134] Even the painting utensils included in his sale reflect his affluence: they included a pigment box in the shape of a cabinet with eleven drawers and a marble top, a porphyry stone for grinding his colours, a mahl stick with an ivory handle and a 'well-conditioned' camera obscura.[135] Comparing his humble beginnings to his comfortable end Boucher provides us with one of the most striking examples of Mercier's observation that by the end of the eighteenth century 'man, more than ever is the *noble* son of his works'.[136]

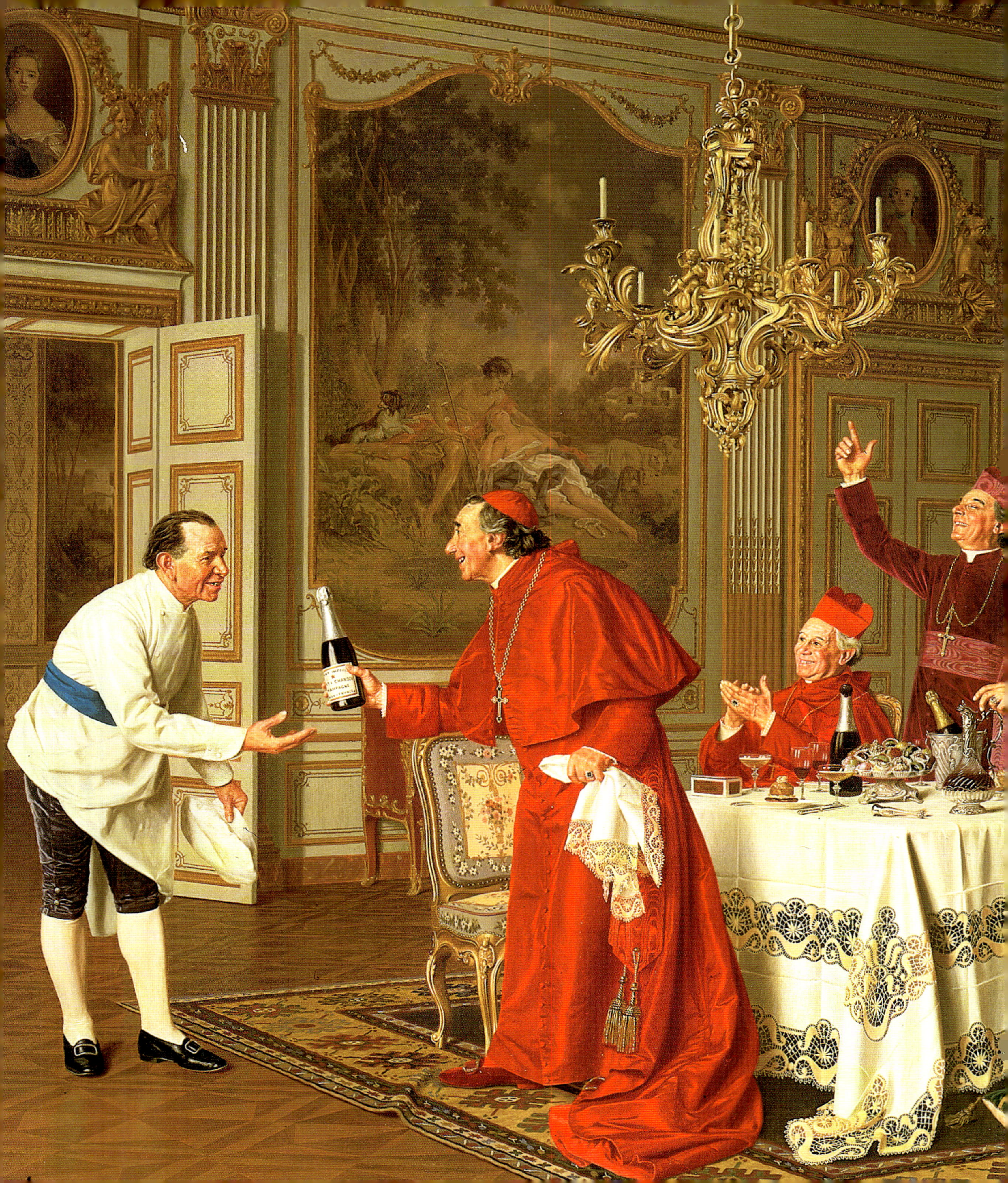

VI

This man unique in his spirit of depravity; who seems to have sharpened his crayon or ground his colours only to charm the eyes of vice GAULT DE SAINT-GERMAIN

Reputation and Reaction: Boucher's Legacy to the Present Day

'I am upset by the death of M. Boucher' Natoire wrote to the marquis de Marigny on 27 June 1770: 'it is a real loss to the Academy, and to me of an old school fellow, to whom I was very close'.[2] The regret at Boucher's death expressed by other friends and colleagues seems to have been profound and genuine. Wille described a poignant last visit to Boucher's collection before its sale in 1771, noting that 'I saw him gradually form this magnificent *Cabinet*, being friends for around thirty years with M. Boucher, whose death I still regret'.[3] Meanwhile Jean-Augustin Jollien des Boulmiers, another friend, ended his obituary of the artist published in the *Mercure de France* by saying 'we can never throw enough flowers on his tomb, which the arts and friendship will continue to cover with tears'.[4] In 1771 two more glowing accounts of the artist's life and work appeared: by Restout in the *Galerie Françoise* and by Bret in the *Nécrologie*.[5] The former emphasised Boucher's 'poetic invention: a rare and precious talent, that he received from nature', while both authors cited *The Setting* and *The Rising of the Sun*, acquired by Monsieur de Saincy at Madame de Pompadour's sale in 1766, as the foremost examples of his art. Boucher was also eulogised in Blondel's *L'Homme du monde Éclairé par les Arts*: 'few artists have composed as many works as he. He had all the talents: and he painted in all the genres … He formed more than one excellent student, yet left no-one who could replace him exactly and compensate us for his loss. He has been universally regretted by both lovers of art and by artists'.[6] Gabriel de Saint-Aubin, meanwhile, paid tribute to his mentor by drawing the cupids and graces weeping hysterically in front of a medallion of the elderly artist as they admired his last works.[7] Even Grimm had to admit that 'in the state in which our School finds itself, his death is a very great loss'.[8]

The Diffusion of Boucher's Idiom

As Blondel observed, none of Boucher's students or followers ever came close to equalling the breadth of their master's talent, but tended to specialise in one or two of the areas formerly treated by him. Julliar, Fragonard and Huet continued to produce landscapes and pastorals, Fragonard also painting memorable examples of the gallant genre, while the exotic was continued in the Russian subjects of Le Prince. A variety of Boucher's followers specialised in mythologies and nudes, including the miniaturist Charlier. Boucher's legacy as a prolific draughtsman was taken in a new direction by Saint-Aubin, while Brenet and Ménageot, although painting in a manner very different from Boucher, specialised in grand histories and religious works. The survival of Boucher's style as an idiom for decorative painting, such as overdoors, is borne out by Taraval's (1729–85) *The Waking of Cupid* (fig.129) and Jollain's (1732–1804) *Sleeping Cupid* (fig.130).[9] These two pictures were in marked contrast to the neo-classical subjects both artists exhibited at the Salon in the 1780s, and were commissioned by the Crown to decorate Queen Marie-Antoinette's bedroom at Marly in 1781. It is worth noting that Boucher's ubiquitous putti

FIG.128 *facing previous page*
ANDREA LANDINI (1847–1912), *The Chef's Birthday*, *c*.1900, oil on canvas, 71.6 × 90.9cm, detail, photo. courtesy of Christie's

FIG.129 *right*
HUGHES TARAVAL (1729–1785), *The Waking of Cupid*, 1781, oil on canvas, 95.5 × 142.7cm, Wallace Collection

FIG.130 *opposite*
NICOLAS-RENÉ JOLLAIN (1732–1804), *Sleeping Cupid*, 1781, oil on canvas, 95.7 × 142.7cm, Wallace Collection

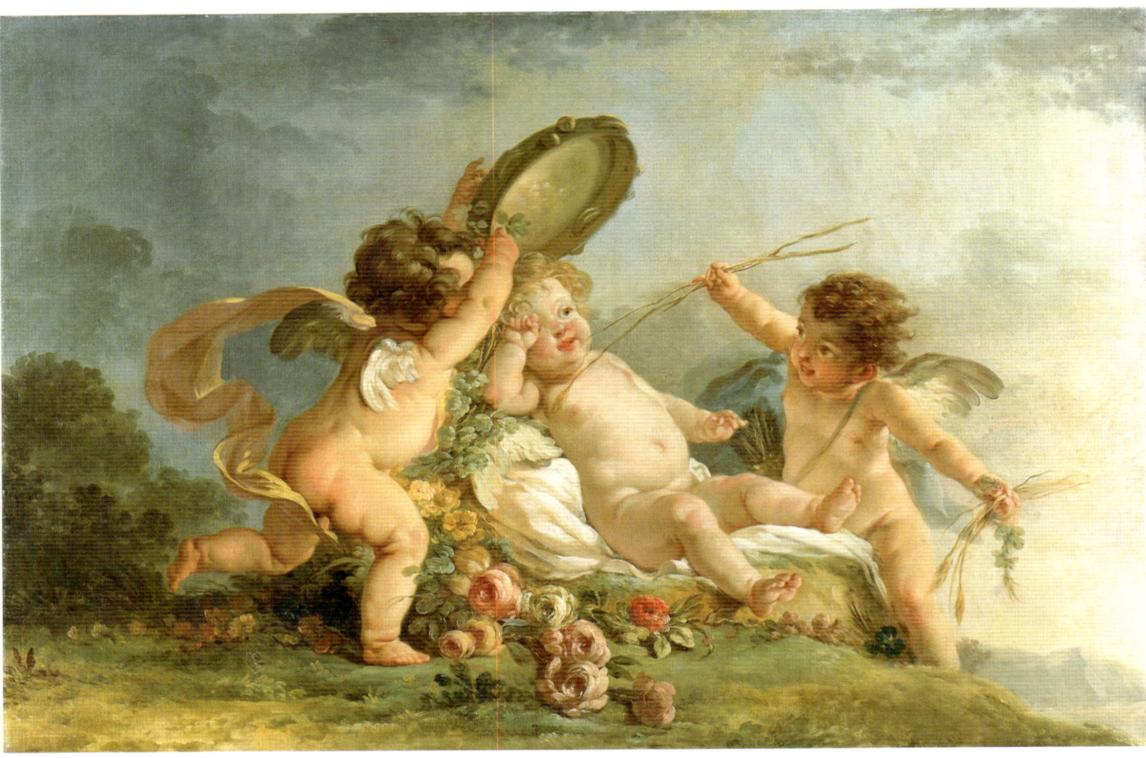

gained even wider currency via Bernard's engraving of Boucher-like *Children* which illustrates the volume of plates on *Drawing* in Diderot and D'Alembert's *L'Encyclopédie*.[10] Meanwhile the small canvas of *Danaë* (fig.131), the daughter of the king of Argos who was seduced by Jupiter in the form of a shower of golden rain, demonstrates the continuing popularity of Boucher's sensual nudes.[11] The composition copies a Boucher drawing and reappears in a miniature in the manner of Charlier in the Wallace Collection.[12] The artist, however, has subtly changed the proportions of the body, making it more elongated and the head smaller, thus recalling the female nudes of Jollain, such as *The Toilette* and *The Bath* in the Musée Cognacq-Jay, Paris.[13]

Boucher's influence on tapestry design was continued by Huet and Le Prince, who provided designs for Beauvais and Aubusson. *The Dance* (fig.132) was woven at Beauvais after designs made by Huet in 1780 for a series of *Pastorals with Blue Drapery and Arabesques*, but its composition is clearly derived from Demarteau's 1769 engraving after Boucher called *The Dance*.[14] This was also copied onto a Sèvres plaque, probably painted by Dodin *c*.1777, which was in turn added in the 1820s to a secretaire by Adam Weisweiler (1744–1820) in the Wallace Collection.[15] Le Prince and Huet's designs for the new textile factory opened by Oberkampf in 1759 on the river Bièvre ensured the wide and lasting diffusion of the Boucher decorative idiom.[16] Their Boucher-inspired shepherds and shepherdesses were reproduced in line designs in blue, red or green on white or cream cotton cloth, derivatives of which continue to delight interior decorators today under the now generic title of *toile de Jouy*. As in the *Boucher Tapestry* series, Boucher's designs, out-moded in the fine arts, continued to be a popular source for the decorative arts, often embellishing neo-classical forms strangely at odds with their Boucheresque decorations. Figure 133 shows a Sèvres garniture of three neo-classical vases, produced about nine years after Boucher's death, decorated with scenes after Boucher, including the *Autumn Pastoral* (see fig.75), *The Schoolmaster* (drawing, Vienna) and the

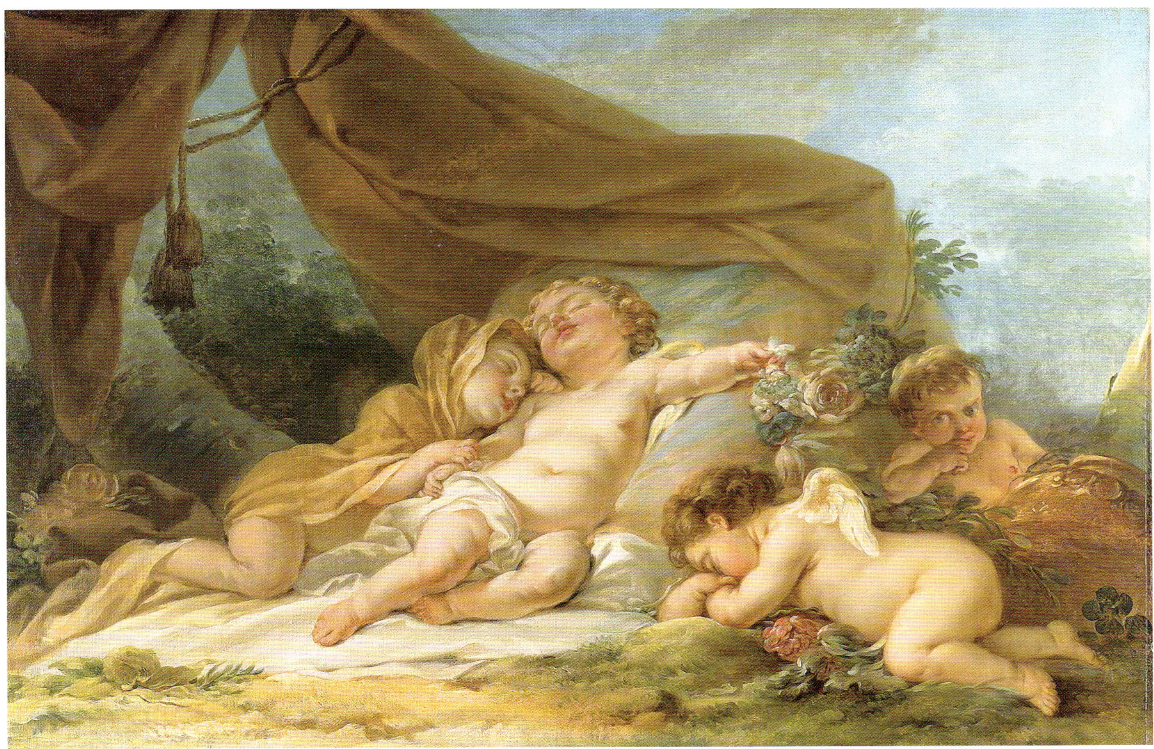

Agreeable Lesson (1748; Melbourne).[17] The Sèvres factory continued to re-use Boucher motifs well after the Revolution, as is shown by a cup and saucer of 1792 in the Wallace Collection, which incorporates designs after Boucher's illustrations to Ovid's *Metamorphoses* (1767–71), the most important source of Boucher designs after his death.[18] Although figurative design was not common in marquetry furniture during the eighteenth century there are nevertheless a few examples which also follow Boucher, including a lacquer secretaire attributed to René Dubois (*c.*1770–75; New York) and a neo-classical commode of *c.*1775 by Christophe Wolff with decoration derived from Huquier's engravings after Boucher's chinoiserie *Senses* and *Elements* (fig.134).[19]

Boucher, Britain and the first three Marquesses of Hertford

Soon after Boucher's death Caraccioli extolled the influence of French culture in Europe, praising its wit and explaining that 'the Frenchman without his lightness would not have charmed Europeans, would not have seduced them'.[20] Boucher, the definitive visual exponent of such *légèreté*, never felt the need to leave Paris or work abroad, but his decorative paintings, exported to Scandinavia and Germany, nevertheless inspired imitations, as seen in a series of overdoors with putti by Johann Heinrich Tischbein (1722–89; Kassel and Schloß Wilhelmsthal).[21] The international taste for gallant mythology, which Boucher did so much to encourage, also lies behind an atypical mythology by Johann Zoffany (1733–1810), *The Triumph of Venus* (fig.135), painted in Trier in 1760 before he moved to Britain where such fanciful subjects never caught on in the fine arts.[22] Otherwise the British, after showing some interest in Boucher's early Dutch and Flemish-inspired cabinet pictures, took virtually no interest in his paintings.[23] The nascent British school was centred on the production of portraits, one of Boucher's least favourite branches of painting, and the two nations were at war for much of the eighteenth century. Anti-French sentiment was rife among artists like Hogarth who

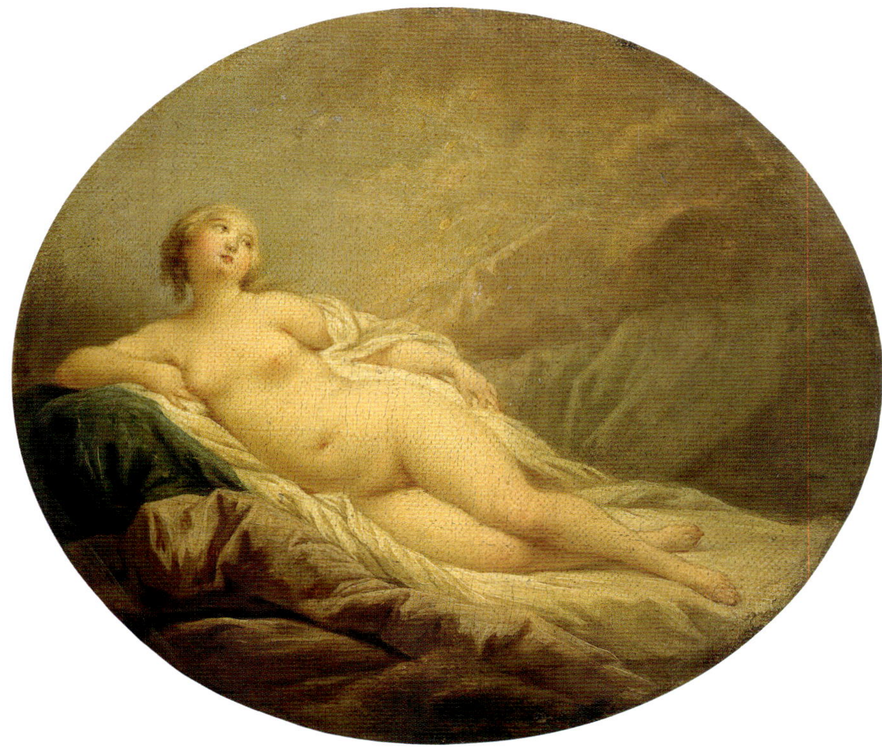

FIG.131 *above*
Attributed to JOLLAIN, *Danaë*, oil on canvas, 19.3 × 22cm, Wallace Collection

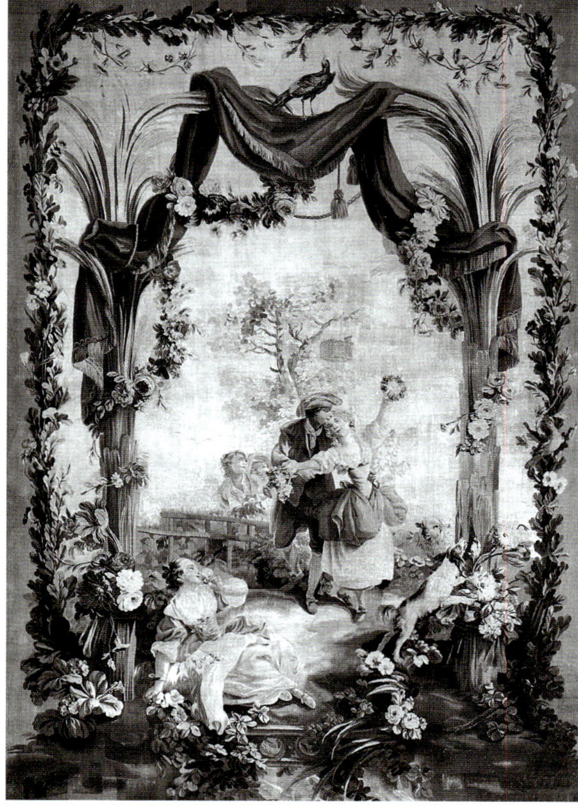

FIG.132 *right*
After JEAN-BAPTISTE HUET (1745–1811), *The Dance*, after 1780, wool and silk Beauvais low warp tapestry, 310 × 212cm, from the series of *Pastorals with Blue Drapery and Arabesques* designed in 1780, Paris, Musée du Petit Palais

were keen to assert the independence of the British School, eventually leading to the foundation of the Royal Academy in 1768.[24]

The 1st Marquess of Hertford (1719–94), one of the founders of the Wallace Collection, served as British Ambassador in Paris 1762–65.[24] There he met Madame de Pompadour in 1763 and described her as 'most polite and obliging, with a great deal more sense and conversation than I had expected'.[26] Lord Hertford would have been familiar with Boucher's work but, despite acquiring the obligatory Canaletto views of Venice like so many others who went on the Grand Tour, he was not tempted to commemorate his Parisian stay with a purchase from Boucher, preferring to commission portraits of his family from Reynolds back in England.[27] Shortly after Lord Hertford's appointment was terminated, but while he was still resident in Paris, he acted as host to Horace Walpole, who took care to visit Boucher's famous collection during his stay. The same year the collector, Charles Rogers, who acquired thirteen drawings by Boucher, also visited the elderly artist in Paris.[28]

In 1768, the year that Boucher relinquished his Directorship of the Academy, Joshua, later Sir Joshua, Reynolds (1723–92) became the first Director of the new Royal Academy in London and also visited Boucher in his studio. We have already noted Reynolds's shock at seeing Boucher painting from imagination. He later noted in his *Discourses* that 'our neighbours, the French, are much in this practice of *extempore* invention, and their dexterity is such as even to excite admiration, if not envy; but how rarely can this praise be given to their finished pictures! The late Director of their Academy, *Boucher*, was eminent in this way'.[29] Although Reynolds did not consider Boucher a good example for the young painters to whom his *Discourses* were directed, he nevertheless conceded that 'even in the lower class of French painters great beauties are often found united with great defects ... The modern affectation of grace in his [Coypel's] works, as well as in those of Boucher and Vatteau [*sic*], may be said to be separated, by a very thin partition, from the more simple and pure

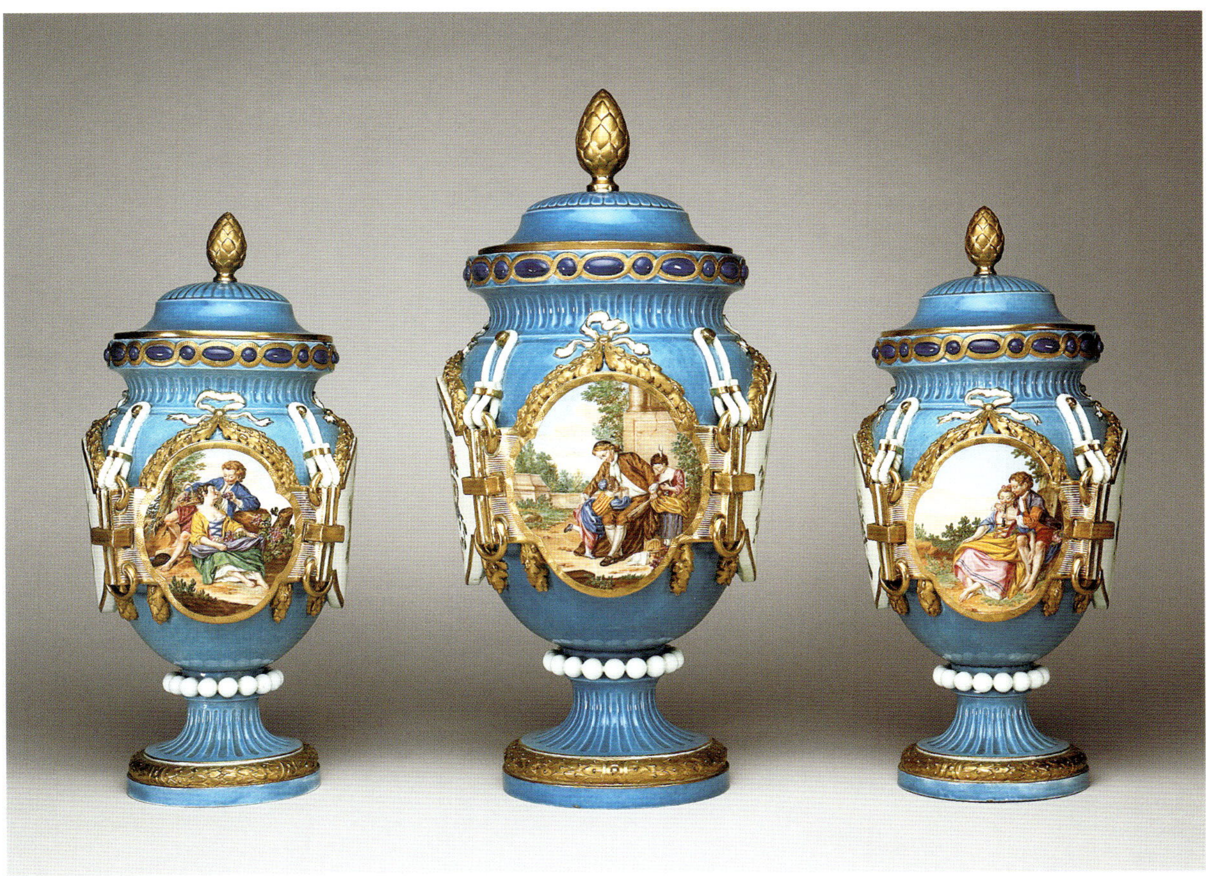

FIG.133 *right*
Garniture of three vases and Covers, *c.*1779, soft-paste Sèvres porcelain, the largest height 42.4cm, width 19.2cm, Wallace Collection

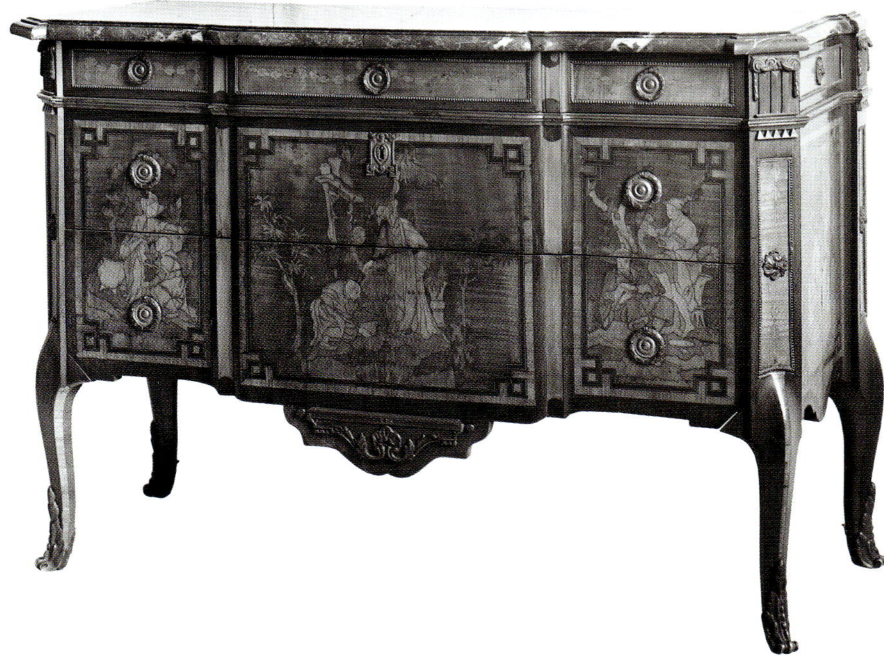

FIG.134 *below*
CHRISTOPHE WOLFF (1720–1795), commode with marquetry panels derived from HUQUIER's engravings after BOUCHER of *The Senses* and *The Elements*, *c.*1775, height 91cm, length 130cm, width 56cm, Paris, Musée des Arts Décoratifs

grace of Correggio and Parmeggiano'.[30] Reynolds was perhaps thinking of *Young Woman with two Cupids and a Vase on the Extrados of an Arch* (fig.136) when he made this comment. The drawing is one of at least five Boucher drawings owned by Reynolds and would have appealed to his love of Italian art, as it appears to have been inspired by a drawing in Boucher's collection by another Italian mannerist, Primaticcio.[31]

In general, the British preferred to take their Boucher watered down via the decorative arts. One of the most prominent examples of this was the success the Gobelins *Boucher Tapestry* enjoyed in England. Figure 137 shows the set commissioned in 1763 by the 6th Earl of Coventry to decorate his tapestry room at Croome Court, Worcestershire. Croome Court was a grand house in the latest neo-classical taste, designed by Lancelot 'Capability' Brown (1718–83) with interiors by Robert Adam

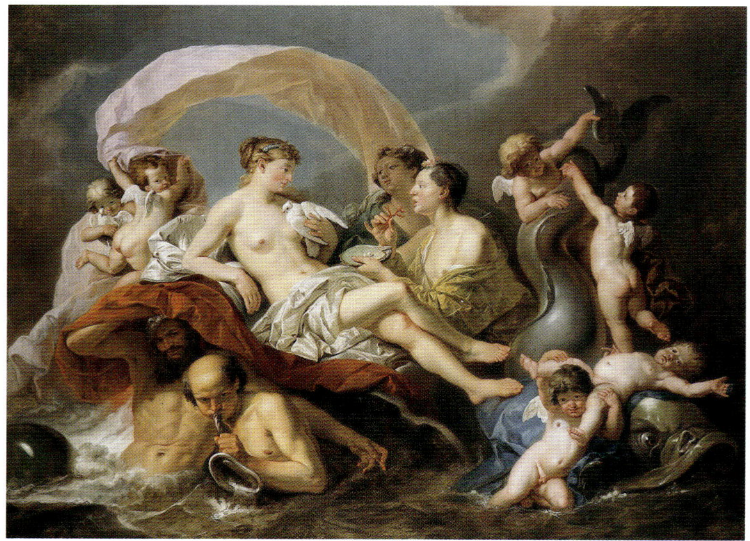

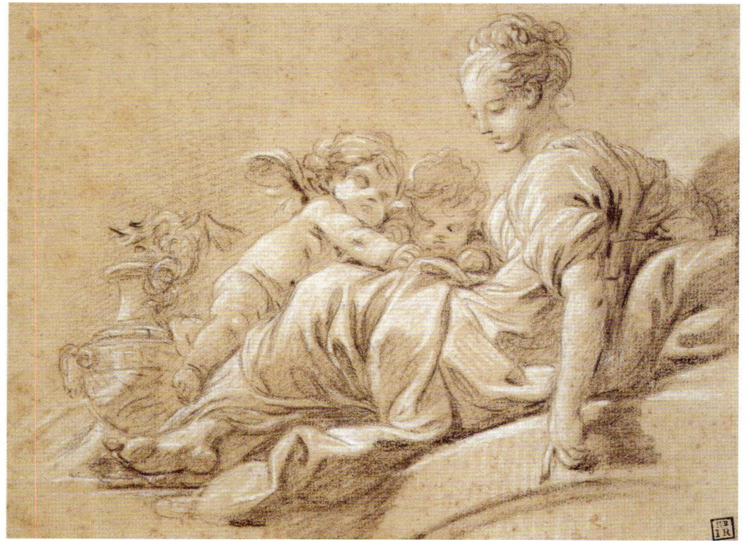

FIG.135
Johann Zoffany (1733–1810), *The Triumph of Venus*, 1760, oil on canvas, 125 × 171cm, Bordeaux, Musée des Beaux-Arts

FIG.136 *above, right*
Boucher, *Young Woman with two Cupids and a Vase on the extrados of an arch*, c.1768, dark red chalk heightened with white, 22.2 × 29.2cm, Boston, Museum of Fine Arts

(1728–92). The tapestries were delivered in 1771 and with their innovative medallion design were considered the perfect complement to Adams's interior, which incorporated a plasterwork ceiling with a central medallion and a matching circular carpet on the floor. Similarly, the ovals of the chair backs echoed those in the tapestries and the seat furniture was covered in matching Gobelins designs. The *Boucher Tapestry* became the ultimate accessory for those wishing to embellish a perfect Adam interior and, of the thirteen sets woven between 1764 and 1789, six went to England.[32] A similar trend is seen in the collecting of Sèvres by the British in the latter part of the eighteenth century. British porcelain manufactories in competition with Sèvres had already adopted Boucher motifs as seen, for example, in a pair of Bow groups, *c*.1748, in the Metropolitan Museum, New York, which are after Aveline's engravings of Boucher's chinoiserie *Fire* and *Air*.

Despite showing no interest in Boucher's paintings, the 2nd Marquess of Hertford (1743–1822) inadvertently helped diffuse Boucher's imagery when his wife acquired a Sèvres cup and saucer, *c*.1770, with figures after Boucher, described in her sitting room at Hertford House in 1834.[33] Such dissemination of Boucher's decorative idiom gathered momentum during the British Regency, when the Prince Regent, the future George IV, and his friend the Earl of Yarmouth (1777–1842), the future 3rd Marquess of Hertford, became keen collectors of Sèvres. The Revolution and the turmoil of the Napoleonic wars that followed dispersed most of the great collections of the *ancien régime*. The 3rd Marquess, the first of his family to show a significant interest in painting, was quick to seize this opportunity by snapping up the sort of Dutch and Flemish 'little masters' that had delighted the French collectors of pre-revolutionary France. He would surely have had many opportunities to buy works by Boucher, but Boucher's reputation was at its lowest ebb, and the 3rd Marquess was little interested in French pictures.

The Critical Backlash

After Boucher's death, Diderot declared: 'I said too many bad things about Boucher, I retract them'.[34] Unfortunately, it was too late for him to reverse the critical tide that his writings had done so much to create. Even before the Revolution prices for Boucher's works were in decline, while the 1770s and 1780s saw the most significant collections of his works dispersed. In 1771, the dealer Le Brun sold a number of drawings by Deshays and Boucher, while Huquier's posthumous sale the following year also contained a considerable quantity of Boucher's drawings.[35] The deaths of

FIG.137
After BOUCHER, MAURICE JACQUES and LOUIS TESSIER (1719–81), *The Boucher Tapestry*, 1763–71, wool and silk high warp Gobelins tapestry, height 330cm, example woven for Croome Court, New York, Metropolitan Museum of Art, Gift of Samuel H. Kress Foundation, 1958 (58.75.1–23)

a series of Boucher's prominent clients led to the dispersal of their collections: Randon de Boisset's collection was broken up in 1777, Sireul's in 1781, the collection of the marquis de Marigny, by then known as the marquis de Ménars, which included the many Bouchers he had inherited from Madame de Pompadour, was sold in 1782, and that of Bergeret followed in 1786.[36] Meanwhile Blondel d'Azaincourt started to sell his Bouchers during his own lifetime.[37] In the year of the Revolution, *The Setting* and *The Rising of the Sun* appeared in the last major eighteenth-century sale of Boucher's work, that of Monsieur de Saincy.[38]

The neo-classicists, led from 1784 by David, were now replacing the generation of artists who had previously stood firm against the critics in their admiration of Boucher's technical skill. The attitude of Julien de Parme (1736–99), as expressed in a letter of 1774, was typical of the new generation. It describes his visit to Watelet's collection, which then contained the *Mercury and Bacchus* and *Rape of Europa* now in the Wallace Collection (figs. 24–25): 'Would you believe that the man had nothing in his collection but Vanloos, Bouchers, Pierres, Viens, Doyens etc… which he finds very beautiful, and I find detestable?'.[39] In 1783, Bachaumont, so laudatory of Boucher in his youth, remarked approvingly that 'in general, true

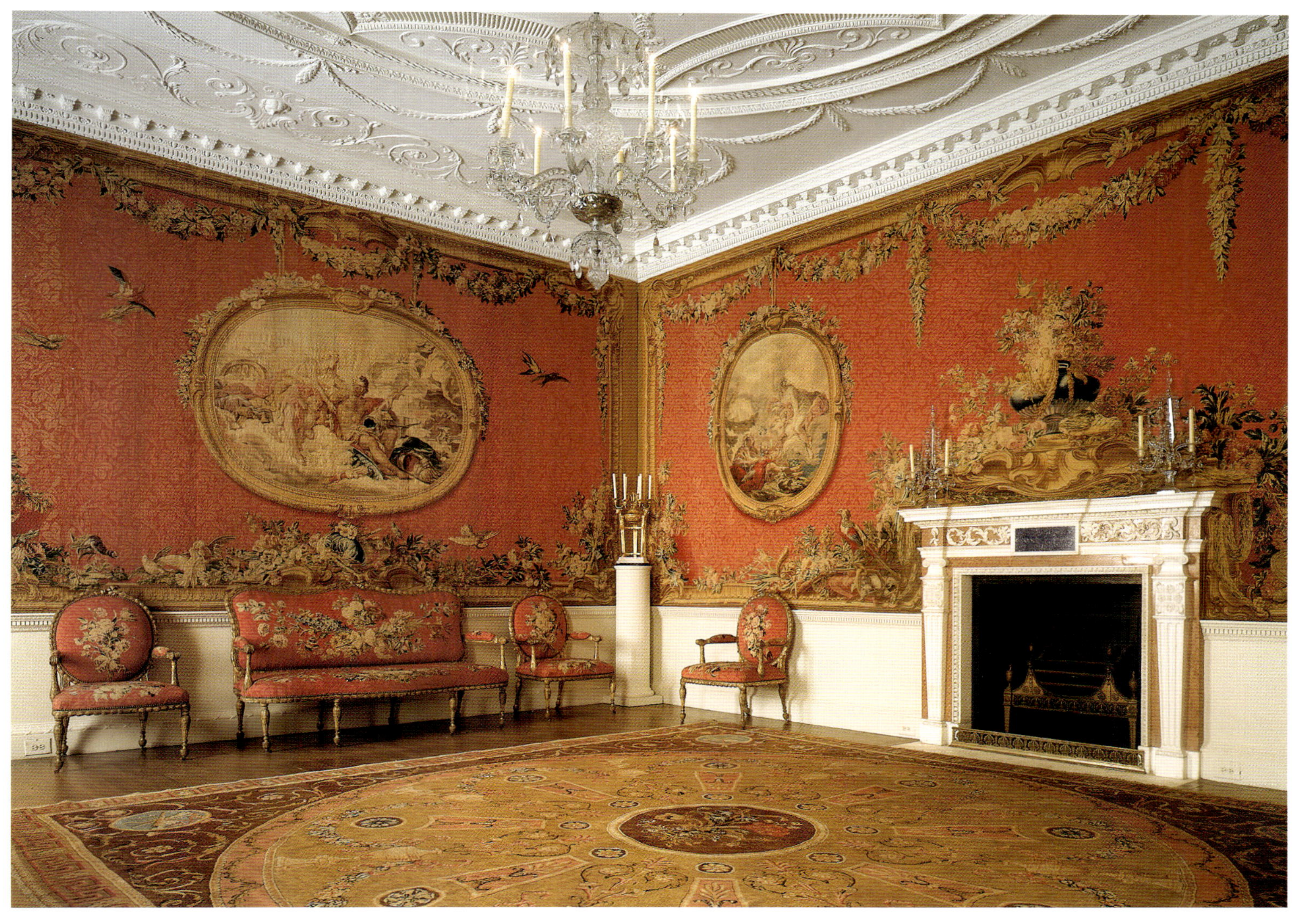

connoisseurs note with satisfaction that the School of Boucher is noticeably disappearing and that in place of its mannered precious style which infected the French school for a long time, at last today good taste in painting and imitation of the antique, even if still distant, is succeeding'.[40]

The rapid decline in her husband's reputation must have been hard on Madame Boucher. Accustomed to living like an aristocrat, her changed situation is shown by Bergeret's having to help her with an annuity of 3,000 *livres* in 1773. This was stopped on Bergeret's death in 1786, as was her royal pension at the Revolution. She apparently survived the Revolution in straitened circumstances but it is not known when she died. The upheavals of this period swept away not only much of the physical context but also the intellectual and social context in which Boucher's art had been produced. Fatally associated with the old régime, Boucher's art was now seen as evidence of its degeneracy. The engraver and expert Basan nevertheless attempted to defend his old friend in 1790, writing that 'this famous artist ... is no longer valued, for no other reason than to have exercised too much of his fecund genius'. The new morality also obliged Basan to claim that Boucher's 'tastes and curiosity for all parts of art and nature, often forced him to produce different pictures which in the bottom of his heart he disapproved of'.[41] Five years later another expert and engraver, Lempereur, while admitting that Boucher's 'taste led him astray, led him beyond limits, and degenerated into a fantasy for fashion which made him lose sight of simple and true beauty', also pointed out his numerous 'good qualities, that many people refuse to acknowledge'.[42]

By the beginning of the nineteenth century, Gault de Saint-Germain observed that 'when pictures by Boucher appear on the market, dealers spend a long time looking for buyers and are forced to sell them at the lowest prices'. To him this was hardly surprising. 'At last appeared Boucher', he wrote in one of the most scathing assessments of the artist, 'whose influence was considerable both on the mores as well as the taste in the arts. This man unique in his spirit of depravity; who seems to have sharpened his crayon or ground his colours only to charm the eyes of vice, was honoured by the palm of genius, and regarded as one of the greatest of talents ... foreigners laughed at the mad admiration the French had for this base trivial man who had lost all idea of truth, shame and delicacy'. The critic also deplored the wide currency Boucher's art was given through engraving and ridiculed his success as a teacher, claiming that 'he did not have students, only victims, who were unable to save themselves from the abyss into which his distractions plunged them'.[43]

Boucher's Rehabilitation in the Nineteenth Century

After the Revolution, Diderot's Salon criticism, a work of art in itself, was published independently and not only admired for its undoubted literary qualities but also as a work of great foresight in view of the critical abyss into which the art of the *ancien régime* had fallen. In the case of Boucher, Diderot's slanderous asides concerning the painter's depravity only served to confirm the prejudices of nineteenth-century commentators, already titillated and shocked by the amoral sensuality of Boucher's pictures. As stories and memoirs were invented to discredit the major political figures of the *ancien régime*, partly to justify the Revolution, partly to explain to a still uncomprehending public how such a bloody event had come about, Boucher was tainted by association. Meanwhile, as women in the nineteenth century came to be regarded as the sacred, but passive, vessels of society's morality, so the behaviour of prominent female figures of the eighteenth century came under particular attack. Boucher's 'feminine' style and close association with Madame de Pompadour, that most potent female symbol of a depraved monarchy, served to undermine his reputation yet further.

Unfortunately, the narrative genius of the nineteenth century makes many of the stories invented during the period too salacious to forget.

Who could fail to be horrified and enthralled by the tale that first appeared in 1806 of Boucher, overcome by the near nudity of the duchesse de Chartres posing as Hebe, seducing her there and then and thus sending her into a downward spiral of nymphomania?[44] Similarly, the duc de Croÿ's aside regarding the King's attraction to a beautiful young model of Boucher's became exaggerated into stories of the painter as royal pander, providing a harem of beauties for Louis XV.[45] The Parc aux Cerfs, in reality a small discreet house with (at most) a couple of occupants at any one time, now became a veritable bordello, with Boucher described as its 'Raphael'. Such emphasis on fictitious details of Boucher's life undermined any serious consideration of his work. For the nineteenth century, Boucher became a symbol of a doomed and decadent regime, as Soyer maintained in 1834: 'The depravity of his morals, the decadence of his taste, the artificiality of his palette, the speciousness of his compositions, the affected character of his heads, his draughtsmanship, and his expressions, all followed step by step the licentious and degenerate course of society under the Regency and the reign of Louis XV'.[46]

Even David, however, had acknowledged the technical mastery of his cousin, exhorting his students to work harder with the words 'one cannot be a Boucher by wishing'.[47] As early as 1812, the expert Henry also pointed out that, if 'during Boucher's lifetime his work was praised with exaggeration, now we have fallen to the opposite extreme, they are blamed too much … In a word, Boucher had a style of his own; that is something'.[48] Ironically the power of Boucher's unabashed female nudes, while continuing to provide ammunition for his detractors, also fascinated nineteenth-century commentators. The shameless creations of 'the Painter of the Graces' seemed to represent a state of sexual innocence and freedom lost to the newly industrialised age. Such playful sensuality inspired the Goncourt brothers to describe Boucher as a 'cheeky Rubens', and it was their brilliantly written and affectionate account of *L'Art du XVIIIème siècle* (*The Art of the 18th Century*), published between 1857 and 1875, which did much to rehabilitate the critical reputation of the art of the *ancien régime*.[49] They describe Boucher's nudes as the visual incarnation of Ovid's *Art of Love* and, while acknowledging their impropriety, could barely contain their excitement in describing them. 'Voluptuousness, that is all the ideal of Boucher … what a nimble hand, what fresh imagination even in indecency, what understanding in composition, in the manner of throwing pretty bodies on rounded clouds with swans' necks! … The severity of the nude is unknown to Boucher … but who has undressed woman better than he? The Venus that Boucher dreamt and painted is only the physical Venus; but how he knows her by heart! … And how he incarnates in this light, aerial and ever-reborn figure, Desire and Pleasure'.[50]

For those who still found the sensuality of his nudes too unsettling, Boucher's pastorals provided a perfect alternative. Despite the disappearance of the fairs, of Favart's charming operettas and the aristocratic theatricals they engendered, the nineteenth century was able to identify with the sentimental aspect of these stories of awakening love, glossing over the ribald jokes of instrumental prowess, and concentrating instead on their sweetness and decorative finesse. In Boucher's shepherds and shepherdesses the nineteenth century found a less troubling outlet for its increasing nostalgia for the *ancien régime*. Thus Gautier enthused over 'that idyllic world invented by Boucher for the use of the eighteenth century – that least rural of centuries, despite its bosky pretences. The sheep are shampooed, the shepherdesses tight-laced with ribbons and quite without that weather-beaten country look and the shepherds are like dancers from the opera. But it is all irresistibly seductive, and the lie is more agreeable than the truth'. While noting that 'for a long-time he was the idol of a century, which preferred the pretty, the beautiful, confusion over style and wit above everything. The idol fell, and the name of Boucher, like that of Van Loo, became an insult in the studios of the classicists', he

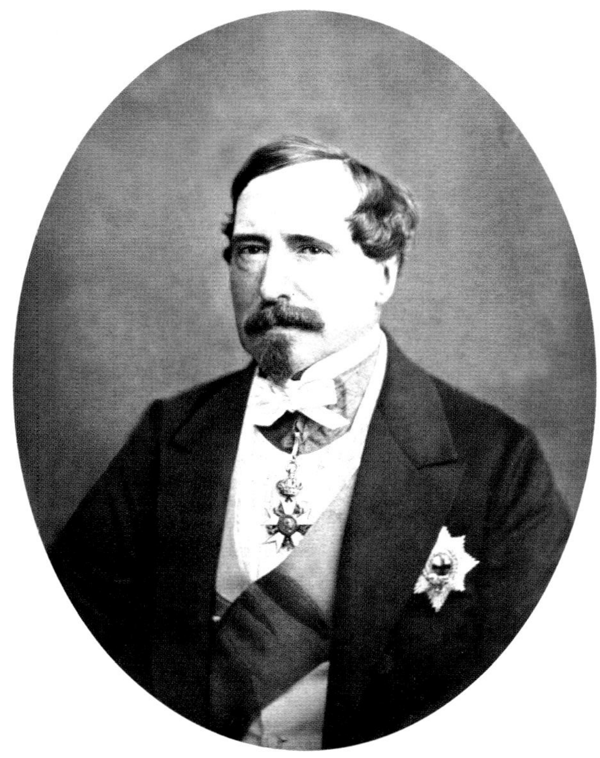

FIG.138
ÉTIENNE CARJAT,
The 4th Marquess of Hertford, c.1860,
photograph,
Wallace Collection

FIG.139 *opposite*
Attributed to BAUDOUIN,
Leda and the Swan,
gouache on ivory,
50 × 72mm (sight),
Wallace Collection

claimed that 'now, one understands everything Boucher is worth'. [51]

In deliberate contradiction to Gault de Saint-Germain, Théodore Lejeune was able write in 1864 that 'this original painter seems to have sharpened his crayon or ground his colours only to charm the eyes.' He goes on to describe 'The reversal of fortune attached to the works of Boucher … for around thirty years his most unremarkable compositions have become intensely sought after and fetch mad prices'.[52] The eighteenth century was again fashionable and Boucher was regarded as its avatar as this famous passage by the Goncourts explains: 'Boucher is one of those men who symbolise the taste of a century, who express it, personify it, and incarnate it. French taste of the eighteenth century is manifest in him in every particular of his character: Boucher remains not only the painter, but the witness, the representative, the type … As the century of Louis XIV was succeeded by that of Louis XV … the ideal of art remained imaginary and conventional; but from majesty this ideal descended to agreeableness. Everywhere spread an elegant refinement, a voluptuous delicacy, which the time called 'the quintessence of the pleasing, the colouring of charms and graces, the embellishment of fêtes and the amours' … The *pretty*, – this, in these hours of light-hearted history, this was the sign and seduction of France. The pretty is the essence and the formula of its genius. The pretty is the tone of its morals. The pretty is the school of its fashions. The pretty, is the spirit of the age – and it is the genius of Boucher'.[53]

The 4th Marquess of Hertford's Passion for Boucher

That the Wallace Collection houses one of the world's greatest collections of Boucher's work is entirely due to the 4th Marquess of Hertford (1800–1870; fig.138).[54] There are twenty-one works by or after Boucher acquired by Lord Hertford in the Wallace Collection today, plus *The Musical Contest* by Fragonard, which was attributed to Boucher when purchased in 1842. Lord Hertford is thought to have owned a further twenty-five works by or after Boucher, including pictures and drawings, which did not form part of Lady Wallace's 1897 bequest to the nation.[55] His illegitimate son, Sir Richard Wallace, completed this collection with the *Jupiter and Callisto* (fig.127) and a copy of *The Birth of Venus* (fig.112), and may also have acquired the two 1754 *Venus* overdoors (figs.108–109). At the same time Hertford also bought a large quantity of Boucher-inspired Sèvres, gold boxes, miniatures and tapestries which, taken together with his paintings, made Boucher the presiding artistic genius of the entire collection. It might at first seem strange that a British aristocrat should manifest such a passion for an artist little appreciated in Britain, but Lord Hertford's family history, which itself reads like an eighteenth-century libertine novel, resulted in his being brought up in France from the age of two. His parents, who had eloped and married against the wishes of the 2nd Marquess and Marchioness of Hertford, escaped the *froideur* of London society by travelling to Paris during the Peace of Amiens in 1802. Unfortunately, Hertford's father was arrested and interned at Verdun when the Peace collapsed the following year. When he emerged from captivity in 1805 it was only to find his wife pregnant by another man (probably Count Casimir de Montrond). The future 4th Marquess of Hertford was subsequently raised in Paris by his adored and cosmopolitan mother, Maria Fagnani, herself the illegitimate daughter of an Italian dancer.

Lord Hertford reached maturity at precisely the moment that Boucher's critical reputation was beginning to recover. Already a select group of collectors, including the miniaturist Daniel Saint (1778–1847), the marquis de Cypierre (1784–1844) and Dr Louis La Caze (1797–1869), had started to collect eighteenth-century French art. The rising prices of such works at the beginning of the nineteenth century are memorably described in Balzac's novel, *Le Cousin Pons*, published in 1847, which tells of the inheritance disputes occasioned by the fabulous art collection of the elderly musician, Pons, picked up for nothing at the beginning of the century and now worth a small fortune. After becoming Marquess in 1842, the new Lord Hertford, now one of the richest men in Europe, but reclusive and neurotic in nature, decided to devote his life to collecting art rather than to pursuing a public career. The French eighteenth century, for men of his generation, symbolised a lost world of aristocratic leisure and finesse which Lord Hertford evidently hoped to recapture by insulating himself against the world, and surrounding himself with the type of art collected by his *ancien régime* counterparts. Nor was he alone in this passion for the eighteenth century, as the acquisitions of other moneyed collectors, including James de Rothschild (1792–1868), the duc de Morny (1811–65) and the Pereire brothers, Emile (1800–75) and Isaac (1806–80) demonstrate. But an extra piquancy was added to Lord Hertford's obsession by his troubled family history and English origins.

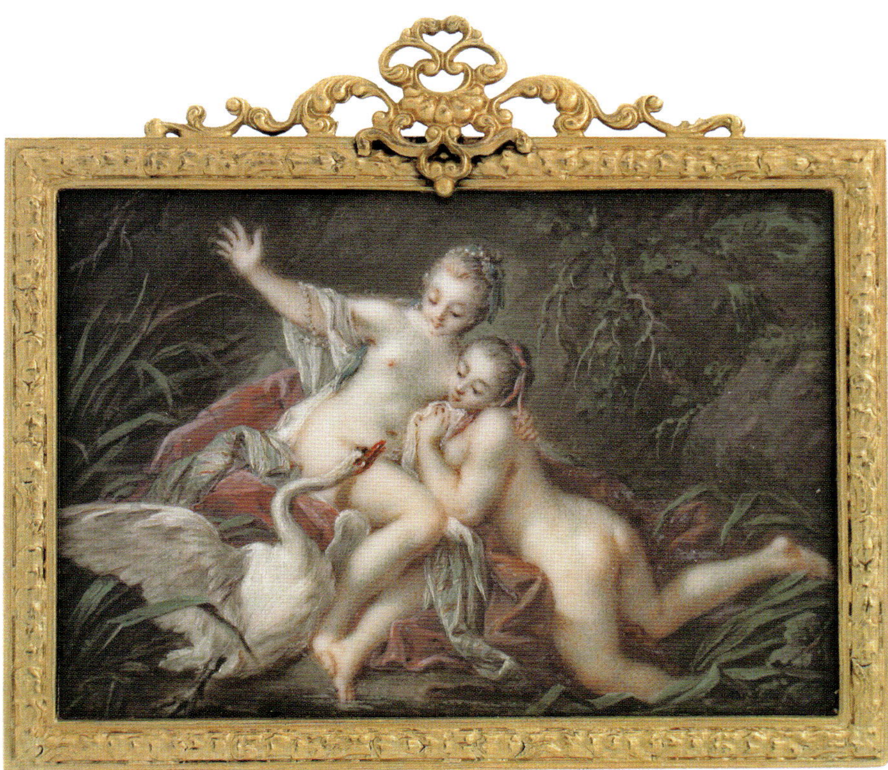

In 1844 Disraeli, writer as well as politician, published his novel *Coningsby*, basing the figure of the dissolute aristocrat, Lord Monmouth, the hero's grandfather, on the well-known rakish character of the recently-deceased 3rd Marquess of Hertford. In one passage Disraeli decribes how to Englishmen of Lord Monmouth's class a knowledge and appreciation of French culture and language was considered an essential for any gentleman. Monmouth 'solemnly adjured [Coningsby] not to neglect his French…there were two educations, one which his position required and one which was demanded by the world. "French, my dear Harry," he continued, "is the key to this second education"'.[56] Disraeli imagined Lord Monmouth's Palladian townhouse in London as decorated in the French taste where 'the walls of the saloon, which were covered with light blue satin, held, in silver panels, portraits of beautiful women painted by Boucher. Couches and easy chairs of every shape invited in every quarter to luxurious repose; while amusement was afforded by tables covered with caricatures, French novels, and endless miniatures of foreign dancers, princesses and sovereigns'.[57] But rather than describing the interiors of the

FIG.140 *below*
The Great Gallery of the 4th Marquess of Hertford's apartment, rue Laffitte, Paris

FIG.141 *opposite*
BOUCHER, *Cupid and the Graces*, 1738, oil on canvas, 141 × 181cm, Lisbon, Calouste-Gulbenkian Foundation

London residences of the 3rd Marquess of Hertford, this passage actually anticipates the atmosphere of sensual luxury, refinement and repose affected by his expatriate son in Paris. Although it is known that the 3rd Marquess collected miniatures of pretty women, it is more likely that his son acquired the large number of Boucher-related miniatures now in the Wallace Collection (fig.139).[58] Figure 140 shows the great gallery of the 4th Marquess's rue Laffitte apartment where Beauvais tapestries from Boucher's *Psyche* series (now in Philadelphia), together with eighteenth-century French paintings and decorative arts, lent his collection its peculiarly Gallic character.[59]

Lord Hertford's letters to his agent in London, Samuel Mawson, provide a further insight into why Boucher, in particular, would have so appealed to him. He claimed 'as you well know I only like pleasing pictures' and was particularly attracted to the fanciful, while disliking difficult or male subjects.[60] The Bouchers he acquired are the type of works also admired by the Goncourts, namely the pastorals of the 1740s and the sensual mythologies of the 1750s; a taste of which, incidentally, Madame de Pompadour would also have approved. Apart from the Derbais pictures (figs.24–25), sometimes in Lord Hertford's time considered to be by Lemoine, he acquired only one other early work, *Cupid and the Graces*, now in Lisbon (fig.141). He also put aside his usual antipathy to non-contemporary drawings and acquired a group of ten coloured drawings, including watercolours, gouaches and red chalk drawings, which must have added to the impression of an eighteenth-century cabinet he was trying to achieve in his rue Laffitte apartment. His keenness to acquire Bouchers and his almost limitless budget were among the factors that contributed to the inflation in the artist's prices in the mid-nineteenth century. Lord Hertford bemoaned this fact himself in 1854 when he described the Madame de Chavagnac sale: 'Four very pretty Dessus de Porte [overdoors] by Boucher or something like him were bought by the Duc de Galliéra, upwards of 10,000fr. very dear, but they knew he was bidding & I know the effect we produce & the price we pay for it'.[61] In contrast,

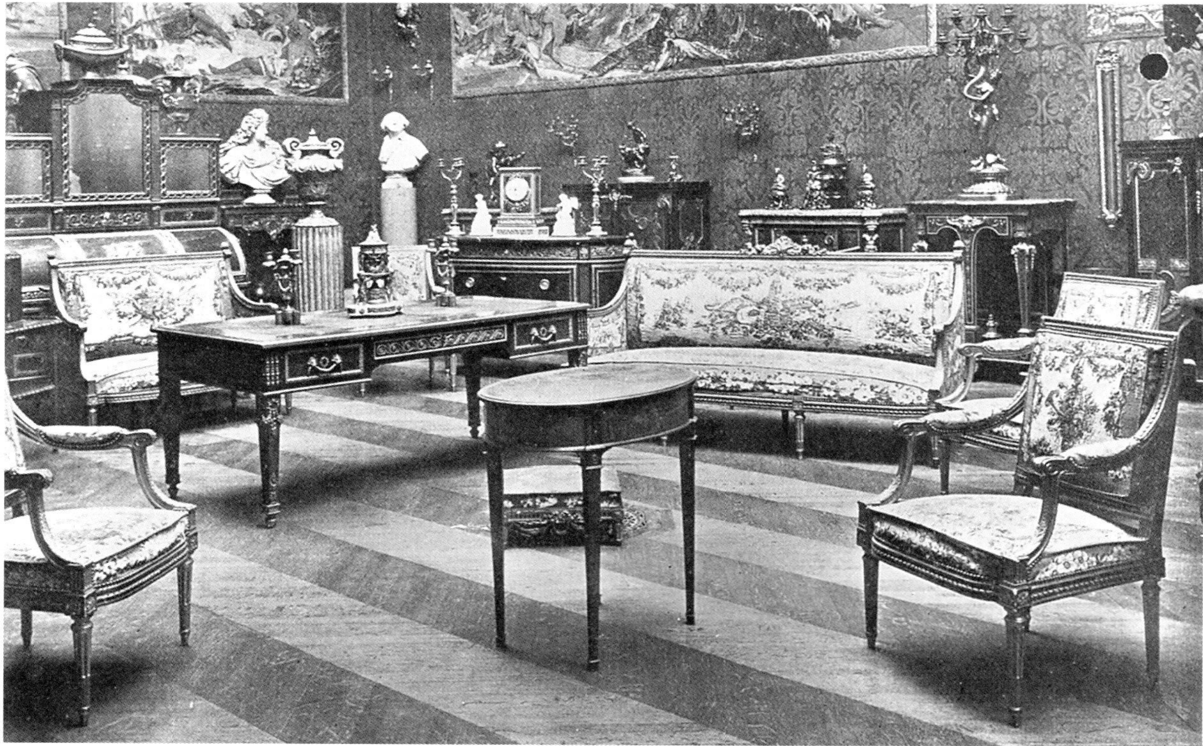

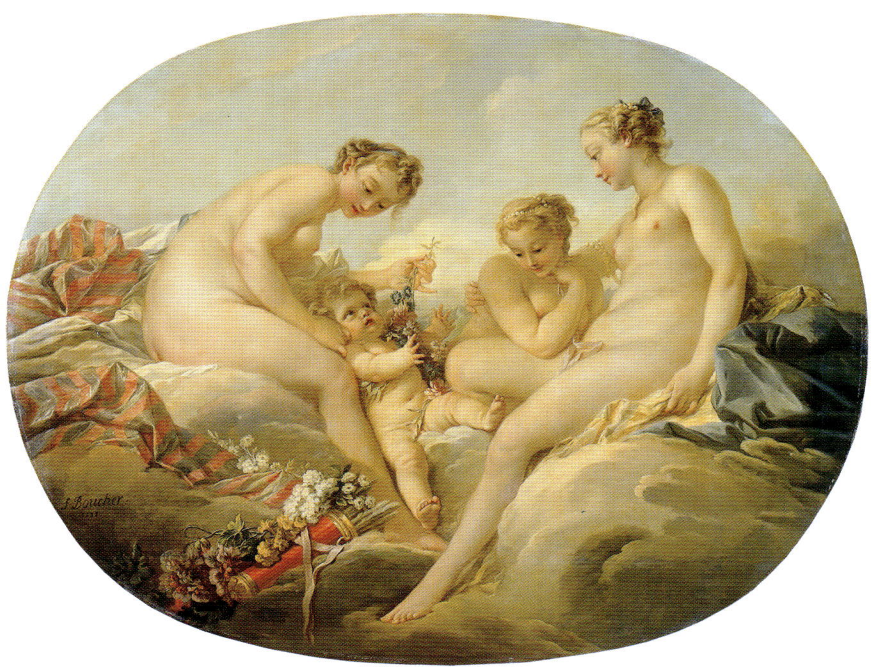

his insouciant manner in describing his acquisitions deliberately apes that of his eighteenth-century predecessors. In the same breath as describing two Desportes hunting pictures as 'a little rubbish for the country', he went on to refer in passing to *Spring* and *Bacchus and Erigone* (figs.70–71) as 'a couple of Bouchers to put over my great doors if I ever finish my Piccadilly house'.[62] Such throw-away comments mask the fact that he was, in fact, very exacting regarding the condition, quality and size of his Bouchers. So, with regard to two large Boucher landscapes Mawson proposed acquiring at the sale of Sir Culling Eardley, Hertford wrote: 'As for the Bouchers if they are those I have seen here & I suspect they are, you must have observed that they are almost completely repainted & in my opinion & on that account not worth having and besides they are much too large'.[63]

Most of Lord Herford's finest Bouchers were bought in the 1850s, and were still considerably cheaper than the Watteau, Pater and Lancret *fêtes galantes* he bought during the same period. His earliest true Boucher acquisitions were the *Mercury and Bacchus* and *Rape of Europa* (figs.24–25), bought in 1843 for the relatively modest sum of 2,820 *francs* (a single small picture by Watteau cost him twice that figure in 1846). In 1855 he had to pay considerably more for *The Setting* and *The Rising of the Sun* (figs.83–4), namely 20,200 *francs*, although the seller, the baron de Comailles, who had acquired the pair for only 380 *francs* in 1827, nevertheless felt they were worth considerably more. Comailles's opinion was confirmed when the Goncourts soon after described them as 'the two triumphal pages of Boucher's art ... They are the greatest effort of the painter, the two great machines of his work. They have excited enthusiasm; they remain breathtaking'.[64] Nonetheless the price of 14,500 *francs* paid by Lord Hertford for *Spring* and *Bacchus and Erigone* scandalised Charles Blanc in 1857: 'thirty years ago one would have got these two canvases for something like 100 *écus* [300 *francs*] ... must one commit such financial follies for such follies of pictures? ... Is it not scandalous that a Boucher costs as much if not more than a Titian?' By 1860 a small pastoral like the *Shepherd and Shepherdess* (fig.105) cost Lord Hertford 4,100 *francs*, nearly four times what each of the Derbais mythologies had cost him twenty years previously.

Lord Hertford's taste for Boucher could only raise the status in which Boucher was generally regarded, especially as he also collected great masterpieces of the Baroque. In the great gallery of the rue Laffitte apartment the *Mercury and Bacchus*, *Rape of Europa*, *Summer and Autumn Pastoral* and *The Setting* and *The Rising of the Sun* (figs.24–25, 74–75, 83–84) were displayed alongside a further twenty-four eighteenth-century French pictures, old masters and contemporary French works. The vertical panels on the theme of *Venus* and *Cupid a Captive* (figs.102–105) were inserted into the panelling of the rotunda and flanked by portraits such as Velazquez's *Lady with a Fan*, Hals's *Laughing Cavalier* and Dutch sea- and landscapes. Meanwhile in Lord Hertford's *maison de plaisance*, Bagatelle, in the bois de Boulogne, Bouchers were used as part of the fixed decoration. *Cupid and the Graces* (fig.141) was set into the ceiling of the west boudoir, where four more Bouchers were set in the walls, helping to explain why such works were not later transported to London by Sir Richard Wallace and were not included in Lady Wallace's bequest. Lord Hertford lent no Bouchers to the Manchester Art Treasures exhibition in 1857 as his Bouchers, apart from *The Milliner* (fig.58), were kept in Paris, not London, and the English public was not noted for its interest in the artist. The Parisian public, however, was treated to a selection of Hertford's eighteenth-century French pictures at Martinet's second *Tableaux de l'école française* exhibition, held in the Boulevard des Italiens in 1860. Lord Hertford's loans included more pictures by Boucher than by any other artist. Although generally admired, their artificiality, perceived immorality and association with the elite still compromised them. In his review of the exhibition, Thoré-Bürger, while admitting that such works would provide excellent decoration for 'a vast room in a château', condemned them for their imaginative departure from nature: although Boucher 'when he consulted nature, when he painted women posing in front of him, is exquisite', in general, like many artists of his time, he could only ever be considered 'a painter of the second rank'.[65]

Larousse's Dictionary, the first part of which was published in Paris in 1865, continued to define Boucher as 'a great talent' but one 'who prostituted himself to a degenerate and corrupt society'. Lord Hertford's well-known love of Boucher probably lay behind the comment that 'the English, they say, are particularly fond of him; that is understandable: the blasé old Lords love libidinous pictures which revive their worn-out senses'.[66] Lord Hertford, who tricked his long-term lover, Madame Oger, into eloping with him by staging a sham marriage, and who was said to have paid a million francs for one night of pleasure with the notorious courtesan, the contessa di Castiglione, was (unsurprisingly) identified as the owner of an even more shocking series of obscene paintings. These were thought to be by Boucher in the nineteenth century and are now attributed to the Boucher pasticheur, Soldini, but were destroyed and are known only from nineteenth-century photographs.[67] The *Couple making love in front of a classical Altar* (fig.142) is the last of the set described, by Charles Blanc, as commissioned by Madame de Pompadour to revive the flagging ardour of Louis XV: 'Boucher immediately composed a little erotic poem in a series of pictures. The first act took place on the grass, naïvely, an idyll, under the branches of a tree with doves circling. In the second picture, the young shepherdess showed how inspiration came to her and by delicate transitions, well managed, the spectator is carried to the final act, a brazen imitation of a bas-relief from the secret museum in Naples'. Blanc explains how 'at the death of Louis XV, when Louis XVI ascended the throne, Maurepas took him to Madame de Pompadour's boudoir. 'These indecencies must disappear' said the new King. The old courtier found it natural to confiscate Boucher's pictures for his own profit, which during the emigration of the nobles [during the Revolution] were taken to Germany by M. de M... Revennes. Recently arrived in France they were bought by an Englishman'. The 'Englishman' is identified in the footnotes as 'Lord Hertford, great lover of pictures, as everyone knows'. It seems that the erotic pastoral series was confused by Blanc with the series of mythological panels, including the raunchy *Mars and Venus*, which had belonged to Thoré-Bürger and which were indeed acquired by Lord Hertford (figs.102–105). For

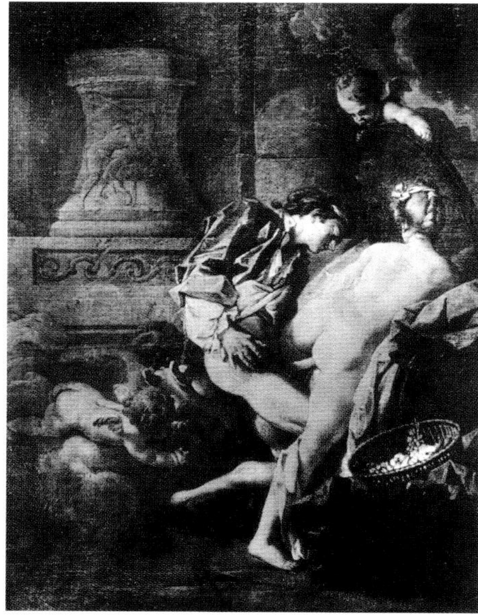

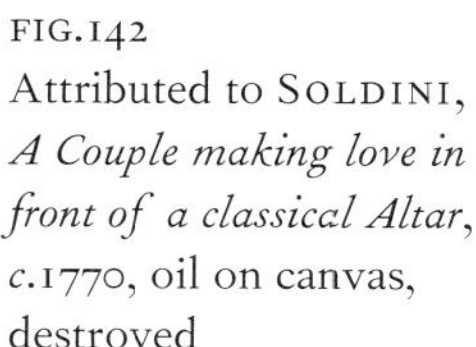

FIG.142
Attributed to SOLDINI, *A Couple making love in front of a classical Altar*, *c.*1770, oil on canvas, destroyed

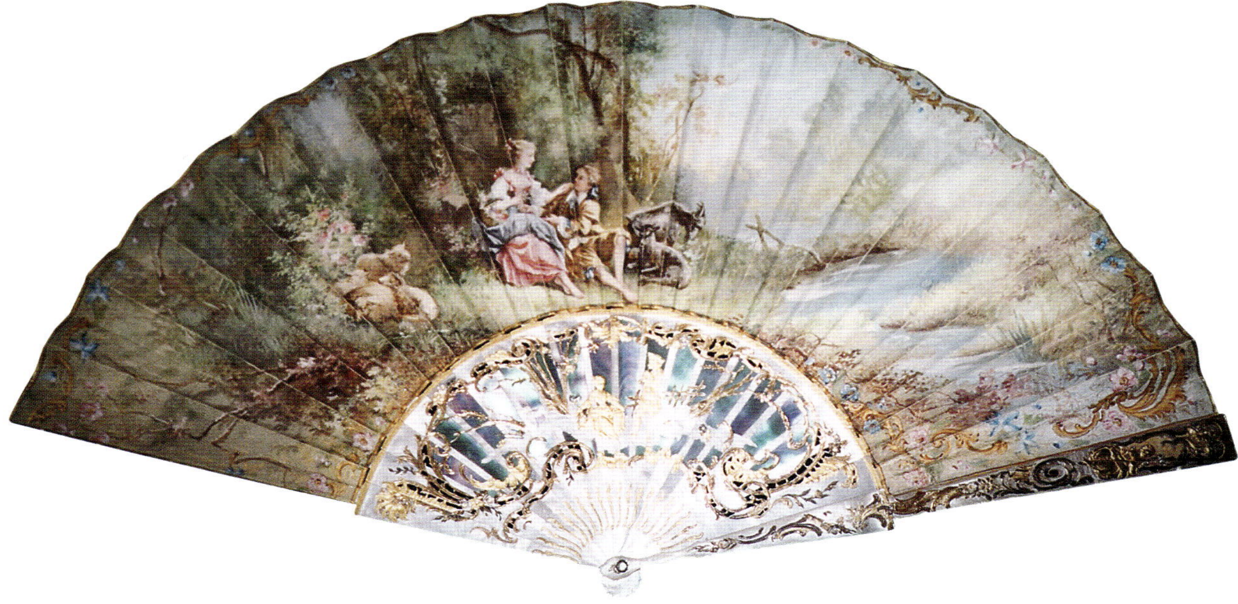

FIG.143
Fan with pastoral scene after BOUCHER, second quarter of the nineteenth century, Paris, Musée de l'Eventail

Blanc goes on to state that 'As for the quality of the paintings, according to M. Thoré from whom we have these strange facts, they are the most beautiful Bouchers in the world'.[68] Apparently the erotic pastorals were eventually sold to an American collector, but returned by the New York customs because of their obscenity and later destroyed by H.M. Customs in Edinburgh![69]

Artistic Reactions to Boucher in the Nineteenth Century

As Boucher's art became more critically accepted and collected, fine and decorative artists, from the mid-century on, began to look to Boucher for inspiration. The link between Boucher and the decorative arts had been noted by Balzac, himself a collector of Sèvres porcelain, when he touchingly described the enthusiasm of the elderly Pons for items such as a 'bonheur-du-jour, a marvel! It executes the designs of Boucher in marquetry with such art … One must kneel before it!'[70] Boucher had been erroneously disparaged by Baron Grimm in the *Correspondance littéraire* as 'a painter of fans', but his pastorals now did begin to appear on fans towards the end of the nineteenth century, replacing Watteau's *fêtes champêtres* as fashionable motifs (fig.143).[71] At the same time Boucher's pastorals inspired textile design, as seen in the shepherd and shepherdess incorporated in elaborate cartouches on brocaded silks produced by Lemire, 1846–49, and exhibited in 1849 among a group of silks called 'Pompadour brocades' (examples in Lyon and the Musée de la Mode, Paris).[72] Boucher pastorals are also endlessly reproduced on tapestries, decorative screens and wall panels such as those by Paul Colin (1838–1916) in the Museum Willet-Holthuysen, Amsterdam. Meanwhile existing eighteenth-century decorative arts were embellished with Boucher-derived designs added in the nineteenth century. Thus a pair of pot-pourri vases and covers of 1756 (with later additions) in the Wallace Collection were further 'prettified' by nineteenth-century additions of pastorals after Boucher.[73]

When Delacroix (1798–1863) came to paint his own Apollo ceiling on the great gallery of the Louvre (fig.144), it is interesting to note that at the same time he expressed his admiration for the aesthetic writings of De Piles and the ideal of overall effect. Accordingly, on 24 February 1850, he wrote in his Journal that 'what De Piles has done for painters only, might be revised to cover all the fine works that survive in human memory'.[74] Although he must have known of Boucher's Apollo ceiling at Fontainebleau, his own ceiling is

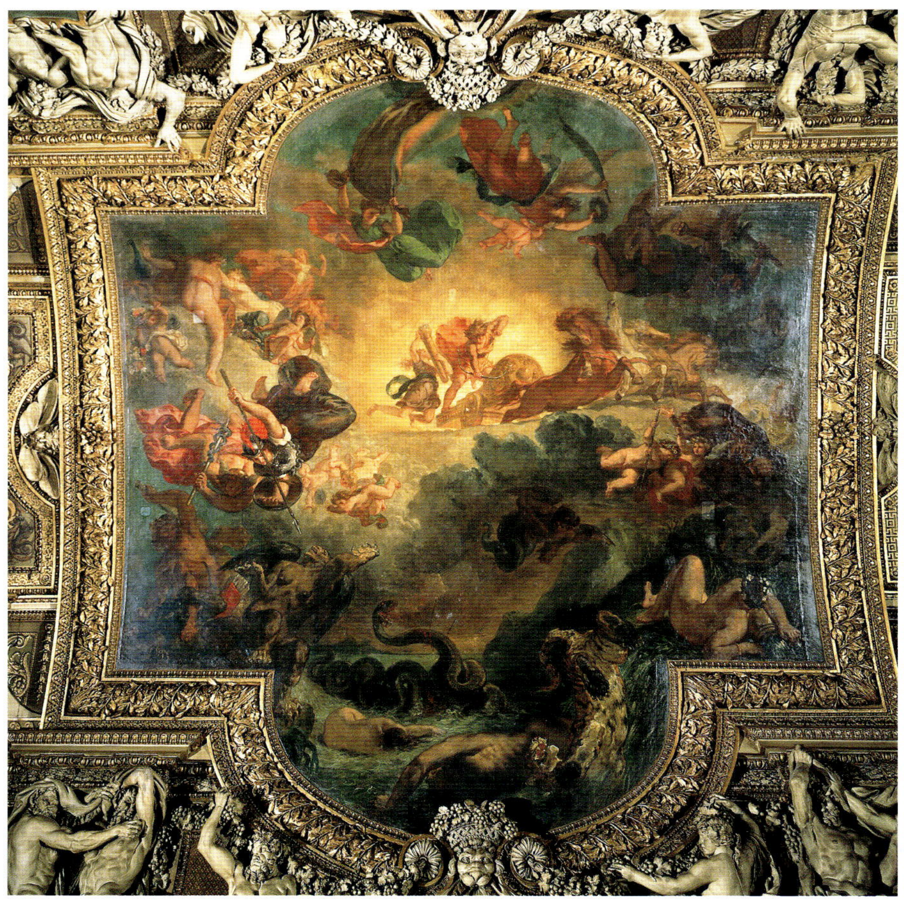

FIG.144
EUGÈNE DELACROIX (1798–1863), *Apollo Vanquishing the Python*, oil on canvas, 800 × 750cm, 1850–1, Paris, Louvre

noticeably more fiery and dramatic. Indeed, he actually criticised Boucher's colouring in 1853, writing that 'Colour is nothing unless it is appropriate to the subject and increases the effect of the picture through the power of the imagination. Let men like Boucher and Vanloo use light and charming tones, etc.'.[75] The same year he described listening to a lecture on the progress of the arts by a M. Ravaisson, which exalted gothic art and attacked the obscene, again typified by the art of Boucher: 'The Saturnalia of Boucher and Voltaire who, according to the professor, showed a distinct preference for immodest paintings, ought to be enough to make us all hate that side of the Antique'. Ravaisson's audience, however, did not entirely agree with his thesis and Delacroix 'after the first part of the lecture … slipped away, perhaps rather disgracefully, but I was encouraged by seeing one or two other people who, like myself, felt that they had been sufficiently edified on the subject of the Beautiful'.[76] In fact, despite Delacroix's reservations, Boucher is one of the few artists cited in his *Plan for a Dictionary of the Fine Arts* of 1857. Under the entry for *Technique*, he notes that 'the most perfect technique is to be found in the works of the greatest masters: Rubens, Titian, Veronese, the Dutch painters' but also planned to have a separate section devoted to Boucher and Vanloo and their 'remarkable methods of execution'.[77] The technical virtuosity of Boucher and Van Loo apparently inspired more and more contemporary French artists to imitate their manner. In 1847 Delacroix recalls visiting the picture dealer Aubry: 'the things I saw at his gallery yesterday give me very little hope for the future of the modern school. They look on Boucher and Vanloo as the great men who should be imitated; but for all their bad taste those painters had real knowledge'.[78] The quintessential expression of this nineteenth-century re-working of the rococo tradition is found in *The Birth of Venus* (fig.145) by Alexandre Cabanel (1823–1889), whose pearly naked Venus born aloft on the turquoise waves clearly pays homage to Boucher (see fig.55).

Boucher and the Belle Époque

As the nineteenth century drew to a close, Boucher-inspired Venuses, nymphs and putti by artists such as Bouguereau (1825–1905) and Chaplin (1825–91) proliferated. The immoral associations of Boucher's art came to be regarded as amusing rather than dangerous in an age when Oscar Wilde could claim that 'all art is immoral'.[79] Decorative artists such as Paul Baudry (1828–86) and Gabriel Ferrier (1847–1914) naturally studied Boucher's example when creating their own Belle-Époque designs, while an artist like Landini (1847–1912), who specialised in depicting dissolute abbés in rococo interiors, often quoted Boucher's paintings to provide an added note of eighteenth-century worldliness and humour. The detail shown in figure 128 shows Landini's clerics disporting themselves before Boucher's *Daphnis and Chloé*

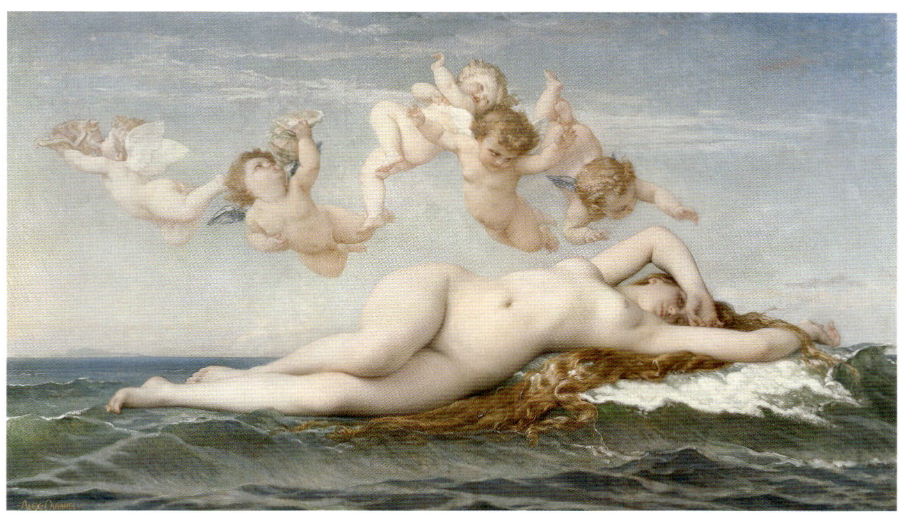

FIG.145
ALEXANDRE CABANEL (1823–1889), *The Birth of Venus*, 1863, oil on canvas, 130 × 225cm, Paris, Musée d'Orsay

(enlarged and reversed; see fig.69) in an imagined interior described as 'the Kings apartments at Fontainebleau'. A series of operas with eighteenth-century themes, including Massenet and Puccini's retellings of *Manon Lescaut* (1884 and 1893 respectively), Tchaikovsky's *Queen of Spades* (1890), Cilea's *Adriana Lecouvreur* (1902) and Richard Strauss's *Der Rosenkavalier* (1911) demonstrate how the rococo revival spread to other arts at the turn of the century.

Proust's *À la recherche du temps perdu* (*In Search of Lost Time*) describes Parisian society at this time: Boucher was now inextricably linked in the popular mind with the aristocratic and the refined. Accordingly the baron de Charlus's pedigree is borne out by his 'archives, furniture, tapestries, and the portraits of his ancestors done by Raphael, Velazquez and Boucher'.[80] The neurasthenic Proust was personally more attracted to the fragile beauty of Watteau than to the healthy optimism of Boucher, and portrays his hero as disappointed to find tapestries after Boucher in the country seat of the Guermantes, instead of the imagined ancestral medieval hangings.[81] He also describes how the aristocratic lure of the *ancien régime* now inspired 'many painters to seek to renew the female portraiture style of the eighteenth century'. Describing his hero's frustration at being unable to reach his girlfriend, Albertine, on the newly-invented telephone, he goes on to express surprise that 'none of our modern Bouchers or Fragonards' had thought to portray their female subjects *Before the Telephone*.[82] Boucher's influence did indeed lend a touch of *ancien régime* glamour to the modern subjects of society artists such as Giovanni Boldini (1842–1931). Boldini's *Reclining Nude on a Day-bed* (fig.146) clearly recalls Boucher's famous *odalisques* (figs.64 and 90), and evokes the rococo through its depiction of a *duchesse brisée*, an eighteenth-century day-bed, and the girl's hairstyle, *à la pompadour*.[83]

The Impressionists, meanwhile, were less attracted by the snobbery concerning Boucher's work than by its formal brilliance. Figure 147 shows a copy by Berthe Morisot (1841–95) after the embracing nymphs in the bottom left corner of Boucher's *Apollo and Issé* (fig.80).[84] Morisot, a leading Impressionist, seems to have had no problems with Boucher's sensual female nudes whose bright colouring and feminine intimacy inspired her to paint at least one other copy after the eighteenth-century master.[85] But perhaps the greatest compliment came from Renoir, who shared Boucher's fascination with the female form. He told Vollard, in an interview recounted in 1919, that Boucher's *Diana Bathing* (1742; Louvre) 'is the first picture which grabbed hold of me and I have continued all my life to love it as one loves one's first loves, even if someone were to tell me unrelentingly that it is not what one should love, that Boucher was only a simple decorator, as if that were a defect! In reality Boucher is one of those men who best understood the female body. He made young buttocks, little dimples, just what was necessary'.[86]

Boucher in the Twentieth Century

The generally negative reaction in England to Boucher's art continued to the end of the nineteenth century, and the homes of prominent collectors of eighteenth-century art, such as the Rothschilds, were often criticised for their lavish and vulgar display. Gladstone's daughter, Mary, 'felt much oppressed with the extreme gorgeousness and luxury' of Ferdinand de Rothschild's home, Waddesdon Manor, while Lady Frances Balfour exclaimed in horror 'Oh! But the hideousness of everything, the showiness! The sense of lavish wealth thrust up your nose!', on seeing Alfred de Rothschild's house, Halton.[87] In such a context Wedmore's 1885 condemnation of Boucher as 'the rose-water Raphael' and the 'bastard of Rubens' is unsurprising.[88] Wedmore nevertheless also acknowledged that 'the eighteenth century in France witnessed the rise … and the fall of a school of art of which the English public remains all but completely ignorant … even Watteau is not to be found within our National Gallery. Here Greuze and Lancret share the task of representing French Art of the period when it was most characteristic. They are unequal to the mission. And until some can join them who will fulfil it better, French eighteenth-century painting will hardly receive its due'.[89] In 1897 that lacuna was spectacularly filled when Lady Wallace, Sir Richard Wallace's French widow, left the contents of the ground and first floors of Hertford House to the British nation on the understanding that the bequest should be named after her husband. A new and more sympathetic response to Boucher's art in England was signalled by Lady Dilke's biography of the artist, published in 1899. Here she stated that 'so great an artist could not wholly go wrong, if he became the 'typical representative of the decadence of art', he was at least of the true race!'[90] In 1900 the Wallace Collection opened to the public, who were able to enjoy, among other treasures, its superb array of Bouchers. Although people flocked to the museum, not all commentators were impressed, with critics finding the Bouchers particularly difficult to appreciate: 'The nation now stands possessed of a much greater number of silly

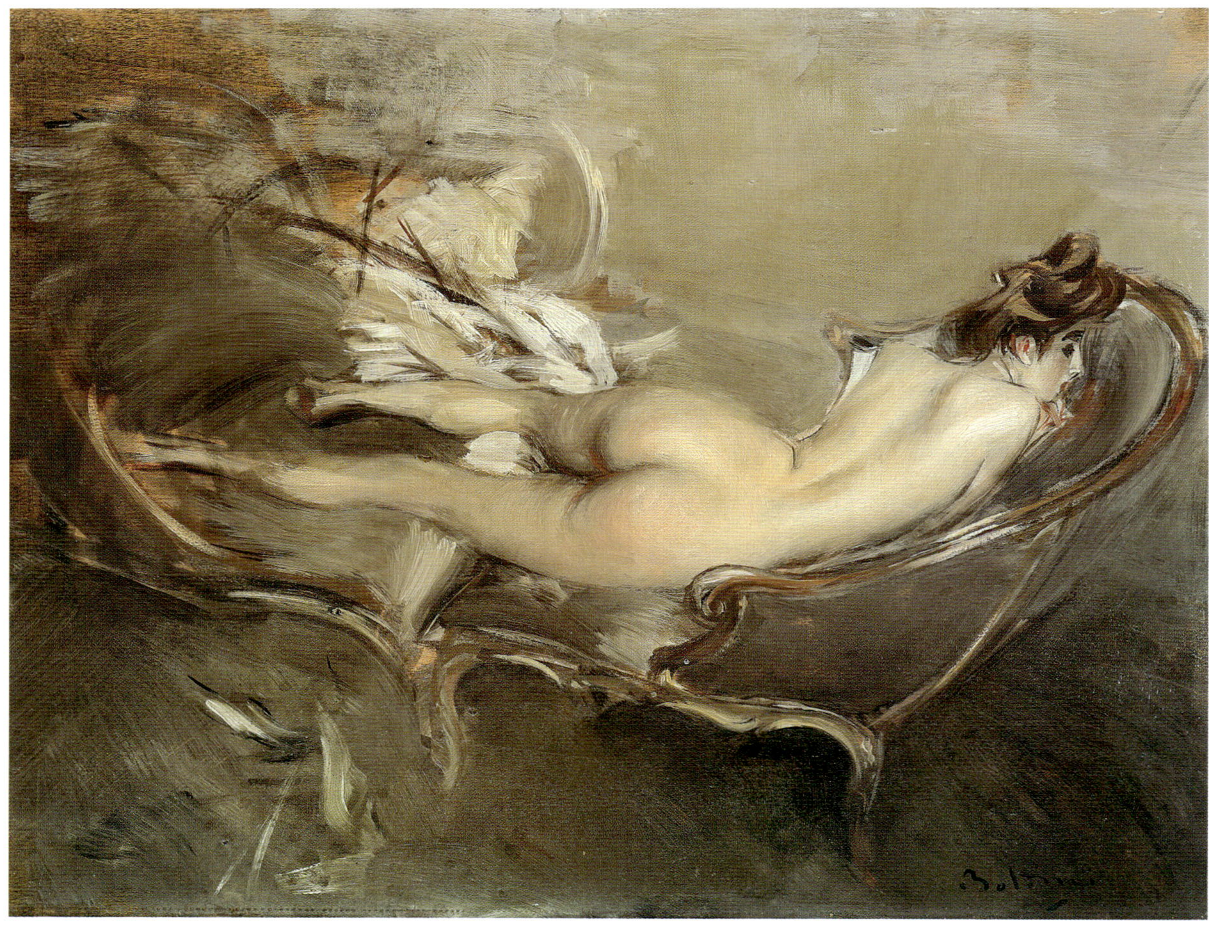

FIG.146
Giovanni Boldini (1842–1931), *A Reclining Nude on a Day-bed*, *c.*1900, oil on panel, 26.6 × 34.3cm, photo courtesy of J.–L. Baroni Ltd

pictures by Greuze than any nation under good instruction ought to wish for. In like manner the public has grown rich in Boucher, much beyond the desires of the judicious'.[91]

The new museum, nevertheless, attracted admiring glances from across the Channel. Pierre de Nolhac singled out the Wallace Collection Bouchers as worthy of especial praise: 'the most fertile, the most famous, the most representative master of the amiable century is represented by at least twenty exquisite works. Even in the Louvre, François Boucher, First Painter to King Louis XV, is not presented as brilliantly as in this new gallery in England'.[92] With the onset of modernism, however, evaluation of Boucher's art in both Britain and France continued to be ambivalent. Already in 1904 Josz had lamented the lack of celebration in Paris to mark Boucher's bicentenary: 'Nevertheless (and so fast) the twelve months of 1903 have passed, and we have forgotten François Boucher ... It is shameful for those who know ... the master so beloved of the young, it is shameful that they did not stir themselves and that they did not have the courage to demand the 'pretty' and serious celebration, in faith, that François Boucher merited. Boucher had nothing ...'.[93] Against the backdrop of the World Wars Boucher's aesthetic of pleasure appeared at best irrelevant and at worst frivolous and vapid. The French historian, Louis Réau, writing in the 1920s, excused Boucher's frivolity by praising his patriotism: 'let us willingly forgive him for imagining that Venus resembles Mlle Murphy rather than a plaster Medici Venus. That his amiable talent lacks elevation one must agree. But let us celebrate this fine painter for staying, even if by habit, faithful to French taste'.[94] Roger Fry,

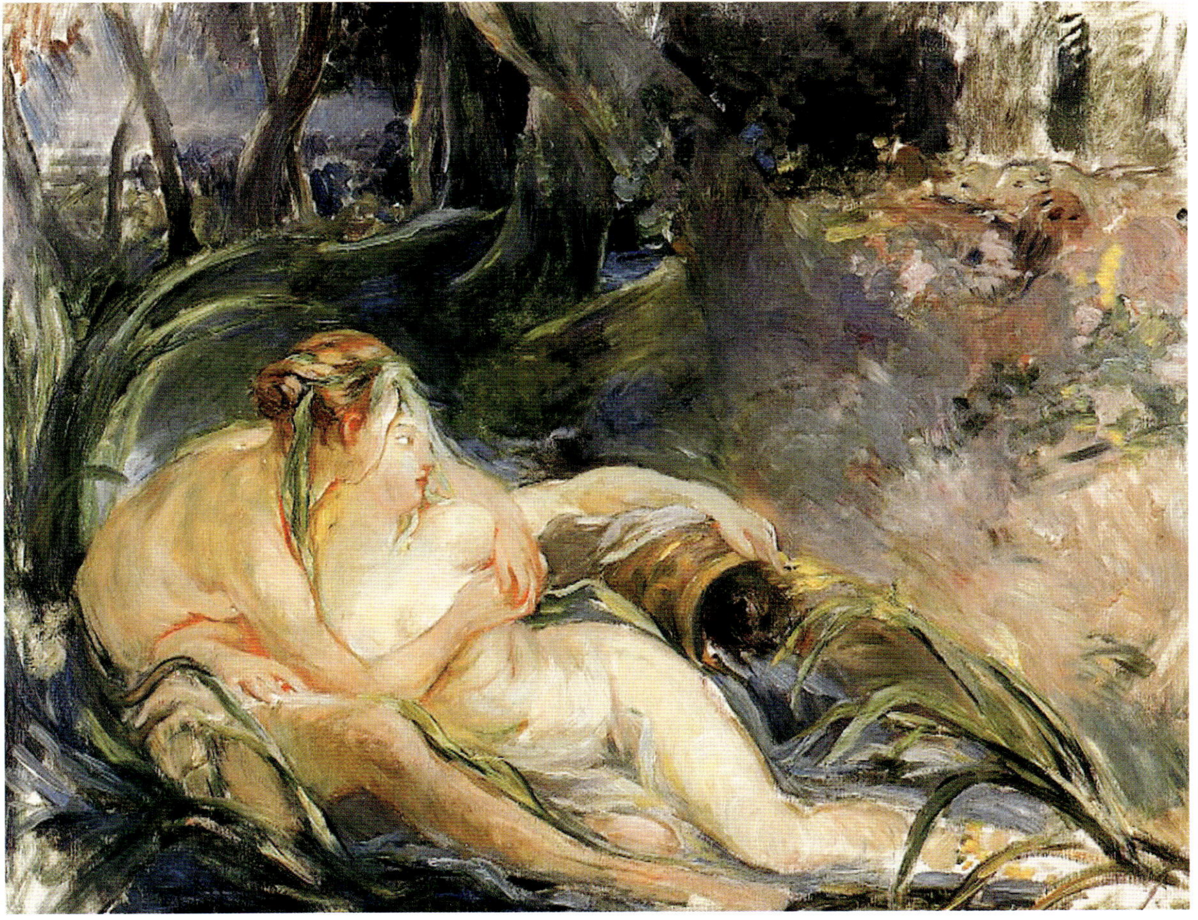

FIG.147
Berthe Morisot (1841–1895), *Two Nymphs Embracing*, 1892, oil on canvas, 63.8 × 79.4cm, photograph courtesy of Sotheby's

FIG.148
Bedroom in the Louis XV Style, New York, 1905, anonymous photograph

FIG.149 *opposite*
SIR GERALD KELLY (1879–1972), *Portrait of Mrs Horace Elgin Dodge*, 1932, oil on canvas, 238 × 124cm, Detroit, Institute of Arts

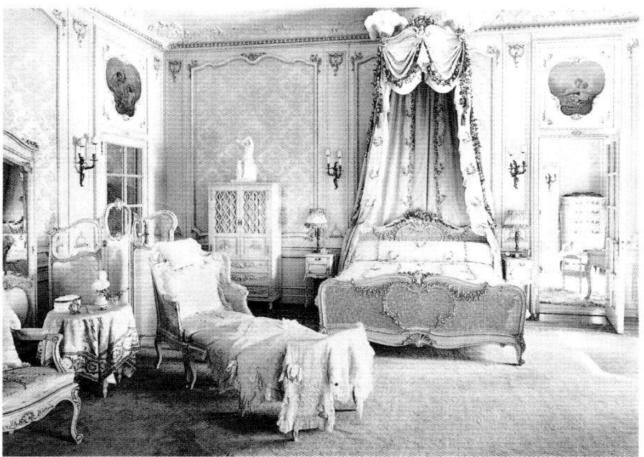

writing in England the following decade, asserted that 'artists like Nattier and Boucher ... looked at life only in order to find the most facile and seductive decorative formula into which its reality could be transposed. They were not in a mood to discover its hidden and unforeseen possibilities. They were content to make their art merely ancillary to the brilliant social life of the day'.[95]

Fresh support for Boucher and the eighteenth-century aesthetic was, however, to be found in the United States. The new American millionaires, in their thirst for European culture and refinement, had no qualms about wholeheartedly embracing the elegance, comfort and conspicuous consumption represented by eighteenth-century France and, in particular, the art of Boucher. Figure 148 shows a bedroom in New York at the beginning of the twentieth century decorated in the fashionable Louis XV style, complete with Boucheresque putti overdoors. Indeed the combination of style and intimacy, so highly prized by the *ancien régime* and by the wealthy gentleman of the nineteenth century, continues to inform chic interiors on the upper East Side today. Moreover, a stream of collectors from Henry Clay Frick to the present day have ensured that a growing number of works by Boucher have found a home in the private collections and museums of the United States. One patron, Mrs Dodge, even carried her enthusiasm for Boucher so far as to have herself depicted as a modern Madame de Pompadour in a portrait (fig.149) that mimics Boucher's portraits of the marquise (see fig.78).

The rise of socialism, the sexual revolution, the cult of the individual and the increasing materialism of European culture in the second half of the twentieth century have all had a bearing on how Boucher has been perceived and interpreted. The biographical approach to his life and work continued in the 1950s and 1960s, with Boucher portrayed as rakish confidante and friend to the Marquise de Pompadour by Nancy Mitford in 1954 and by Ian McInnes in 1965.[96] Boucher was almost too easy a target for the sexual re-interpretations of art in the 1970s. Historians like Michael Levey described the effect of Boucher's works in quasi-pornographic terms where 'man is postulated as the spectator, looking into the pictures as into a vitrine wondering what to buy'.[97] Norman Bryson similarly claimed that 'spatial dislocation in Boucher is the exact mark of sexual availability and in suppressing coherent space through the use of amorphous substances – cloud, water, tinted steam – which cannot be precisely located in space, the body is presented in the minimal form that the [male] erotic gaze most desires: as simply, posture'.[98] More recently, feminist commentators like Eunice Lipton have noted instead the 'insistently feminine' quality of Boucher's work and pointed out that they were intended for the enjoyment of the female as well as the male viewer: 'There is no sexual (and social) tension in Boucher's paintings, I dare say for the reason that there is no gendered 'I' ... There is no place in which to triumph in these paintings, no arenas in which to show off. Male desire is washed up here'.[98]

The 1980s and 1990s were marked by an increasing preoccupation with genre, morality and public responses to art in the eighteenth century. Academics, re-examining the brilliantly written commentaries of Diderot and other Salon critics, often echoed their viewpoints, leading to a similarly negative or, at best, rather flat response to Boucher's artistic achievement, often defined in opposition to Chardin and Greuze. At the same time a parallel response to Boucher's work has co-existed throughout this period, as in the eighteenth century, among those pursuing an empirical and connoisseurial approach to art history. Museum and exhibition curators, auction experts and dealers are still employed, as in Boucher's era, in assembling and ordering factual knowledge about the artist and his work, which they often present in a positive light to help explain or sell the artist to the public or buyer. Boucher's works also continue to attract the attention of wealthy collectors as the high prices fetched by his drawings and paintings prove. The sheer number of fascinating studies on individual aspects of Boucher's vast oeuvre produced by all these different groups has often led to that knowledge remaining restricted to a specialist audience. So, despite the advances in specialised scholarship, many of the sweeping generalisations regarding Boucher's life and art inherited from the nineteenth century have remained largely uncorrected.

In fact it is the salacious and prurient associations surrounding Boucher's art since Diderot that have rendered it fascinating to a new generation of writers and designers. We find that the nineteenth-century image of *ancien régime* decadence, of which Boucher's art appears the manifestation, continues to affect contemporary references to Boucher. Francisco Rebolledo's novel, *Rasero*, is typical: 'That night as he was coming out of the Opéra, after seeing the performance of an unbearable drama by Rameau, he invited the painter François Boucher and a pair of pretty actresses to his house ... the bacchanalia lasted until dawn, when naked, drunk, and overcome by sleep, they lay like rag dolls, some on the bed, others on the carpet'.[100] Had the legend of Louise O'Murphy not been grafted onto the images of Boucher's nymphs it might not have survived to fascinate as in Christopher Logue's autobiography, *Prince Charming*: 'April 1959: A telephone call from someone called George Martin who works at EMI records ... His office is next door to the Wallace Collection so I can combine my seeing him with a view of Miss O'Murphy's bum ... The O'Murphy bum is one of the finest painted. It turns out there were two O' Murphy girls, Victorine and Louise, both painted by Boucher. Lucky man. But whose bum is it?'[101]

Boucher's *Blonde Odalisque* on the cover of Duncan Sprout's novel, *Our Lady of the Potatoes*, another imaginary life of Louise O'Murphy, immediately renders it eye-catching and commercial, as do the other Boucher images used to decorate the array of products shown in Figure 150. Boucher's pastorals, their currency debased through repetition, still prove adaptable as decorations, whether for a Fortnum and Mason's biscuit barrel or a Covent Garden market flower-pot. Timney Fowler's *Boucher Homage* material recalls the original toile de Jouy textiles, while Madame de Pompadour's bathing *Venus* can be

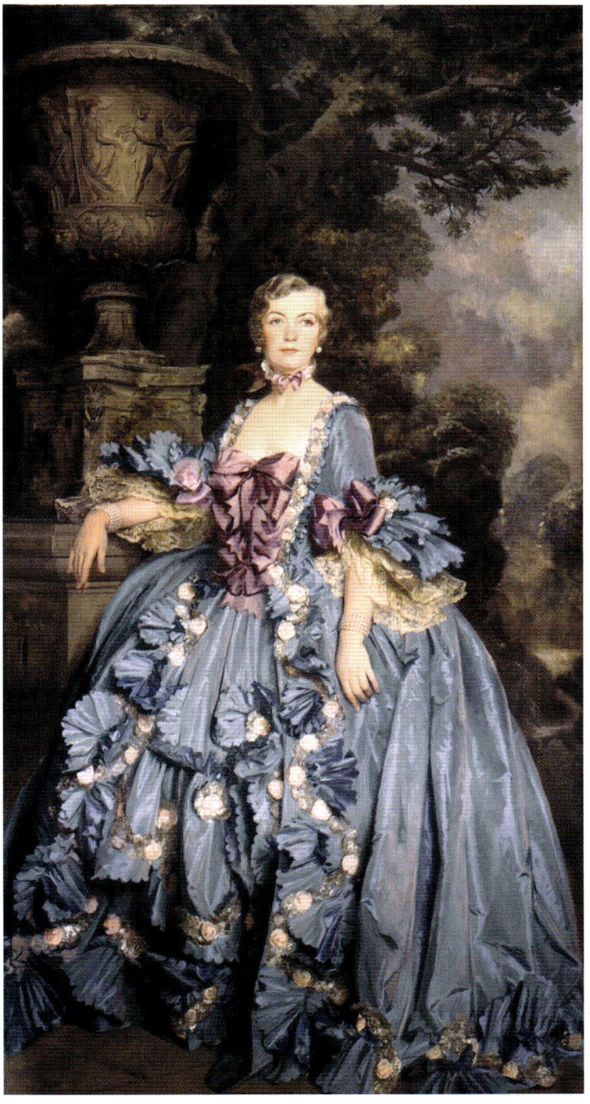

FIG.150
Twentieth-century Boucher-inspired products, including Fortnum and Mason's biscuit-barrel, Timney Fowler *Boucher Homage* material, Valobre Soap, book-covers and Covent Garden market flower-pot

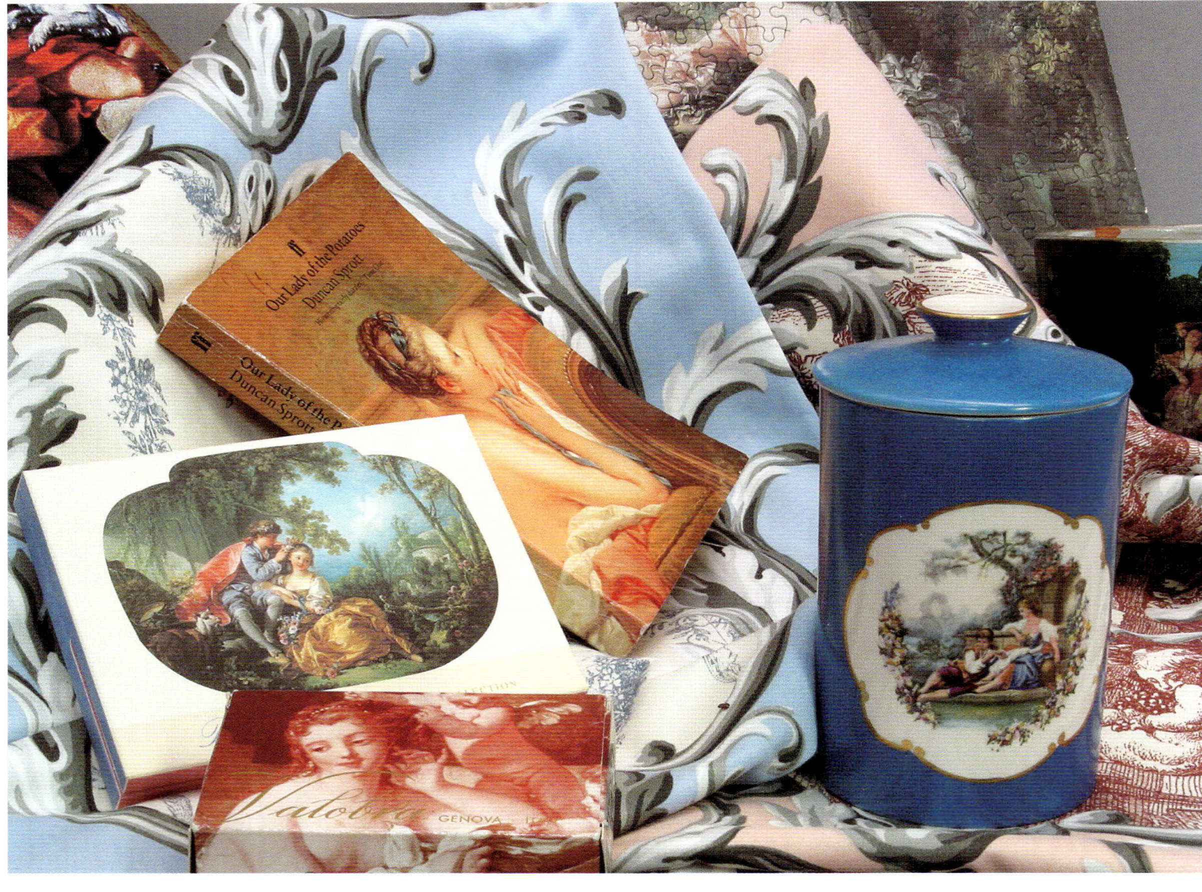

found adorning the packaging for Valobre soap. It is hardly surprising to find that Vivienne Westwood, who once stated that 'fashion is really about being naked', has also been inspired by Boucher. She celebrated the fusion of sex, fashion and art by reproducing Boucher's *Daphnis and Chloé* (fig.69) across a wide variety of products, from T-shirts to scarves to corsets. The latter, when worn, affords the onlooker a view almost as revealing as that enjoyed by Daphnis. Opera and ballet continue to use Boucher pictures for theatrical backdrops or posters. The image of a ballerina asleep in front of the backdrop of Boucher's *Rising of the Sun* (fig.84) was used to advertise English National Ballet's *Sleeping Beauty* of June 2000. But perhaps *Gilded Cabbage* (fig.151) by Antoine Roegiers (1980–) provides one of the wittiest recent responses to Boucher. With a finesse worthy of the Rococo this takes an element from nature, often used to symbolise the female genitalia in Boucher's early rustic canvases, and transforms it through the use of gold paint into a surprising and humorous meditation on the gilded interiors of the eighteenth century.[102]

Nowadays public museums and galleries ensure that the art of François Boucher, originally painted for an elite, can be enjoyed by a wider audience. Whatever one's viewpoint one can stroll into the Wallace Collection during opening hours and contemplate its incomparable collection of Bouchers. Museums and galleries now fulfil the public role formerly taken by the Salon and the churches of eighteenth-century Paris. Like their eighteenth-century forebears, however, their institutional character does not always create the most sympathetic environment for enjoying Boucher's work. Boucher still appears more at home in private, so viewers are often more impressed by Boucher's art when they meet it in the context of a house museum like the Wallace Collection or the Frick Collection. The intimate nature of Boucher's art also makes it harder to display in the context of a large monographic exhibition. Nevertheless, as may be seen at the Wallace Collection, individual works by Boucher can stand alongside the greatest productions of the Western European tradition.

Boucher Today

It is hardly Boucher's fault that contemporary concerns often make us more alert to sex and materialism in Boucher's art than to its overall artistic merit. Few artists have matched Boucher's extraordinary ability to paint nudes so seductive that the viewer is prompted to examine and comment on the model before the work of art. Their undeniable power continues to disturb those who feel that art should have supposedly more profound aims than the pursuit of love and pleasure. Similarly, a moralising interpretation of the subjects of Boucher's paintings also distracts from a considered appraisal of his technical ability. This is all the more ironic in view of the stress on formal autonomy and individual artistic vision that has informed most art criticism since the end of the nineteenth century. We find it perfectly acceptable for Matisse to believe that: 'Art must carry in itself its complete significance and impose itself upon the beholder even before he can identify the subject matter'.[103] The absence of conflict in Boucher likewise finds an echo in Matisse's belief that art should be an 'art of balance devoid of troubling or depressing subject matter … a soothing, calming influence on the mind, rather like a good armchair which provides relaxation from physical fatigue'.[104] The distinction between art and nature, and the importance of artistic imagination promulgated by writers and artists as diverse as Nietzsche – 'Art is nothing but Art, we have art so as not to die from truth', Picasso – 'we all know that Art is not truth. Art is a lie that makes us realise truth', or Francis Bacon – 'art is what man adds to nature', are now widely accepted.[105] Such views more than vindicate Boucher's approach, where technical brilliance is combined with an imagination so intense that it creates an artistic reality as identifiable and individual as anything created by Matisse, Picasso or Bacon. Paradoxically, as in his own day, it is perhaps the exceptional breadth of Boucher's vision that makes the scope of his achievement so difficult to grasp. There are as many different Bouchers today as there are aesthetic, academic, political and economic approaches, each version of Boucher reflecting the different agendas and interests in much the same way as Boucher's vision of China reflected those of the elite of eighteenth-century France. If one agrees with William Blake's belief that 'exuberance is beauty', one can only admire Boucher's diversity and confidence. But this also encourages a tendency to disappear into exploration of the byways of the fine and decorative arts in the eighteenth century, causing us to lose sight of the overall ambition and brilliance of Boucher's contribution to the history of Western art. The sun rises rather than sets in Boucher's joyful canvases in the Wallace Collection, providing a great burst of light to illuminate the European mythological tradition; a last flowering of absolutist confidence and Enlightenment optimism untenable after the *Gotterdämmerung* of the French Revolution. Helped by a greater understanding of Boucher's own age, with the layers of subsequent re-interpretation removed, Boucher's breathtaking divine visions still have the power to seduce. In these days of media emphasis on disaster, war and conflict we can still turn to Boucher, remembering Voltaire's belief that 'it is not a little thing to give pleasure'.[106]

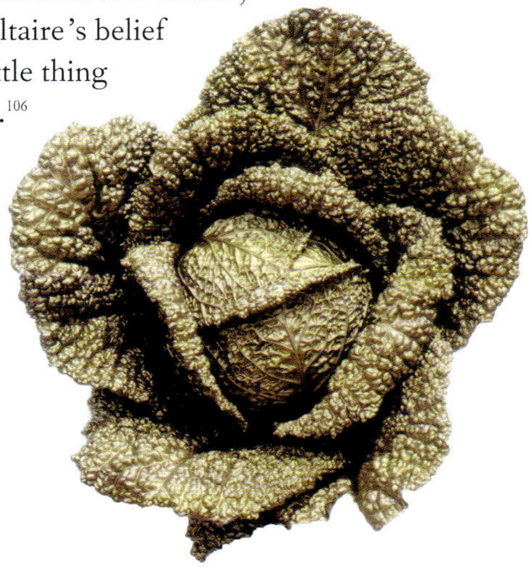

FIG.151
ANTOINE ROEGIERS (1980–), *Gilded Cabbage*, 2003, cabbage covered with gold paint, exhibited in *Rococo & Co.*, Paris, École Nationale Supérieure des Beaux-Arts, 2003

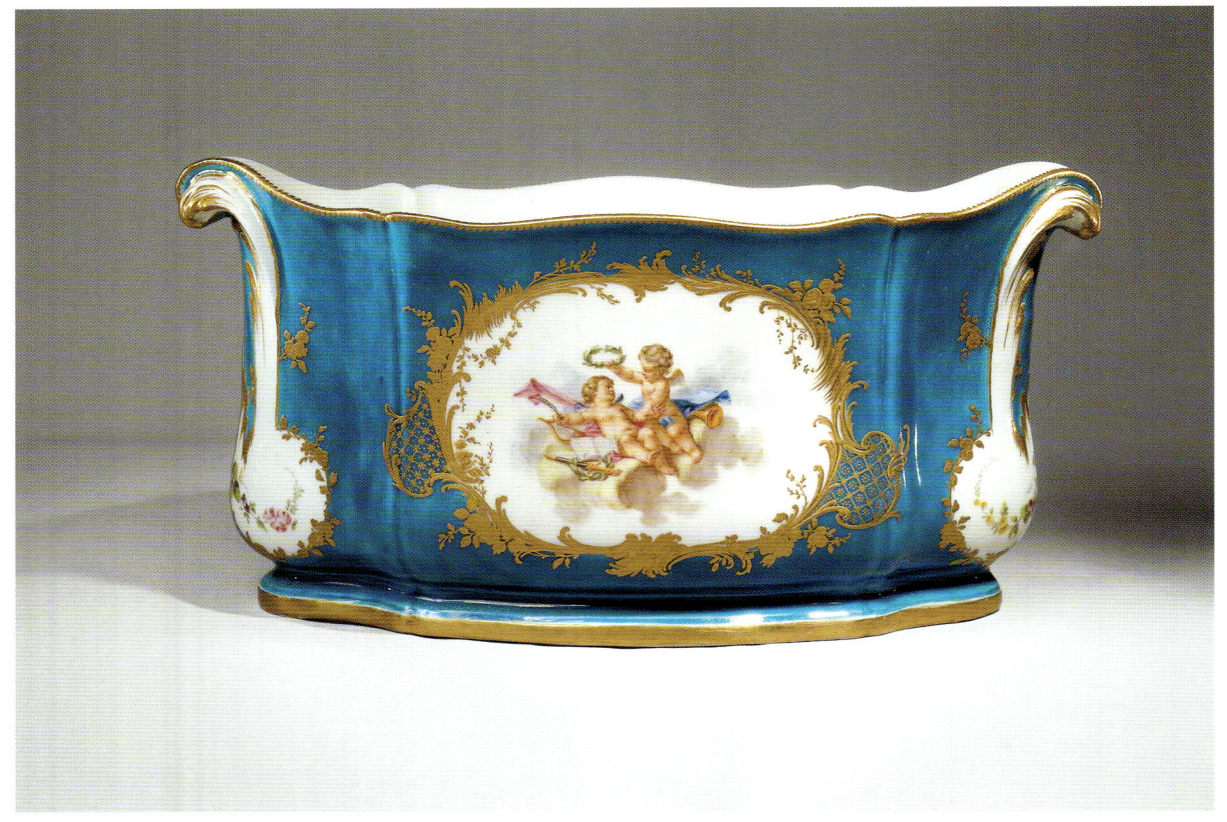

FIG.152
Flower Vase
Vincennes porcelain, 1755–6, decorated with a turquoise-blue ground and painted with cherubs after Boucher from *La Poésie* by G. Demarteau (in same sense, though closer to G.L. Hertel's copy of La Rue's version in the opposite sense). Wallace Collection C214

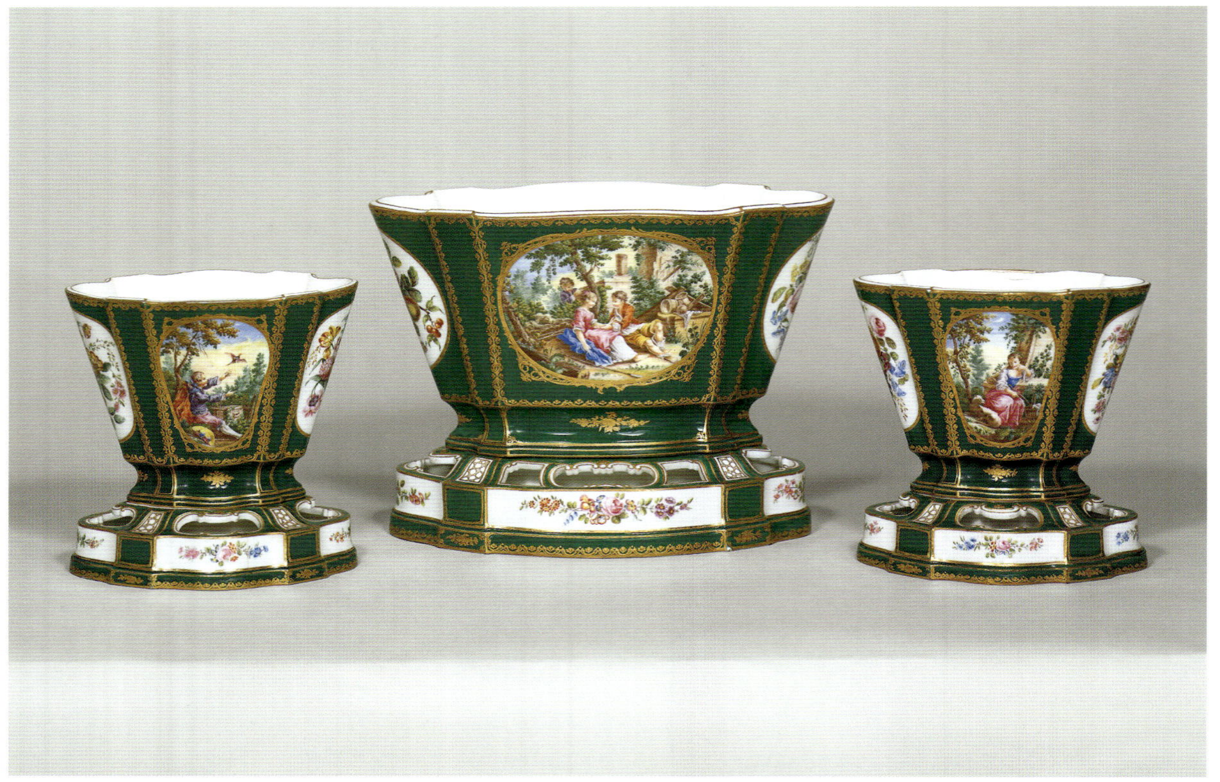

FIG.153
Garniture of Three Flower Pots
Sèvres porcelain, 1762, decorated with a green ground and painted with pastoral scenes after Boucher, including the *Pastorale* by G. Huquier (1736), *Le Pasteur galant* and *Le Pasteur complaisant* by A. Laurant (1742) and *Silvandre, heureux amant, qui ne t'inquiète…* from *Les Amours Pastorales* by C. Duflos (1751–2). Wallace Collection C220–222

Boucher: The Muse for Sèvres Porcelain and Gold Boxes in the Wallace Collection

By Rosalind Savill

The Inspiration

Boucher's effect on the decorative arts in eighteenth-century France is incomparable. A glance through collections anywhere in the world reveals his supreme influence from the late-1740s until the 1790s, and his subjects are the most prolific of any artist on the porcelain and goldsmiths' work in the Wallace Collection. This is due to a perfect combination of circumstances. In about 1750, when he was at the height of his creative powers, his most important patrons Louis XV and Madame de Pompadour were particularly supportive of the burgeoning porcelain factory of Vincennes (later called Sèvres). This enterprise was keen to establish a new, essentially French ceramic style in contrast to the Oriental and Meissen influences that had previously held sway, and so sought inspiration from French artists. Likewise snuff-box enamellers in Paris became increasingly proficient and, instead of simply applying flowers sparingly to the gold, began to illustrate entire pictures within frame-like cartouches created by the goldsmiths, and they needed contemporary subject matter to please their patrons. Boucher was just the catalyst who almost single-handedly could provide the stimulation the decorative arts industries were seeking.

He evolved a style that embodied the spirit of the day in being light-hearted and very human, in being original and contemporary, in contrasting heavenly and earthly themes, in capturing exotic and imaginary worlds, and in being naturally decorative, colourful and appealing. His subjects in the Wallace Collection alone range from playful children (the birdcatchers) to representational cherubs (*The Elements*), from rural landscapes (the mill at Charenton) to urban street sellers (the vinegar seller), from pastorals (*The Grape Eaters*) to mythologies (*Pygmalion*), and from rustic farm subjects (feeding chickens) to exotic chinoiseries (cormorant fishing). They were irresistible, particularly to porcelain and enamel painters, but also to goldsmiths, sculptors, marqueteurs, fan-painters and textile-weavers, and these copies after Boucher established France as the most envied and imitated centre of the arts in Europe.

His designs were chiefly used in two ways: either as sculpted figures in unglazed biscuit porcelain which, after firing, had a smooth marble-like surface, or painted in enamel colours in reserves on porcelain or on gold boxes using either translucent or opaque enamels. Occasionally Boucher's sources were combined with those of other artists on the sides of gold boxes or in garnitures of vases. Sometimes subjects were treated with a fair degree of artistic licence, often being extended or reduced to fit the space given by the shape of the object, or allotted by the goldsmith or the ground-colour painter. The idea of copying an artist's work in eighteenth-century France was more respected than we might imagine today. In 1761 Diderot commented that 'A good copy in enamel is almost regarded as highly as the original' and his views must have been echoed by those enlightened patrons who enjoyed Boucher subjects on everything from their egg cups to grand vases and, if they were snuff takers, even carrying them around in their pockets. They would have prided themselves on possessing their own miniature versions of some of the most fashionable paintings of the day.

Interpretation of the Sources

One of the earliest examples of Boucher inspiring a porcelain painter is a Vincennes glass cooler of about 1747–8 showing one of his engravings after Watteau. The last were some of the subjects from Abbé Banier's new Paris edition of Ovid's *Metamorphoses*, published in 1767–71 but still appearing on Sèvres in 1793, four years after the outbreak of the French Revolution. Generally the subjects were taken from engravings, available through the print sellers in Paris; the Vincennes factory bought twenty-three engravings of children after Boucher in 1752 and at least thirty-seven of varying subjects still survive at the factory. These were either after paintings shown in the *salon* or engraved versions of drawings issued in folios. Among his most popular engravings used in the 1750s and 1760s were the *Pastorale* of 1736, *Cries de Paris* of 1737, *Jeux d'enfants* of 1738, chinoiseries and children from the late-1740s, and the *Amours pastorales* of 1751–2. Even more exciting, and much rarer than the use of engravings, is the number of original drawings and paintings that were used directly. The Vincennes factory commissioned drawings from Boucher himself, largely of children, and one of a young gardener (*Le Petit Jardinier*) has an inscription noting that it was supplied by him on 23 August 1749. The factory's documents reveal that in 1752 he executed thirteen more drawings of children, presumably individuals, as well as designs for three groups of children. But his only recorded payments were for unspecified drawings on 31 December 1754 and on 8 April 1756.

Examples of the factory apparently copying paintings directly include *The Flute Lesson* of 1748 and *The Grape Eaters* of 1749 (also called *The Autumn Pastoral*, in the Wallace Collection) which were modelled as two sculptural groups by 1752, despite the engraving of the former not having been announced until 1758 and no engraving of the latter being recorded. Perhaps Boucher submitted sketches, or the factory sent an artist to copy the original paintings. A similar anomaly arose in 1762 with *The School Master* and *The School Mistress*, both derived from drawings by Boucher, but the latter was not engraved until 1769. Interestingly Falconet, when sculpting the biscuit version of the former, set the action a few moments earlier than Boucher's drawing, perhaps to add a touch of nicety to what may have been an unsuitable subject for Vincennes. In the drawing the girl is shown weeping, her skirts pulled up and she is being beaten by the master whose arm is poised for another blow. But in the biscuit group the master's arm is still at his side and she, well-covered, is imploring him not to punish her. *The Flute Lesson* is often found painted in reserves from the late-1760s, but *The Grape Eaters* and *The School Master* are more rare, yet all three subjects appear on a garniture of vases in the Wallace Collection, probably decorated in 1779 by the painter Caton (see fig.133). The school master is copied from the Falconet group, rather than Boucher's drawing, but the painter has added a humorous touch with the elder girl wearing an ass's ear on her head, the equivalent of a dunce's cap, which is unique to this vase.

Gold-box enamellers also seem to have had access to original subjects as shown by scenes sometimes being in the same sense as the original source rather than in the opposite sense of an engraved version (though a second engraving after the first may have been the source). This is true of two snuff-boxes in the Wallace Collection: one of 1756–7 shows two maternal scenes after Boucher drawings, while the other of 1764–5 shows his painting *Venus Disarming Cupid*. The latter is of special interest because the oval picture was owned by Madame de Pompadour; it was engraved in rectangular form in the opposite sense by Fessard in 1761, and appears in an anonymous drawing of a complete snuff-box design in the Musée des Arts Décoratifs, Paris, where the oval scene is in the same sense as the rectangular engraving. But the box shows the subject in an oval and in the same sense as the original painting, despite the engraving having been available, suggesting perhaps that it was copied directly from Madame de Pompadour's painting.

Children and Cherubs

Boucher's first major contribution to the stylistic development of Vincennes was his series of children. These were divided into two types: either children in colourful clothes pursuing country pursuits or naked winged cherubs set in the clouds, usually representing such themes as *The Elements*, *The Arts* or *The Seasons*, or pursuing various ethereal activities. The children were interpreted by both the sculptors and painters at the factory, probably being produced as free-standing glazed figures from as early as 1748. Usually they were produced as unglazed biscuit figures in a cast of characters displayed in communicating pairs as the table decoration for the dessert course of a meal. Often they were re-workings of Boucher's early-1750s commission with Falconet to provide figures for Madame de Pompadour's Dairy at her Château at Crécy, others had theatrical associations, sometimes after characters in current comic operas performed by the impresario Charles-Siméon Favart. Some were later engraved by Jouaillain so that, as a newspaper announcement of 1763 declared, the engravings would survive the fragile porcelain versions and would provide a lasting record of them.

The first reference to Boucher figures being sold at Vincennes was on 21 November 1752 when eight were bought by the marquis de Courteille, and they remained popular for many years, new figures being added to the range until Falconet left for Russia in 1766. In all over seventy such children were modelled and between two and twenty-one were included in dinner services, often together with pastoral groups after Boucher, between 1758 and 1777. Madame de Pompadour's inventory shows that she had twelve Vincennes children in a dessert service centrepiece with other larger groups after Boucher and Oudry in her pantry (where the dessert was prepared) in the Hôtel de Pompadour in Paris, and at Versailles she had fifty children and five larger groups, this time specified as Sèvres, twenty-five of which she may have bought directly from the factory between 1761 and 1763.

The twenty-three engravings purchased by Vincennes in 1752 were of cherubs, and were far from recent, since the *Jeux d'Enfants* had largely been published 1738. They may already have been the inspiration for Meissen, because the dealer Lazare Duvaux records such decoration on a Meissen cup and saucer on 16 May 1750, and on 15 December 1752 Madame de Pompadour bought a gold and enamelled snuff-box 'with Meissen porcelain cartouches representing children's games' (*'jeux d'enfants'*). While the Vincennes records of decorated pieces only refer to *enfants*, they were generally known as *'enfants de Boucher'* outside the factory, as shown by a pair of vases bought by Madame de Pompadour in 1755 which appear in her inventory at the Château of Saint-Ouen.

When in the early days Boucher's children were interpreted by the painters at Vincennes, they appeared in bright colours of the painter's invention. New artists at the factory would master the difficult enamel colours by working with a single colour, they would then gravitate to a single colour with flesh tones in polychrome and then, finally, to the full polychrome palette. The combination of monochrome and polychrome figures also occurs in enamels on snuff-boxes. Usually the paintings of children are considerably adapted by the time they appear on porcelain, though the gold-box enamellers are more literal in their interpretation of the engraved sources. The porcelain painters invested them with dairy, fishing or gardening equipment, or they blow bubbles, hold hands or exchange doves, and they are usually set in landscapes. A free-hand interpretation by the painter is often witty, as with the version of Boucher's fishing scene *La Pésche* engraved by Le Prince, which appears on a saucer of 1761. It shows the young girl, isolated from her companion and frightened by the addition of a wiggly eel emerging from the huge fishing net above her head.

Rarely (if ever) did the same artist paint both children and cherubs. André-Vincent Veilliard specialised in children, despite the factory admitting in 1755 that he was not good at painting figures, whereas the more able painters, Charles-

Nicholas Dodin and Jean-Louis Morin, both spent their first years at the factory painting cherubs. Where children appear on useful wares such as cups and saucers, tea services (including Madame de Pompadour's blue and green example of 1758–9 in the Wallace Collection, fig.99) and on flower pots, cherubs appear on these and also on the grandest vases and royal commissions of the 1750s, including vases associated with Madame de Pompadour and the inkstand that Louis XV apparently gave to his daughter Madame Marie-Adélaïde.

Chinoiseries, Pastorals and Mythologies

Given the importance placed by the management at Vincennes on creating a French style from about 1750, chinoiseries only had a brief flowering in the early days from 1748–49. These idealised versions after Boucher occasionally recurred in the early-1760s, but differ in style from those examples copied from Chinese porcelain and woodcuts, which also appeared later. Engravings of Boucher's *Scenes of Chinese Life* by Pierre Aveline and *The Elements* by Gabriel Huquier provided sources, especially the *Lady fishing with a Cormorant* which is seen on a Vincennes wine-bottle cooler and, in the Wallace Collection, on a gold box 1749–50. This subject also survives as a drawing in the Sèvres Archives (with an eighteenth-century number and inscribed in a later hand '*F. Boucher*') and Boucher's inspiration for the composition may have come from an Oriental earthenware group of 'A Chinese fisherman with fishing lines and a cormorant beside him' among the Chinese objects in his own collection.

Painted versions of Boucher's pastorals were introduced later than the glazed or biscuit groups, except for a very few examples appearing in a rather Meissen-like style on Vincennes in the late-1740s. They are more usual in the 1760s when they are treated as complete paintings with the figures set in full landscapes with earth and sky. Sometimes the engravings were adapted to the point of idiocy, as with two of Boucher's *Les Amours Pastorales* engraved by Claude Duflos in 1751–2, which appear on a gold box of 1759–60 with the pairs of lovers moved indoors. The pastoral landscapes have been changed to rustic, domestic interiors, but the enameller has failed to adapt his lovers to their new locations so that a shepherdess retains her crook while sitting with her lover on a tree trunk in the middle of a kitchen floor (fig.157). Since other versions of these subjects appear in an interior, the same enameller may be responsible each time. Boucher's actual landscape subjects are rarely seen on decorative arts, though they can appear on the backs of vases or on the sides of snuff-boxes, but figure scenes were always given pride of place.

Mythological scenes became popular at Sèvres in the late-1760s (though perhaps earlier with gold boxes, since Diderot praised a miniature version of *Hercules and Omphale* in 1755), and remained so for the rest of the century. Those after Boucher, being his last area of influence at the factory and derived from his illustrations for the 1767–71 edition of Ovid's *Metamorphoses*, were painted by the most able painters of the day, culminating in the extraordinary quality and complexity of pieces for Louis XVI's great dinner service, begun in 1783 but left incomplete with his execution in 1793 (largely in the Royal Collection at Windsor). Boucher had died before Louis XVI had come to the throne in 1774, yet his classically-inspired subjects were as perfect for this late-eighteenth century service as his cherubs and children had been almost fifty years earlier. In fact he was held in such respect that in 1783 his early *Renaud and Armid*a of 1734 was transported to the Sèvres factory to be copied as a picture on a large plaque (now on a secretaire in the Henry Huntington Collection in San Marino).

Display and Dissemination

Sèvres porcelain and gold boxes enhanced rooms already furnished with the works of Boucher. For example, Madame de Pompadour hung his paintings on her walls and as over-doors, she had his engravings framed and glazed for display and she had Gobelins tapestries woven for her with his subjects of children. Her Grand Salon in the Hôtel de Pompadour in Paris was richly furnished with two large mirrors on the wall opposite the garden reflecting Indian crimson silk curtains and bell cords, a gilded sofa and various chairs covered in Gobelins tapestry with children after Boucher, Gobelins screens with his children's games and with flowers and fables, and nineteen Chinese porcelain vases and a statue of Louis XV. As late as 1779, the princesse de Condé's bedroom in the Hôtel Bourbon-Condé in Paris still had walls hung with crimson-ground Boucher Gobelins tapestries dating from about 1770, against which she displayed on her chest-of-drawers Sèvres rose-ground vases of the 1750s painted with Boucher cherubs.

In addition to inventories and sale catalogues showing that Boucher's subjects were instantly recognisable within his own lifetime, there is also evidence that cautious cataloguers very quickly acknowledged imitators working in the style of Boucher. For example, in Madame de Pompadour's inventory of 1764 figure drawings are described as 'in the taste of Boucher' and, within five years of his death, in the Blondel de Gagny sale of 1776, Sèvres vases were painted not only with 'miniature scenes after François Boucher' but also with 'children in the taste of Boucher'.

His fame spread rapidly throughout Europe, partly disseminated by the many engraved versions of his paintings, but also because decorative arts using his subjects were dispersed abroad. His burst of influence at Sèvres in the 1750s coincided with France entering the Seven Years' War (1756–63), and his cherubs found themselves on vases, a jug and basin and tureens, and his children as biscuit figures, which were given as diplomatic gifts by Louis XV to Austria, Denmark and Russia. Even fourteen years after his death his *Pygmalion* from Ovid's *Metamorphoses* found himself on a magnificent vase presented by Louis XVI to Prince Henry of Prussia (Frederick the Great's younger brother) in 1784 (fig.155). The English also enjoyed Boucher's subjects, the Duchess of Bedford receiving some of his biscuit figures of children and pastoral lovers in the Sèvres service presented to her by Louis XV at the end of the Seven Year's War in 1763, and Lord Melbourne commissioning cherubs (one even holding a copy of *Hamlet*) on his service of 1771. Boucher's international reputation, spread through his engravings, continued to grow as he was copied by most of the European porcelain factories in the eighteenth and nineteenth centuries. But these versions tended to be more slavish replicas, without the individual interpretation of the hand-painted examples of Vincennes and Sèvres or of the enamellers working on gold boxes, where each painter had his own personal touch and where every scene is unique. In the nineteenth century his designs of cherubs, children and pastorals were much copied by fakers and redecorators who saw his style as intrinsic to the unwary collector's idea of rococo Sèvres and goldsmith's work. Even Sèvres itself continued to draw on sources associated with him, for a pair of vases of 1860 at Compiègne is painted with figures of children including the *Dancer* who was then considered to be painted by Boucher for Madame de Pompadour's Boudoir in her Château at Crécy, proving his designs could still be fashionable over a century after he had submitted his first drawings to the factory.

The Muse

One wonders how Boucher reacted to seeing his designs everywhere: in shops, on dinner tables, on fashion accessories, in salons, bedrooms, boudoirs, on furniture, porcelain, textiles and metalwork, in books, trade cards, theatrical scenery, and wall panels. His own sale catalogue shows how he was a passionate consumer and collector of different types of decorative arts, though only two Sèvres biscuit figures can be identified as having been after his own designs. The factory did present him with gifts on three occasions between 1756 and 1758, which included a biscuit figure of a child designed for Louis XV's dinner service, a green-ground basket, and three vases with a turquoise-blue ground, but they were painted (perhaps

FIG.154 *right*
Vase
Sèvres porcelain, *c.*1765, decorated with a blue ground and painted (probably by C.-E. Asselin) with the Savoyard fair scene of *La Lanterne Magique* after Boucher which was modelled as a biscuit group by Falconet in 1757. Wallace Collection C270

FIG.155 *far right*
Vase
Sèvres porcelain, 1781, decorated with a blue ground and painted with *Pygmalion* after Boucher, engraved by N. Lemire for Abbé Banier's edition of Ovid's *Metamorphoses* (Paris 1767–71). Wallace Collection C334

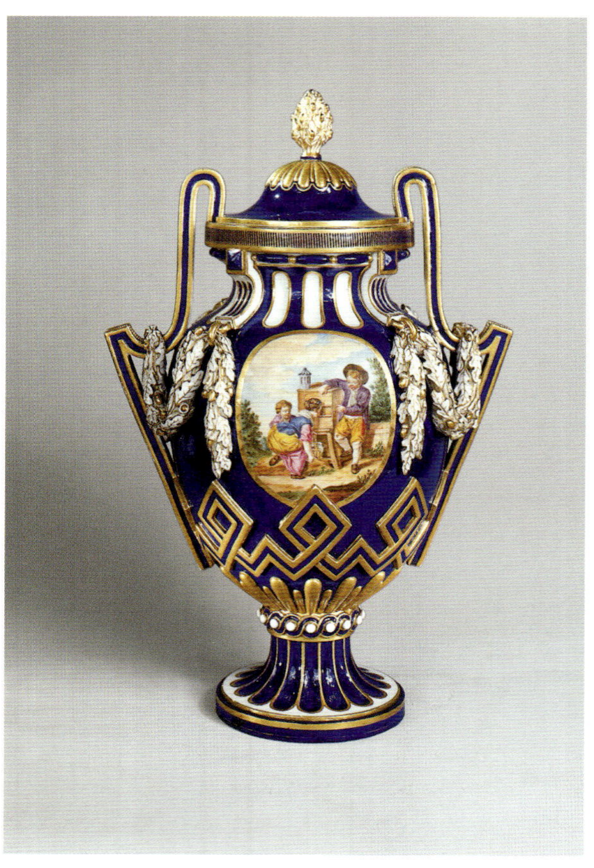

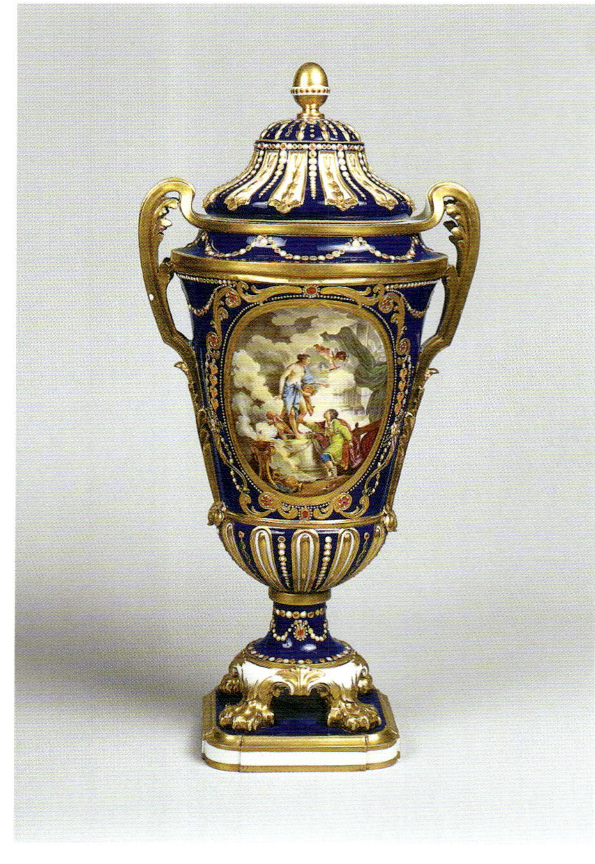

surprisingly) only with flowers. Other sources reveal that he took a practical interest in the applied arts: for example he painted Easter eggs for Louis XV in 1747, he mended a terracotta vase for Louis XV's Finance Minister, Orry de Fulvy, before his death in 1751, he commissioned Duvaux to gild the mounts of two turquoise-blue cups in 1752 (this time asking him to repair one that was broken), and occasionally designed gilt-bronze mounts for his own Chinese porcelain vases. Perhaps this hands-on approach gave him a better understanding of the needs of the painters and decorators of his day.

Another reason for his popularity was his ability to delight almost everyone, as shown by the affectionate foreword to his sale catalogue: 'The abundance of his talent, the richness of his compositions, the elegance of his figures and the smile of his landscapes, justifies his nickname *"peintre des graces"*.' Yet his style, known as '*le goût Boucher*', inevitably had (and still has) its detractors; not least among them the architect Boffrand who once said to Boucher's face: 'How is it possible that a clever man like you can apply himself to painting such foolish things'. But these so-called 'foolish things', their variety and their charm, have made his name synonymous with eighteenth-century France. It was also these qualities that so appealed to the 4th Marquess of Hertford in the nineteenth century and, largely due to him, the Wallace Collection excels not only in the greatest collection of Boucher's paintings in the world, but also in the most representative testimony of his brilliance as the muse for the painters of Sèvres porcelain and gold boxes.

The main sources for this text can be found in the publications listed on p.189.

Appendix

Sèvres Porcelain and Gold Boxes after Boucher in the Wallace Collection

The scenes appearing on the works of art listed below can be recognised in drawings by Boucher or in engravings after him, though alteration and adaptation are not unusual. All the engravings are after Boucher, but only the engraver is named here. When no engraving is cited, the scene is in the style of Boucher (and perhaps derives from lost drawings). They are listed by subject matter, then chronologically.

The works of art are referred to by Wallace Collection museum numbers. For Sèvres Porcelain (C-numbers), see Rosalind Savill, *The Wallace Collection, Catalogue of Sèvres Porcelain*, 3 vols, 1988, for Gold Boxes(G-numbers), see Rosalind Savill, *Gold Boxes in the Wallace Collection*, booklet, 1991. For further reading, see also Rosalind Savill's 'Six enamelled snuff-boxes in the Wallace Collection: some newly identified sources of decoration', *Apollo*, April 1980, vol.CXI, pp.304–9 and 'François Boucher and the porcelains of Vincennes and Sèvres', *Apollo*, March 1982, vol.CXV, pp.162–170.

All the gold boxes are painted in enamel unless qualified as having Sèvres porcelain plaques. The porcelain painter or gold-box enameller is named where known, and the gold-box place of manufacture and maker are recorded.

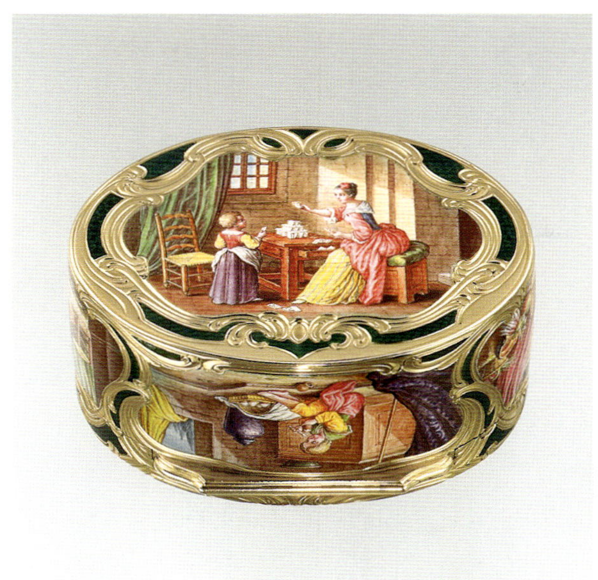

FIG.156 *below, left*
Gold Box
Paris, 1756–7, probably made by N. Hardivilliers and painted in enamels with *Le Petit Ménage* (top) and *Le Château de Cartes* (bottom, as shown) after drawings by Boucher in the Albertina, Vienna, and in a private collection, Paris. Wallace Collection G20

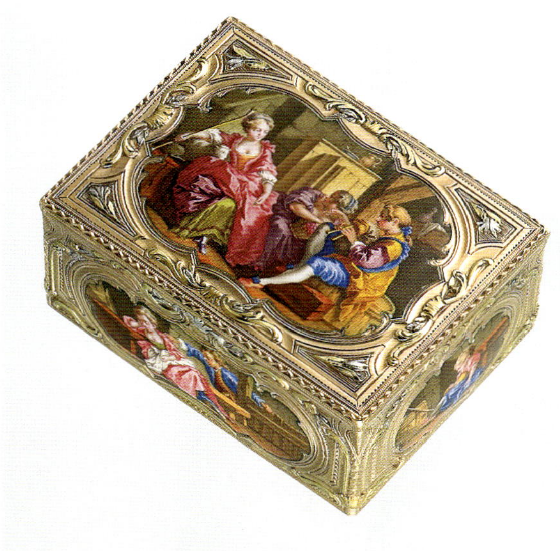

FIG.157 *below, right*
Gold Box
Paris, 1759–60, made by Paul Robert and painted with two of *Les Amours Pastorales* after Boucher, engraved by Claude Duflos (1751–2): *Ce pasteur amoureux chante sur sa musette…*(top, as shown) and *Ne plaignons point le sort de ses bergers…* (bottom). Wallace Collection G30

Cherubs (early: 1750s)

Painted in reserves with no background colour

1755–6

Flower Vase, c214
La Poésie by G. Demarteau (in same sense, though closer to G.L Hertel's copy of La Rue's version in the opposite sense)

Pair of Vases, c241–2
The Four Elements

1756–7

Pair of Vases, c246–7 (painted by C.-N. Dodin)
Quatrième livre de groupes d'enfans (*Deux amours dont un tient une couronne*) by P. Aveline
Cinquième livre de groupes d'enfans (*Deux amours dont un tient des flambeaux*) by J.G. Huquier

1757–8

Garniture of Three Vases, c248–50 (probably painted by C.-N. Dodin)
L'Amour oiseleur
Le Printemps
Quatre amours à la cible by G. Demarteau

Flower Vase, c204 (painted by J.-L. Morin)
Two cherubs with a dove

Jug and Basin, c452–3 (painted by C.-N. Dodin)
Quatrième livre de groupes d'enfans (*Deux amours dont un tient une couronne*) by P. Aveline

Gold Box, c496 (Paris by J. Ducrollay) with Sèvres plaques (probably painted by C.-N. Dodin)
La Poésie by G. Demarteau (in same sense) and by La Rue (in the opposite sense)

1758–9

Inkstand, c488 (probably painted by C.-N. Dodin)
Cherubs

1759–60

Cup and Saucer, c367 (painted by J.-L. Morin)
Cherubs

19th-Century Imitations

Gold Box, c497 with porcelain plaques
Cherubs

Cherubs (late: after 1760)

Usually with coloured backgrounds to the painted reserves

1765

Pair of Vases, c276–7 (painted by C.-N. Dodin)
On one two children deck a goat with bunches of grapes, similar to a Boucher drawing where children deck a donkey with flowers

1766

Saucer from a Tea Service, c391–5 (painted by C.-E. Asselin)
La Terre from Daullé's *Les Eléments* of 1748.
(for the same service, see also Children, Farm Scenes and Pastorals)

1767–70

Cup and Socketed Saucer, c445
Cherubs on clouds

1772

Covered Bowl and Plateau, c434–5 (painted by E. Chabry)
Quatrième livre de groupes d'enfans (*Deux amours dont un tient une couronne*) by P. Aveline
Quatre amours à la cible by G. Demarteau
Cinquième livre de groupes d'enfans (*Deux amours dont un tient des flambeaux*) by J.G. Huquier

Children

1757–8

Flower Pot, c217
Musical children

Tray, c390 (probably painted by A.-V. Veilliard)
La Pésche, by J.-B. Le Prince

1758–9

Tea Service, c384–6 (painted by A.-V. Veilliard)
Rustic children

Tea Service, c401–6 (painted by A.-V. Veilliard)
Rustic children
One subject reminiscent of *Mon moineau est pour Colette* by Crépy

1761

Cup and Saucer, c372
La Pésche, by J.-B. Le Prince

1764

Covered Bowl and Plateau, c428–9 (painted by A.-V. Veilliard)
Four scenes of children in the manner of Boucher

1766

Cup, Sugar Bowl and Teapot from a Tea Service, c391–5 (painted by C.-E. Asselin)
Jeux d'enfants by P. Aveline 1738
Fête de Bacchus
Pescheurs
(for the same service, see also Cherubs, Farm Scenes and Pastorals)

19th-Century Redecoration
TUREEN AND COVER, C467
Rustic children

Domestic scenes

1756–7
GOLD BOX, G20 (Paris probably N. Hardivilliers)
Le Petit Ménage, drawing by Boucher, Albertina, Vienna
Le Château de Cartes, drawing by Boucher, private collection, Paris

1779 (?)
VASE centrepiece of a garniture of three, C264 (probably painted by A. Caton)
Le Maître d'école after the biscuit group of 1762, and after a drawing in the Albertina, Vienna
(for the same set, see also Pastorals)

Farm scenes

1763–4
GOLD BOX, G37 (Paris by M. Coiny)
Le Petit Pasteur by C. Duflos, *Le Mercure de France* 1754
La Petite Fermière by C. Duflos, *Le Mercure de France* 1754

1766
CUP AND TEAPOT from a Tea Service, C391–5 (painted by C.-E. Asselin)
A la ferme by J. Varin.
La petite laitière by F. Jouillain 1757
(for the service, see also Cherubs, Children and Pastorals)

1768 (?)
TRAY/PLAQUE mounted in a Secretaire, C503 (possibly painted by A. Caton)
Farmyard scene

19th-Century Redecoration
POT-POURRI VASE, one of a pair, C239–40
Les poussins engraved by G. Demarteau (in reverse)
(for the pair see Pastorals)

Street scenes

1756–9
GOLD BOX, G23 (Paris by J.-C.-S. Dubos)
Au Vinaigre by Ravenet from *Les Cris de Paris*, *Le Mercure de France* 1737

Fair scenes and Savoyards

1765 (?)
VASE, C270 (probably painted by C.-E. Asselin)
La Lanterne Magique after the biscuit group of 1757, see also *Foire de Campagne* by C.-N. Cochin 1740
1767
BASIN with Jug, C454–5 (painted by C.-E. Asselin)
La Lanterne Magique after the biscuit group of 1757
Tourniquet after the biscuit group of 1757, see also *Foire de Campagne* by C.-N. Cochin 1740

Chinoiseries

1749–50
GOLD BOX, G8 (Paris by H. Cheval)
Five of the six scenes from *Scènes de la Vie Chinoise* by G. Huquier
La Pêche au cormoran
Flûtiste et enfant timbalier
Le Carillon
La Toilette
Chinoise assise tenant un plat…
And the sixth from *L'Eau*, from the *Four Elements* by P. Aveline 1740

Pastorals

1750–60
GOLD BOX, G77 (Berlin, painted enamels by J.G.G. Kruger, op.1755–68)
Les confidences pastorales by C. Duflos 1751
(see also Mythologies)

1759–60
GOLD BOX, G30 (Paris by P. Robert)
Two of *Les Amours Pastorales* by C. Duflos 1751–2:
Ce pasteur amoureux chante sur sa musette…
Ne plaignons point le sort de ses bergers…

1762
GARNITURE OF THREE FLOWER POTS, C220–2
Pastorale by G Huquier 1736
Le Pasteur galant by A. Laurant 1742
Le Pasteur complaisant
Silvandre, heureux amant, qui ne t'inquiète… from *Les Amours Pastorales* by C. Duflos 1751–2

1766
SAUCER from a Tea Service, C391–5 (painted by C.-E. Asselin)
Enfant bergère by Daumont
(for the service see also Cherubs, Children and Farm Scenes)

opposite
BOUCHER,
The Rape of Europa,
*c.*1733–4, oil on canvas,
detail (fig.25), Wallace
Collection

1767 (?)
VASE, C303
(probably painted by C.-N. Dodin)
Bergère garnissant de fleurs son chapeau et berger dormant by G. Demarteau

1769
PAIR OF VASES, C292–3 (painted by C.-N. Dodin)
Les amants surpris by G. Demarteau
La pipée by G. Demarteau

1770
CUP AND SAUCER, C348 (painted by E.-J. Chabry)
L'Ecole de L'Amitié by J.-M. Delattre
Bergère garnissant de fleurs son chapeau et berger dormant by G. Demarteau

1770 (?)
CUP AND SAUCER, C363
La pipée by G. Demarteau
Ce Pasteur amoureux chante sur sa musette… from *Les Amours Pastorales* by C. Duflos 1751–2

1776 (?)
VASE, C318 (painted by C.-N. Dodin)
La Pêche by Beauvarlet

1777 (?)
TWO PLAQUES on a Secretaire, C501
(possibly painted by C.-N. Dodin)
La danse Allemande by G. Demarteau 1769
Le sommeil d'Annette by G. Demarteau 1768

1779 (?)
TWO VASES from a garniture of three, C265–6
(probably painted by A. Caton)
Les Mangeurs de Raisins after the biscuit group of 1752, and after Boucher's painting *The Autumn Pastoral* of 1749 in the Wallace Collection (P482)
L'Agréable leçon after the biscuit group of 1752 and after Boucher's painting in the National Gallery of Victoria, Melbourne
(for the same set, see also Domestic Scenes)

VASE, C330
Pensent-ils à ce mouton? by Madame Jourdan and *Le repos* by J. Bonefoy

19th-Century Redecoration and Imitations
POT-POURRI VASE, one of a pair, C239–40
(redecorated)
Ismène et Daphnis by J.-H. Eberts 1742
(for the pair, see Farm Scenes)

GOLD BOX, G13 (possibly Geneva, though purporting to be Paris, by P.-E. Buron, 1750–1)

Landscapes

1770s
GOLD BOX, G87 (Swiss)
Seconde veue des environs de Charenton engraved by the J.-P. Le Bas in 1747
(see also Mythologies)

Mythologies

1750–60
GOLD BOX, G77 (Berlin, painted enamels by J.G.G. Kruger, op.1755–68)
The Rape of Europa engraved by C. Duflos
Vénus, se préparant pour le jugement de Paris, reçoit d'avance la pomme des mains de l'Amour by J.-B. de Lorraine in 1742
(see also Pastorals)

1764–5
GOLD BOX, G39 (Paris by L.-P. Demay)
L'Amour désarmé by E. Fessard 1761

1770 (?)
VASE one of a pair, C294–5
Vénus sur les eaux by J.-C. Levasseur *c.*1765

1770s
GOLD BOX, G87 (Swiss)
The Rape of Europa engraved by C. Duflos
Rinaldo and Armida engraved by N. Cochin as the frontispiece for Favart's comic opera *Cythère assiégée* in 1748
(see also Landscapes)

1781
VASE from a garniture of three, C334
Pygmalion devient amoureux d'une statue qu'il avoit faite, et Vénus la rend animée by N. Lemire for Abbé Banier's edition of Ovid's *Metamorphoses* (Paris 1767–71)

1792
CUP AND SAUCER, C355 (painted by C.-F. Caron)
Two subjects from Abbé Banier's edition of Ovid's *Metamorphoses* (Paris 1767–71)
Vénus appuyé sur son cher Adonis… by J. Massard
Mars et Vénus… by N. Lemire 1767

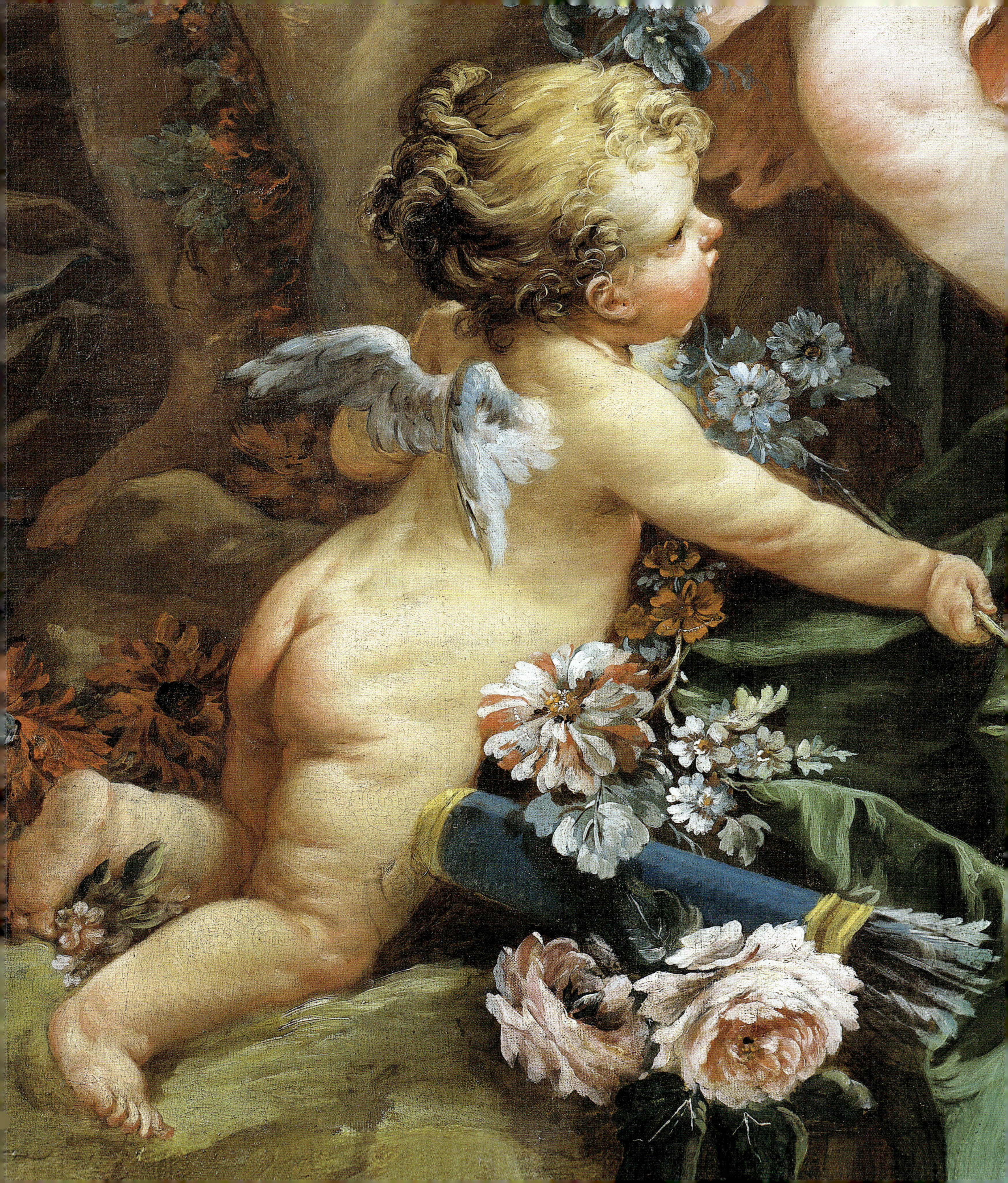

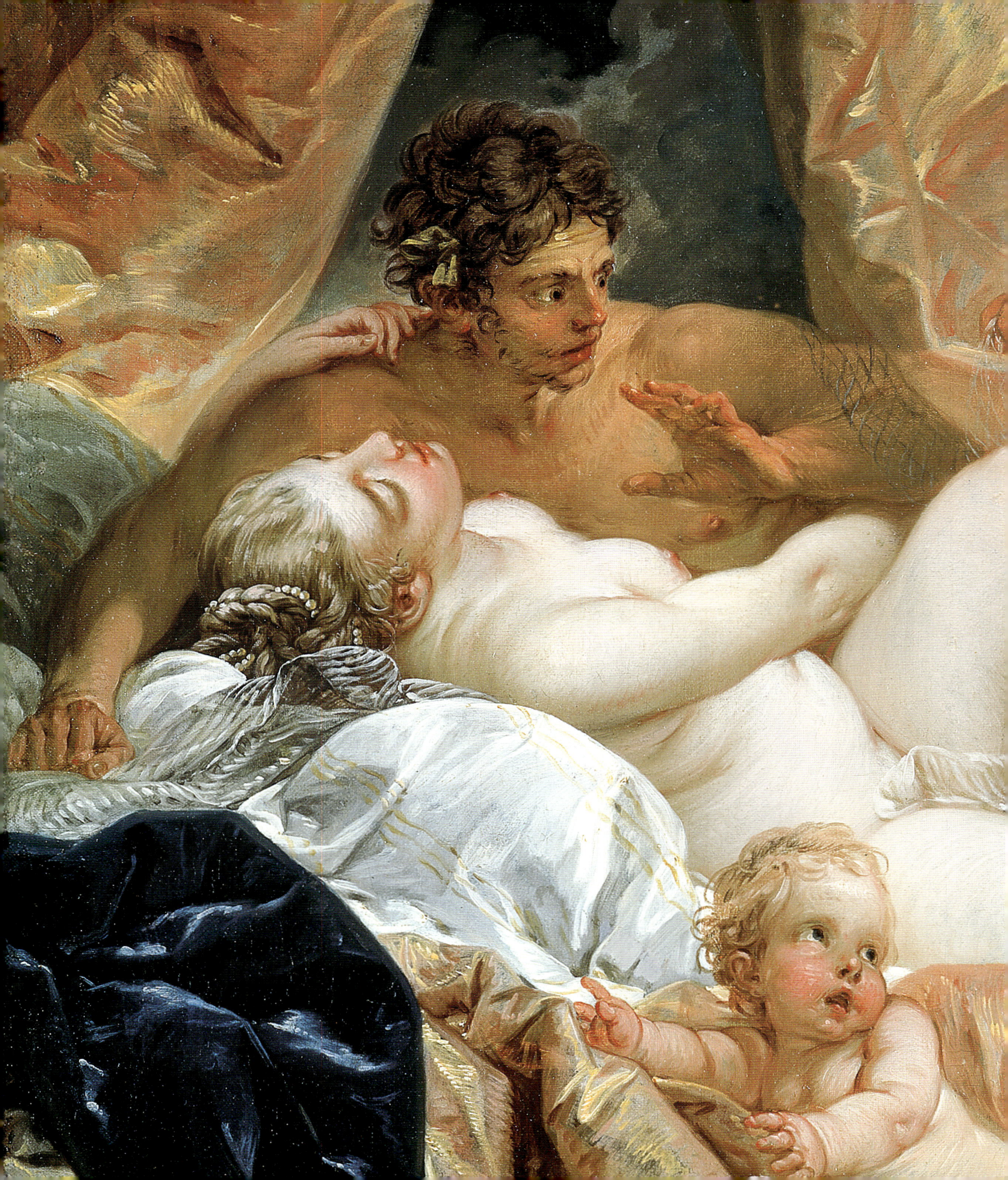

Notes

opposite
BOUCHER,
Mars and Venus, 1754, oil on canvas, detail (fig.102), Wallace Collection

CHAPTER I

1 L.-S. Mercier, *Tableau de Paris*, 12 vols, Amsterdam, 1782–1788, IX, pp.99–104.
2 See catalogue of *Pastels XVIIème et XVIIIème Siècles*, Musée du Louvre, Paris, 1972, no.85.
3 J.-A. J. des Boulmiers, 'Eloge de M. Boucher', *Mercure de France*, September 1770, pp.181–89; cited in A. Ananoff, *François Boucher*, 2 vols., Lausanne-Paris, 1976, document 1075.
4 See the obituaries cited in A. Ananoff, *op. cit.*, documents 1059–84.
5 L.-A. de Bonafons , abbé de Fontenay, *Dictionnaire des artistes ou notice historique et raisonnée des architectes, peintres, graveurs, sculpteurs ...*, 2 vols., Paris, 1776, I, pp.234. The abbé de Fontenay's notice on Boucher largely follows that published by Bret on Boucher's death in 1771; see A. Ananoff, *ibid.*
6 Letter of Mme Geoffrin to Stanislas Poniatowski relating Boucher's suggestion that his unfinished commission for the *Continence of Scipio* be awarded to Vien: see T. Gaehtgens and J. Lugand, *Joseph-Marie Vien, peintre du roi (1716–1809)*, Paris, 1988, pp.180–82.
7 Letter of 1769, see A. Ananoff, *op. cit.*, document 1027.
8 Carl Frederik Scheffer, *Lettres particulières à Carl Gustaf Tessin 1744–1752*, ed. J. Heidner, Stockholm, 1982, pp.124–5.
9 Abbé de Fontenay, *op. cit.*, II, pp.639–40.
10 J.-C. von Mannlich, *Histoire de ma vie*, ed. K. H. Bender and H. Kleber, 2 vols., Trier, 1989, 1993, I, p.155.
11 Evidence for contemporary artists' gambling habits is provided by a letter from the decorative painter Bachelier who was forced to write to an unnamed correspondent because 'Monsieur, I have made quite a considerable bet on the cost it took to erect the bridge of Neuilly. If it is not too indiscreet to ask you what it cost, I would be extremely grateful to know'; see J. Chatelus, *Peindre à Paris au XVIIIe siècle*, Nîmes, 1991, p.319.
12 J.-A. J. des Boulmiers, *op. cit.*, pp.188–9.
13 See A. Laing, 'Boucher: The Search for an Idiom' in A. Laing, exh. cat., *François Boucher 1703–1770*, New York, Detroit, Paris, 1986–7, pp.56–72, in particular p.65.
14 Letter from Mariette, 1731; see B. Schreiber Jacoby, 'New Light on François Boucher's Early Work: A Lost Watercolour Exhibited in Florence by Francesco Maria Gabburri', *Master Drawings*, Autumn 1986, pp.367–77.
15 See J. Chatelus, *op. cit.*, pp.240–45.
16 P. Remy, *Catalogue raisonné des Tableaux, Desseins, Estampes, Terres cuites, Lacques, Porcelaines de différentes sortes, montées et non montées; Meubles curieux, Bijoux, Minéraux, Cristillations, Madrepores, Coquilles & autres Curiosités qui composent le Cabinet de Feu M. Boucher, Premier Peintre du Roi*, Paris, 1771.
17 Abbé de Fontenay, *op. cit.*, p.232–4.
18 Letter from the artist Pierre, 25 May 1788, Arch. Nat. 01 1914, cited in A. Ananoff, *op. cit.*, document 1147.
19 For documentary evidence concerning Boucher's early life, see G. Brunel, *Boucher*, London, 1986, pp.24–36.
20 P. J. Mariette, *Abecedario*, ed. Ph. de Chennevières and A. de Montaiglon, 6 vols., Paris, 1851–60, I, p.165.
21 She did not know how to sign her name when required to do so as a witness at Boucher's marriage in 1733: see G. Brunel, *ibid.*
22 J. Hillairet, *Evocation du Vieux Paris*, 3 vols., Paris, 1952–54, I, pp.199–201 and J. Hillairet, *Dictionnaire Historique des rues de Paris*, 2 vols., Paris, 1986, II, pp.621–3.
23 Diderot, for example, was the son of a cutler and Beaumarchais, the son of a watchmaker.
24 For introductions to the Enlightenment and to eighteenth century thought in general see M. Fumaroli, *Quand l'Europe parlait français*, Paris, 2001; B. Darbeau, *Les Lumières, Anthologie*, Paris, 2002; A. Dupront, *Qu'est-ce que les Lumières?*, ed. Paris, 1996; J. de Viguerie, *Histoire et Dictionnaire du Temps des Lumières 1715–1789*, Paris, 1995; A.de Maurepas and F. Brayard, *Les Français vus par eux-mêmes, le XVIIIe siècle*, Paris, 1996.
25 For a brief resumé of the main historical and artistic currents in the reigns of Louis XIV, XV and XVI see J. Hedley, 'French painting in the Ancien Régime from Louis XIV to the French Revolution' in M. Hilaire, O. Zeder and J. Zutter, exh. cat. *French Paintings from the Musée Fabre*, Montpellier, Canberra, 2003–4, pp.62–91. For general histories of France in the eighteenth century see, for example, G. Chaussinand-Nogaret, *La vie quotidienne des Français sous Louis XV*, Paris, 1979; P. Gaxotte, *Le Siècle de Louis XV*, ed. Paris, 1997; P. Goubert, *The Ancien Régime, French Society 1600–1750*, ed. London, 1997; E. Le Roy Ladurie, *L'Ancien Régime, I, 1715–1770*, Paris 1991; D. Roche, *Le Peuple de Paris*, Paris, 1982. For a more general overview of Europe see N. Davies, 'Lumen, Enlightenment and Absolutism, *c.*1650–1789' in *Europe, A History*, London, 1997, pp.577–674.
26 J. Ingamells, *The Wallace Collection Catalogue of Pictures*, 4 vols., London, 1985–92, III, p.122.
27 See T. Crow, *Painters and Public Life in Eighteenth Century Paris*, New Haven and London, 1985.
28 See P. Hughes, *The Wallace Collection Catalogue of Furniture*, 3 vols., London, 1996, III, pp.1179–92.
29 Quoted in P. Sollers, *Liberté du XVIIIème, Paris*, 1996, p.150.
30 See M. Fumaroli, *ibid.*
31 Entry for 20 September 1719, in J. Buvat, *Journal de la Régence* (1715–23), ed. E. Campardon, 2 vols., Paris, 1865, I, pp.445–7.
32 See J. Hellegouarc'h, *L'Esprit de société. Cercles et 'salons' parisiens au XVIIIe siècle*, Paris, 2000.
33 See S. Cohen, *Art, Dance and the Body in French Culture of the Ancien Régime*, Cambridge, 2000, pp.209–41; J. A. Plax, *Watteau and the Cultural Politics of Eighteenth-Century France*, Cambridge, 2000, pp.108–53.
34 Crébillon *fils*, *Les égarements du coeur et de l'esprit*, 1736–8.
35 As noted by L.-S. Mercier, *Tableau de Paris*, ed. Paris 1990.
36 6–7000 per annum mid-century; see E. Le Roy Ladurie, *op. cit.*, p.46.
37 Quoted in M. Fumaroli, *op.cit.*, p.419.
38 L.-S. Mercier, *op.cit.*, ed. Paris, 1990, pp.159–63.
39 Montesquieu, *op. cit.*, letter 106.
40 See D. Roche, *op. cit.*, p.442.
41 23 February 1745, E.-J.-F. Barbier, *Chronique de la Régence et du règne de Louis XV (1718–1763) ou Journal de Barbier*, 8 vols., ed. Paris, 1857–66, IV, p.19.
42 Montesquieu, *op. cit.*, letter 106.
43 L.-S. Mercier, *op.cit.*, ed. Paris 1990, p.186.
44 See P. Rosenberg, 'The Mysterious Beginnings of the Young Boucher' in A.Laing 1986–7, *op. cit.*, pp.41–55; A. Laing, 'Years of Struggle' in A. Laing, exh. cat., *The Drawings of François Boucher*, New York, Fort Worth, 2003–4; F. Joulie, 'Formation de François Boucher' in F. Joulie and J.-F. Méjanès, exh. cat., *François Boucher, hier et aujourd'hui*, Paris, 2003–4; F. Joulie, 'Formation et culture de François Boucher: "de qui est-il donc le disciple?"' in E. Brugerolles *et al.*, exh. cat. *François Boucher et l'art rocaille*, Paris, Sydney, Ottawa, 2003–6, pp.76–87.
45 See J. Hedley 2003–4, *op. cit.*, pp.69–77.
46 See R. de Piles, *Cours de peinture par principes*, 1708, ed. Nîmes, 1990.

47 See F. Kimball, *The Creation of the Rococo Decorative Style*, New York, ed. 1980, and K. Scott, *The Rococo Interior*, New Haven and London, 1995.

48 For the taste and arrangement of the eighteenth-century picture cabinet see C. Bailey, 'Conventions of the Eighteenth-Century *Cabinet de tableaux*: Blondel d'Azaincourt's *La première idée de la curiosité*', *Art Bulletin*, September, 1987, pp.431–47.

49 See C. Bailey, 'Surveying Genre in Eighteenth-Century French Painting', in C. Bailey *et. al.*, exh. cat., *The Age of Watteau, Chardin, and Fragonard, Masterpieces of French Genre Painting*, Ottowa, Washington, Berlin, 2003–4, pp.2–39; C. Bailey, *Patriotic Taste. Collecting Modern Art in Pre-Revolutionary Paris*, New Haven and London, 2002.

50 See T. Crow, *L'honnête homme et la critique du goût. Esthétique et société au XVIIIe siècle*, Lexington, 1981.

51 See J. Chatelus, *op. cit.*, p.304.

52 See C. Bailey, '"Toute seule elle peut remplir et satisfaire l'attention": The Early Appreciation and Marketing of Watteau's Drawings, with an Introduction to the Collecting of Modern French Drawings During the Reign of Louis XV' in A. Wintermute, exh. cat., *Watteau and his World, French Drawing from 1700 to 1750*, New York, Ottawa, 1999–2000, pp.68–92; and exh. cat., *L'apothéose du geste, l'esquisse peinte au siècle de Boucher et Fragonard*, Strasbourg, Tours, 2003–4.

53 See, for example, M. Stuffmann, 'Les Tableaux de la Collection Pierre Crozat', *Gazette des Beaux-Arts*, July-Sept. 1968, pp.11–144.

54 Entry for 30th September 1720, *Journal de Rosalba Carriera pendant son séjour à Paris en 1720 et 1721*, ed. A. Sensier, Paris, 1865.

55 See R. Neuman, 'Watteau's Enseigne de Gersaint and the Baroque Emblematic Tradition', *Gazette des Beaux-Arts*, Nov. 1984, pp.153–64; M. Morgan Grasselli and P. Rosenberg, exh. cat., Watteau, 1684–1721, Washington, Paris, 1984, pp.447–59; G. Glorieux, *À l'Enseigne de Gersaint*, Seyssel, 2002, pp.72–89.

56 Sirois and his daughter appear in a picture by Watteau in the Wallace Collection; see J. Ingamells, *op. cit.*, III, pp.347–51.

57 L.-S. Mercier, *op.cit.*, ed. Paris, 1990, p.184.

58 See J. Chatelus, *op. cit.*, pp.218–25.

59 Recounted by Diderot in his Salon criticism for 1765, see J. Goodman ed., *Diderot on Art*, 2 vols., New-Haven and London, 1995, I, pp.4–5.

60 See A. Laing 1986–7, *op. cit.*, no.1.

61 For the Academy, organisation, prizes and teaching see exh. cat., *Les Peintres du Roi*, Tours, Toulouse, 2000.

62 Restout, *Galerie Françoise*, 1771, p.1, cited in A. Ananoff, *op. cit.*, document 1081.

63 See C. Bailey, 'An Early Masterpiece by Boucher Rediscovered: *The Judgement of Susannah* in the National Gallery of Canada', National Gallery of Canada Review, I, 2000, pp.11–34.

64 See J. Ingamells, *op. cit.*, III, pp.248–50.

65 P. J. Mariette, *op. cit.*, I, p.165.

66 Almanach littéraire 1778, cited in A. Ananoff, *op. cit.*, p.143; see also J. Ingamells, *op.cit.*, III, p.243–8.

67 P. J. Mariette, *op. cit.*, I, p.165.

68 Sale of Claude Gaspard de Sireul, Paris, 3 Dec. 1781, lot 28; see also *L'apothéose du geste*, *op. cit.*, p.13.

69 P. J. Mariette, *op.cit.*, I, p.165.

70 C.-N. Cochin, *Mémoires inédits*, ed. Paris, 1880, p.100.

71 *Ibid.*, pp.80–1.

72 Cited in J. Chatelus, *op. cit.*, p.152; see also P. Dorbec, 'L'Exposition de la jeunesse au XVIIIe siècle {premier article}', *Gazette des Beaux-Arts*, June 1905, p.456–470.

73 *Mercure de France*, June 1725, p.1402.

74 A. Laing 1986–7, *op. cit.*, no.4.

75 See P. Rosenberg, in A. Laing 1986–7, *op.cit.*, p.49.

76 Blondel de Gagny sale, 10 November 1776, under lot 240.

77 Advertisement in *Mercure de France* of February 1742, describing the print-seller, M. Boucher, in the Place du Louvre. Boucher's father had been described as a draughtsman at the time of his marriage in 1698 and was living in the Place du Louvre at the time of his death in 1743.

78 P.-J. Mariette, *op.cit.*, I, pp.165–6.

79 See J.-A. J. des Boulmiers, *op. cit.*, pp.188–89; G. Brunel, *ibid.*; E. Pagliano, 'Boucher, une lecture de La Fontaine et de quelques autres', *Revue de l'Art*, 2003, no.141, pp.47–56.

80 D.-P.-J. Papillon de La Ferté, *Extrait des différens ouvrages publiés sur la vie des peintres*, vol.II, Paris, 1776, p.660.

81 See P. Jean–Richard, *L'Oeuvre gravé de François Boucher dans la Collection Edmond Rothschild*, Paris, 1978, pp.92–3.

82 See F. Joulie and J.-F. Méjanès, *op. cit.*, pp.24–9.

83 G. Glorieux, *op. cit.*, pp.153–59.

84 See A. Laing 1986–7, *op. cit.*, no.8 and *L'apothéose du geste*, *op. cit.*, no.16.

85 P.-J. Mariette, *op. cit.*, I, p.166; for Jean de Jullienne's engravings commissioned after Watteau see E. Dacier and A. Vuaflart, *Jean de Jullienne et les graveurs de Watteau au XVIIIe siècle*, Paris, 3 vols., 1922 and 1929; M. Roland Michel, 'Prints after paintings – Jean de Jullienne and the Tombeau de Watteau' in *Watteau an Artist of the Eighteenth Century*, London, 1984, pp.260–77.

86 P. Jean-Richard, *op. cit.*, nos.33–163.

87 *Ibid.*, nos.164–175.

88 A suggestion first made by Christian Michel, see G. Glorieux, *op. cit.*, p.170.

89 See E. Brugerolles *et al.*, *op. cit.*, no.12.

90 See M. Morgan Grasselli and P. Rosenberg, *op. cit.*, nos.88, 114–6 and J. Ingamells, *op. cit.*, III, pp.370–72.

91 See B. Schreiber Jacoby, 'A Landscape Drawing by François Boucher after Domenico Campagnola', *Master Drawings*, Autumn 1979, pp.261–72; P. Rosenberg and L.-A. Prat, *Antoine Watteau 1684–1721, Catalogue raisonné des dessins*, Milan, 1996, III, R98; M. Morgan-Grasselli and P. Rosenberg, *op. cit.*, nos.139–42. For similar Boucher drawings see A. Laing 2003–4, *op. cit.*, nos.86, 87 and F. Joulie and J-F. Méjanès, 2003–4, *op. cit.*, nos. 27–29.

92 P. Jean-Richard, *op. cit.*, no.40.

93 See A. Laing 1986–7, *op. cit.*, no.7.

94 See P. Führing, *Juste-Aurèle Meissonnier, 1695–1750*, Turin and London, 1999.

95 For Gersaint's attempts to capitalise on Watteau's productions via print and the decorative see also G. Glorieux, *op. cit.*, pp.179–234.

96 See P. Jean-Richard, *op. cit.*, nos.396, 1216.

97 See Boucher's denouncement of Duflos basing prints on clandestine drawings after his compositions by his least able students printed in the *Mercure de France*, March, 1755, pp.145–6 with defence in May issue, pp.131–33.

98 Private collection; A. Laing 1986–7, *op.cit.*, pp.114–7.

99 Thanks to Jennifer Tonkovich of the Pierpont Morgan Library, New York, for helping with these identifications.

100 P.-J. Mariette, *op. cit.*, III, pp.15–16.

101 A. Laing 2003–4, *op. cit.*, no.4.

102 A.–N. Dezallier d'Argenville, 'Lettre sur le choix et l'arrangement d'un Cabinet Curieux …', *Mercure de France*, June 1727.

103 An inspiration often noted by contemporaries such as Papillon de La Ferté: 'Boucher can be compared to Albani in his graceful subjects, and to Benedetto Castiglione, when he treats animals'; see D.-P.-J. Papillon de La Ferté, *op. cit.*, p.660 and abbé de Fontenay, *op. cit.*, p.232.

104 Letter of Vleughels to the duc d'Antin, 27 May 1728 cited in A. de Montaiglon ed., *Correspondance des directeurs de l'Académie de France à Rome avec les Surintendants des bâtiments*, 18 vols., Paris, 1887–1912, VII, p.420.

105 Letter of Vleughels to the duc d'Antin, 3 June 1728, cited in A. de Montaiglon, *op. cit.*, p.423.

106 D.-P.-J. Papillon de La Ferté, *op. cit.*, II, Paris, 1776, p.657.

107 P.-J. Mariette, *op. cit.*, p.165.

108 See F. Joulie in E. Brugerolles, *op. cit.*, pp.81–87; F. Joulie and J.-F. Méjanès, *op. cit.*, pp.33–51; A. Laing 2003–4, *op. cit.*, pp.56–9.

109 J.-C.von Mannlich, *op.cit.*, p.211.

110 See R.J.A te Rijdt, exh. cat., *De Watteau à Ingres Dessins français du XVIIIe siècle du Rijksmuseum Amsterdam*, Amsterdam, Paris, 2003, no.29, pp.97–100; for Vleughels's own plein-air sketches see *The Gate* (1723; whereabouts unknown), illustrated in P. Rosenberg, *From Drawing to Painting, Poussin, Watteau, Fragonard, David and Ingres*, Princeton, 2000, p.108, fig.131.

111 See A. Laing 1986–7, *op. cit.*, p.59, fig.40.

112 See R. Shoolman Slatkin, 'Abraham Bloemaert and François Boucher: Affinity and Relationship', *Master Drawings*, Autumn 1976, pp.247–260; F. Joulie and J.-F. Méjanès, *op. cit.*, pp.48–9, 52–6; A. Laing 2003–4, *op. cit.*, pp.54–5. For a drawing after figures in the same sketch book by Subleyras (1699–1749) see E. Brugerolles, *op. cit.*, no.52.

113 See P. Jean-Richard, *op. cit.*, nos.176–86.

114 D.-P.-J. Papillon de La Ferté, *op. cit.*, p.657.

115 A fine three-crayon chalk study for the cow on the right is in the Musée des Beaux-Arts, Dijon.

116 See B. Hercenberg, *Nicolas Vleughels peintre et directeur de l'Académie de France à Rome (1668–1737)*, Paris, 1975.

117 See M. P. Eidelberg, 'Watteau, Lancret, and the Fountains of Oppenort', *Burlington Magazine*, 1968,

pp.447–56; E. Brugerolles *et al.*, *op. cit.*, p.87.

118 See A. Laing, exh. cat., *In Trust for the Nation, Paintings from National Trust Houses*, London, 1995–96, no.72.

119 See A. Laing 1986–7, *op. cit.*, no.13; C. Bailey, exh. cat., *Les Amours des Dieux. La peinture mythologique de Watteau à David*, Paris, Philadelphia, Fort Worth, 1991–2, no.42.

120 See C. Bailey 1992, *op. cit.*, no.30.

121 See J. L. Bordeaux, *François Lemoyne and his Generation*, Paris, 1984, no.P47.

122 See exh. cat., *Les peintres du roi*, *op. cit.*, no.29; C. Bailey 1991–2, *op. cit.*, no.33.

123 For female academies done by Boucher's compatriots in Rome see P. Rosenberg, exh. cat., *Subleyras 1699–1749*, Paris, Rome, 1987, no.59.

Chapter II

1 J. F. de Bastide, *La petite maison*, first published in vol.II of *Le Nouveau Spectateur*, Paris, 1758–60, ed. Paris, 1993, p.41, n.1.

2 24 November 1731, A. de Montaiglon ed., *Procès-Verbaux de l'Académie Royale de Peinture et Sculpture 1648–1793*, 10 vols., Paris, 1875–92, vol.V.

3 See X. Salmon, exh. cat., *Jean Marc Nattier 1685–1766*, Versailles, 1999–2000.

4 J. Ingamells, *op. cit.*, III, pp.64–7, 78–80.

5 P.-J. Mariette, *op. cit.*, I, p.165.

6 D.-P.-J. Papillon de La Ferté, *op. cit.*, p.658.

7 As listed as a pair under item 56 of the *Inventaire après le décès de Mr. Derbais*, 2 Mars 1743, Minutier Central, LIX, 230: document first discovered by G. Brunel, *ibid.*

8 See A. Laing 'La Re-Naissance de Vénus: une oeuvre des débuts de Boucher retrouvée à Paris', *Revue de l'Art*, 1994, pp.77–81; A. Laing 1986–7, *op. cit.*, nos. 17–18; C. Bailey 1991–2, *op. cit.*, nos.43–4.

9 See Ingamells, *op. cit.*, III, pp.243–50.

10 C. Bailey 1991–2, *op. cit.*, no.4–5.

11 *Ibid.*, no.38 and M.-C. Sahut, exh. cat., *Carle Vanloo, premier peintre du Roi (Nice, 1705–Paris, 1765)*, Nice, Clermont-Ferrand, Nancy, 1977, no.39.

12 See N. Garnier, *Antoine Coypel*, 1661–1722, Paris, 1989, no.75; I. S. Nemilova, *Catalogue of French Eighteenth-Century Paintings in the Hermitage* (in Russian), Leningrad, 1985, no.37.

13 See pictures on the same theme painted by Pierre Jacques Cazes in 1727 (Barnard Castle) and Watteau, known through Philippe Mercier's engraving; see G. Macchia and E. C. Montagni, *L'opera completa di Watteau*, Milan, 1968, no.54.

14 Veronese's original picture, *c.*1580, had been in the Palazzo Ducale, Venice, since 1713, but a copy was listed in the Regent's collection in Paris; see also J. Hedley 2002–3, *passim*; J.-L. Bordeaux, *op. cit.*, no.P55; I. S. Nemilova, *op. cit.*, no.151.

15 J. Thuillier, exh. cat., *Vouet*, 1990–91, no.55 and compare Cortona's frescoes for the Palazzo Barberini, Rome and *The Golden Age* fresco for the Palazzo Pitti, Florence. Watteau's picture belonged to the portraitist Aved in the eighteenth century, see G. Macchia and E.C. Montagni, *op. cit.*, no.56.

16 I. S. Nemilova, *op. cit.*, no.151.

17 The seated girl with her back to us is taken from Boucher's own *Judgement of Susannah* (fig.7); a figure which Bailey compares to similar figures in Bassano's pastorals; see C. Bailey 2000, *op. cit.*, p.15–17, fig.7.

18 See F. Joulie and J.-F. Méjanès, *op. cit.*, no.20.

19 See D. Sutton, exh. cat., *François Boucher*, Tokyo, Kumamoto, 1982, nos.19, 131 and A. Ananoff, *op. cit.*, no.2.

20 A counterproof is taken by dampening the surface of a chalk drawing, which is then pressed onto a second sheet so as to leave an impression. The counterproof is printed in reverse and, although fainter than the original, can be worked up to make it appear stronger.

21 For example, see P. Jean-Richard, *op. cit.*, no.192.

22 D.-P.-J. Papillon de La Ferté, *op. cit.*, p.660.

23 See P. Perrot, *Le Travail des apparences, Le corps féminin XVIIIe–XIXe siècle*, Paris, 1984, pp.69–70.

24 Marquis de Caraccioli, quoted in P. Perrot, *op. cit.*, p.68.

25 See Legros de Rumigny, *L'art de la coëffure des dames françoises*, Paris, 1768; A. Bloemaert, *Tekenboek*, Amsterdam, 1640, plate 150.

26 Sold Christie's London, 4 July 2000, lot 165.

27 Letter of 1737, see A. Ananoff, *op. cit.*, document 130; A. Laing 1986–7, *op.cit.*, p.159. See also R. Ingrams, 'Bachaumont: A Parisian Connoisseur of the Eighteenth Century', *Gazette des Beaux-Arts*, June 1970, pp.11–28.

28 P.-J. Mariette, *op. cit.*, I, p.165.

29 See C. Duclos, *Considérations sur les moeurs de ce siècle*. Paris, 1751, pp.232–4.

30 See C. Rollin, *Traité des études*, Paris, 1726, re-published seven times before the Revolution.

31 C. Michel, *La Nature et les Moeurs: Thoughts on the Reception of Genre Painting in France*, unpublished paper given at CASVA conference on French genre painting, Washington, Dec. 2003.

32 J.-J. Rousseau, *Narcisse, ou l'amant de lui même*, Paris, 1753, I, 289.

33 Anonymous, *L'Isle du mariage*, Opéra Comique, 1733.

34 Supposedly invented around 1670 by Dom Perignon, a monk in the Champagne region, champagne became the fashionable drink during the Regency; expensive, its consumption was limited to the Court, aristocracy and wealthy elite.

35 Voltaire, *Dialogues et entretiens philosophiques*, Dialogue 25.

36 Voltaire, *Le Mondain*, Paris, 1736, line 28.

37 See J. Ingamells, *op. cit.*, I, pp.210–11; J.-L. Bordeaux, *op. cit.*, nos. P39, P40, P41; P. Remy, *op. cit.*, lot 628.

38 D.-P.-J. Papillon de La Ferté, *op. cit.*, p.660.

39 Paris, Louvre, Département des Objets d'Art OA 2223 and OA 7683.

40 P. Jean-Richard, *op. cit.*, nos.247–8.

41 In studies of the marriage settlements of other artists of the period only thirty-one out of thirty-eight wives received doweries of more than 5000 livres: see G. Brunel, *ibid.*

42 J.-C. von Mannlich, *op.cit.*, I, p.56.

43 Cited in R. Ingrams, *op.cit.*, p.18.

44 Abbé de Fontenay, *op. cit.*, I, p.232–4.

45 A signed drawing by Madame Boucher after her husband is in Stockholm, miniatures by her are listed in the La Live de Jully sale (Paris, 5–16 March, 1770, lot 139) and in the Blondel d'Azaincourt sale of 1783, and an engraving by her after a drawing by Boucher is in the Louvre; see P. Bjurström, *Catalogue of the French Drawings in the Nationalmuseum, Eighteenth Century*, Stockholm, 1982, no.869.

46 See A. Laing, 'Trois lettres de François Boucher et de sa femme à l'auteur dramatique Favart', *Archives de l'Art Français*, 1988, pp.20–2.

47 See G. W. Lundberg, *Roslin liv och verk*, Malmö, 1957, nos.133 and 138.

48 See Brunel, *ibid.*

49 See A. Laing 1986–7, *op.cit.*, pp.160–2; *Les peintres du roi* 1648–1793, *op.cit.*, pp.150–2.

50 24 November 1731, A. de Montaiglon, *Procès-Verbaux*, *op. cit.*, vol.V.

51 See N. Garnier, *op. cit.*, no.97; J. Hedley 'Charles de La Fosse's 'Rinaldo and Armida' and 'Rape of Europa' at Basildon Park', *The Burlington Magazine*, April 2002, pp.204–212; C. Bailey *et al.*, exh. cat., *The First Painters of the King: French Royal Taste from Louis XIV to the Revolution*, New York, New Orleans, Columbus, 1985–6, pp.72–5. A 1993 recording of the opera, conducted by Philippe Herreweghe, is available on Harmonia Mundi.

52 Cited in V. Doria, *Tocqué*, Paris, 1929, p.5.

53 See C. Michel, 'Boucher professeur à l'Académie royale de Peinture et de Sculpture', in E. Brugerolles *et al.*, *op. cit.*, pp.94–101.

54 For Boucher's generation see P. Rosenberg, 'Boucher et la génération de 1700' in E. Brugerolles *et al.*, *op. cit.*, pp.172–79.

55 Letter Cochin to Marigny, 18 July 1765, cited in A. Ananoff, *op. cit.*, document 892.

56 See P. Lemoine, *Guide to the Museum and National Domain of Versailles and Trianon*, Paris, 2002, pp.57–60.

57 See, for example, E. Le Roy Ladurie, *passim*.

58 See P. Conisbee, *Painting in Eighteenth-Century France*, Oxford, 1981, pp.35–72 and J. Locquin, *La peinture d'Histoire en France de 1747 à 1785*, Paris, 1912, reprinted 1978.

59 See exh. cat., *Charles-Joseph Natoire*, Troyes, Nîmes, Rome, 1977, no.53.

60 Voltaire, *Correspondance*, 6 December, 1755.

61 A. Houdar de La Motte, 1719.

62 See M. Roland Michel, *Lajoue et l'art Rocaille*, Paris, 1982.

63 D.-P.-J. Papillon de La Ferté, *op. cit.*, p.660.

64 See for example P. Remy, *op. cit.*, lots 817 and 819: mounted vases after Boucher's own designs including one with handles made of twisting serpents, with masques, satyrs heads and garlands in gilded bronze. Cochin writing of Meissonnier on his death said that 'he invented contrasts, that is to say he banished symmetry' which is born out by a pair of candlesticks in the Wallace Collection, with silvered putti holding gilt bronze stems that twist around them in serpentine curves, deriving from three engravings of *Chandeliers de sculpture en argent* of 1728 later included in the *Oeuvre de Meissonnier* published by Huquier; see P. Hughes, *op. cit.*, III, pp.1204–09.

65 See E. Brugerolles *et al.*, *op. cit.*, no.25.
66 See P. Jean-Richard, *op. cit.*, nos.872–75.
67 See exh. cat., *Geist und Galanterie; Kunst und Wissenschaft in 18. Jahrhundert aus dem Musée du Petit Palais, Paris*, Bonn, 2002–3, no.153.
68 Thanks to F. Joulie for providing this information.
69 See P. Jean-Richard, *op. cit.*, nos.230–46, 1090–97, 1098–1123, 1125–33, 1135–59, 1164–76, 1257–1311, 1334–38, 1516–21 and A. M. Priore, 'François Boucher's Designs for Vases and Mounts', *Studies in the Decorative Arts*, Spring-Summer, 1996, pp.2–51.
70 See E. Brugerolles *et al.*, *op. cit.*, no.67.
71 Paul Henri, Baron d'Holbach, *Système de la Nature*, London, 1780, Part I, Chapter I.
72 Introduction to the section on Conchology in A.-J. Dezallier d'Argenville, *L'Histoire Naturelle éclaircie dans deux de ses parties principales, la Lithologie et la Conchyliologie*, Paris, 1742, pp.195–230.
73 See V. Droguet, X. Salmon and D. Véron-Denise, exh. cat., *Animaux d'Oudry, Collections des ducs de Mecklenbourg Schwerin*, Fontainebleau, Versailles, 2003–4, pp.135–202.
74 'a nerve goes from the brain, it turns around the eyes, the mouth and passes over the heart, it descends to the generative organs, and from this arises the fact that sight is the fore-runner of pleasure'; Voltaire, *Dialogues et entretiens philosophiques*, Dialogue 25.
75 See C. R. Hill, 'The Cabinet of Bonnier de La Mosson' (1702–1744), *Annals of Science*, 43 (1986), pp.147–74.
76 See K. Scott, *op. cit.*, pp.167–76; see also Lajoue's witty rococo cartouche which depicts a tiny crab crawling out of a shell surrounded by seaweed and Neptune's trident; E. Brugerolles *et al.*, *op. cit.*, no.74.
77 See G. Glorieux, *passim*.
78 *Ibid.*, p.360.
78 P. Remy, *op. cit.*, lots 1116–1807.
80 *Ibid.*, lots 1808–1814; for comparable Enlightenment collections in England see K. Sloan ed., *Enlightenment, Discovering the World in the Eighteenth Century*, London, 2003.
81 J.-C. von Mannlich, *op. cit.*, p.56.
82 *Ibid.*, p.156.
83 A.-J. Dezallier d'Argenville, *Conchyliologie nouvelle et portative*, Paris, 1767, pp.312–13; for another description of Boucher's cabinet see A.-J. Dezallier d'Argenville, *L'Histoire Naturelle…*, *op.cit.*, ed. 1780, p.236.
84 Lot 1021 also lists 'sixteen tables of differing size with glass tops for displaying shells'.
85 See 'Les cabinets scientifiques' in J. Queneau and J.-Y. Patte, *La France au Temps des Libertins*, Paris, 2001, pp.38–45.
86 P. Remy, *op. cit.*, lots 623, 975.
87 A.-J. Dezallier d'Argenville, 1727, *op.cit.*
88 Fréron's reaction to Gersaint's 1745 sale catalogue of Antoine de La Roque's collection, quoted in J.Chatelus, *op. cit.*, p.286.
89 See D. Bernard-Folliot, 'Le comte de Tessin à Paris 1739–1742', *Gazette des Beaux-Arts*, January 1985, pp.33–6.
90 F. Metra, *Correspondance secrète, politique et Littéraire*, 18 vols., London, 1787–90.
91 Letter of Natoire to Duchesne, 6 February 1754; A. de Montaiglon, *Correspondance*, *op. cit.*, XI, pp.12–13.
92 J.-F. Blondel, *L'Homme du monde Éclairé par les Arts*, 2 vols., ed. J.-F. Bastide, Paris, 1774, I, p.19.
93 *Ibid.*, pp.89–91.
94 See, for example, J.-F. Blondel, *L'Architecture des Maisons de Plaisance*, 2 vols., Paris, 1738. See also J. Garms, 'La première moitié du XVIIIe siècle', in J.-P. Babelon, *Le château en France*, Paris, 1986, pp.321–5; K. Scott, *passim*; F. Kimball, *op. cit.*
95 See X. Salmon, exh. cat., *Les chasses exotiques de Louis XV*, Amiens, Versailles, 1995–6, nos.18–21.
96 See V. Droguet, X. Salmon and D. Véron-Denise, *op. cit.*, no.61.
97 Decree of October 1722, cited in C. Bailey *et al.*, 2003-4, *op.cit.*, p.24.
98 See F. Vidrion, *La Vénerie royale au XVIIIe siècle*, Paris, 1953 and P. Salvadori, *La Chasse sous l'Ancien Régime*, Paris, 1996.
99 See A. Laing 1986–7, *op. cit.*, no.27 and C. Bailey *et al.*, 2003–4, *op. cit.*, no.51.
100 See L. Dussieux *et. al.*, *Mémoires Inédits sur la vie et les ouvrages des Membres de l'Académie Royale*, 2 vols., Paris, 1854, II, pp.374–6; J. Badin, *La Manufacture de Tapisseries de Beauvais depuis ses origines jusqu'a nos Jours*, Paris, 1909 and M. Fenaille, *État général des tapisseries de la Manufacture des Gobelins*, 5 vols., Paris, III, and IV, 1903–23. For the fabrication of low-warp and high-warp tapestries see Diderot and D'Alembert, *Receuil de Planches sur les sciences, les Arts Libéraux et les Arts méchaniques avec leur explication*, XIX, *Tapisserie des Gobelins*, Paris, 1762.
101 Abbé de Fontenay, *op. cit.*, pp.232–4.
102 See E. Standen, 'Fêtes Italiennes: Beauvais Tapestries after Boucher in the Metropolitan Museum of Art' and R. Shoolman Slatkin 'The Fêtes Italiennes: Their Place in Boucher's Oeuvre', *Metropolitan Museum Journal*, 12, 1978, pp.107–39. For how a room might appear decorated in the Fêtes Italiennes series see B. Pons, *Grands décors français 1650–1800*, Dijon, 1995, p.144.
103 See, for example, A. Laing 2003–4, *op. cit.*, no.21. A coloured gouache drawing of a dance in a park, with Didier Aaron in 2003, also relates to the *Fêtes Italiennes* series.
104 D.-P.-J. Papillon de La Ferté, *op. cit.*, p.658.
105 M. Fenaille, *op. cit.*, IV, (1912), p.226.
106 See C. Gouzi, 'Un prestigieux décor peint, l'hôtel de Soubise à Paris', *L'Estampille-L'Objet d'Art*, March 2001, pp.54–63; M. Le Blanc, 'Ordre social et architecture privée. Les stratégies de la représentation au palais Soubise (1704–1757)', in T. Gaehtgens *et al.*, *L'art et les normes sociales au XVIIIe siècle*, Paris, 2001, pp.63–77.
107 See *Charles-Joseph Natoire*, *op. cit.*, pp.61–64.
108 See A. Laing 1986–7, *op. cit.*, nos.31–2.
109 See P. Stein and M. Tavener Holmes, exh. cat., *Eighteenth-Century French Drawings in New York Collections*, New York, 1999, no.12, where drawings and tapestries are compared.
110 B. Pascal, *Pensées*, published posthumously, 1668, translation A.J. Kreilsheimer, London, 1995, p.8.
111 See P. Rosenberg ed., *Vie Anciennes de Watteau*, Paris, 1984, p.22; *Monkey Painter* after Watteau engraved by Desplaces, see G. Macchia and E.C. Montagni, *op. cit.*, no.67.
112 'On Eloquence' in J. Locke, *An Essay on Human Understanding*, London, 1690.
113 *The Neapolitan Shepherd*, known from a 1752 engraving by Daullé; see A. Laing 1986–7, *op.cit.*, no.22.
114 F. Joulie and J.-F. Méjanès, *op. cit.*, nos.16 and 30 and A. Laing 1986–7, *op. cit.*, no.23.
115 Boucher's camera obscura is discussed in the Favart correspondence already mentioned and listed as lot 1082 of his sale catalogue. See also J.-C. von Mannlich, *op.cit.*, p.157.
116 Sir Joshua Reynolds, *Discourse on Art*, ed. R. R. Wark, New Haven and London, 1997, p.225.
117 See A. Laing 1986–7, *op. cit.*, no.22.
118 See J. Hedley, *Jan Steen at the Wallace Collection*, London, 1996–7, no.2 and for the Dutch emblematic tradition in general, S. Schama, *The Embarrassment of Riches*, London, 1991.
119 See M. P. Eidelberg, 'The Case of the Vanishing Watteau', *Gazette des Beaux-Arts*, July-August, 2001, pp.15–40, see p.26.
120 See A. Laing 1986–7, *op. cit.*, no.28.
121 See P. Jean-Richard, *op. cit.*, no.1520.
122 L.-S. Mercier, *op. cit.*, ed. Paris, 1990, p.183.
123 See C. Leribault, *Jean-François de Troy 1679–1752*, Paris, 2002, no.P203.
124 See P. Jean-Richard, *op. cit.*, nos.402–52.
125 Engraved by Larmessin as one of the series of thirty-eight engravings after Lancret, Pater, Eisen, Boucher and Le Clerc illustrating the tales of La Fontaine. This particular incident is recounted in Book III, Tale 6. Other examples of compositions by Pater and Lancret related to the Larmessin series are in the Wallace Collection; see J. Ingamells, *op. cit.*, III, pp.226–7, 292–3. For the engravings after Boucher by Larmessin see P. Jean-Richard, *op. cit.*, nos.1250–55 and for a different contemporary approach to the same subject see P. Rosenberg 1987, *op. cit.*, nos.28–9.
126 Voltaire, *Défense du Mondain ou L'Apologie du Luxe*, 1736, lines 53–58.
127 Voltaire *Défense du Mondain*, lines 69–72.
128 See A. Laing 1986–7, *op. cit.*, no.33.
129 See, for example, P. Remy, *op. cit.*, lots 83, 687, 702–813 and 1863.

Chapter III

1 A. Piron, *Placet à Mr de Tourneant* [sic] *Directeur des bâtiments, aux fins d'obtenir pour Mr B(oucher) Professeur de l'Académie Royale de Peinture, un logement au Louvre vacant par la mort de Mr Coustou Sculpteur*, February, 1746; cited in A. Ananoff, *op. cit.*, document 255.
2 A.-J. Dezallier D'Argenville, 1780, *op. cit.*, Part I, p.236.
3 See P. Grate, *French Paintings II Eighteenth Century*, Stockholm, 1994, no.81 and D. Bernard-Folliot, *ibid.*
4 See Carl Gustaf, comte de Tessin, *Lettres inédites*, ed. G. von Proschwitz, Paris,

Stockholm, 1983, letter of 22 July 1740.

5 Cited in P. Grate, *op. cit.*, p.54.

6 See T. Crow 1985, *op. cit.*, p.11.

7 Carl Gustaf, comte de Tessin, *op. cit.*, letter of 1755.

8 J.-F. Blondel 1774, *op. cit.*, I, p.15.

9 *Ibid.*, p.18.

10 A. Laing 1986–7, *op.cit.*, p.66.

11 See J. Hedley, *Van Dyck at the Wallace Collection*, London, 1999, p.93.

12 St Luke was traditionally identified as the patron saint of artists shown at an easel painting a vision of the Madonna and Child.

13 L.-G. Baillet de Saint-Julien, *Lettre sur la peinture, sculpture, et architecture, A M****, [Paris], 1748, 2nd edition 1749 publ. Amsterdam, Part III, p.98.

14 C. L. de Saint-Yves, *Observations sur Les Arts, Et sur quelques morceaux de PEINTURE & de SCULPTURE, exposés au Louvre en 1748*, Leiden, 1748, p.29–30.

15 A. Piron, *ibid.*

16 L.-S. Mercier, *op. cit.*, ed. 1990, p.97.

17 Cited A. Ananoff, *op. cit.*, document 161; for the illustrations designed by Boucher and engraved by Chedel see P. Jean-Richard, *op. cit.*, nos.468–78.

18 See A. Laing 1986–7, *op. cit.*, no.38; R. Rand, exh. cat., *Intimate Encounters, Love and Domesticity in Eighteenth-Century France*, Hannover (New Hampshire), Toledo, Houston, 1997–98, no.12, and C. Bailey *et al.*, 2003–4, *op. cit.*, no.52.

19 See C. Leribault. *op.cit.*, no.P114a

20 L.-S. Mercier, *op. cit.*, 1782–88, VI, p.149.

21 One of Marivaux's best-known plays is called the *Surprise de l'amour*, or *Surprise of Love*, first published in 1722.

22 See F. Joulie and J.-F. Méjanès, *op. cit.*, no.26. Compare, for example with Watteau's study of a seated woman in a New York private collection illustrated in M. Morgan-Grasselli and P. Rosenberg, *op. cit.*, no.85.

23 Restif de La Bretonne, *Les Nuits de Paris*, ed. Paris, 1990, p.919.

24 *Ibid.*

25 Montesquieu, *Lettres Persanes*, Letter 99.

26 L.-S. Mercier, *op.cit.*, ed. Paris, 1990, p.97.

27 G. Brunel, *ibid.*

28 See X. Salmon 1999–2000, *op. cit.*, no.31.

29 See P. Remy, *op. cit.*, lot 943.

30 See *ibid.*, lots 802 and 822 and G. Brunel, *ibid.*

31 J.-F. Blondel 1774, *op.cit.*, I, p.2.

32 Carl Gustaf, comte de Tessin, *op. cit.*, letter of February 1745.

33 Boucher received commissions for decorative overdoors for Christiansborg Castle, Copenhagen, in 1741, for the Royal Palace, Stockholm, in 1744, and for the Castle of Amalienborg, Copenhagen, in 1755. See P. Lespinasse, 'Les voyages de Hårleman et du Tessin en France (1732–1742) et leurs conséquences du point de vue de l'influence française en Suède', *Bulletin de la Société de l'Histoire de l'Art Français*, 1910, pp.276–298; P. Lespinasse, 'Le portraitiste Roslin et les artistes suédois en France', *Bulletin de la Société de l'Histoire de l'Art Français*, Part I, 1926, pp.182–213, Part II, 1951, pp.234–297; L. Réau, *Histoire de l'expansion de l'art français*, Paris, 1931; J. P. Marandel, 'Boucher and Europe', in A. Laing 1986–7, *op. cit.*, pp.73–88.

34 For the Wallace Collection picture see J. Ingamells, *op. cit.*, III, pp.83–5. For the Stockholm picture see A. Laing 1986–7, *op. cit.*, no.51; P. Grate, *op. cit.*, no.89; R. Rand, *op. cit.*, no.13; C. Bailey *et al.*, 2003–4, *op. cit.*, no.54.

35 Letter of 17/27 October 1745 cited in A. Ananoff, *op. cit.*, document 249.

36 For comparable genre pictures by *Chardin* painted for Tessin and Louisa Ulrika of Sweden see P. Rosenberg, exh. cat., *Chardin*, Paris, Cleveland, Boston, 1979, nos.88 and 90 and P. Rosenberg, exh. cat., *Chardin*, Paris, Düsseldorf, London, New York, 1999–2000, nos.63–64.

37 See Arch. Nat. O1 1921B, 1747 cited in A. Ananoff, *op. cit.*, document 279.

38 Montesquieu, *op. cit.*, letter 110.

39 See P. Perrot, *op.cit.*, pp.33–7 and V. Cochet, 'Le fard au XVIIIe siècle image, maquillage, grimage', in D. Rabreau ed., *Imaginaire et création artistique à Paris sous l'Ancien Régime (XVIIe–XVIIIe siècles)*, Paris, 1998, pp.103–115.

40 L.-A. Caraccioli, *La Critique des dames et des messieurs à leur toilette*, Paris, 1770, pp.3–4.

41 E. and J. de Goncourt, *L'Art du XVIIIe siècle*, 3 vols., Paris, 1895, vol.I, p.244.

42 See G. Glorieux, *op. cit.*, pp.263–93.

43 *Ibid.*, pp.170–75.

44 *Ibid.*, p.266.

45 Preface to *Bajazet*, 1676.

46 See M. Jarry, *Chinese Influences in European Decorative Arts of the Seventeenth and Eighteenth Centuries*, Fribourg, 1981, pp.9–14.

47 See M. Roland Michel, 'Exoticism and Genre Painting in Eighteenth Century France', in C. Bailey *et al.*, 2003–4, *op. cit.*, pp.106–118.

48 For the Enlightenment response to foreign cultures see K. Sloan, *op. cit.*, pp.224–75; a recording of *Les Indes Galantes*, directed by William Christie in 1991, is available on Harmonia Mundi.

49 See P. Remy, *op. cit.*, lots 631–637, 684–5, 696, 745–63, 773, 807–813, 868–78.

50 *Ibid.*, lots 702–44.

51 *Ibid.*, lots 649–58.

52 *Ibid.*, lots 659–84, 697. The appeal of such *pagodes* to an eighteenth-century audience is conveyed by the delightful sketches of Boucher's pupil, Gabriel de Saint-Aubin, in the 1769 sale catalogue of L.-J. Gaignat; see E. Dacier, *Catalogues de ventes et livrets de Salons illustrés par Gabriel de Saint-Aubin*, XI, Paris, 1921, pp.67–70.

53 P. Remy, *op. cit.*, lots 882–897.

54 *Ibid.*, lots 901–5.

55 *Ibid.*, lots 686–99.

56 *Ibid.*, lots 941–95.

57 See 'Importation and Imitation' in C. Sargentson, *Merchants and Luxury Markets; The Marchands Merciers of Eighteenth-Century Paris*, London, 1996, pp.62–96; and F. Joulie, 'Boucher et les arts décoratifs' in F. Joulie and J.-F. Méjanès, *op. cit.*, pp.84–90 and nos.38–40.

58 A. Fraisse, *Livre des dessins chinois*, Paris, 1735, preface.

59 R. Sayer, *The Ladies Amusement*, London, 1750, preface.

60 J. Bean, *15th–18th Century French Drawings in the Metropolitan Museum of Art*, New York, 1986, no.26.

61 See P. Remy, *op. cit.*, lots 517–22.

62 See P. Jean-Richard, *op. cit.*, nos.230–34.

63 See E. Brugerolles *et al.*, *op. cit.*, no.71, ill.1.

64 See P. Jean-Richard, *op. cit.*, nos. 12–20, 198–202, 230–34, 254, 1125–34, 1140–41, 1208–1215, 1455. Huquier's son also published a series of engravings after Boucher's Chinese Tapestry designs, Crozat de Thiers and Watelet engraved plates after Boucher chinoiserie and Demarteau published chinoiserie designs by Boucher in the 1760s: see P. Jean-Richard, *op. cit.*, nos.777, 1082–88, 1164–70, 1608–10, 1625.

65 See R. Savill, 'Six enamelled snuff-boxes in the Wallace Collection', *Apollo*, CXI, 1980, pp.304–9.

66 Copied after Huquier fils's engraving onto a glass cooler (*sceau à verre*; 1745–50; Musée des Arts Décoratifs, Paris); see A. Laing 1986–7, *op. cit.*, no. 93.

67 See M. Jarry, *op. cit.* pp.15–32.

68 See A. Laing 1986–7, *op. cit.*, no.43; D. Sutton, *op. cit.*, no.30. Compare also *L'Apothéose du geste*, *op. cit.*, no.31.

69 A Chinese headress, metal mirror and parasol, for example, are all listed in Boucher's sale catalogue P. Remy, *op. cit.*, lots 699, 947, 992; see also J. Nieuhof, *L'Ambassade de la Compagnie Orientale des Provinces Unies vers L'Empereur de la Chine ...*, Leyden 2 vols, 1665, French translation published by J. L. Charpentier; A. Kirchner, *La Chine d'Athanase Kirchnere illustré de plusieurs monuments sacrés que profanes ... avec un Dictionnaire*, Amsterdam, 2 vols, 1670; A. Montanus, *Ambassades vers les empereurs du Japon*, Amsterdam, 1680.

70 See P.-F. Bertrand, 'La seconde 'Tenture chinoise' tissée à Beauvais et Aubusson. Relations entre Oudry, Boucher et Dumons', *Gazette des Beaux-Arts*, November 1990, pp.173–84; the Aubusson series, which included a set of matching seat covers, was first on the loom in 1754.

71 See A. Laing 1986–7, *op. cit.*, no.91.

72 See P. Henri Bernard-Maitre, 'Les tapisseries chinoises de François Boucher à Pékin', *Bulletin de la Société d'Histoire de l'Art Français*, 1981, pp.9–10.

73 C. L. de Saint-Yves 1748, *op. cit.*, pp.28–29.

74 See P. Remy, *op. cit.*, lot 611.

75 'Everything there is simply order and beauty/ luxury, peace and sensual indulgence' from Charles Baudelaire, 'L'invitation au voyage' – 'Spleen et idéal', *Les fleurs du mal*, Paris, 1857, no.56.

76 See A. Laing 1986–7, *op. cit.*, no.48.

77 See M. Morgan Grasselli and P. Rosenberg, *op. cit.*, nos. 45–49 and P. Jean-Richard, *op. cit.*, nos.84, 92.

78 See M. Roland Michel in C. Bailey *et al.*, 2003–4, *op. cit.*, p.111.

79 See J. Ingamells, *op. cit.*, III, pp.234–37, 255–57, 265–67. For Turkish influence on painting in general see A. Boppe, 'Les 'Peintres de Turcs' au XVIIIe siècle', *Gazette des Beaux-Arts*, July and September 1905, Part I, pp.43–54, Part II, pp.220–30.

80 See A. de Herdt, exh. cat., *Dessins de Liotard*, Geneva, Paris, 1992, no.70 and P. Jean-

Richard, *op. cit.*, nos.878–98.

81 See P. Remy, *op. cit.*, lots 698, 832–37 and 973.

82 See P. Stein, 'Madame de Pompadour and the Harem Imagery at Bellevue', *Gazette des Beaux-Arts*, January 1994, pp.29–44.

83 See P. Frankl, 'Boucher's Girl on a Couch', in *Essays in Honour of Erwin Panofsky*, New York, 1961, pp.138–52.

84 See J. Ingamells, *op. cit.*, III, pp.370–2.

85 Crébillon *fils*, *Le Sopha*, Paris, 1742, Introduction.

86 D. Vivant Denon, *Point de lendemain*, first published in Dorat, *Mélanges littéraires, ou Journal des Dames*, Paris, 1777 ed. Michel Delon, Paris, 1995, p.60.

87 Diderot, *Salons*, 1767, III, ed. J. Seznec, Oxford, 1983, p.252.

88 Restif de La Bretonne, *op. cit.*, p.921.

89 See A. Laing 1986–7, *op. cit.*, nos.34–35.

90 For examples of Oudry's French landscape motifs see H. Opperman, exh. cat., *J.-B. Oudry 1686–1755*, Fort Worth, 1983, nos.27–28, 44–45.

91 See F. Joulie and J.-F. Méjanès, *op. cit.*, nos.32–3; H. Opperman, *op. cit.*, nos.68–71. For a description of Arcueil see Hurtaut and Magny, *Dictionnaire historique de la Ville de Paris et de ses environs*…, Paris, 1779, I, pp.288–9.

92 See A. Laing 1986–7, *op. cit.*, no.46.

93 See N. Coural, *Les Patel: Paysagistes du XVIIe siècle*, Paris, 2001, pp.15.

94 P.Remy, *op. cit.*, lot 40.

95 See J. Ingamells, *op. cit.*, IV, pp.276–8.

96 C. L. de Saint-Yves, *op. cit.*, p.171.

97 Undated letter, *c.*1750, see A. Laing 1986–7, *op.cit.*, p.64.

98 The list of productions at the Opéra for which we know Boucher provided designs include: Destouches's *Issé* (1742), Lully's *Persée* (1746), *Atys* (1747), *Armide* (1761), *Thesée* (1765), Rameau's *Castor and Pollux* (1764) and Laujon's ballet *Sylvie* (1766). His productions at the Opéra Comique included Favart's *L'ambigu de la Folie, ou Le Ballet des Dindons* (1744) and Noverre's *Les Fêtes Chinoises* (1754). He also provided tapestry cartoons for the *Fragments d'Opéra* series woven at Beauvais from 1752. See also E. G. Landau, '"A Fairytale Circumstance": The Influence of Stage Design on the Work of François Boucher', *Bulletin of the Cleveland Museum of Art*, November 1983, pp.360–78.

99 H.-L. Le Kain, *Mémoire visant à limiter le nombre d'entrées gratuites à la Comédie-Française*.

100 See M. Ledbury 'Intimate Dramas: Genre Painting and New Theater in Eighteenth-Century France' in R. Rand, *op. cit.*, pp.52–3.

101 J. Monnet, *Supplément au roman comique, ou Mémoires de Jean Monnet*, 2 vols., London , 1772, II p.116.

102 An idea of such architectural designs can be seen in drawings in the École des Beaux-Arts and Louvre; see E. Brugerolles *et al.*, *op. cit.*, no.30 and F. Joulie and J.-F. Méjanès, *op. cit.*, no.45.

103 L-G. Baillet de Saint-Julien, *op. cit.*, Part I, pp.49–52.

104 See J. de La Gorce, 'Décors et Machines à l'Opéra de Paris au temps de Rameau Inventaire de 1748', in *Recherches sur la Musique Française Classique*, vol.XXI, 1983.

105 L-G. Baillet de Saint-Julien, *op. cit.*, Part III, p.100.

106 J.-C. von Mannlich, *op.cit.*, p.45.See also positive accounts of Boucher's designs for the revival of Armida quoted in C. Malherbe, 'Les costumes et décors d'Armide', *Bulletin de la Société de l'Histoire du Théâtre*, April 1902, pp.28–32. Despite Mannlich's comments and *pace* an article by Ananoff, 'Propos sur trois dessins de François Boucher', *Gazette des Beaux-Arts*, May-June 1982, pp.211–13, it would appear that Boucher only designed sets and supervised the design of costumes by artists such as Bocquet.

107 C. L. de Saint-Yves, *op. cit.*, p.26.

108 D.-P-J. Papillon de La Ferté, *op. cit.*, p.660. For a detailed discussion of the iconography of Boucher's pastorals see A. Laing, Boucher et la pastorale peinte', *Revue de l'Art*, 1986, no. 73, pp.55–64.

109 See J. Ingamells, *op. cit.*, III, pp.31–32.

110 J.-B. Gresset, *Le Siècle Pastoral*, 1748.

111 A recording of Rameau's *Les Fêtes d'Hébé*, directed by William Christie in 1997, is available on Erato.

112 See J. Ingamells, *op. cit.*, III, pp.54–56, 59–61 and D. Sutton, *op. cit.*, nos. 37–9.

113 Crébillon *fils*, *La Nuit et le Moment*, Paris, 1755.

114 A.-F. (abbé) Prévost, *Manon Lescaut*, 1731; for the growth of *sensibilité* in the eighteenth-century novel see V. Mylne, 'Sensibility and the Novel', in J. Cruickshank, *op. cit.*, pp.45–61.

115 Luc de Clapiers, marquis de Vauvenargues, *Introduction à la connaissance de l'esprit humain*, Paris, 1746.

116 A recording of *Le Devin du Village*, directed by René Clemencic 1991, is available on Nuova Era.

117 F. and C. Parfaict, *Dictionnaire des Théâtres de Paris*, 7 vols., Paris, 1756, III, p.70.

118 L.-G. Baillet de Saint-Julien, *op. cit.*, Part III, p.98.

119 C. L. de Saint-Yves, *op. cit.*, p.26.

120 See J. Ingamells, *op. cit.*, III, pp.61–63, 81–82, 273–74, 277–79, 282–83.

121 See J. Hellegouarc'h, *op.cit.*, pp.108–9, 111.

122 See A. Ananoff, *op. cit.*, document 322.

123 See C. Bailey *et al.*, 2003–4, *op. cit.*, no.55.

124 The motif of the boy in a straw hat appears in Watteau's *Gilles and his Family* in the Wallace Collection and in *The Indiscreet One* (Rotterdam): see J. Ingamells, *op. cit.*, III, pp.347–51 and M. Morgan Grasselli and P. Rosenberg, *op. cit.*, no.31.

125 Hurtaut and Magny, *op.cit.*, pp.572–3.

126 See R. Savill, *The Wallace Collection Catalogue of Sèvres Porcelain*, 3 vols., London, 1988, I, p.228 and A. Laing 1986–7, *op. cit.*, no.100.

127 See P. Jean-Richard, *op. cit.*, nos. 1142–59.

128 C. L. de Saint-Yves, *op. cit.*, p.165.

129 Abbé Desfontaines, *Jugement sur quelques ouvrages nouveaux*, Paris, 1744, I, p.109. From the end of the 1740s and particularly from the 1760s onwards the number of works condemning luxury increased; see, for example: J.-J. Rousseau, *Discours sur les Lettres et les Arts*, 1750 and *Discours sur l'Inégalité*, 1755; Marquis d'Argenson, 'Against the arts, against Luxury' in *Mémoires*, *op. cit.*, V; Marmontel, *Bélisaire*, 1766.

130 Jean Baptiste Boyer, marquis d'Argens, *Lettres juives*, Paris, 1738, *lettre* CXCVII.

131 D. Diderot, *La Promenade d'un Sceptique*, 1747, cited in A. Ananoff, *op. cit.*, document 280.

132 Voltaire, *Le Siècle de Louis XIV*, The Hague, 1751.

133 C. L. de Saint-Yves, *op. cit.*, pp.24–25.

134 E. La Font de Saint-Yenne, 'Réflexions sur quelques causes de l'État présent de la peinture en France, avec un Examen des principaux Ouvrages exposés au Louvre, 1746' in E. Jollet ed., *La Font de Saint-Yenne. Oeuvre critique*, Paris, 2001, p.68.

135 E. La Font de Saint-Yenne, *Réflexions sur quelques causes de l'état présent de la peinture en France*, The Hague, 1747, pp.16–17.

136 C. L. de Saint-Yves, *op. cit.*, pp.152–3.

137 *Ibid.*, p.161.

138 J.-B. abbé Le Blanc, *Lettre sur l'exposition des ouvrages de peinture et de sculpture de l'année 1747, et en général sur l'utilité de ces sortes d'expositions, à Monsieur R.D.R.*, place of publication unrecorded, 1747, pp.52–58.

139 L.-G. Baillet de Saint-Julien, *op. cit.*, part II, p.59.

140 See A. Ananoff, *op. cit.*, documents 304, 306, 309.

141 Engraving by Le Bas after a drawing by Boucher (lost) based on a drawing by Rosa (Munich); see F. Joulie and J. F. Méjanès, *op. cit.*, p.14.

142 Quoted in A. Laing 1986, *ibid.*

143 *Liste des meilleurs Peintres, Sculpteurs, graveurs et architectes des académies Royales de Peinture, Sculpture et architecture, suivant leurs Rangs à l'académie*, 1750, listed in R. Ingrams, *op. cit.* p.26.

144 C. L. de Saint-Yves, *op. cit.*, p.29.

Chapter IV

1 *Journal Encyclopaedique*, 1757.

2 Quoted in J. Chatelus, *op. cit.*, p.127.

3 Recent biographies of Madame de Pompadour include C. Pevitt Algrant, *Madame de Pompadour, Mistress of France*, New York, 2002 and D. Gallet, *Madame de Pompadour ou le Pouvoir féminin*, Paris, 1985.

4 E. La Font de Saint-Yenne 1747, *op.cit.*, p.33

5 See X. Salmon ed., exh. cat., *Madame de Pompadour et les arts*, Versailles, Munich, London, 2002–2003.

6 A comment made by the marquise de Merteuil, in Choderlos de Laclos, *Les liaisons dangereuses*, Paris, 1782.

7 See A. Ananoff, *op. cit.*, document 406.

8 See J. Ingamells, *op. cit.*, III, pp.37–40.

9 *Ibid.*, no.23.

10 See X. Salmon ed. 2002–3, *op. cit.*, nos.24, 46 and J.-F. Méjanès, *Maurice-Quentin Delatour, La Marquise de Pompadour*, Paris, 2002.

11 Cited in J. Ingamells, *ibid.*

12 See A. Ananoff, *op. cit.*, no.332; for another version in a private collection see J. Cailleux, exh. cat., *François Boucher Premier Peintre du Roi 1703–1770*, Paris, 1964, no.50; Louis-Philippe Égalité voted for the death of his own uncle, Louis XVI in 1793.

13 See A. Ananoff, *op. cit.*, documents 410, 414, 419. See also A. Gordon and T. Hensick, 'The picture within the picture, Boucher's 1750 Portrait of Madame de Pompadour identified', *Apollo*, February 2002,

pp.21–30.
14 See, for comparison, X. Salmon ed.2002–3, *op. cit.*, nos.25–30.
15 *Ibid.*, no.132.
16 *Ibid.*, no.63.
17 See M. L. R., *Curiosités de Paris, Paris*, 3 vols., 1778, II, p.269 and J. Cordey, *Inventaire des biens de madame de Pompadour rédigé après son décès*, Paris, 1939, nos.1420–23.
18 See X. Salmon ed. 2002–3, *op. cit.*, no.131.
19 *Ibid.*, nos.34–37.
20 See P. Jean-Richard, *op. cit.*, nos. 1478–1513.
21 See X. Salmon ed. 2002–3, *op. cit.*, no.117.
22 Compare, for example, Vien, *Offering to Venus* (1762; private collection) in T. Gaehtgens and J. Lugand, *op. cit.*, no.183 and Greuze, *Offering to Love* (1767; Wallace Collection) in J. Ingamells, *op. cit.*, III, pp.202–205.
23 See A. Laing 1986–7, *op. cit.*, nos.54–56, C. Kayser *et al.*, exh. cat., *De Chasse et d'Épée, Le décor de l'appartement du Roi à Marly 1683–1750*, Marly, 1999, p.101, and J. Flack, 'The Apotheosis of Aeneas: a lost Royal Boucher rediscovered', *Burlington Magazine*, December 1977, pp.829–33.
24 See A. Laing 1986–7, *op. cit.*, no.58.
25 O1 1921B. f09, cited in A. Ananoff, *op. cit.*, document 392.
26 See P. Biver, *Histoire du château de Bellevue*, Paris, 1933.
27 For a discussion of the significance of Carle Van Loo's decorations for Madame de Pompadour's bedchamber see P. Stein, *passim*.
28 See F. Joulie, 'Boucher décorateur: dessins pour la Manufacture de Beauvais', *Revue de Louvre*, October, 1988, pp.320–24.
29 See J. Ingamells, *op. cit.*, III, pp.68–78.
30 Arch. Nat. O1 1922, cited in A. Ananoff, *op. cit.*, document 278.
31 See Arch. Nat. O1 1921B, 1747, 31 December 1748, and 28 September 1749; cited in A. Ananoff, *op. cit.*, documents 279, 361, 388.
32 See J. Vittet, 'Commandes et achats de Madame de Pompadour aux Gobelins et à la Savonnerie', X. Salmon ed. 2002–3, *op. cit.*, pp.367–79.
33 See letter of Cozette, administrator of the Gobelins, to Monsieur de Vandières, 3 July 1753, Arch. Nat. O1 2036, cited in A. Ananoff, *op. cit.*, document 532.
34 See P. Biver, *op. cit.*, p.48.
35 *Ibid.*, p.4 and for a description of the King's bedchamber see pp.54–57.
36 The fact that the seventeenth-century French audience were more than aware of the classical distinction between Téthys and Thétis is borne out by the discussion of the two different characters in I. Baudoin, *Mythologie ou explication des fables*, Paris, 1627, pp.845–7.
37 Engraved by Le Pautre, *Vue du fonds de la Grotte de Versailles orné de trois groupes de marbres…*, published in A. Félibien, *Description de la Grotte de Versailles*, Paris, 1679; see also L. Lange, 'La grotte de Thétis et le premier Versailles de Louis XIV', *Art de France*, I, 1961, pp.133–48.
38 See M. Stuffmann, 'Charles de La Fosse et sa position dans la peinture française à la fin du XVIIe Siècle',*Gazette des Beaux Arts*, July–August 1964, pp.43, 103, no.31.
39 She performed the piece in January 1750; see *Recueil des Comédies et ballets représentés sur le théâtre des petits appartements pendant l'hiver de 1747–50*, 4 vols., Paris, 1750 and P. Beaussant, 'Le théâtre de la Pompadour' in Les plaisirs de Versailles: *Théâtre et musique*, Paris, 1996, pp.165–89.
40 See M. Stuffmann 1964, *op. cit.*, pp.71–73, 100, nos.17–18 and G. Van der Kemp, *Versailles*, Paris, 1978, p.172.
41 C.-L. de Saint-Yves, *op. cit.*, pp.27–8.
42 Voltaire 1751, *op. cit.*
43 See T. Puttfarken's introduction to R. de Piles, *op. cit.*, pp.5–18.
44 R. de Piles, *op. cit.*, pp.74–5.
45 See J. Chatelus, *op. cit.*, p.85 ss.
46 See R. Démoris, 'Le comte de Caylus et la peinture. Pour une théorie de l'inachevé', *Revue de l'Art*, 2003, no.142, pp.31–43 and M. Fumaroli 'Paris à l'Aube des Lumières: L'abbé Conti et le comte de Caylus' in M. Fumaroli, *op. cit.*, pp.29–66.
47 D.-P-J. Papillon de La Ferté, *op. cit.*, p.660.
48 Thanks to Nicolas Joly for letting me study photographs of these two unpublished sketches. They may be compared to other studio copies of Boucher oil sketches such as those of *The Death of Meleager* and *The Birth of Pyrrhus* (Clermont-Ferrand and Alberquerque, New Mexico); see *L'Apothéose du geste*, *op. cit.* nos.17B, 18B.
49 See M. Vidal, 'Conversation as a Literary and Painted Form: Madeleine de Scudéry, Roger de Piles and Watteau in F. Moureau and M. Morgan Grasselli ed., *Antoine Watteau: le peintre, son temps et sa légende*, Paris and Geneva, 1987, pp.173–79 and M. Vidal, *Watteau's Painted Conversations*, New Haven and London, 1992.
50 See R. Schoolman Slatkin, exh. cat., *François Boucher in North American Collections: 100 Drawings*, Washington, Chicago, 1973–74, p.89; Nattier and Picart's 1707 engraving after Rubens *Le Gouvernement de la reine* illustrated in X. Salmon 1999–2000, *op. cit.*, p.42 and S. Laveissière, exh. cat., *Le Classicisme Français*, Dublin, 1985, no.20.
51 Similar figures appear in Pietro da Cortona's *Rape of the Sabines* and ceiling of the Barberini Palace (Rome).
52 *List of The best Painters, Sculptors, engravers and architects of the Royal academies of Painting Sculpture and Architecture, 1750*, in R. Ingrams, *ibid.*
53 See F. Joulie and J.-F. Méjanès, *op. cit.*, pp.103–112, E. Brugerolles *et al.*, *op. cit.*, nos. 31–32, A. Clarke ed., exh. cat., *Mastery and Elegance. Two Centuries of French Drawings from the collection of Jeffrey E. Horvitz*, Harvard, Ontario, Paris, Edinburgh, New York, Los Angeles, 1998–2000, no.60.
54 C.-H. Watelet and P. C. Levesque, *Encyclopédie méthodique: Beaux-Arts*, 2 vols., Paris and Liège, 1788, I, p.520.
55 See A. Laing 2003–4, *op. cit.*, no.33.
56 See A. Ananoff, *op. cit.*, no.121 and P. Rosenberg and M. C. Stewart, *French Paintings 1500–1825, The Fine Arts Museum of San Francisco*, San Francisco, 1987, pp.114–16.
57 J.-C. von Mannlich, *op. cit.*, p.196.
58 See, for example, drawings for the naiads bottom right in the Louvre and Washington illustrated in A. Ananoff, *op. cit.*, no.423/5, fig.1205 and M. Morgan Grasselli, exh. cat., *Drawings from the Chanler Collection*, Washington, 1982, no.5.
59 See F. Joulie and J.-F. Méjanès, *op. cit.*, no.3 and P. Jean-Richard, *op. cit.*, no.622.
60 J.-C. von Mannlich, *op. cit.*, p.196.
61 See A. Laing 1986–7, *op. cit.*, no.61 and G. Sainty and A. Wintermute, exh. cat., *François Boucher his Circle and Influence*, New York, 1987, no.44.
62 Letter Monsieur de Vandières to Natoire 19 February 1753, Arch. Nat. O1 1940, cited in A. de Montaiglon, *Correspondance*, *op. cit.*, X, pp.438–39.
63 Andrea de Nerciat, *Felicia ou mes fredaines*, London(?), 1775, I, p.15.
64 Emmanuel, duc de Croÿ, *Journal inédit* (1718–1784), 2 vols., Paris, 1906–7, I, p.199.
65 E. and J. de Goncourt, *Madame de Pompadour*, Paris, 1888, p.116.
66 J.-C. von Mannlich, *op. cit.*, p.196.
67 See F. Joulie and J.-F. Méjanès, *op. cit.*, no.62.
68 J.-C. von Mannlich, *op.cit.*, p.157.
69 Christie's, London, 6 July 1987, lot 53 then with Kate de Rothschild.
70 P. Remy, *Catalogue des Tableaux originaux de différens Maîtres …de feue Madame la marquise de Pompadour*, Paris, 28 April 1766 ss., lot 14.
71 See P. Jean-Richard, *op. cit.*, no.456 and A. Laing 2003–4, *op. cit.*, no.76.
72 C. Samoyault-Verlet, 'Précisions iconographiques sur la Salle du Conseil de Fontainebleau', *Revue du Louvre*, 1974, no.4–5, pp.287–91.
73 See M. Stuffmann, *ibid.*
74 See P. Remy 1771, *op. cit.*, lots 56–67, 339–343. The Apollo ceiling modello is listed under lot 63 and fetched the respectable sum of 225 livres, despite the low prices of the other works by La Fosse, deemed unfashionable by 1771.
75 See E. Pagliano. *op. cit.*, pp.49–50.
76 Such as I. Baudoin, *Iconologie ou explication nouvelle de plusieurs images, emblèmes et autres figures hiéroglyphiques des vertus, des vices, des arts …*, Paris, 1644.
77 See J.-M. Pérouse de Montclos, *Fontainebleau*, Paris, 1998, pp.103–9 and J.-P. Samoyault, *Guide du musée national du château de Fontainebleau*, Paris, 1991, pp.131–3.
78 See A. Laing 1986–7, *op. cit.*, no.57.
79 See A. Ananoff, *op. cit.*, p.49, figs.92–99.
80 L.-G. Baillet de Saint-Julien, *op. cit.*, Part III, p.99.
81 C.-L. de Saint-Yves, *op. cit.*, p.27.
82 See P. Biver, *op. cit.*, pp.60–62.
83 Including, for example, a coloured oil sketch in the Metropolitan Museum, New York, a grisaille oil sketch with Agnews in 2000, and drawings in Vienna and Rotterdam; see P. Stein and M. Tavener Holmes, *op. cit.*, no. 52; A. Laing 2003–4, *op. cit.*, nos.60–61, .
84 L.-G. Baillet de Saint-Julien, *Lettre sur la Peinture à un amateur*, Geneva, 1750, p.7.
85 Count von Kaunitz-Rietburg, 'Mémoire sur la Cour de France, 1752', pub. Vicomte du Dresnay, *Revue de Paris*,

VI, p.454.

86 See, for example, *The Sleep of the Infant Jesus* (1758; Moscow) in exh. cat., *French Paintings from the U.S.S.R. Watteau to Matisse*, London, 1988, no.7 and *Saint John The Baptist* (*c*.1754–6; Minneapolis), *The Rest on the Flight to Egypt* (1757; Saint Petersburg), *The Infant Jesus Blessing Saint John the Baptist* (1758; Florence) discussed in X. Salmon ed. 2002–3, *op. cit.*, nos.67–69.

87 *Journal encyclopaedique*, 1757, pp.702–4.

88 Abbé de Fontenay, *op.cit.*, pp.232–4.

89 J.-F. Blondel 1771, *op. cit.*, pp.10–11.

90 Piganiol de La Force, *Description Historique de la Ville de Paris et de ses environs*, 10 vols., ed. Paris, 1765, cited in P. Biver, *op. cit.*, pp.56–58.

91 See P. Biver, *op. cit.*, pp.43–45.

92 See C. Velut, *La Rose et l'Orchidée*, Paris, 1993, p.86.

93 See A. Corbain, *Le Miasme et la Jonquille*, Paris, 1982.

94 Letter of 1737; see R. Ingrams, *op.cit.*, p.18.

95 It is not known which of Madame de Pompadour's châteaux the *Seasons* adorned but they passed to her brother on her death and are listed in his sale catalogue in 1782; see *The Frick Collection An Illustrated Catalogue of Paintings*, 2 vols., New York, 1968, II, pp.24–33 and C. Bailey, 'Pastorals and Genre Paintings: Françcois Boucher's Four Seasons', *The Frick Collection Members' Magazine*, Spring/Summer 2004, pp.4–7.

96 See exh. cat., *La France et la Russie au Siècle des Lumières*, Paris, 1986–87.

97 Emmanuel, duc de Croÿ, *op. cit.*, I, p.93.

98 Cited in M. Maurette, *La Vie privée de Madame de Pompadour*, Paris, 1951, p.132.

99 See X. Salmon ed. 2002–3, *op. cit.*, nos.168–9.

100 See J. Vitet, *op. cit.*, pp.369–70 and X. Salmon ed. 2002–3, *op. cit.*, nos.158–62.

101 E.-J.-F. Barbier, *op. cit.*, IV, pp.401–29.

102 For a discussion of Chardin's very different approach to the depiction of children see K. Scott, 'Child's Play' in C. Bailey *et al.*, 2003–4, *op.cit.*, pp.90–103.

103 For changing attitudes regarding the representation of children in the period see C. Kayser, exh. cat., *L'enfant chéri au siècle des Lumières*, Marly, Cholet, 2003.

104 See, for example, *The Little Farm Girl*, 1752, oil on canvas, Sotheby's, New York, 19 May 1994, lot 79, or *Shepherd Boy playing Bagpipes*, *c*.1754, oil on canvas see E.M. Zafran, *French Paintings in the Museum of Fine Arts, Boston*, Boston, 1998, no.41.

105 See X. Salmon ed. 2002–3, *op. cit.*, nos.164–67.

106 See A. Laing, 'Madame de Pompadour et 'les Enfants de Boucher'', in X. Salmon ed. 2002–3, *op. cit.*, pp.41–49 and *The Frick Collection*, *op. cit.*, pp.8–23. A related screen, one leaf of which bore the fleur-de-lys of the Royal House of France, was also sold by Christie's London, 30 July, 1988, lot 144.

107 See A. Ananoff, *op. cit.*, document 384bis; R. Savill, 'François Boucher and the Porcelains of Vincennes and Sèvres', *Apollo*, March, 1982, pp.162–70; A. Fay-Hallé, 'The Influence of Boucher's Art on the Production of the Vincennes-Sèvres Porcelain manufactory', in A. Laing 1986–7, *op. cit.*, pp.345–50.

108 See P. Jean-Richard, *op. cit.*, nos.933–37 and F. Joulie and S. Schwartz, 'Falconet dans l'orbite de Boucher ou une amicale admiration', in exh. cat. *Falconet à Sèvres ou l'art de plaire 1757–1766*, Sèvres, 2002, pp.47–59.

109 See R. Savill 1988, *op. cit.*, II, pp.617–21.

110 See P. Remy, *op. cit.*, lots 839–865.

111 Emmanuel, duc de Croÿ, *op. cit.*, I, p.148.

112 See J.-M. Pérouse de Montclos, *op.cit.*, pp.105–9.

113 Quoted in A. Dupront, *op. cit.*, p.331.

114 J.-F. de Bastide, *op. cit.*, pp.40–1.

115 *Ibid.*, pp.44–5

116 See T. Crow, 'La critique des Lumières dans l'art du dix-huitième siècle, *Revue de L'Art*, 1986, no.73, pp.9–16 and M. Fried, *Absorption and Theatricality*, Berkeley, Los Angeles, London, 1980, pp.35–39.

117 C.-N. Cochin, *Lettre d'un amateur en réponse aux critiques qui ont paru sur l'exposition des tableaux*, undated, pp.3–10, cited in A. Ananoff, *op. cit.*, document no.550.

118 Paul Henri Baron d'Holbach, *op. cit.*, Part II, Chapter I.

119 J. Gautier Dagoty, *Observations sur l'histoire naturelle sur la physique et sur la peinture avec des planches imprimées en couleur*, Paris, 1753, pp.77–78.

120 *Ibid.*, pp.81–2; see also M. Baxandall, 'The Rococo-Empiricist shadow' in *Shadows and Enlightenment*, New Haven and London, 1995, pp.76–117.

121 J. Gautier Dagoty, *op. cit.*, p.85.

122 *Ibid.*, p.83.

123 See J. Gautier Dagoty, *Des extraits faits dans quelques Ouvrages Publiques, concernant l'Exposition des Tableaux de cette année 1753*, Paris, 1754, p.9.

124 See E. La Font de Saint-Yenne, *Sentiments sur quelques ouvrages de la peinture, sculpture, et gravure écrits à un particulier en province*, (1753) cited in E. Jollet ed., *op. cit.*, pp.286–89.

125 P. Perrot, *op. cit.*, pp.23–9.

126 E. La Font de Saint-Yenne, *Sentiments sur quelques ouvrages de la peinture, sculpture, et gravure écrits à un particulier en province*, ed. Paris, 1754, p.195.

127 See J. Vitet, *op. cit.*, pp.368–69 and X. Salmon ed. 2002–3, *op. cit.*, no.137.

128 See J. Vitet, *op. cit.*, pp.369–70 and X. Salmon ed. 2002–3, *op. cit.*, nos.158–62.

129 Cited in *Observations périodiques sur la physique, l'histoire naturelle et les arts*, Paris, 1756–7.

130 See P. Gaxotte, *op.cit.*, p.167.

131 See T. Crow, *op. cit.*, p.11 and C. Sargentson, 'Estimated Incomes in France 1726–1790' in *op. cit.*, p.XI.

132 G. Brunel, *ibid.*

133 *Ibid.*

134 J.-C. von Mannlich, *op. cit.*, p.156.

Chapter V

1 Destouches, *Le Glorieux*, 1732.

2 Shakespeare, *Love's Labour's Lost*, Act II, Scene I, l.15.

3 Subject described in Ovid, *Heroides* XVI, 57–88 and Lucian, *Dialogues of the Gods*, XX.

4 See J. Ingamells, *op. cit.*, III, pp.42–45, 49–54.

5 Ovid, *Metamorphoses* VI, 171–89.

6 J.-C. von Mannlich, *op. cit.*, pp.195–6.

7 Bret, *Nécrologie*, 1771, cited in A. Ananoff, *op. cit.*, document 1082.

8 Cited in A. Ananoff, *op. cit.*, document 684.

9 See J. Ingamells, *op. cit.*, III, pp.47–49.

10 Anacreon, Ode XXX.

11 See C. Gouzi, *op. cit.*, p.58.

12 See, for example, A. Laing 1986–7, *op. cit.*, nos.65–67, 83–85.

13 See J.-A. J. des Boulmiers, *ibid.*

14 Bret, *ibid.*

15 J. Ingamells, *op. cit.*, III, pp.35–36, 40–41.

16 *Ibid.*, pp.85–89.

17 Abbé de Fontenay, *op. cit.*, pp.232–4.

18 Restout, *ibid.*

19 Bret, *ibid.*

20 See Prevost and Bernard, 'Peinture, Atelier, Palette et Pinceaux', in Diderot & D'Alembert, *op.cit.*, 1771, Pl.I.

21 *Réponse à la lettre critique sur les tableaux exposés au Salon en l'année 1757*, cited in A. Ananoff, *op. cit.*, document 682, p.78.

22 See A. Laing, 'François Boucher his Circle and Influence', *Apollo*, January 1988, pp.50–51 and G. Sainty and A. Wintermute, *op. cit.*

23 P. Remy, *op. cit.*, lots 89–92.

24 Boucher's maternal grandparents were great-great grandparents of David on his mother's side: see A. Schnapper, exh. cat., *David*, Paris-Versailles, pp.558, 560.

25 A. de Montaiglon, *Correspondance*, *op. cit.*, XII, pp.91.

26 A. Ananoff, *op. cit.* document 790.

27 See A. Ananoff, *op. cit.*, documents 874–75.

28 See Restout, *ibid.*, and A. Ananoff, *op. cit.*, document 1067.

29 P. Remy, *op. cit.*, lot 1075.

30 J.-C. von Mannlich, *op.cit.*, pp.139, 155–157.

31 Bret, *ibid.*

32 See P. Rosenberg, exh. cat., *Fragonard*, Paris, New York, 1987–8, pp.178–79.

33 Bret, *ibid.*

34 H. Opperman, *op. cit.*, no.72.

35 See V. Droguet, X. Salmon and D. Véron-Denise, *op. cit.*, pp.25–6.

36 See M. Wilson, *The National Gallery Schools of Painting: French Paintings before 1800*, London, 1985, no.38; A. Laing 2003–4, *op. cit.*, no.90 and also the discussion in F. Joulie and J.-F. Méjanès, *op. cit.*, no.34.

37 P. Remy, *op. cit.*, lot.559; see also M. Rosenthal and M. Myrone ed., exh. cat., *Gainsborough*, London, Washington, Boston, 2002–2003, no.11 and 28 for a discussion of Gainsborough's early etchings and engravings.

38 Bret, *ibid.*

39 See exh. cat., *François Boucher*, Manchester, 1984, P8 and A. Laing 1986–7, *op. cit.*, no.82.

40 See F. Joulie and J.-F. Méjanès, *op. cit.*, no.34, fig.5; Frankfurt, Städelsches Kunstinstitut, Inv.1059; Hamburg, Kunsthalle, Inv.1551–219, and P. Remy, *op. cit.*, lots 270–75.

41 See, for example, landscape by Robert, Christie's, London, 13 December 1991, lot 61 and Christie's, New York, 13 December 2000, lot 58, and 26 October 2001, lot 321. Thanks to A. Laing and P. Raison for this information.

42 See, for example, N. Simmons, 'Le paysagiste Nicolas Jacques Julliar (1719–1790). Catalogue sommaire de son oeuvre', *Bulletin de la Société de l'Histoire de l'Art Français*, 1993, pp.149–68; P. Rosenberg 1987–8, *op. cit*; P. Jean– Richard, *op. cit.*,

nos.264–72 and 1340–43.
43 Thanks to A. Laing for this information; the prints were discovered in the 1980s in Schloß Charlottenburg.
44 See J.-G. Wille, *Mémoires et journal*, 2 vols, ed. Paris, 1857, I, p.424.
45 A. Laing 1986–7, *op. cit.*, nos.79–80.
46 See A. Ananoff, *op. cit.*, documents 869–872.
47 J.-C. von Mannlich, *op. cit.*, p.157.
48 Letter from Pierre to the marquis de Marigny, 14 November 1771, A. N. O1 1912, cited in A. Ananoff, *op. cit.*, document 1095.
49 See J. Ingamells, *op. cit.*, III, pp.45–47; for another version commissioned by Caroline Luise, Margravine of Baden, see A. Laing 1986–7, *op. cit.*, no.71.
50 Sold Christie's, London, 11 December 1992, lot 33.
51 J. Ingamells, *op. cit.*, III, pp.167–9.
52 With Julius Böhler, Munich, 1973.
53 P. Rosenberg 1987–8, *op. cit.*, nos.5–6.
54 See J. Ingamells, *op. cit.*, pp.161–5 and P. Stein and M. Tavener Holmes, *op. cit.*, no.76.
55 Quoted in C. Bailey *et al.*, 2003–4, *op. cit.*, p.15.
56 Hazard's description quoted in J. Cruickshank, *op. cit.*, p.90.
57 Although it is not listed at Bellevue in 1757, the La Live de Jully sale catalogue of 1764 lists a reduction in marble of Falconet's *Cupid* saying that 'This item ... was executed in large scale by the author for the château of Bellevue'.
58 J. Wilhelm, 'Le salon du graveur Gilles Demarteau peint par François Boucher et son atelier avec le concours de Fragonard et de J.-B. Huet', *Bulletin du Musée Carnavalet*, 1975, no.1, pp.6–20.
59 See Ananoff, *op. cit.*, document 371.
60 See V. Droguet, X. Salmon and D. Véron-Denise, *op. cit.*, p.25.
61 H. Walpole, *The Letters of Horace Walpole 4th Earl of Orford*, 16 vols., ed. London, 1904, VI, p.294–5.
62 See E. Brugerolles *et al.*, *op. cit.*, no.69.
63 E.-F. Gersaint, *Catalogue raisonné des diverses curiosités du cabinet de feu M. Quentin de Lorangère*, Paris, 1744, p.38.
64 C.-F. Joullain, *Réflexions sur la peinture et la gravure*, Paris, 1786, p.31.
65 See M. Morgan Grasselli ed., exh. cat., *Colorful Impressions*, Washington, 2003–4.
66 *Ibid.*, no.19.
67 K. Smentek, 'Sex and Sensibility: The Market for Genre Prints on the Eve of the Revolution', unpublished paper given at the CASVA conference, Washington, December 2003.
68 See for example the increased number of prints advertised after Boucher in the *Mercure de France* in the 1760s and 1770s; E. Deville, *Index du Mercure de France 1672–1832*, Paris, 1910, pp.27–28.
69 *Mercure de France*, April 1762, pp.156–7.
70 Abbé de Fontenay, *op. cit.*, pp.232–4.
71 E.-F. Gersaint 1744, *op. cit.*, p.18.
72 Christie's, London, 13 December 1984, lot 156.
73 E.-F. Gersaint 1744, *op. cit.*, p.19.
74 See, for example, R. Schoolman Slatkin 1973–74, *op. cit.*, nos.5–6, 63, 77, 80 and 84.
75 Restout and Bret, *ibid.*
76 See J. Chatelus, *op. cit.*, pp.62–68.
77 See J. Ingamells, *op. cit.*, III, pp.117–18.
78 See, for example, G. Reynolds, *Wallace Collection Catalogue of Miniatures*, London, 1980, nos.51–67.
79 Article published in *Observations périodiques sur la physique, l'histoire naturelle et les arts*, 1756–7.
80 *Mercure de France*, January 1767.
81 See J. Chatelus, *op. cit.*, p.321.
82 Restout, *ibid.*
83 Quoted in J. Hellegouarc'h, *op.cit.*, pp.108–9.
84 L.-S. Mercier, *op.cit.*, ed. 1782–88, XI, pp.39–42.
85 Preface to P. Remy, *op. cit.*
86 See J. Chatelus, *op. cit.*, pp.293–7.
87 Quoted in *ibid.*, p.291.
88 See D.Diderot, *Salons, 1759–61–63*, I, ed. J. Seznec and J. Adhémar, Oxford, 2nd ed. 1975, p.62.
89 D. Diderot, *op.cit.*, 1767, III, ed. J. Seznec, Oxford, 2nd ed., 1983, p.53.
90 For example Abbé Coyers, *Discours*, 1754, or C.J.-F. Hénault, *Nouvel abrégé chronologique de l'Histoire de France*, 1768.
91 J.-J. Rousseau, *Discours*, 1750.
92 J.-J. Rousseau, *Émile, ou l'Éducation*, 1762.
93 J.-J. Rousseau, *Julie, ou la Nouvelle Héloïse*, 1761.
94 L.-S. Mercier, *op. cit.*, 1782–88; chap.88 and 535.
95 See M.-C. Sahut, N. Volle, *Diderot et l'Art de Boucher à David. Les Salons: 1759–1781*, exh. cat., Paris, 1984–5; J. Goodman ed., *Diderot on Art*, 2 vols, New Haven and London, 1995.
96 D. Diderot, *op. cit.* 1759–61–63, p.233.
97 *Ibid.*, p.112.
98 *Ibid.*, p.205.
99 Quoted in D. Diderot, *Oeuvres esthétiques*, ed. Paris, 1959, p.459.
100 D. Diderot, *Salons, 1765*, II, ed. J. Seznec, Oxford, 12 ed., 1979, pp.75–6.
101 *Ibid.*, p.80.
102 D. Diderot, *op. cit.*, 1767, p.252.
103 D. Diderot, *Salons, 1769–1771–1775–1781*, IV, ed. J. Seznec, Oxford, 1967, p.67.
104 Poem written in 1768 on p.199 of *Recueil des Poésies de M. Sedaine*, London-Paris, 1760, in Musée Condé, Chantilly.
105 See *L'Apothéose du geste*, *op. cit.*, no.55 and A. Laing 1986–7, *op. cit.*, no.75.
106 See A. Laing 1986–7, *op. cit.*, no.68 and E. M. Zafran, *op. cit.*, no.42. Mariette also noted that Boucher's freedom of handling, or *manière libertine*, derived from the example of Castiglione; J.-P. Mariette, *op. cit.*, II, 95.
107 See, for example, F. Joulie and J.-F. Méjanès, *op. cit.*, no.66.
108 See P. Remy, *op. cit.*, lots 111–12; P. Rosenberg 1987–8, *op. cit.*, no.10; Sotheby's Monaco, 26 June 1983, lot 487.
109 See P. de Nolhac, *Boucher Premier Peintre du Roi*, Paris, 1925, p.194, and *L'Apothéose du geste*, *op. cit.*, no.61.
110 Restout, *ibid.*
111 See J. Chatelus, *op. cit.*, pp.218–225.
112 Letter of Bachaumont, cited in A. Ananoff, *op. cit.*, document 902.
113 D. Diderot, *op. cit.*, 1765, p.76.
114 Published in the *Mercure de France*, September 1765, pp.148–50.
115 A. de Montaiglon, *op. cit.*, *Correspondance*, XII, p.91.
116 H. Walpole, *op. cit.*, pp.299, 352.
117 The correspondence between Madame Geoffrin and King Stanislas concerning the commission is recounted in T. Gaehtgens and J. Lugand, *op. cit.*, nos.204–7.
118 Related drawings are in Detroit, New York and a private collection; see P. Stein and M. Tavener Holmes, *op. cit.*, no. 56; F. Joulie and J.-F. Méjanès, *op. cit.*, no.74 and A. Laing 2003–4, *op. cit.*, no.83.
119 See B. Schreiber Jacoby, 'Boucher's Late Brown Chalk Composition Drawings', *Master Drawings*, Autumn, 1992, pp.255–86.
120 D. Diderot, *op. cit.*, *1767*, p.87.
121 Letter from Diderot to Falconet, 6 September 1768, see D. Diderot, *Oeuvres complètes*, Pars, ed. 1875–77, 20 vols., vol.XVIII, p.301.
122 See P. Jean-Richard, *op. cit.*, no.793 and F. Joulie and J.-F. Méjanès, *op. cit.*, no.77.
123 Baron Grimm, *Correspondance littéraire*, 15 December 1756, quoted in M. Fried, *op.cit.*, p.161.
124 See comte de Caylus, *Recueil d'Antiquités*, 1752; Winckelman, *Thoughts on the Imitation of Greek Works of Art in Painting and Sculpture*, 1755, and *Monumenti Antichi Inedite*, 1767; Piranesi, *Le Antichità Romane*, 1756, and *Le pitture Antiche d'Ercolano e Cantorini*, begun in 1757.
125 See A. Schnapper, *op. cit.*, pp.162–71.
126 See A. Laing 2003–4, *op. cit.*, no.82.
127 See P. Jean-Richard, *op. cit.*, no.788.
128 See, for example, P. Jean-Richard, *op. cit.*, nos. 466–67, 951–52, and E. Brugerolles *et al.*, *op.cit.*, no.33.
129 See P. Remy, *op. cit.*, lots 1022–24.
130 J. Ingamells, *op. cit.*, III, pp.57–59.
131 See A. Ananoff, *op. cit.*, documents 707–09.
132 Restout, *ibid.*
133 P. Remy, *op. cit.*, lots 1077–82.
134 See G. Brunel, *ibid.*
135 P. Remy, *op. cit.*, lots 1077–82.
136 L.-S. Mercier, *op. cit.*, ed. 1782–88, VIII, p.267.

Chapter VI

1 P.-M. Gault de Saint-Germain, *Les trois siècles de la peinture en France*, Paris, 1808.
2 A. de Montaiglon, *op. cit.*, *Correspondance*, vol.XII, pp.278–79.
3 J. G. Wille, *op. cit.*, entry for 19 February 1771.
4 J.-A. J. des Boulmiers, *ibid.*
5 Both cited in A. Ananoff, *op. cit.*, documents 1081–82.
6 J.-F. Blondel 1774, *op.cit.*, II, p.295.
7 See E. Dacier, *Gabriel de Saint-Aubin, peintre, dessinateur et graveur 1724–1780*, 2 vols., Paris-Bruxelles, 1929–31, II, no.88.
8 Cited in A. Ananoff, *op. cit.*, document 1067.
9 J. Ingamells, *op. cit.*, III, pp.215–16, 332–4.
10 Diderot and D'Alembert, op. cit, 1763, pl.XXII.
11 J. Ingamells, *op. cit.*, III., p.90.
12 See G. Reynolds, *op. cit.*, no.73.
13 See T. Burollet, *Musée Cognacq-Jay, Peintures et Dessins*, Paris, 1980, nos.59–60.
14 See *Geist und Galanterie*, *op. cit.*, nos.185–86; P. Jean-Richard, *op. cit.*, no.769.
15 See R. Savill, *op. cit.*, II, pp.871–76; P. Hughes, *op. cit.*, II, pp.1012–19.
16 See J.-M. Tuchscherer, exh. cat., *(La) Toile de Jouy. Dessins et Cartons de Jean-Baptiste Huet (1745–1811)*, Mulhouse, 1970.
17 See R. Savill, *op. cit.*, I, pp.222–233.

18 See R. Savill, *op. cit.*, I, pp.520–21.

19 See D. O. Kisluk-Grosheide, 'A Japanned Secretaire in the Linsky Collection with decorations after Boucher and Pillement', *Metropolitan Museum Journal*, 1986, pp.139–47. and M. Jarry, *op. cit.*, pp.192–93.

20 L.-A. de Caraccioli, *L'Europe française*, Paris, 1776, chapt. XXXIV, 'De la légèreté'.

21 See also J. P. Marandel, *ibid.*, pp.73–88.

22 See R. Rapetti, *Le Musée des Beaux-Arts de Bordeaux, Guide de Collections*, Bordeaux, 1987, pp.41–42.

23 See A. Laing, 'Playful Perfection, Boucher in Britain', *Country Life*, 5 June 1986, pp.1566–68.

24 See J. Hedley, 'L'Influence française sur l'art du portrait anglais au XVIIIe siècle', in X. Salmon ed., *De Soie et de Poudre, Portraits de Cour dans l'Europe des Lumières*, Versailles, 2004, pp.103–134.

25 For the history of the Wallace Collection see P. Hughes, *The Founders of the Wallace Collection*, London, 1992.

26 Letter 1st Marquess of Hertford to Walpole 28 October 1763; see H. Walpole, *Correspondence*, London, 1974, XXXVIII, p.218.

27 For the picture collecting of the Marquesses of Hertford and Sir Richard Wallace see S. Duffy and J. Hedley, *The Wallace Collection's Pictures; An Illustrated Catalogue*, London, 2004, pp.xvii–xxxix.

28 See A. Laing 2003–4, *op. cit.*, no.14.

29 J. Reynolds, *op.cit.*, pp.224–5.

30 J. Reynolds, *op. cit.*, p.108.

31 See R. Schoolman-Slatkin, 'A Note on a Boucher Drawing', *The Burlington Magazine*, October 1973, pp.676–7; A. Laing 2003–4, *op. cit.*, no.55. Other Boucher drawings owned by Reynolds include a drawing in the British Museum, two listed in A. Ananoff, *L'Oeuvre dessinée de François Boucher (1703–1770)*, Paris, 1966, nos. 274 and 828, and a drawing that was with William Brady, New York, 1990.

32 See E. Harris, 'Robert Adam and the Gobelins', *Apollo*, April 1962, pp.100–106; E. Harris, 'The Moor Park Tapestries', *Apollo*, September 1967, pp.180–89.

33 R. Savill, *op. cit.*, II, pp.537–39.

34 Cited in Lady Dilke, *French Painters of the XVIIIth Century*, London, 1899, p.57.

35 Le Brun sale, Paris, 23 December 1771; Huquier sale, Paris, 9 November 1772.

36 Randon de Boisset sale, Paris, 27 February 1777; Sireul sale, Paris, 3 December 1781; Ménars sale, Paris, 3 March 1782; Bergeret sale, Paris, 24 April 1786.

37 First sale Paris, 10 February 1783.

38 M. de Saincy sale, Paris, 29 April 1789.

39 Letter 9 May 1774 to André Lens, cited in P. Rosenberg, exh. cat., *Julien de Parme*, Rancate, Parma, 1999–2000, pp.17–22.

40 L.P de Bachaumont, 'Sur les peintres, sculptures et gravures exposées au Salon du Louvre, le 25 août, 1783' in B. Fort ed., *Les Salons des 'Mémoires Secrets'* 1767–1787, Paris, 1999, p.255.

41 Catalogue of the sale of the comte d'Orsay, 14 April 1790, cited in A. Ananoff, *op. cit.*, document 1149.

42 Manuscript description by Lempereur, dated 1795, cited in A. Ananoff, *op. cit.*, document 1152.

43 P.-M. Gault de Saint-Germain, *op. cit.*, pp.224–27.

44 E. Guénard, Mme Broissin de Méré, *Le Palais-Royal, ou Mémoires Secrets de la Duchesse d'Orléans, Mère de Philippe par M.D.F****, 2 vols., Hamburg, 1806, I, pp.73–78.

45 A rumour first circulated just after the Revolution in 1796 by A. E. N. Fantin-Desodoards, *Louis Quinze*, 1796, 4 vols., II, pp.214–6, and more widely circulated by J. D. Fiorillo, *Geschichte der zeichnenden Künste von ihrer Wiederauflebung bis auf die neuesten Zeiten*, Göttingen, 5 vols, 1798–1808, III, pp.369–70.

46 L. C. Soyer, 'François Boucher' in *Encyclopédie des Gens du Monde*, III, Paris, 1834, p.762.

47 Cited in A. Ananoff, *op. cit.*, document 1179.

48 Samson Sale, Paris, 27–28 October 1812, lot 16; cited in A. Ananoff, *op. cit.*, document 1158.

49 E. and J. de Goncourt 1888, *op. cit.*, p.116.

50 E. and J. Goncourt 1895, *op. cit.*, I, pp.209–10.

51 T. Gautier, 'Le Musée du Louvre' in *Paris-Guide*, Paris, 1867, pp.403–5.

52 Writing in 1864; cited in A. Ananoff, *op. cit.*, document 1173.

53 E. and J. de Goncourt 1895, *op. cit.*, I, p.195–96.

54 See J. Ingamells, *op. cit.*, III, pp.9–17.

55 *Ibid.*, pp.384–85.

56 B. Disraeli, *Coningsby or the New Generation*, London ed. 1927, p.213.

57 *Ibid.*, pp.17–18.

58 See G. Reynolds, *op. cit.*, no. 77.

59 See P. Hughes, *op. cit.* III, pp.1535–63.

60 See J. Ingamells ed., *The Hertford Mawson Letters*, London, 1981, nos.44, 20, 35.

61 Madame de Chavagnac Sale, Paris, 20 June 1854; see J. Ingamells 1981, *op. cit.*, no.47.

62 *Ibid.*, no.77.

63 *Ibid.*, no.98.

64 E. and J. de Goncourt 1895, *op. cit.*, I, p.227.

65 See W. Thoré-Bürger, 'Exposition de tableaux de l'école française, tirés de collections d'amateurs', *Gazette des Beaux-Arts*, 15 September 1860, pp.342–4.

66 Entry on Boucher in P. Larousse, *Grand dictionnaire universel du XIXe siècle*, December 1865.

67 Thanks to Alastair Laing for suggesting the attribution; the entire series is reproduced in the 'Carnet Secret' in J. Queneau and J.-Y. Patte, *op.cit.*; see also J. Ingamells 1981, *op. cit.*, no.103.

68 C. Blanc, *Peintres des fêtes galantes*, Paris, 1854, pp.79–80.

69 See A. Ananoff, *op. cit.*, document 1200.

70 H. de Balzac, *Le Cousin Pons*, ed. Paris, 1973, pp.57–58.

71 Grimm 1753, cited in P. de Nolhac 1925, *op. cit.*, p.139; thanks to Madame Hoguet for information on fan design.

72 See exh. cat., *L'Art de la soie Prelle 1752–2002 des ateliers lyonnais aux palais parisiens*, Paris, 2002–2003, nos.137–38.

73 See R. Savill, *op. cit.*, II, pp.130–35.

74 *The Journal of Eugène Delacroix*, ed. H. Wellington and transl. L. Norton, London, 1951, p.111.

75 *Ibid.*, p.168.

76 *Ibid.*, pp.179–80.

77 *Ibid.*, p.331.

78 *Ibid.*, p.77.

79 O. Wilde, 'The Critic as Artist: Part II', from *Intentions*, London, 1891.

80 M. Proust, *À l'ombre des jeunes filles en fleur*, Paris, 1st ed. 1918, ed.1987, p.621.

81 M. Proust, *Le Côté de Guermantes*, Paris, 1st ed. 1920, ed. 1987, p.33.

82 M. Proust, *La Prisonnière*, Paris, 1st ed. 1923, ed. 1987, p.90.

83 See D. Garstang, exh. cat., *Jean-Luc Baroni Ltd., Master Paintings and Sculpture*, New York, 2003, no.22.

84 See M.-L. Bataille and G. Wildenstein, *Berthe Morisot, Catalogue des Peintures, Pastels et Aquarelles*, Paris, 1961, no.320.

85 See *L'Apothéose du geste*, *op. cit.*, p.66.

86 A. Vollard, *La Vie et l'Oeuvre de Pierre-Auguste Renoir*, Paris, 1919.

87 Cited in J. Banham, S. Macdonald, J. Porter, *Victorian Interior Design*, London, 1991, p.204.

88 *Notes (no.17) by Mr Wedmore on French Eighteenth-Century Art Illustrated by a Collection of Engravings*, Fine Art Society Exhibition no.34, London, 1885, p.3. Thanks to B. Lasic for this reference.

89 *Ibid.*, p.11.

90 Lady Dilke, *op. cit.*, p.51.

91 *The Pall Mall Gazette*, 14 August 1900.

92 P. de Nolhac, 'Les Bouchers de la Collection Wallace', *Les Arts*, December,1902, p.2.

93 V. Josz, 'A propos du bi-centenaire de la naissance de F. Boucher', *Mercure de France*, February, 1904, pp.538–39.

94 L. Réau, *Histoire de la peinture française au XVIIIe siècle*, 2 vols., 1925–6, Paris, 1925, I, p.44.

95 R. Fry, *Characteristics of French Art*, London, 1932, p.72.

96 N. Mitford, *The Marquise de Pompadour*, London, 1954; Ian McInnes, *Painter, King and Pompadour, François Boucher at the Court of Louis XV*, London, 1964.

97 W. G. Von Kalnein and M. Levey, *Art and Architecture of the 18th Century in France*, London, 1972, p.113.

98 See N. Bryson, *Word and Image, French Paintings of the Ancien Régime*, Cambridge, 1981, pp.94–98.

99 E. Lipton, 'Women, Pleasure and Painting (e.g. Boucher), *Genders*, No. 7, Spring, 1990, p.75.

100 The novel won the Pegasus prize for literature in 1995; F. Rebolledo, *Rasero*, London, 1996, p.67.

101 C. Logue, *Prince Charming*, London, 1999, p.241.

102 See exh. cat., *Rococo & Co.*, Paris, École des Beaux-Arts, 2003, pp.44–5.

103 'Notes d'un peintre' (1908) in D. Fourcade, *Écrits et propos sur l'art*, Paris, 1972, p.30.

104 *Ibid.*

105 'Two Statements by Picasso' in D. Ashton, *Picasso on Art*, 1972.

106 Voltaire, *Correspondance*, 8 January 1740.

Suggested Further Reading

In addition to the sources, articles and specialist works mentioned in the footnotes, the following provides a list of books and catalogues concerning Boucher in general and Boucher in the Wallace Collection.

A. Ananoff
L'Oeuvre dessiné de François Boucher (1703–1770), 1 vol., Paris, 1966.

A. Ananoff
François Boucher, 2 vols., Lausanne-Paris, 1976.

A. Ananoff
L'Opera completa di Boucher, Milan, 1980.

J. Badin
La Manufacture des tapisseries de Beauvais depuis ses origines jusqu'à nos jours, Paris, 1909.

E. Brugerolles *et al.*, exh. cat., *Boucher et l'art rocaille*, Paris, Sydney, Ottawa, 2003–6.

G. Brunel
Boucher, London, 1986.

J. Cailleux
exh. cat., *François Boucher Premier Peintre du Roi* 1703–1770, Paris, 1964.

E. Dacier and A. Vuaflart
Jean de Julliene et les graveurs de Watteau au XVIIe siècle, 4 vols., Paris, 1921–29.

D. Diderot
Salons, ed. J. Seznec and J. Adhémar, 4 vols., Oxford, 1967–83.

S. Duffy and J. Hedley
The Wallace Collection's Pictures: A Complete Illustrated Catalogue, London, 2004.

M. Fenaille
État général des tapisseries de la manufacture des Gobelins, III, Paris, 1904 and IV, Paris, 1907.

E. and J. de Goncourt
L'Art du XVIIIe siècle, I, Paris, 1895.

J. Goodman ed.
Diderot on Art, 2 vols., New Haven and London, 1995.

M. Hilaire and P. Rosenberg
Boucher 60 chefs-d'oeuvre, Fribourg, 1986.

J. Ingamells
The Wallace Collection Catalogue of Pictures, III, French before 1815, London, 1989.

P. Jean-Richard,
L'Oeuvre gravé de François Boucher dans la Collection Edmond de Rothschild, Paris, 1978.

F. Joulie and J.-F. Méjanès
exh. cat., *François Boucher, hier et aujourd'hui*, Paris, 2003–4.

A. Laing
exh. cat., *François Boucher 1703–1770*, New York, Detroit, Paris, 1986–7.

A. Laing
exh. cat., *The Drawings of François Boucher*, New York, Fort Worth, 2003–4.

Manchester
exh.cat., *François Boucher*, Manchester, 1984.

J. C. von Mannlich
Histoire de ma vie, ed. K. H. Bender and H. Kleber, 2 vols., Trier, 1989.

A. Michel
François Boucher, with a catalogue raisonné by Soulié and Mason, Paris, 1906.

P. Remy
Catalogue raisonné des Tableaux, Desseins, Estampes, Terres cuites, Lacques, Porcelaines de différentes sortes, montées et non montées; Meubles curieux, Bijoux, Minéraux, Cristillations, Madrepores, Coquilles & autres Curiosités qui composent le Cabinet de Feu M. Boucher, Premier Peintre du Roi, Paris, 1771.

G. Reynolds
Wallace Collection Catalogue of Miniatures, London, 1980.

G. S. Sainty and A. P. Wintermute
exh. cat., *François Boucher, His Circle and Influence*, New York, 1987.

M.-C. Sahut and N. Volle
exh. cat., *Diderot et l'Art de Boucher à David, Les Salons: 1759–1781*, Paris, 1984.

X. Salmon ed.
exh. cat., *Madame de Pompadour et les Arts*, Versailles, Munich, London, 2002–3.

R. Savill
The Wallace Collection Catalogue of Sèvres Porcelain, 3 vols., London, 1988.

B. Schreiber-Jacoby
François Boucher's Early Development as a Draughtsman, 1720–1734, New York-London, 1986.

D. Sutton
exh. cat., *François Boucher*, Tokyo, Kumamoto, 1982.

Index

Fig. nos. in square brackets

Photographic Credits

The Royal Collection © 2004, Her Majesty Queen Elizabeth II, fig.15; Amiens, Musée de Picardie, cliché Marc Jeanneteau, figs.29, 40; Amsterdam, © Rijksmuseum, fig.19; Barnard Castle © The Bowes Museum, fig.65; Belton House (Lincolnshire), © The National Trust, fig.21; Berlin, Schloß Charlottenburg, © Stiftung Preußische Schlösser und Gärten Berlin-Brandenburg /photographer: Jörg P.Anders, fig.6; Besançon, Musée des Beaux-Arts et d'Archéologie, cliché Charles Choffet, fig.62; Bordeaux, © Musée des Beaux-Arts / cliché Lysiane Gauthier, fig.135; Boston (USA), Photograph © 2004 Museum of Fine Arts, fig.136; Cambridge, Reproduction by permission of the Syndics of the Fitzwilliam Museum, figs. 13, 81; Chicago, © The Art Institute, fig.48; Cincinnati, © Art Museum, fig.26; Copenhagen, © The David Collection / photographer: Pernille Klemp, fig.95; Detroit, The Institute of Arts, fig.149; Dalmany House, By Courtesy of Earl and Countess of Rosebery, fig.63; Douai, © Musée de la Chartreuse / photographer: Hugo Maertens, fig.124; Genoa, © Galleria di Palazzo Bianco, fig.18; Houston, © Sarah Campbell Blaffer Foundation, fig.30; Le Mans, Musée de Tessé, © Cliché Musées du Mans, fig.123; Lisbon, © Calouste-Gulbenkian Foundation, fig.141; London, By permission of the British Library, fig.72; London, © The British Museum, figs. 12, 14, 16, 50; London, © Christie's Images Limited, fig.28, 49, 121, 128; London, © The National Gallery, fig.113; London, © The Natural History Museum, fig.54; Louisville (Kentucky), © collection of the Speed Art Museum, fig.20; Lyon, Musée des Beaux-Arts, Studio Basset, fig.94; Madrid, © Museo Thyssen-Bornemisza, fig.56; Manchester, © Manchester Art Gallery, fig.114; Moscou, Pushkin Museum, fig.22; Munich, © Alte Pinakothek, figs. 68, 90; Munich, © Schloß Nymphenburg, fig.31; New York, By Courtesy of J.-L.Baroni Ltd, fig.147; New York, © Cooper-Hewitt, National Design Museum, Smithsonian Institution / photographer Matt Flynn, fig.43; New York, Copyright The Frick Collection, figs. 97, 98; New York, The Metropolitan Museum of Art, Photograph © 1982, fig.42, Photograph © 1984, fig.60, Photograph © 1993, fig.96, Photograph © 1996, fig.137, Photograph © 1998, figs. 46, 118; New York, © The Pierpont Morgan Library, fig.5; New York, By Courtesy of Sotheby's, fig.146; Ottawa, © National Gallery of Canada, fig.7; Paris, cliché Bibliothèque Nationale de France, figs. 2, 59; Paris, Collection Frits Lugt, Institut néerlandais, fig.57; Paris, © Ecole Nationale Supérieure des Beaux-Arts, fig.11, 35, 37; Paris, Hôtel Soubise, cliché Atelier photographique du Centre historique des Archives nationales, fig.44; Paris, © cliché Institut national d'histoire de l'art, bibliothèque (collections Jacques Doucet), fig.38; Paris, cliché du Mobilier National, fig.100; Paris, Musée Carnavalet, © PMVP/ cliché Lifermann, fig.119; Paris, Musée Cognacq –Jay,© PMVP/ cliché Lifermann, fig.47; Paris, Musée de l'Eventail, fig.143; Paris, Musée des Arts Décoratifs/Photo Laurent-Sully Jaulmes–Tous droits réservés,fig.126, Tous droits réservés, fig.133; Paris, Musée du Louvre, © photo RMN, figs. 1, 33, 34, 76 ; © photo RMN – R.G.Ojeda, fig.9; © photo RMN – J.G. Berizzi, figs.32, 78, 89; © photo RMN – Gerard Blot, figs. 45, 84; © photo RMN – Arnaudet, figs. 52, 64; © photo RMN – Georges Fessy, fig.92; © photo RMN – Lagiewski, fig.93; © photo RMN – G.Blot / C.Jean, fig.144; © photo RMN – Hervé Lewandowski, fig.145; Paris, Musée du Petit-Palais, © PMVP/ cliché Pierrain, fig.36, fig.132; Paris, By permission of Antoine Roegiers, fig.151; Quimper, © Musée des Beaux-Arts, fig.125; Saint Omer, © musée de l'Hôtel Sandelin, Ph. Beurtheret, fig.10; Springfield (Massachusetts), © Museum of Fine Arts, fig.66; Stockholm, © The National Museum of Fine Arts, figs. 17, 55; Tours, Musée des Beaux-Arts, cliché Patrick Boyer, figs. 27, 79; Waddesdon, © The Rothschild Collection (The National Trust), fig.51; Washington, Image © 2004 Board of Trustees, National Gallery of Art, figs. 87, 120; Weimar, © Stiftung Weimarer Klassik und Kunstsammlungen, fig.85.